HEALTH POLICY ISSUES

SEVENTH EDITION

HEALTH POLICY ISSUES

AN ECONOMIC PERSPECTIVE

PAUL J. FELDSTEIN

AUPHA

Health Administration Press, Chicago, Illinois

Association of University Programs in Health Administration, Washington, DC

Your board, staff, or clients may also benefit from this book's insight. For information on quantity discounts, contact the Health Administration Press Marketing Manager at (312) 424-9450.

Library of Congress Cataloging-in-Publication Data

Names: Feldstein, Paul J., author.
Title: Health policy issues : an economic perspective / Paul J. Feldstein.
Description: Seventh edition. | Chicago, Illinois : Health Administration Press (HAP) : Washington, DC ; Association of University Programs in Health Administration (AUPHA), [2019] | Includes bibliographical references and index.
Identifiers: LCCN 2018034249 (print) | LCCN 2018035093 (ebook) | ISBN 9781640550117 (ebook) | ISBN 9781640550124 (xml) | ISBN 9781640550131 (epub) | ISBN 9781640550148 (mobi) | ISBN 9781640550100 (print : alk. paper)
Subjects: LCSH: Medical economics—United States. | Medical policy—Economic aspects—United States. | Medical care—United States—Cost control. | Medical care, Cost of—United States.
Classification: LCC RA410.53 (ebook) | LCC RA410.53 .F455 2019 (print) | DDC 338.4/736210973—dc23
LC record available at https://lccn.loc.gov/2018034249

The paper used in this publication meets the minimum requirements of American National Standard for Information Sciences—Permanence of Paper for Printed Library Materials, ANSI Z39.48-1984. ∞™

Acquisitions editor: Janet Davis; Project manager: Andrew Baumann; Manuscript editor: Janice Snider; Cover designer: James Slate; Layout: Cepheus Edmondson

Found an error or a typo? We want to know! Please e-mail it to hapbooks@ache.org, mentioning the book's title and putting "Book Error" in the subject line.

Health Administration Press
A division of the Foundation of the American
   College of Healthcare Executives
300 S. Riverside Plaza, Suite 1900
Chicago, IL 60606-6698
(312) 424-2800

Association of University Programs
   in Health Administration
1730 M Street, NW
Suite 407
Washington, DC 20036
(202) 763-7283

To Colette, Lauren, Kip, and Poppy

BRIEF CONTENTS

DETAILED CONTENTS

LIST OF EXHIBITS

PREFACE

Being an economist, I believe an economic approach is very useful, not only for understanding the forces pressing for change in healthcare, but also for explaining why the health system has evolved to its current state. Even the political issues surrounding the financing and delivery of health services can be better understood when viewed through an economic perspective—that is, the economic self-interest of participants.

For these reasons, I believe an issue-oriented book containing short discussions on each subject and using an economic perspective is needed. The economic perspective used throughout is that of a "market" economist—namely, one who believes markets (in which suppliers compete for customers on the basis of price and quality) are the most effective mechanisms for allocating resources. Of course, at times markets fail or lead to outcomes that are undesirable in terms of equity. Market economists generally believe that government economic interventions—no matter how well intentioned or carefully thought out—can neither replicate the efficiency with which markets allocate resources nor fully anticipate the behavioral responses of the economic agents affected by the intervention. In cases of market failure, market economists prefer solutions that fix the underlying problem while retaining basic market incentives rather than replacing the market altogether with government planning or provision.

Healthcare reform has been an ongoing process for decades. At times, legislation and regulation have brought about major changes in the financing and delivery of medical services. At other times, competitive forces have restructured the delivery system. Both legislative and market forces will continue to influence how the public pays for and receives its medical services. Any subject affecting the lives of so many and requiring such a large portion of our country's resources will continue to be a topic of debate, legislative change, and market restructuring. I hope this book will help to clarify some of the more significant issues underlying the politics and economics of healthcare.

Changes in the Seventh Edition

Many revisions and additions have been made in this seventh edition. The book consists of 38 chapters, a glossary, 116 exhibits, and extensive references lists. In addition to updating the exhibits (including several new exhibits) and adding recent references, the book has been revised (some sections rather extensively) and updated, using recent data, adding new research findings relevant to various sections, and including new sections in some chapters.

Three chapters have been added: chapter 30, "Should Profits in Healthcare Be Prohibited?", chapter 32, "Health Associations and the Political Marketplace," and chapter 38, "The Affordable Care Act: Did It Achieve Its Goals?"

The Affordable Care Act (ACA), the most significant health policy enacted in many years, affected all aspects of the healthcare financing and delivery system. Many people and institutions have been affected by this legislation, including physicians, hospitals, other healthcare providers, insurers, employers, employees, unions, the uninsured, and the states as well as the federal government. Any book on health policy must discuss the ACA.

The ACA, however, is so complex and its reach so extensive that it is impossible to cover it in one or two chapters. Instead, the ACA is discussed in those chapters in which particular aspects of the legislation are relevant. ACA policies and their implications are repeated in several chapters. The reason for this is twofold. First, instructors generally do not assign all 38 chapters to their students. Second, some chapters would be incomplete if particular aspects of the ACA were not included. For example, the ACA made important changes to the health insurance market and to Medicaid eligibility. Thus, these changes and their consequences are discussed in both chapter 7 and chapter 9.

The following chapters were significantly revised or include important new sections. The three new chapters for this seventh edition are also described below.

Chapter 10: How Does Medicare Pay Physicians?

Included in this chapter is a new section on MACRA (the Medicare Access and CHIP Reauthorization Act), which describes and analyzes the likely consequences of the new Medicare physician payment system starting in 2019.

Chapter 14: Physician Malpractice Reform

The emphasis in this chapter has been changed from a discussion of the recurrent malpractice crises and why malpractice premiums have risen to the objectives of the malpractice system, proposed reforms, and their likely effectiveness, including a new illustrative exhibit.

Chapter 23: Who Bears the Cost of Employee Health Benefits?

This chapter has been extensively revised and emphasizes how the costs of various mandates are shifted to employees.

Chapter 25: The High Price of Prescription Drugs
A new section is included that analyzes the shortage of generic drugs. It is surprising that the supply of generic drugs, inexpensive copies of drugs that have lost their patent protection, cannot be increased quickly when the demand for such drugs exceeds the available supply. The reasons for these recurrent shortages and appropriate public policies are discussed.

Chapter 30: Should Profits in Healthcare Be Prohibited?
This chapter is new. Many people have questioned the role of profits and the adverse incentive effects of making a profit in healthcare. The different definitions of profits used by accountants and economists are discussed, including when "excess" profits are beneficial to society, as well as appropriate government regulation when excess profits are generated by certain types of behavior. This chapter also examines why not-for-profit hospitals and insurers must earn a profit. Examples of the consequences of prohibiting profits are given, and the importance of profits in providing incentives for developing treatment and cost-reduction innovations is discussed.

Chapter 31: The Role of Government in Medical Care
A new section titled "Political Markets Compared with Economic Markets" discusses the similarities and differences between the two types of markets.

Chapter 32: Health Associations and the Political Marketplace
This new chapter discusses the types of legislation demanded by different health associations. Understanding the economic self-interest of association members and their policy preferences gives us insight into why the financing and delivery of medical services has evolved the way it has. Also discussed are the types of legislation and regulation favored (and opposed) by politically powerful health associations.

Chapter 33: Medical Research, Medical Education, Alcohol Consumption, and Pollution: Who Should Pay?
An appendix titled "Inframarginal Externalities in Medical Education" has been added to this chapter. The appendix describes the circumstances in which individuals receive sufficient private benefits from becoming physicians that medical education subsidies are unnecessary.

Chapter 35: Employer-Mandated National Health Insurance
In addition to various updates of exhibits, data, and commentary, this chapter includes a discussion of the ACA's employer mandate.

Chapter 38: The Affordable Care Act: Did It Achieve Its Goals?

This new chapter examines an important objective of the ACA: reducing the number of uninsured. The chapter elaborates on several ACA issues covered in other chapters and provides new materials and exhibits regarding the ACA's approaches for reducing the number of uninsured. Sufficient time has passed and data have become available to allow analyses of the effectiveness of these ACA approaches: Medicaid eligibility expansion, employer mandate, small-business tax credit, individual mandate, and subsidies within the health insurance exchanges. Suggested legislative changes are presented that could increase the number of insured. Bipartisan political support is essential to enacting legislation that expands insurance coverage.

Instructor Resources

This book's Instructor Resources include a test bank, PowerPoint slides, discussion points for the book's end-of-chapter discussion questions, additional questions and discussion points, teaching tips, chapter overviews, and a transition guide to the new edition. For the most up-to-date information about this book and its Instructor Resources, go to ache.org/HAP and browse for the book's title or author name. This book's Instructor Resources are available to instructors who adopt this book for use in their course. For access information, please email hapbooks@ache.org.

Acknowledgments

I thank Glenn Melnick, Thomas Wickizer, Jerry German, Jeff Hoch, and several anonymous reviewers for their comments. For this seventh edition, I also thank Elzbieta Kozlowski for all her assistance, particularly the collection of data and construction of the exhibits.

Paul J. Feldstein
Encinitas, California

THE RISE OF MEDICAL EXPENDITURES

The rapid growth of medical expenditures since 1965 is as familiar as the increasing percentage of US gross domestic product (GDP) devoted to medical care. Less known are the reasons for this continual increase. The purpose of this introductory chapter is threefold: (1) to provide a historical perspective on the medical sector; (2) to explain the rise of medical expenditures in an economic context; and (3) to set forth criteria for evaluating the Patient Protection and Affordable Care Act (ACA), which has been the most significant healthcare legislation since Medicare and Medicaid.

Before Medicare and Medicaid

Until 1965, spending in the medical sector was predominantly private—80 percent of all expenditures were paid by individuals out of pocket or by private health insurance on their behalf. The remaining expenditures (20 percent) were paid by the federal government (8 percent) and the states (12 percent) (see exhibit 1.1). Personal medical expenditures totaled $35 billion and accounted for approximately 6 percent of GDP—that is, six cents of every dollar spent went to medical services.

EXHIBIT 1.1
Personal Health Expenditures by Source of Funds, 1965 and 2016

Source of Funds	1965 $ (Billions)	1965 %	2016 $ (Billions)	2016 %
Total	34.7	100.0	2,834.0	100.0
Private	27.6	79.5	1,479.5	52.2
Out-of-pocket	18.2	52.4	352.5	12.4
Insurance benefits	8.7	25.1	993.8	35.1
All other	0.7	2.0	133.2	4.7
Public	7.1	20.5	1,354.5	47.8
Federal	2.8	8.1	1,093.8	38.6
State and local	4.3	12.4	260.7	9.2

Source: Data from Centers for Medicare & Medicaid Services (2017b).

Two important trends are the increasing role of government in financing medical services and the declining portion of expenditures paid out of pocket by the public. As shown in exhibit 1.1, the government paid 47.8 percent of total medical expenditures in 2016; the federal share was 38.6 percent and the states contributed 9.2 percent. Meanwhile, the private share dropped to 52.2 percent (from 79.5 percent in 1965); of that amount, 12.4 percent was paid out of pocket (from 52.4 percent in 1965).

The Greater Role of Government in Healthcare

Medicare and Medicaid were enacted in 1965, dramatically expanding the role of government in financing medical care. Medicare, which covers the aged, initially consisted of two of its current four parts—Part A and Part B. Part A is for hospital care and is financed by a separate (Medicare) payroll tax on the working population. Part B covers physicians' services and is financed by federal taxes (currently 75 percent) and by a premium paid by the aged (25 percent). Medicare Part C and Part D have since been added. Part C is a managed care option, and Part D is a prescription drug benefit—financed 75 percent by the federal government and 25 percent by the aged. Parts B, C, and D are all voluntary programs.

Medicaid is for the categorically or medically needy, including the indigent aged and families with dependent children who receive cash assistance. Each state administers its own program, and the federal government pays, on average, more than half of the costs. The ACA, enacted in 2010 and implemented in 2014, expanded Medicaid eligibility from 100 to 138 percent of the federal poverty level (FPL). The federal government reimburses states that choose to expand Medicaid for up to 90 percent of their costs for the newly eligible enrollees.

The rapid increase in total national health expenditures (NHE) is illustrated in exhibit 1.2, which shows spending on the different components of medical services over time. Since 2000, NHE per capita has risen from $4,884 to $10,365. During this time frame, hospital care and physician and clinical services—the two largest components of medical expenditures—surged from $416 billion to $1.083 trillion and from $291 billion to $665 billion, respectively. These data indicate the enormous amount of US resources flowing into healthcare.

In 2016, $3.338 trillion (or 17.9 percent of GDP) was spent on medical care in the United States.[1] From 2000 to 2016, these expenditures climbed by about 9 percent per year. Since peaking in the early part of the decade, the annual rate of increase in NHE has been declining, although it remains above the rate of inflation. These expenditures continue to rise as a percentage of GDP.

EXHIBIT 1.2
National Health Expenditures, Selected Calendar Years, 1965–2016 (in Billions[a] of Dollars)

	1965	1970	1980	1990	2000	2010	2016
Total national health expenditures	$42.0	$74.9	$255.8	$724.3	$1,377.2	$2,598.8	$3,337.5
Health services and supplies	37.2	67.1	235.7	675.6	1,289.6	2,456.1	3179.8
Personal healthcare	34.7	63.1	217.2	616.8	1,165.4	2,196.0	2834.0
Hospital care	13.5	27.2	100.5	250.4	415.5	822.3	1082.5
Physician and clinical services	8.6	14.3	47.7	158.9	290.9	512.6	664.9
Dental services	2.8	4.7	13.4	31.7	62.3	105.9	124.4
Other professional care	0.5	0.7	3.5	17.4	37.0	69.9	92.0
Home health care	0.1	0.2	2.4	12.6	32.4	71.6	92.4
Nursing home care	1.4	4.0	15.3	44.9	85.1	140.5	162.7
Drugs, medical nondurables	5.9	8.8	21.8	62.7	152.5	304.3	390.8
Durable medical equipment	1.1	1.7	4.1	13.8	25.2	39.9	51.0
Other personal healthcare	0.7	1.3	8.5	24.3	64.5	129.1	173.3
Program administration and net cost of private health insurance	1.8	2.6	12.0	38.8	81.2	184.4	263.7
Government public health activities	0.6	1.4	6.4	20.0	43.0	75.6	82.2
Research and construction	4.7	7.8	20.1	48.7	87.6	142.7	157.5
Research	1.5	2.0	5.4	12.7	25.5	49.2	47.7
Construction	3.2	5.8	14.7	36.0	62.1	93.5	109.8
National health expenditures per capita	$210	$356	$1,112	$2,851	$4,884	$8,410	$10,365

Source: Data from Centers for Medicare & Medicaid Services (2017b).
[a]Except for per capita data.

The Relationship Between NHE and GDP

The growth in medical expenditures over time can be illustrated by comparing the rate of increase in NHE per capita to the rate of change in GDP per capita. (To show the relationship between the two series more clearly, a five-year moving average of the rates of change is used.) If NHE per capita is rising faster than GDP per capita, the former is becoming a larger share of GDP. If the two series are moving together, then changes in the economy and health spending are closely related. Exhibit 1.3 shows the relationship between the two series from 1965 to 2016.

The only major divergence between NHE per capita and GDP per capita began in the mid-1990s. Medical expenditures increased at a slower rate because of the growth of managed care (which emphasized utilization management) and price competition among providers participating in managed care provider networks. By the end of the 1990s, managed care's cost-containment

EXHIBIT 1.3
Changes in National Health Expenditures and Gross Domestic Product per Capita, 1965–2016

Note: Five-year moving averages.

Source: Data from the Centers for Medicare & Medicaid Services (2017b).

approaches lost support because of public dissatisfaction with managed care's restrictions on access to specialists, lawsuits against managed care organizations (MCOs) for denial of care, government legislation, and a tight labor market that led employers to offer their employees more health plan choices. As a result, medical expenditures rose at a more rapid rate.

The decline in the annual NHE rate increase from about 2008 to 2013 (exhibit 1.3) can be attributed to the Great Recession, slow economic recovery, high unemployment levels, a large number of uninsured, a decrease in the number of employers paying for employee health insurance, and the rapid spread of high-deductible health plans (Fuchs 2013).

NHE is likely to rise at a slightly faster rate in the coming years as the economy continues to recover; more baby boomers become eligible for Medicare; new technology and specialty drugs that improve the quality of life (but are higher in cost) are developed; and increased demand occurs as a result of the ACA's Medicaid eligibility expansion and subsidies for low-income enrollees on health insurance exchanges.

By 2025, federal, state, and local governments are expected to increase their share of total NHE, which is expected to reach $2.6 trillion (almost doubling from $1.5 trillion in 2016) and to consume an even greater portion of GDP (19.9 percent) (Centers for Medicare & Medicaid Services 2017c, table 16). Exhibit 1.4 shows where healthcare dollars come from and how they are distributed among different types of healthcare providers.

EXHIBIT 1.4
The Nation's Healthcare Dollar, 2016

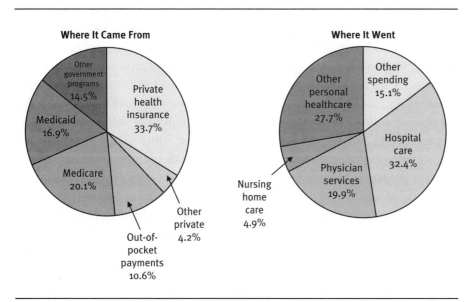

Where It Came From

Other government programs 14.5%

Private health insurance 33.7%

Medicaid 16.9%

Medicare 20.1%

Out-of-pocket payments 10.6%

Other private 4.2%

Where It Went

Other spending 15.1%

Other personal healthcare 27.7%

Hospital care 32.4%

Physician services 19.9%

Nursing home care 4.9%

Notes: "Other personal healthcare" includes dental care, vision care, home health care, drugs, medical products, and other professional services. "Other spending" includes program administration, net cost of private health insurance, government public health, and research and construction.

Source: Data from the Centers for Medicare & Medicaid Services (2017b).

Changing Patient and Provider Incentives

Medical expenditures equal the prices of services provided multiplied by the quantity of services provided. The rise of expenditures can be explained by looking at the factors that prompt medical prices and quantities to change. In a market system, the prices and output of goods and services are determined by the interaction of buyers (the demand side) and sellers (the supply side). We can analyze price and output changes by examining how various interventions change the behavior of buyers and sellers. One such intervention was Medicare, which lowered the out-of-pocket price the aged had to pay for medical care. The demand for hospital and physician services went up dramatically after Medicare was enacted, spurring rapid price increases. Similarly, government payments on behalf of the poor under Medicaid stimulated demand for medical services among this population. Greater demand for services multiplied by higher prices for those services equals greater total expenditures.

Prices also go up when the costs of providing services increase. For example, to attract more nurses to care for the higher number of aged patients, hospitals raised nurses' wages and then passed this increase on to payers in the form of more expensive services. Increased demand for care multiplied by higher costs of care equals greater expenditures.

While the government was subsidizing the demands of the aged and the poor, the demand for medical services by the employed population also was increasing. The growth of private health insurance during the late 1960s and 1970s was stimulated by income growth, high marginal (federal) income tax rates (up to 70 percent), and the high inflation rate in the economy. The high inflation rate threatened to push many people into higher marginal tax brackets. If an employee were pushed into a 50 percent marginal income tax bracket, half of his salary in that bracket would go to taxes. Instead of having that additional income taxed at 50 percent, employees often chose to have the employer spend those same dollars, before tax, on more comprehensive health insurance. Thus, employees could receive the full value of their raise, albeit in healthcare benefits. This tax subsidy for employer-paid health insurance stimulated the demand for medical services in the private sector and further boosted medical prices.

Demand increased most rapidly for medical services covered by government and private health insurance. As of 2016, only 3 percent of hospital care and 8.9 percent of physician services were paid out of pocket by the patient; the remainder was paid by a third party (Centers for Medicare & Medicaid Services 2017b). Patients had little incentive to be concerned about the price of a service when they were not responsible for paying a significant portion of the price. As the out-of-pocket price declined, the use of services increased.

The aged—who represent almost 16 percent of the population and use more medical services than any other age group—accounted for 35.4 percent of all hospital stays as of 2015 (Agency for Healthcare Research and Quality 2017). Use of physician services by the aged (Medicare), the poor (Medicaid), and those covered by tax-exempt employer-paid insurance also increased as patients became less concerned about the cost of their care. Historically, advances in medical technology have been another factor stimulating the demand for medical treatment. New methods of diagnosis and treatment were developed; those with previously untreatable diseases gained access to technology that offered the hope of recovery. New medical devices (e.g., imaging equipment) were introduced, and new treatments (e.g., organ transplantations) became available. New diseases (e.g., AIDS) also increased demand on the medical system. Reduced out-of-pocket costs and increased third-party payments (both public and private)—in addition to an aging population, new technologies, and new diseases—drove up prices and the quantity of medical services provided.

Providers (hospitals and physicians) responded to the increased demand for care, but the way they responded unnecessarily increased the cost of providing medical services. After Medicare was enacted, hospitals had few incentives to be efficient because Medicare reimbursed hospitals their costs plus 2 percent for serving Medicare patients. Hospitals, predominantly not-for-profit, consequently expanded their capacity, invested in the latest technology, and duplicated facilities and services offered by nearby hospitals. Hospital prices rose faster than the prices of any other medical service.

Similarly, physicians had little cause for concern over hospital costs. Physicians, who were paid on a fee-for-service basis, wanted their hospitals to have the latest equipment so they would not have to refer patients elsewhere (and possibly lose them). They would hospitalize patients for diagnostic workups and keep them in the hospital longer than necessary because it was less costly for patients covered by hospital insurance, and physicians would be sure to receive reimbursement. Outpatient services, which were less costly than hospital care, initially were not covered by third-party payers.

In addition to the lack of incentives for patients to be concerned with the cost of their care and the similar lack of incentives for providers to supply that care efficiently, the federal government imposed restrictions on the delivery of services that increased enrollees' medical costs. Under Medicare and Medicaid, the government ruled that insurers must give enrollees free choice of provider. Insurers such as health maintenance organizations (HMOs) that precluded enrollees from choosing any physician in the community were violating the free choice of provider rule and, thus, were ineligible to receive capitation payments from the government. Instead, HMOs were paid fee-for-service, reducing their incentive to reduce the total costs of treating a patient. Numerous state restrictions on HMOs, such as prohibiting them from advertising, requiring HMOs to be not-for-profit (thereby limiting their access to capital), and requiring HMOs to be controlled by physicians, further inhibited their development. By imposing these restrictions on alternative delivery systems, however, the government reduced competition for Medicare and Medicaid patients, forgoing an opportunity to reduce government payments for Medicare and Medicaid services.

The effects of higher demand, limited patient and provider incentives to search for lower-cost approaches, and restrictions on the delivery of medical services were escalating prices, increasing use of services, and resulting in greater medical expenditures.

Government Response to Rising Costs

As expenditures under Medicare and Medicaid increased, the federal government faced limited options: (1) raise the Medicare payroll tax and income taxes on the working population to continue funding these programs; (2) require the aged to pay higher premiums for Medicare, and increase their deductibles and copayments; or (3) reduce payments to hospitals and physicians. Each of these approaches would cost successive administrations and Congress political support from some constituents, such as employees, the aged, and healthcare providers. The least politically costly options appeared to be number 1 (increase taxes on employees) and number 3 (reduce payments to hospitals and physicians). The aged have the highest voting participation rate of any age group, as well as the political support of their children, who are relieved of the financial responsibility to pay their parents' medical expenses.

Federal and state governments used additional regulatory approaches to control these rapidly rising expenditures. Medicare utilization review programs were instituted, and controls were placed on hospital investments in new facilities and equipment. These government controls proved ineffective as hospital expenditures continued to escalate through the 1970s. The federal government then limited physician fee increases under Medicare and Medicaid; as a consequence, many physicians refused to participate in these programs, reducing access to care for the aged and the poor. As a result of providers' refusal to participate in Medicare, many Medicare patients had to pay higher out-of-pocket fees to be seen by physicians.

In 1979, President Carter's highest domestic priority was to enact limits on Medicare hospital cost increases; a Congress controlled by his own political party defeated him.

The 1980s

By the beginning of the 1980s, political consensus was lacking on what should be done to control Medicare hospital and physician expenditures, and private health expenditures also continued to rise. By the mid-1980s, however, legislative changes and other events imposed heavy cost-containment pressures on Medicare, Medicaid, and the private sector.

Legislative and Government Changes

President Nixon wanted a health program that would not increase federal expenditures. The result was the Health Maintenance Organization Act of 1973, which legitimized HMOs and removed restrictive state laws impeding the development of federally approved HMOs. However, many HMOs decided not to seek federal qualification because imposed restrictions, such as having to offer more costly benefits, would have caused their premiums to be too high to be competitive with traditional health insurers' premiums. These restrictions were removed by the late 1970s, and the growth of HMOs began in the early 1980s.

To achieve savings in Medicaid, the Reagan Administration removed the free-choice-of-provider rule in 1981, enabling states to enroll their Medicaid populations in closed provider panels. As a result, states were permitted to negotiate capitation payments with HMOs for care of Medicaid patients. The free choice rule continued for the aged; however, in the mid-1980s, Medicare patients were permitted to voluntarily join HMOs. The federal government agreed to pay HMOs a capitated amount for enrolling Medicare patients, but less than 10 percent of the aged voluntarily participated. (As of 2016, 34 percent of the 48 million aged were enrolled in Medicare HMOs, referred to as Medicare Advantage plans [Centers for Medicare & Medicaid Services 2017a].[2])

Federal subsidies were provided to medical schools in 1964 to increase the number of students they could accommodate, and the supply of physicians expanded. The number of active physicians grew from 146 per 100,000 civilian population in 1965 to 195 per 100,000 in 1980; it reached 233 per 100,000 by 1990 and 321 per 100,000 in 2013 (American Medical Association 1991, 2015). The greater supply created excess capacity among physicians, dampened their fee hikes, and made attracting physicians—and therefore expanding—easier for HMOs.

A new Medicare hospital payment system was phased in during 1983. Under the new system, hospitals were no longer to be paid according to their costs. Fixed prices were established for each diagnostic admission (referred to as diagnosis-related groups [DRGs]), and each year Congress set an annual limit on the amount by which these fixed prices per admission could increase. DRG prices changed hospitals' incentives. Because hospitals could keep the difference if the costs they incurred from an admission were less than the fixed DRG payment they received for that admission, they were motivated to reduce the cost of caring for Medicare patients and to discharge them earlier. Length of stay per admission fell, and occupancy rates declined. Hospitals also became concerned about inefficient physician practice behaviors that increased the hospitals' costs of care.

In addition, in 1992 the federal government changed its method of paying physicians under Medicare. A national fee schedule (referred to as resource-based relative value system [RBRVS]) was implemented, and volume expenditure limits were established to cap the total rate of increase in physician Medicare payments. The RBRVS also prohibited physicians from charging their higher-income patients a higher fee and accepting the Medicare fee only for lower-income patients; they had to accept the fee for all or none of their Medicare patients. Medicare patients represent such a significant portion of a physician's practice that few physicians decided not to participate; consequently, they accepted Medicare fees for all patients.

To contain increases in Medicare expenditures during this period, the federal government imposed price controls and expenditure limits on hospital and physician payments for services provided to Medicare patients.

Private Sector Changes

In addition to the government policy changes of the early 1980s, important events were occurring in the private sector. The new decade started with a recession. To survive the recession and remain competitive internationally, the business sector looked to reduce labor costs. Because employer-paid health insurance was the fastest-growing labor expense, businesses pressured health insurers to better control the use and cost of medical services. Competitive pressures forced insurers to increase the efficiency of their benefit packages by including lower-cost substitutes for inpatient care, such as outpatient surgery. They raised deductibles and copayments, intensifying patients' price sensitivity. Patients had to receive prior authorization from their insurer before being admitted to a hospital, and insurers reviewed patients' length of stay while patients were in the hospital. These actions greatly reduced hospital admission rates and lengths of stay. In 1975, the number of admissions in community hospitals was 155 per 1,000 population. By 1990, it had fallen to 125 per 1,000 and continued to decline thereafter, dropping to 104 per 1,000 in 2015. The number of inpatient days per 1,000 population declined even more dramatically—from 1,302 in 1977 to 982 in 1990 to 565 in 2015 (American Hospital Association 2017).

Because of the implementation of the DRG payment system, the changes to private programs, and a shift to the outpatient sector facilitated by technological change (both anesthetic and surgical techniques), hospital occupancy rates decreased from 76 percent in 1980 to 63.5 percent in 2015 (American Hospital Association 2017).

Antitrust Laws

The preconditions for price competition were in place: Hospitals and physicians had excess capacity, and employers wanted to pay less for employee health insurance. The last necessary condition for price competition occurred in 1982, when the US Supreme Court upheld the applicability of antitrust laws to the medical sector. Successful antitrust cases were brought against the American Medical Association for its restrictions on advertising; against a medical society that threatened to boycott an insurer over physician fee increases; against a dental organization that boycotted an insurer's cost-containment program; against medical staffs that denied hospital privileges to physicians because they belonged to an HMO; and against hospitals whose mergers threatened to reduce price competition in their communities.

The applicability of antitrust laws, excess capacity among providers, and employer and insurer interest in lowering medical costs brought about profound changes in the medical marketplace. Traditional insurance plans lost market share as managed care plans, which controlled utilization and limited access to hospitals and physicians, grew. Preferred provider organizations (PPOs) were formed and included only physicians and hospitals willing to discount their prices. Employees and their families were offered price incentives in the form of lower out-of-pocket payments to use these less expensive providers. Large employers and health insurers began to select PPOs on the basis of their prices, use of services, and treatment outcomes.

Consequences of the 1980s Changes

The 1980s disrupted the traditional physician–patient relationship. Insurers and HMOs used utilization review to control patient demand, emphasize outcomes and appropriateness of care, and limit patients' access to higher-priced physicians and hospitals by not including them in their provider networks. They also used case management for catastrophic illnesses, substituted less expensive settings for costlier inpatient care, and influenced patients' choice of drugs through the use of formularies.

The use of cost-containment programs and the shift to outpatient care lowered hospital occupancy rates. The increasing supply of physicians—particularly specialists—created excess capacity. Hospitals in financial trouble closed, and others merged. Hospital consolidation increased. Hospitals' excess capacity was not reduced until years later when the demand for care began to exceed the available supply of hospitals and physicians. Until then, hospitals and physicians continued to be subject to intense competitive pressures.

Employees' incentive to reduce their insurance premiums also stimulated competition among HMOs and insurers. Employers required employees to pay the additional cost of more expensive health plans, so many employees chose the lowest-priced plan. Health insurance companies competed for enrollees primarily by offering lower premiums and provider networks with better reputations.

The 1990s

As managed care spread throughout the United States during the 1990s, the rate of increase in medical expenditures declined (see exhibit 1.3). Hospital use decreased dramatically, and hospitals and physicians agreed to large price discounts to be included in an insurer's provider panel. These cost-containment approaches contributed to the lower annual rate of increase. However, although price competition reduced medical costs, patients were dissatisfied. The public wanted greater access to care, particularly less restriction on referrals to specialists. Public backlash against HMOs emerged. HMOs lost several lawsuits for denying access to experimental treatments, and Congress and the states imposed restrictions on MCOs, such as mandating minimum lengths of hospital stays for normal deliveries. Consequently, cost-containment restrictions weakened, and increases in prices, use of services, and medical expenditures reaccelerated.

The 2000s

The excess capacity that weakened hospitals in their negotiations with insurers dried up during the 2000s. Financially weak hospitals had closed. Because consolidation reduces the number of competitors in an area, the number of hospital mergers—which enhance bargaining power—increased. As hospital prices rose, so did insurance premiums. Previous approaches, such as decreased hospital use and price discounts, could no longer achieve large cost reductions. Instead, insurers tried to develop more innovative, less costly ways of managing patient care.

Newer approaches to cost containment included high-deductible health plans, reliance on evidence-based medicine, and chronic disease management. Insurers' method of shifting a larger share of medical costs to consumers is referred to as *consumer-driven healthcare*. In return for lower health insurance premiums, consumers pay higher deductibles and copayments. Consumers then presumably evaluate the costs and benefits of spending their own funds on healthcare. Another approach to lowering medical costs is to use evidence-based medicine, which relies on scientific evidence and analysis of large data sets to determine the effect of different physician practice patterns on costs and medical outcomes. Other insurers emphasize disease management to provide chronically ill patients, who incur the most medical expenditures, with preventive and continuous care. This approach not only improves the quality of care but reduces costly hospitalizations.

Pay-for-performance programs also have been developed to lower costs and improve care. Insurers pay higher amounts to physicians and other healthcare providers if they provide high-quality care, which is usually defined on the basis of process measures developed by medical experts. Insurers also make report cards available to their enrollees. Report cards are a means of describing hospitals and medical groups in the insurer's provider network according to medical outcomes, preventive services, and patient satisfaction scores to enable enrollees to make informed choices about the providers they use.

In the latter half of the decade, rising premiums and increased unemployment (resulting from the Great Recession) prompted people to drop their health insurance or switch to plans that charged lower premiums, such as high-deductible plans. Many Americans became concerned that premiums would continue increasing, making insurance even less affordable. The recession, a decrease in the number of insured, and the switch to high-deductible health plans slowed rising healthcare expenditures (see exhibit 1.3).

In 2015, Congress again revised Medicare payments to physicians with passage of The Medicare Access and CHIP Reauthorization Act (MACRA). The law's provisions are being phased in and will become fully effective for all physicians by 2019. MACRA is the most substantive change in physician reimbursement since Medicare was enacted. Congress had previously been reluctant to enforce the accumulated sustainable growth rate (SGR) cuts, which would have reduced Medicare payments to physicians. The SGR formula was eliminated with passage of MACRA. The new law attempts to change physician incentives by moving payments away from fee-for-service toward financial accountability for the care they provide. Another objective of MACRA is to move physicians into alternative payment systems that require them to bear financial risk. (MACRA is discussed more completely in chapter 10.)

It is too early to judge how physicians will adjust to the new Medicare payment system, which requires them to submit a great deal of data. This requirement may force many physicians to decide to become employees of hospitals and insurers.

The Affordable Care Act

The most significant health policy event of the current decade was the 2010 enactment and 2014 implementation of the ACA. Although implementation was fraught with website and enrollment problems, the legislation, which did not receive bipartisan support and has proved to be controversial, has led to important changes in the financing and delivery of medical services. Sufficient time has elapsed to examine the extent to which the ACA has achieved its stated objectives. Consequently, it should be judged according to three criteria.

The first criterion is whether it reduced the number of uninsured, presumably the major goal of the legislation. Before the ACA was enacted, about 50 million Americans did not have health insurance. Several approaches were used to decrease the number of uninsured. The ACA expanded Medicaid eligibility from 100 to 138 percent of the FPL. (However, not all states chose to expand their Medicaid eligibility levels.) Federal and state health insurance exchanges were established, primarily for those who purchase insurance in the individual market. In addition, premium tax credits and cost-sharing subsidies were provided on a declining scale to those with incomes between 138 and 400 percent of the FPL. The legislation included an individual mandate that required everyone to buy insurance or pay a penalty. An employer mandate was imposed that required employers to offer health insurance to their employees or pay a penalty of $2,000 per employee. Small employers (those with fewer than 50 full-time employees) were exempted from this mandate and, instead, were offered a tax credit for providing health insurance to their employees.

In 2010, when the ACA was enacted, the Congressional Budget Office estimated that these steps to increase insurance coverage, expand Medicaid, provide health insurance exchange subsidies, include individual and employer mandates, and provide tax credits for small employers would increase the number of insured by 23 million, leaving 21 million Americans uninsured by 2016. By 2016, however, only 16 million people gained insurance, leaving 28 million uninsured (Congressional Budget Office 2017, 9).

The second criterion relates to cost. The Obama administration and Congressional Democrats expected the ACA to increase the demand for health insurance and, consequently, the demand for medical services without raising the costs of care. In fact, the ACA was expected to "bend the cost curve down," "decrease premiums by $2,500 a year for a family of four," and "not add a dime to the deficit." These promises were made by President Obama in promoting the legislation's benefits to the middle class. The Congressional Budget Office initially calculated the projected cost over a ten-year period and estimated that it would be budget neutral for this period. Budget neutrality was to be achieved by increasing ACA taxes for the entire ten-year period but delaying spending for several years (from 2010 to 2014). Whether the ACA succeeds in reducing the rate of increase in medical expenditures, reducing family premiums, and achieving budget neutrality at the end of the decade will determine if it has met this second objective.[3]

The third criterion is whether people who already had insurance were able to keep the coverage they had, as President Obama promised. He stated numerous times, "If you like your healthcare plan, you can keep your healthcare plan" and "if you like your doctor, you can keep your doctor." What made these promises doubtful was that the ACA made numerous changes to the health insurance market, such as mandating "essential" (i.e., more comprehensive) health benefits, requiring a smaller difference in premiums between older and younger individuals on the health insurance exchanges, establishing gender equality in premium ratings, and initiating a new health insurance tax on premiums for those buying insurance on the exchanges. Additional regulations, as well as subsidies, were imposed on health insurers.

Did these and other changes to the health insurance market, particularly to the individual market, affect the ability of those currently insured to keep their health plans?

These criteria for evaluating the ACA are discussed in chapter 38, "The Affordable Care Act: Did It Achieve Its Goals?"

Finally, any evaluation of the ACA should be based on a comparison—not with the previous healthcare system, but with other proposed healthcare reform approaches in achieving the same objectives. Chapter 36 discusses several of these approaches, including the refundable tax credit.

Summary

The forces that increase demand and the costs of providing care have not changed. The population is aging (the first of the baby boomers retired in 2011), technological advances enable early diagnosis, and new treatment methods are emerging—all of which stimulate increased demand for medical services. Of these three developments, new technology is believed to be the most important force behind rising expenditures. For example, expensive new prescription drugs that extend life and alleviate pain have been brought to market. In addition, the number of people receiving organ transplants, the introduction of new equipment, and the use of imaging tests have grown dramatically. The cost of providing medical services is also rising as more highly trained medical personnel are needed to handle advanced technology and as wage rates increase to attract more nurses and technicians to the medical sector.

The ACA has further increased demand for medical care. More people have become eligible for Medicaid, and many previously uninsured individuals buying insurance on the exchanges receive government subsidies. Everyone is required to have insurance under the legislation's individual mandate (in 2019, the penalty for this mandate ends as a result of legislation passed in December 2017), and under the employer mandate, most employers are required to provide insurance for employees or pay a fine. However, the ACA provides no additional patient or provider incentives to encourage them to be more efficient in use of medical services.

The developing shortage of physicians is a growing concern. The demand for physician services is increasing faster than the supply of physicians, and access to care, as indicated by increased waiting times for a physician appointment, has declined. As the costs of financing expansions of Medicaid eligibility and new exchange subsidies increase, the already large federal deficit is likely to grow even faster. The federal government is under great pressure to reduce the rising deficit and the burden of increasing premiums faced by the middle class. Will the government rely more on regulatory (provider price controls) or competitive approaches to reduce medical expenditures and premium increases?

Innovative approaches to reducing healthcare costs are more likely to be adopted in a system that has price incentives to do so (i.e., enrollees have a financial incentive to choose less costly health plans, and health insurers compete for enrollees on the basis of premiums, access to care, and quality) than in a regulated system. Any regulatory approach that arbitrarily seeks to reduce the rate of increase in medical expenditures will result in reduced access to both medical care and new technology.

The United States spends more on healthcare than any other country; nevertheless, a scarcity of funds exists to provide for all of our medical needs and population groups, such as the uninsured and those on Medicaid. Therefore, choices must be made.

The first choice is to determine how much we, as a society, should spend on medical care. What approach should we use to make this choice? Should individuals decide how much they want to spend on healthcare, or should the government decide the percentage of GDP that goes toward healthcare? Our second choice is to identify the best way to provide medical services. Would competition among health plans or government regulation and price controls bring about greater efficiency? The third choice is to determine how rapidly medical innovation should be introduced. Should regulatory agencies evaluate each medical advance and decide whether its benefits exceed its costs, or should the evaluation of those benefits and costs be left to the separate health plans competing for enrollees? Our fourth choice is to specify how much should be spent on those who are medically indigent and how their care should be provided. Should the medically indigent be enrolled in a separate medical system (e.g., Medicaid), or should they receive subsidized tax credits to enroll in competing health plans?

These choices can be better understood when we are more aware of the consequences of each approach (such as which groups benefit, and which groups bear the costs). Economics clarifies the implications of different approaches to these decisions.

Discussion Questions

1. What are some of the reasons for the increased demand for medical services since 1965?
2. Why has employer-paid health insurance been an important stimulant of demand for health insurance?
3. How did hospital payment methods in the 1960s and 1970s affect hospitals' investment policies and incentives to improve efficiency?
4. Why were HMOs and managed care not more prevalent in the 1960s and 1970s?
5. What choices does the federal government have to reduce greater-than-projected Medicare expenditures?
6. What events during the 1980s in both the public and private sectors made the delivery of medical services price competitive?
7. What three criteria have been proposed to evaluate the success of the ACA?

Notes

1. GDP represents the total value of all goods and services produced in a given year. GDP is also equal to the total income received by the resources—employees, management, and capital—that produced those goods and services.

2. Medicare does not place a limit on a Medicare patient's total out-of-pocket expenses. Consequently, the out-of-pocket medical payments for low-income aged have forced many people to rely on Medicaid. Medicare Advantage plans provide enrollees with additional benefits and a limit on out-of-pocket expenses (Medicare2017.org 2017).

3. As shown in exhibit 1.3, the slowdown in medical expenditures started before the ACA was enacted and was the result of many factors; it should not be attributed solely to the legislation. Proponents of the ACA claim that part of the slowdown in medical expenditure increases was a result of the legislation. However, Chandra, Holmes, and Skinner (2013) reported that the decline started several years before enactment of the ACA (as shown in exhibit 1.3), and that most of the ACA's cost-control measures did not begin until several years after its 2010 passage. In addition, Ryu and colleagues (2013) discuss the reasons for the decline in medical expenditure increases. More recently, Dranove, Garthwaite, and Ody (2016) concluded that economic conditions, not the ACA, accounted for most of the reduction in healthcare spending during the 2009–2011 period.

References

Agency for Healthcare Research and Quality. 2017. "HCUP Fast Stats—Trends in Inpatient Stays." Healthcare Cost and Utilization Project. Updated November. www.hcup-us.ahrq.gov/faststats/NationalTrendsServlet.

American Hospital Association. 2017. *Hospital Statistics, 2017 Edition.* Chicago: American Hospital Association.

American Medical Association. 2015. *Physician Characteristics and Distribution in the United States, 2015 Edition.* Chicago: American Medical Association.

———. 1991. *Physician Characteristics and Distribution in the United States, 1991 Edition.* Chicago: American Medical Association.

Centers for Medicare & Medicaid Services. 2017a. "Medicare Enrollment Dashboard." Accessed August 23. www.cms.gov/Research-Statistics-Data-and-Systems/Statistics-Trends-and-Reports/CMSProgramStatistics/Dashboard.html.

———. 2017b. "National Health Expenditure Data, Historical." Modified January.https://www.cms.gov/Research-Statistics-Data-and-Systems/Statistics-

Trends-and-Reports/NationalHealthExpendData/NationalHealthAccounts Historical.html.

———. 2017c. "National Health Expenditure Data, Projected." Modified January. www.cms.gov/Research-Statistics-Data-and-Systems/Statistics-Trends-and-Reports/NationalHealthExpendData/NationalHealthAccountsProjected.html.

Chandra, A., J. Holmes, and J. Skinner. 2013. "Is This Time Different? The Slowdown in Healthcare Spending." National Bureau of Economic Research Working Paper No. 19700. Published December. http://papers.nber.org/papers/W19700.

Congressional Budget Office (CBO). 2017. *CBO's Record of Projecting Subsidies for Health Insurance Under the Affordable Care Act: 2014 to 2016.* Published December. www.cbo.gov/system/files/115th-congress-2017-2018/reports/53094-acaprojections.pdf.

Dranove, D., C. Garthwaite, and C. Ody. 2016. "Why Healthcare Spending Has Slowed." *Kellogg Insight.* Published February 1. https://insight.kellogg.north western.edu/article/why-healthcare-spending-has-slowed.

Fuchs, V. R. 2013. "The Gross Domestic Product and Health Care Spending." *New England Journal of Medicine* 369 (2): 107–9.

Medicare2017.org. 2017. "Close the Medicare Coverage Gap." Accessed December 11. www.medicare2017.org.

Ryu, A., T. Gibson, M. McKellar, and M. Chernew. 2013. "The Slowdown in Health Care Spending in 2009–11 Reflected Factors Other Than the Weak Economy and Thus May Persist." *Health Affairs* 32 (5): 835–40.

HOW MUCH SHOULD WE SPEND ON MEDICAL CARE?

The United States spends more on medical care than any other country—17.9 percent of its gross domestic product in 2016—and this percentage is expected to continue to grow. Can we afford to spend this much of our resources on medical care? Why do we view the growth of expenditures in other areas (e.g., the automotive industry) more favorably than the growth of expenditures in healthcare? Increased medical expenditures create new healthcare jobs, do not pollute the air, save rather than destroy lives, and alleviate pain and suffering. Why shouldn't society be pleased that more resources are flowing into a sector that cares for the aged, the poor, and the sick? Medical care would seem to be a more appropriate use of a society's resources than cars, electronics, or other consumer products, yet increased expenditures on these goods do not prompt the concern that growth in healthcare spending causes.

Are we concerned about rising medical costs because we believe we are not receiving value for our money—that more medical services and technologies are not worth the cost when compared with other potential uses of those resources? Or is there a fundamental difference of opinion among members of society regarding the rate at which medical expenditures should increase?

To answer these questions, we must define what we consider an appropriate expenditure; only then can we evaluate whether we are spending too much on medical care. If we determine that we are spending too much, how must public policy change to achieve the right expenditure level?

Consumer Sovereignty

The appropriate amount of health expenditure is based on a set of values and the concept of economic efficiency. Resources are limited, so they should be used for what consumers believe to deliver the most value. Consumers decide how much to purchase on the basis of their perceptions of the value they expect to receive and the price they have to pay, knowing that buying one good or service means forgoing other goods and services. Consumers differ greatly in the value they place on medical care and what they are willing to forgo to receive that care. In a competitive market, consumers receive the full benefits of their purchases and, in turn, pay the full costs of those benefits. If the benefits received from the last unit used (e.g., the last visit to a physician) equal the cost of that unit, the quantity consumed is said to be optimal. If more or fewer services are consumed, the benefits received are said to be greater or less than the cost of that service.

Consumer sovereignty is most easily achieved in a competitive market system. Through their purchases, consumers communicate their desires regarding goods and services. In response, producers use their resources to produce the goods and services consumers desire. If producers are to survive and profit in competitive markets, they must use their resources efficiently and produce the goods and services for which consumers are willing to pay; otherwise, they will be replaced by producers that are more efficient and in tune with what consumers want.

Some people believe that consumer sovereignty should not determine how much we as a society spend on medical care. Patients lack information and have limited ability to judge their medical treatment needs. Other concerns are the quality of care patients receive and the quantity of care that is appropriate.

Consumer sovereignty may be imperfect, but the alternatives are equally imperfect. If medical care were free to all and physicians (paid on a fee-for-service basis or salaried) decided the quantity of medical care to provide, the result would be "too much" care. Physicians are likely to prescribe services as long as they perceive them to be even slightly beneficial to their patients because the physicians are not responsible for the cost of that care.

The inevitable consequence of a free medical system is a government-imposed expenditure limit to halt the provision of too much care. Although physicians still would be responsible for determining who receives services and for which diagnoses, "too little" care likely would be provided, as is sometimes the case in government-controlled health systems such as those in Canada and Great Britain. Medical care would be rationed, and waiting times and age would become criteria for allocating resources.

No government that funds healthcare spends sufficient resources to provide all the care demanded at the going price. Like individuals, governments make trade-offs between the benefits received from additional health expenditures and the cost of those expenditures. However, the benefits and costs to the government are different from those consumers consider in their decision-making processes. To the government, *benefit* means the political support it gains by increasing health expenditures, and *cost* means the political support it loses when it raises taxes or shifts resources from politically popular programs to fund additional medical services.

Let us, therefore, assume that consumer sovereignty will continue to guide the amount we spend on medical care. Having consumer sovereignty as a guide, however, does not mean that the United States is spending the right amount on medical services. This judgment is influenced by another factor: economic efficiency.

Economic Efficiency

Efficiency in the Provision of Medical Services

If medical services were produced in an inefficient manner, medical expenditures would be excessive. For example, rather than treating a patient for ten days in the hospital, a physician might be able to achieve the same outcome and same level of patient satisfaction by treating the patient in the hospital over fewer days, sending the patient home, and having a visiting nurse complete the treatment. Similarly, it might be possible to treat the patient in an outpatient setting rather than in the hospital. Physicians' practice patterns vary greatly across the country, causing medical expenditures to vary widely with no apparent difference in outcomes. Unless providers have appropriate incentives to be efficient, economic efficiency in providing medical services is unlikely to be achieved.

When hospitals were paid on a cost-plus basis, they had an incentive to raise their costs. Subsequent events changed those incentives, and since the early 1980s both the federal government and the private sector have been pressing for greater efficiency of the delivery system. Cost-based payment to hospitals under Medicare gave way to fixed payment based on diagnosis-related groups. Price competition has escalated not just among hospitals and physicians but also among insurance companies, which must compete on the basis of premiums in the sale of group health insurance. Preferred provider organizations, health maintenance organizations, and managed care systems have expanded their market share at the expense of traditional insurers. Hospitalization rates have declined as utilization review mechanisms have increased, and the trend toward implementing case management for catastrophic illness and monitoring providers for appropriateness of care and medical outcomes has grown.

Few would contend that the provision of medical services is as efficient as it could be. Waste exists in the healthcare system, and it is difficult to define (Brook 2011; Lallemand 2012). Is waste any medical intervention that provides no medical benefit, or is it a medical intervention in which the potential for a negative outcome exceeds the potential for the patient to benefit? (Fuchs 2009). Economic waste occurs when the expected benefits of an intervention are less than the expected costs. Remember that waste is also a provider's income.

The current movement by managed care plans, Medicare Advantage, and accountable care organizations (ACOs) away from fee-for-service and toward episode-based payment and capitation is changing provider incentives. Providers now have a financial incentive to focus on coordination of care and management of chronic diseases, resulting in less use of costly inpatient settings, greater use of physician extenders, and better outcomes at a lower cost. It will take a number of years, however, for these new payment schemes and outcomes to become widespread throughout the medical care system. Despite the difficulty in defining and reducing waste, the emphasis on cost containment and the growth of managed care are efforts to decrease inefficient use and delivery of medical services.

Inefficiency, although important, is not the main cause for concern about the rise of medical expenditures.

Efficiency in Use of Medical Services

Inefficiencies in the use of medical services result when individuals do not have to pay the full cost of their choices; they consume too much medical care because their use of services is based on their out-of-pocket price, and that price is less than the cost of providing the service. Consequently, the cost of providing the service exceeds the benefit the patient receives from consuming additional units of the service. The resources devoted to providing these additional services could be better used for other services, such as education, that would provide greater benefits.

The effect of paying less than the full price of a service is easy to understand when the concept is applied to some other consumer product, such as automobiles. If the price of automobiles were greatly lowered for consumers, they would purchase more automobiles (and more expensive ones). To produce these additional automobiles, manufacturers would use resources that could have been used to produce other goods. Similarly, if the price for services is decreased, people will use more services. Studies have shown that patients who pay less out of pocket have more hospital admissions, visit physicians more often, and use more outpatient services than patients who pay higher prices (Feldstein 2011). This relationship between price and use of services also holds for patients classified by health status.

Inefficient use is an important concept in healthcare because the price of medical services has been artificially lowered for many consumers. The government subsidizes medical care for the poor and the aged under Medicaid and Medicare. Those eligible for these programs use more services than they would have if they had to pay full price. Although the purpose of these programs is to increase the use of medical services by the poor and the aged, the artificially low prices also promote inefficient use—for example, when a patient uses the more expensive emergency department rather than a physician's office in a nonemergent situation.

A greater concern is that the working population contributes to use inefficiency. An employer-purchased health plan is not considered taxable income for employees. If an employer gave the same amount of funds to an employee in the form of higher wages, the employee would have to pay federal and state income taxes as well as Social Security tax on the additional income. Because employer-purchased health insurance is not subject to these taxes, in effect the government subsidizes the purchase of health insurance and, when the employee uses that insurance, the purchase of medical services. Employees do not pay the full cost of health insurance; it is bought with before-tax dollars, as opposed to almost all other purchases, which are made with after-tax dollars.

The greatest beneficiaries of this tax subsidy are employees in higher income tax brackets. As discussed in chapter 1, rather than receive additional income as cash, which is then subject to high taxes (in the 1970s, the highest federal income tax bracket was 70 percent), these employees choose to receive more of their additional wages in the form of more health insurance coverage. Instead of spending after-tax dollars on vision and dental services, they can purchase these services more cheaply with before-tax dollars. The price of insurance is reduced by employees' tax bracket; as a result, they purchase more coverage than they otherwise would have, and the additional coverage is worth less to employees than its full cost.

With the purchase of additional coverage, the out-of-pocket price paid for medical services declined, prompting the increased use of all medical services covered by health insurance. As employees and their families became less concerned about the real cost of medical services, few constraints limited the growth in medical expenditures. Had the inefficient use of medical services (resulting from the tax subsidy for the purchase of health insurance) been less prevalent, medical expenditures would have risen more slowly.

Inefficiencies in the provision and use of medical services are legitimate reasons for concern about the amount spent on medical care. Public policy should attempt to eliminate these government-caused inefficiencies. However, other, less valid reasons for concern exist.

Government and Employer Concerns over Rising Medical Expenditures

As payers of medical expenditures, federal and state governments and employers are concerned about growing medical costs. State governments pay half the costs of caring for the medically indigent in their state, while the federal government pays the remaining half. Medicaid expenditures have gone up more rapidly than any other state expenditure and, to avoid raising taxes, caused states to reduce funding for other politically popular programs. At the federal level, the government is also responsible for Medicare (acute medical services for the aged). The hospital portion of Medicare (Part A) is financed by a specific payroll tax that has been raised numerous times, and the physician and prescription drug portions (Parts B and D) are financed with general income taxes. Medicare expenditures have also risen rapidly.

As a result of the Affordable Care Act (ACA), government subsidies have greatly increased to pay for expanded Medicaid eligibility and for those whose income is between 138 and 400 percent of the federal poverty level and who buy health insurance on healthcare exchanges.

As shown in exhibit 2.1, federal health spending as a proportion of total federal spending is skyrocketing—from 12 percent in 1985 to 20 percent in 1995 to 30.9 percent in 2015 and to a projected 30.9 percent in 2021. The oldest of the baby boomers began retiring in 2011 and became eligible for Medicare, which will dramatically boost Medicare expenditures over the coming years. Unless the federal government can reform Medicare and reduce its growth rate, the Medicare payroll tax on the working population will be sharply raised to prevent the Medicare trust fund from going bankrupt. Funding Part B, Part D, and the subsidies under the ACA will require raising income taxes, adding to an already large federal deficit, or reducing funding for other federal programs.

Thus, even if inefficiencies did not exist in the provision or use of medical services, large increases in Medicare and Medicaid enrollments and expenses—together with the additional costs to finance the ACA subsidies—will lead to federal expenditures that exceed the government's ability to pay for them. The consumer products comparison presented earlier can be applied here: If the government purchased 50 percent of all automobiles, it would become concerned with the price and use of automobiles and the associated expenditures. The pressure to continue funding Medicaid, Medicare, and the new healthcare entitlements through higher taxes or greater budget deficits is driving the federal government to seek ways to limit medical spending increases.

Similarly, unions and employers are concerned with the rise in employee medical expenditures for reasons other than the inefficiencies in the provision or use of services. The business sector's spending on health insurance premiums

		1965	1975	1985	1995	2005	2015	2021[a]
EXHIBIT 2.1 Federal Spending on Health, Fiscal Years 1965–2021 (in Billions of Dollars)	Total federal spending	118.2	332.3	946.3	1,515.7	2,472.0	3,688.3	5,124.2
	Federal health spending	3.1	29.5	117.1	307.1	614.0	1,138.4	1,584.8
	Medicare	n/a	12.9	65.8	159.9	298.7	546.2	856.1
	Medicaid	0.3	6.8	22.7	89.1	181.7	349.8	474.4
	Veterans Administration	1.3	3.7	9.5	16.4	28.8	61.9	72.4
	Other	1.5	6.1	19.1	41.7	105.0	180.5	287.0
	Federal health spending as a percentage of total federal spending	2.6%	8.9%	12.4%	20.3%	24.8%	30.9%	30.9%

[a]Projected data.

Note: n/a = not applicable.

Source: Data from Office of Management and Budget (2017, tables 1.1 and 15.1).

has increased over time, both as a percentage of total employee compensation and as a percentage of business profits. Health insurance, when offered, is part of an employee's total compensation. Employers are interested only in the total cost (income) of an employee, not in the form of the income (i.e., wages or health benefits). Thus, the employee bears the cost of rising health insurance premiums because higher premiums mean lower cash wages. Large unions, whose members receive generous health benefits, want to slow the rate of growth of medical expenditures because they have seen more of their compensation gains spent on health insurance than paid out as wages.

Large employers were seriously affected by the Financial Accounting Standards Board ruling (Employee Benefit Research Institute 1992). Starting in 1993, employers that promised medical benefits to their retirees were required to list these unfunded liabilities on their balance sheets. Employers previously paid their retirees' medical expenses only as they occurred and did not set aside funds (as is done with pensions). By having to acknowledge these liabilities on their balance sheets, many large corporations, such as automobile companies, have seen their net worth decline by billions of dollars. Furthermore, because these companies have to expense a portion of these future liabilities each year (not only for their present retirees but also for future retirees), they have to report lower earnings per share. If employers were to reduce the rate of increase in their employees' medical expenditures, the net worth of companies with large unfunded retiree liabilities would rise, as would their earnings per share.

These differing reasons for concern over rising medical expenditures are important to recognize. Which concern should drive public policy—the government's desire not to raise revenues to fund its share of medical services, unions' and employers' interest in lowering employee and retiree medical expenses, or society's desire to achieve the appropriate rate of increase in medical expenditures? The interests of government, unions, and large employers have little to do with achieving an appropriate rate of growth. Instead, their particular political and economic burdens drive their proposals for limiting increases in medical expenditures.

Approaches to Limiting Increases in Medical Expenditures

The United States should strive to reduce inefficiencies in both the provision and use of medical services. Inefficiencies in provision, however, are decreasing as managed care plans are forced to compete for enrollees on the basis of price. The large variations in physicians' treatment patterns should decrease as more information on outcomes becomes available through the analysis of large insurer data sets. Vigilant application of antitrust laws is needed to ensure that healthcare markets remain competitive and that providers, such as hospitals and ACOs, do not monopolize their markets. Inefficiencies in use are also declining as managed care plans control use of services through utilization management and patient cost sharing. As these inefficiencies are reduced, the growth rate of medical expenditures will approximate the "correct" rate of increase.

Naturally, the public would like to pay lower insurance premiums and out-of-pocket costs and still have unlimited access to healthcare and the latest medical technology. As in other sectors of the economy, however, choices must be made.

Medical expenditures have consistently grown faster than inflation, sometimes several times faster and sometimes by just several percentage points. Exhibit 2.2 shows the annual percentage change in national health expenditures and the consumer price index since 1965. During the mid-1990s, expenditures moderated as managed care enrollment rose. By the late 1990s, however, they

EXHIBIT 2.2

Annual Percentage Changes in National Health Expenditures and the Consumer Price Index, 1965–2016

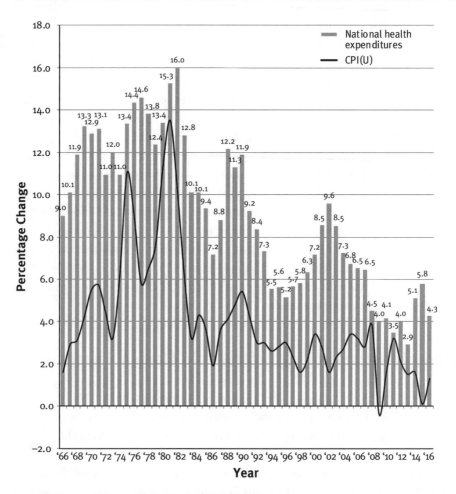

Note: CPI(U) = consumer price index for all urban consumers.

Sources: Data from Bureau of Labor Statistics (2017); Centers for Medicare & Medicaid Services (2017).

increased more rapidly as a result of the backlash against managed care and the consequent relaxation of managed care's cost-containment methods. In the past decade, expenditures have moderated as the economy experienced problems (e.g., the Great Recession) and unemployment and the number of uninsured surged. In the foreseeable future, medical expenditures are expected to continue rising faster than inflation and will be driven by higher incomes, medical advances, federal health reform subsidies, and a greater number of elderly people.

Some politicians believe they will receive the public's political support by proposing additional discounts on drug prices for the aged, managed care regulations that give enrollees freer access to specialists and other healthcare providers, and arbitrary limits on the amount by which medical expenditures and premiums can increase. What would be the consequences of limiting expenditure and premium increases to a rate lower than what would otherwise occur in an aging population and a technologically advanced healthcare system?

The United States is undergoing important demographic changes. The population is aging and will require more medical services, both to relieve suffering and to cure illnesses. Furthermore, the most important reason for the rapid rise in medical expenditures has been the tremendous advances in medical science. Previously incurable diseases can now be cured, and other illnesses can be diagnosed and treated at an earlier stage. Although cures remain elusive for some diseases (e.g., AIDS and various cancers), life for those with these diseases can be prolonged with expensive drugs. Limiting the growth of medical expenditures to an arbitrarily low rate will decrease investment in new medical technologies and restrict the availability of medical services.

Proposed cost-containment methods can reduce the rate of increase. Insurers and payers could impose higher out-of-pocket payments; managed care organizations could require physicians to follow evidence-based medicine guidelines and disease management protocols; or plans could restrict enrollees to using only participating primary care providers, specialists, and hospitals.

The middle class, however, appears unwilling to make these trade-offs; it wants both lower expenditures and unlimited access. (Politicians are responding to these concerns by indicating their willingness to regulate broader access to providers and services, but without acknowledging the higher premiums that would result.) Significantly lowering the rate of increase and funding universal access, however, will require more than implementing these cost-containment measures. To achieve these ends, services and technology will have to be made less available to many people (Fuchs 1993).

Some politicians have led the public to believe these trade-offs are not necessary; they claim that by eliminating waste in the healthcare system, universal coverage can be achieved and everyone can have all the medical care they need at a lower cost. Such rhetoric merely postpones the time when the public realizes it must make the unpleasant choice between spending and access.

Summary

Who should decide how much is to be spent on medical care? All countries face this basic question, and they have made different choices. In some countries, the government determines the allocation of resources among the medical sectors and controls medical prices. When the government makes these decisions, the trade-offs between cost and access are likely to be different from those that consumers would make.

In the United States, consumer sovereignty has been the guiding principle in allocating resources; consumers (except those enrolled in Medicare and Medicaid) determine the amount of their income to be spent on medical services. Yet, consumers have not always received value for their money. Inefficiencies in the medical sector, inappropriate provider incentives, and certain government regulations have made medical services more costly. Furthermore, subsidies for the purchase of health insurance (tax-exempt, employer-paid health insurance) have resulted in greater use of services. Thus, the debate over the appropriate amount to be spent on medical services is likely to be clarified only when these two issues—consumer sovereignty and efficiency of the current system—are separated.

Discussion Questions

1. How does a competitive market determine the types of goods and services to produce, the costs to produce those goods and services, and who receives them?
2. Why do economists believe the value of additional employer-paid health insurance is worth less than its full cost?
3. Why do rising medical expenditures cause concern?
4. Why do inefficiencies exist in the provision and use of medical services?
5. Why are unions and the government concerned about rising medical expenditures?

References

Brook, R. H. 2011. "The Role of Physicians in Controlling Medical Care Costs and Reducing Waste." *Journal of the American Medical Association* 306 (6): 650–51.

Bureau of Labor Statistics. 2017. "Databases, Tables, and Calculators, by Subject." Accessed August. http://data.bls.gov.

Centers for Medicare & Medicaid Services. 2017. "National Health Expenditure Data, Historical." Accessed December. www.cms.gov/Research-Statistics-Data-and-Systems/Statistics-Trends-and-Reports/NationalHealthExpendData/NationalHealthAccountsHistorical.html.

Employee Benefit Research Institute. 1992. "An EBRI Special Report." EBRI Issue Brief 124. Published March. www.ebri.org/pdf/briefspdf/0392ib.pdf.

Feldstein, P. J. 2011. "The Demand for Medical Care." In *Health Care Economics*, 7th ed., 114–38. Albany, NY: Delmar.

Fuchs, V. R. 2009. "Eliminating Waste in Health Care." *Journal of the American Medical Association* 302 (22): 2481–82.

———. 1993. "No Pain, No Gain—Perspectives on Cost Containment." *Journal of the American Medical Association* 269 (5): 631–33.

Lallemand, N. C. 2012. "Reducing Waste in Health Care." *Health Affairs* health policy brief. Published December 13. www.healthaffairs.org/healthpolicybriefs/brief.php?brief_id=82.

Office of Management and Budget. 2017. *Fiscal Year 2017 Historical Tables: Budget of the U.S. Government.* Accessed August. www.govinfo.gov/content/pkg/BUDGET-2017-TAB/pdf/BUDGET-2017-TAB.pdf.

DO MORE MEDICAL EXPENDITURES PRODUCE BETTER HEALTH?

Themes United States spends more per capita on medical services than other countries, yet our health status is not proportionately better. In fact, many countries that have lower per capita medical expenditures also have lower infant mortality rates and higher life expectancies. Is our medical system less efficient at producing good health than these other countries, or are medical expenditures less important than other factors affecting health status?

Medical Services Versus Health

Medical services are often mistakenly considered synonymous with health. When policymakers talk of "healthcare" reform, they mean reform of the financing and delivery of medical services. Medical services consist of not only the diagnosis and treatment of illness, which can lead to improved health, but also the amelioration of pain and discomfort, reassurance of healthy but worried people, and heroic treatments for the terminally ill. One indication that the primary objective of government's medical spending is to treat illness—and not, more broadly, to improve the nation's health status—is that 22.5 percent of all medical expenditures ($721 billion in 2015) are spent on just 1 percent of the population.[1] Furthermore, 37.2 percent of those in that top 1 percent are older than age 65. Increased medical expenditures, therefore, may have relatively little effect on a nation's health status.

Generally, the United States is acknowledged to have a technically superior medical system for treating acute illness. (For a brief but excellent discussion of criteria used to evaluate a country's health system, see Fuchs [1992].) All financing and payment incentives have been directed toward this goal, and physician training has emphasized treatment rather than prevention of illness. Public policy debates regarding medical services have been concerned with two issues: (1) equity—namely, whether everyone has access to medical services and how those services should be financed, and (2) efficiency—namely, whether medical services are produced efficiently. Knowing how to provide a medical treatment efficiently, however, is not the same as knowing how to produce health efficiently.

In contrast to policy regarding medical services, health policy has been less well defined. The goal of health policy presumably should be to improve the population's health status or increase its life expectancy; consequently, we should be concerned with the most efficient ways to improve that status. Assuming policymakers recognize this goal, they should understand that devoting more resources to medical care is just one way to improve health and is unlikely to be the most efficient way to do so.

The more accurate the definition of health, the more difficult it is to measure. Health is a state of physical, mental, and social well-being. More simply, it is the absence of disease or injury. Empirically, it is defined by negative measures, such as mortality rates, work days lost to sickness, or life expectancy. Measures of health can be broad (e.g., age-adjusted mortality rates) or disease specific (e.g., neonatal infant mortality rates within the first 27 days of life and age-adjusted death rates from heart disease). The advantage of using such crude measures is that they are readily available and probably are correlated with more comprehensive definitions of health. Unavailability of morbidity or quality-of-life measures, however, does not mean they are unimportant or should be neglected in analyses.

Health Production Function

To determine the relative importance of medical expenditures in decreasing mortality rates, economists use the concept of *health production function*. A health production function examines the relative contribution of each factor that affects health to determine the most cost-effective way to improve health. For example, mortality rates are affected by use of medical services, environmental conditions (e.g., the amount of air and water pollution), education levels (which may indicate knowledge of disease prevention and an ability to use the medical system when needed), and lifestyle behaviors (e.g., smoking, alcohol and substance abuse, diet, and exercise).

Each of these determinants of health has differential effects. For example, medical expenditures may initially cause mortality rates to drop significantly, as when a hospital establishes the first neonatal intensive care unit (NICU) in its community. Beds will be limited, so the first low-birth-weight infants admitted to the NICU will be the most critically ill and most likely to benefit from medical care and continuous monitoring. As NICUs are added to the community, the neonatal infant mortality rate will decline by a smaller percentage. With a larger number of NICU beds, some beds may be unused or the infants admitted to those beds will not be as critically ill or high risk. Therefore, investment in *additional* NICU beds will have a smaller effect on infant mortality.

Exhibit 3.1 illustrates the relationship between increased medical expenditures and improvements in health status. Higher expenditures produce a curvilinear effect rather than a constant effect on improved health. The marginal (additional) improvement becomes smaller as more money is spent. As shown in exhibit 3.1, an initial expenditure to improve health, moving from point A to point B, has a much larger marginal benefit (effect) than subsequent investments, such as moving from point C to point D. The increase from point H_1 to point H_2 is greater than the increase from H_3 to H_4.

This same curvilinear relationship holds for each determinant of health. Expenditures to decrease air pollution (e.g., by installing smog-control devices on automobiles) would reduce the incidence of respiratory illness. Additional spending by automobile owners (e.g., having their smog-control devices tested once a year rather than every three years) would further reduce air pollution. The reduction in respiratory illness, however, would not be as great as that produced by the initial expenditure to install smog-control devices. The reduction in respiratory illness resulting from additional expenditures to control air pollution gradually declines.

Most people probably would agree that additional lives could be saved if more infants were admitted to NICUs (or respiratory illness further decreased if smog-control inspections were conducted more frequently). More intensive monitoring might save a patient's life. However, the same funds could be spent on prenatal care programs to decrease the number of low-birth-weight infants or on education programs to prevent teen pregnancy. The true "cost" of any program to decrease mortality is the number of lives that could have been saved if the same funds had been spent on another program.

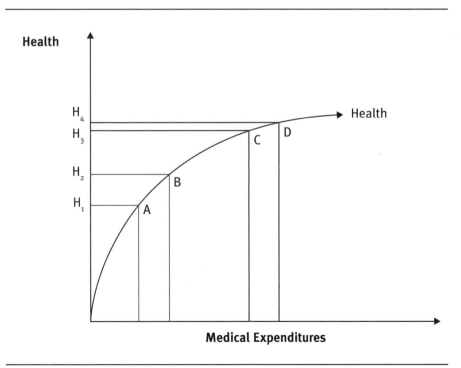

EXHIBIT 3.1
Effect of Increased Medical Expenditures on Health

Physicians, hospitals, dentists, and other healthcare professionals all want more government expenditures to decrease the unmet needs among their populations. However, the government cannot spend all that would be necessary to meet all medical, dental, mental, and other needs. To do so would mean forgoing the opportunity to address other needs (e.g., welfare and education) because resources are limited. At some point, saving all the lives that medical science is capable of saving becomes too costly in light of forgone opportunities. Reallocating the same funds to apprehend drunk drivers or improve highways might save even more lives.

Deciding which programs should be expanded to improve health status requires a calculation of the cost per life saved for each program that affects mortality rates. Looking at the curve in exhibit 3.1, assume that an additional medical expenditure of $1 million results in a movement from point H_3 to point H_4, or from point C to point D, saving 20 lives. The same $1 million spent on an education program to reduce smoking may result in a movement from H_1 to H_2, or from point A to point B, saving an additional 40 lives from lung cancer. The expenditure for the smoking reduction program results in a lower cost per life saved ($1 million ÷ 40 = $25,000) than the cost per life saved from spending the funds on more medical services ($1 million ÷ 20 = $50,000). Continued expenditures on smoking cessation programs result in a movement along the curve. After some point, fewer lung cancer deaths will be prevented and the cost per life saved will rise. A lower cost per life saved could then be achieved by spending additional funds on other programs (e.g., stronger enforcement of drunk driving laws).

Crucial to the calculation of cost per life saved is knowing (1) the marginal benefit of the program—that is, where the program (e.g., medical treatments or smoking cessation) lies on the curve shown in exhibit 3.1, and (2) the cost of expanding that program. The costs per life saved by each program can be compared by dividing the cost of expanding each program by its marginal benefit.

The enormous and rapidly rising medical expenditures in the United States likely have placed the return on medical services beyond point D. Further improvements in health status from continued medical expenditures are very small. The cost of expanding medical treatments has also become expensive. Consequently, the cost per life saved through medical services is much higher than that for other programs.

Improving Health Status Cost-Effectively

Numerous empirical studies have found that additional expenditures on medical services are not the most cost-effective way to improve health status. Medical programs have a much higher cost per life saved than do nonmedical programs. Researchers have concluded that changing lifestyle behaviors offers the greatest promise for reducing mortality rates at a much lower cost per life saved (Fuchs 1992).

The leading contributors to decreased mortality rates over the past 40 years have been the decline in neonatal infant deaths and heart disease–related deaths.

Neonatal Infant Mortality Rate

The neonatal mortality rate represents about two-thirds (66 percent in 2015) of the overall infant mortality rate; the decline in the overall rate has been attributed primarily to the decline in the neonatal rate (Centers for Disease Control and Prevention 2017a). For many years, the neonatal mortality rate had declined steadily; however, starting in the mid-1960s the rate began to plummet. As shown in exhibit 3.2, the rate for whites declined from 19.4 per 1,000 live births in 1950 to 3.3 in 2015, while the rate for African Americans declined from 27.8 in 1950 to 7.4 in 2015. During that period, more NICUs were established, government subsidies were provided for family planning services for low-income women, maternal and infant nutrition programs expanded, Medicaid was initiated and paid for obstetric services for low-income women, and abortion was legalized.

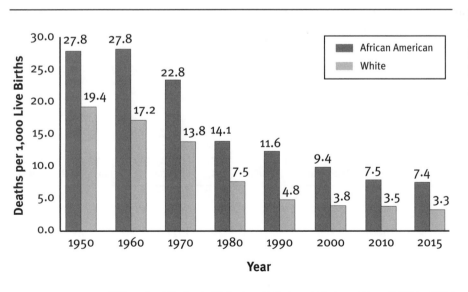

EXHIBIT 3.2
Neonatal Mortality Rates by Race, 1950–2015

Source: Data from Centers for Disease Control and Prevention (2017a, table 11).

Corman and Grossman (1985) found that higher education levels and subsidized nutrition programs were the most important factors in reducing the neonatal mortality rate among whites. The availability of abortion, followed by more NICUs and higher education levels, were the most important factors among African Americans.

Simply knowing the reasons for the decline in neonatal mortality, however, is insufficient in deciding how to spend money to reduce deaths; it is important to know which programs are the most cost-effective. Joyce, Corman, and Grossman (1988) determined that, for whites, teenage family planning programs, NICUs, and prenatal care saved 0.6, 2.8, and 4.5 lives, respectively, per 1,000 additional participants. The corresponding costs of adding 1,000 participants to each of these programs (in 2017 dollars) were $288,000, $32,123,000, and $415,000, respectively. To determine the cost per life saved by expanding each of these programs, the cost of the program was divided by the number of lives saved. As shown in exhibit 3.3, the cost per life saved was $480,000 ($288,000 ÷ 0.6) for teenage family planning, $11,472,000 for NICUs, and $92,000 for prenatal care, the most cost-effective program.

Thus, reducing the potential number of women in high-risk pregnancies and the number of unwanted births (e.g., by providing teenage family planning programs and prenatal care) offers a greater potential for more favorable birth outcomes than investing in additional NICUs.

Heart Disease Mortality Rate

Cardiovascular disease is the leading cause of death in the United States. However, between 1970 and 2015, the mortality rate from heart disease decreased from 362 per 100,000 to 197.2 per 100,000, faster than the rate from any other cause (Centers for Disease Control and Prevention 2017b). Improvements in medical technology (e.g., coronary bypass surgery, coronary care

EXHIBIT 3.3
Cost per Life
Saved Among
Three Programs
to Reduce
Neonatal
Mortality
(Whites)

	Number of Lives Saved per 1,000 Additional Participants	Cost of Each Program per 1,000 Additional Participants (2017 $ in thousands)	Cost per Life Saved (2017 $ in thousands)
Teenage family planning	0.6	$288	$480
Neonatal intensive care units	2.8	$32,123	$11,472
Prenatal care	4.5	$415	$92

Note: 2017 dollar calculations performed by the author using the CPI(U) inflation rate.

Source: Joyce, Corman, and Grossman (1988).

units, angioplasty, clot-dissolving drugs) and changes in lifestyle (e.g., smoking cessation, regular exercise, a low-cholesterol diet) contributed to this decline.

One study estimated that the development and use of new treatment techniques over time accounted for about one-third of the decrease in cardiovascular disease–related deaths; the remaining two-thirds of this decline was attributed to preventive measures, such as new drugs to control hypertension and lower cholesterol levels and help with smoking cessation (Cutler and Kadiyala 2003). These lifestyle changes, however, are not seen uniformly across the US population; those with more education are more likely to undertake them. Many other studies that examined deaths from heart disease have reached a similar conclusion: Lifestyle changes are more important—and much less expensive—than medical interventions in improving health.

Causes of Death by Age Group

Perhaps the clearest indication that lifestyle behavior is an important determinant of mortality is the causes of death by age group. As shown in exhibit 3.4, the top causes of death for young adults (aged 15 to 24 years) are accidents (particularly automobile), suicide, and homicide. For the middle age group (25 to 44 years), the major causes are accidents, cancer, heart disease, suicide, and homicide. For those in late middle age (45 to 64 years), cancer and heart disease are the leading causes of death.

After examining data by cause of death, Fuchs (1974, 46) concluded that medical services have a smaller effect on health than the way in which people live: "The greatest potential for reducing coronary disease, cancer, and the other major killers still lies in altering personal behavior."

Relationship of Medical Care to Health over Time

The studies discussed in this chapter show that the marginal contribution of medical care to improved health is relatively small. Improvements in health status can be achieved in a less costly manner through changing lifestyle factors. Over time, however, major technological advances have occurred in medical care, such as new drugs to lower cholesterol levels and blood pressure, diagnostic imaging, less invasive surgery, organ and tissue transplantations, and treatment for previously untreatable diseases. Few would deny that these advances have reduced mortality rates and increased life expectancy.

Cutler and Richardson (1999) reconciled these seemingly conflicting findings by separating medical care's effect *at a point in time* from its technological contribution *over time*. The authors illustrate the relationship between the total contribution of medical care to health and greater quantities of medical care (exhibit 3.5). Comprehensive health insurance and fee-for-service physician

EXHIBIT 3.4
Leading Causes
of Death by Age
Group, 2015

Age Group	Leading Causes of Death	Deaths per 100,000
15–24	All causes	69.5
	Accident	28.5
	Suicide	12.5
	Homicide and legal intervention	10.8
	Cancer	3.4
	Heart disease	2.3
25–44	All causes	147.1
	Accident	44.4
	Cancer	17.2
	Heart disease	16.4
	Suicide	16.4
	Homicide and legal intervention	9.2
	Chronic liver disease/cirrhosis	4.4
45–64	All causes	633.2
	Cancer	189.3
	Heart disease	132.2
	Accident	48.8
	Chronic liver disease/cirrhosis	26.4
	Pulmonary disease	25.9
	Diabetes mellitus	24.2
	Cerebrovascular disease	20.7

Source: Data from Centers for Medicare & Medicaid Services (2017b).

payments reduce both the patient's and the physician's incentive to be concerned with the cost of care, resulting in movement of the healthcare system to point A, where the marginal contribution of medical care to health is very small. Additional medical care expenditures enhance health, but at a decreasing rate.

Eventually, however, medical advances shift the health production function upward. The level of health has improved, and the number of patients treated has risen, but the marginal contribution of medical care is still low—at point B. Too many patients whose need for treatment is doubtful are treated with the new technology, or excess capacity occurs as too much of the new technology is made available. Thus, although the public believes the medical

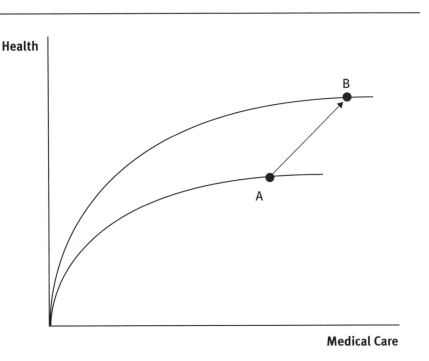

EXHIBIT 3.5
Relationship
Between
Medical Care
and Health

Source: Reprinted with permission from David Cutler and Elizabeth Richardson, "Your Money and Your Life: The Value of Health and What Affects It," in *Frontiers in Health Policy Research*, vol. 2, ed. Alan Garber (Cambridge, Mass.: MIT Press, 1999), pp. 99–132, figure 5–6.

care they receive today is much more valuable than treatments offered 30 years ago, the healthcare system remains inefficient; the marginal benefit of additional medical expenditures is low (Skinner, Staiger, and Fisher 2006).

Summary

If expenditures on medical services have been shown to be less cost-effective in reducing mortality rates than changes in lifestyle behavior, why does the United States spend a growing portion of its resources on medical care?

First, health insurance coverage has been comprehensive—with low deductibles and small copayments—so that individuals faced a very low out-of-pocket price when they went to the hospital or a specialist. Consequently, patients used more medical services than they would have if they had to pay a greater portion of the cost. The expression "the insurance will cover it" is indicative of patients' and providers' lack of incentive to be concerned about cost. The public also has had little incentive to compare prices among providers, because the costs incurred in searching for less expensive providers exceed any savings on already low copayments. Given these low copayments and the incentives inherent in fee-for-service payments to providers, it is not surprising that enormous resources are spent on treating patients in their last year of life. Rapidly rising medical expenditures and limited reductions in mortality rates are the consequences of this behavior.

Second, the primary objective of government medical expenditures has not been to improve health status and decrease mortality rates. Medicare benefits the elderly, and approximately half of Medicaid expenditures are spent for care of the elderly in nursing homes. The purpose of much government-funded medical care has been to help the aged finance their medical needs. Were the government's objective to improve the nation's health, the types of services financed and the age groups that would benefit most from those expenditures would be very different. (One factor to consider is that the aged have the highest voting participation rates of any age group and perhaps have become the most politically powerful group in US society.)

Although medical expenditures have a relatively small marginal effect on health, it would be incorrect to conclude that the government should limit all increases in medical spending. To an individual, additional medical services may be worth the extra cost even when they are not subsidized. As incomes go up, people are more willing to purchase medical services to relieve anxiety and pain—services that are not lifesaving but are entirely appropriate personal expenditures. From society's perspective, financing medical services for those with low income is also appropriate. As a society becomes wealthier, its members and government become more willing to spend on non-lifesaving medical treatments. These "consumption" versus "investment" types of medical expenditures are appropriate as long as everyone recognizes them for what they are.

When a government attempts to improve the health of its low-income populations (using the concept of health production function), expenditures should be directed toward the most cost-effective programs (i.e., those that result in the lowest cost per life saved). Allocating funds in this manner achieves a greater reduction in mortality rates for a given total expenditure than is possible with any other allocation method. The health production function is used more often by employers and health plans that face financial pressures to reduce their medical costs.[2] Employers' use of health-risk appraisal questionnaires recognizes that employees' health can be improved less expensively by changes in lifestyle behavior. Incentives given to employees who stop smoking, lose weight, and exercise enable employers to retain a skilled workforce longer while reducing medical expenditures. Health plans' emphasis on reducing per capita medical costs has led them to identify high-risk groups that can benefit from measures to prevent illness and costly medical treatments.

The recognition by the government, employers, health plans, and individuals that resources are scarce and that their objective should be to improve health status rather than use additional medical services will lead to new approaches to enhance health. The health production function should clarify the trade-offs between different programs and improve the allocation of resources.

Discussion Questions

1. How can the health production function allocate funds to improve health status?
2. Why does the United States spend an ever-growing portion of its resources on medical services, although they are less cost-effective than other methods in improving health status?
3. How can employers use the health production function to decrease their employees' medical expenditures?
4. Describe the health production function in decreasing deaths from coronary heart disease.
5. Describe the health production function in decreasing deaths among young adults.

Notes

1. $721 billion = 22.5% × total national health expenditures of $3,205 billion. In 2015, 50.8 percent of total medical expenditures were for 5 percent of the population. The elderly represented 41.9 percent of those on whom a great amount of money was spent (Soni 2017).
2. See chapter 22 on comparative effectiveness research for further discussion of cost-effectiveness applied to quality-adjusted life years.

References

Centers for Disease Control and Prevention. 2017a. *Health, United States, 2016: With Chartbook on Long-Term Trends in Health.* Published May. www.cdc.gov/nchs/data/hus/hus16.pdf.

———. 2017b. "National Vital Statistics System: Mortality Tables." Published September 29. www.cdc.gov/nchs/data/dvs/lcwk3_hr_2015.pdf.

Corman, H., and M. Grossman. 1985. "Determinants of Neonatal Mortality Rates in the US: A Reduced Form Model." *Journal of Health Economics* 4 (3): 213–36.

Cutler, D. M., and S. Kadiyala. 2003. "The Return to Biomedical Research: Treatment and Behavioral Effects." In *Measuring the Gains from Medical Research:*

An Economic Approach, edited by K. M. Murphy and R. H. Topel, 110–62. Chicago: University of Chicago Press.

Cutler, D. M., and E. Richardson. 1999. "Your Money and Your Life: The Value of Health and What Affects It." In *Frontiers in Health Policy Research*, vol. 2, edited by A. Garber, 99–132. Cambridge, MA: MIT Press.

Fuchs, V. R. 1992. "The Best Health Care System in the World?" *Journal of the American Medical Association* 268 (19): 916–17.

———. 1974. *Who Shall Live?* New York: Basic Books.

Joyce, T., H. Corman, and M. Grossman. 1988. "A Cost-Effectiveness Analysis of Strategies to Reduce Infant Mortality." *Medical Care* 26 (4): 348–60.

Skinner, J., D. Staiger, and E. Fisher. 2006. "Is Technological Change in Medicine Always Worth It? The Case of Acute Myocardial Infarction." *Health Affairs* 25 (2): w34–w47.

Soni, A. 2017. Agency for Healthcare Research and Quality—Medical Expenditure Panel Survey. Personal correspondence with the author, September 8.

4

IN WHOSE INTEREST DOES THE PHYSICIAN ACT?

Physicians have always played a crucial role in the delivery of medical services. Although only 23.5 percent of personal medical expenditures in 2016 were for physician services, physicians control the use of a much larger portion of total medical resources (Centers for Medicare & Medicaid Services 2017). In addition to their own services, physicians determine admissions to the hospital; lengths of stay; the use of ancillary services and prescription drugs; referrals to specialists; and even the necessity for services in nonhospital settings, such as home care. Any public policies that affect the financing and delivery of medical services must consider physicians' responses to those policies. Their knowledge and motivation will affect the efficiency with which medical services are delivered.

The physician's role has been shaped by two important characteristics of the healthcare system. First, only physicians are legally permitted to provide certain services. Second, both patients and insurers lack the necessary information to make many medically related decisions. The patient depends on the physician for diagnosis and treatment and has limited information regarding the physician's qualifications or those of the specialist to whom the patient is referred. This lack of information places the patient in a unique relationship with the physician: The physician becomes the patient's agent (McGuire 2000).

The Perfect Agent

The agency relationship gives rise to a major controversy in the medical economics literature. In whose best interest does the physician act? If the physician were a perfect agent for the patient, he or she would prescribe the mix of institutional settings and the amount of care based on the patient's medical needs, ability to pay for medical services, and preferences. The physician and the patient would behave as if the patient were as well informed as the physician. Traditional insurance, once the prevalent form of health plan coverage, reimbursed the physician on a fee-for-service basis; neither the physician nor the patient was fiscally responsible or at risk for using the hospital and medical services.

Before the 1980s, Blue Cross predominantly covered hospital care; all inpatient services were covered without any patient cost sharing. Although hospital stays are costlier than outpatient care in terms of resources used, patients paid less to receive a diagnostic workup in the hospital than in an outpatient setting. Although doing so was an inefficient use of resources, the physician acted in the patient's interest and not the insurer's. Similarly, if a woman wanted to stay a few extra days in the hospital after giving birth, the physician would not discharge her before she felt ready to return home.

As the patient's agent, the physician prescribed the quantity and type of services based on their value to the patient and the patient's cost for that care. As long as the value exceeded the cost, the physician would prescribe it. By considering only the services' costs and benefits to the patient, the physician neglected the costs to society and the insurance company.

Insurance and the role of the physician as the patient's agent led the physician to practice what Fuchs (1968) referred to as the *technologic imperative*. Regardless of how small the benefit to the patient or how costly to the insurer, the physician prescribed the best medical care technically possible. Consequently, heroic measures were provided to patients in the last few months of their lives, and inpatient hospital costs rose rapidly. Prescribing "low-benefit" care was a rational economic decision because it still exceeded the patient's cost, which was virtually zero with comprehensive insurance.

Supplier-Induced Demand or the Imperfect Agent

The view of the physician as the patient's agent, however, neglects the physician's economic self-interest. As shown in exhibit 4.1, large increases in the total number of physicians and the number of physicians relative to the population have occurred since the 1970s. The number of physicians has tripled since 1970, and the physician-to-population ratio has doubled. The standard economic model, which assumes the physician is a perfect agent for the patient, predicts that growth in supply—other things (e.g., higher consumer income) being equal—results in a decline in physician fees and, consequently, in physician income.

Increases in the physician-to-population ratio, however, did not lead to decreases in physician income. This observation led to the development of an alternative theory of physician behavior. Physicians are believed to behave differently when their own income is adversely affected. In addition to being patients' agents, physicians are suppliers of a service. Under fee-for-service payment, physicians' income depends on how much service they supply. Do physicians use their information advantage over patients and insurers to benefit themselves? This model of physician behavior is referred to as *supplier-induced demand*.

EXHIBIT 4.1
Number of Active Physicians and Physician-to-Population Ratio, 1950–2013

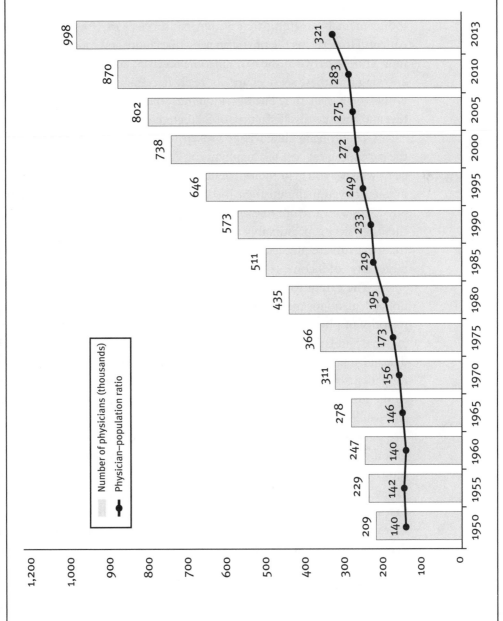

Sources: Data from American Medical Association (1982, 2012, 2015); US Census Bureau (2012, 2016).

The supplier-induced demand theory assumes that if the physician's income falls, the physician will use her role as the patient's agent to prescribe additional services. The physician provides the patient with misinformation to influence the patient to demand more services, thereby adding to the physician's income. In other words, the physician becomes an *imperfect agent*.

Physicians who are imperfect agents might rationalize some demand inducement by arguing that additional services or tests would benefit the patient. However, as the physician prescribes more and more services, he or she must choose between the extra income received and the psychological cost of knowing that these services are not really necessary. At some point, the former is not worth the latter. The physician must make a trade-off between increased revenue and the dissatisfaction of deliberately providing too many services.

Thus, one might envisage a spectrum of demand inducement that reflects the psychological cost to the physician. At one end of the spectrum are physicians who act solely in their patients' interests; they do not induce demand to inflate or even maintain their income. At the other end of the spectrum are physicians who attempt to earn as much money as possible by inducing demand; these physicians presumably incur little psychological cost. In the middle of the spectrum are physicians who induce demand to achieve or maintain some target level of income (referred to as the *target income theory*).

The extent to which the physician is willing and able to generate additional demand for medical services is controversial. Few people believe that the majority of physicians generate demand for services solely to maximize their income. Similarly, few people would disagree that physicians are able to induce demand. Thus, the choice is between the concept of physicians as perfect agents for patients and physicians as imperfect agents who induce demand according to the target income theory. The issue is how much demand physicians can and will induce.

Demand inducement is limited to some extent by the patient's recognition that the additional medical benefits are not worth the time or cost of returning to the physician. The patient's evaluation of these benefits, however, varies according to the treatment prescribed. Patients may easily determine that monthly office visits are not worth their time; however, they may have more difficulty evaluating the benefits of certain surgical services. Presumably, demand inducement is more likely to occur for services about which the patient knows the least; consequently, patients are more concerned about inducement in such cases.

Many studies have attempted to determine the extent of demand inducement (e.g., Feldstein 2011, 270–72), but the magnitude of the problem remains unresolved. A recent study found that once information from a clinical trial regarding the ineffectiveness of a certain type of knee surgery was presented to surgeons, the number of such procedures declined; however, the decline was smaller in physician-owned surgery centers (Howard, David, and Hockenberry 2016).

Evidence shows that cities and counties that have many physicians (in relation to the population) also have high per capita use of physician services. This relationship, however, may merely indicate that physicians establish their practices where the population has a high rate of insurance coverage and, thus, where the demand for their services is great. The positive correlation between the number of surgeons and the number of surgeries has been used as empirical support for the supplier-induced demand theory. Furthermore, studies have found that rates of procedures such as tonsillectomies and hysterectomies are higher when physicians are paid fee-for-service than through other incentives (e.g., those available to physicians in a health maintenance organization [HMO]).

Increase in Physician Supply

The growth in physician supply since the 1970s illustrates the importance of knowing which model of physician behavior—perfect agent or imperfect agent (operating under supplier-induced demand)—is prevalent. As a perfect agent, the physician would consider only the patient's medical and economic interests when prescribing a treatment, regardless of the possibility that her income may decline because the greater supply of physicians may decrease the number of patients she sees.

On the other hand, as an imperfect agent, the physician facing a great supply of competitors would generate demand to prevent his income from falling. Total physician expenditures also would rise as more physicians, each with fewer patients, attempt to maintain their income. Thus, whether one believes in the standard economic model (perfect agent) or the supplier-induced demand model (imperfect agent), a larger number of physicians leads to opposite predictions of their effect on physician prices and income.

Insurers' Response to Demand Inducement

Insurers recognize that under fee-for-service payment, physicians act as patients' perfect agents or as imperfect agents. In either case, the value of the additional services prescribed is lower than the insurer's cost for those services. Consequently, insurance premiums in a fee-for-service environment are higher than those for managed care plans, which theoretically attempt to relate the value of additional medical treatments to the resource costs of those services. Because of the higher relative premium for fee-for-service plans, more of the insurer's subscribers switched to managed care in the 1990s. Since about 2000, insurance companies have developed mechanisms to overcome physicians' information advantage over both insurers and patients.

Insurers, for example, have implemented second-opinion requirements for surgery. Once a physician recommends certain types of surgery of questionable medical necessity (e.g., back surgery), a patient may be required to obtain a second opinion from a list of physicians approved by the insurance company. Another approach is the creation of preferred provider organizations. Physicians who maintain lower fees, recommend fewer medical services, and are considered to be of high quality are selected by insurers. Utilization review is yet another approach. Before being admitted to the hospital or undergoing a surgical procedure, a patient must receive the insurer's approval; otherwise, the patient is subject to a financial penalty. The length of stay in the hospital is also subject to the insurer's approval.

These cost-containment approaches are insurers' attempts to address the imbalances in physician and patient incentives under a fee-for-service system. Furthermore, they ensure that the patient receives appropriate care (when the physician acts to increase his own income) and that the resource costs of a treatment are considered along with its expected benefits.

HMO Incentives by Imperfect Agents

The growth of HMOs and capitation payment provides physicians with income-raising incentives that are opposite those of the traditional fee-for-service approach. HMOs typically pay medical groups annual capitation payments per enrollee and may reward their physicians with profit sharing or bonuses if their enrollees' medical costs are lower than their annual capitation payments. What are the likely effects of the two models of physician behavior—perfect agent and imperfect agent—on an HMO's patients?

In an HMO setting, a perfect-agent physician would continue to provide the patient with appropriate medical services. Regardless of the effect of profit sharing on her income or pressures from the HMO to reduce use of services, the perfect agent would be primarily concerned with protecting patients' interests and providing them with the best medical care, so there is little likelihood of underservice. In an HMO, the physician does not need to be concerned about whether the patient's health plan covers the medical cost in different settings. HMO patients are also responsible for fewer deductibles and copayments. Thus, the settings chosen for the patient's treatment are likely to be less costly for both the patient and the HMO.

The possibility that patients would be underserved in an HMO exists among imperfect-agent physicians (those who attempt to boost their own income). HMO physicians have an incentive to provide fewer services to patients and to serve a large number of patients. HMO physicians who are primarily concerned with the size of their income are more likely to respond to profit-sharing incentives. At times, a physician (who may even be salaried) may succumb to an HMO's pressures to reduce use of services and thereby become an imperfect agent.

If HMO patients believe they are being denied timely access to primary care physicians, specialist services, or needed technology, they are likely to switch physicians or disenroll at the next open-enrollment period. A high dissatisfaction rate with certain HMO physicians could indicate that their patients are underserved. An HMO should be concerned about underservice by its physicians. Although the HMO's profitability will improve if its physicians provide too few services, an HMO that limits access to care and fails to satisfy its subscribers risks losing market share to its competitors.

The more knowledgeable that subscribers are regarding access to care provided by different HMOs, the greater will be the HMO's financial incentive not to pressure its physicians to underserve patients. Instead, it will monitor physicians to guard against underservice. Gathering information on HMOs and their physicians and how well enrollees are served is costly (in terms of time and money) for individuals. It is less costly for employers to gather this information, make the information available to employees, and even limit the HMOs from which employees can choose.

Informed Purchasers

Informed purchasers are necessary if the market is to discipline imperfect agents. An HMO's reputation is an expensive asset that can be damaged by imperfect agents underserving their patients. Performance information and competition among HMOs for informed purchasers should prevent organizations from underserving their enrollees. The financial, reputation, and legal costs of underservice should mitigate the financial incentives to underprescribe in an HMO.

Both insurers and HMOs lack information about a patient's diagnosis and treatment needs. Thus, the insurer's or HMO's profitability depends on the physician's knowledge and treatment recommendations. Depending on the type of health plan and the incentives physicians face, a potential inefficiency exists in the provision of medical services. Physicians may prescribe too many or too few services. When they prescribe too many services, the value to the patient may not be worth the costs of producing the additional services. Prescribing too few services is also inefficient in that patients may not realize that the value of the services and technology they did not receive (and for which they were willing to pay) was greater than their physician led them to believe.

To decrease these inefficiencies, insurers who pay physicians on a fee-for-service basis have instituted cost-containment methods.

Medicare, a fee-for-service insurer for physician services for the aged, has not yet undertaken similar cost-containment methods to limit supplier-induced demand. Until Medicare institutes such mechanisms, imperfect agents will be able to manipulate the information provided to their aged patients, change the visit coding to receive higher payment, and decrease the time spent per visit with these patients. (See chapter 10 for a discussion of the new Medicare physician payment system.)

Monitoring of physician behavior in HMOs and other managed care settings has increased. Physicians who were previously in fee-for-service systems and boosted their income by prescribing too many services are being reviewed to ensure that they understand the change in incentives. Once they are aware of the new incentives, these imperfect agents must continue being monitored to ensure that they do not underserve their HMO patients.

The market for medical services is changing. Insurers and large employers are attempting to overcome physicians' information advantage by profiling physicians according to their prices, use and appropriateness of their services, and treatment outcomes. These profiles provide imperfect agents with less opportunity to benefit at the expense of the insurer. Information on physician performance is available on the internet, and some states (e.g., New York) publish data on physician and hospital performance (e.g., risk-adjusted mortality rates for different types of surgery).[1] Demand inducement, to the extent that it exists, will diminish. One hopes that with improved monitoring systems and better measures of patient outcomes, physicians will behave as perfect agents, providing the appropriate quantity and quality of medical services by considering the costs and benefits of additional treatment.

Insurers serving millions of enrollees maintain very large data sets, and information technology allows insurers to use these data sets to analyze different treatment methods and physician practice patterns. These data will enable insurers to determine which physicians deviate from accepted medical norms.

Not all insurers or employers, however, are engaged in these informational and cost-containment activities. Those who are not are at a disadvantage with regard to the physician and the HMO. Insurers and employers who are less knowledgeable regarding the services provided to their enrollees and employees pay for overuse of services and demand-inducing behavior by fee-for-service providers, as well as underservice by HMO physicians. Medicare and Medicaid, whose payment methods are primarily fee-for-service, are also limited in cost-containment activities to reduce demand inducement. At some point, such purchasers will realize that investing in more information will lower their medical expenditures and improve the quality of care provided.

Summary

Under fee-for-service payment, the inability of patients and their insurers to distinguish between imperfect agents and perfect agents has led to the growth of cost-containment methods. The changes occurring in the private sector and in government physician payment systems must take into account the different types of physicians and the fact that, unless physicians are appropriately monitored, the response by imperfect agents will make achieving the intended objectives difficult.

Discussion Questions

1. Why do physicians play such a crucial role in the delivery of medical services?
2. How might a decrease in physician income, possibly the result of an increase in the number of physicians, affect the physician's role as the patient's agent?
3. What are some ways in which insurers seek to compensate for physicians' information advantage?
4. What forces currently limit supplier-induced demand?
5. How do fee-for-service and capitation payment systems affect the physician's role as the patient's agent?

Note

1. Information on websites and reports on physician and hospital performance are from www.consumerhealthratings.com/index. php?action=showSubCats&cat_id=30. That website includes links to different state reports, such as the following:
   - Massachusetts: Adult Coronary Artery Bypass Graft Surgery in the Commonwealth of Massachusetts: Hospital Risk-Standardized 30-Day Mortality Rates, Fiscal Year 2014 Report—www.mass.gov/ files/documents/2017/12/14/cabg-fy2014.pdf
   - New Jersey: Cardiac Surgery in New Jersey, 2013—www.state.nj. us/health/healthcarequality/documents/cardconsumer16.pdf
   - New York: Adult Cardiac Surgery in New York State, 2012–2014 (ratings of hospitals and surgeons)—www.health.ny.gov/statistics/ diseases/cardiovascular/heart_disease/docs/2012-2014_adult_ cardiac_surgery.pdf

Additional Reading

Mitchell, J. M. 2010. "Effect of Physician Ownership of Specialty Hospitals and Ambulatory Surgery Centers on Frequency of Use of Outpatient Orthopedic Surgery." *Archives of Surgery* 145 (8): 732–38.

References

American Medical Association. 2015. *Physician Characteristics and Distribution in the US, 2015 Edition.* Chicago: American Medical Association.

————. 2012. *Physician Characteristics and Distribution in the US, 2012 Edition.* Chicago: American Medical Association.

————. 1982. *Physician Characteristics and Distribution in the US, 1981 Edition.* Chicago: American Medical Association.

Centers for Medicare & Medicaid Services. 2017. "National Health Expenditure Data." Modified December 21. http://cms.gov/Research-Statistics-Data-and-Systems/Statistics-Trends-and-Reports/NationalHealthExpendData/index.html.

Feldstein, P. J. 2011. *Health Care Economics*, 7th ed. Albany, NY: Delmar.

Fuchs, V. R. 1968. "The Growing Demand for Medical Care." *New England Journal of Medicine* 279 (4): 190–95.

Howard, D., G. David, and J. Hockenberry. 2016. "Selective Hearing: Physician-Ownership and Physicians' Response to New Evidence." National Bureau of Economic Research Working Paper No. 22171. Published April. www.nber.org/papers/w22171.

McGuire, T. G. 2000. "Physician Agency." In *Handbook of Health Economics*, vol. 1A, edited by A. J. Culyer and J. P. Newhouse, 461–536. New York: North-Holland Press.

US Census Bureau. 2016. *Monthly Population Estimates for the United States: April 1, 2010 to December 1, 2017: 2016 Population Estimates.* Published December. www2.census.gov/programs-surveys/popest/tables/2010-2016/national/totals/na-est2016-01.xlsx.

————. 2012. *Statistical Abstract of the United States.* Various editions. www.census.gov/library/publications/time-series/statistical_abstracts.html.

RATIONING MEDICAL SERVICES

N o country can afford to provide unlimited medical services to everyone. Although few would disagree that waste exists in the current system, all medical needs in the United States could not be fulfilled even if that waste were eliminated and those resources were redirected. A large, one-time savings would result from eliminating inefficiencies, but, driven by population growth, an aging population, and advances in medical technology, medical expenditures would continue to increase faster than inflation. As new experimental treatments (e.g., bevacizumab, a tumor-starving drug used for cancer treatment) are developed—no matter how uncertain or small their effect—making them routinely available to all who might benefit would be costly. The resources needed to meet all our medical needs—including prescription drugs, mental health services, long-term care, dental care, and vision care as well as acute, chronic, and preventive services—would be enormous.

The cost of eliminating all medical problems, no matter how small, means forgoing the benefits of spending those resources on other needs, such as food, clothing, housing, and education. Forgoing these other needs is the real cost of fulfilling all our medical needs. Because no country can afford to spend unlimited resources on medical services, each must choose some mechanism to ration or limit access to medical care.

Rationing is done by one of two methods: (1) government nonprice rationing and (2) rationing by market-determined price.

Government Rationing

The first and most frequently used method is nonprice rationing, whereby the government limits access to goods and services. During World War II, for example, food, gasoline, and other goods were rationed; their prices were kept artificially low, but people could not buy all they wanted at the prevailing price. Similarly, in the 1970s, a gasoline shortage developed when the government kept the price of gasoline below its market price. The available supply was effectively "rationed" because people had to wait long hours at gasoline stations. Although they were willing to pay higher prices, they were not permitted to do so because gas prices were set by the government.

This type of rationing is also used to allocate medical services in countries such as Great Britain. The British government sets low prices for medical services and limits expenditures on those services. Because there is a shortage of services at their prevailing prices, these scarce services are explicitly allocated according to a person's age (e.g., denying kidney transplants to those over a certain age) or by setting a value on a human life to determine whether costly treatments should be provided (Cox 2010; Harris 2008). In Canada, rationing is implicit as a patient may wait months or up to a year for certain surgical procedures, such as hip replacements (Barua and Ren 2016).

In the United States, only Oregon has proposed such an explicit system of rationing medical services. In contrast to other states, which provide unlimited medical services to a small portion of the poor, the Oregon legislature decided to limit Medicaid recipients' access to expensive procedures (e.g., organ transplantations) and to increase Medicaid eligibility for more low-income individuals (Baicker et al., 2013). The state ranked all medical services according to the outcomes that could be expected from treatment (e.g., "prevents death with full recovery") and according to their effect on quality of life. Because of the unlikelihood that the state budget will ever be sufficient to fund all medical procedures for the poor, those procedures at the lower end of the rankings would not be funded.

Rationing by Ability to Pay the Market-Determined Price

Among the general population in the United States, medical services are not rationed so explicitly. Instead, a different method of rationing is used: Everyone who can afford to pay the market-determined price has access to the goods and services. No shortages of services exist for those who are willing to pay (either out of pocket or through insurance). Those who are unable or unwilling to pay the market-determined price (e.g., low-income individuals and those without health insurance) receive fewer medical services than those with higher incomes.

Medical services involve a great deal of discretionary use. Empirical studies show that a 10 percent increase in income leads to an approximate 10 percent increase in medical expenditures (Congressional Budget Office 2008). As income rises, the amount spent on medical services increases proportionately. This relationship between income and medical spending exists not only in this country but also across all countries. As shown in exhibit 5.1, the higher the country's income, the greater its medical expenditures.

This observed relationship between income and medical expenditures suggests that as people become wealthier, they prefer to spend more to receive additional medical and higher-quality care. In addition, they make greater use of specialists and are willing to pay to avoid waiting to receive those services.

EXHIBIT 5.1

Health
Spending
and Personal
Income in
Various
Countries, 2016

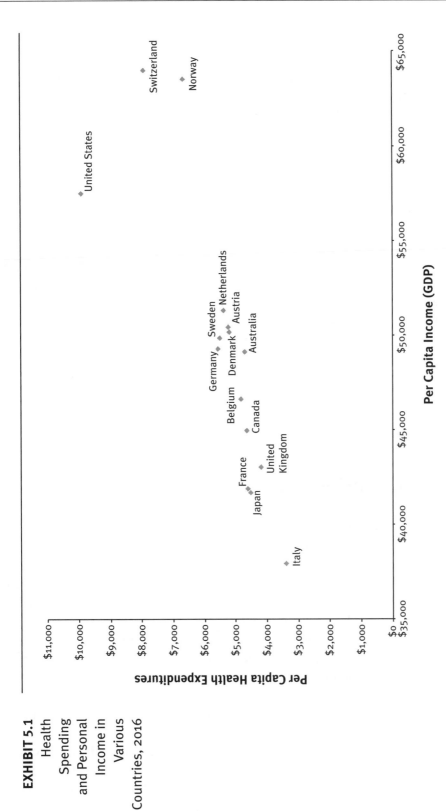

Notes: GDP = gross domestic product.

All values are in US dollars measured in GDP purchasing power parities.

Source: Data from Organisation for Economic Co-operation and Development (2017).

Decision Making by Consumers of Medical Services

Understanding why people use medical services requires more than knowing whether they are ill. Also important are their attitudes toward seeking care, the prices they must pay for such care, and their income.

Whether rationing is based on ability to pay or on government expenditure limits, patients are faced with prices they must pay for medical services. These prices may be artificially low (as in Great Britain or Canada) or may reflect the cost of providing services (e.g., in a market-oriented system in the United States). Regardless of how they are determined, prices are an essential ingredient in consumer decision making.

Consumers spend (allocate) their money on the basis of the value they place on different needs, their income, and the prices of different choices. They are faced with an array of options, each of which offers additional benefits and carries a different price. Consumers decide on the basis of not just the additional benefits they would receive but also the cost of obtaining those benefits. In this manner, prices enable consumers to decide to which services they will allocate their income.

Of course, making one choice means forgoing others. Similarly, as the prices of goods and services increase or decrease, consumers are likely to reallocate their money. An increase in income allows consumers to buy more of everything.

Marginal Benefit Curve

Exhibit 5.2 illustrates the relationship between use of services and the cost to the patient. The marginal benefit curve shows that the additional (marginal) benefit the patient receives from additional visits declines as use of services increases. For example, a patient concerned about her health will benefit greatly from the first physician visit. The physician will take the patient's history, perhaps perform some diagnostic tests, and possibly write a prescription. A follow-up visit will enable the physician to determine whether the diagnosis and treatment were appropriate and provide reassurance to the patient. The marginal benefit of that second visit will not be as high as the benefit of the first visit. More return visits without any indication of a continuing health problem will provide further reassurance, but the value to the patient will be much lower than that of the initial visits.

How rapidly the marginal benefit curve declines depends on the patient's attitude toward seeking care and the value he places on that additional care. For some patients, the marginal benefit curve will decline quickly after the initial treatment; for others, the decline will be more gradual.

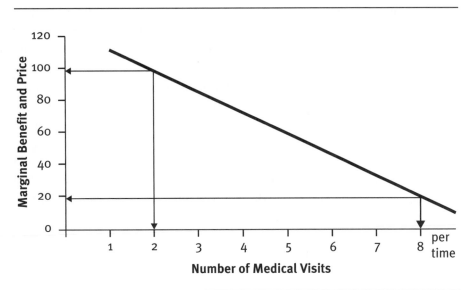

EXHIBIT 5.2
Relationship Among Prices, Visits, and Marginal Benefit of an Additional Visit

The actual number of patient visits is determined by the cost to the patient for each visit. Given the patient's marginal benefit curve and a price per visit of $100, as shown in exhibit 5.2, the marginal benefit to the patient of the first visit exceeds the cost of $100. The patient will demand a total of two visits because the marginal benefit of that second visit equals the cost of the visit. If the patient makes more than two visits, the value received from the third visit would be less than its cost.

Thus, the demand for medical services is determined by the value to the patient (either real or imagined) of those visits and the patient's cost for each visit. When the cost is greater than the value, the patient will not return for an additional visit; he could receive greater value for his money by spending it on other goods and services.

Health insurance reduces the patient's costs for medical care. Although the insurer pays the physician (or hospital) the full price, the patient pays a lower, out-of-pocket price. For example, if the charge for a physician's office visit is $100 and health insurance pays 80 percent, the "real" cost to the patient is $20, the out-of-pocket price. As the patient's cost for an office visit declines from $100 to $20, the patient will increase the number of visits.

The patient will make more visits until the additional (marginal) value received from the last visit is only $20. The patient's decision to use medical services is based solely on a calculation of her own costs (copayment) and the perceived value of those additional visits. Although the real cost of each visit is $100, the patient's cost for additional visits is only $20. The value to the patient of additional visits is less than the full $100 cost of those visits, and the consequence is too much medical care.

In using medical services, the patient usually incurs travel and waiting costs. The importance of these costs differs among patients. Typically, retired people have low waiting costs, whereas working mothers have high waiting costs. To predict use of services, travel and waiting costs (as well as out-of-pocket payments) must be weighed against the marginal benefit of another visit. A medical system that has high out-of-pocket payments and low waiting costs will have different usage patterns from a system that relies on low prices but high waiting costs.

An important empirical question is this: How rapid is the decline in value of additional services to the patient? If the first visit is worth more than $100 and the second visit is worth only $10, little if any overuse of medical services will occur. If, however, a second visit is worth $100 to the patient and the value of subsequent visits declines slowly, the patient will make many visits before the value of a visit falls below $20.

Price Sensitivity

Research on the relationship between the patient's out-of-pocket price and use of medical services indicates that for some medical services, the decline in value of additional services is gradual. In general, a 10 percent increase in price of medical services leads to a 2 percent reduction in use of services (Morrisey 2005). Price sensitivity varies according to the type of medical service. Mental health services are quite price sensitive; a 10 percent reduction in price leads to a 10 percent increase in use of services. Hospital services are the least price sensitive; hospital admissions would rise by about 1.5 percent in response to a 10 percent decrease in price. Lowering the price of physician services by 10 percent boosts use by about 2 percent. Higher-income groups are generally less price sensitive than lower-income groups. Nursing home services are price sensitive; reducing prices by 10 percent leads to an increase in use of about 10 percent (Morrisey 2005). This finding suggests that including long-term care as part of national health insurance will result in large increases in nursing home use and expenditures.

The Medicare drug benefit is administered by private prescription drug plans (PDPs), which use copayments when enrollees require prescription drugs. These copayments serve two purposes. First, by requiring a lower copayment for generic drugs, Medicare enrollees are more likely to switch to generics from brand-name drugs, thereby lowering drug expenditures and reducing the cost of the private drug plan. According to estimates by Hoadley and colleagues (2012), every 10 percent increase in the use of generic, rather than brand-name, statins would reduce Medicare costs by about $1 billion annually. Second, the authors found that setting a low copayment for generic statin drugs—and even eliminating the copayment altogether—had a large effect on encouraging Medicare enrollees to use the generic statin to treat their high cholesterol, thereby minimizing costly hospital stays.

Medicare beneficiaries' price sensitivity when choosing among competing private PDPs is such that a 10 percent increase in a PDP's premium would lead to a 14.5 percent decrease in that plan's enrollment (Frakt and Pizer 2010). An important reason for such a high degree of price sensitivity is that beneficiaries can select a PDP without disrupting their doctor–patient relationship. When Medicare beneficiaries choose among competing health plans, which might require a change in the doctor–patient relationship, an increase of $10 in a plan's monthly premium decreases the plan's market share by between 2 and 3 percentage points (Buchmueller et al. 2013).

The price sensitivity faced by individual physicians, hospitals, and other providers is much greater than that of the overall market because each provider is a possible substitute for other providers. For example, although a 10 percent overall price decrease leads to a 2 percent increase in overall use of physician services, if an *individual* physician raises (or lowers) his price by 10 percent, and other physicians do not change their prices, that physician will lose (or gain) a large number of patients—approximately 30 percent.

Similarly, greater price sensitivity exists toward any single health plan than toward health insurance in general. When employees have a choice of health plans and must pay an out-of-pocket premium (copremium) for these plans, their choice of health plan is very price sensitive. One study found that a difference in health maintenance organization (HMO) copremiums of as little as $5 to $10 a month would cause about 25 percent of the HMO's enrollees to switch to the less costly HMO (Strombom, Buchmueller, and Feldstein 2002).

Moral Hazard

The behavior of patients who use more medical services because their insurance lowers their out-of-pocket cost of those services is known in the insurance industry as *moral hazard*. This term means that having insurance changes a person's behavior, and the cost to the insurance company rises. Those with insurance (or more comprehensive insurance) use more services, see more specialists, and incur higher medical costs than do those who do not have insurance (or have less comprehensive insurance), and the value patients and their physicians place on many of these additional services is lower than their full costs.

Indemnity insurance also places an annual limit—referred to as a *stop loss*—on a patient's responsibility for out-of-pocket payments. If a patient has a serious illness, that out-of-pocket maximum (e.g., $5,000) is reached fairly early in the treatment process. After that point, the patient and her physician (assuming fee-for-service payment) have an incentive to try all types of treatments that may provide some benefit to the patient, no matter how small.

The expression "flat-of-the-curve medicine" indicates the use of all medical technology, even when the benefit to the patient is extremely small. The only cost to the patient is nonfinancial—the discomfort and risk associated with the treatment. Not surprisingly, medical expenditures for those who are seriously ill are, therefore, extraordinarily high. Patients in such circumstances have everything available to them that modern medicine can provide.

The problem of moral hazard has long plagued health insurers, as it results in excessive use, increased cost of medical care, and higher insurance premiums. Until the 1980s, insurers controlled moral hazard primarily by requiring patients to pay a deductible and, once the deductible was met, to cover part of the cost with a copayment.

In the 1980s, insurers began to use more aggressive methods to control overuse of medical services, such as prior authorization for hospital admissions, utilization review once the patient was hospitalized, and second surgical opinions. Unless prior authorization was received, the patient was liable for part of the hospitalization cost (and often the patient's physician had to justify the procedure to the insurer). Requirements to obtain a second surgical opinion were an attempt to provide the patient and the insurer with more information regarding the value of the recommended surgical procedure.

These cost-containment or rationing techniques are often referred to as *managed care*. Managed care methods also include case management (which minimizes the medical cost of catastrophic medical cases) and preferred physician panels (which exclude physicians who overuse medical services). These provider panels are marketed to employer groups as less costly, thereby offering enrollees lower out-of-pocket payments and insurance premiums if they restrict their choice of physician to members of the panel.

In addition to changing patient incentives and relying on managed care techniques, moral hazard can also be controlled by changing physicians' incentives. HMOs are paid an annual fee for providing medical services to their enrolled populations. The out-of-pocket price to the enrollee for use of services in an HMO is low; consequently, usage rates are expected to be high. Because the HMO bears the risk that its enrollees' medical services will exceed their annual payments, the HMO has an incentive not to provide excessive amounts of medical services. An HMO patient, on the other hand, must be concerned with receiving too little care. HMO physicians ration care on the basis of their perception of the benefits to patients and the full costs to the HMO of further treatment. Because HMO enrollees have low copayments, the onus (and incentives) for decreasing moral hazard—hence rationing care—is placed on the HMO's physicians.

These approaches by insurers and HMOs to minimize moral hazard attempt to match the additional benefit of medical services to their full cost.

Copayments and financial penalties for not receiving prior authorization are incentives to change the patient's behavior. In an HMO, the physicians are responsible for controlling moral hazard.

Summary

Important differences exist between government rationing of medical services and the rationing that occurs in a competitive market. In a price-competitive system, consumers differ in the value they place on additional medical services; however, those who place a higher value on additional services can always purchase more. As their income increases, consumers may prefer to spend more of their income on medical care than on other goods and services. If an HMO is too slow to adopt new technology or too restrictive regarding access to medical services, its enrollees can switch to another HMO or to indemnity insurance, pay higher premiums, and receive more services. Under government rationing (as occurs in a single-payer system), even if a patient places a higher value on additional medical services than does the government and is willing to pay the full cost of those services, he will still be unable to purchase them.

Medical services must be rationed because society cannot afford to provide all the medical services that would be demanded at zero prices. Which rationing mechanism should be used? Should people pay for additional services and voluntarily join an HMO or another managed care plan, or should the government decide on the availability of medical resources? The first, or market, approach permits subscribers to match their costs to the value they place on additional services. Only when the government decides on the costs and benefits of medical services, and does not permit individuals to buy services beyond that level, will availability be lower than desired by those who value medical services more highly. The choice of rationing technique—relying on the private sector versus the government—is essential for determining how much medical care will be provided, to whom, and at what cost.

Regardless of which rationing approach is taken, knowledge of price sensitivity is important for public policy and attaining efficiency. If the government wants to increase the use of preventive services—such as prenatal care, mammograms, and dental checkups—for underserved populations, would lowering the price (and waiting cost) of such services achieve that goal? If insurers raise the out-of-pocket price for some visits, would that decrease the use of low-value care? If stimulating competition among health plans is the goal, how great a difference in premiums would cause large numbers of employees to switch plans? If consumers are to be able to match the benefits and costs of medical services, as well as face the costs of their decisions, they will be more discriminating in their choice of health plan and use of services.

Discussion Questions

1. What determines how many physician services are demanded by an individual?
2. What is moral hazard, and how does it increase the cost of medical care?
3. In what ways can moral hazard be limited?
4. Assume that medical services are free to everyone but that the government restricts the supply of services so that physician office visits are rationed by waiting time. Which population groups would fare better?
5. How would you use information on price sensitivity of medical services for policy purposes (e.g., to increase the use of mammograms)?
6. Discuss: The high price sensitivity of insurance copremiums indicates that if employees had to pay (out of pocket) the difference between the lowest-cost health plan and any other insurance, market competition among health plans would be stimulated.

References

Baicker, K., S. Taubman, H. Allen, M. Bernstein, J. H. Gruber, J. P. Newhouse, E. C. Schneider, B. J. Wright, A. M. Zaslavsky, and A. N. Finkelstein. 2013. "The Oregon Experiment: Effects of Medicaid on Clinical Outcomes." *New England Journal of Medicine* 368 (18): 1713–22.

Barua, B., and F. Ren. 2016. *Waiting Your Turn: Wait Times for Health Care in Canada, 2016 Report*. Fraser Institute. Published November 23. www.fraser institute.org/sites/default/files/waiting-your-turn-wait-times-for-health-care-in-canada-2016.pdf.

Buchmueller, T., K. Grazier, R. Hirth, and E. Okeke. 2013. "The Price Sensitivity of Medicare Beneficiaries: A Regression Discontinuity Approach." *Health Economics* 22 (1): 35–51.

Congressional Budget Office. 2008. *Technological Change and the Growth of Health Care Spending*. Published January 31. https://www.cbo.gov/sites/default/files/110th-congress-2007-2008/reports/01-31-techhealth.pdf.

Cox, P. 2010. "United Kingdom: Rationing Health by Cost." PRI's The World. Published December 15. http://rationinghealth.org/united-kingdom-rationing-bycost/uprint.

Frakt, A., and S. Pizer. 2010. "Beneficiary Price Sensitivity in the Medicare Prescription Drug Plan Market." *Health Economics* 19 (1): 88–100.

Harris, G. 2008. "British Balance Benefit Versus Cost of New Drugs." *New York Times*. Published December 2. www.nytimes.com/2008/12/03/health/03nice.html.

Hoadley, J., K. Merrell, E. Hargrave, and L. Summer. 2012. "In Medicare Part D Plans, Low or Zero Copays and Other Features to Encourage the Use of Generic Statins Work, Could Save Billions." *Health Affairs* 31 (10): 2266–75.

Morrisey, M. 2005. *Price Sensitivity in Health Care: Implications for Health Care Policy*. NFIB. Published July. www.nfib.com/Portals/0/PriceSensitivity.pdf.

Organisation for Economic Co-operation and Development. 2017. *OECD Health Statistics 2017*. Updated November 10. www.oecd.org/els/health-systems/health-data.htm.

Strombom, B., T. Buchmueller, and P. Feldstein. 2002. "Switching Costs, Price Sensitivity, and Health Plan Choice." *Journal of Health Economics* 21 (1): 89–116.

6

HOW MUCH HEALTH INSURANCE SHOULD EVERYONE HAVE?

Why do some people have health insurance that covers almost all their medical expenditures, including dental and vision care, while others do not? Why does the government subsidize the purchase of private health insurance for those with high income? Has health insurance stimulated the growth in medical expenditures, or has it served as protection against the rapid rise in medical expenses? The answers to these questions are important in explaining the rapid increase in medical expenditures and understanding healthcare reform issues.

The purpose of health insurance is to enable people to eliminate uncertainty and the possibility of incurring a large medical expense. Buying health insurance converts the possibility of a large loss into a certain but small loss. Insurance spreads risk among a large number of people; when each person pays a premium, the aggregate amount of the premiums covers the large losses of relatively few people.

Definitions of Insurance Terms

Several terms need to be defined. *Indemnity insurance* pays the healthcare provider or the patient a fixed amount (or a percentage of the bill), requiring the patient to pay any balance of the cost for medical treatment. When the insured patient has a *service benefit* policy, he receives all the services needed at no additional cost, regardless of the amount the insurer pays the provider. Current health insurance policies typically contain indemnity and service benefit features. Physician services and out-of-hospital services are usually treated with indemnity insurance features, whereas hospital admissions are usually paid for as a service benefit.

The difference between the provider's charge and the insurance payment is paid by means of deductibles and copayments. A *deductible* is a given dollar amount that the patient will have to spend before the insurer will pay any medical expenses. Typically, indemnity policies require an insured family to spend between $500 and $1,000 of their own money before the insurer will start paying part of their medical bills.[1] A deductible lowers the insurance premium because it eliminates the many small medical expenses most families have each year. The insurer is also able to lower its administrative costs by eliminating the processing for a large number of small claims.

The effect of a deductible on an insurance premium is illustrated in exhibit 6.1. As shown, a large percentage of families have relatively small medical expenses, while a small percentage of families have very large (referred to as *catastrophic*) expenses. Eliminating the area designated as a deductible would reduce the overall amount spent on medical care, thereby reducing the insurance premium.

When a patient pays a percentage of the physician's bill (e.g., 20 percent), this is referred to as *cost sharing* or *coinsurance*. (The term *copayment* has been used to indicate a specific dollar amount, such as $20, paid by the patient.) Coinsurance provides the patient with an incentive to be sensitive to physicians' charges, perhaps by shopping around, as the patient will have to pay part of the bill. The patient will also have an incentive to use fewer services because he will have to balance the value of an additional visit against its cost (coinsurance). Coinsurance also reduces the insurer's share of medical expenses, as shown in exhibit 6.1.

Indemnity policies are typically 80/20 plans, meaning that the insurer pays 80 percent of the bill and the patient pays 20 percent. These policies also contain a *stop loss*, which places an overall limit on the patient's out-of-pocket expenses. For example, once a patient has paid a deductible and copayments that add up to, say, $2,000, the insurer pays 100 percent of all remaining expenses during that year. Without a stop loss, unlimited coinsurance or copayments

EXHIBIT 6.1
Deductibles, Coinsurance, and Catastrophic Expenses

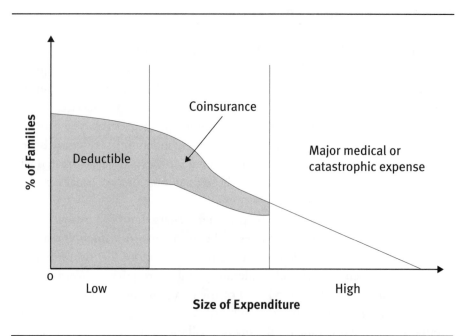

could become a financial hardship. Coinsurance typically applies to out-of-hospital services considered discretionary.[2]

Only a small percentage of individuals and families incur catastrophic claims (see exhibit 6.1). The definition of a catastrophic expense depends on the patient's family income, as a $2,000 expense may be catastrophic to some families but not to others; however, few policies define catastrophic expense this way. Insurance policies that cover only catastrophic medical expenses are referred to as *high-deductible insurance plans*.

The amount of medical expenditures paid out by the insurance company is called the *pure premium*. The pure premium for a group of people with the same risk level (age and sex) represents their expected medical cost—that is, the probability that they will need medical services multiplied by the cost of those services. For example, if the probability of person A needing surgery (given her age and sex) is 5 percent and the cost of the surgery (if needed) is $50,000, she (and others in her risk group) would have to pay a pure premium of $2,500 a year—$50,000 × 0.05. If she chooses not to buy insurance, theoretically she would have to put aside $50,000 to pay for that possible medical expense. However, she may not be able to put aside such a large amount—or even larger amounts (e.g., the amount needed for an organ transplant)—or she may not want to tie up her funds. Insurance offers person A an alternative: It permits her to pay a premium that is equivalent to budgeting for an uncertain medical expense.

When everyone in a particular group has the same chance of becoming ill and incurring a medical expense, each person is considered to be in the same risk class and is charged the same pure premium. The *actual premium* charged, however, is always greater than the pure premium because the insurer has to recover its administrative and marketing costs and earn a profit. This difference between the pure and actual premium is referred to as the *loading charge*. (Another way to indicate the size of the loading charge is to use the *medical loss ratio*, which is the percentage of the collected premiums an insurance company pays out for medical expenses—typically 85 percent. The remaining 15 percent is the loading charge.)

Insurance Purchase Decision Making

The size of the loading charge often explains why people buy insurance for some medical expenses but not for others. If people could buy insurance at the pure premium, they would buy it for almost everything because its price would reflect, on average, what they would likely spend anyway. However, when people are charged more than the pure premium, they must decide whether they want to buy insurance or self-insure—that is, bear the risk themselves.

The higher the loading charge relative to the pure premium, the less insurance people will buy. For example, part of the loading charge is related to the administrative cost of processing a claim, which does not differ much for small and large claims. Small claims, therefore, have higher loading costs (relative to their pure premium) than do large claims. People are more willing to pay a high administrative cost for a large claim than for a small claim.

In the person A example in which the pure premium is $2,500 a year, even if the insurance company charged her $2,600 a year ($100 more than the pure premium), she would probably buy the insurance rather than bear the risk herself. However, her decision probably would be different if she were required to pay the same loading charge with a smaller expected medical expense. For example, let's say she is considering dental coverage. She knows her family will probably need dental care in the coming year, and it will cost $200. The insurance company offers a dental policy for $200 pure premium, plus the $100 administrative cost. Buying insurance for dental care is like prepaying the amount she would otherwise spend, plus a 50 percent loading charge. In the second case, she would rather bear the small risk herself than buy insurance.

This discussion suggests that people are more likely to buy insurance for large, unexpected medical expenses than for small medical expenses (for a more complete discussion of the factors affecting the demand for health insurance, see Feldstein [2011]). This is the pattern typically observed in the purchase of health insurance. A hospital admission and the physician expenses connected with it, such as the surgeon's and anesthesiologist's fees, are covered more completely by insurance than are expenses for a physician office visit. Thus, an important characteristic of good insurance is that it covers large catastrophic expenses. People are less able to afford the catastrophic costs of a major illness or an accident than they are front-end or first-dollar coverage, which are typically small expenses with relatively high loading charges.

Tax-Free, Employer-Paid Health Insurance

Surprisingly, however, many people have insurance against small claims such as dental visits, physician office visits, and vision services. How can we explain this?

Advantages

The predominant source of health insurance coverage for people under age 65 years is through the workplace. As of 2016, 87 percent of all private health insurance was purchased by the employer on behalf of the employee (US Census Bureau 2017, table HI01). This occurs because the federal tax code does not consider employer-paid health insurance as part of the employee's taxable income; it is exempt from federal, state, and Social Security taxes.

Until the early 1980s, marginal tax rates for federal income taxes were as high as 70 percent. Throughout the late 1960s and 1970s, inflation increased, pushing employees into higher marginal tax brackets. Social Security taxes have also risen steadily; as of 2018, the employer and employee each pay 6.2 percent of the employee's wage up to a maximum wage of $128,400 (US Social Security Administration 2017). In addition, the employee and employer each pay a Medicare tax of 1.45 percent on all earned income, for a combined total of 7.65 percent on the employee and employer. Starting in 2013, the Affordable Care Act (ACA) increased Medicare payroll taxes to 2.35 percent (only for the employee part) for individuals earning more than $200,000 and families earning more than $250,000. These high-income individuals and families also have to pay an additional 3.8 percent Medicare tax on all unearned income, such as investment income, dividends, and capital gains.

Marginal federal tax rates, which had declined since the 1980s, have risen again. Effective 2018, the highest federal marginal tax rate was increased to 37 percent for individuals earning more than $500,000 and families earning more than $600,000. Thus, the marginal tax rate on investment income for those with high income is now 40.8 percent (37 + 3.8 = 40.8).

Employees and their employers have a financial incentive for additional compensation in the form of health insurance benefits rather than cash income. The employer saves its share of Social Security taxes, and employees do not have to pay federal, state, or Social Security taxes on additional health insurance benefits.

For example, assume employee B is in a 30 percent tax bracket, has to pay 5 percent state income tax and 7 percent Social Security tax, already has basic hospital and medical coverage, and is due to receive a $1,000 raise. Employee B would be left with only $580 (0.30 + 0.05 + 0.07 = 0.42 subtracted from 100 percent = 0.58 × $1,000) after taxes to purchase for his family dental care and other medical services not covered by insurance. Alternatively, the employer could use the entire $1,000 to purchase additional health insurance, and no taxes would be paid on it. This additional insurance would likely cover employee B's dental care and other previously uncovered medical expenses, which could easily add up to more than the $580 he would receive if simply given a $1,000 raise.

As employees move into higher tax brackets, the higher loading charge on small claims is more than offset by using before-tax income to buy health insurance for those small claims. Using the example of dental care, the choice is between spending $200 of after-tax income on dental care or buying dental insurance for $300 ($200 dental expense plus $100 loading charge). Spending $200 on his family's dental care would require employee B to earn $350 in before-tax income (30 percent federal tax, 5 percent state tax, and 7 percent Social Security tax). However, if his employer uses that same $350 to purchase dental benefits for him, the premium—including the $100 loading charge—would be more than covered, leaving him $50 to buy even more insurance. Tax-free, employer-purchased health insurance provides a financial incentive to purchase health insurance for small claims.

Another way to view the tax subsidy for health insurance is to consider that if an employee saves 40 percent when buying health insurance, the price of insurance to that employee has been cut by 40 percent. Studies indicate that the purchase of insurance has an approximate proportional relationship to changes in its price (Cutler and Reber 1998). Thus, a 40 percent price reduction would be expected to increase the quantity of insurance purchased by 40 percent.

The advantages of tax-free, employer-purchased health insurance stimulate the demand for comprehensive health insurance coverage, particularly among higher-income employees. More services not traditionally thought of as insurable—such as a dental visit, an eye examination, and all small routine expenditures—have become part of the employee's health insurance.

Consequences

Employer-paid health insurance became tax exempt during World War II, when the federal government agreed not to consider it as an increase in an employee's income. This move came in response to wage and price controls and to prevent a West Coast shipbuilder's union from striking for higher wages. The growth in employer-paid health insurance increased rapidly in the late 1960s when inflation rose and more employees were pushed into higher marginal tax brackets. The greater comprehensiveness of tax-exempt, employer-purchased health insurance has had important consequences.

First, too many services have been covered by health insurance. Administrative costs increased as insurers had to process many small claims that a deductible would have excluded. A $20 prescription drug claim and a much larger medical expense cost the same to process. Second, as insurance became more comprehensive, patients' concern with the prices charged for medical services decreased. Physicians, hospitals, and other healthcare providers could more easily raise their fees because patients were covered by insurance—that is, someone else was paying. Similarly, as out-of-pocket medical expenses declined, patients increased use of those services, sought more referrals to specialists, and underwent more extensive medical imaging and testing.

The growth of health insurance and medical technology was intertwined. Expensive technology, which increases the cost of a medical service, causes people to buy health insurance to protect themselves from those large, unexpected medical expenses. At the same time, the availability of insurance to pay for expensive technology stimulates its development. When comprehensive insurance removes any concern that insured individuals may have about the cost of their care, they (and physicians acting on their behalf) want access to the latest technology as long as it offers some benefit, no matter how small. The benefits of that technology to patients outweigh their out-of-pocket costs for using it. Because insurance has been available to pay the costs of expensive technology, such as transplants, financial incentives existed to develop benefit-producing technology. Thus, medical technology was stimulated by, and, in turn, stimulated the purchase of health insurance.

Conversely, cost-reducing approaches generated little interest because employers could pass on higher insurance costs to employees in the form of reduced wages or to consumers in the form of higher prices. Furthermore, the after-tax value of savings to employees from stringent cost-containment measures was small. If, for example, insurance premiums could be reduced by $300 by limiting employees' choice of physician, the inconvenience to the employee and his family associated with changing physicians would probably not be worth the after-tax savings of $150.

The lack of concern over the price of medical services and greater use of those services caused medical expenditures to sharply increase, which, in turn, caused health insurance premiums to rapidly rise. Higher insurance premiums meant smaller wage increases, but this was not obvious to employees because the employer was paying most of the insurance premium.

Hundreds of billions of dollars in tax revenues have been lost because of employer-paid health insurance. The value of this tax subsidy was forecast to be $402 billion in 2017 in forgone federal, Social Security, and state taxes simply because employer-paid health insurance is not considered part of the employee's taxable income (Conover 2017).

These lost tax revenues primarily benefit high-income employees because they are in higher tax brackets. As shown in exhibit 6.2, the higher an employee's income, the greater the value of excluding employer-purchased health insurance from income. This $402 billion in lost tax revenues is equivalent to a huge subsidy for the purchase of health insurance to those who can most easily afford it. In comparison, in 2017 the federal government spent $381 billion on Medicaid, a means-tested program for the poor (Congressional Budget Office 2017).

Exhibit 6.3 shows the distribution of the value of the exclusion from income of employer-purchased health insurance. Families with an income of $100,000 or greater in 2010 (26 percent of all families) received 40.6 percent of the federal portion of this tax subsidy for the purchase of health insurance.

Finally, tax-free, employer-paid health insurance reduced employees' incentive to choose lower-cost health plans. Many employers paid the entire premium for any plan the employee selected (or contributed more than the premium of the lowest-cost plan offered); as there was no visible cost to the employee, her incentive was to choose the most comprehensive plan with the easiest access to primary care physicians and specialists.

EXHIBIT 6.2
Value of Tax
Exclusion for
Employer-
Paid Health
Insurance by
Income Level,
2008

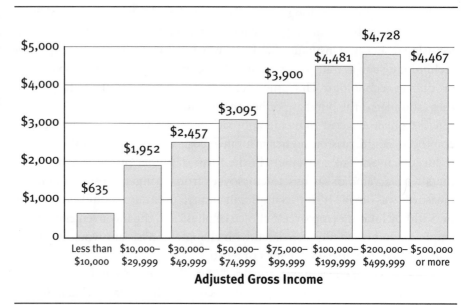

Adjusted Gross Income

Source: Data from Appleby (2009), based on Joint Committee on Taxation calculations of Medical Expenditure Panel Survey data.

EXHIBIT 6.3
Distribution
of Employer-
Paid Health
Insurance Tax
Exclusion by
Income, 2010

Income Level	Tax Exclusion (Billions of Dollars)	Percentage of Total
Less than $20,000	8.1	3.0
$20,000–$29,999	11.3	4.2
$30,000–$39,999	16.7	6.2
$40,000–$49,999	20.8	7.8
$50,000–$74,999	49.3	18.3
$75,000–$99,999	54.0	20.0
$100,000–$149,999	60.0	22.3
$150,000 or more	49.2	18.3
Total	**269.6**	**100.0**

Source: Data from Sheils (2009, figure 1).

Limitation of Tax-Free Status

To encourage competition among health plans on the basis of access to services, quality, and premiums, employers will have to require employees to pay the additional cost of a more expensive health plan. The employee will then evaluate whether the additional benefits of that plan are worth its additional costs. Unless a limit is placed on the tax-free employer contribution, many employees will continue to select health plans on the basis of their benefits without regard to premiums. Competition among health plans based on premiums, reputation, and access to services will not occur until employees have a greater financial stake in these decisions.

Not surprisingly, economists favor eliminating, or at least setting a maximum on, the tax-exempt status of employer-paid health insurance. Individuals with higher income would no longer receive a subsidy for purchase of health insurance. Instead, increased tax revenues would come from those who have benefited most—namely, those with higher income (Clemans-Cope, Zuckerman, and Resnick 2013). These funds then could be used to subsidize health insurance for those with lower income. Employees using after-tax dollars would be more cost conscious in their use of services and choice of health plans.

The ACA imposes a 40 percent tax on "Cadillac" health insurance (amounts greater than $27,500 a year for a family and $10,200 for an individual) starting in 2018. Unions who had negotiated comprehensive health benefits with their employers, however, opposed this provision of the legislation and were able to delay imposition of the tax until 2018. (Starting in 2022, the value of a Cadillac health plan—set at $27,500 a year for a family—will be adjusted for inflation.) While the ACA tax on Cadillac plans was designed to raise revenue so that subsidies could be provided for other parts of the ACA, an unintended consequence is that it will likely reduce rising medical costs. If healthcare spending continues to increase faster than inflation, the percentage of employer-sponsored health plans subject to the Cadillac tax is estimated to increase from 26 percent in 2018 to 42 percent by 2028 (Claxton and Levitt 2015).

With the election of President Donald Trump, who favors changing, if not repealing the ACA, it is highly likely that changes will be made to the ACA. Legislative aspects of the ACA will be difficult to change unless there is a bipartisan consensus to do so. However, regulatory aspects of the ACA can be changed by the new administration. For example, the president has expanded religious exemptions to employer plans that require coverage of birth control. The administration has also stated that short-term (e.g., three-month) health insurance policies, which are much less costly than ACA qualified plans and include fewer benefits, can be purchased for a year. In addition, the Trump administration has repealed the penalty for the individual mandate to buy health insurance. The Cadillac tax, however, will be difficult to revoke because it would require Congress to do so.

Employer-sponsored health plans will undergo changes to avoid the Cadillac tax. However, lowering premiums by decreasing the broad benefits included in the ACA will require legislative change. Instead, the likely approach for avoiding the Cadillac tax will be threefold.

First, high-deductible health plans will become more prevalent. Deductibles will become much higher and the number of small claims paid by insurers will decrease, thereby decreasing administrative costs and insurance premiums. Out-of-pocket expenses will increase and become a greater financial burden on older employees and those who are chronically ill, many of whom will find that the deductibles and out-of-pocket expenses exceed their ability to pay. As employees become more price sensitive, they will have a greater incentive (i.e., lower premiums and copayments) to use a restricted provider panel and join tightly managed care plans, such as health maintenance organizations (HMOs), in which the decision to use services is made by the provider rather than the patient.

Second, insurers will seek to lower their premiums by using narrow (limited) provider networks. These networks rely on hospitals and physicians who are willing to discount their fees in return for a greater number of patients. Enrollees' choice of providers will be greatly reduced.

Third, several large employers are currently using *reference pricing* to reduce their employees' treatment costs and to improve treatment outcomes. An employer (or insurer) determines the maximum price it will pay the provider for an employee's medical treatment, such as a hip replacement. The reference price is usually based on the treatment price at high-quality hospitals. If the employee goes to another hospital for treatment, he pays the difference between the reference price and the hospital's price. As more employers use reference pricing, employee price sensitivity and provider competition will reduce treatment prices.

Because the Cadillac tax will require patients to bear more out-of-pocket expenses for their care, patients will become more price sensitive. Employees may choose to join HMOs to lower their out-of-pocket expenses, thereby delegating the decision to restrict use of services to their managed care plan; in either case, use of services and medical spending will likely decline. In addition, the basis for making treatment decisions will change. Employees (and physicians in managed care plans) will have to consider the costs of their treatment choices.

Although unions, employers, insurers, and healthcare providers will likely exert strong political pressure to overturn the Cadillac tax, legislators may find it difficult to do so because the lost federal tax dollars will be difficult to replace, particularly if additional funds are needed for health reform changes.

Summary

Health insurers play a valuable role in society. Assume a person is at risk for an operation costing $100,000. How many people are able to pay that amount? Insurers pool risks; thus, a person can pay an insurance premium and eliminate the uncertainty that arises from whether she will incur a large expenditure if she becomes ill. Insurance reduces a person's risk of incurring a large financial loss.[3]

However, health insurance also provides protection against relatively small losses, such as physician office visits and dental care. People buy insurance against such small losses because health insurance is subsidized; employer-paid health insurance is tax exempt. Employees purchase more comprehensive health insurance because of this tax subsidy. Those with higher incomes are the primary beneficiaries of this tax subsidy because of their higher marginal tax bracket.

Tax-exempt employer-purchased health insurance has distorted consumers' choices in healthcare and diminished consumer incentives to be concerned with the cost of medical care. Reducing or limiting this tax subsidy may not only provide more funds to assist those with lower income, but also may result in consumers being more price sensitive in their choice of health plans and use of medical services.

Discussion Questions

1. How is a pure premium calculated?
2. What does the loading charge consist of?
3. How does the size of the loading charge affect the type of health insurance purchased?
4. Why does employer-purchased health insurance result in more comprehensive coverage?
5. What are the arguments in favor of eliminating (or placing a cap on) the tax-exempt status of employer-purchased health insurance?
6. How has health insurance affected the development of medical technology, and how has medical technology affected the growth of health insurance?

Notes

1. Insurers typically rely on a provider network, referred to as in-network providers (INP). These providers have agreed on a negotiated price for their services from the insurer. An insured person, however, may decide to use an out-of-network provider (ONP) for medical services. The size of patients' deductibles will vary depending on which type of provider they use. For example, assume the deductible for both INPs and ONPs is $1,000. If a patient uses an ONP for a procedure and is charged $1,500, and the allowable charge for that procedure by an INP is $800, the patient will have met only $800 of his deductible. Therefore, the patient is responsible for the $800 deductible payment plus the

difference between the provider's allowable charge and the ONP's price, which is $700 ($1,500 − $800 = $700). Because the $1,000 deductible hasn't been satisfied, the patient owes the full $1,500. Once the deductible has been met, if the patient continues to use ONPs, he will owe the difference between the ONP price and the insurer's allowable amount. Consequently, patients have a strong disincentive to use an ONP.

2. Insurers use copayments to make patients price sensitive and to discourage the use of medical services that provide little benefit. Patients then must consider the costs and benefits of the additional services. For some medical services, however, copayments may increase medical costs and worsen a patient's health. For high-valued drugs, for example, a copayment may discourage a patient at risk for heart disease and stroke from taking his prescribed medications. In these circumstances, not only is it appropriate to waive the copayment, but it is also in the insurer's (and the patient's) interest to monitor the patient to make sure he is taking his medications. Total medical costs for the patient will be lower than if a copayment is imposed on such high-valued medical services. For more on value-based insurance design, see Fendrick and Chernew (2006).

3. In addition to pooling risks, insurers can decrease their premiums by performing two tasks. First, to decrease the probability of a large loss occurring, insurers can encourage preventive measures among their insured populations. Second, if an expensive procedure is needed, insurers can lower the cost by selecting physicians and hospitals that are higher quality and less costly.

References

Appleby, J. 2009. "How Congress Might Tax Your Health Benefits." *Kaiser Health News*. Published June 8. https://khn.org/news/taxes/.

Claxton, G., and L. Levitt. 2015. "How Many Employers Could Be Affected by the Cadillac Plan Tax?" Kaiser Family Foundation issue brief. Published August. http://files.kff.org/attachment/issue-brief-how-many-employers-could-be-affected-by-the-cadillac-plan-tax.

Clemans-Cope, L., S. Zuckerman, and D. Resnick. 2013. "Limiting the Tax Exclusion of Employer-Sponsored Health Insurance Premiums: Revenue Potential and Distributional Consequences." Urban Institute. Published May. www.urban.org/sites/default/files/publication/23606/412816-limiting-the-tax-exclusion-of-employer-sponsored-health-insurance-premiums-revenue-potential-and-distributional-consequences.pdf.

Congressional Budget Office. 2017. "Detail of Spending and Enrollment for Medicaid for CBO's January 2017 Baseline." Accessed September. www.cbo.gov/sites/default/files/recurringdata/51301-2017-01-medicaid.pdf.

Conover, C. 2017. "Why Tax Reform Should Address Incomprehensible and Indefensible Inequities in Health Subsidies." *Forbes*. Published July 30. www.forbes.com/sites/theapothecary/2017/07/30/why-tax-reform-should-address-incomprehensible-and-indefensible-inequities-in-health-subsidies.

Cutler, D., and S. Reber. 1998. "Paying for Health Insurance: The Trade-Off Between Competition and Adverse Selection." *Quarterly Journal of Economics* 113 (2): 433–66.

Feldstein, P. 2011. "The Demand for Health Insurance." In *Health Care Economics*, 7th ed., 139–69. Albany, NY: Delmar.

Fendrick, M., and M. Chernew. 2006. "Value-Based Insurance Design: Aligning Incentives to Bridge the Divide Between Quality Improvement and Cost Containment." *American Journal of Managed Care* 12 (Special Issue): SP5–SP10.

Sheils, J. 2009. *Ideas for Financing Health Reform: Revenue Measures That Also Reduce Health Spending—Statement for the Senate Committee on Finance*. Published May 12. http://finance.senate.gov/imo/media/doc/John%20Sheils.pdf.

US Census Bureau. 2017. "Health Insurance Coverage Status and Type of Coverage by Selected Characteristics: 2016." *Current Population Survey (CPS) Annual Social and Economic (ASEC) Supplement*. Updated February 13, 2018. www.census.gov/data/tables/time-series/demo/income-poverty/cps-hi/hi-01.2016.html.

US Social Security Administration. 2017. "2018 Social Security Changes." Accessed March 26, 2018. www.ssa.gov/news/press/factsheets/colafacts2018.pdf.

7

WHY ARE THOSE WHO MOST NEED HEALTH INSURANCE LEAST ABLE TO BUY IT?

We have all heard stories of individuals who were sick and needed open-heart surgery, for example, but no insurance company would sell them health insurance. Until the Affordable Care Act (ACA) required insurers to sell health insurance to anyone willing to buy it, health insurance seemed to be available only to those who did not need it. Why did health insurance companies deny coverage to those who were sick and needed it most? To understand these issues, one must recognize how insurance premiums are determined and how health insurance markets work.

The Different Private Health Insurance Markets

In 2016, 87 percent of private health insurance for nonelderly Americans was purchased through the workplace (down from 92 percent in 2000). (The percentages show the population covered by employment-based health insurance as a percentage of the population covered by private health insurance.) Private nongroup coverage has increased to 14 percent from 7 percent in 2000. (The percentages show the population covered by direct-purchase health insurance as a percentage of the total nonelderly population.) Employer coverage has declined from 69 percent in 2000 to 61 percent in 2016. (The percentages show the population covered by employment-based health insurance as a percentage of the total nonelderly population.) (US Census Bureau 2017a; 2017b, table HIA-6) (see exhibit 7.1). As discussed in chapter 6, employer-purchased health insurance provides important tax advantages to employees. Insurance purchased with before-tax dollars is equivalent to a reduction in the price of insurance compared with buying insurance with after-tax dollars. This tax subsidy is not available to those buying insurance in the individual insurance market.

Those purchasing insurance in the individual market tend to be self-employed, students, retirees not yet eligible for Medicare, unemployed, between jobs, or employed but not offered insurance through their employer (or choose not to accept it). Before the ACA, individual insurance was typically purchased through a broker, directly from a health plan, or on the internet. As part of the ACA, health insurance exchanges were established in many states primarily to serve those in the individual insurance market. Exchanges are organizations

EXHIBIT 7.1
Sources
of Health
Insurance
Coverage of
US Nonelderly
(Younger Than
65 Years)
Population in
2016

Market Segment	Population (Millions)	Percentage of Total Nonelderly Population
Employment-based	164.9	60.8
Individual (direct purchase)	37.9	14.0
Medicaid	58.9	21.7
Medicare	7.5	2.8
Military-related healthcare	10.9	4.0
Uninsured	27.5	10.1

Note: Numbers may not add to totals because individuals may receive coverage from more than one source.

Source: Data from US Census Bureau (2017a, table HI-01).

that offer a choice of health plans, certify plans that participate, and provide information to help consumers better understand their options. Federal subsidies are offered to those on the exchange whose income is between 133 and 400 percent of the federal poverty level (FPL).

Determinants of Private Health Insurance Premiums

The insurance premium paid by an individual or an employer on behalf of its employees consists of (1) the loading charge, which represents approximately 15 percent of the premium, and (2) the claims experience of the employee group, which makes up the remaining 85 percent of the premium (see exhibit 7.2). The loading charge reflects the insurance company's marketing costs, administrative costs of handling the insurance claims, and profit. The claims experience of an employee group is the number of claims submitted by members of that group multiplied by the average cost per claim; this amount is also the medical expenditure portion of the premium, referred to as the *medical loss ratio* (MLR; medical claims expense divided by the total premium). Differences in premiums among employee groups and differences in annual premium increases result primarily from differences in claims experience. An experience-rated premium is based on the claims experience of the particular group.

When a new group applies for health insurance, the insurer attempts to estimate the likely claims experience of the group. As shown in exhibit 7.2, the insurer will consider factors that affect the group's medical expenditures, such as the following:

- Types of medical and other benefits provided to the employees and their dependents

EXHIBIT 7.2
Determinants
of Health
Insurance
Premiums

Health Insurance Premiums

Claims Experience
(85 percent)

Loading Charge
(15 percent)

Determinants of Claims Experience
Benefit coverage
State mandates
Demographic characteristics of
    insured population (age,
    sex, and family status)
Industry
Region
Medical inflation rate
Cost-containment policies
• Copayment
• Deductible
• Benefit design
• Utilization review
• Case management
• Preferred provider organization

Determinants of Loading Charge
Administrative costs
Marketing costs
Reserves
Profits

- Types of mandates the state requires to be included in the insurance policy (e.g., hair transplants or in vitro fertilization)
- Average age of the group (older employees have higher medical expenditures than younger employees)
- Proportion of women (women have higher medical expenditures than men)
- Industry in which the firm competes (e.g., physicians, nurses, accountants, and lawyers tend to be heavier users of healthcare than, say, bank tellers)
- Region of the country in which employees are located (hospital costs and physician fees are higher on the West Coast than in the South)
- Estimate of the growth rate of medical inflation

Once an insurer has insured a group long enough to have a history of that group's claims experience, the insurance company will project that claims experience and multiply it by an estimate of the medical inflation rate.

Various approaches can be taken to reduce a group's claims experience. For example, increasing the deductible and the coinsurance rate will decrease employees' use of services; expanding insurance benefits to include lower-cost substitutes for inpatient admissions will reduce treatment costs; and requiring utilization review of hospital admissions, case management of catastrophic cases, and use of preferred provider organizations will lower use rates and provider charges. Thus, the claims experience of a group is related to the characteristics of that group, the medical benefits covered, and the cost-containment methods included in the insurance policy.

The insurer bears the risk of incorrectly estimating the group's medical experience. If the premium charged to that group is too low, the insurer will lose money. In the past, Blue Cross and other insurance companies have lost a great deal of money by underestimating claims experience and the medical inflation rate. An insurer cannot merely increase the group's premiums in the following period to recover its losses because the insurance market is very price competitive. If an insurer says to an employer, "We need to increase our profit this coming year because we lost money on your employees last year," the employer may switch to a competitor, switch to a health maintenance organization (HMO), or self-insure (in which case, the employer bears the risk and uses an insurer to administer and process claims).

Even if the claims experience of two employee groups is similar, one group may have a lower insurance premium because it has a lower loading charge. Large groups have small loading charges because the administrative and marketing costs (which are generally fixed) are spread over a greater number of employees. Furthermore, insurers earn a lower profit when they insure large groups because they fear that, if their profit is too high, the groups will decide to self-insure and bear the risk themselves. Small groups, on the other hand, are less likely to self-insure. If a huge claim were to occur in one year, the financial burden might be too much for a small group to bear. In a large group, huge claims are likely to be offset by premiums from employees making only small claims in a given year. In addition to charging small groups a higher rate, an insurer is likely to maintain a high reserve in case a large claim is made, further increasing the loading charge for small groups. However, the amount of potential profit from a small group is still limited by competition from other insurers and HMOs.

How Health Insurance Markets Work

This brief description of how insurance premiums are determined serves as background to examine why those who are ill have experienced difficulty buying insurance.

Adverse Selection

Assume that person B is without health insurance and requires a heart transplant; he wants to purchase health insurance. If the insurer does not know that he needs expensive medical treatment, his premium will be based on the claims experience of people in a similar age (risk) group. The insurer's lack of information about person B's health status can lead to adverse selection—that is, the insurer enrolls people whose risk level is much higher than the risk level on which their premium is based. This occurs because a person in ill health will attempt to conceal that information so that the insurer will not know of his higher risk.

For example, if 100 people were in a risk group, each with a 1 percent chance of needing a medical treatment costing $100,000, the pure premium for each (without the loading charge) would be $1,000 (0.01 × $100,000). Each year, one member of the group would require a $100,000 treatment. Now, if a person who needs that particular treatment (whose risk is 100 percent) is permitted to join that group at a premium of $1,000 (based on a mistaken risk level of 0.01), that high-risk person receives a subsidy of $99,000 because her premium should have been $100,000. Because the $1,000 premium is based on a risk level of 1 percent, the insurer collects insufficient premiums to pay for the second $100,000 expense and loses $99,000. This example does not differ from one in which a man learns that he has a terminal illness and, without revealing his condition to the insurer, decides to purchase a $10 million life insurance policy to provide for his wife and children.

Insurance enables an individual to protect against uncertainty. Once uncertainty no longer exists, however, the person is not insurable for that particular treatment or situation. If the insurance company knew that person B wanted health insurance to cover the costs of a heart transplant, it would charge a premium that reflected the expected claims experience (i.e., person B's premium would be equal to the cost of the heart transplant plus a loading charge).

We all favor subsidizing those who cannot afford a needed yet expensive treatment. Similarly, we favor subsidies to poor individuals and families. However, isn't it more appropriate for the government, rather than the insurer, to provide these subsidies? When insurers are made to bear such losses, they will eventually be forced out of business unless they can protect themselves from people who withhold information and claim to be in lower risk groups.

To protect themselves against adverse selection, the insurer could raise its enrollees' premiums, but then many low-risk subscribers—who would be willing to pay $1,000 but not $2,000 for a 1 percent risk—would drop their insurance. As more low-risk subscribers drop out, premiums for remaining subscribers would increase further, causing still more low-risk enrollees to drop out. Eventually, large numbers of low-risk people would be uninsured, despite their willingness to pay an actuarially fair premium based on their (low) risk group.

Before the ACA, an insurer attempted to learn as much as possible about the individual's health status. Examining and testing a person who wants to buy health insurance is a means of equalizing the information between the two parties. Another way insurers protected themselves against adverse selection was by stating that the person's insurance coverage would not apply to preexisting conditions—medical conditions known by the patient to exist and to require treatment. Similarly, an insurer might have used a delay-of-benefits clause or a waiting period; for example, obstetric benefits would not be covered until a policy had been in effect for ten months. Large deductibles also discourage high-risk people because they realize they will have to pay a large amount of their medical care expenses themselves.

Insurers were less concerned about adverse selection when selling insurance to large groups with low employee turnover. In such groups, the employer provides health insurance as a tax-free benefit (subsidized by the government); the total group includes low-risk employees as well as high-risk employees. Typically, people join large companies primarily for reasons other than health insurance coverage. Once in the employer group, employees cannot drop the group insurance when well and buy it when ill.

Thus, for insurance companies, adverse selection has been a greater concern when individuals or small groups (with typically higher turnover) want to buy insurance. For example, an insurer might be concerned that the owner of a small firm might hire an ill family member so that she could receive insurance benefits. Thus, employees with preexisting medical conditions would be denied coverage.

Some state and local governments attempted to assist people with pre-existing conditions by prohibiting insurers from using tests to determine, for example, whether someone was HIV positive. Rather than subsidize care for such individuals, governments tried to shift the medical costs to the insurer and its other subscribers. This is an inequitable way of subsidizing care for those with preexisting conditions. A fairer approach would be for government to use an income-related tax to provide the subsidy or to establish a high-risk pool that includes subsidies for those with a preexisting condition. Another consequence of government regulations that shift the cost of ill individuals to insurers and their subscribers is that insurers relied on other types of restrictions not covered by the pre-ACA regulations, such as delay of benefits and exclusion of certain occupations, industries, or geographic areas to protect themselves.

Healthy people may not have had health insurance for several reasons. An insurance premium that is much higher than the individual's expected claims experience renders that insurance too expensive. For example, if an employee was not part of a large insured group, he was charged a higher insurance premium because the insurer suspected he was a higher risk. When individuals buy insurance, they must do so with after-tax dollars because tax-exempt employer-paid health insurance only applies when an employer purchases the coverage for the employee. The loading charge is also higher for individuals and those in small groups because the insurer's administrative and marketing costs are spread over fewer enrollees, leading to a higher premium. Furthermore, state insurance mandates that require expensive benefits or the inclusion of more practitioners in all insurance sold in that state resulted in higher premiums; consequently, fewer people were willing to buy such insurance. (Large firms that self-insure are exempt from costly state mandates.) Many individuals and members of small groups also lacked insurance coverage because premiums were too high relative to their income. They would rather rely on Medicaid if they become ill. Others can afford to purchase insurance but choose not to; if they become ill, they become a burden on taxpayers because emergency departments and hospitals cannot refuse to treat them.

Medicare was concerned that adverse selection would occur in two of its voluntary programs: Part B (physician and outpatient services) and Part D (prescription drugs). Because the programs are voluntary (and are subsidized 75 percent), the government was concerned that people would wait until they needed the services and then join the program; the programs would then have a smaller risk pool of predominantly sicker people, resulting in adverse selection. To encourage all newly eligible Medicare beneficiaries to enroll in these programs, thereby increasing the risk pool, the monthly premiums were increased the longer an eligible beneficiary delayed enrolling in the programs.

The ACA decreed that the preexisting-condition exclusion could no longer be used by health insurers to deny coverage to those willing to buy insurance. To eliminate the problem of adverse selection—namely, people buying insurance only when they became sick—the ACA required everyone to have health insurance (an "individual mandate") or pay a penalty. Subsidies to purchase insurance or expanded Medicaid eligibility is available to low-income individuals. (Removing the preexisting-condition exclusion eliminates "job lock"; employees could change jobs without fear of losing their health insurance or being denied insurance because of a preexisting condition.)

Despite the ACA's removal of the preexisting condition requirement, adverse selection occurred in the individual insurance markets. The reasons for this are discussed below.[1]

Preferred-Risk Selection

Because insurers want to protect themselves against bad risks, they clearly prefer to insure individuals who are better-than-average risks. As long as different groups and individuals pay the same premium (or premiums that do not fully reflect their risk), insurers have an incentive to engage in preferred-risk selection—that is, seek out those who have lower-than-average risks.

As shown in exhibit 7.3, in 2015, 1 percent of the population incurred 23 percent of total health expenditures (37.2 percent of those in the top 1 percent are 65 years or older). In 1963, 1 percent of the population incurred only 17 percent of total expenditures, which demonstrates the effect that medical

EXHIBIT 7.3
Distribution
of Health
Expenditures
for the US
Population by
Magnitude of
Expenditures,
Selected Years,
1928–2015

Percent of US Population Ranked by Expenditures	1928	1963	1970	1977	1980	1987	1996	2007	2015
Top 1 percent	—	17	26	27	29	28	27	23	23
Top 2 percent	—	—	35	38	39	39	38	33	33
Top 5 percent	52	43	50	55	55	56	55	50	51
Top 10 percent	—	59	66	70	70	70	69	65	67
Top 30 percent	93	—	88	90	90	90	90	89	90
Top 50 percent	—	95	96	97	96	97	97	97	97
Bottom 50 percent	—	5	4	3	4	3	3	3	3

Sources: Adapted with permission from "The Concentration of Health Care Expenditures, Revisited, Exhibit 1," by M. L. Berk and A. C. Monheit, *Health Affairs*, 20 (2), 2001, March/April: 12. Copyright © 2001 Project HOPE—The People-to-People Health Foundation, Inc., All Rights Reserved; 2007 and 2010 data from Yu (2010); Soni (2017).

technology has had on increasing medical expenditures. Five percent of the population incurred 51 percent of total expenditures in 2015. Given this high concentration of expenditures among a small percentage of the population, an insurer could greatly increase its profits and avoid losses by trying to avoid the costliest patients. An insurer able to select enrollees from among the 50 percent of the population that incurs only 3 percent of total expenditures will greatly improve profits. The only way to provide insurers with an incentive to cover the high-risk (hence costly) patients is for them to be paid risk-adjusted premiums. For example, premiums for people in older age groups should be higher than those for people in younger age groups. Insurers would then have an incentive to enroll these patients and manage their care to minimize treatment cost rather than search for low-risk enrollees.

When the premium is the same for all risk groups, insurers attempt to enroll individuals with better-than-average risks. For example, if everyone enrolling with a particular insurer pays the same annual premium, the HMO would prefer those who have lower-than-average claims experience, are in low-risk industries, and are younger-than-average employees. To encourage younger subscribers, the HMO might emphasize services used by younger couples, such as prenatal and well-baby care. Emphasizing wellness and sports medicine programs is also likely to draw a healthier population. Similarly, de-emphasizing tertiary care facilities for heart disease and cancer treatment sends a negative message to older individuals and those at higher risk for these diseases. Placing clinics and physicians in areas where lower-risk populations reside also results in a favorably biased selection of subscribers.

Medicare beneficiaries can decide to join an HMO (Medicare Advantage plan). In the past, if an elderly person decided to change her mind, she could leave the HMO with only one month's notice. (This one-month notice, which was permitted for the aged but not for those in Medicaid HMOs, reflected the greater political power of the elderly.) When some HMOs determined that a Medicare patient required high-cost treatment, they encouraged patients to disenroll by suggesting that they might benefit from more suitable treatment outside the HMO. By eliminating these high-cost subscribers, an HMO could save a lot of money. To discourage some HMOs from using this approach to maintain only the most favorable Medicare risks, Congress repealed the one-month notice in 2003; Medicare beneficiaries can now change health plans only once a year during open enrollment.[2]

Pricing Health Insurance: Community Versus Experience Rating

In a price-competitive health insurance market, insurers establish their premiums based on *experience rating*. Premiums reflect the individual's or group's risk level and are determined as shown in exhibit 7.2. Under experience rating, no incentive exists for insurers to engage in preferred-risk selection; insurers have an incentive to enroll high-risk groups and manage their care because their higher premiums will be based on their expected medical expenses. Those who have low income and cannot afford health insurance should receive government subsidies to buy insurance; it is not the role of insurers or their enrollees to provide subsidies to others.

An alternative approach for pricing health insurance is to require all insurers to *community rate* their subscribers—that is, charge all subscribers the same (or a similar) premium regardless of health status or other risk factors, such as age and sex. The cost of high-risk individuals is spread among all subscribers. The government must mandate the use of community rating; it cannot survive in a price-competitive insurance market. When Blue Cross started in the late 1930s, it used community rating. When commercial health insurers entered the market, they used experience rating. Because Blue Cross charged low-risk groups a premium based on the average community rate, low-risk groups moved to commercial insurers that offered them a lower, experience-rated premium. As more low-risk groups switched insurers, Blue Cross's premiums kept increasing and the insurer had to stop using community rating.

Community rating has serious efficiency and equity issues. It provides insurers with strong profit incentives to select low-risk people while receiving a premium based on the average risk for all groups. Furthermore, with uniform premiums, regardless of risk status, insurers and employers no longer had an incentive to encourage risk-reducing behavior among their subscribers and employees (e.g., by providing smoking cessation and wellness programs). Premiums for employee groups could not be decreased relative to those for other groups that did not invest in such cost-reducing behavior. Skydivers, motorcyclists, and others who engage in risky behavior are subsidized by those who attempt to lower their risks. Experience rating—with higher premiums for those who engage in high-risk activities—would provide them with an incentive to reduce such risky behavior and bear the full cost of their activities. Higher, community-rated premiums result in low-risk individuals dropping their coverage.

When given a choice of community-rated health plans, low-risk individuals will select less costly but more restrictive plans that are less attractive to high-risk individuals. As low-risk individuals leave these costlier plans for less costly but more restrictive coverage, the more generous plans end up with a greater number of high-risk individuals; this appears to have happened in New Jersey (Monheit et al. 2004). Consequently, the premiums in these costlier plans will increase, likely leading to their demise.

Community rating also has serious equity effects. A community-rated system benefits those who are high users of medical services or at high risk and penalizes those who are low users or at low risk. Low-risk enrollees pay higher premiums and high-risk enrollees pay lower premiums than they would under an experience-rated system. Those at high risk are, in effect, subsidized by a tax on those who are low risk. Low users of medical services typically are younger and have lower income than older, high users. Because these subsidies and taxes are based on risk rather than income, low-risk individuals with low income end up subsidizing some high-risk, high-income people.

The Affordable Care Act's Changes to the Individual Health Insurance Market

Among the approaches used in the ACA to expand health insurance coverage to an estimated 30 million uninsured are expanding eligibility for Medicaid and providing subsidies to those who buy individual insurance on *health insurance exchanges*. Although the individual health insurance market is quite small relative to the large group market, the ACA has made several significant changes affecting the financing and delivery of health insurance. The more significant of these changes are analyzed using previously discussed insurance concepts to determine their likely effects.

Health Insurance Exchanges
Under the ACA, most states established a health insurance exchange. A federal exchange was created for states that decided not to set up a state exchange. These insurance exchanges are intended to serve individuals and small employer groups. The exchanges were expected to be a market in which individuals would be able to compare different types of plans and premiums from competing insurers. The individual market in 2016 consisted of about 52 million people and represented about 17.8 percent of the total number of insured people in the United States (52 of 292 million).

Four government-standard health plans are available on the exchanges, ranked from lowest to highest premium (Bronze, Silver, Gold, and Platinum). The Bronze plan covers 60 percent of medical expenses, while the Platinum plan covers 90 percent. Each plan limits its enrollees' out-of-pocket expenses.

Individuals whose income is between 133 and 400 percent of the FPL ($33,948 to $98,400 for a family of four in 2018) are eligible to receive a federal subsidy to purchase insurance (declining with higher income).

Elimination of Preexisting-Condition Exclusion

The ACA eliminated any preexisting-condition exclusions in the sale of health insurance. Insurers are required to sell health insurance to any person regardless of his health status. To ensure that adverse selection would not occur—that is, people buying health insurance just when they become ill—the ACA included an individual mandate. Those not buying insurance are penalized by having to pay a tax.

The elimination of the preexisting-condition exclusion was expected to bring into the insurance market high-cost people previously excluded from the market. However, as long as the individual mandate was required, insurers expected an increase in the demand for insurance by healthy individuals whose lower cost would more than offset the higher costs of those with preexisting conditions.

Insurers, however, were strongly opposed to the weak individual mandate's penalty for not buying insurance (which was $95 or 1% of income for an individual in 2014 and increasing to $695 or 2.5% of income, whichever is greater, in 2018). For an individual at 350 percent of the FPL, the premium for a Silver plan in 2017 (net of a premium tax credit) was $4,029 plus a deductible of $3,609, for a total out-of-pocket payment of $7,638 (18 percent of income) before she would receive insurance benefits. Many believed the value of insurance was not worth the cost.

In 2016, 6.5 million opted to pay the penalty rather than buy insurance. Another 12.7 million claimed an exemption to avoid paying the tax or having to buy insurance. Another 4 million did not check the box on their tax return, thereby refusing to let the Internal Revenue Service (IRS) know if they bought insurance or were paying the tax penalty. The IRS processed their returns as usual (Koskinen 2017). Insurers also have complained that individuals bought insurance, and once they were treated and no longer needed medical services dropped their coverage.

Eliminating the preexisting-condition exclusion and imposing a weak penalty for not buying insurance, along with allowing many exemptions for not having insurance, resulted in adverse selection for insurers. Enrollees on the health insurance exchanges were higher cost than expected because too few young people bought insurance. Insurers incurred large losses, many exited the exchanges, and premiums sharply increased. A private health insurance system cannot survive under these conditions.

An early example of the effects of eliminating the preexisting-condition exclusion is the ACA rule, which took effect in 2010, prohibiting insurers from excluding children under age 19 years who were diagnosed with a preexisting condition. Many parents purchased child-only plans because their small-employers' health insurance policies did not cover children. Concerned that they would experience adverse selection by enrolling large numbers of children with preexisting conditions (and the associated high costs), many insurers stopped selling child-only coverage while other insurers exited the market. Parents who previously had enrolled their children faced much higher premiums and many disenrolled, while other parents were unable to buy child-only plans (Shaffer 2010).

Three additional aspects of the ACA reinforced the adverse selection effects of the weak individual mandate: modified community rating, gender rating of premiums, and required minimum health benefits.

Modified Community Rating

The ACA established rules governing how health insurers are permitted to vary their premiums. Insurers are required to use a modified form of community rating. For each type of health plan, premiums can vary by family status, geography within a state, smoking status, and age. On average, the medical costs of older people not yet eligible for Medicare differ—compared with those in their 20s—by about 6:1. However, the ACA requires that premium differences be no greater than 3:1, much less than the actual cost differences. The effect of the ACA's community rating is the redistribution of insurance costs from the old to the young.[3] (This age-rating rule was supported by AARP because it would lower premiums for older enrollees.) Rather than having the government subsidize the higher costs of those in older age groups, the ACA required young adults to do so.

Many of the uninsured are young adults. They have low income, are healthy, and don't see the need for expensive health insurance. Increasing their premiums through community rating, together with a weak penalty for being uninsured, resulted in many deciding to remain uninsured.

Gender Rating of Premiums

Women, on average, use more healthcare services than do men of the same age. They visit physicians more often and take more prescription drugs. Because of their higher healthcare costs, a young woman's premium in the individual health insurance market would be 50 percent greater than that for a young man. The ACA prohibits using gender rating for individuals (and employers with fewer than 100 employees). (The ACA further requires that contraception and maternity care be considered essential health benefits—even for single men and women past childbearing age—and are to be included in all health plans.)

When costs differ, eliminating gender rating is similar to using a modified community rating. Men subsidize women, regardless of their respective income. (In the price-competitive auto insurance industry, gender rating is not prohibited by the government; young men who, on average, have more accidents and incur higher costs pay larger premiums than do young women.) The effect of the ACA's prohibition of gender rating increases the premiums for men, leading some to forgo buying insurance.

Expanded "Essential" Health Insurance Benefits

The ACA requires insurers to include a broad range of mandated "essential" benefits, the scope of which is greater than typical individual policies previously sold. For example, preventive services with no copayments must be included. (However, Russell [2009] noted that 80 percent of preventive services increase rather than decrease costs.) Also mandated are behavioral health services, contraceptives, maternity care, outpatient prescription drugs, and pediatric dental and vision care. Annual lifetime limits on health benefits are prohibited. The more comprehensive and generous the insurance, the more expensive it is.

Many young adults eligible for the individual market have chosen not to buy insurance on the exchanges because of the higher premiums resulting from community and gender rating and extensive mandated health benefits. The weak individual mandate has enabled them to stay uninsured at a limited expense.

Medical Loss Ratios

Health plan critics claim that insurers' profits are too high and that too little of the premium dollar goes to pay for medical expenses. These critics point to an insurance company's MLR as an indicator of its efficiency and even the quality of care. The higher the ratio, the more of the premium dollar that is paid out for medical services and the lower the administrative expenses. However, use of the ratio as an evaluative measure is misleading. High administrative expenses (hence, a low MLR) can result from a health plan's (1) enrolling a great mix of small groups, which have higher marketing and administrative costs than large groups; (2) having a small enrollment base and therefore having to spread fixed administrative costs over fewer enrollees; and (3) having more insurance products, which are more costly to administer than is a single product.

Additional factors to consider are the method used to pay hospitals and physicians (by capitating providers, the administrative and claims processing expense is shifted to the provider, compared with the fee-for-service approach, in which the insurer retains those functions) and the number of cost-containment and quality review activities undertaken by the insurer. For example, a health plan that merely pays out a large percentage of its premiums (high MLR) with minimal review of its claims is likely to be inefficient and of lower quality than a health plan that has a high administrative expense ratio because it reviews the accuracy of claims submitted by providers, assesses the quality of care provided, and administers patient satisfaction surveys.[4]

In a price-competitive health insurance market, a health plan cannot afford to be inefficient in its administrative functions. If it is inefficient and simply pays all claims submitted, its premiums will be higher, and it will lose market share. An insurer must undertake a cost–benefit analysis to determine whether each of its administrative functions saves money (lower claims cost) or increases purchaser satisfaction (as shown by enrollee satisfaction surveys). To do otherwise places the plan at a competitive disadvantage.[5]

The ACA established limits on MLR rather than waiting for insurer competition to determine the size of those ratios. Health plans were required to have no less than an 80 percent ratio in the individual and small group markets and a minimum ratio of 85 percent in the large group market; otherwise, the insurer must refund the difference to its enrollees. For example, if an insurer has a ratio of 70 percent in the individual market, it is required to refund the difference between 70 and 80 percent to the insured individual (Kaiser Family Foundation 2013).

A regulatory limit on MLR has several unintended consequences. Crucial to whether an insurer can meet the 80 percent MLR in the individual market is the definition of a medical or an administrative expense. Medical expenses include payment of medical claims and quality improvement programs, such as quality reporting and chronic disease management. Administrative expenses include cost-containment programs, such as fraud-and-abuse prevention activities (including medical review and provider auditing). Limiting the funds insurers spend on detecting, recovering, and litigating fraud to increase their MLR to 80 percent will result in higher—not lower—premiums. The elimination of these programs to achieve the prescribed ratios is an unintended consequence of the ACA.

Cicala, Liebera, and Marone (2017) found that minimum MLRs incentivize insurers to raise, rather than lower, their medical expenditures. If an insurer is below the 80 percent MLR, it will increase its claims cost (allow providers to increase prices) to achieve the 80 percent MLR. Rather than refunding the difference between its MLR and the mandated minimum MLR, the insurer can meet the higher ratio by spending more on claims. Further, regulating minimum MLRs for insurers, rather than having the MLRs determined by insurer competition, changes insurers' incentives from trying to minimize premium increases to increasing premiums to attain greater profits while maintaining the same MLR.

In another study, Book (2016) found that the ACA-regulated MLR decreased private insurers' administrative expenses in the individual market, but this decrease was more than offset by higher government administrative expenses. Thus, total administrative costs of the health insurance exchanges increased. By heavily advertising the exchanges, the government essentially subsidized the administrative costs of private insurers. In 2014, the federal government spent, on average, $1,539 per person enrolled in exchange coverage and saved the insurance companies an average of $149 per enrollee by doing so.

The Effect of the Affordable Care Act's Rules on Premiums in the Individual Market

Many young, healthy individuals did not buy insurance. The many mandated essential benefits—together with the community-rated and gender-rated premiums and elimination of the preexisting-condition exclusion—sharply increased premiums. In addition, taxes were increased on insurers, pharmaceutical firms, and medical device companies to help fund the ACA. These taxes were passed on to enrollees in the form of higher premiums. As a result, many young people decided not to buy insurance. They would rather pay a weak penalty tax. Being uninsured was a rational choice for many young adults.

Insurers did not anticipate the degree of adverse selection that occurred and lost a great deal of money. The insured risk pool was biased toward those who are older and have higher risks. To control utilization and lower their costs, health plans used *narrow* provider networks and excluded many high-quality, but costlier, providers. As traditional insurers have exited the market, managed care providers with experience in Medicaid markets have started entering the exchanges. In addition to many exchange markets having few insurers, premiums have increased sharply. In many geographic areas, the exchanges are not financially stable without large government subsidies.

Summary

The individual health insurance market, representing a small percentage of the overall number of privately insured people, has been the cause of much concern. Tax-exempt employer-paid health insurance is unavailable to individuals buying their own coverage, and insurers are concerned with adverse selection when individuals want to buy coverage. As a result, premiums in the individual insurance market are higher than those in the group insurance market, and the demand for insurance is lower.

The ACA made several changes affecting the insurance market, particularly the individual market. Health insurance exchanges were established; four types of health plans became available on the exchanges; federal subsidies were provided to those with low income; the preexisting-condition exclusion was eliminated; and a weak individual mandate was imposed, as were community and gender ratings and mandated health benefits.

Many young adults have not joined the exchanges because of the higher premiums and the weak individual mandate. As a result, premiums have increased sharply. For those with low incomes, large government subsidies have enabled them to buy insurance on the exchanges. Those who are not so heavily subsidized have not joined the exchanges or have had to bear the financial burden of much higher premiums. To protect themselves from adverse selection and large losses resulting from fewer young people joining the exchange risk pool, insurers are offering narrow provider networks, using less costly hospitals. In addition, many insurers have exited the exchanges, resulting in decreased competition in many geographic areas.

Discussion Questions

1. What are the different components of a health insurance premium? If an employer wanted to reduce its employees' premiums, which components could be changed?
2. What is adverse selection, and how do insurance companies protect themselves from it? If the government prohibited insurers from protecting themselves against adverse selection, how would it affect insurance premiums?
3. Why do insurers and HMOs have an incentive to engage in preferred-risk selection?
4. What are some methods by which insurers and HMOs try to achieve preferred-risk selection?
5. What is the difference between experience rating and community rating, and what are some consequences of using community rating?
6. What are some reasons the ACA has caused premiums in the individual health insurance market to be sharply higher?
7. Why have insurers developed narrow provider networks on the health insurance exchanges?

Notes

1. Unrelated to the preexisting condition issue, adverse selection is a concern when people buy a low-cost, less generous health plan and desire to shift to a more comprehensive plan because they have become ill. To prevent enrollees from switching plans immediately, insurers have instituted an annual open enrollment period. The concern over adverse selection remains because those who expect to use more medical services will enroll in more comprehensive plans. Powell and Goldman (2016) found that adverse selection occurred in more comprehensive plans, while healthier individuals (favorable selection) enrolled in the least comprehensive plans. More generous plans, with lower out-of-pocket copayments, also resulted in more moral hazard.

2. This change was a result of the Balanced Budget Act of 1997, which sought to decrease Medicare expenditures. To compensate the aged for no longer being able to change their insurer with a 30-day notice, the government provided them with additional preventive benefits.

3. Proponents of the ACA provision that overcharges the young to subsidize older enrollees claim that, over time, it evens out as today's 25-year-old becomes tomorrow's 55-year-old. This argument has several problems. First, having young people overpay for their insurance (same as an excise tax) encourages more of them to remain uninsured. Second, it is inequitable to require a 25-year-old with student debts to subsidize an older person with potentially greater income and wealth. Third, considering the time value of money, on a present value basis, young adults still end up incurring greater costs than if all age groups paid experience-rated premiums. Fourth, requiring each generation to pay for the previous generation is based on the hope that succeeding generations will honor their commitment, which, as shown by Social Security and Medicare, is unlikely to occur. Few young workers believe the same benefits their taxes support today will be there for them when they retire.

4. Robinson (1997) discusses many of these interpretive problems (and more) with MLRs and demonstrates how these ratios vary greatly within nonprofit and for-profit health plans, as well as for the same health plan located in different states.

5. Expense ratios for private insurers are much larger than they are for Medicare. Rather than being an indication of differences in efficiency, some of the reasons for higher expense ratios among private insurers are as follows:

- Medicare's per capita claim costs are much higher, so their administrative expenses are a smaller proportion of total costs.
- The Centers for Medicare & Medicaid Services, which performs administrative services for Medicare, is generally excluded from the calculation of Medicare's administrative costs.
- Additional costs necessary for the operation of Medicare, such as enrollment and billing, are included in the Social Security Administration's costs. The collection of Medicare payroll taxes by the IRS is not attributed to Medicare.
- Medicare also has lower costs because it relies on price controls and thus does not negotiate with providers or undertake cost-containment and quality improvement functions (e.g., medical management), or it spends too little to reduce fraud and abuse.
- Medicare is exempt from paying state premium taxes and incurring regulatory and compliance costs that affect insurance companies.

Additional Readings

Feldstein, P. 2011. "The Demand for Health Insurance." In *Health Care Economics*, 7th ed., 139–69. Albany, NY: Delmar.

Morrisey, M. A. 2013. *Health Insurance*, 2nd ed. Chicago: Health Administration Press.

References

Berk, M. L., and A. C. Monheit. 2001. "The Concentration of Health Care Expenditures, Revisited." *Health Affairs* 20 (2): 9–18.

Book, R. 2016. "The ACA Exchanges Increased Administrative Costs of Health Insurance." American Action Forum. Published December 21. www.americanaction forum.org/wp-content/uploads/2016/12/2016-12-21-ACA-Admin-Costs. pdf.

Cicala, S., E. M. J. Liebera, and V. Marone. 2017. "Cost of Service Regulation in U.S. Health Care: Minimum Medical Loss Ratios." National Bureau of Economic Research Working Paper No. 23353. Revised July. www.nber.org/papers/ w23353.

Kaiser Family Foundation. 2013. "Summary of the Affordable Care Act." Published April 25. www.kff.org/health-reform/fact-sheet/summary-of-the-affordable-care-act/.

Koskinen, J. 2017. "IRS Commissioner John Koskinen Updated Members of Congress Regarding 2016 Tax Filings Related to Affordable Care Act Provisions."

Published January 9. www.irs.gov/pub/newsroom/commissionerletteraca
filingseason.pdf.

Monheit, A., J. Cantor, M. Koller, and K. Fox. 2004. "Community Rating and Sustainable Individual Health Insurance Markets in New Jersey." *Health Affairs* 23 (4): 167–75.

Powell, D., and D. Goldman. 2016. "Disentangling Moral Hazard and Adverse Selection in Private Health Insurance." National Bureau of Economic Research Working Paper No. 21858. Published January. www.nber.org/papers/w21858.

Robinson, J. C. 1997. "Use and Abuse of the Medical Loss Ratio to Measure Health Plan Performance." *Health Affairs* 16 (4): 164–87.

Russell, L. 2009. "Preventing Chronic Disease: An Important Investment but Don't Count on Cost Savings." *Health Affairs* 28 (1): 42–45.

Shaffer, M. 2010. "Child-Only Left Behind." *National Review.* Published September 29. www.nationalreview.com/2010/09/child-only-left-behind-matthew-shaffer/.

Soni, A. 2017. Agency for Healthcare Research and Quality—Medical Expenditure Panel Survey. Personal correspondence with the author, September 8.

US Census Bureau. 2017a. "Health Insurance Coverage Status and Type of Coverage by Selected Characteristics: 2016." Updated February 13, 2018. www.census.gov/data/tables/time-series/demo/income-poverty/cps-hi/hi-01.2016.html.

———. 2017b. "Health Insurance Historical Tables—HIA Series." Accessed April 2018. www.census.gov/data/tables/time-series/demo/health-insurance/historical-series/hia.html.

Yu, W. W. 2010. Agency for Healthcare Research and Quality—Medical Expenditure Panel Survey. Personal correspondence with the author, August 3.

MEDICARE

In 1965, Congress enacted two financing programs to cover two separate population groups: Medicare for the aged and Medicaid for the poor. As a result, the government's (particularly the federal government's) role in financing personal medical services increased dramatically. Federal and state expenditures represent about 67 percent of total medical expenditures.

Medicare and Medicaid have serious problems. Medicare's financial deficits mean that the program will require substantial changes to survive in the future. Medicaid must be improved if it is to serve all those eligible, and it faces huge financial liabilities as an aging population requires long-term care. Medicaid is discussed in chapter 9.

The Current State of Medicare

Medicare is a federal program that primarily serves the aged. In addition, individuals younger than 65 years who receive Social Security cash payments because they are disabled become eligible for the program after a two-year waiting period. People requiring kidney dialysis and kidney transplants, regardless of age, were added to Medicare in the early 1970s. As shown in exhibit 8.1, in 2016 Medicare covered 48.3 million aged and 8.9 million disabled beneficiaries, for a total of 57.1 million beneficiaries (Centers for Medicare & Medicaid Services 2017c). The elderly population is expected to double over the next three decades (88.8 million in 2040, 92.6 million in 2050).

Medicare consists of four parts, each of which offers different benefits and uses different financing mechanisms. Part A provides hospital insurance (HI), Part B provides supplemental medical insurance (SMI), Part C offers program beneficiaries a greater variety of health plan choices (Medicare Advantage plans), and Part D is prescription drug coverage.

Part A: Hospital Insurance

All seniors are automatically enrolled in Part A when they are age 65 years. Part A covers acute hospital care (up to 90 days for each episode of care), skilled nursing home care after hospitalization (up to 100 days), and hospice care for the terminally ill. If a Medicare patient requires hospitalization, she must pay a deductible

EXHIBIT 8.1

Number of Medicare Beneficiaries, Fiscal Years 1970–2030

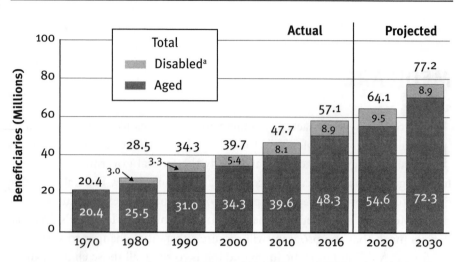

[a]Includes beneficiaries whose eligibility is based solely on end-stage disease.

Note: The disabled became eligible for Medicare in 1973; therefore, no values are included here for the disabled before 1974.

Sources: Data from the Centers for Medicare & Medicaid Services (2017c); Boards of Trustees, Federal Hospital Insurance and Federal Supplementary Medical Insurance Trust Funds (2017, table V.B4).

that is indexed to increase with health costs each year ($1,340 for a hospital stay of 1 to 60 days as of 2018) (Centers for Medicare & Medicaid Services 2017d).

Part A is financed by an earmarked HI payroll tax, which is set aside in the Medicare Hospital Trust Fund. In 1966, this tax was a combined 0.35 percent (0.175 percent each on the employer and employee) on wages up to $6,600. Because Part A expenditures continually exceeded projections, the HI tax and the wage base to which the tax applied were raised. By 1994, the total HI tax grew to a combined 2.9 percent on all earned income.

The Affordable Care Act (ACA) further increased the Medicare payroll tax to a combined 3.8 percent on individuals earning more than $200,000 and families earning more than $250,000. In addition, a 3.8 percent Medicare tax was imposed on all unearned income, such as investment income, dividends, royalties, and capital gains, for the same income groups; these income limits are not adjusted for inflation (Internal Revenue Service 2017).

The Trust Fund is a "pay-as-you-go" fund; current Medicare expenditures are financed by current employee and employer contributions. The HI taxes from current Medicare beneficiaries were never set aside for their own future expenses; instead, they were used to pay for those who were eligible at the time the funds were collected. This approach is in contrast to a pension fund, in which a person sets aside funds to pay for his own retirement. HI taxes on employees and employers have been increased when Medicare actuaries have estimated that the Trust Fund will become insolvent (i.e., when current HI taxes are insufficient to pay current Medicare expenditures).

In 2016, the federal government spent $285 billion on Part A; this amount is estimated to rise to $529 billion by 2026 (Boards of Trustees, Federal Hospital Insurance and Federal Supplementary Medical Insurance Trust Funds 2017). Medicare's expenditures by type of service are shown in exhibit 8.2.

Part B: Supplemental Medical Insurance

Part B pays for physician services, outpatient diagnostic tests, certain medical supplies and equipment, and (since 1998) home health care (previously included in Part A). Medicare beneficiaries are not automatically enrolled in SMI, a voluntary, income-related program, but 95 percent of the elderly pay the premium. In 2018, new Part B beneficiaries pay $134 a month. Single individuals whose annual income is greater than $85,000 or married couples with a combined

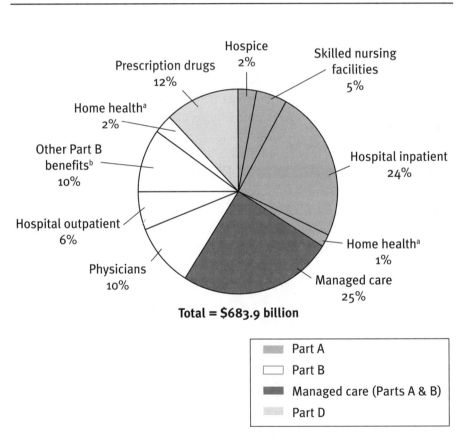

EXHIBIT 8.2
Estimated Medicare Benefit Payments by Type of Service, Fiscal Year 2016

Total = $683.9 billion

[a]Home health services are covered by Part A and Part B.
[b]Other Part B benefits include durable medical equipment, other carrier, other intermediary, and laboratory.
Source: Data from the Centers for Medicare & Medicaid Services (2017b).

income of more than $170,000 pay an additional amount. Beneficiary premiums represent only 25 percent of the program's costs ($72.1 billion in premiums in 2016 out of $289.5 billion in expenditures). Federal tax revenues pay for the remaining 75 percent of Part B expenditures. The aged are also responsible for an annual $183 deductible (in 2018) and a 20 percent copayment for use of Part B services (Centers for Medicare & Medicaid Services 2017d).

In 2007, against much opposition, the Part B premium became income related; seniors earning $80,000 to $100,000 receive a 65 percent premium subsidy, and those earning more than $200,000 receive only a 20 percent premium subsidy. When premiums became income related, only 3 percent of Part B enrollees were affected by the reduced premium subsidies; by 2016, 6 percent of enrollees were affected (Davis 2016, 16). Over time, Medicare has become an increasingly income-related program.

When Part B expenditures exceed projections, there is no concern with insolvency (unlike in the case of the Trust Fund). The federal subsidy simply becomes larger than expected. The federal government's Part B subsidy expenditures increase the size of the federal deficit. In 2016, the federal subsidy for Part B expenditures exceeded $301 billion; this subsidy is estimated to rise to $635 billion by 2027 (Congressional Budget Office 2017a). By way of comparison, Medicare's share of the federal budget was 18 percent ($692 billion) in 2016, and it is expected to increase to 21 percent ($1,390 billion) of all federal expenditures in 2027 (Congressional Budget Office 2017b, tables 1 and 2).

Part C: Medicare Advantage Plans

Since the 1980s, the aged can choose to enroll in a managed care plan—such as a health maintenance organization (HMO) or a preferred provider organization—referred to as *Medicare Advantage* (MA). The MA plan receives a capitation payment from Medicare based on the total Part A, Part B, and Part D expenditures for a Medicare beneficiary in that geographic area (adjusted for age, sex, and Medicaid and institutional status).[1] In return for this capitation payment, the MA plan provides more comprehensive benefits, such as lower out-of-pocket payments and additional services not covered by Part B. The MA plan, which is at risk for providing all the promised benefits in return for the capitation payment, limits enrollees' choice of physicians and hospitals to those in the plan's provider network. Thus, the MA plan has a financial incentive to reduce inappropriate treatment and manage beneficiaries' care in a cost-effective manner.

In 2017, about 19 million elderly—or 33 percent of beneficiaries—were enrolled in MA plans; the remainder were in traditional Medicare, in which the hospitals and physicians are paid on a fee-for-service (FFS) basis and the government regulates prices. Since 2003, the elderly are required to remain in a given health plan for a minimum of one year; previously, they were able to switch health plans with one month's notice.

Part D: Prescription Drug Coverage

In 2003, the Medicare Modernization Act was enacted, which was the largest and most significant change to Medicare since its inception. This legislation provided the aged with a new stand-alone outpatient prescription drug benefit starting in 2006. Part D is a voluntary program, and its cost is heavily subsidized (75 percent) by federal tax revenues. Seniors use more outpatient prescription drugs than does any other age group, and the out-of-pocket financial burden of these drugs was often of greater concern than the costs of hospital and physician services, most of which were covered by Medicare.

At the time of its enactment, the Medicare Trustees estimated that Medicare beneficiaries would pay a monthly premium of $60 a month by 2013. Instead, the monthly premium in 2013 was only $31 a month, on average, not much different than when the program started, which was $32.20 in 2006. The premium is estimated to be only $33.50 in 2018. The reason for the relatively constant Part D premium compared to the Part B premium, which increased from an average of $89 in 2006 to $134 in 2018, is that the drug benefit is provided by private, risk-bearing plans. Beneficiaries are offered a choice of competing plans at different monthly premiums. The result of offering the aged a financial incentive and a choice among competing private plans resulted in the Part D cost to the government being much less than projected, a rarity among government programs.

The design of the new prescription drug benefit was affected by an overall budgetary limit and legislators' desire that all seniors receive some benefit—not limited to just those with very large drug expenses. As shown in exhibit 8.3, after meeting a $405 deductible, the aged must then pay 25 percent of their drug expenses between $405 and $3,750 (so that almost all of the aged would receive some benefit). Then, to remain within the budget limit for this new benefit, the elderly must pay 100 percent of their drug expenses—between $3,750 and $5,000—before the government picks up 95 percent of their remaining drug expenses. As part of the ACA, the size of the "donut hole" was reduced.

Medigap Supplementary Insurance

As of 2013, about 16.9 percent of the aged (mostly middle and high income) also purchase private Medigap insurance to cover the HI and SMI out-of-pocket costs not covered by Medicare. Twelve percent of beneficiaries are covered by Medicaid, 22.6 percent have additional coverage through their previous

EXHIBIT 8.3
Medicare
Prescription
Drug Benefit

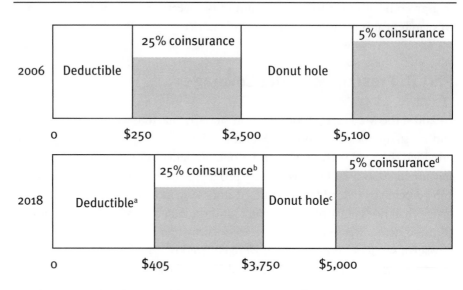

^aSome drug plans do not have a deductible.

^bSome drug plans may have a $10 copay.

^cIn the donut hole, the patient pays 35% for brand-name and 44% for generic drugs.

^dPatients pay some portion (either copays or coinsurance): $8.35 for brand-name drugs or $3.35 for generics (or 5%, whichever is higher).

Source: 2018 data from Centers for Medicare & Medicaid Services (2017b).

employers, 34.5 percent have their out-of-pocket costs covered through their MA plan, and the remaining 13.9 percent have no supplementary coverage (Medicare Payment Advisory Commission 2017, chart 3.1).

These out-of-pocket expenses—the HI and SMI deductibles and the 20 percent SMI copayment—can be a substantial financial burden, as *traditional Medicare does not have any stop-loss limit for out-of-pocket expenses. There is no limit to how much a Medicare patient can spend in a year.* (When their out-of-pocket expenses become too great a financial burden, the low-income aged must fall back on Medicaid.) Medicare is a program primarily for middle- and high-income elderly who can afford Medigap policies. Medigap policies provide the aged with nearly first-dollar coverage, eliminating patients' financial incentives to limit use of services or join managed care plans. MA plans do have an out-of-pocket limit on a person's Medicare expenses.

The Affordable Care Act's Approach to Reducing Rising Medicare Expenditures

The ACA relies on two approaches to reduce the rise in Medicare spending. The first approach was to fund several types of demonstration projects that relied on different payment systems that shift the financial risk of providing care from Medicare to providers. Bundled episode-based payments are a single lump sum payment to cover all the providers involved in the patient's episode of care, such as a hip replacement or heart surgery. Accountable care organizations (ACOs)—the most important of these demonstration projects—are networks of hospitals, physicians, and other providers receiving payment incentives from Medicare for coordinating care for a defined group of Medicare patients. Providers must meet quality and performance targets in return for shared savings for the cost of delivering patient care.

The second approach uses two ways to reduce Medicare provider prices. The first establishes an Independent Payment Advisory Board (IPAB) that decreases provider payments if Medicare spending rises faster than the gross domestic product (GDP) plus 0.5 percent annually. Second, the ACA lowers provider payment updates based on assumed productivity increases, whether or not the productivity increases actually occur.

Accountable Care Organizations

A large number of hospitals, physicians, and insurers have formed ACOs, and it is uncertain how well ACOs will be able to improve care coordination and limit Medicare spending increases. ACOs differ significantly from MA plans in several important ways that are likely to affect the ACO's performance. The designers of the ACO concept believed that traditional FFS Medicare is not as efficient as capitated MA plans and thus wanted to include more Medicare beneficiaries into a different payment system, closer to an HMO. The enrollees whose care the ACO is responsible for managing *do not have to agree* to become part of an ACO as they do when joining an MA plan; they are not informed that they were assigned to an ACO (based on which physicians they use), because they would likely be upset. Thus, the enrollees are still free to go to any provider without a referral or authorization from the ACO; they are not restricted to a closed provider network. However, the ACO is responsible for all of the medical expenditures of their assigned enrollees, including expenses incurred outside the ACO's provider network (Epstein et al. 2014).

The ACO is a very weak form of an HMO. The ACO concept prevents real competition. Patients are not provided with a choice of plans and a financial incentive to choose on the basis of cost, access, gaining additional benefits, and quality. The ACO-assigned enrollee does not benefit if the ACO reduces its cost of caring for the patient as would occur in an HMO. Any cost savings are not passed on to the patient in the form of lower premiums or more benefits.

ACO providers continue to receive FFS payments from Medicare. The difference between ACO payment and traditional Medicare is that, at the end of the year, the ACO is evaluated on the total amount spent on its assigned enrollees and the amount that would have been spent on them in a non-ACO system. Each ACO decides how much risk it is willing to incur—namely, is it willing to participate only in any shared savings it is able to achieve, or is it willing to accept full risk, similar to an MA plan, where it may lose money but could also make money if it succeeds in reducing its enrollees' medical expenditures?

There were 480 ACOs as of 2017 (Centers for Medicare & Medicaid Services 2017a). Most ACOs to date have accepted minimal risk, and ACOs generally have saved Medicare very little money; the cost savings have been concentrated in just a few ACOs (Livingston 2017).

Critics believe the ACO concept is flawed because of the lack of financial incentives among patients and providers. Also, it takes years before physicians, hospitals, and other providers are able to work together in an integrated care environment; before practice patterns are changed; and before care coordination occurs. If, over time, ACO delivery systems are able to achieve the desired integration of services, then changes in enrollee incentives (where the enrollees would share in the cost savings) and provider payment (capitation) are more likely to be instituted and ACOs may evolve into a competitive model.

Reductions in Regulated Provider Prices

The Independent Payment Advisory Board

IPAB consists of 15 appointed members whose task is to recommend policies to reduce Medicare spending if the rate of growth exceeds the annual percentage increase in per capita GDP plus 0.5 percent. With the exception of a few years, Medicare spending has historically exceeded this target goal. The IPAB's recommendations are to be implemented unless Congress can enact policies to achieve the same spending reductions. The IPAB is prohibited from recommending changes that would inflate beneficiaries' premiums, reduce benefits, or increase beneficiary cost sharing. Given its policy constraints, the IPAB would be restricted to reducing provider payments. However, reducing provider payments without changing patient or provider incentives will not improve efficiency or care coordination.

Orszag and Emanuel (2010), two architects of the ACA, claimed that the IPAB was the most important institutional change in the ACA and would result in large decreases in Medicare spending growth. However, little was said regarding its effects on providers and patient access to care.

In February 2018, as part of a large spending bill, the IPAB was repealed by a bipartisan majority of Congress. Legislators did not approve of nonelected bureaucrats having such important authority over Medicare.

Assumed Provider Productivity Increases

Medicare payment rates under the ACA will increase about 1.1 percent more slowly than provider input prices, which include market-based wages and energy and utility costs that are generally outside providers' control. Unless providers can increase their efficiency and productivity, the gap between costs and payments will grow over time. Providers will find it more difficult to provide the same quality and access to care.

In his analysis of the various ACA Medicare payment reductions, Foster (2011, 8), the chief Medicare actuary, stated that the estimated savings from assumed productivity payment decreases may be unrealistic. He also stated that "roughly 15 percent of Part A providers would become unprofitable within the 10-year projection period as a result of the productivity adjustments."

As provider payments grow slower than costs, many providers will become unprofitable and eventually unwilling or unable to treat Medicare beneficiaries; hospitals will be forced to close; and patients' access to care will be jeopardized.

Concerns About the Current Medicare System

Three basic concerns with Medicare are (1) whether its redistributive system is fair; (2) whether it promotes efficiency; and (3) whether its rising expenditures can be reduced given that its deficit is already $34 trillion dollars, and Medicare Trustees estimate that the Health Insurance Trust Fund (Part A) reserves will be depleted by 2029. Will Medicare be available for future generations, and, if so, who will bear the burden of funding this huge deficit?

Redistributive Aspects of Medicare

Does Medicare promote equity in terms of who receives and who finances its subsidies? When a person pays the full cost of the benefits she receives, no redistribution occurs. However, when a person pays less than the full costs of his benefits, he receives a subsidy and other population groups must bear the financial burden of that subsidy. Because Medicare is a pay-as-you-go system, beneficiaries, on average, contributed to it much less than the benefits they receive from it.

Redistribution is based on a societal value judgment that subsidies should be provided to particular groups. Typically, subsidies are expected to go to those with low income and be financed by those with high income. Medicare's redistributive system raises two concerns.

First, Medicare benefits have been the same for all beneficiaries regardless of income. Almost all elderly individuals—96 percent—pay the same Part B premium and, therefore, receive the same subsidy. Medicare has relatively high deductibles and no limit on out-of-pocket expenditures. (An insurance plan should always offer protection against catastrophic expenses.) Nonacute services, such as long-term care, are not covered. Furthermore, those aged requiring home care or nursing home services unrelated to an illness episode typically must rely on their own funds to cover such expenses. Thus, on average, out-of-pocket payments for excluded benefits as a percentage of income exceed 20 percent for the low-income elderly but are less than 6 percent for the high-income aged. Consequently, many low-income seniors find the out-of-pocket expenses a financial hardship, and 12 percent must rely on Medicaid (Centers for Medicare & Medicaid Services 2017b, tables I.1 and I.16).

How equitable is Medicare financing? Medicare beneficiaries do not pay the full costs of the medical services they receive; the aged are subsidized by those who pay state and federal taxes and HI taxes. The subsidy to Medicaid recipients is acknowledged to be welfare, as recipients receive benefits in excess of any taxes they may have paid. As a social welfare program, Medicaid is appropriately financed through the income tax system, whereby those with high income contribute more in absolute and proportionate payments in relation to their income. This is the fairest way to finance a welfare program.

Second, Medicare enrollees currently receive a very large intergenerational transfer of wealth (subsidy) from those currently in the labor force, which is no different from a conventional form of welfare. Several studies have estimated the difference between the Medicare payroll tax contributions made and the average value of the benefits received; the difference is the size of the intergenerational subsidy. As more aged became eligible over the years, they made some payroll contributions to the Trust Fund. In addition to the Part A subsidy is the 75 percent federal subsidy for Part B premiums (which exceeded $293 billion in 2016) and the 75 percent federal subsidy for Part D (which cost $95 billion in 2016) (Congressional Budget Office 2017a).

As shown in exhibit 8.4, a couple who turned 65 years old in 1960 and began receiving Medicare benefits in 1966 receives a $39,000 subsidy over their lifetime. In contrast, a couple who earned an average wage and turned 65 years old in 2015 receives a subsidy of $282,000 ($422,000 – $140,000). Yet another couple with an average income who will turn 65 years old in 2030 is estimated to receive a subsidy of $442,000 ($621,000 – $179,000) over their lifetime. In contrast, a couple who earned a high wage and will turn 65 years old in 2030 is estimated to receive a subsidy of $388,000, less than the $442,000 for a couple with an average income (Steurle and Quakenbush 2015, table 16).

Because the Part B and Part D subsidies are financed from general income taxes, those with high income provide relatively more of the intergenerational subsidy to the aged. With Part A, on the other hand, the subsidy to the aged is financed by a payroll tax on all employees. Thus, an inequitable situation arises. Low-income employees are taxed to subsidize the medical expenses of high-income Medicare beneficiaries.

Payroll taxes are not a desirable method of financing a welfare program. Although the employer and employee each pay half of the HI tax, studies

Year Cohort Turns Age 65 Years	Lifetime Medicare Benefits[a]	Lifetime Medicare Taxes[b]	Lifetime Medicare Subsidy
1960	$ 39,000	0	$ 39,000
1980	$156,000	$ 18,000	$138,000
2015	$422,000	$140,000	$282,000
2030	$621,000	$179,000	$442,000
2050	$965,000	$227,000	$738,000

EXHIBIT 8.4
Two-Earner Couple, Average Wage ($47,800 Each in 2015 Dollars)

[a]Lifetime Medicare benefits represent the amount needed in an account, earning a 2% real interest rate—that is, 2% plus inflation—to pay for those benefits.

[b]Lifetime Medicare taxes are based on the value of accumulated taxes, as if those taxes were put into an account that earned a 2% real rate of interest.

Note: All amounts are presented in constant 2015 dollars.

Source: Data from Steuerle and Quakenbush (2015).

confirm that employees end up paying most of the employer's share of the payroll tax as well (Brittain 1971; Gruber 1994; Summers 1989). When an employer decides how many people to hire and what wage to pay them, it considers all costs for each employee. Imposing any tax or regulatory cost on the employer on the basis of its number of employees is the same as requiring the employer to pay higher wages to employees. Whether the cost of that employee is in the form of wages, fringe benefits, or taxes does not matter to the employer; each is considered a cost of labor. An increase in the employer's HI tax raises the cost of labor.

When the cost of an employee is so high that it exceeds her value to the employer, the employer will discharge the employee—unless it can reduce the employee's wage to the point at which the cost is about equal to the employee's economic value. Typically, when payroll taxes are increased, wages are eventually renegotiated. Raises are smaller than they otherwise would have been because of higher payroll taxes imposed on the employer. Most of these taxes are shifted to employees in the form of lower wages.

A tax per employee imposed on the employer rarely stays with the employer. The part of the tax not passed on to the employee (decreasing wages) is shifted forward to customers (increasing prices of goods and services). For example, most industries are competitive and do not earn excessive profits; otherwise, new firms would enter the industry and compete away those profits. When the HI tax is increased on the employee and the employer, employment contracts cannot be immediately renegotiated. Rather than being forced to reduce its profits and potentially leave the industry, the employer will shift the tax expense to the consumer by raising prices, which is a greater proportionate burden on low-income consumers.

Why is half of the Medicare payroll tax imposed on the employer and half on the employee, even though the employer does not bear any burden of the tax? The reason is related more to a tax's visibility than to who ends up paying it. Politicians would prefer to make employees believe their share of the tax is much smaller than it actually is. Whether the tax is shifted back to the employee or forward to the consumer, the tax is regressive; those with low income pay a greater portion of their income in Social Security taxes than do high-income people. In 1994, the HI payroll tax became proportional to income, and the ACA made the tax progressive. Those with high earnings pay a greater percentage of their income on the tax, as well as pay an additional Medicare tax on unearned income. (These additional Medicare taxes, however, are *not* used to support Medicare; they are used to offset the increased expenditures under the ACA to expand Medicaid and provide subsidies for those under age 65 years who buy insurance on the state health insurance exchanges.)

If society makes the value judgment that it wants to help the poor by providing a welfare benefit, the most equitable way to do so would be to finance those benefits by taxing the rich. The burden of financing Part A, however, has fallen more heavily on those with low earnings. An income tax, which takes proportionately more from those with high income (including the aged), would be a more equitable way to finance benefits to those with low income. Although the retirement income of affluent seniors is not subject to payroll taxes, it is subject to income taxes.

Efficiency Incentives in Medicare

Traditional Medicare was designed to provide limited efficiency incentives to beneficiaries or providers of medical services. The elderly had no incentives to choose less costly hospitals, as the deductible was the same for all hospitals (and hospitals were precluded from competing for the aged by decreasing the deductible), and there were no copayments for inpatient admissions or lengths of stay. To protect themselves from copayments and deductibles, many elderly people buy Medicare supplementary insurance, lessening any incentive they may have to be concerned with higher prices or fewer services.

Physicians under FFS have an incentive to provide more of those services whose regulated fees greatly exceed their costs and few of those services whose regulated fees are less than their costs or not paid for under FFS. Chronic conditions are the costliest forms of care for Medicare patients. For example, diabetes management requires frequent checking of the patient's physical condition and blood sugar level, training the patient in self-management of his disease, discussing lifestyle changes, and ensuring that the patient is taking his medications. Many of the tasks required to manage chronic conditions—such as symptom monitoring, lifestyle changes, and monitoring and adjusting medications—do not require an office visit or even a physician. However, Medicare's FFS system does not pay for many of these services unless the patient is checked by the physician in an office visit. Other forms of patient–physician communication, such as phone calls and emails, are not covered by Medicare FFS. Instead, patients with questions must schedule an appointment and travel to a physician's office.

Hospitals initially were paid according to their costs for caring for an elderly patient. In 1984, Medicare changed hospital payment to a fixed price per admission, but neither hospitals nor physicians have a financial incentive to manage the overall costs of an episode of care for an aged patient or provide preventive services that lead to lower acute medical costs. (Only MA plans—such as HMOs, which are paid on a capitation basis—have such incentives, and more recently ACOs.)

Medicare can best be thought of as a state-of-the-art 1960s health insurance plan, and its design has not changed much since then. Congress modeled Part A after Blue Cross (which paid for hospitalization) and Part B after Blue Shield (which covered physician services). To secure the support of the medical profession, Congress acceded to the profession's demand that physician payment should be FFS and that patients should have free choice of physicians—namely, Medicare beneficiaries should not be required to enroll in HMOs, which would restrict their choice of out-of-network providers. Cost containment and utilization management methods used extensively in the private insurance market are virtually nonexistent in Medicare.

The lack of financial incentives for providers to coordinate care and minimize the cost of care led to rapid increases in the cost of Medicare. In 2016, Medicare spent $679 billion (compared with $1.8 billion in 1966). As Medicare expenditures exceeded government projections, every administration, regardless of political party, increased the HI payroll tax and reduced the rate of increase in hospital payments to treat Medicare patients.

As shown in exhibit 8.5, when Medicare introduced fixed prices per hospital diagnosis-related group (DRG) in the mid-1980s and placed an annual limit on raising the DRG price, hospitals' incentives changed; the rate of increase in Medicare hospital expenditures declined.

In 1997, concerned by the rate of increase in Part A expenditures, Congress enacted several changes intended to keep the Trust Fund solvent. Home health care expenditures, which were growing rapidly, were simply moved from Part A to Part B. This change shifted the financing of home health care from the payroll tax to the income tax. Congress also lowered payments to hospitals and to Medicare HMOs, which caused many HMOs to reduce enrollment of Medicare beneficiaries. (Both changes decreased Part A expenditures, as shown in exhibit 8.5.) To limit the rise of Part B expenditures, in 1997 Congress changed the method by which physicians' fees would be updated annually. Medicare physician fee increases were to be based in part on the percentage increase in real GDP per capita, which is unrelated to the supply of and demand for physician services by Medicare beneficiaries. This method is referred to as the *sustainable growth rate* (SGR). The consequences of the SGR were not felt for several years. While

EXHIBIT 8.5
Growth in Real Medicare Expenditures per Enrollee, Part A, Part B, and Part D, 1966–2016

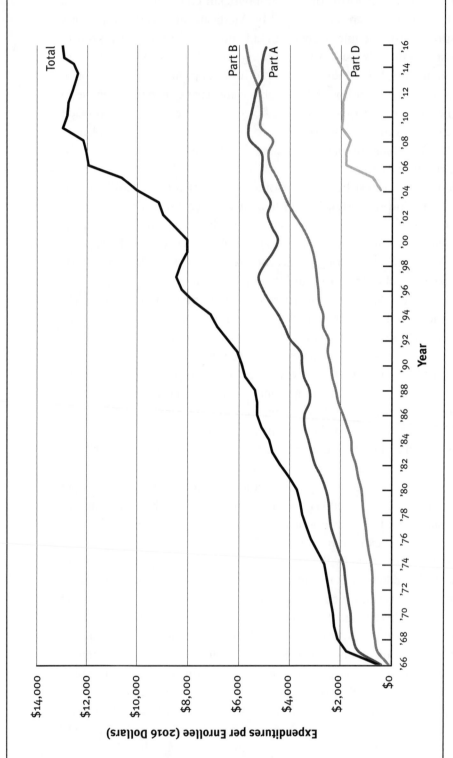

Notes: Values adjusted for inflation using the consumer price index for all urban consumers.
Part A and Part B expenditures exclude the patient deductible.

In 1997, home health care was moved from Part A to Part B. As a result, Part A expenditures per enrollee decreased.

Sources: Data from US Department of Health and Human Services and Social Security Administration (2000); 2000–2016 data from the Boards of Trustees, Federal Hospital Insurance and Federal Supplementary Medical Insurance Trust Funds (2017, tables III.B4, III.C4, III.D3, and V.B4).

Congress was limiting provider payment increases, seniors were receiving additional benefits through the expansion of Medicare coverage for preventive services such as mammograms, Pap smears, and prostate and colorectal screening tests.

Perhaps the clearest indication of Medicare's inefficient design is the wide variation across states in Medicare expenditures per beneficiary with chronic illness, without any difference in life expectancy or patient satisfaction.[2] For example, in 2014 Medicare spent, on average, $43,240 per beneficiary in New Jersey, compared with an average of $34,837 per beneficiary in other states. Patients with chronic illness in New Jersey had an average of 40.1 physician visits during the last six months of their lives, compared with an average of 13.8 visits for similar patients in Utah (or 13.2 visits in Idaho, the lowest in the United States). Hospital days during the last six months of their lives varied from 23 per beneficiary at one medical center in New York City to 4.9 at another medical center in Utah. During the past two years, Medicare spent an average of $79,182 per beneficiary per year at one academic medical center, compared with $32,707 at another academic medical center (Dartmouth Institute for Health Policy & Clinical Practice 2017). Medicare pays for quantity, not quality. Only relatively recently has Medicare tried to pay for quality, not quantity.

The Unsustainable Rise in Medicare Expenditures

The current Medicare program, without improvements, is ill suited to serve future generations of seniors and eligible disabled Americans, nor is it sustainable given its huge and increasing financial deficit.

Medicare's future includes a series of challenges. The number of elderly people is increasing, both in absolute and percentage terms. People are living longer. Medical care costs continue to rise, and technology is driving those costs even higher. Maintaining the solvency of Part A by imposing higher payroll taxes on the working population is politically infeasible and inequitable for low-income individuals. Part B and Part D expenditures will require substantial increases over time in both general revenue financing and premium charges to the elderly. As the reserves in the Medicare Part A Trust Fund are drawn down and as Parts B and D (and Medicaid) general revenue financing requirements continue to grow, pressure on the federal budget will intensify, which will require politically unpopular payroll and income tax hikes and necessitate reductions in other federal programs, such as the military, welfare, education, and the environment.

Medicare expenditures for Parts A, B, and D are expected to increase from 3.8 percent of GDP in 2016 to 5.0 percent by 2027. As a percentage of the federal budget, total Medicare expenditures are estimated to increase from 18 percent to 21 percent by 2027, based on the more pessimistic, but likely, projections (Congressional Budget Office 2017b, tables 1 and 2).

In coming years, the aging of the population will place great pressures on the Trust Fund. In 2011, the first of the 77 million baby boomers (those born between 1946 and 1964) began to retire. In 1960, just 9.2 percent of the population was 65 years or older. In 2017, almost 16 percent of the population was 65 years or older. The number of Medicare recipients will almost double from 51 million in 2017 to 88 million in 2050 (up from 70 million when the last of the baby boomers retire in 2030) (see exhibit 8.6). In 2050, one in five Americans (22 percent) will be 65 years or older.

People older than 65 years have five to six times the medical costs of younger Americans. Large numbers of retirees, combined with increased longevity and more expensive and advanced medical technology, will generate huge

EXHIBIT 8.6
Population Pyramid, United States, 1960, 2017, and 2050

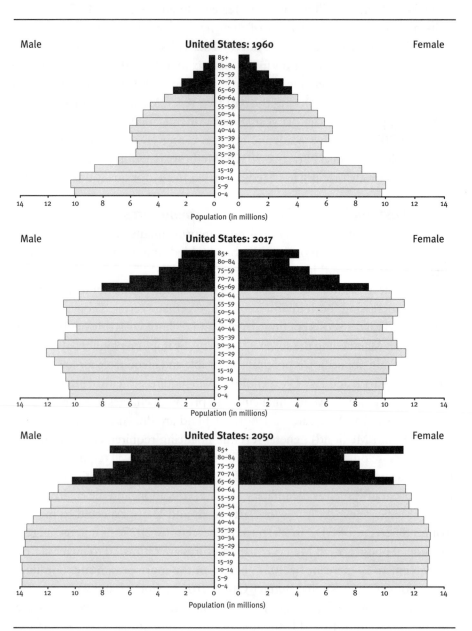

Source: Data from the US Census Bureau (2017).

increases in Medicare spending. The magnitude of this projected shortfall in the Trust Fund is shown in exhibit 8.7.

As of 2016, the Trust Fund (for Medicare Part A) had declining positive cash flows; annual cash flow deficits are expected to grow rapidly as more baby boomers retire. The growing deficits will exhaust the Trust Fund reserves by 2029.[3] (The current cash deficit is financed by previous payroll taxes in excess of outlays. The federal government gave the Trust Fund an IOU and spent the excess payroll taxes as part of general federal expenditures. Now the federal government is using general tax revenues to repay those IOUs, which contribute to the federal deficit.)

The employee base supporting Medicare is eroding. Per elderly person, the number of workers paying taxes and financing the program has steadily declined, increasing the tax burden on each employee. In 1960, there were 5.1 workers per Medicare beneficiary, and in 1970, that number decreased to 3.7 per beneficiary; currently, there are 3.1 workers per beneficiary. By 2030, the number of workers is projected to decline to 2.4 per beneficiary (Boards of Trustees, Federal Hospital Insurance and Federal Supplementary Medical Insurance Trust Funds 2017). Intermediate projections indicate that the HI tax will have to be increased from 2.9 percent to 6.21 percent (Congressional Budget Office 2010). However, as actual experience has been much closer to pessimistic (high-cost) assumptions, the HI tax rate will likely have to be increased to 10.86 percent by 2030.[4] These higher tax rates are only for Part A. In 2016,

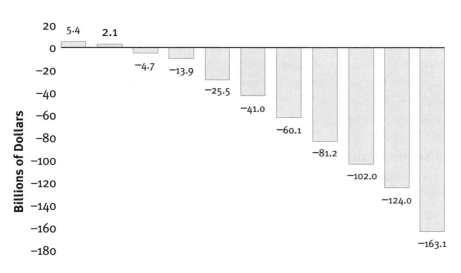

EXHIBIT 8.7
Cash Deficit of the Medicare Hospital Insurance Trust Fund, 2016–2026

Note: Data based on high-cost assumption.

Source: Data from Boards of Trustees, Federal Hospital Insurance and Federal Supplementary Medical Insurance Trust Funds (2017, table III.B5.)

annual federal expenditures were $293 billion for Part A, $301 billion for Part B, and $95 billion for Part D: a total of $689 billion. Projected federal subsidies (expenditures minus premiums) in 2027 for each part of Medicare, in constant dollars, are $547 billion for Part A, $635 billion for Part B, and $205 billion for Part D: a total of $1.387 trillion (Congressional Budget Office 2017a).

Political support for Medicare is likely to decline as the costs to the nonelderly go up, with a consequent increase in intergenerational political conflict. The US political system cannot wait until more baby boomers retire to resolve an issue that involves such a large redistribution of wealth among different groups in society. Those who will become eligible for Medicare in the coming decade have certain expectations about what they will receive from the program. Politicians cannot change Medicare's benefits at the last moment. No presidential candidate will campaign on decreasing Medicare benefits. Any changes will have to be agreed upon in nonelection years and gradually phased in. Yet, the longer Congress waits, the higher will be the payroll tax.

Enacting legislation to decrease Medicare benefits or eligibility in a presidential or congressional election year will be difficult, as Medicare has such widespread political support among the elderly, the near elderly, and their children (who might be faced with an increased financial burden of paying for their parents' medical expenses). Given that a new Medicare system must be phased in, and few nonelection years exist in which to enact such controversial legislation, any changes must be enacted within the first two years after a presidential election.

Proposals for Medicare Reform

Proposals to restructure Medicare should be based on three criteria: equity, efficiency, and a reduction in the rate of increase in Medicare spending. Many approaches have been proposed, and a combination of proposals will likely be used to spread the financial burden.[5] The following are several of the widely discussed proposals.

Raise the Eligibility Age to 67

Similar to one change made to the Social Security system to improve its solvency, raising the age of Medicare eligibility to 67 years (by means of a gradual phase-in over 24 years) would make the eligibility age for Social Security and Medicare the same. With increased life expectancy, people could work longer and maintain their employment-based health insurance.

Reduce the Rate of Increase in Medicare Provider Payments

This approach has been used and is likely to be part of any long-term solution. However, decreasing provider payments will ultimately reduce provider participation and access to care by Medicare beneficiaries.

Increase the HI Tax

This approach, which also has been used, is likely to be part of any proposed solution. Raising the HI tax would increase the financial burden on low-wage workers. However, the HI tax could be made more progressive.

Increase Part B and Part D Premiums and Make Them Income Related

Most elderly people currently pay a premium that covers only 25 percent of Part B and Part D expenditures. (The progressivity of income payments, which has already begun, should continue.) Premiums could be increased over time to cover a higher percentage of these expenses. With this approach, hardship on the low-income aged would be minimized by a greater use of income-related premiums. Equity would be achieved, and the deficit reduced if subsidies to high-income aged were eventually phased out.

Rely on Competition Between Medicare Health Plans

One proposal to increase competition among Medicare health plans is referred to as *premium support*. MA plans would compete directly with the government-administered Medicare FFS on a regional basis, and beneficiaries would select their coverage from the competing options. Government payment to health plans, including FFS plans, would be based on the competing plans' premiums. The government's contribution could be based on the second lowest plan's (risk-adjusted) bid, which would become the new benchmark premium. Thus, a beneficiary would always have access to a plan that requires no additional premium. Beneficiaries choosing a plan whose bid is above the benchmark would have to pay the difference between the benchmark's premium and that of the costlier plan. If a beneficiary chooses a relatively expensive coverage option, the additional premium would be paid entirely by the Medicare enrollee, not the government. If traditional Medicare FFS is not the cheaper plan or the benchmark, beneficiaries would have to pay an additional premium to remain in traditional Medicare.

Competition among Medicare plans, with different premiums and different additional benefits, would provide a powerful incentive for beneficiaries to seek out high-value, low-cost plans, and for plans to compete on premiums, benefits, patient access to providers and satisfaction, and quality. Premium support changes Medicare from a defined (and continually expanding) benefit program—which is an open-ended commitment by the government to pay for promised benefits regardless of their costs—to a defined contribution program, with the government paying a predetermined amount of money (including Parts A, B, and D). This approach is similar to providing a voucher to a health plan. (Older and sicker beneficiaries would receive higher amounts so that health plans would have an incentive to enroll them.) The financial risk of caring for the aged is shifted from the government to the health plan. This approach is similar to the Federal Employees Health Benefits plan.

Proponents of competition in Medicare claim that a defined contribution program will force competing Medicare plans to be efficient and will reduce rising Medicare expenditures.

Currently, MA plans could be much less expensive. However, they have less incentive to reduce their costs, rather than lower their premium or give enrollees a rebate, because the government requires them to provide more generous benefits. With more generous benefits, enrollees use more services and the plan's costs increase.

Proponents of premium support claim that health plan competition would reduce Medicare costs. Jacobson, Neuman, and Damico (2012) found that the best-performing MA HMOs can offer the Medicare benefit package at premiums that are below the cost of FFS in most parts of the United States. MA plans have a greater incentive to innovate to lower costs than do FFS providers, which would get paid less. Part D (a defined contribution program) provides evidence of the effect of Medicare plan competition. Medicare beneficiaries choose among competing private drug plans; as a result, premiums for these plans have stayed relatively constant over time. Plans must cover at least one drug in each specified drug class, but the plans can vary according to whatever else they cover, copays, and premiums.[6] The private drug plans have encouraged generic substitution for branded drugs by reducing copays for generics. The costs of the drug program are 40 percent less than the Medicare actuary's projection (Congressional Budget Office 2014).

A study by Baicker, Chernew, and Robbins (2013) found that greater Medicare managed care penetration (MA) in a market decreased hospital utilization (length of stay) and hospital costs for all seniors, including those in traditional Medicare, as well as for non-Medicare insured patients. The spillover effects of competition were positive on all sectors of the medical care system.

Duggan, Gruber, and Vabson (2018) studied Medicare beneficiaries who were in MA plans but had to switch to FFS Medicare because the MA plan exited the market. Their study design controls for whether the populations enrolled in the two types of plans differed in their health status. After the enrollees were forced to switch to FFS Medicare, their hospital use and hospital charges were higher than those in the MA plan. The authors concluded that greater efficiency occurs when enrollees have a managed care option available.

Allowing alternative health plans to compete is the best way to judge whether traditional Medicare FFS or MA plans are more efficient. To ensure that enrollees have adequate information about the plans, data must become available on each plan's premiums, out-of-pocket payments, quality, waiting times for access to primary care physicians and specialists, and patient satisfaction.

Critics of a defined contribution program claim that many enrollees will have to pay an additional premium if traditional Medicare is not one of the cheaper plans and they want to remain in it. Many Medicare beneficiaries would have to make a trade-off between higher premiums and restrictions on provider choice. Critics are also concerned about the ability of the elderly to make such choices and the difficulty in understanding the differences between competing health plans.

Change Medicare to an Income-Related Program

The defined contribution program could be used to change Medicare to an income-related program. Each recipient would receive premium support, but its value would be determined by the recipient's income. The subsidy would equal the entire premium required to provide a uniform set of benefits for low-income beneficiaries, but wealthy beneficiaries would receive proportionately smaller premium support vouchers. The income-related voucher would be phased in for future Medicare beneficiaries.

An income-related subsidy would reduce the cost of Medicare and the huge intergenerational subsidies from low-income workers to high-income aged. Income-related benefits would also help the low-income aged, who cannot afford the deductibles, cost sharing, and Part B and D premiums and thus must rely on Medicaid for these payments.

Politics of Medicare Reform

The popularity of Medicare among the aged (who have the highest voting participation rates) and their children (who are relieved of the financial responsibility for their parents' medical expenses) means that politicians who attempt to change it without the endorsement of both political parties are at great political risk. Any political party proposing decreased Medicare benefits, higher beneficiary cost sharing or premiums, or the removal of seniors' free choice of providers would lose the votes of the elderly and their children. It has been more politically feasible to impose financial burdens on providers by paying them less and raising employee payroll taxes than increasing the financial burden on the elderly.

Unfortunately, the longer it takes to phase in a system that is equitable and efficient, the greater the political problems will be. Current workers will have to pay higher payroll taxes, intergenerational transfers from low-income workers will increase, beneficiaries will have less access to providers as providers' fees are reduced, and the financial hardship on low-income aged, who cannot afford high out-of-pocket expenditures and rising Parts B and D premiums, will be greater. The sooner the financial burden is shared among the different groups in an equitable manner, the smaller will be future tax increases.

Summary

To make Medicare an equitable and efficient redistribution system, society must recognize the "entitlement" myth of Medicare and acknowledge its large welfare component. Government subsidies should be used primarily to help the low-income elderly. Health plans, including traditional Medicare, should be able to compete for beneficiaries on the basis of price, quality, outcomes, and enrollee satisfaction. Health plans will then have incentives to be efficient and responsive to beneficiary preferences.

The potential political cost of suggesting dramatic solutions to the problems of Medicare is high for either major party. Whatever the combination of approaches selected, a vast redistribution of wealth will result. A bipartisan commission whose recommendations are adopted by Congress has, in the past, resolved such highly visible redistributive problems. The National Bipartisan Commission on the Future of Medicare (created by Congress as part of the 1997 Balanced Budget Act) was unable to reach agreement (by just one vote) on reforming Medicare in 1999.

Whether and when a commission approach will again be used to reform Medicare remains to be seen.

Discussion Questions

1. Which population groups are served by Medicare, what are the different parts of Medicare, and how is Medicare financed?
2. Discuss how Medicare's patient and provider incentives affect efficient use of services.
3. How equitable are the methods used to finance Medicare?
4. How does the Medicare Hospital Trust Fund differ from a pension fund?
5. Why is it necessary to reform Medicare?
6. Why is it politically difficult to reform Medicare?
7. How would patient and provider incentives differ between ACOs and proposals for transforming Medicare into a premium support model?

Notes

1. The MA plans submit a premium bid for insuring Medicare beneficiaries. The government establishes a benchmark premium to decide how much to pay MA plans. The benchmark is the average FFS expenditure for a Medicare beneficiary in that geographic area, adjusted for risk factors. If the MA plan bid exceeds the benchmark premium, the plan receives the benchmark premium. If the plan's bid is below the benchmark, the government pays the plan its bid and gives a rebate of 75 percent of the difference between the plan's bid and the

benchmark premium. The 75 percent rebate must be returned to the plan's enrollees in the form of additional benefits and services. About 90 percent of MA plans receive some rebate.

2. The Dartmouth Atlas Project online report, *The Care of Patients with Severe Chronic Illness*, examined differences in the management of Medicare patients with one or more of twelve chronic illnesses that account for more than 75 percent of all US healthcare expenditures (Center for the Evaluative Health Sciences, Dartmouth Medical School 2006). Among people who died between 1999 and 2003, per capita spending varied by a factor of six between hospitals across the country. Spending was not correlated with rates of illness in different parts of the country; rather, it reflected how intensively certain resources—acute care hospital beds, specialist physician visits, tests and other services—were used in the management of people who were very ill but could not be cured. Since other research has demonstrated that, for these chronically ill Americans, receiving more services does not result in improved outcomes, and since most Americans say they prefer to avoid a very 'high-tech' death, the report concludes that Medicare spending for the care of the chronically ill could be reduced by as much as 30%—*while improving quality, patient satisfaction, and outcomes.*

3. The high-cost estimates assume that the ACA payment reductions will not be implemented in all future years. Medicare actuaries claim that, under current law, Medicare's payments for health services would fall increasingly below providers' costs. "Providers could not sustain continuing negative margins and would have to withdraw from serving Medicare beneficiaries. ... Under such circumstances, lawmakers might feel substantial pressure to override the productivity adjustments, much as they have done to prevent reductions in physician payment rates. In view of these issues, it is important to note that the actual future costs for Medicare are likely to exceed those shown by the current-law projections in this report, possibly by substantial amounts" (Boards of Trustees, Federal Hospital Insurance and Federal Supplementary Medical Insurance Trust Funds 2013, 207).

4. The rate of growth in real wages (because HI is a payroll tax) and life expectancy at retirement are important components of these projections. Pessimistic projections assume a rate of growth in real wages similar to the growth rate in the past 25 years, which is half as large as that used in the intermediate assumption. Advances in medicine, genetics, and biotechnology are also projected to result in a more rapid increase in life expectancy at retirement than the intermediate projections that assume the same rate as that for the past 50 years.

5. The May 2013 issue of *Health Affairs* contains many articles devoted to reducing Medicare's spending growth rate. Also see Kaiser Family Foundation (2013), which includes more than 150 options and the pros and cons of each.

6. The ACA required Part D drug plans to increase the number of drugs within a class to more than one. This change decreased a Part D drug plan's negotiating ability relative to a drug company. Pharmaceutical firms have benefitted at the expense of higher premiums for Medicare beneficiaries.

References

Baicker, K., M. Chernew, and J. Robbins. 2013. "The Spillover Effects of Medicare Managed Care: Medicare Advantage and Hospital Utilization." National Bureau of Economic Research Working Paper No. 19070. Published May. www.nber.org/papers/w19070.pdf.

Boards of Trustees, Federal Hospital Insurance and Federal Supplementary Medical Insurance Trust Funds. 2017. *2017 Annual Report of the Boards of Trustees of the Federal Hospital Insurance and Federal Supplementary Medical Insurance Trust Funds.* Published July 13. www.cms.gov/Research-Statistics-Data-and-Systems/Statistics-Trends-and-Reports/ReportsTrustFunds/Downloads/TR2017.pdf.

———. 2013. *2013 Annual Report of the Boards of Trustees of the Federal Hospital Insurance and Federal Supplementary Medical Insurance Trust Funds.* Published May 31. https://downloads.cms.gov/files/tr2013.pdf.

Brittain, J. A. 1971. "The Incidence of Social Security Payroll Taxes." *American Economic Review* 61 (1): 110–25.

Center for the Evaluative Health Sciences, Dartmouth Medical School. 2006. "The Care of Patients with Severe Chronic Illness: An Online Report on the Medicare Program by the Dartmouth Atlas Project." Dartmouth Atlas of Health Care. Accessed March 30. www.dartmouthatlas.org/downloads/atlases/2006_Chronic_Care_Atlas.pdf.

Centers for Medicare & Medicaid Services. 2017a. "All Medicare Shared Savings Program (Shared Savings Program) Accountable Care Organizations (ACOs)." Published January. www.cms.gov/Medicare/Medicare-Fee-for-Service-Payment/sharedsavingsprogram/Downloads/All-Starts-MSSP-ACO.pdf.

———. 2017b. "CMS Statistics Reference Booklet: 2016 Edition." Modified March 6. www.cms.gov/Research-Statistics-Data-and-Systems/Statistics-Trends-and-Reports/CMS-Statistics-Reference-Booklet/2016.html.

———. 2017c. "Medicare Enrollment Dashboard Data File." Modified February 28. www.cms.gov/Research-Statistics-Data-and-Systems/Statistics-Trends-and-Reports/CMSProgramStatistics/Dashboard.html.

————. 2017d. "2018 Medicare Parts A & B Premiums and Deductibles." Published November. www.cms.gov/Newsroom/MediaReleaseDatabase/Factsheets/2017-Fact-Sheet-items/2017-11-17.html.

Congressional Budget Office. 2017a. "Medicare—Congressional Budget Office's June 2017 Baseline." Published June 29. www.cbo.gov/sites/default/files/recurring data/51302-2017-06-medicare.pdf.

————. 2017b. *An Update to the Budget and Economic Outlook: 2017 to 2027.* Published June. www.cbo.gov/system/files/115th-congress-2017-2018/reports/52801-june2017outlook.pdf.

————. 2014. *Competition and the Cost of Medicare's Prescription Drug Program.* Published July 30. www.cbo.gov/publication/45552.

————. 2010. *The Long-Term Budget Outlook.* Published June 30. www.cbo.gov/ftpdocs/115xx/doc11579/06-30-LTBO.pdf.

Dartmouth Institute for Health Policy & Clinical Practice. 2017. "Care of Chronically Ill Patients During the Last Two Years of Life." Dartmouth Atlas of Health Care. Accessed March 2018. www.dartmouthatlas.org/tools/downloads.aspx?tab=40.

Davis, P. A. 2016. *Medicare: Part B Premiums.* Congressional Research Service. Published August 4. https://fas.org/sgp/crs/misc/R40082.pdf.

Duggan, M., J. Gruber, and B. Vabson. 2018. "The Consequences of Health Care Privatization: Evidence from Medicare Advantage Exits." *American Economic Journal: Economic Policy* 10 (1): 153–86.

Epstein, A., A. K. Jha, E. J. Orav, D. L. Liebman, A.-M. J. Audet, M. A. Zezza, and S. Guterman. 2014. "Analysis of Early Accountable Care Organizations Defines Patient, Structural, Cost, and Quality-of-Care Characteristics." *Health Affairs* 33 (1): 95–102.

Foster, R. S. 2011. "The Estimated Effect of the Affordable Care Act on Medicare and Medicaid Outlays and Total National Health Care Expenditures." Testimony before the House Committee on the Budget, January 26. http://budget.house.gov/uploadedfiles/fostertestimony1262011.pdf.

Gruber, J. 1994. "The Incidence of Mandated Maternity Benefits." *American Economic Review* 84 (3): 622–41.

Internal Revenue Service. 2017. "Affordable Care Act Tax Provisions." Updated August 27. www.irs.gov/affordable-care-act/affordable-care-act-tax-provisions.

Jacobson, G., T. Neuman, and A. Damico. 2012. *Transforming Medicare into a Premium Support System: Implications for Beneficiary Premiums.* Kaiser Family Foundation Medicare Policy. Published October. https://kaiserfamilyfoundation.files.wordpress.com/2013/01/8373.pdf.

Kaiser Family Foundation. 2013. *Policy Options to Sustain Medicare for the Future.* Published January. https://kaiserfamilyfoundation.files.wordpress.com/2013/02/8402.pdf.

Livingston, S. 2017. "Medicare Shared-Savings ACOs Cut $1 Billion in Costs over Three Years." *Modern Healthcare*. Published August 29. www.modernhealthcare. com/article/20170829/NEWS/170829881.

Medicare Payment Advisory Commission. 2017. *A Data Book: Health Care Spending and the Medicare Program*. Published June. http://medpac.gov/docs/default-source/data-book/jun17_databookentirereport_sec.pdf.

Orszag, P., and E. Emanuel. 2010. "Health Care Reform and Cost Control." *New England Journal of Medicine* 363 (7): 601–3.

Steuerle, C. E., and C. Quakenbush. 2015. "Social Security and Medicare Lifetime Benefits and Taxes." Urban Institute. Published September. www.urban.org/sites/default/files/publication/66116/2000378-Social-Security-and-Medicare-Lifetime-Benefits-and-Taxes.pdf.

Summers, L. 1989. "Some Simple Economics of Mandated Benefits." *American Economic Review* 79 (2): 177–83.

US Census Bureau. 2017. "International Data Base." Updated August. www.census.gov/data-tools/demo/idb/informationGateway.php.

US Department of Health and Human Services and Social Security Administration. 2000. *Annual Statistical Supplement, 2000 to the Social Security Bulletin*. Accessed April 9, 2018. www.ssa.gov/policy/docs/statcomps/supplement/2000/supp00.pdf.

MEDICAID

Medicaid is a means-tested welfare program for the poor, providing medical and long-term care to more than 22 percent of the US population. In 1985, the program covered 20 million people, the federal government spent $23 billion on the program, and it represented 2.4 percent of the federal budget. By 2016, Medicaid covered 74 million people (1 in 5 Americans), a greater number than those enrolled in Medicare; total federal expenditures reached $369 billion; and the program's share of the federal budget increased to 9.2 percent (Centers for Medicare & Medicaid Services 2016). Medicaid is the fastest-growing expenditure in the federal budget, and it is the third-largest expenditure in the federal budget. Moreover, these rapidly increasing Medicaid expenditures, which represent a growing financial burden on federal and state budgets, continue to provide insufficient access to care for program beneficiaries.

As a result of the Affordable Care Act (ACA), Medicaid has had a major enrollment expansion. The ACA increased Medicaid eligibility to include single, childless adults and families whose incomes are between 100 and 138 percent of the federal poverty level (FPL) (as of 2017, this meant up to $16,643 for an individual and $33,948 for a family of four). For the first time, these eligibility standards, which are uniform for all states, include childless adults.

The ACA provided full federal financing for those newly eligible (from 100 percent up to 138 percent of the FPL) for the years 2014 to 2016. The federal matching rate then gradually declines from 100 percent for those newly eligible to 90 percent by 2020 and thereafter (Kaiser Family Foundation 2013). Only 31 states plus the District of Columbia, however, chose to take advantage of the ACA's eligibility expansion, despite the ACA's inducement that the federal government would initially pay 100 percent of the medical expenses for those meeting the new eligibility levels.[1]

Exhibit 9.1 shows the number of Medicaid enrollments and expenditures after the ACA reforms. The ACA expanded Medicaid enrollments by about 12 million. The federal government's generous payment rates for those eligible for the Medicaid expansion are indicated by the large increase in federal expenditures compared with state expenditures during that time.

Given the large expected increase in Medicaid enrollment starting in 2014, the government was concerned that the Medicaid population would have limited access to primary care physicians, particularly given that Medicaid pays physicians lower fees than any other payer. Thus, for just two years (covering the 2014 Congressional midterm elections), the ACA required the federal government to pay

EXHIBIT 9.1
Medicaid
Enrollment and
Expenditures,
2013–2017

Year	Enrollment (in Millions)	Expenditures Federal (Billions)	Expenditures State (Billions)	Expenditures Total (Billions)
Historical data				
2013	59.8	$262.7	$192.9	$455.6
2014	65.1	299.3	195.4	494.7
2015	70.0	347.7	204.7	552.3
Projections				
2016	72.2	363.4	212.5	575.9
2017	73.5	368.9	226.6	595.5

Source: Data from Centers for Medicare & Medicaid Services (2016).

the additional cost of making Medicaid fees to primary care physicians equal to Medicare fees. After 2014, Medicaid fees were determined by the states and returned to their previous lower levels, with a consequent sharp drop in physician availability.

Federally Mandated Medicaid Population Groups

Medicaid is administered by each state, but policy is shared with the federal government, which pays the states different matching formulas (between 50 and 74 percent of the costs of the program, based on each state's financial capacity [per capita income]). (This federal matching rate is for those who are eligible according to pre-ACA criteria.) These federal dollars make Medicaid a less expensive approach (than other state programs such as General Assistance) for the states to use in expanding access to medical care by those with low income. Each state Medicaid program must cover certain federally mandated population groups to qualify for federal matching funds.

The first and largest federally mandated population group is composed of those receiving cash welfare assistance (including single-parent families) who were previously eligible for Aid to Families with Dependent Children (AFDC), as well as those low-income aged, blind, and disabled individuals who qualify for Supplemental Security Income. The second group comprises low-income pregnant women and children who do not qualify for cash assistance. The third group includes those considered to be "medically needy" (i.e., individuals who do not qualify for welfare programs but have high medical or long-term care expenses). The fourth and final group consists of low-income Medicare beneficiaries who cannot afford the deductibles, cost-sharing payments, premiums for Medicare Parts B and D, or the cost of services not covered by Medicare.

States may expand eligibility and enroll additional groups (and add services beyond those mandated by the federal government). Thus, wide variations in coverage and eligibility exist among the states. Groups typically added at the state's option include medically needy groups, such as the elderly and people with disabilities; children and pregnant women at a high percentage (e.g., 200 percent) above the FPL; and all uninsured persons with income below a certain level. However, the percentage of the Medicaid-covered population considered poor (less than 100 percent of the FPL) varies greatly by state—from 32 to 68 percent. Just being poor is insufficient to qualify for Medicaid. On average, in 2016, only 52 percent of those classified as poor were enrolled in Medicaid. The percentage of near poor—100 to 199 percent of the FPL—enrolled by states varies from 20 to 50 percent, with an average of 35 percent in 2016 (US Census Bureau 2017).

In 1996, Temporary Assistance to Needy Families (TANF) was enacted to replace AFDC. TANF retains the same eligibility rules as those of AFDC. Before welfare reform, many poor children qualified automatically for Medicaid because their families were receiving AFDC, the national cash benefits program for poor children. Welfare reform ended that link by abolishing AFDC. Because Congress did not want anyone to lose Medicaid eligibility as a consequence of welfare reform, it decreed that states should continue using their old AFDC rules for determining Medicaid eligibility, such as covering pregnant women, the medically needy, and children (if their parents would have qualified for AFDC). Children of women who leave welfare for work are still eligible for Medicaid if their family income remains low enough.

An Illustration of Medicaid Eligibility

Within federal guidelines, states may set their own income-and-asset eligibility criteria for Medicaid. Following is an illustration of how the medically needy qualify for Medi-Cal (Medicaid in California). A person cannot have more than $2,000 in assets ($3,000 if there is a family member older than 60 years), excluding a house, car, and furniture. One's financial assets can be reduced in many legitimate ways to qualify for Medicaid. Money could be spent fixing up one's house, purchasing a new car, or taking a vacation, or it could be put in a special burial account. Selling one's house and giving the cash to one's children will make one ineligible for Medicaid for months. The penalty period for doing so is determined by dividing the amount transferred by the average private pay cost of a nursing home in the state. For example, if a person gave away property to his children worth $100,000 and the monthly cost of nursing home care in California in 2017 was $8,114 (for a semiprivate room; a private room was $9,703), the person would be ineligible for Medicaid benefits for 16 months (Genworth Financial Inc. 2017).

When a couple is involved, special spousal financial protections exist. If a husband enters a nursing home, the wife can remain in their home and is entitled to have a monthly income of $2,981 and $119,220 in financial assets (excluding a primary residence and a car). If the wife's Social Security payments are below $2,981 per month, the husband's Social Security can be used to bring her monthly income to $2,981 (as of 2015) (California Department of Health Care Services 2015). Retirement accounts and other assets can be partially shielded from the government by counting the income from those retirement accounts toward the $2,981 monthly income. For example, if a person has $100,000 in an investment account and withdraws $500 a month, the $500 counts toward his monthly income, but the $100,000 does not count as an asset. A number of states have begun to crack down on various schemes used by some wealthy aged to shield their assets to become Medicaid eligible, such as setting up annuities, trusts, and life contracts.[2] In general, many middle-class elderly become distraught when they find they must spend down their hard-earned assets for a spouse to become eligible for Medicaid.

State Children's Health Insurance Program

A major expansion of Medicaid eligibility occurred in 1997. As part of the 1997 Balanced Budget Act, Congress enacted the State Children's Health Insurance Program (SCHIP). SCHIP was enacted to provide coverage for low-income children whose family income was too high to qualify for Medicaid. Politically, children are considered a vulnerable and more deserving group than other uninsured groups; consequently, this program expansion received bipartisan support. (Medical benefits for children are considered relatively inexpensive when compared with benefits for uninsured adults.) Furthermore, providing coverage to older children (up to age 19 years) was viewed as an expansion of existing Medicaid policies, which extended to infants, younger children, and pregnant women in the late 1980s. This program provided the states with federal matching funds to initiate and expand healthcare assistance for uninsured low-income children up to age 19 years with family income as high as 400 percent of the FPL.

The number of children eligible for public coverage increased dramatically, as did participation rates in SCHIP. The percentage of uninsured children whose family income is between 100 and 200 percent of the FPL (as well as those whose family income is less than 100 percent of the FPL) has declined since 1997. In each of these groups, the percentage of children with public coverage climbed, while the percentage of children with private insurance declined during this period. Not all of the increase in public coverage for poor and low-income children was the result of uninsured children being enrolled in SCHIP. Significant growth in public coverage also resulted from a movement from private insurance to free or low-cost public coverage (referred to as *crowd-out* because public insurance "crowds out" private insurance). Gruber and Simon

(2008) estimated that as many as 60 percent of those newly enrolled in public insurance programs, such as SCHIP, were formerly in private insurance plans.

Bipartisan support for SCHIP was achieved as a result of an ideological compromise on how SCHIP services would be delivered to eligible children. States may either purchase health insurance coverage for eligible children in the private market or include them in the state's Medicaid program.

SCHIP, now called Children's Health Insurance Program (CHIP), was renewed in 2010. A concern with CHIP was that it was originally intended for children from low-income families but has now been extended to include more children from middle-income families who do not qualify for Medicaid. Qualifying income for CHIP in some states is as high as $98,400 for a family of four (e.g., New York in 2017) (Kaiser Family Foundation 2018a); moreover, several states use CHIP funds to cover adults other than expectant mothers.

The ACA requires any child whose parents earn between 100 and 133 percent of the FPL to switch from CHIP to Medicaid. Many children previously enrolled in CHIP and in private health plans, such as Blue Cross, are required to receive their care from Medicaid networks, whose access to and coordination of care is inferior to that provided by private health plans.

The changes in eligibility resulting from the ACA Medicaid expansion and the shift of children from CHIP to Medicaid increased total Medicaid enrollment from 58.9 million in 2012 to 73.5 million by 2017. Medicaid enrollment would have been higher had all states implemented the ACA's Medicaid expansion. (The estimate of 73.5 million represents the total number of individuals enrolled in Medicaid at any point during the fiscal year; however, average enrollment for 2017 was 52 million.)

Medicaid faces serious challenges in ensuring that enrollees have appropriate access to medical services while controlling rising medical costs.

Medicaid Enrollees and Medicaid Expenditures

Broadened eligibility requirements for Medicaid have caused the number of recipients to sharply rise from 20.2 million in 1975 to 60 million in 2013 and to an estimated 70 million by 2017. Most of the previous enrollment growth resulted from federal and state expansions in coverage of low-income children and pregnant women. As of 2015, the major beneficiary groups consisted of low-income children (41 percent); nondisabled low-income adults (pregnant women and adults in families with children receiving cash assistance, 35.5 percent); seniors receiving Medicare who need Medicaid (dual eligibles) to pay for their deductibles, cost sharing, premiums for Medicare Parts B and D, and other services not covered by Medicare (8.2 percent); and blind and disabled individuals receiving acute medical and long-term care services (15.3 percent).

As shown in exhibit 9.2, the distribution of Medicaid expenditures does not match the distribution of Medicaid enrollees. Although 76.5 percent of Medicaid recipients are low-income parents and children, they account for only 44.7 percent of Medicaid expenditures. By comparison, 55.3 percent of Medicaid expenditures are for medical services and institutional care for the aged, people with disabilities, and people with mental handicap (23.5 percent of Medicaid recipients).

Although Medicaid enrollment has increased over time, from about 14 million in the 1970s to 20 million in the 1980s to more than 60 million in 2013 and to 70 million in 2015, the distribution of beneficiary groups has stayed roughly constant during this period. State and federal Medicaid expenditures have increased rapidly and are expected to continue to rise sharply over the next decade. Medicaid represents one of the largest items in state budgets, along with elementary and secondary education expenditures. Federal and state Medicaid expenditures were $41.3 billion in 1985; spending rose to an estimated $552 billion in 2015 and is expected to reach almost a trillion dollars a year ($958 billion) by 2025. During this same period, the number of beneficiaries is expected to grow by 17 percent (see exhibit 9.3).

EXHIBIT 9.2
Percentage Distribution of Medicaid Enrollees and Benefit Payments by Eligibility Status, Fiscal Year 2015

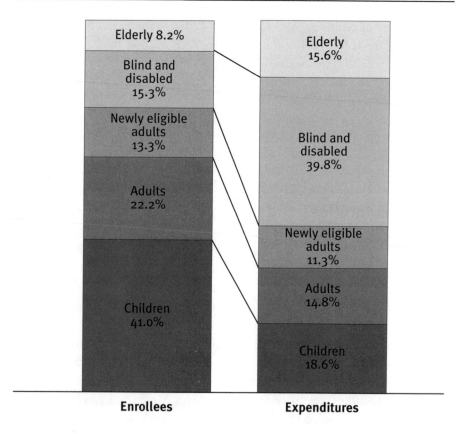

Enrollees

Elderly 8.2%
Blind and disabled 15.3%
Newly eligible adults 13.3%
Adults 22.2%
Children 41.0%

Expenditures

Elderly 15.6%
Blind and disabled 39.8%
Newly eligible adults 11.3%
Adults 14.8%
Children 18.6%

Note: Totals exclude disproportionate-share hospital expenditures, territorial enrollees and expenditures, and adjustments.

Source: Data from Centers for Medicare & Medicaid Services (2016, table 2).

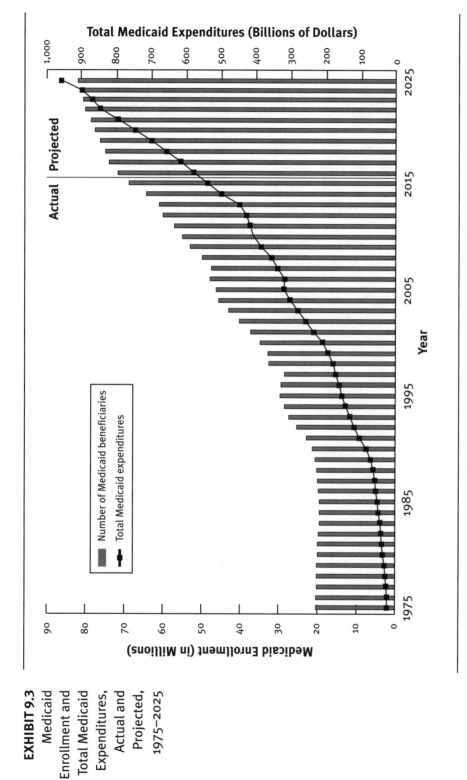

EXHIBIT 9.3
Medicaid Enrollment and Total Medicaid Expenditures, Actual and Projected, 1975–2025

Sources: Data from Centers for Medicare & Medicaid Services (2010, 2016).

Exhibit 9.4 shows the distribution of Medicaid expenditures by type of service. The largest share of Medicaid expenditures is for acute care (74.4 percent), which is made up managed care (43.6 percent), various fee-for-service (FFS) payments (28 percent), and Medicare premiums (2.7 percent). Long-term care (which includes nursing home care and home health care) represents the second-largest category (22.1 percent). Because Medicaid pays providers relatively low rates, payments to disproportionate-share hospitals (3.5 percent) compensate those hospitals that serve proportionately more Medicaid beneficiaries and low-income people.

Medicaid Concerns

Medicaid Eligibility

Although Medicaid is the government's major healthcare financing system for the poor—including low-income families, children, childless adults, elderly, and those requiring long-term care—it is generally perceived to be highly inadequate. The program does not cover a large portion of those with low income. On average, only 52 percent of people below 100 percent of the FPL in the non-Medicaid

EXHIBIT 9.4
Medicaid
Expenditures by
Service, 2015

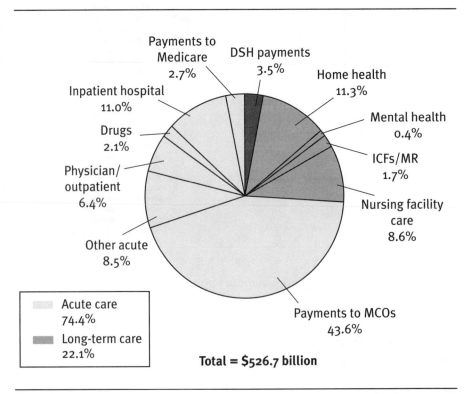

Total = $526.7 billion

Note: DSH = disproportionate-share hospital; ICFs/MR = intermediate care facilities for individuals with developmental disabilities; MCOs = managed care organizations.

Source: Data from Centers for Medicare & Medicaid Services (2017).

expansion states were covered, and only 35 percent of those who are considered poor and near-poor (below 200 percent of the FPL) were covered in 2016. The likelihood of a poor person's being eligible for Medicaid varies greatly by state. States with higher per capita income were more likely to cover a higher percentage of their poor population and provide more generous Medicaid benefits. The percentage of poor eligible for Medicaid varied from 32 to 68 percent among states in 2016. (In 2017, 100 percent of the FPL was $24,600 for a family of four, $16,240 for a couple, and $12,060 for a single person [US Census Bureau 2017; US Department of Health and Human Services 2018].)

When Medicaid eligibility is expanded, newly eligible adults who are employed and have health insurance have an incentive to drop their private insurance and accept the free public insurance. Medicaid is considered less valuable than private insurance (because of the stigma cost and more restricted access to physicians because of low Medicaid reimbursement), but as the cost of private insurance increases, Medicaid becomes a more desirable substitute. Expanded public coverage in some states has displaced existing private coverage with little additional overall gain in coverage, referred to as *crowd-out*. (Part of the private coverage replaced by public coverage may have had relatively limited benefits.) For those who switch from private to public coverage, it would be preferable if they could be partially subsidized to maintain their private coverage rather than being fully subsidized by Medicaid.

Medicaid eligibility has a sharp income limit. Thus, people who are employed and on Medicaid have a disincentive to earn more income such that it would place them above the income limit; they could lose their eligibility once their incomes rise above their state's cutoff level, which could still be below the FPL. Dague, DeLeire, and Leininger (2017) found that increased Medicaid eligibility levels for childless adults resulted in a disincentive to work; they were less likely to return to the labor market. Those newly eligible adults, who pay no premiums and minimal copayments, have a 12 percent relative reduction in employment compared with similar childless adults not eligible for the Medicaid expansion (the latter group was on a Medicaid waiting list).

The potential loss of Medicaid benefits is a disincentive for recipients to accept low-paying jobs. A Medicaid-eligible person must make a trade-off between earning a higher income versus losing all of her benefits (this is referred to as the *notch effect*). Instead, if as people's wages go up, they would lose only a portion of their Medicaid benefits, their incentives toward earning additional income would be reversed. Graduating Medicaid eligibility according to income would provide an incentive for those who want to keep their Medicaid benefits to work more hours and seek higher-paying jobs.

Medicaid Effectiveness

Medicaid is a fragmented FFS system in which care is not coordinated and accountability for outcomes is nonexistent; poor care often results in greater reimbursement for the provider. The traditional program has been shown to be ineffective in improving its beneficiaries' health, compared with those who are uninsured. In 2008, Oregon enrolled an additional 10,000 low-income individuals, chosen by lottery, in its Medicaid system. Baicker and colleagues (2013) compared the health status of those who were selected by lottery with those who were not selected by lottery to be enrolled in Medicaid. The researchers found that Medicaid coverage had no significant effect on the prevalence or diagnosis of hypertension or high cholesterol levels or on the use of medication for those conditions; in addition, no improvement in individuals' diabetes was observed. Medicaid recipients, however, had reduced out-of-pocket expenses, decreased rates of depression, and increased use of preventive and physicians' services. An important finding from this study was that those on Medicaid felt financially relieved about not having to pay for needed medical care.

In a further analysis of the Oregon data, Taubman and colleagues (2014) found that Medicaid coverage significantly increased emergency department (ED) visits by 40 percent per person, compared with ED use by those not selected for Medicaid. The higher numbers of ED visits were for broad types of conditions, including those readily treatable in primary care settings. These findings on ED use by Medicaid recipients are contrary to the expectations of the ACA that as more of the uninsured are enrolled in Medicaid and treated in physicians' offices, costly ED visits would decline, and money would be saved.

The ACA is expanding Medicaid eligibility to many millions of people at a cost of hundreds of billions of dollars. If the program merely expands eligibility, significant changes in participants' health status will not occur. Unless the delivery of Medicaid services is radically transformed, a great deal of money will have been spent with little effectiveness in improving the health of its beneficiaries.

State Funding

Rising Medicaid expenditures have become a great financial burden to the states and the federal government. Continuing to spend an increasing portion of state budgets on Medicaid would require a tax hike or a reduction of expenditures on politically popular programs, such as education and prisons. Each option is politically costly. Instead of making such a politically costly choice, many states have resorted to setting low FFS provider-payment rates.[3] The consequences of reduced provider fees are low provider participation rates, limited access to care, less willingness of a physician to spend much time with a Medicaid patient, a shift away from physician offices to hospital EDs, and a lack of care coordination (Decker 2009; Zuckerman, Williams, and Stockley 2009).

Conflict exists between Medicaid's goals of expanding eligibility, improving access to care, providing coordinated and effective care, and slowing the rate of increase in Medicaid expenditures. Federal financing of Medicaid expansion (and subsidies for the health insurance exchanges) started in 2014. The federal government, however, currently faces a huge deficit, which will increase as a result of expanding federal health expenditures. Unless the federal government can reduce current and future Medicaid (and Medicare) expenditures, it will be unable to reduce its ever-growing deficit.

The Affordable Care Act's Impact on Medicaid

The ACA generously funded those states that expanded Medicaid eligibility for single, childless adults whose incomes are between 100 and 138 percent of the FPL (as of 2017, this meant up to $16,643 for an individual and $33,948 for a family of four). Several studies have been conducted to determine the effect of Medicaid expansion on the patient's health status, access to care, use of services, and financial effects (Antonisse et al. 2018; Miller and Wherry 2017).

A consistent finding in the studies is that those who became newly eligible in the Medicaid expansion states felt less stressed regarding their ability to pay for medical care, and were financially better able to pay for additional follow-up care than were those in nonexpansion states. Beneficiaries in the expansion states did not have significantly greater use of physician services or hospital admissions than the uninsured in nonexpansion states. The researchers noted that in expansion states, increased waiting times were reported for appointments, which delayed receipt of medical care.

These researchers generally concluded that health effects have been minimal, although the study periods have been only a few years. Studies over a longer period are needed to determine whether significant changes in health status occur among Medicaid enrollees compared with comparable groups who have been uninsured.

Medicaid Reforms

Numerous proposals have been made to improve Medicaid's effectiveness in providing care to those with low incomes and to reduce the rise in Medicaid's rapidly increasing expenditures and the financial burden placed on the federal and state governments (McConnell and Chernew 2017; Slavitt and Wilensky 2017). The following are three such proposals, which are not mutually exclusive.

Medicaid Managed Care
Managed care offers Medicaid programs a way to reduce rising Medicaid expenditures and provide coordinated care to enrollees. By paying managed care plans, such as health maintenance organizations (HMOs), a fixed fee per person per

month (i.e., a capitation fee), states can shift their risk for higher expenditures to a managed care plan. In addition, states should be able to monitor how well the managed care plan achieved specific goals, such as immunization rates, preventive care, reduced use of hospital EDs, and so on. Medicaid managed care has become an important approach to providing Medicaid services.

The largest change in the distribution of Medicaid expenditures has been the growth in Medicaid managed care. Almost all states rely on some form of managed care for their Medicaid populations. About 77 percent (as of 2014) of beneficiaries are enrolled in some form of managed care program (Kaiser Family Foundation 2018b). The types of managed care plans vary across states. Initially, many states used primary care case management, whereby beneficiaries are enrolled with a primary care gatekeeper, who does not assume financial risk but receives a monthly fee of about $2 to $3 per enrollee per month and is responsible for coordinating the enrollee's care. Under the primary care case management concept, providers themselves are paid on a FFS basis. In the mid-1990s, many states moved toward contracting with HMOs and paying them a capitated amount for each enrolled Medicaid beneficiary. Under full-risk capitation, the HMO provides a comprehensive range of required benefits that includes preventive and acute care services.

States contract with managed care plans for two reasons. First, the rate of increase in Medicaid expenditures is reduced. Managed care produced substantial savings in the private sector. Similar savings have not occurred in FFS Medicaid programs, in which providers do not have similar incentives to decrease inpatient utilization, use less costly outpatient settings, and minimize unnecessary use of the ED.

Second, managed care plans expand Medicaid enrollees' access to care. To save money, Medicaid FFS programs reduced payments to hospitals and physicians (well below rates paid by other insurers), so that many providers refuse to serve Medicaid patients. Enrollees typically have had to rely on EDs and clinics that predominantly serve large numbers of Medicaid patients. By contracting with managed care plans, the states expect their enrollees to have greater access to primary care providers, receive coordinated care, and spend fewer dollars than they had previously. The percentage of Medicaid beneficiaries enrolled in managed care plans has increased rapidly—from 4.5 percent in 1991 to 77 percent in 2014.

Medicaid managed care programs have a great deal of experience caring for relatively young demographic groups, such as children and working-age adults, similar to their commercial insurance businesses. However, children and nondisabled, low-income adults (who make up 76.5 percent of Medicaid beneficiaries) account for a relatively small share of Medicaid spending (44.6 percent of Medicaid expenditures).

Managed care plans, however, have had less experience in caring for chronically ill and disabled populations, for whom providing managed care is more difficult, but the potential savings of coordinated care are much greater. The aged, blind, and disabled as well as those in nursing homes (23.5 percent of beneficiaries) account for the majority of Medicaid expenditures (about 55.4 percent). Until managed care plans enroll and manage care for the chronically ill, those with severe mental illness, and the institutionalized aged who require long-term care, Medicaid managed care savings will not be very large (Centers for Medicare & Medicaid Services 2016).

If managed care plans are to enroll these costlier Medicaid beneficiaries, states must provide these plans with appropriate financial incentives. State capitation payments should reflect the costs of caring for different types of beneficiaries (risk-adjusted payments). If the payment rate is set too low, managed care plans will be unwilling to enroll high-cost groups. To date, it has been difficult to develop capitation rates that adequately reflect the costs of caring for elderly and chronically ill population groups.

In addition, it is necessary for state Medicaid programs to monitor the care provided and the access to care by beneficiaries in any delivery system, whether it is managed care or traditional FFS. Unfortunately, many states' performance in monitoring the quality of care received by their Medicaid populations has been notoriously inadequate. For budgetary reasons, some states are unwilling to monitor and punish low-performing providers. Nursing home scandals continue to surface, and many Medicaid programs' quality of care and accessibility are inadequate. Private insurers use various monitoring mechanisms and financial incentives, such as pay-for-performance, to reward providers who practice high-quality care. It remains to be seen how well state agencies will use the quality information they receive to similarly reward or penalize Medicaid providers.

Block-Granting Medicaid

Federal law restricts the ability of states to change Medicaid benefits. To make such changes, a state must apply for a federal waiver, which is a time-consuming process. Having the federal government provide block grants to the states based on a fixed amount per Medicaid beneficiary, which would increase by an inflation index, has been proposed as a means of limiting the open-ended financing commitment by federal and state governments. Currently, the federal government matches (by 50 to 73 percent) each state's Medicaid expenditures.

Many state governors would prefer receiving federal block grants in return for greater state flexibility in the design of Medicaid benefits and administration. Fewer restrictions on how states spend Medicaid dollars would enable them to be more innovative in providing care to their Medicaid population; improving access to care; and reducing their Medicaid budgets, which are crowding out state expenditures on education and public safety. Block grants also would improve equity among the states because wealthier states that can afford to spend more receive a greater amount of federal Medicaid funds. The Medicaid benefits received by the poor vary greatly depending on where they live.

Several states have experimented with federal Medicaid waivers, and not all have had favorable outcomes. An important reason for the success of waivers in Rhode Island and Washington has been careful planning and engaging important interest groups, such as the medical societies. Implementation that is too rapid causes confusion among providers and recipients. Low payment rates, failure to adequately adjust risk-based payments, and adverse selection negatively affected the implementation of Tennessee's reforms (Beaulier and Pizzola 2012). Rhode Island, for example, was able to reduce Medicaid costs while increasing patients' access and reducing the use of EDs for routine visits. Rhode Island's Medicaid program reduced admissions to nursing homes by means of better case management programs for patients with asthma, diabetes, and heart problems. Home care subsidies provided long-term care patients with services in their home and in a community-based facility, which saved money for Rhode Island (Lewin Group 2011).

States could mine utilization data to determine patients at high risk and offer preventive services to minimize costly hospital admissions. States could fund nonmedical services, such as supportive housing for the mentally ill; allow Medicare and Medicaid patients to use Medicaid funds for services, such as caregivers, that enable them to remain in their residence rather than enter a nursing home; and permit Medicaid patients to obtain care from nurse practitioners in a retail medical clinic rather than from physicians in the ED. Care management techniques can reduce ED use and improve health outcomes for adults with chronic diseases. Increasing home and community-based services would decrease the number of nursing home users.

Block grants would have to be adjusted by type of Medicaid recipient—child, young adult, person with an addiction-related illness, or patient in a nursing home; otherwise, states could game the system by enrolling more low-cost people, such as children. The federal government's ongoing monitoring of the health outcomes of state programs that receive block grants would alleviate the concern that the poor would be harmed by states not providing necessary services and access to care. Medicaid block grants (per capita) also would be counter-cyclical economic policy. In an economic downturn, as more people qualify for Medicaid, the total block grant would increase—compared with the current situation in which the state receives less tax revenues and cutbacks are made, when instead there should be an increase (Cassidy 2013).

Many state governors have requested waivers providing fewer Medicaid funds in exchange for greater flexibility in how they spend those dollars.

Allowing states to receive block grants with fewer rules and mandates would encourage greater experimentation with approaches to care for the poor, disabled, and elderly populations that are more satisfactory but less expensive. Other states would be able to copy those approaches that improve health outcomes and better meet the needs of their Medicaid populations.

Income-Related Vouchers

Another Medicaid reform proposal is to do away with eligibility levels that have a sharp cutoff and instead include all those with low income by means of an income-related voucher (excluding those in long-term care and disabilities programs). The size of the subsidy would decline as income grows, and the beneficiary would be able to use his voucher to choose among competing managed care plans. Because those receiving a subsidy would lose only a portion of their subsidized voucher as their incomes rise, they would no longer have a disincentive to accept a low-paying job. An income-related voucher would eliminate the large differences among states in the percentage of their populations eligible for Medicaid.[4]

The ACA provides income-related subsidies only to those whose income is between 133 and 400 percent of the FPL and who buy private insurance through the health insurance exchanges. Treating those on Medicaid in the same way would be preferable, as would permitting them to buy private insurance on the exchanges.

An income-related subsidy would improve efficiency (and equity) while reinforcing the movement toward Medicaid managed care, with its emphasis on coordinated care, better access to primary care physicians, and incentives to provide care in less costly settings.

To be effective in promoting competition among health plans, the income-related voucher should be risk adjusted; specifically, chronically ill Medicaid enrollees should receive more valuable vouchers than those who are younger and in better health. Risk-adjusted premiums will induce health plans to compete for chronically ill enrollees and develop disease management programs to better care for them.

When Medicaid beneficiaries have a choice among managed care plans, managed care firms have an incentive to compete for patients. States, however, need to provide their Medicaid population with relevant information about their plan choices.

To the extent that beneficiaries are assigned to a managed care plan, the role of choice in disciplining plan performance is negated.

To reduce Medicaid expenditures, attention must be focused on those groups consuming the largest portion of Medicaid expenditures—namely, the chronically ill. (These groups are also the fastest-growing segment of the Medicaid population.) The challenge for the states in the coming years is to include these vulnerable population groups in managed care, pay managed care plans appropriately for their care, and vigorously monitor the care they receive.

Medicaid's movement to managed care has made survival difficult for many safety-net providers, such as public and not-for-profit hospitals and community clinics that have traditionally served large Medicaid and uninsured populations. These providers rely on disproportionate-share hospital payments and need Medicaid patients if they are to survive. As managed care firms seek less expensive hospital settings and reduce inpatient use, these safety-net providers must become part of a network that competes for Medicaid capitation contracts. Unless they can do so, their financial stability is threatened. The loss of safety-net providers would be unfortunate, as a Medicaid income-related voucher will not likely be enacted in the near future. Until then, those without private insurance or Medicaid coverage will need access to medical care, which is likely to be delivered primarily by safety-net providers.

Summary

Medicaid is a means-tested program that pays for the medical care provided to low-income people. Although state Medicaid programs are federally required to serve designated population groups, states have discretion to include additional medical services and population groups in their programs. Medicaid does not cover all those with low income or all of the uninsured population. Medicaid recipients and their supporters are not able to provide legislators with as much political support as do those supporting Medicare. Thus, the generosity of Medicaid programs (i.e., provider access, eligibility levels, and included services) varies across states. In times of budget difficulties, many states attempt to reduce their deficits by cutting Medicaid eligibility, benefits, and provider payments.

In 2014, the ACA expanded Medicaid eligibility. A major concern is that the greater number of newly and previously eligible beneficiaries greatly increased the demand for physician services, and supply did not similarly increase. Unless state Medicaid programs increase physician fees, beneficiaries will not attain greater access to coordinated care and will have to rely on hospital EDs.

Several approaches have been proposed to increase Medicaid's effectiveness. Providing beneficiaries with the option to use managed care plans will increase their access to care. Managed care plans can lower the costs of caring for Medicaid patients by providing coordinated care and boosting physician productivity. Providing a federal income-related subsidy to all those eligible for Medicaid would improve equity among low-income individuals who live in different states and give them an incentive to earn more without the fear of completely losing their Medicaid eligibility. Block-granting Medicaid to the states in return for fewer federal regulations will permit each state to innovate in how medical services are provided, which, in turn, results in greater patient satisfaction at a lower cost.

An important challenge facing Medicaid reform is how to handle the costliest beneficiaries—people with disabilities and long-term care patients in nursing homes. The current Medicaid system has not performed adequately in this arena, and managed care plans must demonstrate their ability to care for these patients.

The federal government has a huge debt and large annual deficits. The growing number of Medicaid and Medicare patients will further increase federal expenditures and the deficit. The financial markets will soon place great pressure on the federal government to reduce its deficits. Medicaid is an important contributor to federal deficit spending, and its recipients are less politically powerful than Medicare and Social Security beneficiaries. Thus, changes in Medicaid's financing and eligibility are likely to occur.

Discussion Questions

1. Describe the Medicaid program. What are the differences between Medicare and Medicaid?
2. How well does Medicaid achieve its objectives?
3. Why would it be difficult to enroll all of the Medicaid population in HMOs?
4. What are some approaches to reforming Medicaid?
5. What are the arguments for and against having one government program instead of having both Medicare and Medicaid?
6. What changes did the ACA make with respect to the Medicaid program?

Notes

1. States declined to participate in the ACA Medicaid expansion for several reasons. For example, states currently face substantial Medicaid expenditures for currently eligible populations and for growing numbers of aged requiring long-term care services. Accepting the financial burden of newly eligible enrollees, even if it requires only a 10 percent matching rate, may still be too large a financial commitment. These additional expenditures over time may require increasing taxes or reducing funding for other politically popular programs.

2. As part of deficit-reduction legislation in 2005, Congress included limits on the ability of people with homes and assets to get Medicaid to pay their nursing home costs. The legislation toughened rules that prevent individuals seeking to become Medicaid eligible from transferring assets, usually to their children. Examples of these changes include lengthening the period in which states can examine the inappropriate transfer of assets to five years and excluding from Medicaid coverage people whose home equity exceeds $500,000 (previously, a home equity limit did not exist).

3. States have used various financing schemes to inappropriately increase federal Medicaid payments. For example, a state may impose a $100 million tax on its hospitals and then return those funds to the hospitals in the form of Medicaid expenditures. The state then receives federal Medicaid matching funds of $100 million to $200 million, depending on its matching formula. Once the state receives the federal matching payments, it can substitute those funds for its share of future Medicaid spending or even for non-Medicaid purposes (if the state does not return the full amount of the tax payments to the hospitals). Because all states except Alaska game the system by using these "provider taxes" to raise federal Medicaid spending, Congress has been reluctant to close this loophole.

4. To provide income-related subsidies, Medicaid would have to be federalized. States would continue to spend what they currently spend, and the federal government would have to pay for the difference between what is currently spent and what is required for an equal income-related subsidy across all states.

References

Antonisse, L., R. Garfield, R. Rudowitz, and S. Artiga. 2018. "The Effects of Medicaid Expansion Under the ACA: Updated Findings from a Literature Review." Kaiser Family Foundation issue brief. Published March 28. www.kff.org/medicaid/issue-brief/the-effects-of-medicaid-expansion-under-the-aca-updated-findings-from-a-literature-review/.

Baicker, K., S. Taubman, H. Allen, M. Bernstein, J. H. Gruber, J. P. Newhouse, E. C. Schneider, B. J. Wright, A. M. Zaslavsky, and A. N. Finkelstein. 2013. "The Oregon Experiment: Effects of Medicaid on Clinical Outcomes." *New England Journal of Medicine* 368 (18): 1713–22.

Beaulier, S., and B. Pizzola. 2012. "The Political Economy of Medicaid Reform: Evidence from Five Reforming States." Mercatus Center at George Mason

University. Published April. www.mercatus.org/system/files/The-Political-Economy-of-Medicaid-Reform.pdf.

California Department of Health Care Services. 2015. *2015 Comprehensive Brochure: California Partnership for Long-Term Care.* Published March. www.rureadyca.org/sites/default/files/uploads/2015_comprehensive_brochure_5-28-2015.pdf.

Cassidy, A. 2013. "Per Capita Caps in Medicaid." *Health Affairs* health policy brief. Published April 18. www.healthaffairs.org/do/10.1377/hpb20130418.246392/full/.

Centers for Medicare & Medicaid Services. 2017. "Expenditure Reports from MBES/CBES: Financial Management Report for FY 2015." Accessed October. www.medicaid.gov/medicaid/financing-and-reimbursement/state-expenditure-reporting/expenditure-reports/index.html.

———. 2016. *2016 Actuarial Report on the Financial Outlook for Medicaid.* Accessed October 31, 2017. www.cms.gov/Research-Statistics-Data-and-Systems/Research/ActuarialStudies/Downloads/MedicaidReport2016.pdf.

———. 2010. *2010 Actuarial Report on the Financial Outlook for Medicaid.* Accessed October 31, 2017. www.medicaid.gov/medicaid/financing-and-reimbursement/downloads/medicaid-actuarial-report-2010.pdf.

Dague, L., T. DeLeire, and L. Leininger. 2017. "The Effect of Public Insurance Coverage for Childless Adults on Labor Supply." *American Economic Journal: Economic Policy* 9 (2): 124–54.

Decker, S. 2009. "Changes in Medicaid Physician Fees and Patterns of Ambulatory Care." *Inquiry* 46 (3): 291–304.

Genworth Financial Inc. 2017. *Genworth 2017: Cost of Care Survey.* Accessed October. www.genworth.com/about-us/industry-expertise/cost-of-care.html.

Gruber, J., and K. Simon. 2008. "Crowd-Out Ten Years Later: Have Recent Expansions of Public Insurance Crowded Out Private Health Insurance?" *Journal of Health Economics* 27 (2): 201–17.

Kaiser Family Foundation. 2018a. "Medicaid and CHIP Income Eligibility Limits for Children as a Percent of the Federal Poverty Level as of January 1, 2018." Accessed April. www.kff.org/health-reform/state-indicator/medicaid-and-chip-income-eligibility-limits-for-children-as-a-percent-of-the-federal-poverty-level/.

———. 2018b. "Total Medicaid Managed Care Enrollment." Accessed April. www.kff.org/medicaid/state-indicator/total-medicaid-mc-enrollment/.

———. 2013. "Medicaid: A Primer—Key Information on the Nation's Health Coverage Program for Low-Income People." Published March. www.kff.org/medicaid/7334.cfm.

Lewin Group. 2011. *An Independent Evaluation of Rhode Island's Global Waiver.* Published December 6. www.lewin.com/publications/publication/201112060458.html.

McConnell, K. J., and M. E. Chernew. 2017. "Controlling the Cost of Medicaid." *New England Journal of Medicine* 377 (3): 201–3.

Miller, S., and L. R. Wherry. 2017. "Health and Access to Care During the First 2 Years of the ACA Medicaid Expansions." *New England Journal of Medicine* 376 (10): 947–56.

Slavitt, A., and G. Wilensky. 2017. "JAMA Forum: Reforming Medicaid." Published July 11. https://newsatjama.jama.com/2017/07/11/jama-forum-reforming-medicaid/.

Taubman, S. L., H. Allen, B. Wright, K. Baicker, and A. Finkelstein. 2014. "Medicaid Increases Emergency-Department Use: Evidence from Oregon's Health Insurance Experiment." *Science* 343 (6168): 263–68.

US Census Bureau. 2017. "Current Population Survey (CPS)." Accessed April 2018. www.census.gov/cps/data/cpstablecreator.html.

US Department of Health and Human Services. 2018. "HHS Poverty Guidelines for 2018." Accessed April. https://aspe.hhs.gov/poverty-guidelines.

Zuckerman, S., A. Williams, and K. Stockley. 2009. "Trends in Medicaid Physician Fees, 2003–2008." *Health Affairs* 28 (3): w510–w519.

HOW DOES MEDICARE PAY PHYSICIANS?

I n 2017, Medicare spent $70 billion on physician services, which represents about 10 percent of total Medicare expenditures (Congressional Budget Office 2017). However, physicians, through their decisions, affect a much higher percentage of Medicare expenditures. Medicare physician payments represent a significant share of physician incomes, on average, more than 20 percent. Because physician payment has such a large impact on total Medicare expenditures (and on physicians' own incomes), an understanding of how Medicare pays physicians is an important policy issue.

Medicare has used several physician payment systems. In 2015, a new Medicare physician payment system was instituted: the Medicare Access and CHIP Reauthorization Act (MACRA). Why was it necessary to change the payment system? How does the new payment system compare with previous ones? What are the likely effects of this new payment system on access to care by Medicare patients, Medicare expenditures, and physician incomes?

When evaluating past and current Medicare payment systems, it is important to have criteria by which to judge each approach. First, Medicare physician reimbursement should be sufficiently generous to encourage physicians to participate in the Medicare program. Second, physicians should be incentivized to provide their Medicare patients with the appropriate (quality and quantity) care. Third, physicians should use the most cost-effective set of resources (e.g., personnel, technology) and the least costly settings, such as office visits, homes, and institutions. Fourth, physicians should be accountable for the care they provide.

Initial Medicare Physician Payment

When Medicare Part A (which pays for hospital care) was enacted in 1965, Part B (which pays for physician and out-of-hospital services) was included. (Part B is a voluntary benefit for which the aged pay a monthly premium that covers only 25 percent of the total cost of the program.) Physicians were paid on a fee-for-service (FFS) basis and were given the choice of whether they wanted to participate. Physicians could also participate for some medical claims but not for others. When physicians participated, they agreed to accept the Medicare fee for that service, and the patient was responsible for only 20 percent of that fee after the annual deductible was paid.

If a physician did not participate, the patient had to pay the physician's entire charge (which was higher than the Medicare fee) and apply for reimbursement from Medicare. When the government reimbursed the patient, it would pay only 80 percent of the Medicare-approved fee for that service. Thus, a patient who visited a nonparticipating physician had to pay 20 percent of the physician's Medicare-approved fee plus the difference between the approved fee and the actual charges. This difference is referred to as *balance billing*. Medicare patients who saw nonparticipating physicians were also burdened by the paperwork involved with sending their bills to Medicare for reimbursement.

Physicians' fees and Medicare expenditures increased rapidly as demand for medical services increased, and, in 1972, the government placed a limit—referred to as the Medicare Economic Index—on physicians' Medicare fee increases. Physicians' fees, however, continued to rise sharply in the private sector, and as the difference between private-physician charges and the Medicare-approved fees became larger, fewer physicians chose to participate in Medicare. Consequently, more of the aged were balance billed for the difference between their physician's fee and the Medicare-approved fee.

Another consequence of limiting increases in participating physicians' charges was the possibility that physicians would encourage more visits and engage in more testing to raise their Medicare billings (called *induced demand*). Even with limits on physicians' fees, Part B expenditures continued to increase rapidly, as shown in exhibit 8.5 in chapter 8.

Reasons for Adopting the Resource-Based Relative Value Scale

The resource-based relative value scale (RBRVS) physician payment system was enacted by Congress in 1989 (effective as of 1992) for three reasons.

The first and most important reason was the federal government's desire to limit the increase in the federal budget deficit, an issue of great political concern in the early 1990s. Part B expenditures rose from $777 million in 1967 to more than $50 billion by 1992 and were expected to continue to climb. In 2017, Part B expenditures reached $307 billion and are expected to reach $635 billion by 2027 (Congressional Budget Office 2017). As Medicare physician payments continued to increase, the government's portion of the cost of the program—75 percent of the total (again, the aged paid a monthly premium that covered only 25 percent of Part B expenditures)—contributed directly to the growing federal budget deficit. Both Republican and Democratic administrations believed that if the government were to reduce the growing federal deficit, the growth in Part B expenditures had to be slowed. The federal government, however, was constrained in the approaches it could take to limit

Part B expenditures. Given the political power of the elderly, the government was reluctant to ask seniors to pay higher Part B premiums or to increase their cost sharing. Furthermore, the government could not simply limit Medicare physician fees for fear that physicians would decrease their Medicare participation, which would decrease patients' access to care.

The second reason Medicare physician payment was changed was that members of Congress were concerned that unless they ensured that the aged had access to physicians, they would lose their political support at election time. As limits were placed on Medicare physician fee increases, fewer physicians were willing to accept Medicare payment, so more seniors were either charged additional amounts by nonparticipating physicians (balance billed) or, if they could not afford the additional payments, had to face decreased access to physician services. Congress wanted to increase physician participation in Medicare.

Third, many physicians and academicians believed that the previous Medicare payment system was inequitable and inefficient. A recent medical school graduate establishing a fee schedule with Medicare could receive higher fees than could an older physician whose fee increases were limited by the Medicare Economic Index. Physicians who performed procedures such as diagnostic testing and surgery were paid at a much higher rate per unit of physician time than were physicians who performed cognitive services, such as office examinations. Medicare fees for the same procedure varied greatly across geographic areas and were unrelated to differences in practice costs. The FFS payment system encouraged inefficiency by rewarding physicians who performed more services. These inequities and inefficiencies caused differences in physician income and affected their choice of specialty and practice location.

Components of the RBRVS System

Reducing the federal deficit by limiting Part B expenditures, expanding physicians' participation in Medicare, and achieving greater Medicare fee equity among physicians led to the three main parts of the new physician payment system. The inefficiencies inherent in the FFS system were not addressed.

RBRVS Fee Schedule
The first, and most publicized, part of the new payment system was the creation of an RBRVS fee schedule. The RBRVS attempted to approximate the cost of performing each physician service. Its premise was that, in the long run, in a competitive market, the price of a service will reflect the cost of producing that service. Thus, the payment for each physician service should reflect resource costs. However, this cost-based approach to determining relative values was complex,

as it required a great deal of data; relied on interviews; was based on certain assumptions, such as the time required to perform certain tasks; and needed to be continually updated because any of the cost and time elements could change.

Three resource components were used to construct the fee for a particular service. The first—the work component—estimated the cost of providing a service, including the time, intensity, skill, mental effort, and stress involved.[1] The second component consisted of the physician's practice expenses, such as salaries and rent. The third component was malpractice insurance, because its cost varies across specialties. Each component was assigned a relative value that was summed to form the total relative value of the service; the greater the costs and time needed, the higher the relative value unit (RVU). A procedure with a value of 20 was believed to be twice as costly as one with a value of 10.

The actual fee was then determined by multiplying these RVUs by a politically determined conversion factor. For example, "transplantation of the heart" was assigned 44.13 work RVUs, 49.24 practice-expense RVUs, and 9.17 malpractice RVUs, for a total of 102.54 RVUs. The 1992 conversion factor was $31, making the fee for this procedure $3,178 ($31 × 102.54). This fee was then adjusted for geographic location. (The initial conversion factor was set so that total payments under the new system would be the same as those under the previous one—that is, the system was "budget neutral.") A separate conversion factor was used for surgical services, primary care, and other nonsurgical services. (In 1998, a single conversion factor was instituted for all services.) Exhibit 10.1 illustrates how the RBRVS and the conversion factor were used to calculate the fee for a visit to an office located in Los Angeles–Long Beach–Anaheim (Orange County), California.

RBRVS reduced the variation in fees both within specialties and across geographic regions. New physicians received 80 percent of the Medicare fee schedule in their first year, increasing to 100 percent by the fifth year. Medicare fees could still vary geographically by 12 percent less than and 18 percent more

EXHIBIT 10.1
Calculations of Physician Payment Rate Under RBRVS Office Visit (Midlevel), Los Angeles–Long Beach–Anaheim (Orange County), California, 2018

	Relative Value		Geographic Adjustment	Adjusted Relative Value
Physician work	0.97	×	1.05	1.02
Physician expense[a]	1.02	×	1.18	1.20
Professional liability insurance	0.07	×	0.69	0.05
				2.27
			Conversion factor	× 35.99
			Payment rate	$81.70

[a]Nonfacility practice expense.

Note: RBRVS = resource-based relative value scale.

than the average fee, but this variation is greatly reduced from the previous geographic variation. As a result, fees dropped for physicians in California, whereas fees in Mississippi increased by 11 percent.

The RBRVS system reflected the cost of performing 7,000 different physician services, including visits, procedures, imaging, and tests. When constructing the RBRVS fee structure, Harvard professor William Hsiao and colleagues (1988) found that physician fees were not closely related to the resource costs needed to produce those services. In general, cognitive services (e.g., patient evaluation, counseling, and management of services) were greatly undervalued compared with procedural services (e.g., surgery and testing). The RBRVS reduced the profitability of procedures while increasing payment for cognitive services. By changing the relative weights of different types of services, the system caused substantial shifts in payments—and consequently incomes—among physicians. In large metropolitan areas, for example, surgeons' fees declined by 25 percent. Exhibit 10.2 shows the "winners" and "losers" among physician specialties after the new system was introduced.

The Sustainable Growth Rate

The RBRVS approach was still FFS payment, did not differentiate physicians' quality of care, and did not change physicians' incentives to limit volume, mix of services, or total expenditures. Because the government was concerned that physicians would induce demand to offset their lower Medicare fees, the Balanced Budget Act of 1997 included an approach for limiting the rise in overall physician Medicare expenditures.

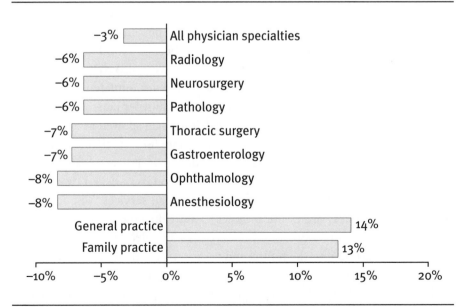

EXHIBIT 10.2
Medicare Physician Fee Schedule Effect on Fees by Specialty, 1992

Source: Data from US Senate Subcommittee on Medicare and Long-Term Care (1991).

The sustainable growth rate (SGR) in Medicare physician expenditures was designed to adjust physician fee updates if physician spending exceeded or was less than a specified target. If volume grew more rapidly than a target rate, Congress would lower the annual fee update the following year. Too rapid an increase in services would result in a smaller fee update. Medicare spending growth for physician services was linked to the general economy—the gross domestic product (GDP)—and was adjusted for several factors. Tying the SGR to GDP per capita represented an affordability criterion—how much the government could afford to subsidize physician Part B expenditures.

The SGR consisted of four elements:

1. The percentage increase in real GDP per capita
2. A medical inflation rate of physician fee increases
3. The annual percentage increase in Part B enrollees (other than Medicare Advantage enrollees)
4. The percentage change in spending for physicians' services resulting from changes in laws and regulations (e.g., expanded Medicare coverage for preventive services).

The SGR formula did not provide any incentives for *individual* physicians to control volume growth. Further, fee changes based on the SGR were unrelated to any changes in the supply of or demand for physician services.

During the late 1990s and early 2000s, physicians received generous fee increases from Medicare (5.4 percent in 2000 and 4.5 percent in 2001). However, the government then revised upward its estimate of previous years' actual physician expenditures and lowered the spending target on the basis of revised GDP data. Physician fees dropped by 5.4 percent in 2002, a decline that was, in part, a correction for fees that had been set too high in previous years because of forecasting errors. Physician fees were also to be decreased in subsequent years in part to recoup excess spending accumulated from averted cuts in previous years and in part because real spending per beneficiary (volume and intensity) on physician services increased faster than allowed under the SGR.

Congress faced a dilemma. It could maintain fiscal discipline and reduce the rapid growth in Medicare physician expenditures by relying on an automatic mechanism, the SGR. By doing so, however, Congress risked dramatically reducing Medicare beneficiaries' access to physician services. The increasing federal deficit was less of a political threat to individual members of Congress. Consequently, Congress overruled each year's scheduled SGR fee reductions, pushed them further into the future, and occasionally increased physicians' fees.

The medical profession, however, became concerned at the size of the accumulated total SGR fee reductions (almost 25 percent) on their income

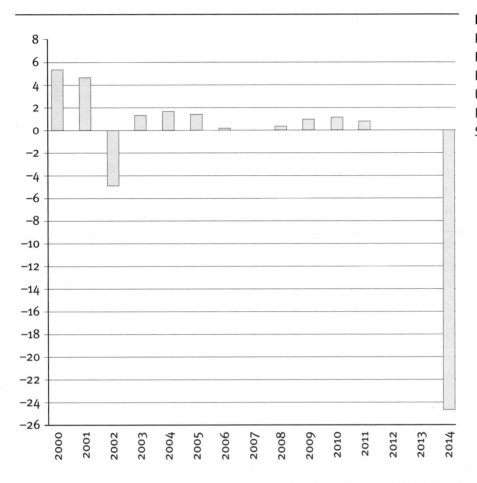

Source: Data from Boards of Trustees, Federal Hospital Insurance and Federal Supplementary Medical Insurance Trust Funds (2013, table IV.B1).

should the fee cuts occur. Exhibit 10.3 shows actual physician updates for the years 2000 to 2013. The sharp decline in physician fees for 2014 shows the accumulated required fee decreases according to the SGR formula.

Balance-Billing Limit

In addition to the use of RBRVS and the SGR, the payment system included limits on the amount physicians can balance bill Medicare patients. Physicians who participated in Medicare were no longer able to participate for some patients but not others. Few physicians are able to forgo Medicare participation, which represents a significant source of revenue. Even physicians who decided not to participate in Medicare were restricted in how much they could charge to treat a Medicare patient; they could not charge a patient more than 109 percent of the Medicare-approved fee.

EXHIBIT 10.3
Recent and Projected Payment Updates for Physician Services

Concerns with the RBRVS Payment System
The SGR Formula Is Unrelated to Demand and Supply Changes

The SGR formula had, for several years, required decreases in physician fees, given that actual expenditure growth exceeded SGR projected physician expenditures. Congress, concerned that decreasing physician fees would lessen the elderly's access to care, postponed these annual fee decreases. Under the law, the accumulated amount of these fee decreases must be recouped by even larger fee reductions in the following year. Although Congress realized that Medicare physician fees would not be cut by such a large amount, they were reluctant to change the SGR formula. To do so would mean that, according to budget rules, Congress would have to raise taxes, reduce other federal spending, or acknowledge a $175 billion increase in the federal deficit over the next ten years. Given the political concern over increasing federal deficits, each Congress preferred to overrule the SGR decrease in fees one year at a time.

The SGR formula, by limiting increases in Medicare physician expenditures, was intended to provide physicians with an incentive to practice more efficiently, thereby not exceeding the overall expenditure limit. However, because the SGR is based on the aggregate Medicare payment for physician services, individual physicians had no incentive to limit their services. In fact, their incentive was to provide more services because the penalty for exceeding the aggregate Medicare spending limit fell proportionately on all physicians. Those physicians who did limit their services were penalized. An overall spending limit cannot be effective unless the incentives are based on the behavior of individual physicians.

The demand for physician services among the elderly continues to rise because of growth in the aged population (many baby boomers started retiring in 2011), advanced technologies, and legislated new benefits. The Affordable Care Act further increased demand for physician services by expanding Medicaid eligibility (to 138 percent of the federal poverty level) and providing subsidies to individuals (whose income is between 138 and 400 percent of the federal poverty level) purchasing health insurance on newly formed state health insurance exchanges.

With the increased demand for physician services, unless Congress permitted physician fee increases, shortages of primary care physicians would occur. As demand by Medicare, Medicaid, and private patients increases, primary care physicians will raise their fees. To the extent that Medicare fees remain lower than rising fees charged to private patients, physicians will find it more profitable to serve a greater number of private patients. If Congress limited Medicare fee increases to save money, the relative profitability of Medicare patients to physicians would continue to decline.

As Medicare fees fall relative to private fees, the only way it remains equally profitable for primary care physicians to continue seeing the same number of

Medicare patients is by "raising" their Medicare fees; such methods include reducing the time spent per Medicare visit, having the patient return more often, or performing more imaging tests (for which the physician receives payment).

As the demand for Medicare services exceeds the amount physicians are willing to supply at Medicare's relatively lower fee, some primary care physicians have begun charging their Medicare patients an annual "concierge" fee of about $2,000. This fee is technically for services not provided under Medicare and provides a concierge patient with greater access to his physician. Because a concierge physician sees fewer patients, the shortage of primary care physicians is exacerbated for those who do not or are unable to pay such a fee. A concierge fee is an indication that the demand for physicians exceeds the supply at the fees Medicare is willing to pay.

The Lack of a Mechanism to Indicate Market Disequilibrium

To determine whether Medicare's physician fees are too low, thereby affecting Medicare patients' access to care, the Medicare Payment Advisory Commission (MedPAC) undertakes several types of surveys. The first is a survey of physicians' willingness to serve Medicare patients; the second is a survey of Medicare patients' access to care. Both surveys take several years to conduct and analyze before the results become available. Because of this delay, MedPAC conducts an annual telephone interview survey of Medicare beneficiaries and privately insured persons aged 50 to 64 years to compare any differences in their access to physician services.

Even though private insurers paid physicians more than Medicare's fees, MedPAC concluded that, as of 2016, Medicare patients generally had adequate access to physician services, and this access was comparable to that of privately insured patients (MedPAC 2017, 100–109).

An indication of market disequilibrium in the Medicare physician market is a 2017 survey conducted by Merritt Hawkins, which found that although the average acceptance rate of new Medicare patients by physicians was 85 percent, wide variations existed in patients' access to care in different physician markets (Miller 2017). For example, the family practice physician acceptance rate for new Medicare patients was 50 percent in Dallas, 40 percent in Denver, and 85 percent in New York City.

Unless the SGR formula was changed, Medicare patients' access to care was likely to decrease. In a normal market situation, rising physician fees would indicate demand growing faster than supply and would indicate the adequacy of Medicare physician fees in different parts of the country. Medicare could then take corrective action. But MedPAC survey data were not current and because balance billing—which acted as a market-driven indicator—was no longer allowed, no automatic mechanism existed to indicate a shortage and, hence, access problems. A survey by the Kaiser Family Foundation (Casillas and Hamel 2015) found that primary care physicians were accepting a greater number of new privately insured patients than new Medicare patients.

Fee Schedules and Physician Incentives

Physician fee schedules result in numerous problems. Certain services are "overvalued"—that is, the fee is too high relative to the cost or difficulty of providing the service. Overvalued services are more profitable than undervalued services (i.e., the fee is too low relative to the cost of providing the service). Thus, imaging and procedure-oriented services have increased more rapidly than services provided by primary care physicians. These differences in fees relative to costs also affect physicians' career choices, as some specialties provide greater rewards than others.

A single committee of the American Medical Association (AMA) decided on the time required for a physician (and different specialties) to perform various procedures, such as colonoscopies. These time requirements became part of the relative values used by Medicare to determine the fee for performing a particular medical service. However, a study determined that the AMA's estimates of the time involved in many procedures were greatly overstated (Whoriskey and Keating 2013). Some physicians in the study performed procedures that, according to the AMA's and Medicare's time estimates, had them working 24, 30, and even 50 hours a day.

Establishing a uniform fee schedule among physicians in the same specialty provides the wrong incentives. In a competitive market in which fees vary, differences in fees for the same service reflect differences in that service. For example, some physicians provide services of higher quality or spend more time listening to the patient's concerns. Although the service code may be nominally similar, the content of that service will vary. The costs of providing that service in terms of the physician's time differ. Medicare uniform fee schedules provide no incentive for physicians (other than their own integrity) to add value to their patients. Medicare initiated a Physician Quality Reporting System to encourage higher quality. However, the quality bonus was so small that it provided minimal incentive for physicians to change their behavior; the bonus was limited to only 0.5 percent of the previous year's Medicare payments to that provider. The physician's cost of collecting quality data likely exceeded any financial return from the program.

Patients are willing to pay more for certain physician attributes, such as their ability to relate to the patient. A uniform fee schedule provides perverse incentives by preventing a physician treating Medicare patients from charging for these extra attributes. Busy primary care physicians can earn a higher income by providing additional visits rather than spending time cultivating these attributes, which are not rewarded.

Medicare Physician Demonstration Projects

Various demonstration projects were undertaken to change physicians' incentives from rewarding volume of services provided (FFS) to improving quality and reducing medical costs (MedPAC 2010). One type of demonstration project was a bundled or episode-based payment—a single payment to a provider to cover all the services related to a specific disease or condition during a specific period. The hospital, specialists, and primary care physicians involved in the patient's treatment received a specified amount (which they had to share) for a patient's episode of care (e.g., a heart attack or joint replacement), including follow-up care. Episode-based payment required physicians and hospitals to more closely coordinate the patient's care. Each participant had an incentive to be concerned with the efficiency and coordination of care among specialists. The participants' quality and cost performance in providing an episode of care could then be evaluated by comparing it with the care provided by other organizations whose participants are paid FFS.

The results of the bundled payment demonstrations were mixed, as discussed in a report by the Lewin Group (2016).

Under pay-for-performance (P4P), physicians meeting certain quality guidelines, such as lower complication rates for knee arthroscopic surgery, received higher payments. P4P offered incentives to physicians that differed from those for FFS, where quality is not rewarded. The National Commission on Physician Payment Reform (2013) also recommended that physician payment for "evaluation and management" services be raised. The current FFS system provides a disincentive for physicians to spend time with patients who have complex chronic conditions; another problem is neglecting illness prevention and disease management. The evidence on P4P demonstrations to date has not shown consistently improved health outcomes (Mendelson et al. 2017).

As indicated by these payment reform demonstration projects, Medicare has attempted to move away from paying traditional FFS to adjusting payments for differences in quality of care and care coordination.

The Medicare Access and CHIP Reauthorization Act (MACRA)

In 2015, Congress, in a bipartisan vote, approved MACRA, a new Medicare physician payment system. The law's provisions were phased in and will become fully effective for all physicians by 2019. MACRA is the most substantive change in physician reimbursement since Medicare was enacted (Findlay 2017).

MACRA had three basic objectives. The first, and most urgent, was to overturn Medicare's SGR formula that would have required reducing physician payments by 21 percent. Each year, Congress, concerned that reducing physician payments would decrease Medicare beneficiaries' access to care, voted (often at the last moment) to postpone required SGR physician pay cuts. As the accumulated pay cuts became larger, physicians' uncertainty regarding their Medicare payments similarly increased. MACRA did away with the SGR formula and the accumulated physician pay reductions.

Second, MACRA is an attempt to reform Medicare physician payment. Previous Medicare physician payment systems provided physicians with the wrong incentives. Physicians were rewarded for the number of visits, tests, and procedures performed, inducing some to provide too little or too much care, and offering little incentive to be concerned with the overall cost and coordination of patients' treatment. In addition, no attempt was made to hold physicians accountable for the care provided (or not provided) or the quality of that care. MACRA proposes to reward (or penalize) physicians based on the value of the care they provide. Physicians' incentives have been changed. Incentives are provided for physicians to provide Medicare patients with the appropriate (quality and quantity) care; for physicians to use the most cost-effective set of resources (e.g., personnel, technology) and the least costly settings, such as office visits, homes, and institutions; and to make physicians financially accountable for the care they provide.

Third, MACRA attempts to transition physicians away from FFS to participating in alternative payment models, referred to as Advanced Alternative Payment Models (APMs). An Advanced APM is an APM that bears financial risk. Examples of Advanced APMs include risk-bearing accountable care organizations (ACOs) and a government-approved patient-centered medical homes model, which is a team-based, primary care model that provides comprehensive and coordinated care in a patient-accessible setting. MACRA hopes to achieve greater physician accountability, greater transparency, quality improvement, and payment reform. These are admirable goals. Whether MACRA can achieve such far-reaching goals has yet to be determined.

Merit-Based Incentive Payment System

To achieve its goals, MACRA relies on two approaches. Physicians are required to choose between two quality-oriented physician payment options. Both payment options rely on quality and performance measures, as well as efforts to improve patient care and limit cost increases. The first approach relies on FFS but is based on a complex system for measuring P4P, known as the Merit-Based Incentive Payment System (MIPS). If physicians do not participate in MIPS or Advanced APMs, Medicare will reduce their fees. (Physician practices that see 100 or fewer Medicare patients are exempt from the MIPS requirements.) MIPS is a data-driven physician payment system designed to incentivize physicians to provide quality comprehensive care to their Medicare patients.

Physicians must document electronically a great deal of data during a patient visit. Performance categories include quality of care, use of electronic health records, clinical improvement activities, and measures of cost and resource use. Based on the physician's metrics, his Medicare payments may be increased or decreased up to 4 percent in 2019 and increasing to 9 percent by 2024. It has been estimated that 90 percent of practicing physicians will participate in MIPS (Findlay 2017). Additional physician performance payments will be balanced by decreased payments to other participating physicians.

Several concerns have been expressed about the implementation of MIPS. A physician's MIPS data will become publicly available. Not only are physicians at financial risk for their MIPS scores (i.e., possible reductions in their Medicare fees), but they may also suffer harm to their professional reputation. They can be publicly judged, which may affect their ability to join other medical groups or Advanced APMs.

MACRA critics have been concerned that MIPS reporting requirements are too extensive. During a patient visit, the physician will have to spend more time recording the necessary patient information to prove she provided value and should not be penalized; consequently, the physician will have little time for patient interaction.

An important consideration (and physician concern) pertains to the metrics used by the government to measure physician performance. Will the government be able to adequately adjust patient health risk in a physician practice—namely, adjust for each patient's health status and the overall mix of patients in a physician's practice?

Physicians are similarly concerned about the accuracy of Medicare's quality metrics. In its report on healthcare quality, the US Government Accountability Office (2016) found that although many quality measures have been collected, payers and providers have not relied on the same measures. Little agreement exists among physicians, providers, insurers, and others regarding the use of different quality measures to evaluate physician performance.

The US Government Accountability Office (2016) also determined that physician participation in electronically collecting MIPS data can be very costly; some studies cited found that overall quality measurement efforts could cost physicians $46,000 per year to comply with MIPS data collection requirements.

Many physicians have been leaving private practice to become hospital employees. It is likely that many small physician practices will find the cost of complying with MIPS so onerous that they will be forced to join larger organizations, including Advanced APMs.

Advanced Alternative Payment Models

Physicians participating in an Advanced APM are exempt from MIPS requirements. They bear financial risk because they are eligible for bonus payments (or penalties) based on their organization's quality performance and its ability to reduce rising Medicare expenditures. Historically, physicians have been reluctant to undertake financial risk, given the possibility of losing money.

Advanced APMs will require physicians to change how medical services are delivered, increase the involvement of care coordinators and other nonphysicians in the care process, and make a sizeable investment in the organization's supporting infrastructure.

Physicians in an Advanced APM are also concerned about Medicare's risk adjustment process and the quality metrics used to measure the value of care provided to the patient. Without proper health risk adjustment and quality measures, Advanced APMs may be unfairly judged on their quality and expenditure metrics.

Exhibit 10.4 illustrates physician payments under MIPS and Advanced APMs.

Currently, the number and types of Advanced APMs available for physicians to join is limited to government-approved patient-centered medical homes and risk-bearing ACOs. To date, Medicare Advantage plans have not been approved as an Advanced APM.

As FFS physicians find that MIPS is too costly and onerous, will enough APMs be available for them to join? It will take time for the government to demonstrate the feasibility of new Advanced APMs before they can be approved. Medicare Advantage plans should be approved as Advanced APMs because such plans bear financial risk and represent a growing percentage (34 percent in 2017) of the Medicare population, who have voluntarily enrolled in these plans.

Will MACRA offer physicians the rewarding professional career they anticipated when becoming a physician? Private-practice FFS physicians face a difficult choice. They can continue practicing FFS and be subject to the burdensome MIPS requirements or they can join Advanced APMs as more become available. Many more physicians likely will become employees of large organizations (Casalino 2017).

MACRA represents a major change in physician payment and delivery systems. Will MACRA be able to achieve its objectives of improving patient care and restraining medical cost increases?

Summary

Medicare's initial physician payment system was based on FFS, as was its replacement, RBRVS. The RBRVS national fee schedule (with expenditure controls, the SGR, and limits on balance billing) attempted to limit federal expenditures for Medicare physician services, improve equity among different medical specialties, and limit Medicare beneficiaries' out-of-pocket payments and Part B premiums, while increasing access to care.

EXHIBIT 10.4

Implementing the Medicare Access and CHIP Reauthorization Act's (MACRA's) Physician Payment Reforms, 2017–2022

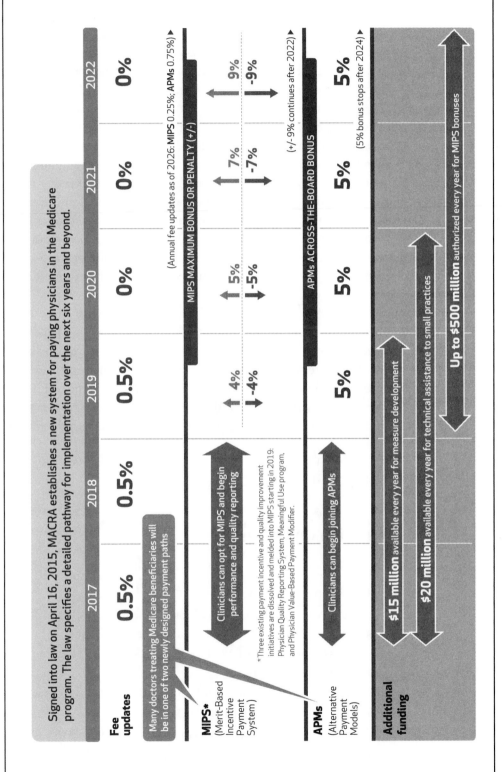

Signed into law on April 16, 2015, MACRA establishes a new system for paying physicians in the Medicare program. The law specifies a detailed pathway for implementation over the next six years and beyond.

	2017	2018	2019	2020	2021	2022
Fee updates	0.5%	0.5%	0.5%	0%	0%	0%

(Annual fee updates as of 2026: **MIPS** 0.25%; **APMs** 0.75%) ▲

Many doctors treating Medicare beneficiaries will be in one of two newly designed payment paths

MIPS* (Merit-Based Incentive Payment System)

Clinicians can opt for MIPS and begin performance and quality reporting

*Three existing payment incentive and quality improvement initiatives are dissolved and melded into MIPS starting in 2019: Physician Quality Reporting System, Meaningful Use program, and Physician Value-Based Payment Modifier.

MIPS MAXIMUM BONUS OR PENALTY (+/-)

	4%	5%	7%	9%
	-4%	-5%	-7%	-9%

(+/- 9% continues after 2022) ▲

APMs (Alternative Payment Models)

Clinicians can begin joining APMs

APMs ACROSS-THE-BOARD BONUS

5%	5%	5%	5%

(5% bonus stops after 2024) ▲

Additional funding

$15 million available every year for measure development

$20 million available every year for technical assistance to small practices

Up to **$500 million** authorized every year for MIPS bonuses

Source: Reprinted with permission from Findlay, S. 2017. "Implementing MACRA." *Health Affairs.* Published March 27. www.healthaffairs.org/do/10.1377/hpb20170327.272560/full/.

RBRVS and the SGR did not achieve the goals deemed appropriate for a physician payment system. A uniform fee schedule continues to reward physicians for scheduling more visits and performing more tests and procedures; provides little incentive for the physician to be concerned with the overall cost and coordination of treatment; and makes no attempt to hold physicians accountable for the care provided (or not provided) or for the quality of that care. A uniform fee schedule also cannot identify a developing shortage in some geographic areas or among certain specialties; neither can uniform fees eliminate such shortages once identified. Unless a national fee schedule is flexible and allows fees for some services, physicians, and geographic regions to grow more rapidly than others, shortages will arise and persist.

The SGR formula for limiting the growth in Medicare physician expenditures was faulty. It did not penalize physicians who overprescribed services, but instead would have reduced all physicians' fees. More importantly, Congress was reluctant to enforce decreases in physician fees when the SGR was exceeded because of concern it would decrease Medicare enrollees' access to physician services.

A new Medicare physician payment system, MACRA, was enacted in 2015 and phased in to include all physicians participating in Medicare. MACRA includes financial incentives to reward (or penalize) physicians based on the value of the care they provide and on their use of the most cost-effective set of resources. Physicians are financially accountable for the care they provide. Physicians have two options under MACRA: be reimbursed on an FFS basis in MIPS or become part of an Advanced APM, which is a risk-based alternative payment system.

Many FFS physicians likely will join Advanced APMs because they will find MIPS burdensome and costly.

Discussion Questions

1. What were the reasons for developing the RBRVS and SGR Medicare physician payment system?
2. In what ways did the RBRVS physician payment system differ from the way in which Medicare initially reimbursed physicians?
3. What were the effects of Medicare's RBRVS payment system on physicians (by specialty)?
4. What were the likely effects of FFS versus episode-based payment?
5. Why did Congress enact MACRA?
6. What are the two ways a physician can participate in MACRA?
7. Discuss two concerns physicians have about MACRA.

Note

1. Two methods were used to estimate the complexity of a task: personal interviews and a modified Delphi technique in which each physician was able to compare her own estimate with the average estimate of physicians in that specialty. Many assumptions were required; for example, in calculating opportunity cost, it was assumed that the years required for training in a specialty were the minimum necessary. Further assumptions were made regarding the lengths of working careers across specialties, residency salaries, the hours worked per week, and an interest rate to discount future earnings.

References

Boards of Trustees, Federal Hospital Insurance and Federal Supplementary Medical Insurance Trust Funds. 2013. *2013 Annual Report of the Boards of Trustees of the Federal Hospital Insurance and Federal Supplementary Medical Insurance Trust Funds.* Accessed September. www.cms.gov/Research-Statistics-Data-and-Systems/Statistics-Trends-andReports/ReportsTrustFunds/Downloads/TR2013.pdf.

Casalino, L. P. 2017. "The Medicare Access and CHIP Reauthorization Act and the Corporate Transformation of American Medicine." *Health Affairs* 36 (5): 865–69.

Casillas, C. G., and L. Hamel. 2015. "Primary Care Physicians Accepting Medicare: A Snapshot." Kaiser Family Foundation issue brief. Published October 30. www.kff.org/medicare/issue-brief/primary-care-physicians-accepting-medicare-a-snapshot/.

Congressional Budget Office. 2017. "Medicare: Congressional Budget Office's June 2017 Baseline." Accessed September. www.cbo.gov/sites/default/files/recurringdata/51302-2017-06-medicare.pdf.

Findlay, S. 2017. "Implementing MACRA." *Health Affairs* health policy brief. Published March 27. www.healthaffairs.org/do/10.1377/hpb20170327.272560/full/.

Hsiao, W. C., P. Braun, D. Yntema, and E. R. Becker. 1988. "Estimating Physicians' Work for a Resource-Based Relative Value Scale." *New England Journal of Medicine* 319 (13): 835–41.

Lewin Group. 2016. *CMS Bundled Payments for Care Improvement Initiative Models 2–4: Year 2 Evaluation & Monitoring Annual Report.* Published August. https://innovation.cms.gov/Files/reports/bpci-models2-4-yr2evalrpt.pdf.

Medicare Payment Advisory Commission (MedPAC). 2017. *Report to the Congress: Medicare Payment Policy.* Published March. http://medpac.gov/docs/default-source/reports/mar17_entirereport.pdf.

————. 2010. "Appendix A: Review of CMS's Preliminary Estimate of the Physician Update for 2011." In *Report to the Congress: Aligning Incentives in Medicare.* Published June. www.aacom.org/docs/default-source/grad-medical-education/jun10_entirereport.pdf.

Mendelson, A., K. K. Kondo, C. Damberg, A. Low, M. Motu'apuaka, M. Freeman, M. O'Neil, R. Relevo, and D. Kansagara. 2017. "The Effects of Pay-for-Performance Programs on Health, Health Care Use, and Processes of Care." *Annals of Internal Medicine* 166 (5): 341–53.

Miller, P. 2017. *2017 Survey of Physician Appointment Wait Times and Medicaid and Medicare Acceptance Rates.* Accessed September 7, 2018. www.merritthawkins.com/uploadedFiles/MerrittHawkins/Pdf/mha2017waittimesurveyPDF.pdf.

National Commission on Physician Payment Reform. 2013. *Report of the National Commission on Physician Payment Reform.* Published March. http://physicianpaymentcommission.org/wp-content/uploads/2012/02/physician_payment_report.pdf.

US Government Accountability Office. 2016. *Report to Congressional Committees: Health Care Quality—HHS Should Set Priorities and Comprehensively Plan Its Efforts to Better Align Health Quality Measures.* Published October. www.gao.gov/assets/690/680433.pdf.

US Senate Subcommittee on Medicare and Long-Term Care. 1991. "Medicare Physician Payment Reform Regulations." Hearing before the Subcommittee on Medicare and Long-Term Care of the Committee on Finance, July 19.

Whoriskey, P., and D. Keating. 2013. "How a Secretive Panel Uses Data That Distort Doctors' Pay." *Washington Post.* Published July 20. www.washingtonpost.com/business/economy/how-a-secretive-panel-uses-data-that-distorts-doctors pay/2013/07/20/ee134e3a-eda8-11e2-9008-61e94a7ea20d_story.html.

THE IMPENDING SHORTAGE OF PHYSICIANS

11

bout every 10 to 20 years, concern arises that the United States is producing either too many or too few physicians. In 1992, the Council on Graduate Medical Education (COGME), which advised the government on the size of the physician workforce and its training, warned that by 2000 a surplus of specialists would occur—as high as 15 to 30 percent of all physicians—as well as a shortage of primary care physicians. Evidence for the belief in a large physician surplus was the rapid growth in the number of active physicians, which increased from 435,000 in 1980 to 573,000 in 1990, to 738,000 in 2000, and to 998,000 in 2013. When adjusted for population, the number of active physicians per 100,000 population (the physician-to-population ratio) increased from 195 in 1980 to 234 in 1990, to 270 in 2000, and to 321 in 2013 (see exhibit 4.1 in chapter 4).

Some researchers, assuming that a large portion of the US population would be enrolled in health maintenance organizations (HMOs), compared the relatively low physician ratio in HMOs to the national physician ratio and claimed that an overall surplus of 165,000 physicians (or 30 percent of the total number of patient care physicians) would occur by 2000. A 30 percent surplus in the number of specialists also was projected.

The projected physician surplus was expected to have adverse effects on physician income—especially specialist income—for many years. To forestall such surpluses, COGME and physician organizations recommended reducing medical school enrollments, decreasing the number of specialists, increasing the number of primary care physicians (from 30 percent to 50 percent of all physicians), and limiting the number of foreign medical school graduates entering the United States.

In 2005, COGME issued a new report warning that an overall shortfall of 85,000 to 95,000 physicians was likely by 2020. A 2012 study by the Association of American Medical Colleges (AAMC) predicted a shortage of 62,900 physicians by 2015, growing to more than 90,000 by 2020 (45,000 primary care physicians and 46,000 surgeons and medical specialists), and creating a deficit of 130,000 physicians by 2025.

The AAMC published its latest forecast of a physician shortage in 2017, using 2015 as the base period (IHS Markit 2017). Acknowledging that several uncertainties affect a forecast, the AAMC projects a range of shortage estimates, as shown in exhibit 11.1. The estimated size of the shortage increases over

EXHIBIT 11.1
Projected Total
Physician
Shortfall Range,
2015–2030

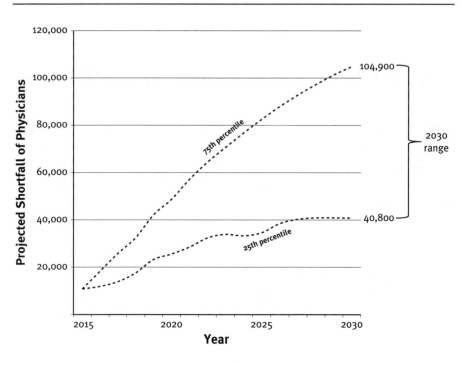

Source: IHS Markit. 2017. 2017 Update: The Complexities of Physician Supply and Demand—Projections from 2015 to 2030. Prepared for the Association of American Medical Colleges. Washington, DC: Association of American Medical Colleges. Published February 28. https://aamc-black.global.ssl.fastly.net/production/media/filer_public/c9/db/c9dbe9de-aabf-457f-aee7-1d3d554ff281/aamc_projections_update_2017_final_-_june_12.pdf.

time, as does the uncertainty of the forecast. By the year 2030, the estimated physician shortage is expected to be between 40,800 and 104,900.

This anticipated shortfall is the result of several factors. The demand for physicians would sharply increase because 30 million uninsured were expected to become insured as a result of the Affordable Care Act (ACA), and because of the growing number of aged, who have the highest need for care. Though the supply of physicians has been rising, more physicians are leaving primary care because of decreased fees, fewer medical students are choosing a primary care specialty because the income is lower than that in other medical specialties, and about one-third of all physicians are expected to retire by 2020. The shortage of primary care physicians is becoming more severe and will adversely affect the most vulnerable members of the population.

The demand for physicians was based on different scenarios, such as changing demographics, the effect on use rates of the growth of managed care, and the degree to which advanced practice registered nurses (APRNs) and physician assistants (PAs) would increase in number and become integrated in providing medical services. Projections of future physician supply were also based on alternative scenarios, such as whether physician retirements would occur sooner or be delayed, the number and characteristics of new physicians entering the workforce, the number of hours worked, and the growth of retail medical clinics. Each of the physician supply scenarios was compared with each demand scenario.

The AAMC's analyses assume that during the baseline period (2015), a physician shortage does not exist, other than in primary care. Further, shortage estimates are based on maintaining the baseline (2015) care use patterns.

The demand for physician services is expected to increase more rapidly than the supply, and the resulting shortage will become larger over time. These shortage estimates are for the nation, and because the distribution of physicians varies greatly in different parts of the country, the physician shortage will be much worse in some geographic areas than in others.

Separate projections have been developed for primary care physicians and for several broad physician specialty categories.

The AAMC is aware that changes may occur in coming years that will affect the estimates of a physician shortage, such as the new administration may make changes to the ACA, Medicaid eligibility may change, and different payment models (and timing of these payment methods) may be introduced.

Concerns over an increasing physician shortage, particularly in primary care, have important policy implications. For example, should medical schools receive increased funding to produce more physicians; should new medical schools also be funded; should training for more APRNs and PAs be expanded; and so on.

Before discussing public policy options, it is best to discuss the basis for these projections of an increasing a physician shortage. Is the magnitude of a possible (low estimate) shortage of 40,800 physicians in 2030, given the size of the physician population at that time, sufficiently large to warrant concern? Could medical services be delivered more efficiently to obviate the need for more physicians? More fundamentally, what is an economic definition of a physician surplus or shortage, and do shortages (and surpluses) have self-correcting mechanisms? If not, what are economists' proposals for correcting a shortage (and surplus)?

Definitions of a Physician Shortage or Surplus

Physician-to-Population Ratio

Different approaches have been used to determine whether a shortage (or surplus) exists in a profession. One approach often taken in the health field is a physician-to-population ratio. This ratio often relies on a value judgment about how much care people should receive or on a professional determination of how many physician services are appropriate for the population.

With this method, the existing physician-to-population ratio typically is compared with the physician-to-population ratio likely to occur in some future period. First, the *supply ratio* is projected by estimating the future population and the likely number of medical school graduates who will be added to the stock of physicians (less the expected number of deaths and retirements). Second, the *physician requirement ratio* is projected by estimating the extent of disease in the population (usually based on survey data), the physician services necessary to provide care for each illness, and the number of physician hours required to provide preventive and therapeutic services. (Some studies attempt to modify the requirements ratio by basing it on utilization rates of population subgroups, such as age, sex, geographic location, and insurance coverage, and multiplying these rates by the future population in each category.) Third, assuming a 40-hour workweek per physician, the number of hours is translated into the number of physicians and a physician-to-population ratio. The same approach is used to determine the number of physicians in each specialty. The difference between the supply ratio and the requirements ratio is the anticipated shortage or surplus.

The Graduate Medical Education National Advisory Committee (the predecessor organization to COGME) also used a physician-to-population ratio methodology to determine the appropriate number of physicians.

This ratio technique has served as the basis for much of the health workforce legislation in the United States and has resulted in many billions of dollars of subsidies from federal and state governments. Nonphysician health professional associations, such as those for registered nurses (RNs), also have used this approach in their quest for government subsidies. However, using a physician-to-population ratio to judge whether a shortage (or surplus) exists has serious shortcomings.

First, use of a ratio—whether based on health professional estimates of the need for services or on the current physician-to-population ratio—as a guideline for determining whether future ratios will be adequate does not consider changes in physician demand. For example, if demand for physicians is growing faster than the supply because of an aging population, an expansion of Medicaid eligibility, new medical advances that encourage the public to use medical care, or an increase in the number of privately insured individuals on state insurance exchanges, then maintaining a particular ratio is likely to result in too few physicians.

Second, the ratio method does not include productivity changes that are likely to occur or could be attained. Adding physician services is possible without increasing the number of physicians. Technology (e.g., health information systems) and personnel with less training can relieve physicians of many tasks; delegation of some tasks would permit the number of physician visits to grow. A smaller physician-to-population ratio would be needed if productivity growth is considered. Conversely, if the percentage of female physicians (who work fewer hours, on average, than male physicians) rises or if physicians prefer an easier lifestyle, will more physicians be needed? The AAMC projects future shortages based on maintaining the "care use patterns" that existed in 2015. Changes in the demand for medical care are considered in its projections. Rather than relying on a simple physician-to-population ratio, the required number of physicians is adjusted by the possible use of APRNs, PAs, and retail clinics.

Third, the ratio technique does not indicate the importance of a surplus or shortage if, in fact, one exists. Is a shortage or surplus of 10,000 physicians significant, or does the number have to reach 200,000 to warrant concern? What are the consequences for physician fees, income, and patients' access to care? Few physician shortage studies examine the costs of decreasing physician shortages of different sizes, compared with the costs of alternative approaches to increase the supply of medical services (e.g., APRNs) or decrease the demand for such services (e.g., use of telehealth and cell phone apps).

Projections of shortages and surpluses using the ratio technique have been notoriously inaccurate. Many assumptions are used in calculating future ratios, and public policies based on inaccurate projections take many years to correct, exacerbating future shortages or surpluses. Two economic approaches have been used to estimate whether a physician shortage or surplus exists. The first is to examine the market for physician services; the second is to estimate the rate of return for having a medical education.

The Market for Physician Services

When analyzing the market for physician services, it is important to distinguish between temporary and static shortages because the appropriate public policy proposals for each are very different.

Temporary Economic Shortages

An economic shortage exists when the demand for physician services exceeds the supply of services—at a given price. Patients are then unable to purchase all the physician services they want at the going market price. The available supply is rationed by patients, who must wait longer to see a physician. This type of shortage may be temporary. Initially, as demand increases, physicians may be unaware that the higher demand is permanent, and they can raise their prices. As physicians conclude that demand will remain high, they can increase their fees and retain at least the same number of patients. Some patients will demand fewer physician visits as fees rise, but overall the number of visits will likely increase.[1] Higher payments provide physicians with an incentive to supply more services. In addition to working longer hours, physicians can hire additional staff to boost their productivity. Market equilibrium is restored when patients can buy all the physician visits they want *at the going market price.*

A temporary shortage is usually resolved when physicians realize they can raise their fees. Approaches that decrease physician demand, such as the growth of retail medical clinics, increases in physician productivity, and use of telehealth, will also reduce temporary shortages.

Static Economic Shortages

A more serious type of economic shortage, referred to as a *static shortage*, occurs when physicians are unable to raise their fees in response to an increased demand for their services. When the government regulates physicians' fees, as occurs under Medicaid and Medicare, it may not realize for some time that a shortage has occurred; the government will then determine how much fees need to be increased to eliminate the shortage. Also, state Medicaid programs may decide not to raise physician fees because doing so will increase the state's deficit. In these cases, the shortage of physician services will persist, and for many Medicaid programs, the shortage becomes permanent. The demand for physician services continues to exceed the supply of such services at the government's regulated physician fees.

Resolving a static economic shortage requires the removal of government price fixing or barriers to entry of new healthcare providers.

Rate of Return on a Medical Education

The second approach for determining the existence of a physician shortage (or surplus) is to determine the rate of return on a medical education. The rate of return is calculated by estimating the costs of that investment and the expected higher financial returns from that investment while discounting the cash flow to the present.

If a person decides to enter medical school, she is in effect making an investment in an education that offers a higher future income. The explicit costs of that investment include tuition, books, and other expenses. Often, the largest part of this investment is an implicit cost, the income that could have been earned had the person taken a job. Both the explicit and implicit costs represent the opportunity cost of a graduate education. The return earned on this investment is the higher income received. Because this income is earned in the future, and future income is valued less than current income, it must be discounted to the present. Does the discounted rate of return on a medical education exceed what the student could have earned had she invested an equivalent amount of money in a savings or bond account? If the rate of return is higher than what could have been earned by investing an equivalent sum of money, a shortage of physicians occurs. If the rate of return is lower than alternative investments or an educational investment for other professions, a surplus exists.[2]

The rate-of-return approach does not imply that every prospective student makes a rate-of-return calculation before deciding on a medical or other graduate education. Many students would become physicians even if future income prospects were low, simply because they believe medicine is a worthwhile profession. However, some students may be equally excited about a career in medicine, business, or computer science. Changes in the rates of return affect these students. High relative rates of return in medicine shift more students to medicine (eventually lowering the rate of return), whereas low relative rates of return shift them to other professions, eventually eliminating the physician surplus.

This approach incorporates all the relevant economic factors, such as likely income lost while pursuing a medical degree and residency training and the longer time to become a specialist (i.e., greater opportunity costs). In addition, differences in likely physician income by specialty and educational costs (e.g., tuition) alter the rate of return on a medical education.[3]

Consequences of an Imbalance in Physician Supply and Demand

What is likely to occur if demand for physicians exceeds supply? A shortage has short-term and long-term consequences. These effects will vary depending on whether the individual demanding the service is a private-pay patient or a publicly funded patient for whom the government regulates the physician's fee.

Private Market for Physician Services
Short-Term Effects of a Physician Shortage
As discussed earlier, a temporary shortage results in an increase in the number of patients seeking physician services. Wait times for appointments will increase. Physicians' bargaining position with insurers will improve, and they will eventually raise their fees. In addition, physicians will likely add staff to increase their productivity so they can see more patients. Physician income also will rise. Equilibrium will be reestablished—similar to what existed before demand increased—as a consequence of the higher physician fees. Patients will pay higher insurance premiums (or out-of-pocket payments), and some patients will not see their physicians as often as they did previously.

Long-Term Effects of a Physician Shortage
Over time, as physician income increases, so will the rate of return on a medical education. That return will exceed the return achieved by professionals with comparable training times, such as professors. The demand for medical education will increase, as will demand for residency positions in specialties

experiencing the largest growth in demand. An important issue is whether medical schools will accommodate the higher demand for a medical education. If medical schools expand and new medical schools open, the supply of US-trained physicians will slowly increase. If not, the applicant-to-acceptance ratio will rise, driving students who desire a medical education to seek that training overseas and then return to the United States for residencies. Eventually, a greater supply of physicians will moderate physician fee increases, and physicians will enter those specialties in which demand has surged. With physician supply growing faster than physician demand, the rates of return will decline to the point that they become comparable to those of other professions.

The market response by patients, physicians, college graduates, and medical schools will result in the elimination of a shortage. The response will not be immediate, as it takes time for patients and physicians to realize that demand has increased; for some college graduates to decide to enter medicine; and for these medical students to graduate and complete their residencies.

Crucial assumptions regarding the long-term response to a shortage in the private market are (1) physician fees are able to increase, (2) the number of medical school spaces expands to accommodate the high demand for medical education, and (3) the number of residency positions in teaching hospitals increases to allow more medical graduates to be trained. Higher physician fees will eliminate any shortage in the market for physician services.

However, if medical school spaces and residency positions do not expand, physicians will continue to earn higher rates of return, particularly in those specialties in which the demand for residencies is greatest.[4] Limited medical school spaces and the inability to gain a residency are entry barriers that have kept physician rates of return high, particularly in specialties with the highest incomes (Nicolson 2003).

Although physician fee increases will eliminate shortages in the private and public physician services markets, shortages will continue to exist in the demand for and supply of medical education. Moreover, expanding the number of medical school spaces will do little to alleviate the shortages unless the number of residency positions also expands. The number of residency positions has not been expanding to accommodate the increasing number of graduates, both US- and foreign-trained, particularly in the most sought-after residencies. Slightly more than 30,000 residency positions are offered each year (National Residency Matching Program 2017). Of the total number of residencies, 59,311 are in general/teaching hospitals and 51,897 are at academic medical centers (Accreditation Council for Graduate Medical Education 2017, figure E.8). Medicare finances the costs of graduate medical education (GME) in two ways: the direct salary costs of GME and the indirect costs that reflect the higher patient costs associated with residency training. Medicare financial support for these residency positions has been declining. In 2013, direct GME payments subsidized 83,000 residents, and 79,000 residents received indirect subsidies (US Government Accountability Office 2017).

Public Market for Physician Services
Short-Term Effects of a Physician Shortage
The public and private markets for physician services are interrelated. Physicians allocate their time according to the relative profitability of serving patients in each market. (This is not meant to imply that all physicians behave in this way, but a sufficient number are willing to shift their services on the basis of the relative profitability of serving Medicare, Medicaid, and private-pay patients [Rice et al. 1999].) Consequently, the effects of a physician shortage on patients depend on the flexibility of physician fees in each market. Markets that permit greater flexibility in fees and entry of new physicians are more likely to resolve a shortage situation than are markets that rely on government-regulated fees, which are slow to adjust to changes in demand and supply.

The main difference between the private and public markets is that the government regulates the price of physician services in public markets (i.e., Medicare and Medicaid). Governments rarely are able to accurately determine the price for physician services and for each specialty so that they can equilibrate supply and demand. In addition to a lack of information about changes in the market for physician services, budget considerations often influence how much the government will spend on physician services.

When a shortage develops in the private market and insurers increase physician fees, physicians will serve fewer Medicare and Medicaid patients unless the government also raises physician fees. Physicians will shift their time to higher-paying private patients. Medicare patients are currently experiencing this difficulty, and the problem is continual for Medicaid patients.

Long-Term Effects of a Physician Shortage
If government fees are not increased sufficiently to match those in the private market, a shortage of physicians may continue indefinitely in the public market. Low out-of-pocket payments by Medicare and Medicaid patients result in high demand, which will continue to exceed the supply of services that physicians are willing to provide at the regulated price. The consequence is increased wait times for appointments, an important deterrent to receiving care. Some physicians can increase their hourly fee by reducing the time spent with each patient, while others engage in "upcoding" (e.g., billing for a comprehensive visit when a brief visit was provided), and still others are unwilling to see new patients.

When regulated fees are below those in the private market, physicians have no incentive to increase the supply of services in the regulated markets. Instead, they will reallocate their time to private patients, in a setting where fees are higher. When regulated fees prevent equilibrium from occurring—such as in some Medicare markets where demand exceeds supply—physicians are able to charge an annual "concierge" fee of $1,500 to $2,000. In addition to same-day appointments and more time per visit for concierge patients, the physician helps the patient negotiate the bureaucratic medical system. To provide more time for concierge patients, physicians reduce the size of their practice from about 2,500 to 600 patients, thereby forcing those unable or unwilling to pay the concierge fee to seek another physician. The growth of concierge medicine will continue in our current multitiered healthcare system, whereby those with high income receive more and timelier care than those with low income.

With decreased access to private physician services, patients in the public market will search for substitutes, such as hospital emergency departments (EDs) and retail medical clinics. More publicly funded patients also will join HMO-type organizations, which are able to attract physicians by paying them a higher rate than government-regulated rates. (More Medicare patients will enroll in Medicare Advantage plans.) These organizations, which are paid an annual amount per enrollee (known as *capitation payment*), can cut costs by using more nonphysicians and providing preventive and disease management services, which reduce costly hospital care.

Economic Evidence on Trends in Physician Demand and Supply

Several measures are used to determine whether a shortage exists and, if so, whether it is temporary or permanent. A shortage in the physician services market is characterized by high fees and physician incomes, lengthy wait times, and high rates of return on a medical education.

A temporary shortage is distinguished from a permanent shortage by whether the supply of physician services is increasing (which is consistent with a temporary shortage). When demand increases, regulatory limits on physician fee hikes result in a permanent shortage for Medicare and Medicaid patients, a shortage that becomes more severe as physicians shift their time to the private sector where they can earn more revenue per visit.

Trends in Physician Fees

In the late 1980s, physician fees rose much more rapidly than did inflation (indicative of demand increasing faster than supply) and more rapidly than in the 1990s, when managed care began having an effect. Exhibit 11.2 indicates that physician fee increases barely exceeded inflation in the previous decade. It has only been in the last several years that physician fees have exceeded low inflation rates.

A growing divergence in fees exists between the private and public markets for physicians, leading to a growing shortage of physician services among

EXHIBIT 11.2

Annual Percentage Changes in the Consumer Price Index and in Physicians' Fees, 1965–2017

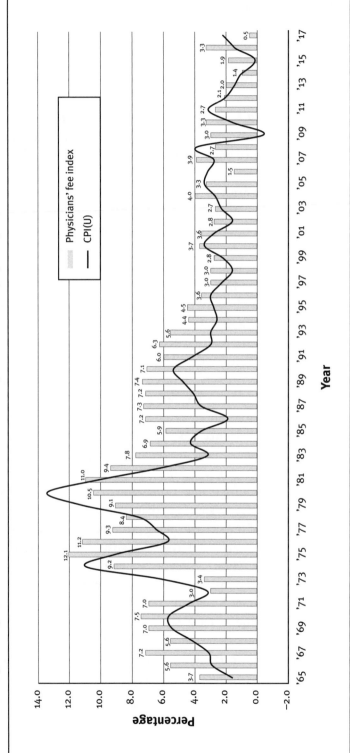

Note: CPI(U) = consumer price index for all urban consumers.

Source: Data from Bureau of Labor Statistics (2018).

Medicare and Medicaid patients. While average private physician fees have increased faster than the rate of inflation in recent years, Medicare physician fees have declined when adjusted for inflation. Physicians have tried to compensate for these declining (inflation adjusted) Medicare fees by increasing the volume of imaging and testing services, thereby raising their Medicare revenue per patient (Medicare Payment Advisory Commission 2017).

Trends in Patient Wait Times and Acceptance Rates

A 2017 physician survey examined how long new patients would have to wait for an appointment with a physician in five medical specialties—family practice, cardiology, dermatology, obstetrics/gynecology, and orthopedic surgery—in 15 major metropolitan markets in the United States (Miller 2017). The survey also asked physicians whether they accepted Medicare and Medicaid patients. A similar survey was conducted in 2004, 2009, and 2014.

Large differences between cities existed in new-patient wait times. Boston had the highest average wait times (45 days) among physician markets studied (the average wait time in Dallas was 12 days). By contrast, Boston's wait time in the 2014 survey was 21 days. Average wait times to see a physician in family medicine, a cardiologist, and a dermatologist increased, but wait times remained about the same for obstetrician/gynecologists and orthopedic surgeons.

The acceptance rate for new Medicaid patients by physicians in all five specialties and in all 15 markets surveyed was 53.0 percent, down from 55.4 percent in 2009. Although physician acceptance rates for new Medicare patients were not included in earlier surveys, the average acceptance rate in 2017 in all five specialties and in all 15 markets was 84.5 percent.

These survey data show that wait times vary widely among specialties and in different markets, indicating that physician shortages are much greater in some parts of the country than in others and in certain specialties. Medicaid patients, in particular, face a shortage that results in severe access problems. The limited number of physicians willing to serve these patients is the result of Medicaid's low physician fees. Physicians have greater financial incentive to serve other patients for whom payments are higher.

Although physician payment rates are higher for Medicare than for Medicaid, the average 84.5 percent acceptance rate for Medicare patients indicates that these patients have access problems in a number of markets. For example, the family practice physician acceptance rate for new Medicare patients was 40 percent in Denver, 47 percent in Seattle, and 50 percent in Dallas. When demand and supply vary around the country, a single government payment system will not fully reflect these different market conditions; shortages are bound to occur in those areas where demand for physicians is increasing faster than the supply and where Medicare fees are not sufficiently flexible to respond to these differences.

Trends in Physician Income

Exhibit 11.3 shows that, over the 2002 through 2016 period, physician incomes rose above the inflation rate by 1 to 2 percent per year. These data also indicate that demand for physician services is increasing faster than the supply.

Trends in Rates of Return on a Medical Education

To determine whether a shortage of physicians exists, and, if so, in which specialties, examining the economic relative rate of return to a medical education is useful. Does an investment in a medical education offer higher returns than other professional educational opportunities or working after graduating from college? High relative rates of return are indicative of a shortage.

A permanent shortage is characterized by high relative rates of return and limited entry into the profession so that the high rates of return persist. (The applicant-to-acceptance ratio for medical schools is further evidence of whether prospective medical students believe the returns to a medical career are more favorable than those for other professions.)

Data on rates of return on a career in medicine are intermittent and available only up to 1997. Different researchers conducted these studies, and

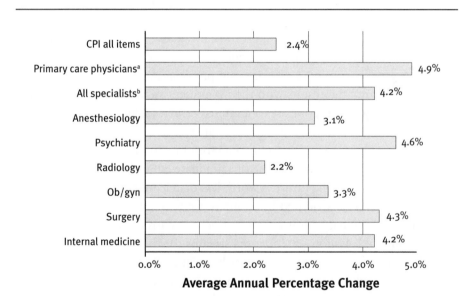

EXHIBIT 11.3
Average Annual Percentage Change in Physicians' Median Salaries from Medical Practice by Specialty, 2002–2016

[a]Primary care physicians group includes family practice, internal medicine, and pediatric/adolescent medicine.

[b]All specialists group includes anesthesiology, cardiology, dermatology, emergency medicine, gastroenterology, hematology/oncology, neurology, obstetrics/gynecology, ophthalmology, orthopedic surgery, otorhinolaryngology, psychiatry, pulmonary medicine, radiology, general surgery, and urology.

Note: CPI = consumer price index.

Source: Data from Medical Group Management Association (2008; 2009, table A; 2017).

their methodologies may not be similar. What do they indicate? Throughout the post–World War II period, rates of return on a medical career were sufficiently high to suggest that a shortage existed. In 1962, the rate of return was estimated to be 16.6 percent. By 1970, it had risen to 22 percent. The rate of return declined slightly between 1975 and 1985, when it was estimated to be 16 percent, still indicative of a shortage (Feldstein 2011).

Rates of return have varied greatly among medical specialties. In 1985, some specialties, such as anesthesiology and surgical subspecialties, earned 40 and 35 percent returns, whereas pediatrics earned a return of only 1.3 percent (indicative of a surplus). During the 1980s, the rate of return on a medical education was more than 100 percent greater than the rate of return on the education of a college professor. In 1994, the rate of return for primary care physicians was estimated to be 15.9 percent and for specialists, 20.9 percent. Weeks and Wallace (2002) calculated that in 1997 the rate of return for primary care physicians was about the same as it was in 1994 at 15.8 percent, but for specialists had declined to 18 percent. These data show that the economic return on a medical career has been quite high, indicating a physician shortage.[5] Using 2009 data, Roth (2011) calculated high rates of return to a medical education that varied greatly depending on specialty. The estimates ranged from 11 to 35 percent, with the majority in the high teens and 20s, clear evidence that a shortage of physicians continued to exist. Vaughn and colleagues (2010) calculated the net present value of going to graduate school for a master of business administration (MBA) degree, becoming a primary care physician, or becoming a cardiologist and compared the results with the net present value of an undergraduate (bachelor's) degree. In contrast to a rate-of-return calculation, in which the discount rate of a future income stream is the rate of return, the calculation of net present value uses a predetermined interest rate to discount future income streams. Because the higher income of a graduate education occurs over time, and a dollar earned in the future is worth less than a dollar earned today, those income streams are discounted by an interest rate to determine the economic value of the additional educational investment in current dollars.

Exhibit 11.4 shows the income streams for the four career paths and illustrates when the income began for each career path and its magnitude at different ages. Based on these data, Vaughn and colleagues (2010) calculated that the net present value from college graduation to age 65 years was $5,171,407 for cardiologists, $2,475,838 for primary care physicians, $1,725,171 for those with an MBA, and $340,628 for those with only a bachelor's degree. Thus, even accounting for the many years of training, the delay in earning an income and for fewer years, as well as the high levels of debt incurred, a medical career (particularly one in cardiology) has a great deal of economic value.

The economic returns of an investment in medical education have been sufficiently high to indicate the existence of a physician shortage. If a surplus

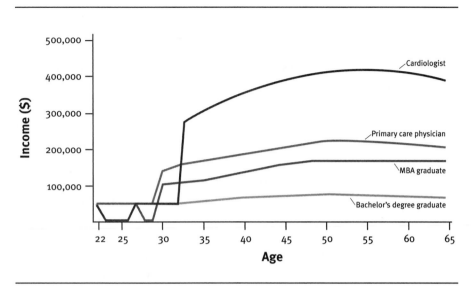

EXHIBIT 11.4
Annual Ordinary
Income
(Before Taxes)
for Various
Professions and
Educational
Attainment
Levels, Ages
22–65 Years

Note: MBA = master of business administration.

Source: Adapted from Vaughn et al. (2010).

had been indicated, the net present value of a medical career would be less than that of a career requiring only a bachelor's or master's degree. Whether or not the investment return on a medical career has fallen in the past several decades, the rate is still sufficiently high to suggest that there are too few physicians. An increase in the supply of physicians would lower the current high returns on medical education investment.

Applicant-to-Acceptance Ratio in Medical Schools

Another indicator of the economic value of a medical career is the demand for medical education. The applicant-to-acceptance ratio has always been greater than 1 (see exhibit 12.1 in chapter 12). After reaching a high of 2.9:1 in 1973, the applicant-to-acceptance ratio steadily declined to 1.6:1 in 1988, rose again in the mid-1990s, and, after declining again and reaching 1.9:1 in 2002, the ratio has increased and was 2.3:1 in 2017. Therefore, an excess demand for a medical education still exists.

Summary of the Evidence on a Physician Shortage

What can one conclude from the data on wait times, physician fees, rates of return, net present value, and the applicant-to-acceptance ratio? A shortage is evident in the physician services market, particularly in some areas. Medicare and Medicaid physician fees have not been increasing, and these patients will experience greater access problems, particularly access to primary care physicians. The ACA, which expanded coverage to an additional 14 million by increasing Medicaid eligibility and providing federal subsidies to those enrolled in state and federal health insurance exchanges, together with the demographic trends resulting in a growing number of elderly, increased the demand for primary care services, thereby lessening access to care, particularly among those receiving Medicaid.

The shortage of physicians has existed for many years. A medical career is an attractive investment. Physician (particularly specialist) income is still sufficiently high to offer a generous economic return on a medical career, relative to other careers available to prospective medical students. A growth in the supply of physicians would reduce these high relative rates of return, making them comparable to the rates of return on other educational investments.

Consistently high returns—particularly for medical specialties such as cardiology—point to barriers that prevent many qualified students from becoming physicians and gaining entry into highly remunerative specialties. These barriers consist of the limited number of medical school spaces, resulting in many US students going overseas to receive a medical education at a substantial expense. Limited expansion of medical residencies also prevents entry into those specialties that have high rates of return. Medical students have strong financial incentives to enter the specialties, not just because of the much higher income potential but also because the higher income enables them to quickly pay off their large medical school loans.

The supply of primary care physicians likely will not expand sufficiently to reduce the physician shortage. Further, under the current fee-for-service payment system, the large differences in returns between primary care physicians and many specialties will continue to exist.

Long-Term Outlook for the Physician Shortage

The demand for physician services is expected to increase sharply in coming years, as described in the AAMC's 2016 report, thereby exacerbating the physician shortage. Exhibit 11.5 shows the increasing role of government in physician payment. Unless Medicare and Medicaid increase physician fees when demand is increasing faster than supply, those with low income (Medicaid) and the aged (Medicare) will experience a significant decrease in access to physician services.

The shortage of physician services in the public markets, however, need not be resolved solely by investing greater sums to produce more physicians. Reducing the shortage of physician services requires two types of approaches: decreasing demand and increasing the supply of services.

Demand Strategies for Reducing the Shortage
Two general approaches can be used to decrease the demand for physician services.

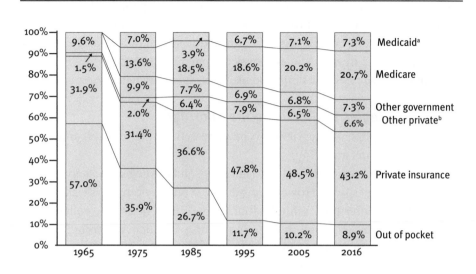

EXHIBIT 11.5
Percentage
Distribution
of Physician
Expenditures
by Source
of Funds,
Selected Years,
1965–2016

ᵃTotal Medicaid (excluding Medicaid expansion).

ᵇThis category includes industrial inplant and other private revenues (such as philanthropy); other private funds in 1965 and 1975 were 1.5% and 2.1%, respectively.

Source: Data from Centers for Medicare & Medicaid Services (2017).

First, patient incentives can be changed by increasing the price patients pay for low-value services. For example, most Medicare enrollees purchase private supplementary health insurance (Medigap) policies. This coverage pays for their Medicare deductibles and copayments, greatly lowering the price they must pay for physician services (some Medigap policies cut the price to zero) and decreasing their price sensitivity to physician fees. With virtually complete coverage for physician services, many elderly patients use an excessive amount of primary care and specialist services. Requiring a copayment for Medicare patients able to afford it will decrease the use of low-value services and increase patients' awareness of the cost of services.

Second, physician incentives can be changed by switching from fee-for-service to a broader payment system, such as capitation or a single fee for an episode of illness. In this way, physicians will use more innovative and less costly approaches to providing care, particularly to the chronically ill. Physicians will have an incentive to identify high-risk patients and manage their care before a costly episode occurs. For example, motivating more patients to control their hypertension will decrease the incidence of stroke. Similarly, foot examinations for patients with diabetes will reduce the number of amputations. Over time, these changes will lead to a decrease in the demand for costly medical services.

Under fee-for-service, higher-quality care may lead to fewer complications, which, in turn, leads to fewer office visits and lower physician income. Under a broader payment system, physicians are rewarded for improving quality and minimizing use of costly services for chronically ill patients. Further, physicians have a greater incentive to assist patients in becoming and remaining healthy and in better managing their conditions, which decreases the demand for services. The new Medicare physician payment system, MACRA, is an attempt to move physicians into the use of broader payment systems.

Supply Strategies for Reducing the Shortage

The supply of physician services can be increased in several ways, and efforts are currently underway.

First, new medical schools are launching, and existing schools are expanding the number of spaces. However, producing a primary care physician requires about 12 years after high school—four years of undergraduate college, four years of medical school, and three to four years of residency training. In addition, innovations in medical education must occur, such as reducing completion time from four years to three years.

However, simply increasing the number of medical school graduates to ease the shortage of physicians will be neither quick nor adequate. Only about 33 percent of physicians are in primary care, which includes internists, family physicians, pediatricians, and geriatricians. Although graduates of foreign medical schools make up about 24 percent of all physicians, they represent about 30 percent of primary care physicians. Unless more residency positions are created, the growing number of graduates of US medical schools will simply replace foreign medical school graduates without adding to the total physician supply (AAMC 2016).

Second, in coming years, physicians will have to boost their productivity by using midlevel practitioners to perform certain tasks when medically appropriate. APRNs, which include nurse practitioners, nurse midwives, nurse anesthetists, and clinical nurse specialists, as well as PAs and similarly trained personnel perform some physician-type services (particularly primary care), and their numbers are likely to grow.[6] In some states, nurse practitioners and PAs are assuming more responsibility for delivering primary care, especially in underserved communities (Conover 2015). In a national survey of physicians and nurse practitioners in primary care practice, Donelan and colleagues (2013, p. 1,898) found that

> [n]urse practitioners were more likely than physicians to believe that they should lead medical homes, be allowed hospital admitting privileges, and be paid equally for the same clinical services. When asked whether they agreed with the statement that physicians provide a higher-quality examination and consultation than do nurse practitioners during the same type of primary care visit, 66.1% of physicians agreed and 75.3% of nurse practitioners disagreed.

Medical associations, however, are strongly opposed to midlevel practitioners expanding their scope of practice and working without the supervision of physicians. Under fee-for-service, physicians and independent nurse practitioners are competitors. Under a broader payment system, physicians and nurse practitioners are in less economic competition for patients.

Third, technological advances are improving the efficiency of physicians' offices, enabling the practice to increase the number of patients seen and to use the physician's time more effectively. Physicians are beginning to prescribe smartphone applications and medical devices, such as a glucose meters and blood pressure monitors, that remind patients to take their medications and manage their chronic diseases (e.g., heart disease, diabetes, asthma). Clinical decision support systems, such as IBM's Watson supercomputer, are being developed that can make more accurate diagnosis and treatment recommendations. Telehealth applications provide easier access to physicians and enable them to respond to patients in a timelier manner (Ashwood et al. 2017).

Fourth, an important response to the shortage has been the rise of retail medical clinics. As of 2013, there were more than 1,400 retail medical clinics, twice as many as six years previously (Robeznieks 2013). When regulated fees cause a shortage, the *effective price*—the out-of-pocket payment for a visit and the value of the wait time to see a physician—to the patient increases. A higher effective price makes patients more willing to use substitutes, for which the out-of-pocket price may be higher but the wait time cost may be lower.

Urgent care centers and retail medical clinics are available every day of the week, and some are open 24 hours a day. A large percentage of the population does not have a primary care physician. Walgreens and CVS Health, for example, have expanded their health services from providing acute episodic care (e.g., giving flu shots and treating sore throats) to managing chronic diseases (e.g., diagnosing and treating patients for asthma, diabetes, and high cholesterol levels). Diagnosis and treatment—areas long controlled by physicians—are now provided by nurse practitioners and PAs, who prescribe tests, make diagnoses, write prescriptions (as state laws allow), and advise patients on managing their conditions at home.

Retail chains have also entered the potentially lucrative business of treating customers with long-term medical problems, which often require prescription drugs or other supplies that can be purchased at these stores. These convenient and relatively low-cost substitutes will eventually take business from physicians by using midlevel practitioners and by controlling referrals to healthcare professionals and hospitals. Whoever controls the entry point to medical services will also determine referrals to other healthcare providers (Ashwood et al. 2016). Also driving the demand for retail clinics are high-deductible health plans offered by employers. Because more employees are choosing these high-deductible plans (which place responsibility on patients for "first dollar" coverage), they have become more cost-conscious purchasers of medical services. In addition, insurers—once skeptical of retail medical clinics—now reimburse for vaccinations and family physicals obtained at these clinics.

Medical associations, such as the American Academy of Family Physicians, are seeking state legislation that limits the scope of services offered by retail medical clinics because these clinics (which use independent nurse practitioners) are providing disease management services that adversely affect physician incomes.

The physician's role will have to change as innovations occur in the payment system; in the technology used to diagnose, treat, and manage illness; in the professions involved in providing services (i.e., midlevel practitioners who desire to become independent practitioners); and in the settings in which services are delivered.

Summary

Regulated fees prevent equilibrium from occurring when demand exceeds supply in Medicare and Medicaid physician services markets. The resulting shortage will cause Medicare and Medicaid patients to endure much longer wait times and experience decreased access to care.

Continual high rates of return on medical education and an increasing applicant-to-acceptance ratio for medical schools are further signals of a physician shortage. Increasing the supply of physicians along with expanding residency positions would lower these high rates of return, making them comparable to the return on other educational investments. This approach is very costly and would take years before the supply of physicians is appreciably increased.

Shortages and surpluses are resolved over time through the adjustment of rising or falling fees. Market imbalances are not resolved quickly, as it takes many years to train physicians. One problem with medical education is that it is highly regulated by the medical profession. It is difficult for entrepreneurs to develop new medical schools with innovative curricula, shorten the required education time for students, and achieve the same outcomes as graduates of traditional medical schools. As long as these restrictions continue, along with an excess demand for a medical education, medical schools will be unresponsive to increased demands for a medical education and to curriculum innovations.

To reduce the shortage of physician services, two approaches should be used. First, decrease the demand for services by providing financial incentives to patients to use fewer less-valued services and to physicians to better manage the care of chronically ill patients. Second, increase the supply of physician services by boosting physician productivity, using more midlevel practitioners, and using more technology that improves physician efficiency.

Whether a shortage or surplus is beneficial depends on whether one is a patient or a physician. A small physician supply raises physician income, whereas greater competition among physicians and the expansion of midlevel practitioners benefit patients by improving access to care.

Discussion Questions

1. Evaluate the use of the physician-to-population ratio as a means of determining a physician surplus or shortage.
2. Describe and evaluate how a rate of return on a medical education would determine the existence of a physician surplus or shortage.
3. What demand and supply trends in the physician services market will affect the income of surgical specialists and primary care physicians?
4. Based on the evidence presented on physician income, physician fees, physician-to-population ratio, and applicant-to-acceptance ratio in medical schools, would you conclude that a physician shortage currently exists?
5. What are alternative approaches for decreasing a shortage in the physician services market?

Notes

1. Typically, physicians require higher fees from insurers, which, in turn, pass these costs to their enrollees in the form of higher health insurance premiums. Insurers may also impose higher cost-sharing amounts on patients seeing a physician.
2. The internal rate of return is the discount rate that, when applied to the future earnings stream, will make its present value equal to the cost of entry into the profession or the present value of the expected outlay or cost stream. A normal rate of return might be similar to the rate of return on a college education or on the return the individual could have received had he or she invested a sum of money comparable to what was spent on a medical education.
3. In the United States, a residency is a three- to seven-year-long on-the-job training in a teaching hospital that medical school graduates must complete before they can practice medicine. Each year, graduates of US medical schools compete with thousands of graduates of osteopathic schools, thousands of US-citizen graduates of international medical schools, and thousands of non–US citizen graduates of international medical schools for a limited number of new residency positions.
4. The belief that increasing funding for graduate medical education (GME) to produce a greater number of residents will reduce a physician

shortage is unfounded, according to Chandra, Khullar, and Wilensky (2014, 2357). They "argue that DME [direct medical education] funding does little to offset the cost of training physicians—that residents essentially pay the full cost of their training, while the DME program simply transfers money to recipient hospitals." Further, they state that "these funds are often used in ways that are difficult to trace, assess, and justify" (Chandra, Khullar, and Wilensky 2014, 2359).

5. Glied, Prabhu, and Edelman (2009) used a novel approach to estimate physician workforce planning. The authors used a human capital model to estimate the societal and private cost of producing a physician service. In doing so, they estimated the opportunity cost of physician time in addition to the explicit costs of becoming a physician. The authors further estimated that the private return on a medical education for a primary care physician is between 7 and 9 percent, which is relatively low compared with the returns to become a specialist.

6. Nurse practitioners are RNs who have completed a postgraduate nursing degree program with a specialization in primary care, acute care, or psychiatric/mental healthcare and sometimes with a focus on pediatrics, adult/gerontology, or women's health. State scope-of-practice laws vary widely in the level of physician oversight required for nurse practitioners: Some states allow nurse practitioners to practice independently, while others prohibit them from diagnosing, treating, or prescribing medications without supervision. Medicare reimburses nurse practitioners 85 percent of the fee received by physicians for the same services.

References

Accreditation Council for Graduate Medical Education. 2017. *GME Data Resource Book 2016–2017*. Accessed April 30, 2018. www.acgme.org/About-Us/Publications-and-Resources/Graduate-Medical-Education-Data-Resource-Book.

Ashwood, J. S., M. Gaynor, C. M. Setodji, R. O. Reid, E. Weber, and A. Mehrotra. 2016. "Retail Clinic Visits for Low-Acuity Conditions Increase Utilization and Spending." *Health Affairs* 35 (3): 449–55.

Ashwood, J. S., A. Mehrotra, D. Cowling, and L. Uscher-Pines. 2017. "Direct-to-Consumer Telehealth May Increase Access to Care but Does Not Decrease Spending." *Health Affairs* 36 (3): 485–91.

Association of American Medical Colleges (AAMC). 2016. "2016 Physician Specialty Report." Accessed April 30, 2018. www.aamc.org/data/workforce/reports/457712/2016-specialty-databook.html.

———. 2012. "Physician Shortages to Worsen Without Increases in Residency Train-ing." Center for Workforce Studies. Accessed April 30, 2018. https://kaiser healthnews.files.wordpress.com/2011/01/md-shortage.pdf.

Bureau of Labor Statistics. 2018. "Databases, Tables, & Calculators by Subject." Accessed April. http://data.bls.gov.

Centers for Medicare & Medicaid Services. 2017. "National Health Expenditure Data." Modified December 21. www.cms.gov/Research-Statistics-Data-and-Systems/ Statistics-Trends-and-Reports/NationalHealthExpendData/index.html.

Chandra, A., D. Khullar, and G. Wilensky. 2014. "The Economics of Graduate Medical Education." *New England Journal of Medicine* 370 (25): 2357–60.

Conover, C. 2015. "A Faster, Better, Cheaper Path to Filling the Doctor Shortage." *Forbes*. Published March 16. www.forbes.com/sites/theapothecary/2015/03/16/a-faster-better-cheaper-path-to-filling-the-doctor-shortage/.

Council on Graduate Medical Education (COGME). 2005. *Physician Workforce Pol-icy Guidelines for the United States, 2000–2020. Sixteenth Report.* Published January. www.hrsa.gov/advisorycommittees/bhpradvisory/cogme/Reports/ sixteenthreport.pdf.

———. 1992. *Improving Access to Health Care Through Physician Workforce Reform: Directions for the 21st Century. Third Report.* Published October. https:// archive.org/details/thirdreportimpro00heal.

Donelan, K., C. DesRoches, R. Dittus, and P. Buerhaus. 2013. "Perspectives of Physi-cians and Nurse Practitioners on Primary Care Practice." *New England Journal of Medicine* 368 (20): 1898–906.

Feldstein, P. J. 2011. "Health Manpower Shortages and Surpluses: Definitions, Mea-surement, and Policies." In *Health Care Economics*, 7th ed., 364–94. Albany, NY: Delmar.

Glied, S. A., A. Prabhu, and N. H. Edelman. 2009. "The Cost of Primary Care Doctors." *Forum for Health Economics & Policy* 12 (1). doi:10.2202/1558-9544.1140.

IHS Markit. 2017. *2017 Update. The Complexities of Physician Supply and Demand: Projections from 2015 to 2030.* Prepared for the Association of American Medi-cal Colleges. Published February 28. https://aamc-black.global.ssl.fastly.net/ production/media/filer_public/c9/db/c9dbe9de-aabf-457f-aee7-1d3d554ff281/aamc_projections_update_2017_final_-_june_12.pdf.

Medical Group Management Association. 2017. *2017 MGMA DataDive Provider Compensation Data.* Englewood, CO: Medical Group Management Association.

———. 2009. *Physician Compensation and Production Survey: 2009 Report Based on 2008 Data.* Englewood, CO: Medical Group Management Association.

———. 2008. *Physician Compensation and Production Survey: 2008 Report Based on 2007 Data.* Englewood, CO: Medical Group Management Association.

Medicare Payment Advisory Commission. 2017. *Report to the Congress: Medicare Payment Policy.* Published March. http://medpac.gov/docs/default-source/ reports/mar17_entirereport.pdf.

Miller, P. 2017. *2017 Survey of Physician Appointment Wait Times and Medicaid and Medicare Acceptance Rates.* Merritt Hawkins. Published September 22. www.merritthawkins.com/news-and-insights/thought-leadership/survey/survey-of-physician-appointment-wait-times/.

National Residency Matching Program. 2017. *Results and Data: 2017 Main Residency Match.* Published April. www.nrmp.org/wp-content/uploads/2017/06/Main-Match-Results-and-Data-2017.pdf.

Nicolson, S. 2003. "Barriers to Entering Medical Specialties." National Bureau of Economic Research Working Paper No. 9649. Published April. www.nber.org/papers/w9649.

Rice, T., S. C. Stearns, D. E. Pathman, S. DesHarnais, M. Brasure, and M. Tai-Seale. 1999. "A Tale of Two Bounties: The Impact of Competing Fees on Physician Behavior." *Journal of Health Politics, Policy and Law* 24 (6): 1307–30.

Robeznieks, A. 2013. "Retail Clinics at Tipping Point: Pharmacies, Chains Answering Demand for Access and Affordability." *Modern Healthcare* 43 (18): 6–7.

Roth, N. 2011. "The Costs and Returns to Medical Education." University of California, Berkeley. www.econ.berkeley.edu/sites/default/files/roth_nicholas.pdf.

US Government Accountability Office. 2017. *Physician Workforce: Locations and Types of Graduate Training Were Largely Unchanged, and Federal Efforts May Not Be Sufficient to Meet Needs.* Report to Congressional Requesters. Published May. www.gao.gov/assets/690/684946.pdf.

Vaughn, B., S. DeVrieze, S. Reed, and K. Schulman. 2010. "Can We Close the Income and Wealth Gap Between Specialists and Primary Care Physicians?" *Health Affairs* 29 (5): 933–40.

Weeks, W., and A. Wallace. 2002. "The More Things Change: Revisiting a Comparison of Educational Costs and Incomes of Physicians and Other Professionals." *Academic Medicine* 77 (4): 312–19.

WHY IS GETTING INTO MEDICAL SCHOOL SO DIFFICULT?

12

I n 2017, only 22,266 of the 51,680 students who applied to 136 medical schools in the United States were accepted, for an applicant-to-acceptance ratio of 2.3:1. (The number of matriculants was 928 fewer because some applicants were accepted at more than one school.) The ratio—having reached a high of 2.8:1 in 1973—steadily declined to 1.58:1 in 1988; rose again in the mid-1990s; and, after falling again and reaching a low of 1.9:1 in 2002, increased to 2.3:1.

As shown in exhibit 12.1, first-year medical school enrollments grew sharply in the early 1970s, mostly because federal legislation (the Health Manpower Training Act of 1964) gave medical schools strong financial incentives to increase their enrollments. When these federal subsidies phased out, enrollments leveled out. They have remained relatively steady since the early 1980s and have only recently started to rise. Since 2009, 14 new medical schools have opened and several schools have expanded their class size, which will lead to further growth in student enrollment. However, even with greater school capacity, a large excess demand for a medical education will continue.

Many qualified students are rejected each year because of the limited number of medical school spaces. Some rejected students choose to enroll in medical schools in other countries, such as Mexico. Medical schools overseas often charge higher tuition and require longer training periods than do US medical schools, which require four years of college before the four years of medical school. Residency training requires an additional three to seven years of graduate medical education. Unfortunately, academic excellence is not a sufficient qualification for admission to medical school. Other types of graduate-level professional education programs have experienced sharp increases in demand, but not the continual excess demands that medical schools experience. Although every well-qualified student who wants to become a physicist, a mathematician, an economist, or a lawyer cannot realistically expect to be admitted to her first choice in graduate schools, if she has good academic qualifications (as do most medical students), she will likely be admitted to a US graduate school.[1]

The Market for Medical Education in Theory

When medicine is perceived as relatively more attractive than other careers, demand for medical schools exceeds the number of available spaces. If the

EXHIBIT 12.1

Medical School Applicants and Enrollments, 1960–2017

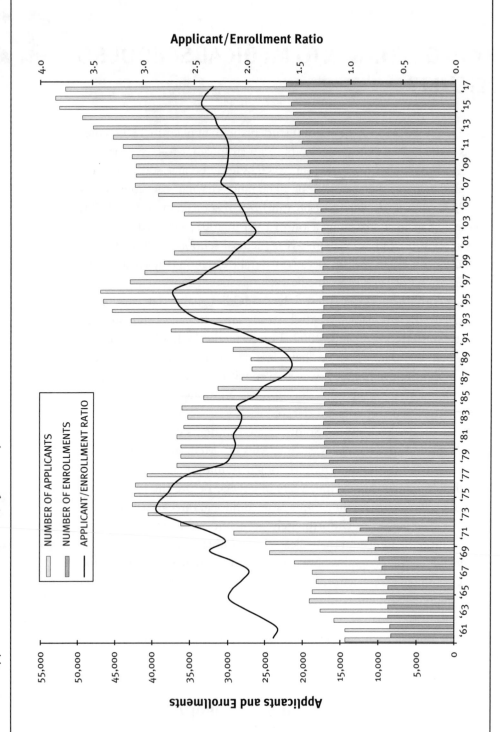

Source: Data from Association of American Medical Colleges (n.d.).

market for medical education were like other markets, this shortage would be temporary while more medical schools are built and existing schools recruit additional faculty members and add physical facilities to meet the greater demand. Over time, the temporary shortage would be resolved as the supply of spaces increases. Crucial in eliminating a temporary shortage is a rise in price (tuition). Higher tuition will serve to ration student demand for the existing number of spaces and provide medical schools with a financial incentive (and the funds) to invest in facilities and faculty so that they can accommodate larger enrollments. Subsidies and loan programs could be made available directly to low-income students faced with high tuition rates.

The Market for Medical Education in Practice

The market for medical education, however, differs from other markets. The medical education industry produces its output inefficiently (at high cost and requiring too many years of a student's time), and the method used to finance medical education is inequitable (large subsidies go to students from high-income families, who then go on to earn high salaries). If medical education were similar to other industries, more efficient competitors would have driven out less efficient competitors and transformed the industry. How has this industry, with its record of such poor performance, been able to survive?

The producers of medical education have been insulated from the marketplace. Tuition, established at an arbitrarily low level, represents less than one-third of the costs of medical education and approximately 3.8 percent (as of 2016) of medical school revenues (Association of American Medical Colleges 2017b, table 1).

Medical schools can maintain low tuition because large state subsidies and research grants offset educational costs. Tuition, being such a small fraction of educational costs and not rising with higher demand, neither serves to ration excess demand among students nor provides an incentive to medical schools to expand their capacity. Medical schools—particularly public ones— do not depend on tuition revenue to even cover their operating expenses. Lacking a financial incentive to expand, medical schools do nothing to alleviate the temporary shortage. Instead, the shortage becomes permanent, which is a far more serious situation.

For-profit businesses respond to greater consumer demands by raising prices and increasing supplies because they want to make more profit. New firms enter industries in which they perceive they can earn more on their investments than they can earn elsewhere. When prices are prevented from rising or barriers exist to new firms entering an expanding market, temporary shortages can become permanent. Typically, barriers to entry are legal rather than economic, and they protect existing firms from competition. Protected firms are better able to maintain higher prices and receive above-normal profit than they would if new firms were permitted to enter the market.

Medical schools, being not-for-profit, are motivated by more "noble" goals, such as the prestige associated with training tomorrow's medical educators. Most medical schools share the goal of having renowned, research-oriented faculty members who teach a few small classes of academically gifted students, who, in turn, will be their successors as super-specialist researchers. Few, if any, medical schools seek acclaim for graduating large numbers of primary care physicians who practice in underserved areas.

Only by maintaining an excess demand for admissions can medical schools choose the type of student who will become the type of physician they prefer (i.e., someone who will meet their prestige goals). The medical school faculty determines both the type of student selected and the design of the educational curriculum; these decisions are not made on the basis of what is needed to train quality physicians efficiently (in terms of student time and cost per student). As long as a permanent shortage of medical school spaces exists, medical schools will continue to "profit" by selecting the type of student desired by the faculty, establishing educational requirements the faculty deems most appropriate, and producing graduates who mirror the faculty's values. The current system of medical education has inadequate incentives for medical schools to respond cost-effectively to changes in the demand for education.

How likely is it that an organization, perhaps a health plan, could start its own self-supporting medical school—one that admits students after only two years of undergraduate training (as is done in Great Britain), with a revised curriculum and residency requirement that combines the last two years of medical school with the first two years of graduate medical education (reducing the graduate medical education requirement by one year, as proposed by the former dean of the Harvard Medical School), and financed either by tuition or by graduates who repay their tuition by practicing for a number of years in the organization (Ebert and Ginzberg 1988). Emanuel and Fuchs (2012, 1143) claimed that the average length of training could be reduced by 30 percent without any loss of physician competence or quality of care. Further, they argued that "there is no evidence that graduates of 6-year programs perform more poorly on standardized board examinations or as practicing physicians." Schools with shorter training times could satisfy the excess demands for a medical education, reduce the educational process by three to four years, and, at the same time, teach students to be practitioners in a managed care environment.[2]

Accreditation for Medical Schools

Not surprisingly, starting new and innovative medical schools is very difficult. The Liaison Committee on Medical Education (LCME 2017) accredits programs leading to the doctor of medicine (MD) degree and establishes the criteria to which a school must adhere to receive accreditation. For example, the LCME specifies a minimum number of weeks of instruction and calendar years (four) in which the instruction is to occur; in addition, an undergraduate education (usually four years) is required for admission to a medical school. Innovations in curricula and changes in the length of time required to become a physician (and to prepare for admission to medical school) must be approved by the LCME. The LCME also states that the cost of a medical education should be supported by diverse sources: tuition, endowment, faculty earnings, government grants and appropriations, the university, and gifts. Through its belief that medical schools should not rely heavily on tuition, the LCME encourages schools to pursue revenue sources and goals unrelated to educational concerns.

To become accredited, medical schools must be not-for-profit. The LCME's accreditation criteria in effect eliminate all incentives for health plans and similar organizations to invest in medical schools in hopes of earning a profit or having a steady supply of practitioners. Private organizations in the United States have no incentive to invest capital to start a new medical school.

The status quo of the current high-cost medical education system would be threatened if graduates of these proposed new medical schools proved to be as qualified as those trained in more traditional schools (as evidenced by their licensure examination scores and performance in residencies offered to them) and could enter practice three years earlier.

To bring about medical education reforms, nine commissions have been set up since the 1960s to recommend changes. In a 1990 survey, medical school deans, department chairs, and faculty members overwhelmingly endorsed the need for "fundamental changes" or "thorough reform" in medical student education (Hendricson et al. 1993). In a review of several published studies, Enarson and Burg (1992) indicated that faculties lack sufficient incentives to participate in reforming medical education programs because promotion and tenure are based primarily on research productivity and clinical practice expertise. "[There is] the relegation of students' education to a secondary position within the medical school." Moreover, "faculty have tended to think of the goals of their own academic specialty and department rather than the educational goals of the school as a whole" (Enarson and Burg 1992, 1142).

Recommended Changes

Not surprisingly, without financial incentives, the not-for-profit sector will fail to respond to increased student demands for a medical education and will not be concerned about the efficiency with which medical education is provided. Instead of relying on innumerable commissions whose proposed reforms largely go unimplemented, three changes in the current system of medical education and quality assurance should be considered: (1) ease the entry requirements for starting new medical schools, (2) reduce medical school subsidies, and (3) place more emphasis on monitoring physician practice patterns.

Ease the Entry Requirements for Starting New Medical Schools

The accreditation criteria of the LCME should be changed to permit other organizations, such as managed care organizations (MCOs) (including those that are for-profit) to start medical schools. A larger number of schools competing for students would pressure medical schools to be more innovative and efficient. With easier entry into the medical education market, greater emphasis could be placed on quality outcomes (by examining and monitoring physicians' practice behavior) than on the process of becoming a physician. Directly monitoring physicians' practice behavior is the most effective way to protect the public from unethical and incompetent physicians.

As more physicians participate in MCOs, and as hospitals and physicians become more integrated, physician peer review will be enhanced. Integrated organizations have a financial incentive to evaluate the quality and appropriateness of care provided by physicians under their auspices, as these organizations compete with similar groups on the basis of premiums, quality of care provided, and access to services. Report cards documenting physician quality of care and patient satisfaction are increasingly required by large employers and consumer groups. Quality assurance of physician services will increase as a result of competition among medical groups, integrated organizations, and health plans.

Reduce Medical School Subsidies

Reducing government subsidies would force medical schools to become more efficient by shortening the time required to earn a medical degree and lowering the costs of providing it. Medical students should not be subsidized to a greater extent than students in other graduate or professional schools. A decrease in state subsidies to medical schools would force them to reexamine their curricula and cut the costs of education. Medical schools that respond merely by raising their tuition to make up the lost revenues will find it difficult to attract a sufficient number of highly qualified applicants once more schools are competing for students. As tuition more accurately reflects the cost of education, applicants will comparison shop and evaluate schools within a range of tuition levels. To be competitive, schools with lesser reputations will need to have correspondingly lower tuition levels. The need to reduce students' educational costs most likely would result in innovative curricula, new teaching methods, and better use of the medical student's time.

To ensure that every qualified student has an equal opportunity to become a physician once subsidies are decreased, more student loan and subsidy programs must be made available. Current low tuition rates in effect subsidize the medical education of all medical students, even those from high-income families. Once these students graduate, they enter one of the highest-income professions. Providing subsidies directly to qualified students according to their family income levels would be more equitable.

Furthermore, the subsidies given directly to students should be in the form of a voucher (to be used only in a medical school). Giving the state subsidies to students would be an incentive for them to select a medical school according to its reputation, total educational costs, and the number of years of education required to graduate from college and medical school. Medical schools would then be forced to compete for students on the basis of these criteria.

Place More Emphasis on Monitoring Physician Practice Patterns

Currently, the process for ensuring physician quality relies wholly on graduating from an approved medical school and passing a licensing examination. Once a physician is licensed, no reexamination is required to maintain that license, although specialty boards may impose their own requirements for admission and maintenance of membership. State licensing boards are responsible for monitoring physicians' behavior and penalizing physicians whose performance is inadequate or whose conduct is unethical. Unfortunately, this approach for ensuring physician quality and competence is completely unreliable.

State licensing boards discipline very few physicians. In 1972, the disciplinary rate was only 0.74 per 1,000 physicians; a number of states did not undertake any disciplinary actions against their physicians. Between 1980 and 1982, the disciplinary rate rose to 1.3 per 1,000 physicians, or about one-tenth of 1 percent of all physicians. Although some improvements in certain states have been observed in recent years, the number of disciplinary actions against physicians varies greatly among states.

As of 2011, the number of disciplinary actions per 1,000 practicing physicians was 5.2 in New York, 5.1 in California, 7.9 in Ohio, 12.7 in Texas, and 8.9 in Colorado. Many states had much lower disciplinary rates. Two states with nearly the lowest serious disciplinary action rates for 2011—Minnesota (2.4 actions per 1,000 physicians) and Massachusetts (2.4 actions per 1,000 physicians)—have been among the bottom ten states for each of the past five years. (The lowest serious disciplinary action rate in 2011 was in Washington state [2.2 actions per 1,000 physicians]) (Carlson 2017).

It is unlikely that Texas, which had 12.7 prejudicial acts per 1,000 physicians in 2011, has a greater percentage of unethical or incompetent physicians or more physicians requiring disciplinary actions than many other states. Instead, the considerable variability among states represents the uneven efforts by the states' medical licensing boards (which are mainly composed of physicians) to monitor and discipline physicians in their states. In fact, even when physicians lose their licenses in one state, they can move to another state and practice; some state medical boards encourage physicians to move to another state in exchange for dropping charges. The public is not as protected from incompetent and unethical medical practitioners as the medical profession has led it to believe.[3]

In 2013, the Federation of State Medical Boards (FSMB) discontinued publishing its annual report (which had been published since 1985) on the number of physician disciplinary actions by each state's medical board. Thus, it has not been possible to update the data provided earlier regarding physician disciplinary actions by state. The FSMB claims that the data have been misused and do not accurately reflect each state's medical board performance. A consumer advocacy group, Public Citizen, claims that the report was discontinued to prevent the group from publishing the rankings of state medical boards that the boards and physicians disliked (Robeznieks 2013).

Monitoring the care provided by physicians through use of claims and medical records data would be a more direct way to assess their competence. State licensing boards also need to devote more resources to monitoring physician behavior. Requiring periodic reexamination and relicensure of all physicians would compel them to update their skills and knowledge. Rather than requiring physicians to take a minimum number of hours of continuing education, states should require reexamination. Individual physicians then would determine the appropriate amount of continuing education they need to pass the examination. (Continuing education by itself is a process measure for ensuring quality, but it does not ensure that physicians actually maintain and update their skills and knowledge base.) Reexamination is a more useful and direct measure to assess whether a physician has achieved the objectives of continuing education.

Periodic reexamination and relicensure would identify an individual physician's areas of proficiency. Currently, all licensed physicians are permitted to perform a wide range of tasks, although they may have insufficient training in some of these tasks. Physicians may designate themselves as specialists whether or not they are certified by a specialty board. At present, any physician can legally perform surgery, provide anesthesia services, and diagnose patients. Reexamination could result in a physician's practice being limited to those tasks for which she continues to demonstrate proficiency. Instead of all-encompassing licenses, physicians would be granted specific-purpose licenses. This process would acknowledge that licensing physicians to perform a wide range of medical tasks does not serve the best interests of the public because not all physicians are qualified to perform all tasks adequately.

Specific-purpose licensure would mean that not all physicians would need to undergo the same educational training; in some specialties, training would take much less time, whereas training to become a super-specialist would take longer. Less extensive educational requirements for family practitioners would lower the cost of their medical education, enable them to graduate earlier, and earn an income sooner. Even with higher yearly tuition, family practitioners would incur a smaller debt and could begin paying it off at least three years earlier.[4] The number of family practitioners would increase because they would incur a much smaller investment (fewer years of schooling and lost income) in their medical education, and that would more than compensate for not receiving an income as high as that of a specialist. When a physician wants an additional specific-purpose license, he can receive additional training and take the qualifying examination for that license. Training requirements for entering the medical profession would be determined not by the medical profession but by the demand for different types of physicians and the lowest-cost manner of producing them.

Summary

The competition among medical schools that would result from reducing their subsidies (or providing subsidies directly to students) and permitting new schools to open would improve the performance of the market for medical education. Easing entry restrictions would make it easier to open nontraditional schools (and innovate in existing schools), allowing more qualified students to be admitted to a medical school. Qualified students would no longer have to incur the higher expense and longer training times involved in attending a foreign medical school.

　　Emphasizing outcome measures and appropriateness of care would better protect the public from incompetent and unethical physicians. Reducing government subsidies to medical schools would force them to be more efficient and innovative in structuring a medical curriculum. Further, distributing subsidies to students according to family income rather than to the medical school (which results in a subsidy for all students) would enhance equity among students receiving a medical education and force medical schools to compete for those students.

Discussion Questions

1. Evaluate the performance of the current market for medical education in terms of the number of qualified students admitted and the cost (both medical education and forgone income) of becoming a physician.

2. The current approach to subsidizing medical schools results in all medical students being subsidized. Contrast this approach with one that

awards the same amount of subsidy directly to students (according to their family income) for use in any medical school.

3. Medical schools are typically interested in prestige. How would medical school behavior change if schools had to survive in a competitive market (with free entry of new competitors) and without subsidies?

4. An important reason that so few family practitioners exist is their much lower economic returns than those for specialists. How would a competitive market in medical education increase the relative profitability of becoming a family practitioner?

5. Currently, the public is protected from incompetent and unethical physicians by the requirement that physicians graduate from an approved medical school, pass a one-time licensing examination, and receive continuing education. What are alternative, lower-cost approaches to protecting the public's interest?

Notes

1. Medical education also differs from other graduate programs in that, once accepted to medical school, a student is virtually assured of graduating. The attrition rate is approximately 2 percent, compared with attrition rates of 50 percent in other graduate programs.

2. About 25 medical schools admit a small number of students who completed only two to three years of college (combined BA/BS/MD programs) (http://theperfectmed.com/programs.html).

3. Improvements have been occurring slowly over time. All states now share formal action information with other states and report disciplinary actions to the National Practitioner Data Bank.

4. The median graduating-student debt level for public and private medical schools in 2017 was $180,000 and $202,000, respectively (Association of American Medical Colleges 2017a).

References

Association of American Medical Colleges. n.d. *Medical School Admission Requirements, United States and Canada.* Various editions. Washington, DC: Association of American Medical Colleges.

———. 2017a. "Medical Student Education: Debt, Costs, and Loan Repayment Fact Card." Published October. https://members.aamc.org/iweb/upload/2017%20 Debt%20Fact%20Card.pdf.

———. 2017b. "Revenues Supporting Programs and Activities at Fully-Accredited U.S. Medical Schools FY2016 ($ in Millions)." www.aamc.org/download/480304/data/fy2016_medical_school_financial_tables.pdf.

Carlson, D. 2017. Summary of 2011 board actions of the Federation of State Medical Boards of the United States, Inc. Personal correspondence with the author, September 5.

Ebert, R. H., and E. Ginzberg. 1988. "The Reform of Medical Education." *Health Affairs* 7 (Suppl. 2): 5–38.

Emanuel, E., and V. Fuchs. 2012. "Shortening Medical Training by 30%." *Journal of the American Medical Association* 307 (11): 1143–44.

Enarson, C., and F. Burg. 1992. "An Overview of Reform Initiatives in Medical Education: 1906 Through 1992." *Journal of the American Medical Association* 268 (9): 1141–43.

Hendricson, W. D., A. F. Payer, L. P. Rogers, and J. F. Markus. 1993. "The Medical School Curriculum Committee Revisited." *Academic Medicine* 68 (3): 183–89.

Liaison Committee on Medical Education (LCME). 2017. *Rules of Procedure.* Published June. http://lcme.org/publications/#Guidelines--amp--Procedures.

Robeznieks, A. 2013. "Where's Doc Disciplinary Data?" *Modern Healthcare* 43 (30): 36–37.

THE CHANGING PRACTICE OF MEDICINE

13

The practice of medicine has changed dramatically since the mid-1980s. For many years, the predominant form of medical practice was solo practice with fee-for-service (FFS) reimbursement. With the increase in medical knowledge and technological advancements, however, more physicians became specialists. Insurer payment and federal education subsidies also encouraged the growth of specialization. The development of managed care changed the practice of medicine; more physicians joined together in increasingly large medical groups. And Medicare physician payment systems are completing the transformation of physicians' practices.

What are the reasons for the shift away from solo and small group practice toward large medical groups? Is the consolidation of medical practices into large groups likely to continue? How are accountable care organizations (ACOs) and the new physician payment system, the Medicare Access and CHIP Reauthorization Act (MACRA), changing how physicians practice?

Types of Medical Groups

Different types of medical groups have formed to serve the varied needs and preferences of practicing physicians. Following is a description of these two basic types.

Single Specialty or Multispecialty Groups

Physicians in these groups share facilities, equipment, medical records, and support staff. Physicians may be paid according to one or more methods: salary plus a share in remaining net revenues, discounted FFS with a share in remaining net revenues, or capitation. Leaving a group practice is difficult for physicians, as they cannot take their patients with them. Any contracts the group has with a health plan belong to the group and include the patients covered by those contracts.

Independent Practice Associations

Physicians who want to be associated with other physicians (on a nonexclusive basis) for the purposes of joint contracting with a health plan will form a loose organization, such as an independent practice association (IPA). These physicians continue to practice in their own offices, see their own patients, hire and pay their own staff, and do their own billing.

When the IPA contracts with a health plan, the IPA physicians are paid on a discounted FFS basis. If an IPA enters into a capitation contract with a health plan, the physicians may be paid a discounted FFS with the possibility of receiving additional amounts if total physician billings are less than the total capitation amount at the end of the year. The IPA may also subcapitate some specialists. As IPAs competed for capitated contracts and assumed financial risk, they began to exercise more oversight of their physicians' practice patterns.

Changes in Size and Type of Medical Groups

Data sources on physicians' practice settings have changed over time. The most recent data reported by the American Medical Association (AMA) are not comparable to data collected previously (up to 2008) by the Center for Studying Health System Change. The most recent data represent the years 2012, 2014, and 2016 and are based on a nationally representative sample of US physicians who were not employed by the federal government and worked at least 20 hours a week (Kane 2017). These surveys indicate the changes in physician practice patterns, but they are less dramatic compared with what has occurred over a longer period. However, the trends in physician practice are still noticeable.

Exhibit 13.1 shows the distribution of physicians by ownership status and type of practice. A decline has occurred in the number of physicians that have an ownership stake in their practice. For the first time, fewer than half of all physicians have such an ownership stake. Similarly, the number of physician employees has been increasing sharply. Additional data in the AMA survey show that younger physicians and female physicians are more likely to be employed.

Exhibit 13.1 also shows that the largest percentage (42.8 percent) of physicians is in single specialty groups, although the percentage has slightly decreased since 2012. Multispecialty groups are the second largest form of practice—24.6 percent—and the percentage has increased slightly since 2012. Physicians classified as direct hospital employees, although only 7.4 percent of the total, have had the largest percentage increase since 2012.

Exhibit 13.2 describes the distribution of physicians by size of practice and by single or multispecialty status. Most physicians work in small practices with ten or fewer physicians. Practices with five or fewer physicians have been declining over time (shown elsewhere in the Kane study). Single-specialty groups are more likely to be in smaller practices than are multispecialty groups.

The AMA data also indicate that hospital ownership of practices is more likely to include those with primary care physicians. Also, primary care practices are more likely to be classified as hospital ownership than are other practices. Further, the growth in hospital acquisition of physician practices appears to be slowing, possibly because hospitals are concentrating on ways to better manage and integrate the physicians they currently employ.

	2012	2014	2016
	N = 3,466	*N* = 3,500	*N* = 3,500
Ownership status			
Owner	53.2%[b]	50.8%[a]	47.1%[a]
Employee	41.8%	43%[a]	47.1%[a]
Independent contractor	5%[b]	6.2%	5.9%
Type of practice			
Solo practice	18.4%	17.1%	16.5%[b]
Single-specialty group	45.5%[a]	42.2%	42.8%[b]
Multispecialty group	22.1%[a]	24.7%	24.6%[b]
Direct hospital employee	5.6%[a]	7.2%	7.4%[a]
Faculty practice plan	2.7%	2.8%	3.1%
Other[c]	5.7%	5.9%	5.7%

EXHIBIT 13.1
Distribution of Physicians by Ownership Status and Type of Practice, 2012–2016

Notes: Significance tests are for year-to-year changes within category. [a] = $p < .01$. [b] = $p < .05$. Indications in the 2012 column are tests for 2012 and 2014; in the 2014 column for 2014 and 2016; and in the 2016 column for 2012 and 2016. [c]Other includes ambulatory surgical center, urgent care facility, HMO/MCO, medical school, and fill-in responses.

Source: Used with permission of the American Medical Association. (C. K. Kane, "Updated Data on Physician Practice Arrangements: Physician Ownership Drops Below 50 Percent," AMA Economic and Health Policy Research, 2017).

Number of Physicians in Practice	Single-Specialty Group	Multispecialty Group
	N = 1,490	*N* = 797
< 5	38.9%	10.4%
5 to 10	32.2%	18.9%
11 to 24	16.5%	18.7%
25 to 49	7.4%	13.4%
≥ 50	5.0%	38.7%

EXHIBIT 13.2
Distribution of Physicians in Single-Specialty and Multispecialty Groups by Practice Size, 2016

Source: Used with permission of the American Medical Association. (C. K. Kane, "Updated Data on Physician Practice Arrangements: Physician Ownership Drops Below 50 Percent," AMA Economic and Health Policy Research, 2017).

In a highly competitive managed care market, physicians in individual and small group practices are at a disadvantage. Therein lies an important explanation for the formation of large medical groups.

Medical Groups as a Competitive Response

Before managed care became dominant in the insurance marketplace, physicians were less concerned with being included in an insurer's provider panel or competing for insurance contracts. The growth in private insurance reduced the out-of-pocket price of physician services paid by private patients. As patients' out-of-pocket payments declined, they became less price sensitive to physicians' fees, and demand increased. Patients had access to all physicians, who were paid according to their established fee schedules. Patients had similar insurance (indemnity) and limited, if any, information about physician qualifications or the fees charged.

Price competition among managed care plans for an employer's enrollees changed all that. To be price competitive, insurers had to reduce the price they paid for their inputs (physician and hospital services) and reduce the quantity of services used. The physician services market in the 1980s consisted of a growing supply of physicians—particularly specialists—and a high proportion of them were in solo or small group practices. Physicians were eager to contract with new managed care health plans. Insurers and health maintenance organizations (HMOs) were able to form limited provider networks by selecting physicians according to whether they were willing to sharply discount their fees in return for a greater volume of patients. Physicians excluded from such networks lost patients.

The growth of managed care had two main effects on physicians. First, managed care forced physicians to deeply discount their fees in return for a greater number of the plan's enrollees. Patients enrolled in managed care plans were required to use providers who were part of their plan's provider network; otherwise, the patient had to pay the full price charged by a nonnetwork provider. For physicians to have access to an insurer's enrollees, the physician had to be part of the insurer's provider network. Managed care plans limited the number of physicians in their provider networks and selected physicians on the basis of their willingness to steeply discount fees (and not overuse medical services).

Second, managed care reduced enrollee access to specialists. Managed care relied on gatekeepers—primary care physicians—to determine whether a patient would receive a referral to a specialist. The growth of managed care increased the demand for primary care physicians and decreased the demand for specialists.

The growth of medical groups was a competitive response to the greater bargaining power of insurers and HMOs. Being part of a medical group—particularly a large group—provided physicians with a competitive advantage over physicians who were not similarly organized. Large medical groups were able to bid for HMO contracts and serve as preferred provider organizations for employers and insurers. Negotiating and contracting with one large medical group is less costly than carrying out separate, time-consuming negotiations with an equivalent number of individual physicians. Tasks performed by the insurer, such as utilization management, can be delegated to the medical group. Thus, in the 1980s and 1990s, large medical groups were better able to compete for patients than were individual physicians and small medical groups.

HMOs were also able to shift their insurance risk to a large medical group by paying that group on a capitation basis instead of a FFS basis. Similarly, a large medical group can spread financial risk over many capitated enrollees and physicians.

Capitation also provided medical groups with financial incentives to be innovative in the delivery of medical services and the practice of medicine. By reducing its costs, the medical group could keep more of the capitation payment and increase its physicians' income. These incentives do not exist in small group practices that are paid FFS. Consequently, several large medical groups developed expertise in managing care and in developing "best-practice" guidelines. In the 1990s, medical groups in California (more so than those in other states) sought more financial risks and rewards by accepting a greater percentage of the HMO premium (Gillies et al. 2003). These medical groups believed that by being responsible for all of the patient's medical services, they could better manage care; further, by reducing hospital admissions, lengths of stay, and payments to hospitals, they could earn greater profits.

Unfortunately, many of these medical groups were inexperienced in managing the financial risks associated with capitation and suffered financially.

Increased Market Power

An employer or a health plan contracting with a large medical group has less reason to be concerned about physician quality. Large medical groups have more formalized quality control and monitoring mechanisms than do independently practicing physicians. Within a large group, physicians refer patients to their own specialists; thus, specialists who are not part of a group are less likely to have access to patients. These contracting, quality review, and referral mechanisms provide physicians in large medical groups with a competitive advantage over physicians who are unaffiliated with such groups.

These advantages resulted in large groups' having greater bargaining power over health plans compared with independent and small group practices. Consequently, large groups were better able to negotiate higher payments and increased market share (receiving a greater portion of the health plan's total number of enrollees).

Large medical groups also have greater leverage over hospitals. Because such groups control large numbers of enrollees, they can determine to which hospitals they will refer patients. Hospitals, in turn, were willing to share some of their capitated revenues with these groups. When hospitals were capitated, a *risk-sharing pool* was formed from part of the hospital's capitation payments, whereby the savings from reduced hospitalization were shared between the hospital and the medical group. These risk-sharing pools enabled physicians in large medical groups to earn more money than they would have earned in independent or small group practices.

Economies of Scale in Group Practice

An obvious reason for moving toward large medical groups in a price-competitive environment is to take advantage of economies of scale. Large groups have lower per-unit costs than do small groups. They also are better able to spread certain fixed costs over more physicians. The administrative costs of running an office (including making appointments; billing patients, government, and insurance companies for services rendered; maintaining computerized information systems to keep track of patients; and employing aides to assist the physician) do not rise proportionately to the increase in the number of physicians. Multispecialty groups also can better provide care coordination to patients and arrange for consultations with other physicians in the group. In addition, they receive volume discounts on supplies and negotiate lower rates on their leases than can the same number of physicians practicing separately or in small groups.

Informational economies of scale also provide large groups with a competitive advantage over small groups or independent practices. A distinguishing characteristic of the physician services market is the lack of information about physicians, including the quality of care they provide, their fees, their accessibility, and the manner in which they relate to patients. Physicians are better able than patients to evaluate other physicians. Evaluating and monitoring member physicians is less costly for the medical group than it is for patients. Being a member of a medical group conveys information to patients regarding quality, giving physicians in that group the equivalent of a brand name.

A new physician entering a market is at a disadvantage (compared with established physicians) because developing a reputation and building a practice take time. Joining a medical group immediately transfers the group's reputation to the new physician. The group's reputation with respect to specialist services that are used less frequently is important to the patient. Multispecialty groups offer greater informational economies of scale than do groups composed of family practitioners.

Medical Groups and Quality of Care

Large medical groups are more likely than physicians in solo or small groups to invest in management and clinical information systems, such as an electronic health record (EHR). Studies have shown that, on average, large multispecialty medical groups deliver higher-quality care and achieve lower annual costs per patient than physicians in solo practice or small groups (Weeks et al. 2010). Large medical groups are likely to use more recommended care management processes for patients with chronic illnesses. Large groups can hire professional management firms to deal with an increasingly burdensome regulatory environment and achieve operational efficiencies by taking advantage of economies of scale.

The growing emphasis by insurers, employers, and Medicare on monitoring systems to measure patient outcomes and satisfaction and the greater interest in pay-for-performance give large medical groups a competitive advantage in attracting patients and receiving bonuses for attaining certain quality benchmarks. Pay-for-performance revenue is likely to become a large share of physician income; thus, medical groups that invest in information technology and can demonstrate improved patient outcomes will receive more physician revenues.

Reversal of Fortunes of Large Multispecialty Groups

The promise of large multispecialty medical groups in managing patient care and being rewarded for accepting greater capitation risk foundered in the late 1990s, particularly in California.

Changing Market Environment

The prosperity created by the economic expansion in the United States in the late 1990s led employees to demand broader provider networks and freer access to specialists from their HMOs. Large medical groups had been using primary care gatekeepers to control specialist referrals and utilization management to control the growth in medical costs. But when the market changed, it was no longer willing to reward large capitated medical groups for strict cost-control measures.

During this time, competition among HMOs led to low premium increases, leaving large groups of capitated enrollees with low capitation rates. Medical groups found themselves in financial difficulty as their costs increased and state and federal governments enacted patient protection measures. These measures included 48-hour hospital stays for normal deliveries, requiring HMOs to allow obstetricians/gynecologists to serve as primary care physicians, and prohibiting limited lengths of stay after a mastectomy. These measures resulted in higher medical costs for these groups.

HMOs were wary of being sued for withholding appropriate treatment even when the HMO had delegated such treatment decisions to its large medical groups. As HMOs began to undertake those decisions themselves, some of the advantages of capitation payment to large groups faded.

Difficulty in Developing a Group Culture

A well-functioning medical group cannot be formed overnight; the group may not coalesce even after years. An important difference between group and nongroup physicians is the willingness of group physicians to give up some autonomy and abide by group decisions. Physicians might not share values or accept the same assumptions regarding their external environment, mission, and relationships with one another. This cultural difference often determines whether physicians will remain in a group. Many physicians are independent and do not want other physicians involved in their practice, whether the issue relates to contracting with certain health plans, reviewing practice patterns, or determining compensation.

A large multispecialty group must create various committees, one of which determines physician compensation. Disputes among physicians over their compensation are an important reason such groups have dissolved. For example, when a multispecialty group is capitated for a large number of enrollees, the group must decide how the primary care physicians and each specialist will share in those capitation dollars. In the past, when specialists had excess capacity and primary care physicians controlled specialist referrals, some groups paid the primary care physicians more than they would have earned under a discounted FFS environment. These funds came from paying specialists less.

Another issue in medical group compensation is how much of each physician's income should be tied to productivity. Productivity incentives decline when a physician's payment is not directly related to his clinical work. More productive physicians may decide to leave if large discrepancies exist between productivity and compensation.

When physicians in a large group share the use of inputs—personnel and supplies—they are less concerned with those costs than they would be in an independent or a small group practice, where their costs are more directly related to their earnings. This lack of efficiency incentives offsets some savings from economies of scale.

Lack of Management Expertise

As medical groups increased in size and number, many lacked adequate management expertise to handle the clinical and financial responsibilities of the group. The groups did not have adequate information systems for tracking expenses and revenues; they lacked actuarial expertise for underwriting risk when they were receiving capitation payments; and they did not have sufficient management expertise in marketing, finance, and contracting. Unfortunately, many medical groups expanded more rapidly than their ability to manage the increased risk and patient volume.

Instead of developing such management expertise, many groups joined for-profit (publicly traded) physician practice management (PPM) companies. These companies promised numerous benefits to a participating medical group, such as including the group in a larger contracting network with health plans, handling its administration, and improving its efficiency. In return for these services, the PPM company received a percentage (e.g., 15 percent) of the group's revenues. However, several publicly traded PPM companies were themselves poorly managed and declared bankruptcy. A further disappointment with these companies was that the cost savings achieved in the medical group and the additional contracting revenue brought to the group were often less than the PPM's 15 percent management fee.

Lack of Capital

Medical groups typically pay out all of their net revenues to their member physicians. Thus, no funds are available to reinvest in expanding the group, such as by establishing new clinics, purchasing expensive diagnostic services, or buying costly hardware and software for information technology. The lack of capital is an important reason expanding medical groups seek partners.

Hospitals generally have been willing to provide the capital for medical groups to expand and develop their infrastructures. In return for such investments, hospitals hope to secure the medical group's inpatient referrals and negotiate joint contracting arrangements with a health plan. The hospital may also manage or become a part owner in a joint management company that contracts with the medical group for medical services.

Medical groups' main concerns in having hospitals as capital partners are that the hospital will somehow gain control of the group, and the hospital may not be the most appropriate facility to which to refer patients. Many hospitals have lost a great deal of money investing in their physician partners because the hoped-for returns have not been realized—particularly when hospitals purchased physician practices, and physician productivity (separated from compensation) declined.

The Outlook for Medical Practice

The organization of medical practice is based on several factors, but one increasing in importance is the method of payment for medical services. FFS payments are likely to increase more slowly under government programs. As major payers, Medicare and MACRA, the new physician payment system, are likely to have a strong impact as they experiment with alternative payment strategies for medical services—away from FFS and toward value-based care and capitation.

Physicians and hospitals will be under intense pressure to control rising healthcare costs while demonstrating to payers that the quality of care provided and the outcomes achieved are measurably improved. Provider organizations will need to better coordinate care for chronic illness, manage the health of their enrolled populations, and ensure easier access to care—while doing so under more stringent payment conditions. It will be increasingly difficult for solo practitioners and small medical practices to compete in this new economic environment.

The Growth of Hospital-Employed Physicians

An important trend is the growth in hospital-employed physicians. In the 1990s period of tightly managed care, excess capacity existed among physicians, the demand for primary care physicians rose as they became gatekeepers and restricted access to specialists, and specialist fees decreased. To increase their referrals and gain market share, hospitals bought medical practices. As managed care became less restrictive and hospitals found they were losing money on their medical groups, hospitals divested the groups. Hospitals have again started to employ physicians. As of 2015, 759,421 physicians were in patient care; the number of physicians employed by community hospitals increased by 61 percent between 2000 and 2015—from 158,000 to 254,000 (American Hospital Association 2017, figure 10; Association of American Medical Colleges 2017). Since 2007, this growth has been more rapid.

The number of independent physicians has been declining over time. Currently, less than half of all physicians (47 percent) own their own practices (Kane 2017). In 2016, 32.8 percent of physicians were in hospital-owned practices or were employed directly by a hospital. These trends are likely to continue and perhaps even accelerate because of the requirements of the new Medicare physician payment system.

Hospitals have several reasons for again employing physicians. An important medical group may be considering moving its admissions to another hospital; the hospital may be trying to enter a new market; the hospital may lack specialists in some services; or the hospital may be trying to preempt competition from specialists who have started their own outpatient services. In addition to capturing physician referrals, hospitals that employ specialists and primary care physicians are likely to have increased negotiating leverage over health plans; if the health plan does not raise the hospital's rates, it may lose both the hospital and its physicians (Casalino 2017).

By employing physicians, hospitals can increase their Medicare payments. When a physician's practice is purchased by a hospital and the physician treats the same patients in the same location as previously, under Medicare Part A, the hospital can charge more for the same service than if the physician is an independent practitioner and bills under Medicare Part B. Medicare's cost of care goes up as does the patient's copayment. For example, "when a Medicare beneficiary receives a certain type of echocardiogram in a doctor's office, the government and the patient together pay a total of $188. They pay more than twice as much—$452—for the same test in the outpatient department of a hospital" (Pear 2013). "From 2010 to 2011 . . . the number of echocardiograms provided to Medicare beneficiaries in doctors' offices declined by 6 percent, but the number in hospital outpatient clinics increased by nearly 18 percent" (Pear 2013). Medicare's financial incentives have resulted in more than tripling the number of hospital-employed cardiologists—from 11 percent in 2007 to 35 percent in 2012 (Pear 2013). Similarly, Medicare pays $1,090 for a colonoscopy performed in a hospital outpatient department, while for the same procedure performed in a physician's office, Medicare pays only $413, a difference of $677 (Physicians Advocacy Institute 2017).

The continued increase in hospital-employed physicians will result in increased spending by Medicare and Medicare patients simply because the physician is employed by a hospital. Although hospitals have sought to employ both primary care physicians and specialists, they are more likely to seek an ownership interest in multispecialty groups (Kane 2017). Multispecialty groups' wider scope of practice and use of primary care physicians are the apparent reasons for hospitals' greater interest in such groups. In addition to providing a strong referral base, hospitals seem to be preparing for changes in payment that shift from FFS to broader arrangements that hold providers accountable for the cost and quality of care provided (O'Malley, Bond, and Berenson 2011).

Physicians, particularly new graduates, have become more receptive to hospital employment because it provides them with regular work hours and eliminates the paperwork, regulations, need to invest in EHRs, and administrative responsibilities of dealing with the government and private insurers. The cost in terms of dollars and physician time related to reporting quality outcomes is quite high. Tai-Seale and colleagues (2017) estimated that primary care physicians spent an average of 3.08 hours on office visits and 3.17 hours on desktop medicine each day. Employment also eliminates the financial risks of operating one's own medical practice. More than half of all physicians work for hospitals and other organizations rather than in private practice.[1]

It is not clear whether hospital-employed (salaried) physicians are more productive than those working in small medical groups or whether their earnings are more directly related to the FFS revenue derived from their productivity.

Once physicians have worked for a hospital, it is difficult for them to open an independent private practice. They would require significant capital to finance renting office space, hiring staff, building a patient base, and developing the information technology and quality compliance systems necessary for dealing with Medicare, Medicaid, and multiple private insurers.

The reasons independent physicians and medical groups join hospitals—namely, an increasing and costly regulatory burden, the desire for regular work hours, and limited market power to increase their fees compared with larger organizations—are unlikely to change in the future.

The Effect of Payment Changes on Medical Practices

Medicare payment changes are likely to have a major effect on the organization of physician and hospital services, decreasing the growth of single-specialty groups while increasing the number of multispecialty groups and hospital employment.

The organization of medical services has been greatly affected by the payment system. FFS encourages the provider to perform more services and shifts the open-ended financial risk of paying for all services to the insurer or to Medicare and Medicaid. When each type of provider (e.g., hospital, primary care physician, specialist, home health agency) is paid FFS, the delivery system is likely to be fragmented. Coordination of services and alignment of providers' incentives are less likely to occur than under a broader payment system.

Capitation payment shifts the financial risk to the provider; the provider receives a fixed payment and must provide all necessary medical services, so its incentive is to perform fewer services. Under a broader payment system, however, the incentive for participating providers to coordinate care is greater to reduce the costs of providing that treatment.

Each type of payment system requires monitoring and quality reporting. Under FFS, monitoring the quality of many unaffiliated providers is more difficult; duplication of services is more likely to occur, and costs are harder to control. Because the incentive under capitation is to provide fewer services, it is also necessary to monitor treatment outcomes, which is easier than measuring the care given by each provider, as is done under FFS. Controlling rising medical costs is less difficult under capitation, as the organization bears the financial risk of exceeding the overall payment per enrollee.

However, until recently, Medicare has continued to rely on FFS physician payment. Although Medicare regulated physician fees using the resource-based relative value scale (RBRVS) system, the sustainable growth rate (SGR) approach failed to limit use of physician services. Medicare found it difficult to reduce rising physician expenditures.

Over time, Medicare has recognized the difficulty in controlling utilization of services and costs under FFS and has tried moving to a broader payment system. One example is the change from paying hospitals according to their costs to a fixed price per admission. The financial risk of the costs per admission shifted from Medicare to hospitals. Hospitals responded by reducing lengths of stay and becoming more efficient. Medicare was better able to control rising hospital costs. However, hospitals had no incentive to be concerned about the costs of treating the patient before admission to the hospital or after discharge.

Medicare began to develop demonstration programs using a broader-based payment system. One such example is episode-based payment, whereby a single fee is paid that includes all the services involved in performing a certain procedure, such as heart surgery or hip replacement. The single payment covered patient services before the stay, during the inpatient stay when the surgical procedure was performed, and after discharge for a specified period. Eventually, the goal was to expand episode-based payment to more types of treatments.

Medicare Advantage (MA) plans, which are similar to HMOs, are paid a risk-adjusted capitation amount for each Medicare enrollee, and the private plans compete against each other, as well as with traditional Medicare FFS. MA enrollees are provided with increased benefits and decreased cost-sharing, in return for enrollees' limiting their access to the plan's provider network. The two political parties differed on the use of private managed care plans rather than encouraging the growth of MA plans. The ACA offered financial incentives to organizations to form ACOs. More of the financial risk of controlling costs was shifted to ACO providers. ACOs are meant to encourage hospitals and physicians to collaborate to manage care and limit rising costs.

Medicare Access and CHIP Reauthorization Act

A new Medicare physician payment system, with important implications for solo practitioners and small physician groups, was enacted in 2015.[2] By enacting MACRA, Congress repealed the unenforced SGR approach for limiting Medicare physician expenditures. MACRA attempts to make physicians accountable for the care they provide. Physicians are rewarded (or penalized) for the value of the care provided to patients rather than for the number of visits, tests, and procedures performed. Importantly, MACRA provides physicians with incentives to transition away from FFS to Advanced Alternative Payment Models (APMs), such as ACOs.

Physicians are given a choice. They can choose the Merit-Based Incentive Payment System (MIPS) or become part of an Advanced APM, an organization that bears financial risk for the care provided to patients. MIPS relies on FFS. During a patient visit, a MIPS physician must document a great deal of information using an electronic health record (EHR), and record data on quality of care, clinical improvement activities, and measures of cost and resource use. Depending on the physician's performance measures, he may receive an increase or a decrease in payments.

Physicians are concerned that they will have to spend more time recording the necessary patient information to document the value provided and to avoid being penalized; they will have little time for patient interaction. Many physicians will find that MIPS requirements are so onerous and costly to implement, they will be forced to participate in an Advanced APM. Advanced APM physicians are exempt from MIPS requirements and are eligible for greater payment increases if their Advanced APM achieves specified spending targets.

Although the overall goal of MACRA—to make physicians accountable for the care they provide—is admirable, it is questionable whether the MIPS approach or pressuring physicians into ACOs is the best way to achieve this goal.

There are fewer than 350 ACOs, too few for large numbers of physicians to transition into, and most ACOs have not yet proved that they are capable of meeting their financial and spending targets. Medicare beneficiaries voluntarily join MA plans; they do not knowingly join an ACO. They are assigned to an ACO without their knowledge; however, because they are in traditional Medicare, patients can go to nonparticipating physicians. Medicare beneficiaries, by law, have free choice of providers. Unlike Medicaid patients, they cannot be made to enroll in a medical organization. This freedom to use nonparticipating providers is a major weakness of the ACO concept. Thus, controlling an ACO patient's medical expenditures can be difficult. It is up to the ACO to try and provide all care within the ACO, so the patient doesn't use other medical services.

To date, MACRA has not included MA plans as qualified Advanced APMs. Doing so would be desirable as about 30 percent of Medicare beneficiaries have voluntarily joined MA plans, which have demonstrated the ability to achieve spending and quality targets.

MACRA is likely to result in many physicians becoming hospital employees and members of larger medical organizations. Individual practicing physicians and small medical groups will find it more costly and burdensome to participate in Medicare.

These broader payment systems, if successful, are likely to transform the delivery of medical services. More multispecialty medical groups will undertake financial risk by becoming ACOs and Advanced APMs. Hospital employment of physicians will increase and enable the hospital to become an ACO or Advanced APM and provide care in a less costly manner. Under this scenario, single-specialty medical groups will be at a disadvantage, as will physicians who own various surgery and imaging centers and those who are not affiliated with a hospital or a multispecialty group. With broader-based payment, the financial risk of rising costs is shifted to providers, and provider incentives for coordinating care and investing in EHRs will increase.

Summary

The organization of medical practices has been changing. Large medical groups have advantages over physicians in solo or small group practices. In addition to being able to hire professional management, achieve economies of scale, and attain greater bargaining leverage with health plans and hospitals, large medical groups can increase their revenues by shifting into their own outpatient settings more services that were previously provided in hospitals.

Medical groups face challenges in coming years. Employers, insurers, and Medicare are placing increased emphasis on monitoring patient outcomes and satisfaction. As payers become more sophisticated and quality is rewarded, large medical groups have an advantage because quality and outcome measures are more accurate for medical groups than for individual physicians. The costs of meeting new Medicare payment rules are lower for large medical groups than for smaller groups. Medical groups will also have to become more proficient in managing chronic illness for an increasingly aged population, while demonstrating improved medical outcomes and patient satisfaction. Large medical groups are better able than small medical groups to invest in the information technology needed to evaluate practice patterns and patient outcomes.

Broader payment systems provide hospitals with incentives to expand their role in the delivery of medical services. The trend toward lower hospital utilization, greater reliance on less costly outpatient services, and movement away from FFS toward capitation has placed hospitals at financial risk for delivering episodes of treatment at a fixed price. To provide coordinated care across all delivery settings, hospitals have been employing more physicians and purchasing medical groups.

The net effect of MACRA will be to hasten the movement of physicians into employment with larger organizations. The number of independently practicing physicians, along with small medical groups, will continue to decline (Casalino 2017).

Many physicians have an opportunity to achieve greater control over their future by understanding the trends affecting changes in the financing and delivery of health services. If physicians are to develop efficient delivery models with improved patient outcomes, it is essential that they participate in organizations that are likely to be in the forefront of these trends. Large multispecialty medical groups, able to take advantage of economies of scale and bear financial risk for a large patient population, can become ACOs and Advanced APMs and be innovators in healthcare delivery. Whether medical groups will be sufficiently entrepreneurial to achieve their promise in developing innovative treatment methods that decrease medical costs while demonstrating improved patient outcomes will not be known for several years.

Discussion Questions

1. Why has the size of multispecialty medical groups increased?
2. Why do large medical groups have market power?
3. Why do medical groups occasionally break up?
4. Describe how an IPA functions.
5. What are the different types of capital partners available to medical groups? What do they expect in return for providing capital?
6. What trends are affecting the way physicians will practice in coming years?

Notes

1. Health plans are also acquiring physician groups to increase their control over physician practices, utilization, and healthcare costs. In 2011, United Health Care purchased the largest physician group in Orange County, California. To date, physicians have preferred to become part of hospitals rather than health plans. The ACA offers incentives for hospitals (as well as insurers and medical groups) to form ACOs to provide healthcare for Medicare enrollees, basing payment on a capitation or a shared-savings model. When the organization is paid on a basis other than FFS, the financial risk is shifted from the payer to the organization. The organization at risk requires physicians to provide coordinated care, reduce hospital admissions (and readmissions), and better manage chronically ill patients to reduce the costs of care.

2. See chapter 10, "How Does Medicare Pay Physicians?," for a more complete discussion of MACRA and references.

References

American Hospital Association. 2017. *Hospital Statistics.* Chicago: American Hospital Association.

Association of American Medical Colleges. 2017. "Number of Active Physicians in the Largest Specialties by Major Professional Activity, 2015." Accessed November. www.aamc.org/data/workforce/reports/458480/1-1-chart.html.

Casalino, L. 2017. "The Medicare Access and CHIP Reauthorization Act and the Corporate Transformation of American Medicine." *Health Affairs* 36 (5): 865–69.

Gillies, R., S. Shortell, L. Casalino, J. Robinson, and T. Rundall. 2003. "How Different Is California? A Comparison of U.S. Physician Organizations." *Health Affairs* (web exclusive): w3-492–502. http://content.healthaffairs.org/cgi/reprint/hlthaff.w3.492v1.

Kane, C. K. 2017. "Updated Data on Physician Practice Arrangements—Physician Ownership Drops Below 50 Percent." American Medical Association policy research perspective. Published May. www.ama-assn.org/sites/default/files/media-browser/public/health-policy/PRP-2016-physician-benchmark-survey.pdf.

O'Malley, A., A. Bond, and R. Berenson. 2011. "Rising Hospital Employment of Physicians: Better Quality, Higher Costs." Center for Studying Health System Change issue brief. Published August. http://hschange.org/content/1230/1230.pdf.

Pear, R. 2013. "Medicare Panel Urges Cuts to Hospital Payments for Services Doctors Offer for Less." *New York Times.* Published June 14. www.nytimes.com/2013/06/15/health/medicare-panel-urges-cuts-to-hospital-payments-for-services-doctors-offer-for-less.html.

Physicians Advocacy Institute. 2017. *Implications of Hospital Employment of Physicians on Medicare & Beneficiaries.* Published November. www.physiciansadvocacy institute.org/Portals/0/assets/docs/PAI_Medicare%20Cost%20Analysis%20 --%20FINAL%2011_9_17.pdf.

Tai-Seale, M., C. W. Olson, J. Li, A. S. Chan, C. Morikawa, M. Durbin, W. Wang, and H. S. Luft. 2017. "Electronic Health Record Logs Indicate That Physicians Split Time Evenly Between Seeing Patients and Desktop Medicine." *Health Affairs* 36 (4): 655–62.

Weeks, W. B., D. J. Gottlieb, D. E. Nyweide, J. M. Sutherland, J. Bynum, L. P. Casalino, R. R. Gillies, S. M. Shortell, and E. S. Fisher. 2010. "Higher Health Care Quality and Bigger Savings Found at Large Multispecialty Medical Groups." *Health Affairs* 29 (5): 991–97.

PHYSICIAN MALPRACTICE REFORM

14

The cost of malpractice insurance has been of long-standing concern to physicians, particularly specialists, for whom the premiums can be very high. The American Medical Association and state medical societies have for many years sought legislative solutions to lower the cost of physician malpractice premiums. Several times in previous decades malpractice "crises" have occurred when annual malpractice premiums sharply increased. During the 1970s, the first of these crises occurred, when some insurers completely withdrew from the malpractice insurance market, while others increased their premiums by as much as 300 percent. Physicians threatened to strike if state legislatures did not intervene. To ensure access to malpractice insurance at the lowest possible rates, some medical societies formed their own mutual insurance companies. In the mid-1980s and in 2002, as premiums again rose rapidly and premiums for some medical specialties increased sharply, medical societies once again pressured federal and state legislatures for malpractice reform—that is, tort changes that would limit malpractice awards and claims filed.

Physicians worry about being accused of malpractice. Even though the cost of the trial may be paid for by their malpractice insurer, the nonmonetary costs of having to defend against a lawsuit—anxiety, loss of time to practice, and a possible loss of one's reputation—can be high. Higher malpractice premiums may also change the distribution of physician specialties. To forestall a possible lawsuit, physicians often practice defensive medicine, providing medical services and tests that might not be necessary. (Mello and colleagues [2010] estimated the costs of defensive medicine to be $55.6 billion, equal to 2.4 percent of total healthcare spending in 2008.)

Lawsuits are not always best for resolving a patient's malpractice issue; the injured patient may have to wait several years before the physician's negligence can be determined and the patient is compensated for her injury.

Understanding the goals of malpractice reform is important to address the needs of an injured patient, while deterring physician negligence. It is often difficult to achieve the correct balance between the interests of the patient and those of the physician. Many state malpractice laws have been less concerned with protecting the patient's interests than with protecting those of physicians.

It is useful, however, to first examine the magnitude of malpractice claims and how they vary among physicians, and by specialty status.

How Malpractice Claims Vary Among Physicians and by Specialty Status

Schaffer and colleagues (2017) examined paid physician malpractice claims from the National Practitioner Data Bank during the period from 1992 to 2014. The following are some of their findings.

- The average paid claim increased by 23 percent (in 2014 dollars) from 1992–1996 to 2009–2014.

- The highest average paid claim was for neurology ($469,222), while the lowest was for dermatology ($189,065).

- The number of paid claims per physician decreased from 20.1 per 1,000 physician-years in the early period to 8.9 per 1,000 physician-years in 2009–2014, a 55.7 percent decline.

- The distribution of paid claims among physician specialties was uneven. One percent of all physicians accounted for 7.6 percent of all paid claims. Ten percent of physicians were responsible for 39.4 percent of all paid claims. The skewed distribution of paid claims occurs within each physician specialty, while each specialty differs from the others in the number of paid claims.

- The reasons a small percentage of physicians incur a large percentage of claims probably vary: Some may be caring for higher-risk patients, whereas others may be providing inadequate care.

- The most common paid claim was for diagnosis error (31.8 percent), followed by surgical errors (26.9 percent), and medication or treatment errors (24.5 percent).

- Although the average number of paid claims declined over time, the average payment per claim increased by 23 percent; again, this percentage varied by specialty.

- Over time, the number of paid claims that were over $1 million increased, representing 7.6 percent of all paid claims; again, the percentages varied by physician specialty. Neurology had the highest percentage of awards greater than $1 million. The authors commented that the large awards may not be the result of greater negligence, but instead likely reflect the debilitating nature of the injury. Laws limiting damages for pain and suffering (noneconomic damages) do not affect the size of actual economic damages.

- The most severe injury, patient death, represented 32.1 percent of paid claims, which varied greatly by physician specialty. Ophthalmologists had the fewest paid claims for patient deaths (2.7 percent), while pulmonologists had the highest (64.8 percent).

Studdert and colleagues (2016) also conducted a study on the prevalence of physician malpractice paid claims. The general nature of their findings is similar to that of Schaffer and colleagues, although their results differ in magnitude. Studdert and colleagues found that 1 percent of physicians incurred 32 percent of paid claims. The skewed distribution of paid claims is further demonstrated by the finding that only 6 percent of physicians had any paid claims over the 10-year period studied. Neurosurgeons had the highest risk of incurring a paid claim, and the risk varied greatly according to the physician's specialty. Of the malpractice claims studied, only one-third were eventually paid. Studdert and colleagues (2016) found that 54 percent of paid claims were the result of serious injury, and about one-third of the paid claims represented a patient's death.

The biggest predictor of whether a physician is more likely to incur a malpractice claim is the number of prior claims on that physician. To better understand the reason for malpractice claims incurred by a hospital's medical staff, it would be more appropriate to examine the claims against the small number of physicians who have the most claims.

Objectives of the Malpractice System

Tort law is the basis for medical malpractice. It entitles an injured person to compensation as a result of someone's negligence. Damages include economic losses (lost wages and medical bills) and noneconomic losses (referred to as *pain and suffering*). Thus, physicians have a financial incentive to provide good treatment and perform only those procedures in which they are competent.

The purposes of tort law are (1) to compensate the victim for negligence and (2) to deter future negligence. How well does the malpractice system fulfill these two objectives? Can legislative reforms achieve them at a lower cost than that of the current system? Physician advocates maintain that too many claims have little to do with negligence (so the insurer will settle to avoid legal expenses that would exceed the settlement cost), and that juries award large sums unrelated to actual damages. Further, *defensive medicine*—additional tests and procedures prescribed by physicians to protect themselves against malpractice claims—adds billions of dollars to the nation's health expenditures.

Patient advocates counter those claims. They argue that physician negligence is more extensive than that reflected in the number of claims filed, large jury awards are infrequent, incompetent physicians must be discouraged from practicing because physicians do not adequately monitor themselves, and defensive medicine is caused by the fee-for-service (FFS) insurance system that rewards physicians for performing more services and eliminates patients' incentives to be concerned about the cost of care.

Compensation of Victims

A 1990 Harvard University study found that too few of those injured by negligence are compensated under the malpractice system (Localio et al. 1991). The authors examined medical records from 1984 in 51 hospitals in the state of New York and determined that almost 4 percent of all patients suffered an injury while in the hospital. Furthermore, one-quarter of those injuries were the result of negligence. Thus, about 1 percent of all patients discharged from New York hospitals in 1984 experienced some type of negligence. Examples of injuries occurring in hospitals are errors in diagnosis, falls, hospital-caused infections, and surgical complications.

Surprisingly, fewer than 2 percent of the patients identified as victims of negligence filed malpractice claims. However, 6 percent of injured patients who had not been victims of negligence filed claims. (Even though the surgeon may not have committed negligence, not all surgical procedures are successful, and the patient could be left with a disability or even die.) According to the Harvard study, half the patients who filed claims eventually received some compensation. Many patients settle within two years without receiving any compensation, and the rest may wait years for compensation. Only about 1 percent of victims of actual negligence ever receive compensation. Of those patients injured through negligence who do not file claims (98 percent of negligence victims), 20 percent have serious injuries—disabilities that last six months or longer—and this figure includes fatalities (Localio et al. 1991).

A later study (involving cases in Colorado and Utah) also found a poor relationship between medical negligence and malpractice claims; 97 percent of those who experienced a medical negligence injury did not sue. Studdert and colleagues (2000) found that the elderly and the poor were least likely to sue for medical negligence. When physicians were sued, the claims were generally for injuries not caused by negligent care. (See Studdert and colleagues [2006] for an additional study on medical negligence and malpractice claims.)

Several reasons account for the low percentage of negligence claims filed. A patient may not know that negligence caused an injury. Some claims may be difficult to prove. Recoverable damages may be less than the litigation costs, particularly in the case of minor injuries.

The cost of administering the compensation system is high, and only a small portion of malpractice premiums is returned to those injured through negligence. Overhead, including legal fees, consumes the major portion of premiums. For every dollar paid into the liability system, 54 cents goes to legal fees and administrative costs (Studdert et al. 2006). Health insurance, on the other hand, returns 80 to 85 percent of the premium for medical expenses. If the sole purpose of malpractice insurance is to compensate those who are negligently injured, more efficient means, at lower administrative costs, exist. A different approach could compensate a greater number of victims and return a greater portion of premiums to those injured.

Deterrence of Negligence

Justification for the current malpractice system must depend, therefore, on how well the system performs its second, more important, purpose: deterring negligence. Compensation tries not only to make whole the injuries suffered by victims of negligence, but also to force negligent healthcare providers to exercise greater caution in future caregiving situations. Concerns exist, however, that not enough injuries are prevented by the current system to justify the high costs of practicing defensive medicine, determining fault, and prosecuting malpractice claims.

The standard of care used in determining negligence is what one would expect from a reasonably competent person who is knowledgeable about advances in medicine and who exercises care. Some cases of malpractice, such as amputating the wrong leg or leaving surgical supplies in a patient's abdomen, are easily established. For other types of physician behavior, however, uncertainties exist in both diagnosis and treatment outcome. Many medical procedures are inherently risky. Even with correct diagnosis and treatment, a patient may die because of poor health conditions, or a baby may be born with a birth defect through no fault of the obstetrician. Physicians differ in the quality of care they provide and in their success rates, but it is difficult—hence costly—to determine whether a specific outcome is a result of physician negligence, poor communication of the risks involved, or the patient's underlying health condition.

The potential for malpractice suits increases the cost of negligent behavior to the physician. Therefore, physicians would be expected to change their behavior and restrict their practices to forestall such costs (i.e., stop performing procedures and tasks for which they lack competence). Preventing malpractice costs time and resources; therefore, physicians should invest their time, training, and medical testing in prevention up to the point at which the additional cost of prevention equals the additional value of injuries avoided (forgone malpractice costs). Too much prevention could occur if a great deal of time and resources (the additional costs) are used to prevent occasional minor injuries. Requiring an injury rate of zero would be too costly for society and would discourage skilled specialists from performing procedures that involve an element of risk of injury but that could benefit the patient.

How Well Does the Malpractice System Deter Negligence?

Is the value to patients of the negligence prevented greater than the costs (i.e., defensive medicine, determining liability, and litigation) of the malpractice system? Experts differ on this issue.

First, critics of the current system claim that physicians are not penalized for negligence, as only 2 to 3 percent of negligence victims file claims. (However, some sources report a rate as high as 20 percent [Gottlieb and Doroshow 2017].)

Second, because only 40 percent of malpractice insurance premiums ($9.36 billion in 2015)—approximately $3.6 billion, or 0.11 percent of total healthcare spending—are returned to victims of negligence, and the remainder is spent on overhead and legal fees, the system is too costly (Public Citizen 2017).

Third, because most malpractice insurance does not experience-rate physicians within their specialties, incompetent physicians are not penalized by having higher premiums; their behavior merely raises premiums for all physicians in that specialty.

Fourth, not all physicians who are sued are incompetent. Although incompetent physicians may be sued more often, competent physicians also may be sued because of occasional errors or because they are specialists who treat more difficult cases. For example, board-certified physicians are sued more often than are other physicians.

Fifth, a characteristic of the current system is the amount of money spent on tests and services that are not medically justified but that help protect physicians from malpractice claims. Physicians overuse tests because the costs of such defensive medicine are borne by patients and insurers, whereas an injury claim could result in physician liability. Thus, physicians can shift the costs of their greater caution to others.

In Defense of the Malpractice System

Defenders of the malpractice system claim that the incentive to avoid malpractice suits changes physicians' behavior and forces them to act with more care. Physicians have limited their scope of practice, they are more conscientious in documenting medical information, and they take the time to discuss with their patients the risks involved in a procedure. Although physician malpractice premiums are not experience-rated, lawsuits are a costly deterrent in terms of the time spent defending against them and the potential damage to the physician's reputation.

The Costs of Defensive Medicine

The costs of defensive medicine are probably overstated because, under a FFS system, excessive testing would occur even if the threat of malpractice were eliminated. Physicians order too many tests because insured patients pay only a small portion of their price. Although the benefits of many tests are less than the costs of performing them, patients want those tests because the benefit to them may be greater than their share of the costs. Physicians are reimbursed on a FFS basis for prescribing extra tests, while physicians in health maintenance organizations (HMOs) have less of an incentive to perform excessive testing. Thus, physicians' use of excessive testing results, in part, from traditional insurance payment systems and a lack of policing of such tests by insurers, not necessarily from malpractice concerns.

The costs imposed by defensive medicine are difficult to measure. Estimates often rely on conjectural surveys of providers, and what one provider may consider defensive medicine may be deemed prudent medicine by another. However, Mello and colleagues (2010) estimated the annual medical liability system costs, including defensive medicine, to be $55.6 billion (in 2008 dollars), equal to 2.4 percent of total healthcare spending.

Physicians with malpractice insurance are not at risk for a large financial loss resulting from a malpractice case. However, a malpractice case imposes other, nonfinancial, costs on a physician. During the time it takes to resolve a malpractice claim (about five years after the incident), the physician is likely to be concerned about the damage to her reputation, the time lost from work, and the general stress of the process. These costs often weigh heavier on the physician's mind than do the possible financial costs, causing her to be defensive in the tests and treatments she prescribes.

A study by Carrier and colleagues (2013) found that physicians who were more concerned about malpractice were more likely to engage in defensive medicine, such as ordering more diagnostic tests than medically necessary, performing more procedures, requiring more visits, and being more likely to hospitalize a patient or refer him to other physicians.

Removing the threat of malpractice leaves few alternatives for monitoring and disciplining physicians. The emphasis on quality control in organized medicine has always been placed on the process of becoming a physician—that is, spending many years on education, graduating from an approved medical school, and passing national examinations. However, once a physician is licensed, he is never reexamined for relicensure. State medical licensing boards do not adequately monitor physicians for the quality of care provided or discipline incompetent physicians. Finally, patients have little or no access to information about physicians' procedure outcomes. Until recently the medical profession actively discouraged public access to such information. Other than filing a malpractice claim, what recourse would a patient have after being injured by an incompetent physician?

Few would disagree that victims of negligence are not adequately compensated. The controversial issues pertain to whether malpractice actually deters negligence and whether alternatives are available for monitoring and disciplining incompetent physicians.

Proposed Changes to the Malpractice System

Many changes have been proposed to correct perceived inadequacies in the malpractice system. Generally, proposals seek to lower malpractice premiums by limiting the size of jury awards for pain and suffering (economic costs for medical expenses and lost wages are not subject to a cap) and the number of claims filed. Both changes would reduce lawyers' incentives to accept malpractice cases.

Damage Caps

Proposals to limit the potential recovery of damages decrease the value of malpractice claims and thereby reduce the number of malpractice claims filed. One study found that malpractice premiums in states with damage caps were 17 percent lower than those in states without damage caps (Thorpe 2004).[1] In 1975, California enacted a $250,000 damage cap on pain and suffering, which has not been updated for inflation. (If adjusted for inflation, the cap would be $1.083 million in 2013 dollars.)

Caps such as those in California lower the amount of malpractice awards that can be used to pay legal fees, as the remainder of the award is for lost wages and medical expenses. Zeiler and Hardcastle (2012) reviewed multiple studies that have estimated the effect of damage caps on malpractice premiums and concluded that little weight can be placed on any one study because of methodological shortcomings. Paik, Black, and Hyman (2017) found that damage caps have no significant impact on Medicare hospital spending, but Medicare physician expenditures are about 4 percent greater with damage caps.

Collateral Offset Rule

Under the collateral offset rule, the amount of an injured party's jury award or insurer's settlement is reduced because of the amounts paid by other sources, such as health insurance and workers' compensation. Proponents of this rule believe additional payments from other sources provide the injured party with much more than he is entitled to. Opponents of this rule believe that unless the injured party collects the full amount of his award, even though he is paid by other sources, the negligent defendant benefits because her liability is reduced. Proposals to reduce awards by amounts paid by other sources would have the same effect as imposing damage caps. Lawyers would have less incentive to bring suits on behalf of patients.

Limits on Attorneys' Fees

Fewer malpractice cases would be brought if a limit were placed on lawyers' contingency fees (currently these can be as high as one-third to one-half of the award). Lawyers accept malpractice cases on the basis of the probability of winning and the size of the likely award. They have less financial incentive to invest their resources in cases whose awards would be small. They are in a competitive market and may represent plaintiffs or defendants in malpractice cases. Defendants pay them an hourly rate. Fewer lawyers would choose to represent plaintiffs if contingency fees were reduced.

Joint and Several Liability

Joint and several liability occurs when an injured person sues multiple defendants and is able to collect the entire award from any of the defendants, regardless of the defendant's degree of fault. Even if a defendant is only 10 percent liable, she may end up paying most of the damages. This rule creates an incentive for the injured party to sue as many defendants as possible to make sure the damages can be paid. Some states have limited a defendant's liability to the individual degree of fault. Limiting a defendant's liability decreases the potential size of the award, which might lessen the defendant hospital's oversight of its staff physicians to avoid malpractice suits.

Special Health Courts

In a special health court, the jury is replaced with a specially trained judge (with both medical and legal training) who is advised by neutral experts. Proponents of this approach claim that proceedings would be expedited (the case would be decided in a matter of months); costs would be dramatically lower than those of the current system, which consumes about 60 percent of the premium for legal fees and administrative costs and takes about five years to resolve a case; and a special health court would provide a system of justice based on accepted medical standards, thereby reducing the need for defensive medicine.

As part of the proposal for special health courts, patient compensation for medical negligence would be decided by a separate administrative agency (which would act as a neutral fact finder) rather than by the current court system (which is adversarial, with each side having its own experts).

If special health courts were adopted, filing a claim would be less costly, a greater number of patients would be able to file claims, and more injured patients would be compensated for medical negligence. The amount of compensation for a patient negligently injured likely would be less given that so many more patients would receive compensation. Although special courts have been used in other areas in which special expertise is needed—such as in tax courts, bankruptcy courts, and family courts—special health courts have not been used in the United States; their implementation is opposed by trial lawyers, who benefit from the current malpractice system.

Evidence-Based Guidelines

The adoption of national (as opposed to local) standards of care has been proposed for judging malpractice suits. Guidelines are written documents of what are considered the best clinical practices for a set of symptoms, type of patient, and a specific disease. Local standards of care differ greatly across the country, leading to wide variations in tests and procedures. Physicians who can demonstrate that they practiced according to well-accepted, evidence-based national guidelines would then be exempt from liability in malpractice lawsuits. The current tort-based malpractice system would not be changed if national guidelines were adopted; however, the evidence used to determine whether a physician was negligent would be based on these national rather than local standards of care.

Frakes (2013) examined geographic variations in physician practice patterns and estimated that if states were to adopt national standards for judging malpractice claims, geographic variations in use of medical services would decrease by 30 to 50 percent. Frakes also found no associated changes in patient health resulting from a shift to national guidelines.

The adoption of national guidelines for malpractice cases is controversial. Critics claim that such guidelines cannot account for the wide variation in patients' conditions and their health problems. (A similar criticism has been leveled against the use of comparative effectiveness research—see chapter 22.)

No-Fault Malpractice

A no-fault system would compensate an injured patient whether or not negligence was involved. In return, patients would forfeit their right to sue. A no-fault system has two main advantages. First, litigation costs would be lower because proving who was at fault for the injury is not necessary, and these savings could be used to increase victim compensation. Second, all injured patients, most of whom could not win malpractice suits because their claims are too small to attract a lawyer's interest or no one is at fault in causing their injuries, would receive some compensation. A no-fault system could include a payment schedule based on the types of injuries that led to loss of income and medical expenses. The schedule could include payment for pain and suffering in cases of severe injury.

A no-fault system, however, has two important problems. First, such a system contains no deterrence mechanism to weed out incompetent providers or encourage physicians to exercise greater caution. Second, because all injuries would be subject to compensation, no clear line would be drawn between injuries resulting from negligence, injuries not resulting from negligence, unfavorable treatment outcomes caused by the patient's health condition and lifestyle, and outcomes of risky procedures (e.g., transplants and delivery of low-birth-weight infants) that are never 100 percent favorable. Compensating patients for all injuries and unfavorable outcomes could be very expensive, given the large number of injuries for which no claims are filed.[2] Who should bear these costs?

Studdert, Brennan, and Thomas (2000) estimated that a no-fault compensation system for patients who are injured from all events (negligent and nonnegligent) would cost more than four times as much as the current tort system.

Enterprise Liability

Deterring physician negligence continues to be difficult. Regulatory approaches, such as state licensing boards for monitoring and disciplining physicians, have performed poorly. One approach that seeks to improve on the malpractice system for deterring negligence is enterprise liability. Changing the liability laws so that liability is shifted away from the physician to a larger entity of which the physician is required to be a part—such as a hospital, medical group, or managed care plan—would place the incentive for monitoring and enforcing medical quality with that larger organization. These organizations would then balance the increased costs of prevention and risk-reducing behavior against the potential for a malpractice claim.

The shift to enterprise liability is already occurring because of market trends and court rulings. The growth of managed care organizations, and the fact that they are liable for physicians they employ or contract with, have increased such organizations' monitoring of physician behavior. Further, the concept of joint and several liability—wherein the physician is the primary defendant but the hospital or managed care plan is also named as a defendant with potentially 100 percent liability for damages (although it may have been only 10 percent at fault)—provides hospitals and HMOs with an incentive to increase their quality assurance and risk management programs. Many physicians, however, perform surgery only in outpatient settings or do not practice within a hospital. Other physicians may have multiple hospital staff appointments, and still others do not belong to large health plans. These physicians would be most affected by such a shift in liability laws because they would lose some of their autonomy as they become subject to greater supervision by larger entities, such as HMOs.

Placing liability for malpractice on a large entity would enable insurers to experience-rate the organization.[3] As more healthcare organizations become experience-rated, they will devote more resources to monitoring their quality of care and disciplining physicians for poor performance. Many organizations—such as HMOs, preferred provider organizations, and large medical groups—have information systems in place to profile the practice patterns of their physicians. Competition on price and quality provides organizations with an incentive to develop quality-control mechanisms. These organizations, rather than regulatory bodies, have the incentives and the ability to evaluate and supervise physicians.

Disclosure, Apology, and Offer Programs

A relatively new approach for resolving malpractice claims that does not require new legislation is referred to as *disclosure, apology, and offer* (Sage et al. 2014). The physician and hospital voluntarily disclose any adverse events and errors, apologize for such injuries and errors, and offer compensation to the patient and family. Further, all hospital and professional fees are waived if the patient received substandard care. Several institutions using this approach state that it has reduced the number of malpractice claims filed against them, as well as the time to settle malpractice cases; it also has eliminated the high costs of defending a malpractice lawsuit, including attorneys' fees, use of expert witnesses, and court costs (which can be as high as $350,000) (Bell et al. 2012). In addition, these institutions claim that defensive medicine by physicians—such as additional laboratory and radiology tests—has also decreased.

Disclosing medical errors, apologizing, and offering compensation are contrary to the approach used by many hospitals and physicians fearful of a malpractice case. Their approach has been to (1) deny that such adverse events and errors have occurred and (2) defend themselves. But such a defensive approach often leads to the filing of a malpractice case because a patient may feel that doing so is the only way to determine the cause of the injury.

An important advantage of the disclosure, apology, and offer approach is that physicians and hospitals can improve patient safety by learning how to prevent similar adverse events. The major elements of this approach include reporting errors, analyzing what occurred, issuing an apology, offering compensation, improving process and performance, and educating professional and support staff.

The Effects of Various Tort Reforms

Many proposals have been made to improve the current tort system, which does not adequately compensate patients injured by medical negligence or act as a deterrent for negligent physicians. Mello, Kachalia, and Studdert (2017) provide an assessment of the effectiveness of proposed malpractice liability reforms on various outcome measures (exhibit 14.1): frequency of malpractice claims and costs, healthcare providers' liability costs, defensive medicine, supply of medical services (including supply of physicians and health insurance coverage rates), and quality of care. In addition, the exhibit indicates the strength of the evidence. Unfortunately, for many of the proposals, the strength of the evidence is moderate or low.

Sage (2014, 2105) sums up the choices presented by Mello, Kachalia, and Studdert (2017) as follows:

> [A]pproaches that accelerate the recognition of errors and the resolution of disputes are likely to further both monetary and nonmonetary goals of malpractice reform. Conventional litigation thrives on delay, producing a host of ill effects. Patients and families are denied critical information and assistance. Timely feedback for safety improvement is impossible. Administrative costs mount. Compensation is withheld but emotional pain and adversarial stress are not. Over the longer term, delay exacerbates actuarial uncertainty for liability insurers and increases the vulnerability of insurance markets. A major advantage of communication-and-resolution programs and most of the other liability reforms evaluated by Mello and colleagues, therefore, is that they save time.

Reform	Key Outcome Measures	
	Evidence Sufficient to Draw Conclusions (Overall Strength of Evidence)	Evidence Too Mixed to Draw Conclusions
Safe harbor rules	Insufficient evidence	Insufficient evidence
Administrative healthcare tribunals (health courts)	Lower overhead costs (M)	
Periodic payment	No change in claims frequency (M) No change in compensation amounts (M) No change in physician supply (M) No change in patient care outcomes (L)	Effect on liability insurance premiums Effect on defensive medicine and healthcare spending
Joint-and-several liability reform	No change in physician supply (H) No change in quality of care (H) No change in compensation amounts (M) No change in liability insurance premiums (M)	Effect on defensive medicine and healthcare spending Effect on litigation costs Effect on health insurance coverage rates
Shorter statutes of limitation	No change in compensation amounts (M) Slower growth of liability insurance premiums (M)	Effect on claims frequency
Apology laws	Insufficient evidence	Insufficient evidence
Attorney fee limits	No change in compensation amounts (H) No change in claims frequency (M) No change in liability insurance premiums (M) No change in physician supply (M)	
Collateral-source rule reform	No change in compensation amounts (H) No change in physician supply (H) No change in quality of care (H)	

(continued)

EXHIBIT 14.1
Levels of Currently Available Evidence Concerning Effects of Proposed Medical Liability Reforms

EXHIBIT 14.1
Levels of
Currently
Available
Evidence
Concerning
Effects of
Proposed
Medical Liability
Reforms
(continued)

Reform	Key Outcome Measures	
	Evidence Sufficient to Draw Conclusions (Overall Strength of Evidence)	**Evidence Too Mixed to Draw Conclusions**
Collateral-source rule reform *(continued)*	No change in claims frequency (M) No change in liability insurance premiums (M) No change in defensive medicine or healthcare spending (M) No change in health insurance coverage rates (L)	
Caps on non-economic damages	Reductions in some types of defensive medicine (H) Substantial reduction in average compensation amounts (H) Modest increase in physician supply (H) Reduction in claims frequency for both paid claims and all filed claims (M) Moderate constraint on growth of liability insurance premiums (M) Disproportionate chilling effect on the number of claims filed by elderly patients (L) Substantial reduction in time to settlement (L)	Effect on healthcare spending Effect on quality of care and patient outcomes Whether reductions in award amounts disproportionately burden elderly claimants Effect on health insurance coverage rates

Note: H denotes high strength of evidence, M moderate, and L low. "Insufficient evidence" indicates that evidence is inadequate to support any conclusions.

Source: Adapted from Mello, Kachalia, and Studdert (2017).

Summary

The current medical malpractice system has several important flaws. First, most patients injured by medical negligence (97 to 98 percent) do not sue and are not compensated for their injuries. Second, given the small percentage of injured patients who sue, physicians' negligent behavior is rarely deterred. Third, the current system is inefficient. A large percentage of the malpractice premium is not used for patient compensation but for legal costs and administrative expense. Further, physicians have an incentive under FFS payment (and insurance that results in low patient copayments) to engage in defensive medicine, prescribing care of doubtful value to decrease the probability of a malpractice lawsuit.

Experts do not agree on malpractice reform. Reform proposals that decrease the size of an award or make filing claims more difficult are addressing the wrong problem. These remedies are directed at reducing the number of claims, but the real problem appears to be that too few bona fide *negligence* claims are brought. Reform should be evaluated in terms of whether it deters negligent behavior and improves victim compensation. Some proposals, such as special health courts and enterprise liability, have academic support. However, enacting reform is a difficult political problem. Proposals often reflect the interests of those who might benefit from the change. Medical societies are often pitted against the trial lawyers' associations (and their respective political parties). The battle for changes in the malpractice system is occurring in almost every state and, because of the opposition of trial lawyers, only demonstration projects were included in the Affordable Care Act. All proposals by whatever interest group should be judged by how well they achieve the two goals of the malpractice system: compensating victims injured by negligence and deterring negligence.

Discussion Questions

1. How well does the malpractice system compensate victims of negligence?
2. How effective is the deterrence function of the malpractice system?
3. Discuss the advantages and disadvantages of no-fault insurance.
4. Do you think the costs of defensive medicine would be reduced under a no-fault system?
5. Evaluate the possible effects of the following on deterrence and victim compensation:
   a. Limiting lawyers' contingency fees
   b. Special health courts
   c. Limiting the size of malpractice awards
   d. Placing the liability for malpractice on the healthcare organization to which the physician belongs

Notes

1. Malpractice liability has affected physicians' participation in a market. Physicians claim that the financial burden of high malpractice premiums has led some to retire early, others to stop performing high-risk procedures, and still others to move to states with lower malpractice

premiums—all of which affect patients' access to medical care. For example, states that capped noneconomic damages in malpractice cases experienced a relatively modest 3.3 percent increase in physician supply compared with states without such caps (Kessler, Sage, and Becker 2005). Rural counties in states with noneconomic damage caps had 3.2 percent more physicians per capita than did rural counties in states without caps. Obstetricians and surgeons, who are considered more vulnerable to lawsuits than other physicians, were most influenced by the presence or absence of caps (Encinosa and Hellinger 2005).

2. The Institute of Medicine and others have issued reports documenting high rates of medical error causing serious harm or death in the United States. Not all of these injuries to patients, however, are believed to be the result of provider negligence. Appropriate systems are lacking to prevent human error (Kohn, Corrigan, and Donaldson 1999).

3. The reason generally given for the lack of experience-rating, except by specialty, is that malpractice suits and awards are unrelated to medical negligence or the physician's history of negligence. Instead, they are related more to the physician's bedside manner. Whether this is correct is debatable.

References

Bell, S. K., P. Smulowitz, A. C. Woodward, M. M. Mello, A. M. Duva, R. C. Boothman, and K. Sands. 2012. "Disclosure, Apology, and Offer Programs: Stakeholders' Views of Barriers to and Strategies for Broad Implementation." *Millbank Quarterly* 90 (4): 682–705.

Carrier, E., J. Reschovsky, D. Katz, and M. Mello. 2013. "High Physician Concern About Malpractice Risk Predicts More Aggressive Diagnostic Testing in Office-Based Practice." *Health Affairs* 32 (8): 1383–91.

Encinosa, W., and F. Hellinger. 2005. "Have State Caps on Malpractice Awards Increased the Supply of Physicians?" *Health Affairs* 24: w5-250–w5-258.

Frakes, M. 2013. "The Impact of Medical Liability Standards on Regional Variations in Physician Behavior: Evidence from the Adoption of National-Standard Rules." *American Economic Review* 103 (1): 257–76.

Gottlieb, E., and J. Doroshow. 2017. *Briefing Book: Medical Malpractice by the Numbers.* Updated December 10. https://centerjd.org/content/briefing-book-medical-malpractice-numbers.

Kessler, D., W. Sage, and D. Becker. 2005. "Impact of Malpractice Reforms on the Supply of Physicians." *Journal of the American Medical Association* 293 (21): 2618–25.

Kohn, L., J. Corrigan, and M. Donaldson (eds.). 1999. *To Err Is Human: Building a Safer Health System.* Washington, DC: National Academies Press.

Localio, A. R., A. Lawthers, T. Brennan, N. Laird, L. Hebert, L. Peterson, J. New-house, P. Weiler, and H. Hiatt. 1991. "Relation Between Malpractice Claims and Adverse Events Due to Negligence." *New England Journal of Medicine* 325 (4): 245–51.

Mello, M. M., A. Chandra, A. A. Gawande, and D. M. Studdert. 2010. "National Costs of the Medical Liability System." *Health Affairs* 29 (9): 1569–77.

Mello, M. M., A. Kachalia, and D. M. Studdert. 2017. "Medical Liability: Prospects for Federal Reform." *New England Journal of Medicine* 376 (19): 1806–8.

Paik, M., B. Black, and D. Hyman. 2017. "Damage Caps and Defensive Medicine, Revisited." *Journal of Health Economics* 51: 84–97.

Public Citizen. 2017. *The Medical Malpractice Scapegoat: Claims That Litigation Is Responsible for Rising Healthcare Costs Crumble Under Scrutiny.* Published February 28. www.citizen.org/sites/default/files/medical-malpractice-scapegoat-report.pdf.

Sage, W. 2014. "Medical Malpractice Reform: When Is It About Money? Why Is It About Time?" *Journal of the American Medical Association* 312 (20): 2103–5.

Sage, W., T. Gallagher, S. Armstrong, J. Cohn, T. McDonald, J. Gale, A. Woodward, and M. Mello. 2014. "How Policy Makers Can Smooth the Way for Communication-and-Resolution Programs." *Health Affairs* 33 (1): 11–19.

Schaffer, A. C., A. B. Jena, S. A. Seabury, H. Singh, V. Chalasani, and A. Kachalia. 2017. "Rates and Characteristics of Paid Malpractice Claims Among US Physicians by Specialty, 1992–2014." *JAMA Internal Medicine* 177 (5): 710–18.

Studdert, D. M., M. M. Bismark, M. M. Mello, H. Singh, and M. J. Spittal. 2016. "Prevalence and Characteristics of Physicians Prone to Malpractice Claims." *New England Journal of Medicine* 374 (4): 354–62.

Studdert, D. M., T. J. Brennan, and E. J. Thomas. 2000. "Beyond Dead Reckoning: Measures of Medical Injury Burden, Malpractice Litigation, and Alternative Compensation Models from Utah and Colorado." *Indiana Law Review* 33 (4): 1643–86.

Studdert, D. M., M. M. Mello, A. A. Gawande, T. K. Gandhi, A. Kachalia, C. Yoon, A. L. Puopolo, and T. A. Brennan. 2006. "Claims, Errors, and Compensation Payments in Medical Malpractice Litigation." *New England Journal of Medicine* 354 (19): 2024–33.

Studdert, D. M., E. J. Thomas, H. R. Burstin, B. I. Zbar, E. J. Orav, and T. A. Brennan. 2000. "Negligent Care and Malpractice Claiming Behavior in Utah and Colorado." *Medical Care* 38 (3): 250–60.

Thorpe, K. 2004. "The Medical Malpractice 'Crisis': Recent Trends and the Impact of State Tort Reforms." *Health Affairs* (web exclusive): w4-20–30.

Zeiler, K., and L. Hardcastle. 2012. "Do Damages Caps Reduce Medical Malpractice Insurance Premiums? A Systematic Review of Estimates and the Methods Used to Produce Them." Georgetown Business, Economics and Regulatory Law Research Paper No. 12-042. Accessed May 2018. http://scholarship.law.georgetown.edu/cgi/viewcontent.cgi?article=2140&context=facpub.

DO NONPROFIT HOSPITALS BEHAVE DIFFERENTLY THAN FOR-PROFIT HOSPITALS?

Hospitals initially cared for the poor, the mentally ill, and those with contagious diseases, such as tuberculosis. Many hospitals were started by religious organizations and local communities as charitable institutions. More affluent patients were treated in their own homes. Things began to change with the development of ether in the mid-1800s, which allowed operations to be conducted under anesthesia. By the late 1800s, antiseptic procedures began to increase the chances of surviving surgery. The introduction of the X-ray machine around the beginning of the twentieth century enabled surgeons to become more effective by improving their ability to determine the precise location for the surgery, and some exploratory surgery was eliminated.

Because of these improvements, hospitals became the physician's workshop. Similarly, the type of patients served by the hospital changed. Hospitals were no longer places in which to die or be incarcerated, but rather places in which paying patients could be treated and then returned to society. The development of drugs and improved living conditions reduced the demand for mental and tuberculosis hospitals, and the demand for short-term general hospitals grew.

The control of private nonprofit hospitals also changed. As more of the hospital's income came from paying patients, reliance on trustees to raise philanthropic funds declined. Physicians, who admitted and treated patients, became more important to the hospital. Because they were responsible for generating the hospital's revenue, physicians' control over the hospital increased.

Most hospitals in the United States are nonprofit, either nongovernmental institutions or controlled by religious organizations. Together, these are referred to as *private nonprofit hospitals*. As exhibit 15.1 shows, the ownership of the majority of hospitals (2,849 of the 4,850 hospitals in 2016) is voluntary, meaning private nonprofit. In 2016, 956 state and local government and 199 federal hospitals were in operation. Investor-owned (for-profit) institutions accounted for 1,035 hospitals. Together, private nonprofit and for-profit hospitals admitted 83.5 percent of patients (68.5 percent and 15.0 percent, respectively).

The main legal distinctions between nonprofit and for-profit hospitals are that nonprofits cannot distribute profits to shareholders, and their earnings and property are exempt from federal and state taxes. They also may receive donations.

Since the mid-1980s, when managed care competition started, debate has ensued over whether nonprofit hospitals are really different from for-profit

EXHIBIT 15.1
Selected Hospital Data, 2016

Type of Hospital	No. of Hospitals	Percentage Change				No. of Beds	No. of Admissions	Distribution of Admissions, %	Occupancy Rate[a]
		1975–85	1985–95	1995–05	2005–16				
Short-term								97.6	
General[b]	4,850	−3.3	−9.8	−5.1	−2.1	781,340	33,439,436	95.1	64.0
State and local government	956	−10.4	−16.5	−17.8	−13.9	112,536	4,040,959	11.5	64.3
Not-for-profit	2,849	0.3	−8.1	−4.3	−3.7	533,368	24,096,781	68.5	65.5
Investor-owned	1,035	3.9	−6.6	15.4	19.2	134,368	5,286,513	15.0	57.9
Federal	199	−10.2	−12.8	−23.8	−7.0	35,050	877,180	2.5	67.3
Long-term[c]	485	−6.3	4.0	−25.8	−17.2	78,184	842,318	2.4	83.6

[a]Ratio of average daily census to every 100 beds.

[b]Short-term general includes community hospitals and hospital units of institutions. Community hospitals consist of state and local government, nongovernment not-for-profit, and investor-owned hospitals.

[c]Long-term includes general, psychiatric, tuberculosis and other respiratory diseases, and all other hospital types.

Sources: Data from American Hospital Association (n.d.): 1986 edition, text table 2; 1996–97 edition, table 3A; 2007 edition, table 2; 2018 edition, table 2.

hospitals. The issues surrounding this debate center on the following questions: Do nonprofits charge lower prices than for-profits? Do nonprofits provide a higher level of quality than for-profits? Do nonprofits provide more charity care than for-profits? Or, as some critics of nonprofits maintain, is there no difference between the two other than the tax-exempt status of nonprofits' surpluses? If the latter position is correct, is continuing nonprofit hospitals' tax advantages and government subsidies justified? Alternatively, if nonprofits provide more charity care and higher-quality service and charge lower prices, will eliminating for-profits enable nonprofits to better serve their communities?

Why Are Hospitals Predominantly Nonprofit?

Several hypotheses have been offered to explain the existence of nonprofit hospitals. The most obvious is that when hospitals were used predominantly as institutions to serve the poor, they depended on donations for funding. However, the possibility of receiving donations does not explain why the majority of hospitals continue to be nonprofit. Donations account for a small percentage of hospital revenue. As public and private health insurance became the dominant source of hospital revenue, the potential for profit increased, as did the number of for-profit hospitals.

Although both public and private insurance have increased, many people remain uninsured. Some believe that only nonprofit hospitals provide uncompensated care to those who are unable to pay. Nonprofit hospitals presumably are willing to use their surplus funds to subsidize both the poor and money-losing services.

A related explanation is the issue of trust. A relationship based on trust is needed in markets in which information is lacking. Patients are not sure what services they need. They depend on the provider for diagnoses and treatment recommendations, and they are not knowledgeable about the skill of the surgeon. The quality of medical and surgical treatments is difficult for patients to judge, and they cannot tell whether the hospital failed to provide care to save costs. In such situations, patients are more likely to rely on nonprofit providers, believing that because they are not motivated by profit, they will not take advantage of a patient who lacks information and is seriously ill.[1]

Another explanation for the predominance of nonprofit status is that the hospital's managers and board of directors want to be part of a nonprofit hospital, where their activities are subject to limited community oversight. The managers and board have greater flexibility to pursue policies that reflect their own preferences, such as offering prestigious but money-losing services even if these services are provided by other hospitals in the community.

Furthermore, nonprofit hospitals are in physicians' financial interest. Being associated with nonprofit organizations allows physicians to exercise greater control over the hospital's policies, services offered, and investments in facilities and equipment. In a for-profit hospital, physicians have less money available for facilities and equipment of their choosing, because surpluses must be distributed to shareholders and the government through payment of dividends and taxes. The hospital's physicians also benefit from the hospital's ability to receive donations and from the trust placed in the hospital by the community.

The importance of trust, the provision of community benefits, and the financial interests of physicians appear to be key reasons for the nonprofit status of hospitals.[2]

Performance of Nonprofit and For-Profit Hospitals

For-profit hospitals have a more precise organizational goal—namely profit—than do nonprofit hospitals. A concern of any organization is monitoring its managers' success in achieving the firm's goals. In a for-profit firm, the objective is straightforward, and the shareholders have an incentive to monitor the performance of managers and replace them if their performance is lacking.

A nonprofit firm has multiple objectives, making it more difficult to monitor its managers. The various stakeholders of the nonprofit hospital—medical staff, board members, managers, employees, and the community—have different and sometimes conflicting objectives as to how the hospital's surplus should be distributed. Should profits be used to subsidize the poor, increase compensation for managers, raise wages for employees, establish prestige facilities, or provide benefits (e.g., low office rent and resources) to medical staff? The board of directors has less incentive to monitor a nonprofit hospital, as it has less financial interest in the hospital's performance and must rely on the managers for information about achieving the hospital's multiple goals. Furthermore, if the nonprofit hospital is not performing efficiently, it may be able to survive on community donations.

Given the differing goals and incentive-monitoring mechanisms of for-profit and nonprofit hospitals, it is important to examine how the behavior of nonprofits differs from that of for-profits.

Pricing

For-profit hospitals attempt to set prices to maximize their profits.[3] Do nonprofit hospitals set lower prices than for-profit hospitals? Three aspects of hospital pricing shed light on how nonprofit hospitals set prices.

Many people believe that nonprofit hospitals set prices to earn sufficient revenues to cover their costs. Nonprofits set prices for private insurers that are below their profit-maximizing prices, but raise those prices when the government lowers the price it pays for Medicare or Medicaid patients. For cost shifting to occur, a hospital (1) must have market power—that is, be able to profitably raise its price and (2) must decide not to exploit that market power before the government reduces its price. (A more complete discussion of cost shifting is provided in chapter 18.)

Evidence of hospital cost shifting is based on data from before the mid-1980s (before managed care competition). With the start of intense price competition among hospitals, insurers became more sensitive to the prices charged by hospitals. Hospitals' market power declined because insurers were willing to shift their volume to hospitals offering lower prices. Any ability of nonprofit hospitals to shift cost disappeared with hospital competition for managed care contracts. Instead, as the government reduced the prices it paid for Medicare and Medicaid patients, hospitals experienced greater pressure to lower their prices to be included in an insurer's provider network.

Second, the pricing practices of nonprofit hospitals regarding uninsured patients have received a great deal of media publicity recently. Large purchasers of hospital services (e.g., health insurers, Medicare, Medicaid) receive deep discounts from a hospital's billed charges—often as high as 50 percent. Uninsured patients were asked to pay 100 percent of the hospital's billed charges. Newspaper articles have described the hardship faced by many patients who do not have the resources to pay their hospital bills. Several lawsuits were filed on behalf of the uninsured against nonprofit hospitals because the hospitals charged the highest prices to those least able to pay and hounded patients for unpaid debts. These lawsuits (several of which have been settled by hospitals) claimed that nonprofit hospitals violated their charitable mission by overcharging the uninsured and sought to have these hospitals' tax-exempt status revoked. The pricing practices of nonprofits with respect to the uninsured appear to be no different from those of for-profits. (New federal rules for hospitals have modified their pricing practices for the uninsured [Pear 2015].)

Third, do nonprofit hospitals increase prices if they merge with other nonprofit hospitals? The number of hospital mergers has grown in recent years. Consolidation of for-profit firms or hospitals in a market causes concern that competition will decline, enabling the hospitals to raise prices. Would a merger of nonprofit hospitals similarly result in higher hospital prices, or are nonprofit hospitals different?

In early court cases in which the merger of nonprofit hospitals was contested by federal antitrust agencies, the presiding judges ruled that nonprofit mergers are different from for-profit mergers. The judges believed that nonprofit mergers were unlikely to result in price increases—even if the hospitals acquired monopoly power—because the boards of directors are themselves local citizens and would not take advantage of their neighbors. Empirical studies, however, contradict the judges' belief that nonprofit ownership limits price increases after a merger (Capps and Dranove 2004; Melnick, Keeler, and Zwanziger 1999).

Researchers found that nonprofits with great market power charge significantly higher prices than do nonprofits in competitive markets. These results suggest that some nonprofit hospitals merge simply to increase their market power and to negotiate higher prices with managed care plans. This type of behavior is no different from the behavior expected of for-profit hospitals.

In October 2005, the Federal Trade Commission (FTC) won an antitrust suit against nonprofit Northwestern Healthcare for a previously consummated hospital merger. The FTC claimed that a hospital merger that occurred in 2000 violated federal antitrust law because the newly created three-hospital system sufficiently boosted its market power to illegally control hospital prices in its market. The FTC's decision was upheld on appeal, and the system hospitals were ordered to negotiate independently with insurers, rather than have Northwestern Healthcare divest itself of one hospital, as the initial decision recommended.

Mergers of nonprofit hospitals are no longer likely to be viewed as different from mergers of for-profit hospitals (Morse et al. 2007).

The FTC (2006) claimed that, as a result of the merger, Northwestern Healthcare used its postmerger market power to impose huge price increases—40 to 60 percent and, in one case, even 190 percent—on insurers and employers.

Quality of Care

Sloan (2000) reviewed several large-scale empirical studies of quality of care received by Medicare beneficiaries in nonprofit and for-profit hospitals. The studies examined various measures of quality, such as the overall care process and the extent to which medical charts showed that specific diagnostic and therapeutic procedures were performed competently. The studies assessed different hospital admissions (e.g., hip fracture, stroke, coronary heart disease, congestive heart failure) and outcome measures (e.g., survival, functional status, cognitive status, probability of living in a nursing home). The study findings showed that teaching hospitals performed better; however, no statistically significant differences were found between nonteaching private nonprofit hospitals and for-profit hospitals.

In an extensive study, McClellan and Staiger (2000) compared patient outcomes for all elderly Medicare beneficiaries hospitalized with heart disease (more than 350,000 per year) in for-profit and nonprofit hospitals between 1984 and 1994. McClellan and Staiger (2000, 4) found that

> [o]n average, for-profit hospitals have higher mortality among elderly patients with heart disease, and . . . this difference has grown over the last decade. However, much of the difference appears to be associated with the location of for-profit hospitals. Within specific markets, for-profit ownership appears if anything to be associated

with better quality care. Moreover, the small average difference in mortality between nonprofit and for-profit hospitals masks an enormous amount of variation in mortality within each of these ownership types. Overall, these results suggest that factors other than for-profit status per se may be the main determinants of quality of care in hospitals.

Charity Care

Nonprofit hospitals have a long tradition of caring for the medically indigent. They were given tax-exempt status and community donations in the belief that they would provide charity care. However, the advent of price competition in the mid-1980s changed their ability to provide the level of charity care some believe is necessary to justify their tax-exempt status. Researchers have examined the extent of charity care provided in terms of (1) hospital conversions (a nonprofit becomes a for-profit) and (2) the effect of greater competitive pressures from managed care.

Concern has arisen that once a hospital converts to for-profit status, its charity care will decline as the profit motive becomes dominant. Various studies, however, have found no difference in provision of uncompensated care once a hospital converts from nonprofit to for-profit status. Norton and Staiger (1994) found that for-profit hospitals are often located in areas with a high degree of health insurance (Medicare, Medicaid, and private). However, once differences in location are accounted for—such as by examining nonprofit and for-profit hospitals in the same market—no difference was found in the volume of uninsured patients treated by the two types of hospitals.

Price competition is expected to negatively affect a nonprofit hospital's ability to provide charity care by decreasing the "profits" or surplus available for such care. As competition reduces the prices charged to privately insured patients, profits decline and, thus, fewer funds are available for charity care. Gruber (1994) found that increased competition among hospitals in California from 1984 to 1988 led to decreased revenues from private payers, decreased net income, and, consequently, less provision of uncompensated care. David Walker (2005), the-then comptroller general of the United States, stated that in four of the five states studied in 2003, state and locally owned hospitals provided an average of twice as much uncompensated care as did nonprofit or for-profit hospitals. In Florida, Georgia, Indiana, and Texas, nonprofits delivered more uncompensated care than did for-profits, but the difference was small. In California, for-profits delivered more uncompensated care than did nonprofits. In a study of uncompensated care in five states, the Congressional Budget Office (2006, 2) found that the cost of uncompensated care as a percentage of hospital operating expenses was much larger in government or public institutions (13 percent) than in nonprofit (4.7 percent) or for-profit (4.2 percent) institutions.

Individual nonprofit and for-profit hospitals, however, varied widely in the amount of uncompensated care they provided. Capps, Carlton, and David (2017) compared the provision of charity care between nonprofit and for-profit hospitals under different competitive conditions. They found that when both types of hospitals achieve greater market power, the amount of charity care or unprofitable services provided is not increased. Both types of hospitals exhibit a similar response to financial incentives.

Overall, competitive pressures result in lower income available for charity care in nonprofit and for-profit hospitals, whereas public hospitals experience higher uncompensated care costs.

The Question of Tax-Exempt Status

Nonprofit hospitals have received tax advantages that obligate them to serve the uninsured. Nonprofits, however, vary greatly in the amount of care they provide to the uninsured. In some cases, the value of the hospital's tax exemption exceeds the value of charity care provided. Consequently, it has been proposed that, in return for their tax-exempt status, nonprofit hospitals should be required to deliver a minimum amount of charity care.

If the tax exemption is to be tied to the value of charity care or community benefits, the measure to be used and the amount of care to be provided must be defined. The following are proposed possible measures:

- *Pure charity care:* care for which payment is not expected and patients are not billed
- *Bad debt:* value of care delivered and billed to patients believed to be able to pay, but from whom the hospital is unable to collect
- *Uncompensated care:* the sum of bad debt and charity care
- *Medicaid and Medicare shortfalls:* the difference between charges and the amount reimbursed by Medicare and Medicaid
- *Community benefits:* the previous items plus patient education, prevention programs, medical research, and provision of money-losing services (e.g., burn units, trauma centers)

Deciding which definition should be used and what percentage of a nonprofit hospital's revenue should be devoted to that measure is an important public policy issue being debated by state and federal governments. For example, if the charity care definition is used, is the amount of free care measured by the hospital's full charges (which few payers actually pay) or the lower prices a health maintenance organization would pay? Further, using the broadest definition of community benefits may result in a hospital's delivering no charity care but relying instead on Medicare and Medicaid shortfalls and some community prevention programs, which also may be viewed as a marketing effort by the hospital.[4] If such a broad definition were used, little difference would be found between many nonprofit and for-profit hospitals.

Many states have begun to engage in limited monitoring of the uncompensated care provided by nonprofit hospitals (see, for example, Day 2006; Reece 2011). Stringent requirements have not been imposed on hospitals to maintain their tax-exempt status. Included as part of the Affordable Care Act is the requirement that nonprofits conduct and submit a community needs assessment, after which their progress toward meeting those needs will be measured every three years. Those nonprofits that achieve little or no progress toward meeting the identified needs in their community will risk losing their tax-exempt status. Nonprofits also are required to ensure that their patients are aware when free or discounted care is available. These conditions are less severe than requiring nonprofits to spend a given percentage of their surplus on charity or uncompensated care.

Summary

In examining whether the behavior of nonprofit hospitals is different from that of for-profit hospitals, one must keep in mind that wide variations in behavior exist within both types of hospitals. Although little difference has been found between ownership type in pricing behavior, quality of care delivered, or even the amount of uncompensated care provided, these comparisons are based on averages.

As price competition among hospitals increases, ownership differences become less important in determining a hospital's behavior regarding pricing, quality of care, and even charity care. In a price-competitive environment, nonprofit and for-profit hospitals must behave similarly to survive; nonprofits will have a smaller surplus with which to pursue other goals.

Ideally, the poor and uninsured should not have to rely on nonprofit or for-profit hospitals for charity care. Expanding health insurance to the uninsured—either through private insurance refundable tax credits or Medicaid—will more directly solve the problem of providing care to the medically indigent. As more people obtain some form of coverage, the tax-exempt status of many nonprofit hospitals is likely to be questioned. Although certain nonprofits, such as teaching hospitals, will continue to provide care to those who remain uninsured, the majority of nonprofit hospitals will have to justify their role in society.

Discussion Questions

1. Discuss the differences and similarities among theories on why many hospitals are nonprofit.

2. Do you agree with the ruling by a federal judge that mergers of nonprofit hospitals should not be subject to the same antitrust laws as mergers of for-profit hospitals?

3. How has price competition affected the ability of nonprofit hospitals to achieve their mission?

4. What conditions should be imposed on nonprofit hospitals to retain their tax-exempt status?

5. In what ways, if any, are nonprofit hospitals different from for-profit hospitals?

Notes

1. The trust relationship between the patient and provider, however, applies more strongly to the patient–physician relationship. The physician diagnoses the illness, recommends treatment, refers the patient to specialists, and monitors the care the patient receives from different providers. Yet, physicians practice on a for-profit basis.

2. An additional explanation for the existence of nonprofit status is that the stochastic nature of the demand for medical services requires hospitals to maintain excess capacity for certain services. It can be very costly for patients if they cannot access hospital care when needed. For-profit hospitals, some believe, would be unwilling to bear the cost of idle hospital capacity. Further, certain hospital services (e.g., emergency departments; trauma centers; neonatal intensive care units; and teaching, research, and care for certain groups [such as drug addicts] that benefit the community) generally lose money and would otherwise not be provided.

3. Lakdawalla and Philipson (2006) claimed that the traditional for-profit analysis of a firm can be used to explain nonprofit hospitals, but with a lower cost structure because of their nonprofit status. The type of services a hospital chooses to offer (in addition to the pricing strategy) will also affect its profitability. Horwitz and Nichols (2009) found that nonprofit hospitals' services vary according to the relative market share of nonprofit, for-profit, and government hospitals in a market. Nonprofits in markets with high for-profit market share were more likely to offer relatively profitable services and less likely to offer

unprofitable services compared with nonprofits in markets with low for-profit penetration.

4. Young and colleagues (2013) surveyed nonprofit hospitals to determine how much they spent on Internal Revenue Service–defined measures of community benefit. They found that hospitals spent, on average, 7.5 percent of their operating expenses on community benefits. On average, more than 85 percent of these expenditures went toward patient care, and almost 50 percent of the 85 percent was used to supplement the low prices paid by government for services provided to Medicaid and other means-tested patients. Community benefit spending not related to patient care was devoted to community health improvement activities and health professions education. Only 1.9 percent of the study hospitals' operating expenditures was spent, on average, on charity care.

References

American Hospital Association. n.d. *Hospital Statistics.* Various editions. Chicago: American Hospital Association.

Capps, C., D. Carlton, and G. David. 2017. "Antitrust Treatment of Nonprofits: Should Hospitals Receive Special Care?" National Bureau of Economic Research Working Paper No. 23131. Published February. www.nber.org/papers/w23131.

Capps, C., and D. Dranove. 2004. "Hospital Consolidation and Negotiated PPO Prices." *Health Affairs* 23 (2): 175–81.

Congressional Budget Office. 2006. "Nonprofit Hospitals and the Provision of Community Benefit." Published December. www.cbo.gov/sites/default/files/cbo files/ftpdocs/76xx/doc7695/12-06-nonprofit.pdf.

Day, K. 2006. "Hospital Charity Care Is Probed." *Washington Post.* Published September 13. www.washingtonpost.com/wp-dyn/content/article/2006/09/12/AR2006091201409.html.

Federal Trade Commission (FTC). 2006. "In the Matter of Evanston Northwestern Healthcare Corporation." Last updated April 28, 2008. www.ftc.gov/sites/default/files/documents/cases/2007/08/070806opinion.pdf.

Gruber, J. 1994. "The Effect of Competitive Pressure on Charity: Hospital Responses to Price Shopping in California." *Journal of Health Economics* 13 (2): 183–212.

Horwitz, J., and A. Nichols. 2009. "Hospital Ownership and Medical Services: Market Mix, Spillover Effects, and Nonprofit Objectives." *Journal of Health Economics* 28 (5): 924–37.

Lakdawalla, D., and T. Philipson. 2006. "The Nonprofit Sector and Industry Performance." *Journal of Public Economics* 90 (8–9): 1681–98.

McClellan, M., and D. Staiger. 2000. "Comparing Hospital Quality at For-Profit and Not-for-Profit Hospitals." In *The Changing Hospital Industry: Comparing Not-for-Profit and For-Profit Institutions*, edited by D. Cutler, 93–112. Chicago: University of Chicago Press.

Melnick, G., E. Keeler, and J. Zwanziger. 1999. "Market Power and Hospital Pricing: Are Nonprofits Different?" *Health Affairs* 18 (3): 167–73.

Morse, M., B. Kevin, R. McCann, and L. Bryant Jr. 2007. "Federal Trade Commission Finds Evanston Northwestern Healthcare Merger Unlawful but Orders 'Separate and Independent Negotiating Teams' Rather Than Divestiture." Published August 17. www.lexology.com/library/detail.aspx?g=a1132f 5c-4483-41e5-a31d-dc832f51f1ea.

Norton, E., and D. Staiger. 1994. "How Hospital Ownership Affects Access to Care for the Uninsured." *RAND Journal of Economics* 25 (1): 171–85.

Pear, R. 2015. "New Rules to Limit Tactics on Hospitals' Fee Collections." *New York Times*. Published January 11. www.nytimes.com/2015/01/12/us/politics/ new-rules-to-limit-tactics-on-hospitals-fee-collections.html.

Reece, M. 2011. "Bill Scrutinizes Nonprofit Property Tax Structure." *Flathead Beacon*. Published February 7. http://flatheadbeacon.com/2011/02/07/ bill-scrutinizes-nonprofit-property-tax-structure/.

Sloan, F. 2000. "Not-for-Profit Ownership and Hospital Behavior." In *Handbook of Health Economics*, vol. 1B, edited by A. J. Culyer and J. P. Newhouse, 1141–73. New York: North-Holland Press.

Walker, D. M. 2005. "Nonprofit, For-Profit and Government Hospital: Uncompensated Care and Other Community Benefits." Testimony before the Committee on Ways and Means, House of Representatives, GAO-05-743T. Publicly released May 26. www.gao.gov/new.items/d05743t.pdf.

Young, G. J., C.-H. Chou, J. Alexander, S.-Y. D. Lee, and E. Raver. 2013. "Provision of Community Benefits by Tax-Exempt U.S. Hospitals." *New England Journal of Medicine* 368 (16): 1519–27.

COMPETITION AMONG HOSPITALS: DOES IT RAISE OR LOWER COSTS?

Current federal policy (the antitrust laws) encourages competition among hospitals. Hospitals proposing a merger are scrutinized by the Federal Trade Commission (FTC) to determine whether the merger will lessen hospital competition in that market; if so, the FTC will oppose the merger. Critics of this policy believe hospitals should be permitted—in fact, encouraged—to consolidate the facilities and services they provide. They claim that the result will be greater efficiency, less duplication of costly services, and higher quality of care. Who is correct, and what is the appropriate public policy for hospitals? Competition or cooperation?

Important to understanding hospital performance are (1) the methods used to pay hospitals (different payment schemes offer hospitals different incentives) and (2) the consequences of having different numbers of hospitals compete with one another.

Origins of Nonprice Competition

After the introduction of Medicare and Medicaid in 1966, hospitals were paid for the costs of services rendered to the aged and poor. Private insurance, which was widespread among the remainder of the population, reimbursed hospitals generously according to their costs or their charges. The extensive coverage of hospital services by private and public payers removed patients' incentive to be concerned about the costs of hospital care. Patients pay lower out-of-pocket costs for hospital care (3.0 percent in 2016) than they do for any other medical service.

Third-party payers (government and private insurance) and patients had virtually no incentive to be concerned about hospital efficiency and duplication of facilities and services. Further, most hospitals are organized as nonprofit (nongovernment) organizations that are either affiliated with religious organizations or controlled by boards of trustees selected from the community. With the introduction of extensive public and private hospital insurance after the mid-1960s, the use of nonprofit hospitals increased. Lacking a profit motive and assured of survival by the generous payment methods, nonprofit hospitals also had no incentive to be efficient. Consequently, the costs of caring for patients rose rapidly.

Exhibit 16.1 illustrates the dramatic growth in hospital expenditures from the 1960s to 2015. After Medicare and Medicaid were enacted in 1966, hospital expenditures rose by more than 16 percent per year, which was primarily attributable to sharp increases in hospital prices (as shown in exhibit 16.2). Price increases moderated during the early 1970s, when wage and price controls were imposed, but then continued once the controls were removed in mid-1974. Hospital expenditure growth was less rapid in the mid-to-late 1980s as Medicare changed its hospital payment system and price competition increased. The rate of increase in hospital expenditures and hospital prices continued to slow during the 1990s.[1] These declines, discussed later, are indicative of the changes that have occurred in the market for hospital services.

In the late 1960s, the private sector also did not encourage efficiency. Although services such as diagnostic workups could be provided less expensively in an outpatient setting, BlueCross paid for such services only if they were provided as part of a hospital admission. Small hospitals attempted to emulate medical centers by having the latest in technology, although those services were used infrequently.

Because cost was of little concern to patients or purchasers of services, it did not matter whether large organizations had lower costs per unit and higher-quality outcomes than those of small facilities. The greater the number of hospitals in a community, the more intense was the competition among nonprofit hospitals to become the most prestigious. Hospitals competed for physicians by offering the same medical services available at other hospitals to maximize the physicians' productivity and to discourage them from referring patients elsewhere. This wasteful form of nonprice competition was characterized as a "medical arms race" and caused the rapid rise in hospital expenditures.

As the costs of nonprice competition ballooned, federal and state governments attempted to change hospitals' behavior. Regulations were enacted to control hospital capital expenditures; hospitals were required to have certificate-of-need (CON) approval from a state planning agency before they could undertake large investments. According to proponents of state planning, controlling hospital investment would eliminate unnecessary and duplicative investments.

Unfortunately, no attempts were made to change hospital payment methods, which would have changed hospitals' incentives to undertake such investments.

Numerous studies concluded that CON had no effect on limiting the growth in hospital investment. Instead, CON was used in an anticompetitive manner to benefit existing hospitals in the community, which ended up controlling the CON approval process. Ambulatory surgery centers (unaffiliated with hospitals) did not receive CON approval for construction because they would

EXHIBIT 16.1
Trends in
Hospital
Expenditures,
1966–2015

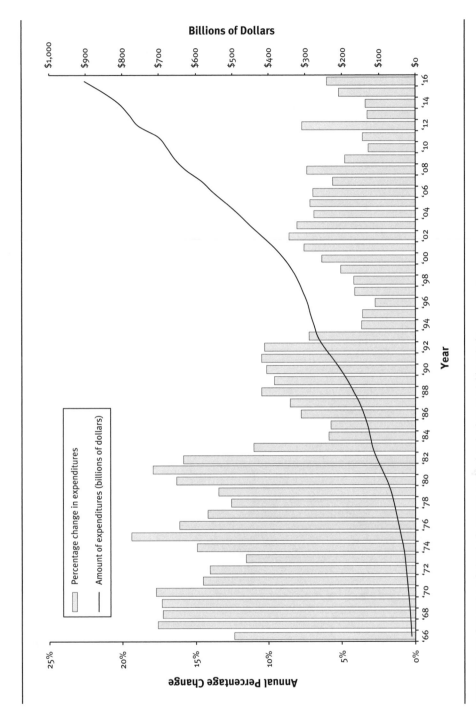

Note: Data are for total nonfederal, short-term general and other special hospitals.

Source: Data from American Hospital Association (2018, table 1).

EXHIBIT 16.2

Annual Percentage Changes in the Consumer Price Index and the Hospital Room Price Index, 1965–2017

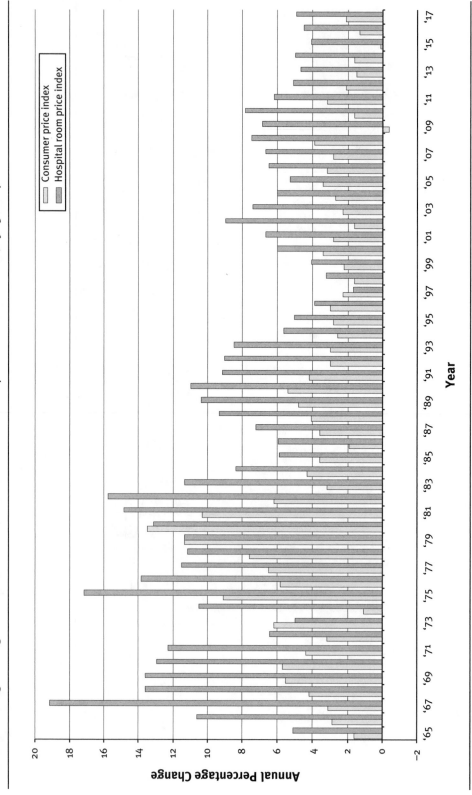

Note: Because of changes in Bureau of Labor Statistics coding, data after 1996 are for hospital services.

Source: Data from Bureau of Labor Statistics (2018).

take away hospital patients; health maintenance organizations (HMOs), such as Kaiser, found entering a new market difficult because they could not receive CON approval to build a hospital; and the courts found that the CON process was used in an "arbitrary and capricious manner" against for-profit hospitals attempting to enter the market of an existing nonprofit hospital (Salkever 2000).

Transition to Price Competition

Until the 1980s, hospital competition was synonymous with nonprice competition, and it was wasteful and led to rapidly rising expenditures.

During the 1980s, hospital and purchaser incentives changed. Medicare began to pay hospitals a fixed price per admission, which varied according to the type of admission. This new payment system—referred to as *diagnosis-related groups (DRGs)*—was phased in over five years starting in 1983. Faced with a fixed price, hospitals now had an incentive to reduce the costs of caring for aged patients. In addition, hospitals reduced lengths of stay for aged patients, which caused declines in hospital occupancy rates. For the first time, hospitals became concerned with their physicians' practice behavior. If physicians ordered too many tests or kept patients in the hospital longer than necessary, the hospital lost money, given the fixed DRG price.

Pressure to reduce hospital costs also came from private insurers, primarily because employers became concerned about the rising costs of insuring employees. Insurers changed their insurance benefits to encourage patients to undergo diagnostic tests and minor surgical procedures in less costly outpatient settings. Insurers instituted utilization review to monitor the appropriateness of inpatient admissions, which further reduced hospital admissions and lengths of stay. These changes in hospital and purchaser incentives reduced hospital occupancy rates from 76 percent in 1980 to 67 percent by 1990; as of 2015, the rate was about 63 percent. The decline in occupancy rates was much more severe for small hospitals (with fewer than 50 beds), where rates fell to below 50 percent (American Hospital Association 2018, table 2). As occupancy rates fell, hospitals became willing to negotiate price discounts with insurers and HMOs that could deliver many patients to their hospitals. This initiated price competition among hospitals by the late 1980s.

Price competition does not imply that hospitals compete only on the basis of the lowest price. Purchasers are also interested in the characteristics of a hospital, such as reputation, geographic location in relation to patients, facilities and services available, patient satisfaction, and treatment outcomes. In recent years, as mergers have taken place and price competition has lessened, hospitals' market power has expanded (relative to that of health insurers), and hospital prices (adjusted for inflation) have risen rapidly (see exhibit 16.2).

Price Competition in Theory

How did hospitals respond to this new competitive environment in which purchasers demand lower prices? Let us examine two hypothetical situations.

In the first situation, only one hospital exists in an area; it has no competitors, and no substitutes for inpatient services are available. The hospital is a monopolist in providing services and has no incentive to respond to purchaser demands for lower prices, quality information, and patient satisfaction. The purchaser has no choice but to use that one hospital. If the hospital is not efficient, it can pass on the resulting higher costs to the purchaser. If patients are dissatisfied with the services or the hospital refuses to provide outcomes information, the purchaser and patients have no choice but to use the hospital. (Obviously, at some point, it becomes worthwhile for patients to incur large costs to travel to a distant hospital or facility.) When only one hospital serves a market, that hospital is unlikely to achieve high performance. It has little incentive to be efficient or to respond to purchaser and patient demands.

In the second situation, many hospitals—perhaps ten—serve a geographic area. Now assume a large employer in the area is interested, on behalf of its employees, in not only high-quality care and high patient satisfaction, but also in low hospital costs. Further, assume each of the ten hospitals is equally accessible to the employees in terms of short travel distances and availability of physician appointments. How are hospitals likely to respond to this employer's demands?

At least several of the ten hospitals would be willing—in return for gaining many new patients from the employer—to negotiate on prices and accede to demands for information on quality and patient satisfaction. As long as the price the hospital receives from the employer is greater than the direct costs of caring for the employees, the hospital will make more money than it would if it did not accept this business. Further, unless each hospital is as efficient as its competitors, it cannot hope to obtain such a contract. A more efficient hospital is always able to charge less money. Similar to competing on price is competing on willingness to provide information about treatment outcomes. Because hospitals rely on purchaser revenues to survive, they must respond to purchaser demands. If Hospital A is not responsive to these demands, other hospitals will be, and Hospital A will soon find that it has too few patients to remain in business.

When hospitals compete on quality, satisfaction, price, and other purchaser demands, their performance is opposite that of a monopoly provider. In price-competitive markets, hospitals have an incentive to be efficient and respond to purchaser demands. What if, instead of competing with one another, the ten hospitals agree among themselves not to compete on price or provide purchasers with any additional information about quality or patient satisfaction? The outcome would be similar to a monopoly situation. Prices would be higher, and hospitals would have less incentive to be efficient. Patients would be worse off because they would pay more, and quality and patient satisfaction would be lower because employers and other purchasers would be unable to select hospitals based on these criteria.

The more competitive the market, the greater the benefits to consumers. For this reason, society seeks to achieve competitive markets through its antitrust laws. Although competitive hospitals might be harmed and driven out of business, the evaluation of competitive markets is based on their effect on consumers rather than on any competitors in that market. Antitrust laws are designed to prevent hospitals from acting anticompetitively.

Price-fixing agreements, such as those described earlier, are illegal because they reduce competition. Barriers that prevent competitors from entering a market are also anticompetitive. If two hospitals in a market can restrict entry into that market (perhaps through use of regulations such as CON approval), they will have greater monopoly power and be less price competitive and less responsive to purchaser demands. Mergers may be similarly anticompetitive. For example, if nine of the ten hospitals merged, leaving only two organizations, the degree of competition would be less than if ten are operating independently. For this reason, the FTC examines hospital mergers to determine whether the consolidation is eliminating competition in the market.

Price Competition in Practice

The previous discussion provides a theoretical basis for price competition. To move from price competition's theoretical benefits to reality, two questions must be considered. First, does any market have enough hospitals for price competition to occur? Second, is there any evidence about the actual effects of hospital price competition?

The number of competing hospitals in a market is determined by the cost–size relationship of hospitals (economies of scale) and the size of the market (the population served). A large hospital—for example, one with 200 beds—is likely to have lower average costs per patient than a hospital with the same set of services but only 50 beds. In a large hospital, some costs can be spread over a greater number of patients. For example, the costs of an administrator, an X-ray technician, and imaging equipment (which can be used more fully in a large organization) do not change whether the hospital has 50 or 200 patients. These economies of scale, however, do not continue indefinitely; at some point, the high costs of coordinating services begin to exceed the gains from being large. Studies generally have indicated that hospitals in the range of 200 to 400 beds have the lowest average costs.

If the population in an area consists of only 100,000, only one hospital of 260 beds is likely to survive (assuming 800 patient days per year per 1,000 people and 80 percent occupancy). If more than one hospital is in the area, each has higher average costs than does one large hospital; one of the hospitals may expand, achieve lower average costs, and be able to set its prices lower than those of the other hospital. An area with a population of 1 million is large enough to support three to six hospitals in the 200- to 400-bed range.

Hospital services, however, are not all the same. The economies of scale associated with an obstetrics facility are quite different from those associated with organ transplant services. Patients are less willing to travel great distances for a normal delivery than for a heart transplant. The costs of traveling to another state for a transplant represent a smaller portion of the total cost of that service than do the costs of traveling to another state for childbirth (and the travel time is less crucial). Thus, the number of competitors in a market depends on the particular service. For some services, the relevant geographic market served may be relatively small, whereas for others the market may be the state or region.

As of 2015, approximately 85 percent of hospital beds were in metropolitan statistical areas (MSAs). An MSA may not be indicative of the particular market in which a hospital competes. For some services, the travel time within an MSA may be too great, whereas for other services (organ transplants), the market may encompass multiple MSAs. However, the number of hospitals in an MSA provides a general indication of the number of competitors in a hospital's market. As shown in exhibit 16.3, 212 MSAs (48 percent) have fewer than four hospitals, and 85 MSAs (19 percent) have four or five hospitals. The remaining MSAs (33 percent) have six or more hospitals; however, that 33 percent contains 73 percent of the hospitals located in metropolitan areas. Therefore, most hospitals in MSAs (73 percent) are in MSAs with six or more hospitals. Even in an MSA with few hospitals, competition still occurs, and substitutes for the hospitals' services (e.g., outpatient surgery) are often available, which reduce the hospitals' monopoly power.

When few specialized facilities exist in a market (because of economies of scale and the size of the market), the relevant geographic market is likely to be much larger because the highly specialized services are generally not of an emergency nature, and patients are willing to travel farther to access them. Insurers negotiate prices for transplants, for example, with several regional *centers of excellence*—hospitals that perform a high number of transplants and experience good outcomes. Thus, price competition among hospitals appears to be feasible. As insurers and large employers have become concerned about the costs of hospital care and better informed about hospital prices and patient outcomes, hospitals are being forced to respond to purchaser demands and compete according to price, outcomes, and patient satisfaction. Exhibits 16.1 and 16.2 show how competition lowered the rate of increase in hospital expenditures and prices during the

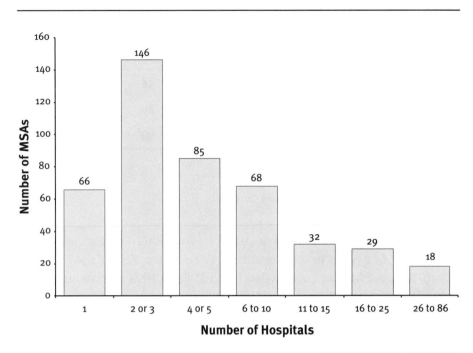

EXHIBIT 16.3
Number of
Hospitals in
Metropolitan
Statistical
Areas, 2016

Note: MSA = metropolitan statistical area.

Source: Data from American Hospital Association (2018, table 8).

late 1990s. As hospitals competed to be included in provider panels of managed care plans, they had to become more efficient and discount their prices.

Several studies have been published on the effects of hospital price competition. The research findings support traditional economic expectations regarding competitive hospital markets. The change to hospital price competition has not been uniform throughout the United States. Price competition in California developed earlier and more rapidly than in other areas. Bamezai and colleagues (1999) classified hospitals in California according to whether they were in a high- or low-competition market and whether the managed care penetration was high or low. Hospitals in more competitive markets (controlling for other factors) were found to have a much lower rate of increase in the costs per discharge and per capita than were hospitals in less competitive markets.

Bamezai and colleagues (1999) also found that an increase in managed care penetration reduced the rise in hospital costs (see exhibit 16.4). The decrease in costs, however, was much greater for hospitals in more competitive markets. Also, regardless of the degree of managed care penetration, competition was important in slowing hospital cost increases. These findings imply that hospital mergers that decrease competition are likely to result in higher hospital prices. Melnick, Chen, and Wu (2011) confirmed these findings in a subsequent study showing that greater market concentration leads to higher hospital prices.[2]

EXHIBIT 16.4
Hospital Cost
Growth in the
United States
by Level of
Managed Care
Penetration and
Hospital Market
Competitiveness,
1986–1993

Level of Managed Care Penetration	Level of Hospital Competition		% Difference
	Low	High	
Low	65	56	16[a]
High	52	39	33[a]
% difference	25[a]	44[a]	67[b]

[a] % difference = [(High − Low)/Low].
[b] [Low/Low (65) − High/High (39)] / [High/High (39)].
Source: Calculations by Glenn Melnick, Rand Corporation.

Other studies have reached similar conclusions using different methods and data on specific types of hospital treatment. For example, Kessler and McClellan (2000) analyzed Medicare claims data (from 1985 to 1994) for patients admitted to the hospital with a primary diagnosis of a heart attack. They found that before 1991, hospital competition based on the latest technology led to higher costs and, in some cases, lower rates of adverse health outcomes. After 1990, hospital price competition led to substantially reduced costs and rates of adverse outcomes. Patients had lower mortality rates in the most competitive markets.

Chandra and colleagues (2016, 2110) also described the benefits of market competition. They found that "higher quality hospitals have higher market shares and grow more over time. The relationship between performance and allocation is stronger among patients who have greater scope for hospital choice, suggesting that patient demand plays an important role in allocation. Our findings suggest that healthcare may have more in common with 'traditional' sectors subject to market forces than often assumed."

After the consumer backlash against managed care in the late 1990s and early 2000s, health plans broadened their provider networks to give enrollees more provider choices. As insurers included more hospitals in their networks, their bargaining power over hospitals decreased (Dranove et al. 2008). Reinforcing this shift in relative bargaining power was the decrease in the number of hospitals. Hospital closures and mergers resulted in fewer hospitals competing within a market.[3] Consequently, hospital prices increased much more rapidly. Insurers' reliance on broad provider networks coupled with the decreased number of competing hospitals enabled hospitals to maintain their relative bargaining power over insurers.

Cooper and colleagues (2015, 3) estimated the effect of hospital consolidation on hospital prices:

Measures of hospital market structure are strongly correlated with higher hospital prices . . . even after controlling for . . . [many demand and cost factors] . . . We estimate that monopoly hospitals have 15.3 percent higher prices than markets with four or more hospitals. Similarly, hospitals in duopoly markets have prices that are 6.4 percent higher and hospitals in triopoly markets have prices that are 4.8 percent higher than hospitals located in markets with four or more hospitals.

Many economists believe the steady erosion of competition in hospital markets (almost one-half of all hospital markets are considered highly concentrated) is resulting in higher prices. In addition, the recent trend toward hospitals employing more practicing physicians is further decreasing hospital competition (Gaynor, Mostashari, and Ginsburg 2017).

Summary

The controversy over whether hospital competition results in higher or lower costs is based on studies from two periods. When hospitals were paid according to their costs, nonprice competition occurred and resulted in rapidly rising hospital costs. Medicare's switch to fixed-price hospital payment and managed care plans' switch to negotiated prices changed hospitals' incentives. Hospitals had incentives to be efficient and compete on price to be included in managed care plans' provider panels. Consequently, hospital costs and prices rose less rapidly in more competitive markets. Public policies (e.g., antitrust laws) that encourage competitive hospital markets will be of greater benefit to purchasers and patients than will policies that enable hospitals to increase their monopoly power.

As enrollment in managed care plans rose, the demand for hospital care fell. Hospitals developed excess capacity and were willing to discount their prices to be included in insurers' limited provider networks. As a result, hospital prices declined. With excess capacity, some hospitals closed, and many merged with financially stronger hospitals. Under public pressure to expand their provider networks, insurers were less able to offer hospitals a greater volume of patients in return for heavily discounted prices. With fewer hospital competitors in a market and insurers' willingness to contract with more hospitals, the relative bargaining positions of hospitals and insurers changed. Hospitals' market power increased—as did their prices, which have been higher than in the 1990s, when managed care limited provider networks and hospitals had excess capacity.

Discussion Questions

1. Why did hospital expenditures rise so rapidly after Medicare and Medicaid were introduced in 1966?
2. What changes did Medicare DRGs cause in hospital behavior?

3. What is the likely response of hospitals when only one hospital is in a market, compared with their response when ten hospitals are competing for a large employer's employees?

4. What determines the number of competitors in a market? Apply your answer to obstetrics and to transplant services.

5. What are some anticompetitive hospital actions that the antitrust laws seek to prevent?

Notes

1. Starting in the mid-1980s, hospital price increases—as calculated in the consumer price index (CPI)—were greatly overstated because the CPI measured "list" prices rather than actual prices charged. The difference between the two became greater with the increase in hospital discounting (Dranove, Shanley, and White 1991). To correct this discrepancy, the Bureau of Labor Statistics, in constructing the CPI, began to use data on actual hospital prices in the early 1990s.

2. In 2006, the British government tried to introduce competition by allowing patients to choose among hospitals and providing them with information on hospital quality and timeliness of care. Gaynor, Moreno-Serra, and Propper (2013) found that patients discharged from hospitals in more competitive markets were less likely to die, had shorter lengths of stay, and incurred no more costs than patients in less competitive markets.

3. An example of the effect of fewer competing hospitals on hospital prices is the study by Wu (2008), who analyzed hospital closures between 1993 and 1998 and found that as the number of competitors decreased, competitors located near the closed hospitals improved their bargaining position over insurers. As these hospital markets became more concentrated, hospitals were able to raise their prices more than could those in less concentrated markets. In 2015, Trish and Herring found that the degree of hospital competition and insurer competition within a market affects insurance premiums.

References

American Hospital Association. 2018. *Hospital Statistics.* Chicago: American Hospital Association.

Bamezai, A., J. Zwanziger, G. Melnick, and J. Mann. 1999. "Price Competition and Hospital Cost Growth in the United States: 1989–1994." *Health Economics* 8 (3): 233–43.

Bureau of Labor Statistics. 2018. "Consumer Price Index Databases, All Urban Consumers (Current Series)." Accessed January. www.bls.gov/cpi/data.htm.

Chandra, A., A. Finkelstein, A. Sacarny, and C. Syverson. 2016. "Health Care Exceptionalism? Performance and Allocation in the US Health Care Sector." *American Economic Review* 106 (8): 2110–44.

Cooper, Z., S. Craig, M. Gaynor, and J. Van Reenen. 2015. "The Price Ain't Right? Hospital Prices and Health Spending on the Privately Insured." Health Care Pricing Project. Published May. www.healthcarepricingproject.org/papers/paper-1.

Dranove, D., R. Lindrooth, W. White, and J. Zwanziger. 2008. "Is the Impact of Managed Care on Hospital Prices Decreasing?" *Journal of Health Economics* 27 (2): 362–76.

Dranove, D., M. Shanley, and W. White. 1991. "How Fast Are Hospital Prices Really Rising?" *Medical Care* 29 (8): 690–96.

Gaynor, M., R. Moreno-Serra, and C. Propper. 2013. "Death by Market Power: Reform, Competition and Patient Outcomes in the National Health Service." *American Economic Journal: Economic Policy* 5 (4): 134–66.

Gaynor, M., F. Mostashari, and P. Ginsburg. 2017. "Health Care's Crushing Lack of Competition." *Forbes*. Published June 28. www.forbes.com/sites/realspin/2017/06/28/health-cares-crushing-lack-of-competition/.

Kessler, D., and M. McClellan. 2000. "Is Hospital Competition Socially Wasteful?" *Quarterly Journal of Economics* 115 (2): 577–615.

Melnick, G., Y. Chen, and V. Wu. 2011. "The Increased Concentration of Health Plan Markets Can Benefit Consumers Through Lower Hospital Prices." *Health Affairs* 30 (9): 1728–33.

Salkever, D. 2000. "Regulation of Prices and Investment in Hospitals in the U.S." In *Handbook of Health Economics*, vol. 1B, edited by A. J. Culyer and J. P. Newhouse, 1489–535. New York: North-Holland Press.

Trish, E. E., and B. J. Herring. 2015. "How Do Health Insurer Market Concentration and Bargaining Power with Hospitals Affect Health Insurance Premiums?" *Journal of Health Economics* 42: 104–14.

Wu, V. 2008. "The Price Effect of Hospital Closures." *Inquiry* 45 (3): 280–92.

THE FUTURE ROLE OF HOSPITALS

Hospitals have traditionally been the center of the healthcare delivery system. Before Medicare and Medicaid were implemented in 1965, hospital expenditures represented 40 percent of total healthcare expenditures. During the late 1960s and the 1970s, the growth of Medicare, Medicaid, and private insurance stimulated the demand for hospital services. By 1975, 46 percent of healthcare expenditures were for hospital services. Although hospital expenditures have continued to increase, hospitals' share of total healthcare expenditures declined to 32 percent in 2016. Will the traditional role of the hospital continue to decline, or will hospitals expand their role beyond treating inpatients and become responsible for a greater portion of the spectrum of care?

From Medicare to the Present

During the post-Medicare period (1966 to early 1980s), hospitals were reimbursed for their costs, engaged in nonprice competition to attract physicians, and quickly adopted new technology. Facilities and services grew rapidly, and hospitals were the largest and fastest-increasing component of healthcare expenditures.

Starting in the mid-1980s, the financial outlook for hospitals changed. Medicare introduced diagnosis-related groups (DRGs), which changed Medicare payment from a cost basis to a fixed price per admission (by type of admission). Hospitals realized that reducing their costs and patients' lengths of stay raised their net income because they could keep the difference between the DRG price and the cost of caring for Medicare patients. Under pressure from employers, insurers introduced managed care with its cost-containment measures, such as utilization review; second surgical opinions; and lower-cost substitutes to inpatient care, including ambulatory surgery and outpatient diagnostic testing. To reduce treatment costs, managed care shifted services out of the most expensive setting—the hospital—and toward outpatient and step-down facilities, such as skilled nursing facilities, rehabilitation units, and home health care.

Hospitals experienced excess capacity as they cut Medicare patients' lengths of stay and as private cost-containment measures reduced hospital use.

With excess capacity, hospitals were willing to compete on price to be included in managed care preferred provider organizations. Managed care competition, hospitals' excess capacity, and the resulting pressures on hospitals to compete on price led to bankruptcies, mergers, declining profit margins, and a distressed hospital industry. The DRG Medicare payment system and managed care's utilization management methods left the industry with too much excess capacity. The financial survival of many hospitals was in doubt.

Exhibit 17.1 describes the changes that occurred in the hospital industry. The number of hospitals and beds, average length of stay, and occupancy rates all declined during the 1980s and 1990s. With the movement to less expensive settings, outpatient visits and surgeries sharply rose. These trends have continued to the present time. Inpatient use of hospitals has continued to decline.

To increase admissions, hospitals bought physicians' practices, thereby increasing physician referrals. However, employed physicians, with their changed incentives, became less productive, so hospitals abandoned the practice. Hospitals were not adept at managing physicians' practices, and physicians were suspicious of working too closely with hospitals. Hospital–physician relationships have been a continual concern of hospitals, especially because physician-owned outpatient surgery centers brought physicians into competition with hospitals.

By the late 1990s, hospital profitability gradually returned. Financially troubled hospitals closed or merged with other hospitals. To survive and prosper, hospitals adopted strategies that emphasized monopolization of the market. Mergers between competing hospitals increased, and large multihospital systems developed. The number of hospital competitors in a market decreased. The Federal Trade Commission (FTC), concerned that mergers were creating monopoly

EXHIBIT 17.1
US Community Hospital Capacity and Utilization, 1975–2015

Year	Number of Hospitals	Number of Staffed Beds (Thousands)	Inpatient Admissions (Thousands)	Average Length of Inpatient Stay (Days)	Average Inpatient Occupancy Rate (%)	Outpatient Visits (Thousands)
1975	5,875	942	33,435	7.7	74.9	190,672
1980	5,830	988	36,143	7.6	75.6	202,310
1985	5,732	1,001	33,449	7.1	64.8	218,716
1990	5,384	927	31,181	7.2	66.8	301,329
1995	5,194	873	30,945	6.5	62.8	414,345
2000	4,915	824	33,089	5.8	63.8	521,404
2005	4,936	802	35,239	5.6	67.3	584,429
2010	4,985	805	35,149	5.4	64.6	651,424
2015	4,862	783	33,261	5.5	63.5	722,121

Source: Author's analysis based on data from American Hospital Association (2018, table 1).

power that enabled hospitals to raise their prices, brought several antitrust suits against mergers. The FTC, however, lost every merger case. The judges in these cases believed that nonprofit hospitals were different from for-profits in that the nonprofits would not exploit their market power by raising prices.

The managed care backlash, which occurred in the late 1990s, resulted in health plans expanding their provider networks, thereby providing enrollees with more choice. With broader networks, insurers were less able to guarantee hospitals increased patient volume in return for large price discounts. The weakening of managed care's cost-containment methods reinforced hospitals' bargaining power over insurers.

Hospital consolidation, the reduction in hospital bed capacity, and the demise of managed care's limited provider networks in the late 1990s led to higher prices for hospital services and increased hospital profitability. As shown in exhibit 17.2, hospital profit margins reached a high in 1996 and 1997. They then declined for several years as Medicare reduced hospital payments to postpone bankruptcy of the Medicare Trust Fund. Profit margins increased throughout most of the past decade, reaching a high in 2007. A deep recession, large numbers of uninsured, and bad debts reduced profit margins in 2008. In 2009, hospitals' finances began to improve, and in 2014 the highest total margins (8.3 percent) were reached in more than 30 years.

Hospitals have increased their market power as a result of mergers, decreased excess capacity, and insurers' reliance on broad provider networks (White, Bond, and Reschovsky 2013). These changes enabled hospitals to increase their prices and profitability. Hospitals' market power has limited insurers' ability to reduce growing hospital expenditures, one of the fastest-rising components of insurance premiums.

These changing trends, which have affected hospitals since the 1960s, are shown in exhibit 17.3, which describes the annual rate of increase in hospital expenditures (adjusted for inflation). Medicare and Medicaid led to a large increase in spending growth rates in the late 1960s. Thereafter, annual growth rates have been on a generally downward trend. Although spending growth rates rose after the sharp drops during the managed care boon, expenditure growth rates decreased as the United States entered a severe recession, unemployment remained high, the percentage of employees with employer-paid health insurance declined, and more employees chose high-deductible health plans with lower premiums.

In recent years, annual growth rates in hospital expenditures appeared to stabilize. Although the number of hospitals, the number of staffed beds, and occupancy rates have declined, and admissions have remained approximately stable, hospital outpatient visits have sharply increased. Although hospitals are receiving a smaller share of the healthcare dollar, they have been quite profitable, as indicated by their total and net margins.

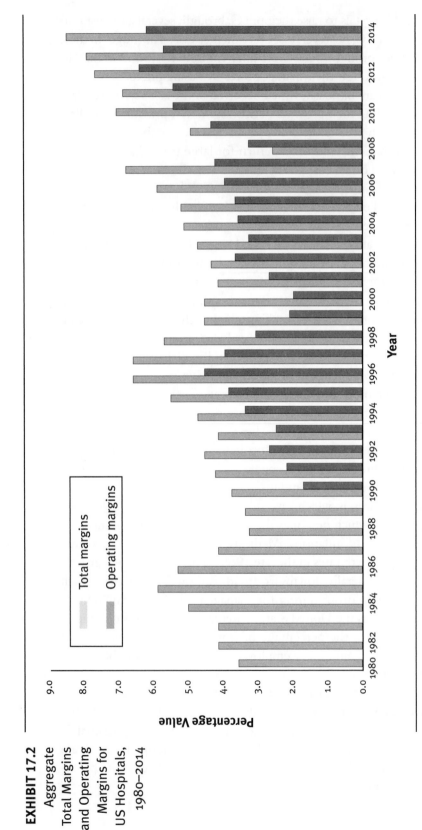

EXHIBIT 17.2
Aggregate
Total Margins
and Operating
Margins for
US Hospitals,
1980–2014

Notes: Total margin is calculated as the difference between total net revenue and total expenses divided by total net revenue. Operating margin is calculated as the difference between operating revenue and total expenses divided by operating revenue. Data on operating margin before 1990 are not available.

Sources: Data for 1980–1989 are author's calculations from American Hospital Association (n.d.); 1990–2014 data are from American Hospital Association (2016, table 4.1).

EXHIBIT 17.3
Annual Rate
of Increase
in Hospital
Expenditures,
Actual and
Trend, GDP
Price Deflated,
1961–2016

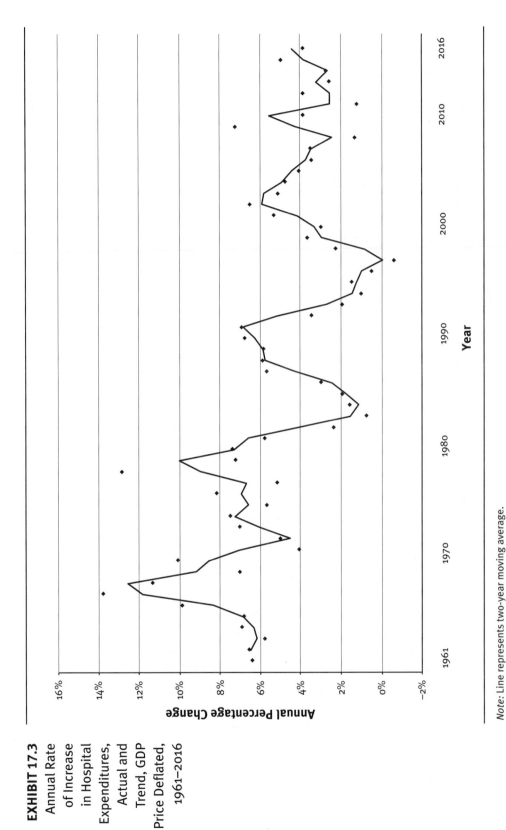

Note: Line represents two-year moving average.

Sources: Author's calculations based on data from Centers for Medicare & Medicaid Services (2018); gross domestic product (GDP) data from Office of Management and Budget (2018, table 10.1).

Hospitals face an uncertain future. The federal and state governments (through Medicare and Medicaid) are major payers of hospital services, and both face severe financial deficits. The privately insured sector is declining, and the Affordable Care Act (ACA) is also likely to significantly affect hospital revenues and hospitals' future role. Will hospitals be able to generate sufficient funds to replace aging buildings, upgrade their facilities, purchase the latest technology, and continue to play an important role in the delivery of medical services?

The Hospital Outlook

Forecasting the industry outlook over the next five to ten years requires an analysis of trends affecting hospital costs and revenues (subdivided into hospital payment [price] and utilization). The hospital's margin (profit) is the difference between revenues and costs. Further, the actions of the two major payers of hospital care—government (Medicare and Medicaid) and private insurers—should be considered, along with the likely consequences of the ACA. Lastly, two scenarios can be envisioned: the status quo and a new role for hospitals.

Hospital Costs: The Public and Private Sectors

The greatest certainty regarding hospitals is that their costs will continue to grow faster than inflation. Two drivers warrant discussion. First is increasing labor costs. Salaries and benefits are the largest component of hospital costs, making up 53 percent of hospitals' overall expenses. The supply of and demand for registered nurses (RNs) determine their wages. Although the recession that began in 2008 caused many RNs who had left the workforce to return, and although nursing school enrollments are up, this increase in the supply of nurses (which has exceeded the demand) has limited raises in nurse wages in the past several years. However, as many baby boomers become eligible for Medicare and, thus, demand more medical services, and as the number of "old-old" elderly goes up, the demand for RNs will also grow. Although RNs work predominantly in hospital settings, they also work in other care settings—from outpatient facilities, to home health care, to hospices. RNs represent 28.6 percent of hospital personnel, and their wages are likely to rise in coming years (2015 data from American Hospital Association [2017], table 2). (See chapter 24 for a more complete discussion of the nurse labor market.)

Economists consider new technology—including equipment, technicians, and expensive drugs—as the second most important reason for rising medical costs. In addition, hospitals are making large investments in information technology (IT) such as electronic health records, which capture patient information related to visits with primary care physicians and specialists, laboratory tests, prescription refills at pharmacies, and use of hospitals and outpatient facilities in the communities. Further, hospitals are investing large sums in clinical IT to streamline clinical decision making, promote quality, and reduce medication errors. These investments, while likely to improve quality and reduce costs, will require nonprofit hospitals to incur debt, which will add to their cost structure.

The costs of caring for patients will continue to rise. Whether hospitals will have the revenue to cover these costs depends on future utilization and payments from the public and private sectors.

Hospital Revenues

Hospital revenues are calculated by multiplying price times quantity—namely utilization. Several factors likely to affect trends in hospital utilization are considered in the following sections, followed by a discussion of likely changes in hospital payment.

Hospital Utilization
The Public Sector
The population is aging. In 2011, the oldest of the baby boomers became eligible for Medicare, and 40 million people began shifting from private insurance to Medicare. While Medicare discharges per enrollee (a measure of hospital use) have been decreasing in recent years, outpatient services per enrollee have been sharply increasing as more surgical procedures are performed in outpatient settings (Centers for Medicare & Medicaid Services 2017). Both trends are likely to continue.

The ACA, enacted in 2010, expanded coverage for the uninsured starting in 2014 (Kaiser Family Foundation 2013). About 11 million people enrolled in Medicaid as a result of the expanded eligibility levels (to 138 percent of the federal poverty level [FPL]), and about 10 million people (between 133 and 400 percent of the FPL) received subsidies for private coverage purchased on health insurance exchanges.[1] As a result of the ACA, many hospitals experienced an increase in demand for their services; patient revenues increased and uncompensated care costs for the uninsured decreased (Cunningham, Garfield, and Rudowitz 2015).

The Private Sector
Hospital utilization by privately insured patients is likely to decline as the baby boomers (a high-risk/user group) become eligible for Medicare. To limit increases in private insurance premiums, insurers will continue to examine approaches to decrease hospitalization, the costliest component of medical care. Hospitals will become more dependent on inpatient utilization from the expanding public sector.[2]

Hospital Payment

How hospitals are paid—and how much—has a significant effect on revenues. Individual hospitals cannot negotiate with the government over the price Medicare pays for services. Instead, hospital associations negotiate politically with legislators who determine Medicare's annual rate increases. Medicaid payment is determined at the state level. Price negotiation with private insurers depends on hospitals' relative bargaining power. Thus, hospital prices are determined in both a competitive and a political marketplace.

Public Payers

Hospital payment sources have changed over time. Government now accounts for about 52 percent of hospital revenue (see exhibit 17.4). Hospitals receive about 88 percent of their average costs of treatment for Medicaid patients and 87 percent for Medicare patients (see exhibit 18.1). Lower government payment-to-cost ratios for Medicare and Medicaid enrollees reduce hospital profitability.

Medicaid will continue to be constrained in its payments to hospitals. States—which pay about half the costs of Medicaid on average (the remainder

EXHIBIT 17.4
Sources of Hospital Revenues by Payer, Selected Years, 1965–2016

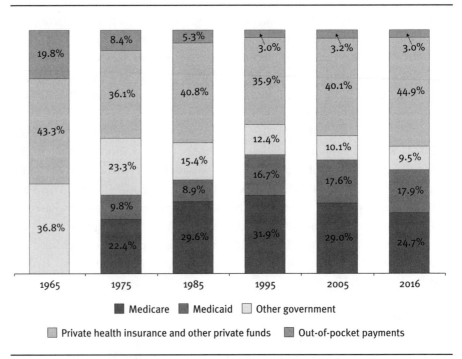

Legend: Medicare · Medicaid · Other government · Private health insurance and other private funds · Out-of-pocket payments

Note: Medicaid includes State Children's Health Insurance Program (SCHIP) and Medicaid SCHIP expansion. Other government includes workers' compensation, Department of Defense, maternal/child health, Veterans Administration, vocational rehabilitation, temporary disability, and state/local hospitals and school health.

Source: Author's calculations based on data from Centers for Medicare & Medicaid Services (2018).

is paid by the federal government)—have difficulty financing rising Medicaid expenditures. Under the ACA, the federal government pays for most of the cost of expanding the Medicaid-eligible population. States, however, will bear some financial liability for this larger population. (As of 2017, many states had not decided whether they were going to expand Medicaid eligibility.) Medicaid payments have not kept up with rising hospital costs and are unlikely to do so in the future. The increasingly large number of low-income aged requiring long-term care will place additional pressures on state Medicaid programs to limit hospital and other provider payments.

The Impact of the ACA on Medicare Hospital Payments

The ACA lowers Medicare hospital payments in several ways. The ACA also established an Independent Payment Advisory Board (IPAB) that must recommend payment reductions for hospitals and other Medicare providers if the per capita growth rate in Medicare spending exceeds the per capita growth rate of gross domestic product (GDP) plus 1 percent, which is lower than the historic spending average. The IPAB's recommendations will have the force of law if Congress is unable to enact alternative measures to achieve the same spending reduction. (The IPAB was repealed by Congress in 2018.) In addition, the ACA reduces hospital payments if a patient is readmitted for what is known as a *preventable hospital readmission*.[3] The hospital is now at financial risk for the appropriateness and quality of care received by patients in settings other than the hospital.

An ACA change with substantial financial consequences for the hospital is a change to the DRG price update. Under the Medicare hospital DRG system, Congress annually decided the percentage increase in the DRG price, which is supposed to be based on technical factors, such as hospital input price increases and productivity changes. The ACA, however, bases the DRG update on an assumed increase in hospital productivity (regardless of whether the productivity increase actually occurs). These assumed productivity improvements, which will reduce the DRG price update, will occur automatically in coming years and cannot be modified or rescinded, except through new legislation.

Medicare's chief actuary has testified that the ACA's hospital payment cuts will, over time, result in Medicare hospital rates being much lower than Medicaid rates and that many hospitals will be forced into bankruptcy (Foster 2011, 7–8).

Accountable Care Organizations and Episode-Based Payment

The ACA also included several new voluntary Medicare payment models—accountable care organizations (ACOs) and bundled payments for an episode of illness—with the goal of reducing medical costs and providing coordinated care for a defined group of Medicare beneficiaries. The intent of coordinated care is to ensure that patients—especially the chronically ill—receive appropriate care when needed while avoiding unnecessary duplication of services. ACOs may be organized by insurers, hospitals, medical groups, and other providers. Payment varies according to the financial risk the ACO is willing to bear. Minimum financial risk involves a shared savings program whereby the ACO accepts responsibility for the overall quality and cost of caring for a defined group of Medicare fee-for-service (FFS) beneficiaries and shares in any cost savings. A model including greater risk requires the ACO to share both savings and losses.

One problem with the ACO model is that Medicare FFS patients are not informed that they have been assigned to an ACO and can seek care anywhere, even outside the ACO. Medicare patients have no financial incentive to seek care only from the ACO; they can still go to any hospital or specialist. The ACO, however, may incur penalties based on patients' cost of care, regardless of who delivers it and where.

Episode-based (or bundled) payment pays hospitals and physicians a single price for all the services included in a particular diagnosis; the financial risk is shifted from the payer to the provider. The payment is made to an organization, such as a hospital, which then divides the payment among the participating providers. Episode-based payment changes providers' incentives so they have incentives to innovate, coordinate care, reduce costs, and improve quality.

Geisinger Health System (Danville, PA) uses a bundled payment model as follows: For cardiac procedures, bundled payment includes the costs of the physician visit at which surgery is determined to be necessary, all hospital costs for the surgery and related care for 90 days after the surgery, and cardiac rehabilitation. Any associated complications and treatment are also the provider's financial responsibility. Because of this bundled payment model, since 2006 Geisinger has experienced a 21 percent decrease in surgical complications and a 44 percent decrease in readmissions; in addition, the average length of stay has been reduced by half a day (Paulus, Davis, and Steele 2008). Geisinger has expanded this model beyond cardiac procedures; it is now applied to hip replacement procedures, cataract surgery, obesity surgery, prenatal care, and cardiac catheterization.

Expanding episode-based payment to many more diagnoses is difficult. Patients frequently are treated for multiple chronic conditions, and bundled payment, which has a single-condition focus, may not be best for these patients. Changes in government payment policy, such as the move away from Medicare's DRG system and toward a broader system, occur slowly. Until such changes occur (if they do occur), hospitals will continue to be motivated to increase admissions.

Private Payers

Hospital prices are referred to as *charges*. However, few purchasers of hospital services pay full (100 percent) charges.[4] Almost all payers receive discounts on charges. Hospitals may discount their charges by up to 50 percent. Most insured patients are insensitive to the prices hospitals charge because they typically do not pay any out-of-pocket costs when they are admitted to the hospital. (Only 3.1 percent of hospital revenue is paid out of pocket by patients, which is lower than any other insured service.) The insurer negotiates a prearranged price with the hospital, which has separate contracts with many health plans.

Insurers attempt to include in their network those providers preferred by their enrollees, and who are willing to give steep price discounts in return for a greater volume of the insurer's enrollees. The insurer's ability to shift patients to competing hospitals determines its hospital discount. Its ability to shift patients is limited by the degree of hospital competition in a market. In markets with only one hospital, the hospital is a monopolist and can exercise its market power by charging more than hospitals charge in markets made up of multiple similar hospitals.[5] In competitive markets, insurers can shift their enrollees to lower-cost (but equal-quality) hospitals. The greater the number of hospitals competing on price, the lower the hospital's price markup and the greater the hospital discount (Ho 2009).

Because a large percentage of the population is enrolled in Medicare and Medicaid, hospitals try to serve more privately insured patients, whose payment rates are higher (see exhibit 18.1). However, private insurers are under competitive pressure to reduce rising premiums. Hospitals with little market power face difficult price negotiations with insurers and will continue to be pressured to limit their price increases. Only those hospitals with strong market power will receive high FFS payments—from a shrinking private sector, however.

The Current Hospital Outlook

Hospital Consolidation

A great deal of hospital consolidation has been occurring over the past two decades. Increased hospital spending in recent years is the result of higher hospital prices charged to commercial insurers, not because patients are using hospitals more (see exhibit 18.1). A major contributor to these higher prices is ongoing hospital consolidation. Before 2008, the FTC was unable to prevent hospital mergers. The agency was overruled by the courts because judges believed that if nonprofit hospitals gained market power, they would not raise their prices. Studies conducted after 2008 by healthcare economists demonstrating that increased consolidation led to higher hospital prices enabled the FTC to be more successful in blocking anticompetitive hospital mergers.

After reviewing the research literature, Gaynor and Town (2012) concluded that hospital consolidation generally results in higher hospital prices. When hospital mergers occur in markets that are already consolidated, price increases exceed 20 percent. A second important finding is that physician–hospital consolidation was primarily for the purpose of gaining greater bargaining power over insurers and did not lead to more integration. Unless greater integration occurs, physician–hospital consolidation does not lead to improved quality or reduced costs.[6]

Cooper and colleagues (2015) also found that when hospitals face less competition, they are able to negotiate higher prices with private insurers. The prices charged by hospitals with monopoly power are, on average, 15 percent higher than prices in markets with four or more hospitals. Further, variations in hospital prices explain, to a large extent, why geographic variations exist in private health insurance expenditures. By contrast, geographic variations in Medicare expenditures are caused primarily by differences in quantity of services.

The ACA provides broader payment for ACOs and illness episodes, which encourages hospital consolidation and vertical integration between hospitals and physicians. Hospitals are employing greater numbers of physicians and purchasing more physician practices. Part of the reason for hospital employment of physicians is that Medicare physician fees are much higher when billed as a hospital outpatient visit than when billed as a visit at a freestanding physician's practice. Similarly, the Medicare fee for a magnetic resonance imaging test performed by a hospital is several times greater than the fee for the same test performed at a freestanding physician's practice. Medicare should pay the same price regardless of whether the service is performed in a hospital facility or the private physician's office.

Hospitals are moving more of their services to outpatient settings. As new technologies allow patients to be treated less invasively, more inpatient procedures can be performed more effectively in an outpatient setting. About 60 to 70 percent of all surgeries are now being performed in an outpatient setting, and outpatient services represent about 50 percent of hospital revenue (American Hospital Association 2018, table 3). To remain competitive, hospitals need to offer their services in wider geographic areas and at convenient locations for patients. Patients do not want to travel to a large hospital in an urban center for all the services they need.

Hospital consolidation and physician integration enable hospitals to raise prices, gain greater leverage with suppliers and pharmaceutical firms, and have better access to capital. A major strategy of hospitals has been, and will continue to be, to gain market power. Mergers, clinics and facilities located in a larger geographic area, and physician integration are key components of this strategy. These hospital systems are positioned to bill higher prices in an FFS market that will eventually shrink, and, as government and private payers seek to use less of the costliest components of care, be better able to compete as broader payment systems become more prevalent.

Expansion of Medicaid and Enrollment on ACA Health Insurance Exchanges

The ACA expanded coverage by broadening Medicaid eligibility and offering income-related subsidies on health insurance exchanges. Although Medicaid pays hospitals less than private payers do, and insurers offering coverage on exchanges are using narrow provider networks to limit their costs, hospitals have fared well in the past several years, and their total and net margins have increased. Uncompensated care costs have declined as millions of previously uninsured received coverage from state Medicaid expansions, and premium and cost-sharing subsidies encouraged many previously uninsured to enroll in ACA health insurance exchanges.

Changing Payment Systems

Hospital payment has changed over time. When Medicare was enacted in 1965, it paid hospitals according to the hospitals' costs of treating patients. Realizing that cost-based payment provides incentives for inefficiency and duplication of facilities and services, Medicare shifted to prospective payment—a fixed price per diagnosis—starting in 1983. The ACA also changed Medicare hospital payments. Greater efficiency incentives could be achieved by including a better continuum of care within that fixed price. Demonstrations using bundled or episode-based payment, payment to ACOs, and disallowing reimbursement to hospitals for preventable readmissions within 30 days of discharge are forms of prospective payment that incentivize the provider to keep the patient out of the hospital. This form of payment is in contrast to FFS, a retrospective fee that pays the provider once the patient is ill.

These ACA demonstration projects are a step toward capitation, which is a single annual payment per enrollee for all their medical services. Medicare already uses capitation for Medicare Advantage plans, which enroll about 28 percent of Medicare enrollees. Kaiser and health maintenance organizations (HMOs) have long relied on capitation in the private sector. Rather than giving Medicare beneficiaries an incentive to use Medicare Advantage plans, the government encouraged demonstration projects that offer enrollees or providers few financial incentives to limit high costs. Critics doubt that these ACO Medicare demonstrations will lead to large savings.

The assumption underlying the ACA's approach to limiting rising government hospital expenditures was the imposition of price controls, such as the ACA's assumed hospital productivity increases (hence, lower payments) and the IPAB's limits on Medicare expenditure increases to GDP plus 1 percent.

Hospital Strategies

Hospitals face various possible scenarios. The underlying assumptions of each scenario are that (1) under the ACA (according to the Medicare actuary), hospitals will receive less and less payment from Medicare; (2) to minimize utilization of inpatient admissions—the most expensive component of care—public and private payers will seek to have more care provided in less costly settings, such as outpatient centers or patients' homes; and (3) accelerating the shift from inpatient to outpatient care is the gradual change in payment systems by all types of payers (i.e., away from FFS and toward episode-based or capitation reimbursement).

FFS does not necessarily promote coordination of care, high-quality outcomes, or efficient use of services. Poor medical performance is not penalized; in fact, providers may receive additional revenues. Organizations that cut unnecessary services and shift patients to lower-cost settings earn lower revenues under FFS. The financial risk and additional cost of complications and hospital readmissions under FFS is shifted from providers to insurers (and enrollees, in the form of higher insurance premiums). Thus, reforming the delivery system requires reforming the payment system.

Capitation is a single payment per enrollee for all medical services (however, patients may be required to make copayments for some services). The broader the payment system, the greater the organization's incentive to be innovative in reducing medical costs, such as by understanding and anticipating the healthcare needs of its risk pool of enrollees and by preventing illness. Under episode-based payment and capitation, hospitals and physicians have an incentive to form integrated organizations. Further, measurement of quality and care outcomes is easier than under FFS. As Medicare payments for hospitals and physicians are lowered over time, broader payment systems offer providers an opportunity to deliver care in a more efficient and effective manner while enhancing their revenues.

A new trend in Medicare reimbursement is paying for value, not just volume of services. Hospitals and healthcare organizations can deliver care, but if their quality metrics do not meet specified levels, they will receive less payment for services, which could severely impact revenues. Hospitals must invest in personnel and technology to ensure that their care meets or exceeds specified standards.

Moving from FFS to capitation and value-based care will be difficult for hospitals and physicians; they will need to align their financial incentives, learn how to provide coordinated care, and invest in and develop sophisticated IT systems to become a fully integrated organization. This approach will take time.

Status Quo Scenario

Hospitals that continue to rely on inpatient admissions as their major source of revenue under FFS payment will experience declining admissions and falling payments. The annual Medicare DRG payment updates will become insufficient to cover rising hospital costs. Similarly, Medicaid hospital payments will be inadequate to cover the full costs of caring for patients. Consequently, hospital margins will decline, and hospitals will not be able to raise the capital needed to purchase the latest technology. In time, hospitals will no longer receive sufficient government funds to pay competitive wages and will have to reduce their staffing ratios. Eventually, publicly funded patients' access to care will be limited, and quality of care slowly will deteriorate.

Hospitals that have consolidated and increased their market power will be positioned to raise their rates to private insurers. Faced with high hospital prices and regulatory and competitive limits on premium rate increases, insurers likely will develop narrower hospital and provider networks (as they did during the 1990s) and try to shift more services to outpatient settings.

Under the status quo scenario, hospitals will seek to become larger, and those with market power will perform better than those without such pricing power. However, even for these hospitals, the expenditure growth rate will decline. As insurers direct their enrollees to outpatient services, hospitals will be used mostly for the very sick and for trauma cases.

A New Role for Hospitals

To become successful under the new payment systems, hospitals must develop new relationships with physicians. In the past, hospitals depended on physicians for admission referrals and to receive higher Medicare payments for outpatient services (e.g., surgery, imaging tests) when billed by the hospital rather than by independent physicians. When payment is based on an episode of care or on capitation, hospitals need physicians to be able to provide coordinated care to reduce medical costs and improve patient outcomes. Physician and hospital incentives must be aligned to achieve these desired outcomes.

Under FFS, insurers and the government bear the risk. As hospitals form ACOs and engage in broader payment systems, risk is transferred from the payer to the ACO. Data are essential for managing risk, understanding costs of caring for different types of patients, and accepting risk-based contracts. "Because insurers pay claims for all doctor visits, lab tests, and other care, they get a full view of their members. Hospital systems say they need direct access to [those] data, which they can get by offering their own plans, to manage patients better, avoiding duplication and detecting and treating problems early to head off pricey procedures later" (Mathews 2012). Only then will hospitals be able to manage the population health of their enrollees, anticipating and preventing illness particularly among the chronically ill.

Several hospital systems have developed their own health plans, offering HMOs that rely on their own hospitals and physicians, while limiting enrollees' access to out-of-network providers. Whether hospital systems develop their own health plans or continue to contract with insurers, hospital must adapt to new public and private payment changes. To survive the trend toward less inpatient care and toward population health, hospitals must think of themselves as health systems, an integrated organization with a capability for data analytics, able to accept risk contracts, rely on physicians to coordinate care, expand outpatient capabilities in multiple locations, and provide—in addition to acute care—home health care and telehealth services at times convenient to the working population.

To control both cost and quality, the hospital/health system needs to become vertically integrated and achieve greater control over the entire continuum of care—from wellness and prevention to acute care and to post-acute services such as home health care.

Summary

Hospital fortunes have changed over time. Managed care and Medicare DRG payment greatly reduced hospital utilization, created excess capacity, and weakened hospitals' bargaining power over insurers. Over time, hospital capacity decreased, mergers occurred, and managed care broadened its provider networks; hospitals consolidated and used their increased bargaining power over insurers to raise prices and enhance profitability.

The future presents threats and opportunities. Technological developments have enabled a greater number of complex procedures to be performed in an outpatient setting. Payment systems also have provided incentives to perform more services in outpatient settings. A gradual but dramatic reduction in hospital rates for Medicare patients will occur as a result of the ACA. Hospitals' growing reliance on government payment is likely to result in a slower growth rate in hospital expenditures. As the number of publicly insured individuals increases, hospital competition for the diminishing pool of privately insured patients will intensify. Changes in payment systems offer the potential for greater revenues to those hospitals and physicians able to integrate their services over the entire continuum of care. Hospitals unable to do so will rely on FFS and a shrinking revenue base. Because of changing payment systems and the need to coordinate care, hospitals are employing physicians and purchasing physician practices. Broader payment systems require integrated delivery organizations to manage risk (as they become similar to insurers) and collect enrollee data to anticipate and reduce preventable illnesses.

Payment system changes will result in many disruptive innovations in the delivery of medical services. In a $3 trillion industry, huge financial rewards are available to those who can cut costs while improving patient outcomes and satisfaction. Providers traditionally have concentrated on their own role in caring for the sick. Will hospitals be able to think in terms of the entire continuum of care? Will hospitals be able to think in terms of managing the health of a population? The future of hospitals will be determined by how well they can work with physicians to deliver coordinated care while reducing rising medical costs and improving patient outcomes. Many hospitals will experience difficulty in adjusting to new payment systems.

Discussion Questions

1. What is the outlook for hospital cost increases?
2. How has Medicare hospital payment changed over time?
3. What are the likely economic assumptions hospitals should consider in developing their future strategies?
4. Why do hospital mergers increase hospitals' bargaining power over insurers?
5. What are two hospital strategies for responding to new payment system changes?

Notes

1. The income of an individual at 138 percent and 400 percent of the FPL in 2018 is $16,643 and $48,240, respectively. For a family of four, the respective income levels are $33,948 and $98,400.

2. Hospitals are expanding their emergency departments (EDs) as a place for lower-acuity patients to access care 24 hours a day, seven days a week. A RAND study found that EDs are now responsible for about half of all inpatient admissions and accounted for all growth in admissions between 2003 and 2009 (the period studied) (Gonzalez Morganti et al. 2013). The growth in hospital admissions has stagnated. It was previously believed that EDs served mainly the uninsured, but this is no longer the case. Insured patients are also using EDs (which may lead to an admission), and they have become a new source of revenue for the hospital.

3. Under the ACA, hospitals will receive lower Medicare payments if a patient is readmitted to the hospital within 30 days for one of five specified diagnoses (heart attack, heart failure, pneumonia, chronic obstructive pulmonary disease, and hip and knee arthroplasty). For example, after being discharged from the hospital for hip replacement surgery, a Medicare patient receives care in a skilled nursing facility and then continues her recovery at home, using physical therapy services and visiting her physician. The hospital's spending per beneficiary would be based on all these costs. Consequently, the hospital must coordinate all elements of care, including the possibility that the patient develops an infection and has to be readmitted to the hospital.

4. Although few payers pay full charges, hospitals attempt to collect 100 percent of their charges from those who have not negotiated a discounted price. Individuals most likely to be billed full charges are automobile accident victims brought to the hospital by an ambulance.

At that point, neither the accident victim nor his auto insurance company is in a position to negotiate a discounted rate from the hospital. Billing auto insurance companies full charges is very profitable for hospitals.

5. By merging, hospitals decrease the number of competitors with which the insurer can contract, and their new demand curve will be less price elastic, enabling them to raise prices and increase total revenue. The term *price elasticity of demand* is the percentage change in quantity demanded with a 1 percent change in price. When the percentage change in quantity demanded exceeds the percentage change in price, the good or service is considered to be price elastic. For example, if the price decreases by 5 percent and the quantity demanded increases by 10 percent, the price elasticity equals –2. If the percentage change in price is greater than the percentage change in quantity, the service is *price inelastic* (e.g., price increases by 5 percent and quantity demanded decreases by 2 percent). Price elasticity is important in determining the effect of a change in price on revenue. When a service is price inelastic, increasing the price will raise total revenue; decreasing the price will lower total revenue. Conversely, when the demand for a service is price elastic, increasing the price decreases total revenue. Price elasticity is mainly determined by the similarity of substitutes. A hospital with good substitutes (i.e., comparable hospitals) will have a price-elastic demand curve; if it raises prices, its total revenue will decrease.

6. Hospitals often claim that their merger will achieve greater efficiency and hence lower prices. Economies of scale occur when a firm's output increases by a greater proportion than the increase in its input cost; average total cost per unit, therefore, decreases as output increases. Large firms' unit costs are lower than those of small firms. Economies of scope occur when it is less expensive for a firm to produce multiple related services (or products) than it is for the services (or products) to be produced separately by different firms. An example is when a physician who undertakes stem cell research also provides stem cell therapy. In this case, it is less costly to provide the research and therapy together than separately by different firms. When economies of scope exist, multiproduct (service) firms are more efficient than single-product (service) firms. Economies of scale are unrelated to economies of scope.

References

American Hospital Association. n.d. *Hospital Statistics.* Various editions. Chicago: American Hospital Association.

———. 2018. *Hospital Statistics, 2018 Edition*. Chicago: American Hospital Association.

———. 2017. *Hospital Statistics, 2017 Edition*. Chicago: American Hospital Association.

———. 2016. "Trends in Hospital Financing." Chapter 4 in *TrendWatch Chartbook: Trends Affecting Hospitals and Health Systems*. Accessed April 2018. www.aha.org/guidesreports/2017-12-11-trendwatch-chartbook.

Centers for Medicare & Medicaid Services. 2018. "National Health Expenditure Data." Last modified January. www.cms.gov/Research-Statistics-Data-and-Systems/Statistics-Trends-and-Reports/NationalHealthExpendData/NationalHealth|AccountsHistorical.html.

———. 2017. "CMS Program Statistics: Medicare Utilization." Last modified June 21. www.cms.gov/Research-Statistics-Data-and-Systems/Statistics-Trends-and-Reports/CMSProgramStatistics/2015/2015_Utilization.html#Medicare Outpatient Facility.

Cooper, Z., S. Craig, M. Gaynor, and J. Van Reenen. 2015. "The Price Ain't Right? Hospital Prices and Health Spending on the Privately Insured." Health Care Pricing Project. Published May. www.healthcarepricingproject.org/papers/paper-1.

Cunningham, P., R. Garfield, and R. Rudowitz. 2015. "How Are Hospitals Faring Under the Affordable Care Act? Early Experiences from Ascension Health." Kaiser Family Foundation issue brief. Published April 30. www.kff.org/health-reform/issue-brief/how-are-hospitals-faring-under-the-affordable-care-act-early-experiences-from-ascension-health/.

Foster, R. 2011. "The Estimated Effect of the Affordable Care Act on Medicare and Medicaid Outlays and Total National Health Care Expenditures." Testimony Before the House Committee on the Budget, January 26. http://budget.house.gov/uploadedfiles/fostertestimony1262011.pdf.

Gaynor, M., and R. Town. 2012. "The Impact of Hospital Consolidation—Update." Robert Wood Johnson Foundation. Published June. www.rwjf.org/content/dam/farm/reports/issue_briefs/2012/rwjf73261.

Gonzalez Morganti, K., S. Bauhoff, J. Blanchard, M. Abir, N. Iyer, A. Smith, J. Vesely, E. Okeke, and A. Kellermann. 2013. *The Evolving Role of Emergency Departments in the United States*. RAND Corp. Accessed April 2018. www.rand.org/content/dam/rand/pubs/research_reports/RR200/RR280/RAND_RR280.sum.pdf.

Ho, K. 2009. "Insurer–Provider Networks in the Medical Care Market." *American Economic Review* 99 (1): 393–430.

Kaiser Family Foundation. 2013. "Summary of the Affordable Care Act." Published April 25. www.kff.org/health-reform/fact-sheet/summary-of-the-affordable-care-act/.

Mathews, A. W. 2012. "Hospital Systems Branch Out as Insurers." *Wall Street Journal*. Published December 16. www.wsj.com/articles/SB10001424127887324677204578183041243834084.

Office of Management and Budget. 2018. "Historical Tables." Accessed January. www.whitehouse.gov/omb/historical-tables/.

Paulus, R., K. Davis, and G. Steele. 2008. "Continuous Innovation in Health Care: Implications of the Geisinger Experience." *Health Affairs* 27 (5): 1235–45.

White, C., A. Bond, and J. Reschovsky. 2013. "High and Varying Prices for Privately Insured Patients Underscore Hospital Market Power." HSC Research Brief No. 27. Published September. www.hschange.org/CONTENT/1375/.

COST SHIFTING

The theory of cost shifting has often been used as the basis for public policy proposals, such as an employer mandate and the Affordable Care Act (ACA). Employers and insurers point to cost shifting as one reason for the rise in employees' health insurance premiums. When one purchaser—whether Medicare, Medicaid, or the uninsured patient—does not pay the full charges, many believe that hospitals and physicians raise their prices to those who can afford to pay, namely those with private insurance. Cost shifting is considered unfair, and its elimination is, in large part, why large employers (whose employees have health insurance) favor the mandate that all employers provide their employees with health insurance. One rationale for the ACA set forth by President Obama was that those with insurance pay higher premiums to cover the costs of the uninsured who rely on the emergency department for care that can be delivered in other, much less expensive, settings.

Those who concur with the cost-shifting hypothesis believe that the ACA slows Medicare payment updates to hospitals to finance, in part, expanded Medicaid eligibility and provide subsidies to those buying health insurance on state exchanges. These lower hospital payments will, for many hospitals, reduce Medicare prices below the costs of caring for these patients. Will hospitals shift costs to private insurers to make up for these lower payments, resulting in much higher private health insurance premiums?

Evidence of cost shifting is based on the observation that different payers pay different prices for similar services (see exhibit 18.1). Private payers have always had higher payment-to-cost ratios (higher price markups) than have Medicare and Medicaid, and Medicare has generally paid more than Medicaid. The payment-to-cost ratios for all three payers have changed over time. Exhibit 18.1 suggests that when Medicare and Medicaid have low payment-to-cost ratios (which result in low profit margins for providers), private payers have high price-to-cost ratios. Still to be examined, however, is whether the relationships are causal—that is, whether low public payment–cost relationships lead to high private payment-to-cost ratios.

Although the logic of cost shifting may seem straightforward, it provokes troubling questions. For example, can a hospital or physician merely increase prices to those who can pay to recover losses from those who do not pay? If the provider can shift costs, why do hospitals complain about the uncompensated care they are forced to provide? Further, if providers can offset their losses by

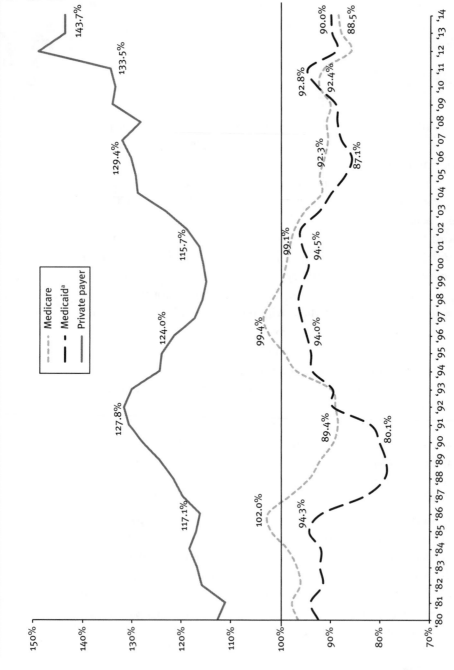

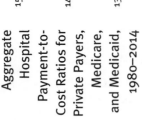

EXHIBIT 18.1
Aggregate
Hospital
Payment-to-
Cost Ratios for
Private Payers,
Medicare,
and Medicaid,
1980–2014

aIncludes Medicaid disproportionate-share payments.

Note: Private payer data available until 2014.

Sources: 1980–2014 data from American Hospital Association (2016a, table 4.4); 2015 data from American Hospital Association (2016b); 2016 data from American Hospital Association (2017).

raising prices to those with insurance, why have they not done so and thereby earned greater profits?

To better understand cost shifting, we must discuss (1) the provider's objective when it prices its services and (2) how different objectives result in different pricing strategies.

Setting Prices to Maximize Profits

Organizations typically price their services to maximize profits—that is, to make as much money as possible. This is the simplest objective to start with in analyzing hospital and physician price setting. Assume that the hospital has two sets of patients: those who can pay and those who cannot pay for services. Exhibit 18.2 illustrates how a profit-maximizing price is set for the insured group of patients. The relationship between price (P) and quantity (Q) is inverse, meaning the lower the price, the more units are likely to be purchased. Total revenue (TR) is price multiplied by quantity. As the price is decreased, more units will be sold, and TR will increase; after some point, however, the greater number of units sold will not offset the lower price per unit and TR will actually decline. The effect on TR when price is lowered and more units are sold is shown by the TR curve in exhibit 18.3.

To determine the price and output that result in the largest profit, we must also know the costs of producing that output. Total cost (TC) consists of two parts: (1) fixed costs, which do not vary as output changes (e.g., rent for an office or depreciation on a building), and (2) variable costs, which do

Price (P), $	Quantity (Q)	Total Revenue (TR), $	Total Cost (TC), $	Profit, $	TC_2, $	$Profit_2$, $
11	1	11	9	2	11	0
10	2	20	13	7	17	3
9	3	27	17	10	23	4
8	4	32	21	11	29	3
7	5	35	25	10	35	0
6	6	36	29	7	41	−5
5	7	35	33	2	47	−12
4	8	32	37	−5	53	−21
3	9	27	41	−14	59	−32

EXHIBIT 18.2
Determining the Profit-Maximizing Price

EXHIBIT 18.3
Profit-
Maximizing
Price With
and Without
a Change in
Variable Cost

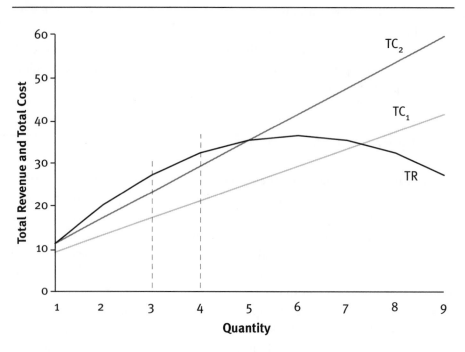

vary. For this example, fixed costs are assumed to be $5 and variable costs are constant at $4 per unit. The difference between TR and TC is profit. According to exhibit 18.2, the largest amount of profit occurs when the price is $8 and output equals four units. At that price, TR is $32, TC is $21 ($5 fixed cost plus $16 variable costs), and profit is $11. According to exhibit 18.3, the greatest difference between the total cost line (TC) and TR (profit) occurs at four units of output.

Raising or lowering the price will only reduce profits. If the hospital decreases its price from $8 to $7, it will have to cut the price on all units sold. The hospital's volume will increase; TR will rise from $32 to $35, or $3. Because the variable cost of the extra unit sold is $4, the hospital will lose money on that last unit. The profit at a price of $7 will be $10. Similarly, if the hospital raises its price from $8 to $9, it will sell one fewer unit, reducing its variable cost by $4 but forgoing $5 in revenue (see exhibit 18.4).[1] Changing the price once it is at the profit-maximizing price lowers the hospital's profit.

Exhibit 18.2 illustrates several important points. First, establishing a profit-maximizing price means the price is set so that the additional revenue received is equal to the additional cost of serving one more patient. When the change in TR is equal to the change in TC, choosing any other price will result in less profit.

Second, if the hospital's fixed costs increase from $5 to $11, the hospital should not change its price; if it does, it will make even less profit. With

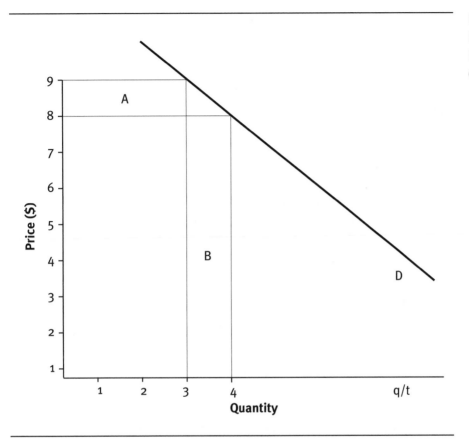

EXHIBIT 18.4
Effect on Total
Revenue of a
Change in Price

an increase in fixed costs, profit will decline by $6 at every quantity sold. At a price of $8, the hospital will make a total profit of $5; TR is $32, while TC is now $27 ($11 plus $16). If the hospital raised its price to $9 to compensate for the higher fixed costs, TR will be $27, TC will be $23 ($11 plus $12), and total profit will fall to $4. Thus, changes in fixed costs should not affect the hospital's profit-maximizing price.

Third, if the hospital's variable costs changed—perhaps because nurses' wages or the cost of supplies increased—the hospital will find it profitable to change its price. For example, if variable costs rise by $2 and the price–quantity relationship is unchanged, the largest profit will occur at a price of $9 (TR $- TC_2 =$ Profit$_2$ in exhibit 18.2). The higher variable cost is shown in exhibit 18.3 as TC_2. The distance between TR and TC_2 (which is profit) is greatest at three units of output. If the price per unit remains at $8 when variable costs increase to $6 per unit, the addition to TR from producing four rather than three units is only $5. The hospital will lose money on that last unit, the cost of which is $6. Thus, by raising the price and producing fewer units, the higher TR slightly exceeds the additional cost of producing that last unit. Hospitals, therefore, will be expected to raise their prices as their variable costs increase.

Similarly, if variable costs decrease, the hospital will realize more profit by lowering the price.

Fourth, hospitals also will be expected to change the price they charge if the relationship between price and quantity were to change. The price–quantity relationship is a measure of how price sensitive purchasers are to changes in the hospital's price. When the price is changed and quantity changes by a small percentage, purchasers are not very price sensitive; the demand for the hospital's service is *price inelastic*. Conversely, when quantity changes by a greater percentage than the change in price, purchasers are said to be more price sensitive; the demand is *price elastic*. As the demand for the hospital's services becomes more price sensitive (price elastic), the hospital will be expected to lower its price, even if there is no change in its costs.[2]

For example, if five hospitals exist in a market and each is considered to be a relatively good substitute for the others in terms of location, services, reputation, medical staff, and so on, each hospital's demand is considered to be very price sensitive. In competing to be included in different HMO and insurer provider networks, each hospital will compete on price. If just one hospital lowers its price, it will cause large increases in that hospital's patient volume. Similarly, raising its price when the other hospitals do not will cause that hospital to lose a large portion of its market share.

Conversely, a hospital that is the sole community provider or has the only trauma unit, for example, faces a less price-sensitive demand for its services or its trauma unit. The hospital's prices will be higher than they would be if good substitutes were available for its services. If the hospital is already charging a profit-maximizing price to its paying patients, and the variable costs of serving paying patients have not changed, the hospital will make even less profit by further increasing prices to paying patients. Referring to exhibit 18.2, if the hospital raises its price from $8 to $9 simply because other patients did not pay, the hospital will forgo profit. Assuming the hospital wants to make as much money as possible from those who can afford to pay, the hospital will not raise its price to those patients unless there is a change in variable costs or in the price–quantity relationship. Because neither factor changes when another group of patients pays less, it will not make sense for the hospital to charge its paying patients more.

Based on this explanation of how a profit-maximizing price is set, changes in prices can be explained by changes in the variable costs of caring for patients or by a change in the price-sensitivity relationship facing a hospital (or a physician).

Contrary to what many people believe, when the government lowers the price it pays for Medicare or Medicaid patients, physicians will likely *reduce* the prices they charge to higher-paying patients. For example, assume that a physician serves two types of patients: private patients and Medicaid patients. The government determines the price charged to Medicaid patients, whereas the physician sets the price for private patients. Traditionally, the price received by the physician for treating private patients is higher than that received for treating Medicaid patients. The physician presumably allocates her time so that revenues per unit of time are the same, regardless of the types of patients served. To produce equal returns when the prices for Medicaid and private patients differ, the physician may spend less time with the Medicaid patient.

If the government further decreases the price it pays for Medicaid patients, the physician is likely to decide that she can earn more by shifting some time away from Medicaid patients and toward caring for more private patients. As more physicians limit the time they spend with Medicaid patients and allocate more time to the private market, the supply of physician time in this market grows. With an increase in supply, physicians will be willing to reduce their prices to attract more private patients. Assuming limited demand creation by physicians, a lower price for Medicaid patients is likely to result in *lower* physician fees for private patients.

Assuming that the objective of hospitals and physicians is to make as much money as possible, these two examples suggest that prices for private patients will be unchanged or reduced when another payer—government—pays the provider less.

Origins of Claims of Cost Shifting

Based on the earlier discussion, why do private purchasers of medical services claim they are being charged more to make up for the lower prices paid by the government? The belief that cost shifting is occurring may simply be an artifact of trends over time in rising hospital prices and uncompensated care. Hospitals may appear to be raising prices to compensate for lower prices charged to other patients, but hospital prices to private payers have increased for two reasons: (1) variable costs have increased as expenses for wages and supplies have risen and (2) changes in the hospitals' payer mixes—growth in the proportion of patients who are less price sensitive—may have enabled them to raise their markups on services to certain types of private patients. This association between rising prices and uncompensated care does not necessarily indicate a causal relationship.

However, a logical explanation, unrelated to cost shifting, does exist for why some purchasers pay more for the same service than do other purchasers. Some purchasers may be more price sensitive than others. In the past, private patients had either indemnity insurance or Blue Cross hospital coverage; because hospitals had a close relationship with Blue Cross (hospitals started and controlled Blue Cross), Blue Cross was charged a lower price than were indemnity insurers. The price–quantity relationship for those with indemnity insurance represented the average relationship for everyone in the indemnity plan. However, as employers began offering different types of health plans, such as health maintenance organizations (HMOs), preferred provider organizations (PPOs), and managed care, in addition to the traditional indemnity plan, and as employees had to pay varying premiums and copayments under these plans, the price–quantity relationships of these plans differed. Those with indemnity insurance could choose whatever hospital and physicians they desired. Other plans, however, were more restrictive in determining the providers their subscribers could use. HMOs and PPOs were likely to bargain with providers for lower prices in return for directing their subscribers to these approved providers.

Faced with different price–quantity relationships with different purchasers, hospitals began charging different prices to each type of payer. These prices take into consideration the price sensitivity of each of these insurance plans. Patients remaining in the traditional indemnity plan are charged the highest prices because they are not restricted in their use of providers. Their insurers cannot promise to direct them to particular hospitals and are least able to negotiate lower hospital prices. It is the willingness of an insurer to shift its enrollees to another hospital that results in the greater price sensitivity.

Price Discrimination

Charging according to what the market will bear is not really cost shifting, but rather simply charging a profit-maximizing price to each group; this is price discrimination. Services for which purchasers are willing to pay more have higher markups. Airlines charge higher prices for first-class seating and lower prices for 21-day advance purchases, for example. Movie theaters charge lower prices for matinees and to senior citizens. Each of these industries is setting prices according to different groups' willingness to pay; each group has a different price–quantity relationship.

Hospital pricing is no different. Hospitals placing a proportionately higher markup on laboratory tests or drugs used by inpatients than on the room-and-board fee are engaging in price discrimination. Patients who must pay part of the bill themselves can more easily compare hospital room-and-board rates before they enter the hospital; therefore, hospitals have to be price competitive on their room rates. Once a patient is hospitalized, however, he has little choice in what he pays for services rendered in the hospital. The price–quantity relationships for inpatient services are quite insensitive to prices charged. Hospitals do not face any competition for laboratory tests or other services provided to their inpatients. Thus, their markup for these services is much higher.

Price discrimination is an important reason some purchasers can pay lower hospital prices. A large employer or an HMO willing to direct its employees or enrollees to a particular hospital will receive a lower price for the same service than will a small employer with only 10 employees negotiating with the same hospital. The hospital's price–quantity relationship is more price sensitive when the hospital negotiates with a large purchaser than when the hospital deals with a small employer. The small employer does not pay higher prices because the large purchaser pays a lower price. The small employer pays more because the hospital is less concerned about losing 10 patients than losing 1,000 patients from a large purchaser.

Even if the government increased its payments to hospitals for treating Medicare patients, the price to the small employer is not reduced because the price–quantity relationship for these patients (who are less price sensitive) is unchanged. Only if the small employer becomes part of a large purchasing group (which is willing to offer a hospital a greater volume of patients in return for lower prices) can that small employer receive a lower hospital price. Different prices to different purchasers are related to how price sensitive the purchasers are rather than to what other purchasers are paying. As the insurance market has become more segmented with HMOs, PPOs, self-insured employer groups, traditional indemnity-type insurance plans, and so on, hospitals have developed different pricing strategies for each group.

Empirical evidence supports the view that hospital prices are not raised to some purchasers when prices are reduced to large purchasers. Dranove and White (1998) found that hospitals that had a higher proportion of Medicaid patients (20 percent or more of their budgets) did not increase prices to other paying patients when Medicaid decreased its reimbursement; if anything, hospitals lowered their prices to private payers.[3] Research reinforces the finding that hospital cost shifting is minimal, if at all. White (2013) found that when Medicare cut its payment rate by 10 percent, hospital rates charged to private payers were *reduced* by 3 to 8 percent. By lowering the prices charged to private payers, hospitals attempt to attract a greater volume of higher-paying patients.

Conditions Under Which Cost Shifting Can Occur

Under certain circumstances, however, cost shifting may occur. Some hospitals may have a different pricing objective—they do not price to maximize their profits. These hospitals may voluntarily forgo some profits to maintain good community relationships. When hospitals do not set profit-maximizing prices, increases in uncompensated care or fixed costs may cause the hospital to raise its prices to those groups who have more ability to pay. For example, *average cost pricing* occurs when a hospital sets its price by relating it to the average cost of caring for all its patients. If one payer (e.g., the government) decides to pay the hospital less, the average price goes up for all other payers. For cost shifting to occur, the hospital must have bargaining or market power that it has not used; the purchasers of hospital (or physician) services must be relatively insensitive to the higher prices. If the purchasers switch to other providers or use fewer services as a result of the provider's cost shifting, the provider's revenues and profits decline.

Does cost shifting explain why private patients are paying higher medical prices today? Purchasers have become more price sensitive since the mid-1980s. Given the increased competitive market in which providers find themselves, they are likely unwilling to forgo profits by not setting profit-maximizing prices. Forgoing profits means the hospital has no better use for those funds. Two ways in which the hospital could use those higher profits are to purchase new equipment or to start new services to increase its revenues. The medical staff, an important constituency within the hospital, also desires new equipment and facilities. Paying higher wages makes it easier to attract needed nursing and technical personnel. Hospitals could enhance their community image and market themselves by providing screening and health awareness programs to their communities. Further, additional funds could always be used to provide care to those in the community who cannot afford it and who are not covered by public programs.

The benefits to the hospital of forgoing profit on some payer groups are unlikely to exceed the benefits to the hospital of using that forgone profit in other ways. By not setting profit-maximizing prices, the hospital's decision makers place a greater weight on benefiting some purchaser group than on using those funds for other constituencies. One type of cost shifting occurs when the government pays hospitals a fixed price for inpatient care of Medicare patients but reimburses outpatient services on a cost basis.

If the hospital has $100 in indirect administrative costs to allocate between inpatient units (paid according to a fixed-price diagnosis-related group) and outpatient units (paid on a cost basis), the hospital will select a cost-allocation method that optimizes its payment from the government—namely, the method that allocates a greater portion of the $100 to outpatient units.

Another type of cost shifting occurs when the government shifts its costs to employers. For example, when the government requires all employers to buy health insurance for their employees, the government's Medicaid expenditures for employees and their dependents who are otherwise eligible for Medicaid are reduced.

The Direction of Causality

Payment-to-cost ratios for all three payers—private, Medicare, and Medicaid—have fluctuated over time (see exhibit 18.1). It appears that the payment-to-cost ratios between public (Medicare and Medicaid) and private payers are inversely related; when public ratios decline (low or negative profit margins), private ratios rise (high profit margins). However, the causality likely goes in the opposite direction—when private payment-to-cost ratios increase, public payment-to-cost ratios decrease.

Stensland, Gaumer, and Miller (2010) found that as hospitals gain market power, they are better able to increase their prices to private payers and, hence, increase their profits. Because nonprofit hospitals cannot distribute their profits to shareholders, the funds are used to expand services, invest in new technology, add staff, purchase physician practices, provide greater patient amenities, and so on. The expenditure of these "profits" increases hospital costs per discharge. The higher costs per discharge affect patients of all payer types—public as well as private. With higher hospital costs per discharge and fixed Medicare and Medicaid prices, the price-to-cost ratio of public payers declines; that is, the higher hospital costs and the same payment result in lower margins from public payers.

Stensland, Gaumer, and Miller (2010) also determined that more profitable hospitals had higher costs per discharge than did less profitable hospitals, and that the former also had lower Medicare payment-to-cost ratios. The opposite was also found: Hospitals under financial stress had lower costs per discharge and higher Medicare margins.

Over time, hospitals' market power has changed, leading to different private and public payment-to-cost ratios. During the early 1980s, the payment-to-cost ratios for private payers, Medicare, and Medicaid were relatively close; the economy-wide recession was ending; and Medicare was beginning to shift from cost-based payment to fixed prices per admission. The late 1980s and early 1990s was a period of economic growth, and hospital private payment-to-cost ratios rose. Managed care had its greatest effect in the mid-to-late 1990s; hospitals developed excess capacity; intense price competition developed among hospitals seeking to be included in managed care's provider networks; hospitals reduced their costs to remain competitive; and managed care plans negotiated large price discounts from hospitals. Private payment-to-cost ratios declined.

In the past decade, hospital mergers have increased (Kaufman Hall 2017). And as broadened managed care provider networks have lessened insurers' bargaining power, hospitals have gained greater market power. Hospital price markups have increased rapidly (as shown in exhibit 18.1), returning to the situation that existed before the managed care period of the 1980s and early 1990s.

We should examine changes in hospital payment-to-cost ratios for each payer with respect to trends in hospitals' market power. Contrary to what many believe—that low Medicare and Medicaid payments lead to increases in hospital prices to private payers—the causality goes in a different direction: Hospitals' market power and their ability to raise prices to private payers result in a higher cost structure, which, with fixed public prices, leads to lower public payment-to-cost ratios.

Summary

The cost-shifting hypothesis has important policy implications regarding how the ACA has relied on reductions in Medicare hospital payment updates to finance its insurance coverage expansions. Will lower Medicare hospital payments cause private insurance premiums to increase faster than would otherwise occur?

In the past, when insurance premiums were paid almost entirely by the employer and managed care was not yet popular, hospitals probably were less interested in making as much money as possible. Many hospitals were reimbursed according to their costs, and they could achieve many of their goals without having to set profit-maximizing prices. However, as occupancy rates declined and hospitals were left with excess capacity, price competition increased, HMOs and PPOs entered the market, and hospitals could no longer count on having their costs reimbursed—regardless of what those costs were. Hospital profitability declined. Hospitals that had not set prices to make as much money as possible began to do so. Some cost shifting occurred during this transition period.

Today, differences in hospital prices for different payer groups are more likely the result of price discrimination than cost shifting. The difference between these two explanations is significant. Cost-shifting proponents believe that unless government payments to hospitals and physicians are increased, private payers (e.g., insurers and employers) will have to pay higher prices for healthcare. Economists, however, predict that with lower government-provider payments, medical prices to private payers will decrease, not increase. As the payment for one type of patient is reduced, physicians can earn more money by shifting some time away from these less profitable patients. The supply of physician time in the private market will increase, resulting in lower prices to private payers.

In addition, as hospitals gain market power through mergers, they will be able to price discriminate and raise their prices to private payers. Because nonprofit hospitals cannot distribute their profits, they use them to increase the hospital's cost structure by adding new facilities and services. These higher costs per discharge affect all payers. Thus, while hospitals can raise their payment-to-cost ratios to private payers, higher costs per discharge and fixed government payments result in lower public payment-to-cost ratios.

Discussion Questions

1. Explain why an increase in a hospital's fixed costs or an increase in the number of uninsured cared for by the hospital will not change the hospital's profit-maximizing price.

2. Why would a change in a hospital's variable costs change the hospital's profit-maximizing price?

3. Why are hospitals able to charge different purchasers different prices for the same medical services?

4. Under what circumstances can cost shifting occur?

5. How does cost shifting differ from price discrimination?

Notes

1. Exhibit 18.4 is another way to illustrate how a change in price affects TR. Price is shown along the vertical axis, and quantity (number of units sold each month or year) is shown along the horizontal axis. When the price is $9 per unit, three units are sold. When price is reduced to $8, four units are sold. Cutting the price from $9 to $8 results in a decrease in TR of $1 for each of the three units that would have been sold at $9. This loss of $3 is shown by area A. However, lowering the price to $8 gains $8 for that additional unit sold, shown as area B. The difference between area A (loss of $3) and area B (gain of $8) is $5, which is the increase in TR from selling one additional unit. Increasing the price from $8 to $9 has the opposite effect—a loss of $5 in TR.

2. The effect of price sensitivity (economists use the term *price elasticity*) on hospital prices and markups (percentage increase in price over cost) is based on the following formula:

$$\text{Price} = \frac{\text{MC}}{1 - \dfrac{1}{\text{price elasticity}}}$$

MC is the marginal cost of producing an additional unit and is assumed to be equal to the average variable cost. For simplicity, assume MC = $1,000. Thus, if a hospital believes the price sensitivity of a particular employee group is such that a 1 percent increase (decrease) in the hospital's price leads to a 2 percent decrease (increase) in admissions, the hospital's markup—applied to its average variable costs—is 100 percent:

$$\frac{\$1,000}{1 - \dfrac{1}{2}} = \frac{\$1,000}{\dfrac{1}{2}} = \$1,000 \times \frac{2}{1} = \$2,000.$$

If use of services is more price sensitive, such that a 1 percent price increase (decrease) leads to a 3 percent decrease (increase) in admissions, the markup is 50 percent:

$$\frac{\$1,000}{1-\frac{1}{3}} = \frac{\$1,000}{\frac{2}{3}} = \$1,000 \times \frac{3}{2} = \$1,000. \times 1.5 = \$1,500.$$

If the hospital's variable costs of serving patients were the same in both examples, the prices charged to each employee group could vary greatly depending on their price sensitivity. Even those hospitals that have few good substitutes and a less price-elastic demand for their services will always price in the elastic portion of their demand curve. For an explanation, see Browning and Zupan (2014, 313).

3. Dranove, Garthwaite, and Ody (2013) analyzed whether nonprofit hospitals increased their prices (cost shifted) as a result of large endowment losses caused by the 2008 recession. The authors reasoned that the losses of endowment revenue would be no different from decreased Medicare or Medicaid revenue. They found that the average hospital did not cost shift; only 10 percent of the hospitals studied that likely had some market power raised their prices compared with what would have occurred in the absence of their financial losses.

Additional Reading

Morrisey, M. 2003. "Cost Shifting: New Myths, Old Confusions, and Enduring Reality." *Health Affairs* (web exclusive): w3-489–w3-491.

References

American Hospital Association. 2017. "Underpayment by Medicare and Medicaid Fact Sheet." Published December. www.aha.org/system/files/2018-01/medicare medicaidunderpmt%202017.pdf.

———. 2016a. "Trends in Hospital Financing." Chapter 4 in *TrendWatch Chartbook 2016: Trends Affecting Hospitals and Health Systems.* Accessed April 2018. www.aha.org/research/reports/tw/chartbook/2016/2016chartbook.pdf.

———. 2016b. "Underpayment by Medicare and Medicaid Fact Sheet." Published December. www.aha.org/system/files/2018-02/2016-dec-medicaremedicaid underpmt.pdf.

Browning, E., and M. Zupan. 2014. *Microeconomics: Theory and Applications*, 12th ed. New York: John Wiley & Sons.

Dranove, D., C. Garthwaite, and C. Ody. 2013. "How Do Hospitals Respond to Negative Financial Shocks? The Impact of the 2008 Stock Market Crash." National Bureau of Economic Research Working Paper No. 18853. Published February. www.nber.org/papers/w18853.pdf.

Dranove, D., and W. White. 1998. "Medicaid-Dependent Hospitals and Their Patients: How Have They Fared?" *Health Services Research* 33 (2, Part I): 163–85.

Kaufman Hall. 2017. "Hospital Merger and Acquisition Activity Continues to Climb According to Kaufman Hall Analysis." Published April 19. www.kaufmanhall.com/news/hospital-merger-and-acquisition-activity-continues-climb-according-kaufman-hall-analysis.

Stensland, J., Z. Gaumer, and M. Miller. 2010. "Private-Payer Profits Can Induce Negative Medicare Margins." *Health Affairs* 29 (5): 1045–51.

White, C. 2013. "Contrary to Cost-Shift Theory, Lower Medicare Hospital Payment Rates for Inpatient Care Lead to Lower Private Payment Rates." *Health Affairs* 32 (5): 935–43.

CAN PRICE CONTROLS LIMIT MEDICAL EXPENDITURE INCREASES?

I n the continuing debate over how to limit rising medical expenditures, supporters of regulation—such as those who favor a single-payer system— propose placing controls on the prices physicians and hospitals charge. To prevent hospitals and physicians from circumventing such controls by simply performing more services, they also would impose an overall limit (also known as *global budget*) on total medical expenditures.

Price controls and global budgets may seem to be obvious approaches for limiting rising medical expenditures, but the potential consequences should be examined before placing almost one-fifth (17 percent) of the US economy (more than $3.3 trillion a year, as of 2016) under government control. The healthcare industry in the United States is larger than the economies of most countries. An announcement in any country that price controls would be imposed on the entire economy would seem incredible to all who have observed the past communist economies of Eastern Europe and Russia. Widespread shortages occurred, many of the goods produced were of shoddy quality, and black markets developed.

These countries have recognized the inherent failures of a controlled economy, and they have moved toward developing free markets. Why should we think healthcare is so different that access to care, high quality, and innovation can be better achieved through price controls and regulation than by relying on competitive markets? What consequences are likely if price controls are imposed on medical services?[1]

Effect of Price Controls in Theory

Imbalances Between Supply and Demand
Imbalances between demands for care and supply of services will occur. The demand for medical services and the cost of providing those services are constantly changing. Prices bring about an equilibrium between the demanders and suppliers in a market. Prices reflect changes in the demand for or costs of producing a service. When demand grows (perhaps because of an aging population or rising income), prices increase. Higher prices cause consumers to curtail some of their demand, but suppliers respond by offering more

services. Higher prices serve as a signal (and an incentive) to suppliers that greater investment in personnel and equipment is needed to meet the increased demand (Baumol 1988).

When regulators initially place controls on prices, they are assuming that the conditions that brought about the initial price—namely, the demands for service and the costs of producing that service—will not change. However, these conditions do change for many reasons, so the controlled price is no longer an equilibrium price. The problem with price controls is that demand is constantly changing, as is the cost of providing services. Although regulators often allow some increases in prices each year to adjust for inflation, seldom if ever are these price increases sufficient to reflect the changes in demand or costs that are occurring. When prices are inflexible, an imbalance between demand and supply occurs.

Not only do the demand for and costs of producing services change, but the product itself—medical care—is also continually changing, which complicates the picture for regulators. For example, the population is aging, and older individuals consume more medical care. Diseases such as cancer require extensive testing, treatment, and prolonged care. Technology continues to improve. Since the mid-1990s, transplants have become commonplace. Diagnostic equipment has reduced the need for many exploratory surgeries. Very low-birth-weight infants can now survive. Such ongoing advances raise the demand for medical services and require greater use of skilled labor, expensive monitoring equipment, and new imaging machines.

Unless regulators are aware of these changes in the medical product and technology, their controlled prices will be below the costs of providing these services. How will the demand be met? Imbalances will undoubtedly occur because regulators cannot anticipate all the changes in demand, costs, and technology.

Excess Supply

At times, regulators may set prices too high, which occurs when healthcare providers are able to increase their productivity. Surgeons took longer to perform certain procedures, such as heart surgery or transplants, when the procedures were first developed. As surgeons became more experienced in performing these surgeries, their time per procedure decreased and their surgical patients' outcomes improved. Yet, for many years, the Medicare price per procedure did not drop as the surgeon's productivity rose. In a competitive market, productivity gains are quickly translated into lower consumer prices.

Medicare, which regulates physician fees, relied on a single committee of the American Medical Association (AMA) to determine the time required for a physician (and different specialties) to perform various procedures, such as colonoscopies, under the resource-based relative value system. These time requirements become part of the relative values used by Medicare to determine the fee for performing a particular medical service. However, Whoriskey and Keating (2013) determined that the AMA's estimates of the time involved in many procedures were greatly overstated. Some physicians in the study performed procedures that, according to the AMA's and Medicare's time estimates, have them working 24, 30, and even 50 hours a day.

Productivity increases lead to decreases in the cost of a service. However, when fees are controlled, it is difficult for the price controller to know when and by how much productivity has increased. As the cost of performing a service declines and the price received for that service remains unchanged (or does not match the decline in costs), the profit per unit of surgeon's time grows; the surgeon responds to that incentive by performing more profitable procedures. The same incentive exists for other medical services for which the price exceeds the costs, such as diagnostic and imaging services.

The failure of price controllers to accurately change prices in response to changes in physician productivity results in more of these procedures being performed; in some patients receiving too many procedures, such as colonoscopies; in higher medical costs; in patients and/or private and public insurers paying too much; and in demand being distorted for certain physician specialties because these specialists' income is greater than that for other specialists. (Medical students have a financial incentive to enter procedure-oriented specialties that become more profitable as a result of increased productivity and "sticky" prices.)

Service Shortages

Shortages are the inevitable consequence of price controls. Demand for medical services is continually growing, yet price controls limit the expansion of supply. To expand its services, a hospital or a medical group must be able to attract additional employees—by raising wages that lure skilled and trained employees away from their current employers. As wages increase, trained nurses who are not currently employed as nurses will find returning to their profession financially attractive, and more people will choose a nursing career as its salary becomes comparable to that of other professions. However, if hospitals cannot increase wages because they cannot raise prices, they will not be able to hire the nurses and other staff needed to expand their services.

In addition, price controls actually cause a reduction in services, which exacerbates the shortage over time. As prices and wages grow throughout the economy, price controls in the healthcare sector make it difficult for hospitals and medical groups to pay competitive wages and high supply costs. Hospitals must hire nurses and technicians, buy supplies, pay heating and electric bills, and replace or repair equipment. If the salary of hospital accountants, for example, is not comparable to that of accountants working in other settings, fewer accountants will choose to work in hospitals (or those who accept lower wages may not be as qualified as those who do not). As medical costs increase faster than the permitted price growth, hospitals and medical groups will be unable to retain their existing labor forces and provide their current services. When costs per patient rise faster than government-controlled prices, hospitals, outpatient facilities, and physician practices are faced with two choices: (1) care for fewer but more costly patients or (2) care for the same number of patients but devote fewer resources to each patient.

Eliminating all waste in the current system would only lead to a one-time savings. If rising expenditures are caused not by waste but by new technologies, aging of the population, and new diseases, medical costs will still rise faster than the rate at which hospitals and other providers are reimbursed under price controls. Providers will then be faced with the same two choices: (1) care for fewer patients or (2) devote fewer resources to each patient and, thus, deliver low-quality service.

Price controls on medical services cause the demand for medical services to exceed the supply. The out-of-pocket price the patient pays for a physician visit, a magnetic resonance imaging (MRI) test, ultrasound imaging, or laboratory tests will rise more slowly than if the price were not controlled. (The "real," or inflation-adjusted, price to the patient is likely to fall.) Consequently, although patient demand for such services is high, suppliers cannot expand their services if the cost of doing so exceeds the fixed price. In fact, over time, the shortage will become even more severe because the fixed price will cover fewer services. We have seen this occur when rent controls are imposed on housing, such as in New York City. The demand for rent-controlled housing continually exceeds its supply, and the supply of existing housing decreases as the costs of upkeep exceed the allowable increases in rent, thereby causing landlords to abandon entire city areas.

Shift of Capital Away from Price-Controlled Services
As profitability is reduced on services subject to price control, capital investment will eventually shift to areas that are not subject to control and in which investors can earn higher returns. Less private capital will be available to develop new delivery systems, invest in computer technology for patient care management, and conduct research and development on breakthrough drugs. Price controls on hospitals cause hospital investment to decline and capital to move into unregulated outpatient services and home health care. Should all health services become subject to controls, capital will move to nonhealth industries and to geographic regions without controls.

Effect of Price Controls in Practice

Medicaid
Price controls have been tried extensively in the United States and other countries. Shortages and decreased access to care, which typify the Medicaid program,

are caused by price controls. Once a patient is eligible for Medicaid, the price he has to pay for medical services is greatly reduced, increasing his demand for such services. Government Medicaid payments to physicians are fixed, however, and below what they can earn by treating non-Medicaid patients. Low provider payments have decreased the profitability of serving Medicaid patients and resulted in a shortage of Medicaid services. In 2013, 31 percent of physicians were unwilling to accept Medicaid patients (Hing, Decker, and Jamoom 2015). As the difference in prices grows for Medicaid patients and those with private medical insurance, more of the physician's time shifts toward caring for private patients, thereby exacerbating the shortage of medical services faced by Medicaid patients.

Medicare

Hospitals are also subject to price controls on the payments they receive from Medicare. When fixed prices per diagnostic admission were introduced in 1984, hospitals began to "upcode" their Medicare patients' diagnoses to maximize reimbursements. Consequently, Medicare hospital payments rose sharply, and 75 percent of the increase was attributed to "code creep" (Sheingold 1989). Eventually, the federal government reduced Medicare payments so much that more than two-thirds of all hospitals lost money caring for Medicare patients. After a few years of losses, payments were raised. The failure of Medicare diagnosis-related group payments to accurately measure the severity of a patient's illness has led some hospitals to "dump" on other hospitals those Medicare patients whose costs exceed their payments. Congress has enacted legislation to penalize hospitals that engage in dumping.

In the early 1970s, Medicare limited how rapidly physician fees could rise under the program. As the gap between Medicare fees and private fees widened, physicians stopped participating in Medicare and billed their patients directly. To prevent this, Congress changed the rules in the 1990s. Physicians are no longer able to participate for some but not all of their Medicare patients by billing them the balance between what Medicare paid and the physician's typical fee; instead, physicians must participate for all or none of their Medicare patients.

When price controls and Medicare fee reductions were imposed in 1992, physicians who experienced the greatest reduction in fees also experienced the largest increases in service volume (Nguyen 1996). For example, radiologists' fees dropped by 12 percent, while their volume rose by 13 percent. Similarly, urologists' fees dropped by 5 percent, while their volume rose by 12 percent. These specialists were apparently able to create demand among their Medicare fee-for-service patients.

Until recently, Medicare used the sustainable growth rate (SGR) to limit increases in Medicare physician payments. The SGR includes, as one of its major components, the growth in gross domestic product (GDP), and is based on the assumption that total Medicare physician expenditures should not rise faster than GDP. The growth in GDP, however, does not accurately reflect changes in the supply of and demand for Medicare physician services. Consequently, Medicare fees for primary care physicians have lagged behind those in the private insurance sector, and each year fewer and fewer primary care physicians are willing to accept new Medicare patients.

When Medicare limited the rise in premiums for health maintenance organizations (HMOs), a number of HMOs dropped out of the Medicare HMO market. Medicare Advantage plans were subsequently given significant premium incentives in 2003 to reenter the Medicare market. (Their new payments were about 14 percent higher than the cost of treating comparable risk-adjusted patients in traditional Medicare.)

The Affordable Care Act (ACA) established the Independent Payment Advisory Board (IPAB) to achieve savings in Medicare when Medicare expenditures exceeded the rate of growth in per capita GDP plus 1 percent. The IPAB—by law and for political reasons—was prohibited from submitting proposals that would raise beneficiaries' out-of-pocket costs or premiums, change Medicare benefits, or change Medicare eligibility. Because of the law's constraints on how the IPAB could limit Medicare costs, reducing provider payments was the most likely approach to be used by the government.

The IPAB (repealed in 2018 before it became effective) would have decreased access to care in two ways. First, by lowering the prices Medicare pays for certain procedures and drugs, it would have become unprofitable for physicians to perform procedures the IPAB believed to be too costly, although such procedures may provide valuable benefits to Medicare beneficiaries. Second, by reducing overall provider payments to achieve its cost-containment goal, the IPAB would have lowered Medicare fees far below Medicaid fees (which already have caused access problems for Medicaid enrollees) and the fees paid by private health insurers.

The ACA also imposes price reductions on hospitals on the basis of assumed (debatable) productivity increases. Medicare's chief actuary reported that, by 2019, these payment reductions will result in operating losses for 15 percent of hospitals, skilled nursing facilities, and home health agencies. By 2030, 25 percent of those providers will sustain losses, and by 2050, that number will rise to 40 percent (Foster 2011). Because these price controls force many hospitals and other providers into bankruptcy, access to care and quality will be greatly diminished. To date, however, these hospital and disproportionate share hospital payment reductions, which would have had severe financial effects, have been postponed.

Rationing

Under price controls, as demand for medical services exceeds supplies, what criteria will be used to ration the supplies that are available? Undoubtedly, emergency cases would take precedence over elective services, but how would elective services be rationed? In some countries, such as Canada and Great Britain, where age is a criterion, individuals above a certain age often face barriers in accessing hip replacement, kidney dialysis, heart surgery, and other services. Thus, both quality of life and life expectancy are reduced.

Waiting Lists

Typically, waiting lists are used to ration elective procedures. In countries that rely on this approach, such as Canada and Great Britain, waiting times for surgical procedures—whether for cataracts or open-heart surgery—vary from six months to two years.[2] Delays are costly in terms of reduced quality of life and life expectancy. When resources are limited, acute care has a higher priority than preventive services. A lower percentage of women older than 50 years are screened for breast cancer in countries where price controls and global budgets are used than in the United States (Organisation for Economic Co-operation and Development 2017).

Those who can afford to wait—that is, those with lower time costs, such as the retired—are more likely to receive physician services than are those with higher time costs. Access to nonemergency physician services is determined by the value patients place on their time. Waiting is costly in that it uses productive resources (or enjoyable time). A large, but less visible, cost is associated with waiting. Suppose the out-of-pocket price of a physician's office visit is limited to $10, but the patient must take three hours off work to see the physician. If the patient earns $20 an hour, the effective cost of that visit is $70. The "lower" costs of a price-controlled system never explicitly recognize the lost productivity to society or the value of that time to the patient. Patients with high time costs are willing to pay not to wait, but they do not have that option. They cannot buy medical services at a price that reflects the value to them, which is greater than the government's price.

The effects of price controls are often a great burden on those with low income and those who do not know how to "work the system." Specialists frequently see those with connections more quickly, and those with high income can travel elsewhere to receive care.[3] For example, in 2010, the premier of Newfoundland went to the United States for heart surgery at his own expense (Wallace 2010).

Deterioration of Quality

As the costs of providing medical services increase faster than the controlled price, providers may reduce the resources used in treatment, resulting in a deterioration of quality. A physician may prefer a highly sophisticated diagnostic test such as an MRI, but to conserve resources she may order an X-ray instead. The value to the patient of a diagnostic test may exceed its cost, but an overall limit on costs will preclude performing many cost-beneficial tests or procedures. Experience with Medicaid confirms these concerns regarding quality of care. Large numbers of patients are seen for very short visits in Medicaid "mills." Such short visits are more likely to lead to incorrect diagnoses and treatment. Similarly, in Japan, where physicians' fees are controlled, physicians see many more patients per day than do US physicians and spend 30 percent less time with each patient.[4]

When controlled prices do not reflect quality differences among hospitals or physicians, suppliers have less incentive to provide higher-quality care. If all physicians are paid the same fee, the incentive to invest the time to become board certified is reduced. In a price-controlled environment with excess demand, even low-quality providers can survive and prosper. Similarly, drug and equipment manufacturers have no incentive to invest in higher-quality products if such products cannot be priced to reflect their higher value.

Gaming the System

Price controls provide incentives for providers to try to "game" the system to increase their revenues. For example, physicians paid on a fee-for-service basis are likely to decrease the time devoted to each visit, which enables them to see more patients and bill for more visits. Less physician time per patient represents a more hurried visit and presumably lower-quality care. Physicians are also likely to "unbundle" their services; by dividing a treatment or visit into its separate parts, they can charge for each part individually. For example, separate visits may be scheduled for diagnostic tests, obtaining the results of those tests, and receiving medications. Price controls also provide physicians and hospitals with an incentive to upcode the type of services they provide—that is, to bill a brief office visit as a comprehensive examination.

Gaming the system results in higher regulatory costs because a larger bureaucracy is needed to administer and monitor compliance with price controls. C. Jackson Grayson (1993), who was in charge of price controls imposed in the United States in 1971, stated, "We started Phase II [from 1971 to 1973] with 3½ pages of regulations and ended with 1,534." Gaming is also costly to patients. Multiple medical visits, which enable the physician to bill for each visit separately, increase patient travel and waiting times, an inefficient use of patients' resources that may discourage them from using needed services.

Global Budgets

To ensure that gaming does not increase total expenditures, an expenditure limit (global budget) often is superimposed on price controls. Included in a global budget are all medical expenditures for hospital and physician services, outpatient and inpatient care, health insurance and HMO premiums, and consumer out-of-pocket payments. Unless the global budget is comprehensive, expenditures and investments will shift to unregulated healthcare sectors. Additional controls will then be imposed to prevent expenditure growth in these areas, and monitoring compliance with the controls becomes even more costly.

What happens under global budgets when demand for certain providers or managed care organizations increases? The more efficient health plans cannot raise prices to attract more physicians and facilities to meet increased enrollment demands. Thus, the public is precluded from choosing the more efficient, more responsive health plans that are subject to overall budget limits. Limiting a physician's total revenue discourages the use of physician assistants and nurse practitioners who could boost the physician's productivity. Once a physician has reached the overall revenue limit, what incentive does he have to continue treating patients? Why not work fewer hours and take longer vacations?

What incentives do hospitals or physicians have to develop innovative, less costly delivery systems—such as managed care, outpatient diagnostics and surgery, or home infusion programs—if the funds must be taken from existing programs and providers? Efficient providers are penalized if they cannot increase expenditures to expand, and patients lose the opportunity to be served by more efficient providers.

To remain within their overall budgets, hospitals will undertake actions that decrease efficiency and access to care. Hospitals adjust to stringent budget limits by keeping patients longer, as this requires fewer resources than does performing procedures on more patients. Strict budget limits will result in greater delays in admitting patients, and patients will have less access to beneficial but costly technology. Hospitals in the Netherlands, under the country's previous global budget payment system (now changed to a more price-competitive system), typically reached the end of their budget in late fall and, consequently, sharply reduced the number of new admissions, causing long waiting times.

Global budgets are based on the assumption that the government knows the exact amount of medical expenditures needed for the nation.[5] However, a correct percentage of GDP that should be spent on medical care has never been determined, and the fact that many countries spend less than the United States spends does not tell us which country we should emulate or what services we should forgo. Medical expenditures rise for many reasons. No accurate information exists as to how much of that growth is attributable to waste, new diseases, an aging population, and new technology. The quality of healthcare will deteriorate, and long waiting times for treatment will result if price controls and global budgets are set too low. In 1997, Medicare's payment system to physicians was based on the premise that total Medicare physician expenditures should be tied to growth in the economy (adjusted for the number of Medicare beneficiaries)—the SGR. Even Congress admitted that the SGR payment system was badly flawed and consistently refused to implement the formula's payment reductions. In 2015, Congress enacted a new Medicare physician payment system that does not include the SGR's overall limit on physician expenditures.

Whether US politicians would permit a strict global budget to continue in the face of shortages and complaints about access to medical services is doubtful. More likely, they would respond to their constituents' complaints and relax the budget limit. In fact, this has happened in other countries, such as Canada, when access to medical services became too limited because of price controls and global budgets. Great Britain, for example, permits "buyouts." A private medical market is allowed to develop, and those with high income who can afford to buy private medical insurance jump the queue to receive medical services from private providers. To the extent that buyouts are permitted, medical expenditures will increase more rapidly and a two-tier system will evolve. If a buyout is envisaged, the rationale for price controls and global budgets is questionable.

Summary

Price controls and global budgets provide the appearance of limiting rising prices and expenditures. In reality, however, they lead to cheating and a reduction in quality, impose large costs on patients and providers, and do little to improve efficiency.

Consumers and producers respond to prices. When government sets prices below costs, hospital and physician economic incentives are to reduce the supply of services. Regulators should not assume that producers will go against their economic incentives.

If the purpose of regulation is to improve efficiency, eliminate inappropriate services, and decrease the costly duplication of medical technology, government policies should provide incentives to achieve these goals. Such incentives are more likely to occur in a system in which purchasers make cost-conscious choices and providers must compete for those purchasers. Competitive systems provide motivation for both purchasers and providers to weigh the benefits and costs of new medical technology. When patients are willing to pay not to wait and to gain access to new technology, medical expenditures will increase faster, but the rate of increase will be more appropriate.

Discussion Questions

1. Why do price controls cause shortages, and why do these shortages increase over time?

2. Why do price controls require hospitals to make a trade-off between quality of medical services and number of patients served?

3. What are the various ways in which a provider can "game" the system under price controls?

4. What costs do price controls impose on patients?

5. What are the advantages and disadvantages of permitting patients to buy out of the price-controlled medical system?

6. How might the IPAB have reduced patient access to care?

Notes

1. For a more complete discussion of this subject, see Pope (2013).

2. The Fraser Institute (www.fraserinstitute.ca) collects data annually on waiting times in each of the Canadian provinces, by procedure, and on waiting time for a referral from a general practitioner to a specialist.

3. The "true" price a patient faces is not just the out-of-pocket price she may have to pay but also the cost of the time spent waiting (or what she could have been doing had she received the care without waiting). For example, a person needing cataract surgery may be unable to drive while waiting six months for such surgery. The cost to the person of being unable to drive may be worth a great deal. Thus, the out-of-pocket price and the foregone benefits of waiting may be sufficiently high that the person prefers to pay for a substitute service whose out-of-pocket price is high but whose waiting cost is low. A Canadian waiting for cataract or cancer surgery may decide, as many have, that the higher out-of-pocket price of such care in another country (such as the United States) is less expensive, all things considered.

4. In 1991, Japanese physicians saw an average of 49 patients a day, and 13 percent saw 100 patients a day (Ikegami 1991). The US average was 22 patients per day in 1996. Another study (Ohtaki, Ohtaki, and Fetters 2003) analyzed the amount of time spent by Japanese and US physicians and found that Japanese physicians spent 30 percent less time with each patient. Konrad and colleagues (2010) conducted a survey of physicians in three countries with similar physician-to-population ratios and determined the amount of time spent with each patient. Physicians in Germany, Britain, and the United States were allocated 16, 11, and 18 minutes per patient, respectively, but they actually spent 12, 20, and 36 minutes, respectively, with each patient. The physicians believed the time allocated was insufficient.

5. Another expenditure control mechanism is healthcare certificate-of-need (CON) laws, which control capital expenditures on health services and facilities. The rationale for CON laws was that government planning would result in an appropriate and efficient allocation of resources and reduce rising healthcare costs. Economic studies have been unable to find any evidence that CON regulations, which are currently imposed in 37 states, have reduced healthcare expenditures. Instead, such regulations have been found to be used politically by self-interested providers to prevent competitors from entering a market (Mitchell 2016, table 1).

References

Baumol, W. 1988. "Containing Medical Costs: Why Price Controls Won't Work." *Public Interest* 93 (Fall): 37–53.

Foster, R. S. 2011. "The Estimated Effect of the Affordable Care Act on Medicare and Medicaid Outlays and Total National Health Care Expenditures." Testimony Before the House Committee on the Budget, January 26. Accessed April 2018. http://budget.house.gov/uploadedfiles/fostertestimony1262011.pdf.

Grayson, C. J. 1993. "Experience Talks: Shun Price Controls." *Wall Street Journal*, March 29, A14.

Hing, E., S. Decker, and E. Jamoom. 2015. "Acceptance of New Patients with Public and Private Insurance by Office-Based Physicians, United States, 2013." Centers for Disease Control and Prevention. NCHS Data Brief No. 195. Published March. www.cdc.gov/nchs/data/databriefs/db195.pdf.

Ikegami, N. 1991. "Japanese Health Care: Low Cost Through Regulated Fees." *Health Affairs* 10 (3): 87–109.

Konrad, T. R., C. L. Link, R. J. Shackelton, L. D. Marceau, O. von dem Knesebeck, J. Siegrist, S. Arber, A. Adams, and J. B. McKinlay. 2010. "It's About Time: Physicians' Perceptions of Time Constraints in Primary Care Medical Practice in Three National Healthcare Systems." *Medical Care* 48 (2): 95–100.

Mitchell, M. D. 2016. "Do Certificate-of-Need Laws Limit Spending?" Mercatus Center working paper. Published September. www.mercatus.org/system/files/mercatus-mitchell-con-healthcare-spending-v1a.pdf.

Nguyen, X. N. 1996. "Physician Volume Response to Price Controls." *Health Policy* 35 (2): 189–204.

Ohtaki, S., T. Ohtaki, and M. Fetters. 2003. "Doctor–Patient Communication: A Comparison of USA and Japan." *Family Practice* 20 (3): 276–82.

Organisation for Economic Co-operation and Development. 2017. *OECD Health Statistics 2017*. Updated November 10. www.oecd.org/els/health-systems/health-data.htm.

Pope, C. 2013. "Legislating Low Prices: Cutting Costs or Care?" *Backgrounder* No. 2834. Heritage Foundation. Published August 9. www.heritage.org/sites/default/files/2017-12/bg2834.pdf.

Sheingold, S. 1989. "The First Three Years of PPS: Impact on Medicare Costs." *Health Affairs* 8 (3): 191–204.

Wallace, K. 2010. "Newfoundland Premier in U.S. for Surgery." *Canadian Medicine*. Published February. www.canadianmedicinenews.com/2010/02/in-news-newfoundland-premier-in-us-for.html.

Whoriskey, P., and D. Keating. 2013. "How a Secretive Panel Uses Data That Distort Doctors' Pay." *Washington Post*. Published July 20. www.washingtonpost.com/business/economy/how-a-secretive-panel-uses-data-that-distorts-doctors-pay/2013/07/20/ee134e3a-eda8-11e2-9008-61e94a7ea20d_story.html.

THE EVOLUTION OF MANAGED CARE

20

An important policy debate relates to the organization and delivery of medical services—namely, should the United States rely on regulation or on market competition to achieve efficiency in the provision of medical services? Market competition can take different forms; one was the emergence and rapid growth of managed care organizations during the 1980s and 1990s. What effect has managed care competition had? Has managed care improved efficiency and reduced the rate of increase in medical expenditures? What happened to patient satisfaction and quality of care? To examine these issues, we must discuss what is meant by "managed care," why it came about, the evidence on how well it has performed, and how it is evolving.

Why Managed Care Came About

Managed care was a market response to the wasteful excesses of the past, which resulted in rapidly rising medical costs in a system widely believed to be inefficient. Traditional indemnity health insurance, with its comprehensive coverage of hospitals and small patient copayments for medical services, lessened patient concerns with hospital and medical expenses. Physicians were paid on a fee-for-service (FFS) basis and were not fiscally responsible for hospital use, which they prescribed. New medical technology was introduced rapidly because the insurer paid for its use and cost; insurers merely passed the higher cost on to employers.

The lack of incentives for insurers, patients, physicians, and hospitals to concern themselves with costs led to their rapid rise. Insured patients demanded too many services, physicians paid on a FFS basis benefited from supplying more services, and hospitals competed for physicians by making available to them the latest technology so their patients would not have to be referred to other hospitals and physicians. Advances in medical technology and the lack of cost incentives led to nonprice competition among hospitals; technology was adopted no matter how small its medical benefits or how infrequently it would be used. This behavior led not only to higher costs but also to lower quality, as studies demonstrated that hospitals that performed a smaller volume of a particular procedure had worse outcomes than those that performed a larger volume of the same procedure (Hughes, Hunt, and Luft 1987).

As large employers sought to reduce the rapid increases in health insurance premiums, physicians, hospitals, and traditional health insurers were not responsive to their cost concerns. Instead, entrepreneurs recognized the potential for reducing medical system inefficiencies and created health maintenance organizations (HMOs), utilization review firms, and preferred provider organizations (PPOs). These innovators, who aggressively marketed their approaches to large employers, were rewarded for their efforts.

What Is Managed Care?

Managed care embodies a variety of techniques and types of organizations. Financial incentives, negotiation of large provider discounts, limited provider networks, physician gatekeepers, utilization management, disease management, and drug formularies are some of these techniques.

Managed care health plans were successful in interfering with the traditional physician–patient relationship because employees were willing to switch from traditional insurers in return for lower premiums. Managed care plans contracted with those physicians and hospitals willing to discount their prices, which was a precondition for joining the plan's limited provider network. Because physicians and hospitals had excess capacity in the 1980s and 1990s, they were willing to discount their prices in return for increased patient volume (Wu 2009). The patient's choice of primary care physician was restricted to those in the plan's provider panel, as were the specialists to whom the patient could be referred and the hospitals in which the patient could be admitted. Decisions about whether to hospitalize a patient, length of stay, specialist referrals, and types of drugs prescribed—formerly made by the physician—were now influenced by the managed care plan.

Managed care techniques have changed over time. First-generation approaches were quite restrictive. Managed care plans relied on selective contracting, which limits the provider panel to hospitals and physicians who are willing to discount their prices and are appropriate users of medical services; a gatekeeper model; and stringent utilization review. An enrollee in a managed care plan chose a primary care physician from among a panel of physicians who would manage the patient's care and control diagnostic and specialist referrals (this is the gatekeeper model). The primary care physician often performed some tasks previously carried out by specialists. Utilization review includes prior authorization for hospital admission, concurrent review (i.e., the patient's length of stay is reviewed to make sure it does not exceed what is medically necessary), and retrospective review (to ensure that appropriate care was provided).

The initial sources of managed care savings were lower hospital use (the most expensive component of care) and deep provider price discounts. The

HMOs could shift large numbers of enrollees to those providers who competed to be included in the HMO's provider panel; the HMOs were able to achieve cost savings relatively easily and without changing the practice of medicine.

To achieve more reductions in medical costs, managed care had to become more innovative and effective in managing patient care. So-called second-generation managed care approaches rely more heavily on changing physicians' practice patterns, such as identifying high-risk enrollees early, decreasing the variation in physicians' utilization patterns, reducing inappropriate use of services, and substituting less costly in-home services for continued care in the hospital. Managed care plans are accessing large data sets on physicians' treatment patterns around the country and using information technology to analyze those data to determine which treatment decisions lead to better outcomes. Moreover, integrated and coordinated care and disease management can decrease medical costs and improve patient outcomes.

Some managed care plans (particularly in California) have shifted more of the capitation payment, hence risk, to physicians and hospitals; providers are thereby given an incentive to innovate in the delivery of medical services. Furthermore, with the shifting of risk from employers to HMOs, large employers place greater emphasis on report cards. Because managed care plans and their providers have a financial incentive to deliver fewer services under capitation, both the plans and providers must be continuously monitored for patient satisfaction and medical outcomes. Health plans and their providers are being held accountable for the health status of their enrolled populations.

Types of Managed Care Plans

Managed care health plans vary in the degree to which they use a select network of providers and limit access to specialists. Typically, the more restrictive the managed care plan, the lower its premium. The most restrictive type of managed care plan is an HMO, which offers the most comprehensive health benefits. An HMO relies on a restricted provider network, and the patient is responsible for the full costs of going to nonnetwork providers. Cost control is achieved through stringent utilization management, financial incentives to physicians, and limited access to providers.

Managed FFS indemnity insurance plans include a PPO, which is a closed provider panel. Providers are paid FFS, and enrollees have a financial incentive (lower copayment) to use the PPO providers rather than out-of-network providers. Costs are controlled through utilization management, patient copayments, and discounted fees from PPO providers.

Specialist referrals also vary. In an HMO, the primary care physician must refer the patient to a specialist. In a PPO, the patient may self-refer to a specialist, but the copayment is lower if the specialist is in the PPO.

Traditional HMOs began to offer a point-of-service option in the early 1990s to counter the growing popularity of PPOs. A point-of-service plan is an HMO that permits its enrollees to use nonparticipating providers if enrollees are willing to pay a high copayment (e.g., 40 percent) each time they use such providers.

Exhibit 20.1 shows the market share for each type of health insurance plan for the working population and how that share has changed over time. In the early 1980s, managed care was just beginning to grow. Traditional indemnity insurance, with free access to all providers (unmanaged care), was the dominant form (95 percent) of health insurance. Since then, the distribution of different types of health plans has changed rapidly. In the past 10 years, the high-deductible health plan with a savings option (HDHP/SO) has experienced the most rapid growth of any type of plan. To lower their insurance premiums, enrollees are willing to bear more of their front-end medical costs by having a large deductible. By 2017, traditional insurance had virtually disappeared, and various types of managed care had become the predominant form of insurance.

The premium in a typical managed care plan is allocated as shown in exhibit 20.2. In this example, the ABC Managed Care Health Plan retains 15 percent of the premium to cover expenses associated with marketing, administration, and profit. About 35 percent of the premium is allocated for hospital and other medical facility expenses, 40 percent is set aside for physician services, and 10 percent is spent on for pharmacy and ancillary services. Use of services by enrollees outside the plan's area and certain catastrophic expenses may also be included in the health plan's retained 15 percent.

Providers in each of these budgetary groups may be paid in several ways. Some managed care plans (e.g., Kaiser Health Plan) place their physicians on a salary, others pay discounted FFS, and still others capitate their physicians. (Capitation means to pay an annual amount to the physician group for each enrollee for whom they are responsible. Capitated medical groups are primarily found in California.) For each of these payment arrangements, the organization that is at financial risk withholds a certain percentage of the budget allocated to the providers to ensure that sufficient funds are available to pay for all necessary services. Funds remaining at the end of the year are divided among the members of that provider group.

When medical groups and hospitals are capitated, a shared risk pool exists. Part of the hospital's capitated payment is set aside to be shared with the medical group so that it has an incentive to reduce use of the hospital.

How Has Managed Care Performed?

Managed care did not spread equally to all parts of the country or to all population groups. It moved more rapidly into those areas with high healthcare

EXHIBIT 20.1
The Trend
Toward
Managed Care

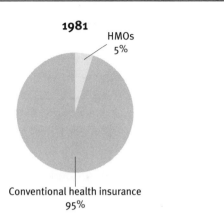

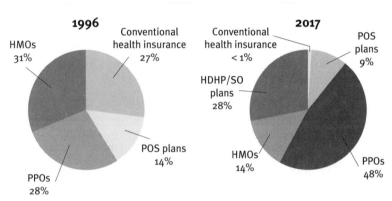

Notes: HMO = health maintenance organization: an organization that provides comprehensive healthcare services to a voluntarily enrolled membership for a prepaid fee. HMOs control costs through stringent utilization management, payment incentives to their physicians, and restricted access to their providers.

PPO = preferred provider organization: a third-party payer contracts with a group of medical providers who agree to furnish services at negotiated fees in return for prompt payment and increased patient volume. PPOs control costs by keeping fees down and curbing excessive service through utilization management.

POS = point of service: an HMO that permits its enrollees to access nonparticipating providers if the enrollees are willing to pay a high copayment each time they use such providers.

Conventional health insurance: a plan that permits patients to go to any provider, with the provider paid on a fee-for-service basis. The patient typically pays a small annual deductible plus 20 percent of the provider's charge, up to an annual out-of-pocket limit of $3,000.

HDHP/SO = high-deductible health plan with savings option: a consumer-driven health plan that works like a PPO plan with in-network and out-of-network benefits for covered services. Patients can see a specialist without a referral. Selection of a primary care physician is not required. HDHP plans have higher annual deductibles and out-of-pocket maximums but lower premiums. Patients with HDHP plans can set up a tax-deductible health savings account.

Sources: Data from Kaiser Family Foundation and Health Research & Educational Trust (2017); KPMG Peat Marwick (1982).

EXHIBIT 20.2
How an HMO
Allocates the
Premium Dollar

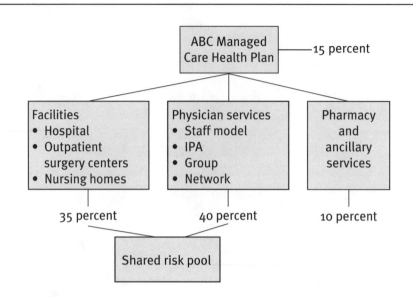

Types of HMOs
Staff model: An HMO that delivers health services through a physician group that is controlled by the HMO unit.

IPA: An HMO that contracts directly with physicians in independent practices.

Group: An HMO that contracts with one independent group practice to provide health services.

Network: An HMO that contracts with two or more independent group practices.

costs, where the potential for cost reductions was greatest. Managed care plans were more likely to enter urban than rural areas. They were introduced in the West, particularly California, earlier than in the East or Southeast, and a greater percentage of the population was enrolled in these plans compared with populations in the East or Southeast. Workers employed in large firms moved more rapidly into managed care than did individuals on Medicare or Medicaid, who had limited price incentives to enroll in managed care plans.

While the privately insured are almost all in some form of managed care, only 33 percent of the 57 million aged were in Medicare managed care plans (referred to as Medicare Advantage plans) as of 2016; the percentage has been increasing over time (Centers for Medicare & Medicaid Services 2017b). The high percentage of individuals on Medicaid who are in managed care (75 percent) represent those who are not in nursing homes or disabled.

To assess the performance of managed care competition, population groups subject to managed care should be compared with comparable populations not in managed care. Thus, earlier studies compared managed care plans with traditional FFS plans in the private sector. Such comparisons of the privately insured are more difficult to conduct today. Instead, current studies evaluate the performance of managed care plans by comparing enrollees in Medicare Advantage plans with those in traditional Medicare.

The Issue of Biased Selection

A concern with all studies of managed care is the issue of "biased selection." Managed care plans initially attracted younger enrollees, those new to an area, and fewer individuals who were chronically ill—people who did not have long-standing physician relationships. If HMOs and managed care plans enrolled a healthier population group, a comparison of their performance with traditional health insurers would be biased. Better health outcomes and lower healthcare costs in an HMO would be related more to the population enrolled than to its performance. Thus, crucial to any study examining whether managed care plans are better at controlling growth in costs and improving treatment outcomes is the ability to control for lower-risk groups enrolled in managed care.

A wide variety of studies have been conducted on the performance of HMOs, managed care plans, and traditional insurers serving the privately insured (Glied 2000). Following is a summary of the results of these earlier studies and of those plans serving Medicare enrollees (which have controlled for biased selection).

Rise in Health Insurance Premiums

Managed care competition worked in the following manner. As managed care plans entered a market and enrolled a significant number of members, hospitals and physicians competed on price to be included in the managed care plan's provider network. Given their excess capacity and need for more patients, providers were also willing to accept utilization review, which decreases hospital use. These cost savings (discounted prices and lower hospital use rates) enabled the managed care plan to lower its premium relative to those of non–managed care health plans. When employees are required to pay the additional cost of more expensive health plans, studies show that premium differences as small as $5 to $10 a month will cause 25 percent of a health plan's employees to switch (Buchmueller and Feldstein 1996). Employees are very price sensitive. Therefore, health plans must be very price competitive.

To prevent further losses in their market share, indemnity, non–managed care insurers adopted managed care techniques, such as utilization review and use of PPOs, to limit the rise in premiums. Managed care plans not only reduced their own medical costs but, by their competitive effect, forced other insurers to adopt managed care techniques to reduce their costs and remain price competitive.

Managed care competition dramatically slowed the rise in health insurance premiums, particularly during the mid-1990s. Exhibit 20.3 shows the national trend in employer-paid health insurance premiums and the annual

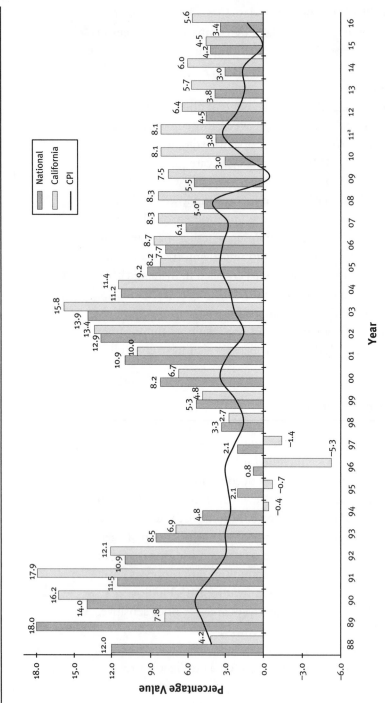

EXHIBIT 20.3
Annual Percentage Increase in Health Insurance Premiums for the United States, California, and the CPI, 1988–2016

[a]2011 national percentage increase is estimated.

Notes: CPI = consumer price index. In 2008, Kaiser/HRET changed its method for reporting the US annual percentage premium increase. Before 2008, percentage increase was calculated as the average of percentage changes in premium for a family of four in the largest plan of each plan type. Since 2008, percentage increase reflects the overall percentage increase in premium for family coverage using the average of the premium dollar amounts for a family of four in the largest plan of each plan type and weighted by covered workers.

Sources:

1. National data: 1988–2007 data from Kaiser Family Foundation and Health Research & Educational Trust (2007); 2008–2016 data from Kaiser Family Foundation and Health Research & Educational Trust (2017).

2. California data: 1988–2012 data from Whitmore and Gabel (2017).

3. CPI data: Bureau of Labor Statistics (2017).

percentage change in the consumer price index. Also included are premium data from California, where managed care competition began earlier and was more extensive than in the rest of the country. Clearly, as managed care market share increased (see exhibit 20.1), insurance premiums rose more slowly. (In California, the managed care effect was even more pronounced. During the mid-1990s, health insurance premiums in California actually declined.)

A major source of the early savings from managed care was reduced hospital use, which is shown in exhibit 20.4. Hospital patient days per 1,000 population declined from 1,302 in 1977 to 565 by 2015. Also shown is the earlier and larger decline in hospital use rates in California; rates there declined from 996 to 426 per 1,000 population over the same period. New York, which had a higher hospital use rate than the national average, also saw a decline, although at 762 in 2015, it was still much higher than the national average and almost twice as high as that in California.

Hospital admissions per 1,000 population have also fallen, although not as dramatically as patient days. Admission rates in 1978 were 162 nationally, 147 in New York, and 141 in California. By 2015, rates had declined to 104, 112, and 83, respectively.

As a result of managed care, hospitals' share of total medical expenditures declined. The decline in hospital use rates in California indicates that reductions in hospital use are still possible in other parts of the country.

The sharp decrease in hospital use rates and admissions explains why hospitals have been forced to expand their outpatient services to make up for the revenue losses from declining inpatient use. Technological changes and insurer coverage for lower-cost outpatient diagnostic services and surgery have prompted the move toward greater use of outpatient care.

One-Time Versus Continual Cost Savings

Managed care achieved the easiest cost reductions, such as decreased hospital days, substitution of less costly settings for costly inpatient stays, and lower provider prices. These reductions, however, are one-time cost savings, even though they occur over a period of years and are instituted at different times in different parts of the country. An important policy question is whether managed care competition is only able to produce these one-time savings or whether it can achieve continual cost reductions.

The two most important factors that determine the rate at which medical expenditures will increase are demographics—an older population has more costly care needs—and the development and adoption of new medical technology. Whether managed care can achieve continual cost reductions will depend on whether it is able to innovate in managing the care of the aged and chronically ill, as well as reduce the rate of new technology diffusion while encouraging the development of cost-reducing technology.

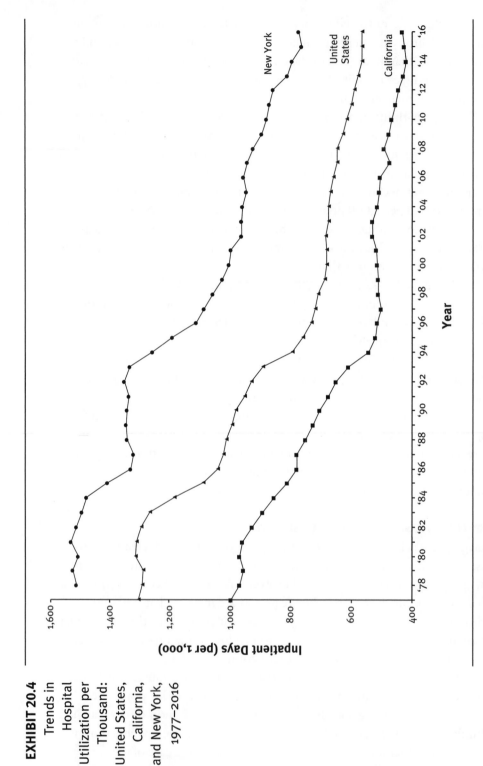

EXHIBIT 20.4
Trends in Hospital Utilization per Thousand: United States, California, and New York, 1977–2016

Source: Utilization data from American Hospital Association (n.d.).

Under unmanaged FFS indemnity insurance, new technology was adopted if it provided some additional benefit, no matter how small, and regardless of its cost. There was little financial incentive to develop cost-reducing technology. For managed care to produce continual savings, new technology must be justified on the basis of its costs as well as its benefits. To the extent that investment in technology can be directed to reducing the use of more costly procedures, using less invasive procedures, enabling care to be provided in the home or in an outpatient setting, and preventing the need for costly acute care, continual reductions in medical costs are possible.[1]

The results of several studies have shown that managed care has slowed the rate at which new technology has been adopted. Mas and Seinfeld (2008) studied the adoption of 13 medical technologies by hospitals over the period 1982–1995. They found that higher levels of managed care market share were associated with lower levels of hospitals' adoption of medical technology. The researchers also found that managed care has achieved continual reductions in the cost of medical care.

Managed care achieved one of its main goals: It reduced the rise in healthcare expenditures. Without managed care, insurance premiums would have increased more rapidly. Higher insurance premiums make health insurance less affordable; consequently, the number of uninsured would have been greater because the demand for insurance is inversely related to its price. Furthermore, the lower rate of increase in insurance premiums resulted in a redistribution of income from hospitals and physicians (an important reason for their opposition to managed care) to employees. Lower health insurance premiums meant that a firm's employees had greater take-home pay. Lower premiums also meant, however, that less revenue was available for physicians, hospitals employed fewer people, and their wages increased more slowly.

Patient Satisfaction and Quality of Care

Any evaluation of managed care performance should be broader than just examining whether it results in lower insurance premiums. Managed care competition (and any system for organizing the delivery of medical services) should also be evaluated on whether it promotes efficiency (the rate at which premiums increase), desired treatment outcomes, and patient satisfaction.

Many studies have examined member satisfaction in managed care plans (Glied 2000). These studies typically compared the most restrictive form of managed care, an HMO, with less restrictive forms or with non–managed care insurance plans. Measures of patient satisfaction typically include waiting times for an appointment, the ability to obtain referrals to a specialist, and travel times to a panel provider. The study results typically show a high degree of member satisfaction in HMOs. Such studies, however, have limited usefulness because most people do not have health problems and therefore do not make costly demands on the HMO.

More recent surveys attempted to measure satisfaction of chronically ill patients and those with serious health problems. Such studies have examined access to care by those with low incomes, those who are HIV positive, and those who are chronically ill. The results of these studies are mixed. Some found no significant differences between health plans, whereas some found greater patient satisfaction in HMOs compared with other health plans, and others found lower patient satisfaction in HMOs. In traditional, unmanaged health plans, the patient has easier access to specialists and fewer restrictions on hospital use. In managed care plans, however, coordination of care is better for those with chronic illness; otherwise, a chronically ill patient can be hospitalized multiple times, increasing the managed care plan's costs (Sipkoff 2003). Early managed care plans lacked experience in caring for those with chronic illness, and, as a result of anecdotal stories of access problems, regulatory restrictions were placed on these plans; this situation has changed in most managed care plans.

With regard to the quality of care in managed care versus traditional insurance plans, the empirical literature suggests little difference between the two. Some studies indicate that traditional insurance may perform better for those who have serious health conditions, particularly low-income individuals. Given the large number of managed care plans and the different types of such plans, generalizations regarding patient satisfaction and treatment outcomes are difficult to make. How the providers are paid (FFS, salary, or capitation), who is at financial risk, the type of decision-making structure, and the managed care culture of the medical group are likely to be more important determinants of patient satisfaction and outcomes than is the type of health plan.

To the extent that risk-adjusted premiums are used to pay for high-risk patients and those who have serious illnesses, a higher capitation rate paid by the employer to the health plan provides managed care plans with an incentive to compete for such patients, improve their access to care, and innovate in devising new treatment methods. An example of these types of managed care plans are Medicare demonstration projects that pay such firms risk-adjusted premiums to care for special needs populations, such as the frail elderly. The HMO has an incentive to provide the necessary services, including preventive care, to keep their enrollees in the community rather than admitted to nursing homes.

Medicare Advantage HMOs Versus Traditional Medicare

Landon and colleagues (2012) analyzed enrollees' utilization patterns in Medicare Advantage HMOs and in traditional FFS Medicare during the 2003–2009 period to determine whether differences in patterns reflected more integrated care received by HMO enrollees. Utilization rates in several major categories, including emergency departments and ambulatory surgery, were 20 to 30 percent lower in Medicare Advantage HMOs during each of the years studied. Further, enrollees in Medicare Advantage HMOs underwent more coronary bypass surgeries than did patients in traditional Medicare. The authors concluded that "overall, Medicare Advantage HMO enrollees might use fewer services and be experiencing more appropriate use of services than enrollees in traditional Medicare."

Landon and colleagues (2015, 559) compared enrollees in Medicare Advantage plans and traditional Medicare who had diabetes or cardiovascular disease. They found that Medicare Advantage plans used fewer resources to care for patients, and their quality of care was higher. They concluded that Medicare Advantage "plans that are more established, nonprofit, and/or larger generally had lower resource use and better relative quality than did smaller, newer, for-profit HMOs or preferred provider organizations."

Curto and colleagues (2017) compared healthcare spending between Medicare Advantage plans and traditional FFS Medicare. They found that Medicare Advantage plans spend about 25 percent less than traditional Medicare plans, after adjusting for enrollees in the same county with the same risk score. The authors also reported that Medicare Advantage plans encourage substitution to less costly care (e.g., using primary rather than specialist services and less inpatient and more outpatient surgery) and use a variety of utilization management approaches.

Managed Care's Spillover Effect

Medicare Advantage plans have different financial incentives than providers in traditional Medicare. Medicare Advantage plans receive a risk-adjusted payment per enrollee from Medicare for providing at least the same coverage as does traditional Medicare. More efficient Medicare Advantage plans (i.e., they can provide the same coverage for less money than the Medicare payment) can provide their enrollees with greater coverage, thereby increasing their market share over traditional Medicare. Medicare Advantage plans, however, also have a "spillover" effect. When Medicare Advantage plans improve their efficiency in delivering medical care to their enrollees, these improvements are adopted by the same providers when caring for their non-Medicare Advantage plan patients.

Baicker, Chernew, and Robbins (2013) found that as the market share of Medicare Advantage plans in an area increases, their providers begin to adopt the same approaches when caring for traditional Medicare patients, as well as younger, privately insured patients. The growth of Medicare Advantage plans has led to a decrease in intensity of care and, hence, lower hospitalization costs and a decrease in length of stay for non-Medicare patients.

The Change in Managed Care

In the late 1990s, managed care began to undergo changes. Several events occurred that resulted in a loosening of managed care's more restrictive cost-containment measures.

Economic Prosperity of the 1990s

In the late 1990s, the US economy was expanding, the stock market was reaching new highs, "dot-com" companies were the craze, and firms had difficulty attracting and retaining skilled employees. During that prosperous period, employees wanted health plans that were less restrictive with respect to specialist referrals and that offered broader provider networks. Given the tight labor market, employers were more concerned with keeping their employees than with the costs of healthcare and were willing to pay higher insurance premiums for more generous health plans. Enrollment growth in HMOs, the most restrictive type of plan, began to decline, and PPO plans became more popular.

As health plans restructured themselves to accommodate employees' demands, the health plans had more difficulty controlling medical costs. Changing from limited to broad provider networks meant that health plans had less leverage over the provider to negotiate large price discounts. The removal of physician gatekeepers meant an increase in self-referrals to specialists and more procedures. Less utilization review by health plans also led to greater use of medical services. Greater use of specialists, more procedures, and reliance on FFS payment over a broad provider network not only made coordinating and monitoring patient care more difficult but also increased the cost of care and, consequently, premiums.

Furthermore, to the extent that managed care plans have broader provider networks and providers participate in multiple health plans, holding the health plan accountable for the performance of its providers is difficult. Similarly, a single health plan has difficulty collecting data from providers, monitoring their performance, and changing their practice patterns. The broader the provider network and the fewer the restrictions placed on specialist referrals, the less control health plans have over providers.

Higher Prices for Hospitals, Physicians, and Prescription Drugs

The structure of the healthcare industry was also changing during the late 1990s. To improve their bargaining power with fewer but larger health plans, hospitals and physicians began merging and consolidating into fewer, larger organizations. Hospital mergers within a market meant fewer competitors with which the health plan could negotiate discounts. Also, excess capacity among hospitals was reduced as a result of hospital closures and mergers. Therefore, hospitals were able to charge health plans higher prices. Drug costs began to increase sharply as new, more effective drugs became available, and as pharmaceutical companies stimulated demand with direct-to-consumer advertising. Health plans were forced to increase premiums to pay for these higher costs.

Regulation of Managed Care

By the end of the 1990s, a backlash by providers and patients forced many managed care plans to abandon the strict cost-containment methods, such as use of gatekeepers and specialist referral requirements, and adopt less restrictive policies. Increased government regulation of managed care occurred for several reasons:

- Widespread media attention was given to certain cases of denial of care by HMOs.
- The public wanted increased access to specialists (without paying more).
- The American Medical Association wanted to redress the balance of power between managed care plans and physicians; physicians' bargaining power would increase if limited provider networks could be opened to all physicians, thereby allowing patients greater choice of physician ("any willing provider" laws).
- Some were opposed to managed care because they wanted a single-payer system, and regulation would eliminate managed care's success in reducing medical costs.

Legislators saw an opportunity to gain visibility by holding hearings on HMO practices and receive the public's support by enacting legislation making certain managed care practices illegal (e.g., outpatient mastectomies and "drive-through deliveries").

Legislators did not discuss the trade-offs between legislating freer access to care and the increased premiums that would result. The public was led to believe that increased access would come at no additional cost, and Congress and the states responded by increasing regulation. To the extent that government intervenes in the practice of medicine (establishing minimum lengths of stay and determining which procedures can be performed in an outpatient setting) and regulates how managed care plans structure their delivery systems, treatment innovation is inhibited and health insurance premiums will increase by more than they would otherwise.

In October 1999, a class-action lawsuit requesting billions of dollars in damages was filed against a managed care firm (Humana), alleging that by using cost-containment methods, the firm reneged on its promise to pay for all medically necessary care. Although the lawsuit was dismissed three years later, along with similar suits against other managed care plans, managed care plans relaxed their cost-containment methods.

Recent Developments in Managed Care

As managed care's stringent cost-containment methods and limited provider networks were loosened, premiums began increasing rapidly in the late 1990s. Employers and employees once again became concerned with rising premiums. Employers started shifting a greater portion of the insurance premium to their employees and pressured managed care firms to better control rising healthcare costs.

Narrow Provider Networks

Health insurers incurred large financial losses by participating in the Affordable Care Act's health insurance exchanges. Their enrolled population turned out to have much greater medical expenses than they anticipated. The financial penalty for not complying with the individual mandate was too low, and many healthy young people decided not to enroll in the exchanges. As a result, insurers suffered from adverse selection, and they had to sharply increase their premiums. Many other insurers left the market.

To control their enrollees' medical costs, the remaining insurers on the exchanges resorted to using narrow provider networks. The narrow networks limited insurers' premium increases, but enrollees had limited access to higher-quality providers. The adverse selection problems that occurred on the insurance exchanges were mainly limited to the exchanges and did not affect the much larger employer market.

Additional Cost-Containment Approaches

Managed care has also been developing innovative cost-control approaches for managing care and reducing medical costs. Approaches being used today include the early management of diseases such as diabetes, hypertension, and congestive heart failure, as these diseases can lead to catastrophic medical expenses (Berenson et al. 2008). Managing chronic illness requires development of clinical guidelines or protocols, clinical integration and coordination of care, and early identification and treatment of high-risk patients. With the aging of the population, managed care firms are learning how to manage chronic care needs for which they are at financial risk.

Assisting in the development of innovative approaches are computer information systems and large databases, which can revolutionize practice patterns. Large data sets that track specific diseases over long periods will enable providers to determine which variations in treatment methods result in the most desired patient outcomes; this information could be used to promote changes in physicians' practice patterns. Information technology and analysis of large amounts of data also will enable managers to increase efficiency by better understanding their enrollees' medical costs, as well as improve clinical outcomes and quality of care. Provider performance will be evaluated in terms of patient outcomes, satisfaction, and cost of care.

Report Cards

In the past, consumers had little or no information by which to judge the quality of providers or the quality of care they received. The development of managed care made it possible to evaluate patient satisfaction and treatment outcomes of enrolled population groups. By having limited provider panels of physicians and hospitals, together with a defined group of enrollees, a managed care plan can obtain information on the practice patterns of and patient satisfaction with its providers, as well as on the care received by enrollees.

Under pressure from employer coalitions for more information about managed care plans and their participating providers, managed care plans have provided data to independent organizations for developing report cards. These report cards include information about patient satisfaction, quality process measures, and outcomes data on health plans and their participating providers. When these report cards are made available to employees during open enrollment periods, the information influences their choice of health plan (Kolstad and Chernew 2009). Publicly available information increases pressure on health plans and their providers to compete on satisfaction and outcome measures as well as on premiums. Employees can then make a more informed decision regarding the trade-off between lower premiums and desirable plan characteristics.

Consumers' use of report cards and public information about physician and hospital performance, however, has been lower than anticipated (Shaller, Kanouse, and Schlesinger 2014). No consistent evidence exists that consumer behavior has changed as a result of access to information about provider performance. Research is ongoing to determine how to increase consumer awareness and use of such performance data.

Pay-for-Performance

Incentive-based provider payments, referred to as *pay-for-performance (P4P)*, began around 2000. Insurers typically pay physicians and hospitals for providing services, and little if any attempt has been made to reward providers who deliver higher-quality services or who reduce treatment costs. This is beginning to change. Although quality of medical care is difficult to measure, medical experts agree that certain standards should be met for preventive care and specified diagnoses (Rosenthal et al. 2005). Although the measures used for incentive payments are not standardized across different health plans, three types of measures are being used: (1) clinical quality, including childhood immunization rates, breast cancer and cervical cancer screening rates, and measures related to the management of chronic diseases, such as diabetes and asthma; (2) patient satisfaction measures; and (3) measures related to investment in information technology that enables clinical data integration.

Managed care plans that have a large market share (and therefore greater bargaining power over providers) initiated the P4P experiments. Incentive payments to providers represent 1 to 5 percent of a provider's total revenue. P4P is still in its early stages. Medical societies have generally been opposed on grounds that the quality measures are not fully developed, and that P4P incentives imply that providers are not delivering high-quality care. Although incentive payments have been widely adopted by health plans, studies examining their impact have found mixed results depending on the size of the incentive bonus, the competitiveness of the market, and the financial situation of participating providers (James 2012).

More recent studies have not found consistently positive results from P4P programs (Mendelson et al. 2017, 341). These authors reported that such programs "may be associated with improved processes of care in ambulatory settings, but consistently positive associations with improved health outcomes have not been demonstrated in any setting."

In 2015, Congress enacted a new Medicare physician payment system that requires more extensive data from physicians and relies more heavily on P4P (see chapter 10, "How Does Medicare Pay Physicians?").

P4P programs will continue to evolve; the size of the incentive payment will likely increase, standards for judging providers will become uniform across health plans and medical groups, and FFS physicians will have to invest more in information technology to provide the data by which they will be measured.

Accountable Care Organizations

The Affordable Care Act included funds for experimenting with new provider payment systems. One such approach was to encourage providers to organize as accountable care organizations (ACOs), which would provide primary care, specialty services, and inpatient care for a defined population of Medicare beneficiaries. An ACO and its physicians would be responsible for the overall care of their Medicare beneficiaries, include adequate participation of primary care physicians, provide coordinated care, promote evidence-based medicine, and report on their quality and costs of care. ACOs that meet their quality and cost thresholds would share in the cost savings they achieve for the Medicare program. The hope was that ACOs would transform not only the Medicare system but also the delivery of medical services in the private sector, improving the quality of care and reducing rising medical costs.

To become an ACO, hospitals have been consolidating and employing physicians to provide integrated and coordinated care to Medicare enrollees. However, unlike Medicare Advantage plans, Medicare enrollees do not choose to join an ACO and they receive no financial incentive to do so. In fact, they are unaware that they have been assigned to an ACO. Medicare patients incur no financial penalty if they use providers unaffiliated with the ACO. Many believe that this distinction between the ACO and Medicare Advantage plans is a fatal flaw in the ACO concept.

As of 2017, 480 ACOs were in the Medicare program, serving about 9 million beneficiaries (about 16 percent of all Medicare beneficiaries) (Centers for Medicare & Medicaid Services 2017a).

Early studies on the effectiveness of ACOs are not promising, and little evidence exists of their ability to reduce costs or improve quality. In their study of the Medicare Shared Savings Program, Kury, Baik, and McDonald (2017, 724) "found that the care patterns for ACO beneficiaries shifted away from some costly types of care, but at the expense of increased utilization of other types, increased imaging and testing expenditures, and increased medication use, with overall net greater increase in cost instead of smaller increase."

Sullivan (2017), a critic of the ACO concept, stated the following:

> CMS [Centers for Medicare & Medicaid Services] has now conducted three demonstrations of the 'accountable care organization,' and all of them have failed. The Physician Group Practice (PGP) Demonstration, which ran from 2005 to 2010, raised Medicare costs by 1.2 percent. The Pioneer ACO program, which ran from 2012 through 2016, cut Medicare spending by three- or four-tenths of a percent on average over its first four years. And the Medicare Shared Savings Program (MSSP), which began in 2012 and may lumber on indefinitely, has raised Medicare costs by two-tenths of a percent on average over its first four years.

Critics of the ACO concept are also concerned that permitting combinations of hospital and physician groups to form large ACOs may lessen competition, thereby increasing prices to the private sector.

Population Health

There is a growing recognition among health policy analysts and managed care plans that improving an enrolled population's health requires more than emphasizing the delivery of medical services. The social determinants of health, in addition to enrollees' medical needs, are important contributors to health outcomes and reducing medical costs. The lack of adequate assistance in the patient's home is likely to increase use of the emergency department by chronically ill patients.

Similarly, patients with alcoholism or other behavioral problems will experience greater hospital utilization. Identifying patients at risk, regardless of whether the increased risk derives from medical, social, economic, or behavioral factors, is necessary for developing innovative approaches to providing the necessary services to reduce use of costly medical services and improve the patient's health.

Managed care organizations are beginning to collect a great deal of data on the medical and nonmedical needs of their enrolled population. To better allocate their scarce resources to improve enrollees' health and reduce medical costs, such firms need to develop the analytic skills to use these huge data sets to manage an enrolled population's health (Fraze et al. 2016).

Summary

Health insurance premiums increased sharply as a consequence of the economic prosperity that led to employee demands for less restrictive health plans in the 1990s, hospital mergers and physician consolidations that led to higher provider prices, increased drug prices, regulations imposed on managed care plans, and advances in medical technology. Managed care plans have demonstrated less ability to control costs today than they had previously.

Employers and employees are searching for new approaches to limit their premium increases. Employers are shifting more of the insurance premium to employees, and health plans are developing new cost-containment strategies, such as disease management and reliance on evidence-based medicine. Under pressure from employers, health plans are using report cards to enable employees to make more informed choices regarding health plans and participating providers. Health plans are also beginning to use incentive-based payment to encourage participating providers to improve quality of care and patient satisfaction, as well as to increase use of information technology to integrate clinical data.

A recent trend affecting the growth of managed care plans is use of consumer-driven health plans. These high-deductible plans, sold at lower premiums, shift more of the financial risk to consumers and require them to become better informed about their purchases of healthcare services and choice of providers.

The market is responding to rising premiums by placing greater emphasis on consumer cost sharing to hold down costs and use of services.

Discussion Questions

1. What is managed care, and what are managed care techniques?

2. When managed care enrollment increases in a market, how does it affect other insurers and providers?

3. Why did managed care occur?

4. What are the different types of managed care plans?

5. What are report cards, and what effects are they expected to have on managed care competition?

6. How has the growth of managed care affected the performance of the medical sector?

Note

1. On balance, new technology has led to increased, not decreased, medical expenditures. However, increased medical expenditures resulting from new technology are not the same as inflation in medical costs. The medical treatment received is different and improved. Furthermore, as long as the public is willing to pay for these enhanced benefits, an increase in medical costs is appropriate.

Additional Reading

Dranove, D. 2000. *The Economic Evolution of American Health Care: From Marcus Welby to Managed Care.* Princeton, NJ: Princeton University Press.

References

American Hospital Association. n.d. *Hospital Statistics.* Various editions. Chicago: American Hospital Association.

Baicker, K., M. Chernew, and J. Robbins. 2013. "The Spillover Effects of Medicare Managed Care: Medicare Advantage and Hospital Utilization." National Bureau of Economic Research Working Paper No. 19070. Published May. www.nber.org/papers/w19070.

Berenson, R., M. Hash, T. Ault, B. Fuchs, S. Maxwell, L. Potetz, and S. Zuckerman. 2008. *Cost Containment in Medicare: A Review of What Works and What Doesn't.* AARP Public Policy Institute. Published December. http://assets.aarp.org/rgcenter/health/2008_18_medicare.pdf.

Buchmueller, T., and P. Feldstein. 1996. "Consumers' Sensitivity to Health Plan Premiums: Evidence from a Natural Experiment in California." *Health Affairs* 15 (1): 143–51.

Bureau of Labor Statistics. 2017. "CPI—All Urban Consumers." Accessed May 2018. https://data.bls.gov/timeseries/CUUR0000SA0.

Centers for Medicare & Medicaid Services. 2017a. "Fast Facts: All Medicare Shared Savings Program (Shared Savings Program) Accountable Care Organizations (ACOs)." Published January. www.cms.gov/Medicare/Medicare-Fee-for-Service-Payment/sharedsavingsprogram/Downloads/All-Starts-MSSP-ACO.pdf.

———. 2017b. "Medicare Enrollment Dashboard Data File." Accessed April 2018. www.cms.gov/Research-Statistics-Data-and-Systems/Statistics-Trends-and-Reports/CMSProgramStatistics/Dashboard.html.

Curto, V., L. Einav, A. Finkelstein, J. D. Levin, and J. Bhattacharya. 2017. "Healthcare Spending and Utilization in Public and Private Medicare." National Bureau of Economic Research Working Paper No. 23090. Published January. www.nber.org/papers/w23090.

Fraze, T., V. A. Lewis, H. P. Rodriguez, and E. S. Fisher. 2016. "Housing, Transportation, and Food: How ACOs Seek to Improve Population Health by Addressing Nonmedical Needs of Patients." *Health Affairs* 35 (11): 2109–15.

Glied, S. 2000. "Managed Care." In *The Handbook of Health Economics*, edited by J. P. Newhouse and A. J. Culyer, 707–53. New York: North-Holland Press.

Hughes, R., S. Hunt, and H. Luft. 1987. "Effects of Surgeon Volume and Hospital Volume on Quality of Care in Hospitals." *Medical Care* 25 (6): 489–503.

James, J. 2012. "Pay-for-Performance." *Health Affairs* health policy brief. Published October 11. http://healthaffairs.org/healthpolicybriefs/brief_pdfs/health policybrief_78.pdf.

Kaiser Family Foundation and Health Research & Educational Trust. 2017. *Employer Health Benefits 2017 Annual Survey*. Published September. http://files.kff.org/attachment/Report-Employer-Health-Benefits-Annual-Survey-2017.

———. 2007. *Employer Health Benefits 2007 Annual Survey*. Published September. https://kaiserfamilyfoundation.files.wordpress.com/2013/04/76723.pdf.

Kolstad, J. T., and M. E. Chernew. 2009. "Quality and Consumer Decision Making in the Market for Health Insurance and Health Care Services." *Medical Care Research and Review* 66 (1 Suppl): 28S–52S.

KPMG Peat Marwick. 1982. *Survey of Employer-Sponsored Health Benefits*. Amstelveen, Netherlands: KPMG Peat Marwick.

Kury, F. S. P., S. H. Baik, and C. J. McDonald. 2017. "Analysis of Healthcare Cost and Utilization in the First Two Years of the Medicare Shared Savings Program Using Big Data from the CMS Enclave." *AMIA Annual Symposium Proceedings*. Published February 10. www.ncbi.nlm.nih.gov/pmc/articles/PMC5493183/.

Landon, B. E., A. M. Zaslavsky, R. C. Saunders, L. G. Pawlson, J. P. Newhouse, and J. Z. Ayanian. 2015. "A Comparison of Relative Resource Use and Quality in Medicare Advantage Health Plans Versus Traditional Medicare." *American Journal of Managed Care* 21 (8): 559–66.

———. 2012. "Analysis of Medicare Advantage HMOs Compared with Traditional Medicare Shows Lower Use of Many Services During 2003–09." *Health Affairs* 31 (12): 2609–17.

Mas, N., and J. Seinfeld. 2008. "Is Managed Care Restraining the Adoption of Technology by Hospitals?" *Journal of Health Economics* 27 (4): 1026–45.

Mendelson, A., K. Kondo, C. Damberg, A. Low, M. Motúapuaka, M. Freeman, M. O'Neil, R. Relevo, and D. Kansagara. 2017. "The Effects of Pay-for-Performance Programs on Health, Health Care Use, and Processes of Care: A Systematic Review." *Annals of Internal Medicine* 166 (5): 341–53.

Rosenthal, M., R. Frank, Z. Li, and A. Epstein. 2005. "Early Experience with Pay-for-Performance." *Journal of the American Medical Association* 294 (14): 1788–93.

Shaller, D., D. E. Kanouse, and M. Schlesinger. 2014. "Context-Based Strategies for Engaging Consumers with Public Reports About Health Care Providers." *Medical Care Research and Review* 71 (5 Suppl): 17S –37S.

Sipkoff, M. 2003. "Health Plans Begin to Address Chronic Care Management." *Managed Care*. Published December 1. www.managedcaremag.com/archives/2003/12/health-plans-begin-address-chronic-care-management.

Sullivan, K. 2017. "Would ACOs Work If They Were Turned into HMOs?" *Health Care Blog*. Published June 8. http://thehealthcareblog.com/blog/2017/06/08/would-acos-work-if-they-were-turned-into-hmos/.

Whitmore, H., and J. Gabel. 2017. "California Employer Health Benefits: Prices Up, Coverage Down." California Health Care Foundation. Published March 14. www.chcf.org/publication/california-employer-health-benefits-prices-up-coverage-down/.

Wu, V. 2009. "Managed Care's Price Bargaining with Hospitals." *Journal of Health Economics* 28 (2): 350–60.

HAS COMPETITION BEEN TRIED—AND HAS IT FAILED—TO IMPROVE THE US HEALTHCARE SYSTEM?

21

Critics claim that market competition has been tried but has failed to improve the US healthcare system. Healthcare costs are rising rapidly, and per capita healthcare spending is the highest in the world, yet many Americans are without health insurance. More of the middle class are finding that health insurance has become too expensive, life expectancy is lower than that in other countries, and the infant mortality rate is higher than that in some countries with lower per capita healthcare expenditures. In other words, is it time to try something different? Specifically, is it time for more government regulation and control of the healthcare system? "Some say that competition has failed, I say that competition has not yet been tried." Alain Enthoven (1993, 28) wrote that statement in 1993, and it continues to be correct today.

This chapter discusses how medical markets differ from competitive markets, why making medical markets more competitive is desirable, what changes are needed to bring about greater competition, whether competitive markets are responsible for the growing numbers of uninsured, and what role the government plays in a competitive medical care environment.

Criteria for Judging Performance of a Country's Medical Sector

The health of a population, as measured by life expectancy or infant mortality rates, is not solely the consequence of the country's medical system. How people live and eat are more important determinants of life expectancy than whether they have good access to medical services when they become ill. Life expectancy is related to a number of factors, such as smoking, diet, marital status, exercise, drug use, and cultural values. Although universal access to health insurance is desirable, studies have shown that medical care has a smaller effect on health levels than do personal health habits and lifestyle (see chapter 3). Therefore, assessing the medical care system on measures that are affected more by lifestyle factors is inappropriate. After all, the financing and delivery of medical services has been based on treating people when they are ill and not on keeping them well.

Several healthcare organizations in the United States have gone beyond treating people when they become ill and have tried to lower costs by preventing illnesses that are expensive to treat. Reducing hip fractures among the elderly and instituting monitoring mechanisms for diabetes patients, for example, have been shown to prevent more costly treatments later. The financial incentives for these organizations differ from the typical fee-for-service payment incentives used predominantly in the United States and other countries.

Assuming the purpose of a medical care system is more narrowly defined—that is, treating those who become ill—what criteria should be used to evaluate how well that system performs? The criteria should be the same as those used to evaluate the performance of other markets, such as housing, food, automobiles, and electronics—markets that produce necessities and luxuries. The following are the performance criteria of a medical care system:

1. *Information.* Do consumers have sufficient information to choose the quantity and type of services based on price, quality, and other characteristics of the services being supplied?
2. *Consumer incentives.* Do consumers have incentives to ensure that the value of the services used is not less than the cost of producing those services?
3. *Consumer choices.* Does the market respond to what consumers are willing to pay? If consumers demand more of some services, will the market provide more of those services? If consumers differ in how much they are willing to spend or want different types of services, will the market respond to those varied consumer demands?
4. *Supplier incentives.* Do suppliers of goods and services have an incentive to produce those goods and services (for a given level of quality) at the lowest cost?
5. *Price markups.* Do the prices charged by suppliers for their services reflect the costs of production? (This occurs when suppliers compete on price to supply their services.)
6. *Redistribution.* Do those who cannot afford to pay for their medical services receive medically necessary services?

To the extent that the medical sector approximates the first five criteria, the system will produce its output efficiently, and medical costs will rise at a rate that reflects the cost of producing those services.[1] The type of services available, as well as the new medical technology adopted, will be based on what consumers are willing to pay.

Competitive markets—compared with monopoly markets or markets with government controls on prices and investment—come closest to achieving the first five criteria. Competitive markets are the yardstick by which all markets are evaluated, and they underlie the antitrust laws. Proponents of competition believe the same benefits can be achieved by applying competitive principles to medical care. Competitive markets, however, do not help those unable to afford the goods and services produced. It is government's role, not the market's, to subsidize those with low income so that they can receive the necessary amounts of food, housing, and medical services. When adequate subsidies in the form of vouchers for health insurance are provided, through a competitive market, to those with low income, providers have incentives to produce those services efficiently, and patients have a greater choice when using them.

Market forces are powerful in motivating purchasers and suppliers. The search for profits is an incentive for suppliers to invest a great deal of money to satisfy purchaser demands. Suppliers innovate to become more efficient, develop new services, and differentiate themselves from competitors, thereby increasing their market share and becoming more profitable. Incentives exist in both competitive and regulated markets. The incentives appropriate to a competitive market are those for which both the purchaser and the supplier bear the cost and receive the benefits of their actions. When a purchaser's and a supplier's costs and benefits are not equal, the market becomes less competitive and its performance suffers.

How Medical Markets Differ from Competitive Markets

The Period Before Managed Care

Before managed care began to grow in the 1980s, health insurance coverage was predominantly traditional indemnity insurance. Patients had little or no out-of-pocket cost when they used medical services, and hospitals and physicians were paid on a fee-for-service basis. Information about providers was nonexistent, as it was prohibited by medical and hospital associations, and accrediting agencies (e.g., The Joint Commission) did not make their findings public. Insurance companies merely passed higher provider costs on to employers, who paid their employees' insurance premiums. Medicare and Medicaid greatly reduced their beneficiaries' concern regarding medical prices. Medicare paid hospitals according to their costs, and physicians were paid on a fee-for-service basis. Medicaid paid hospitals and physicians fee-for-service.

Regulatory policies at the state and federal levels, enacted at the behest of provider groups, led to greater market inefficiency. Restrictions were imposed on any form of advertising; on the tasks different healthcare professionals were permitted to perform; on entry into markets by new hospitals and free-standing outpatient surgery centers; on health maintenance organizations (HMOs), which were required to be nonprofit; and on which healthcare providers were eligible for payment under Medicare, Medicaid, and even Blue Cross and Blue Shield. Neither patients nor physicians had any incentive to be concerned about

EXHIBIT 21.1

Trends in
Payment
for Medical
Services,
1960–2016

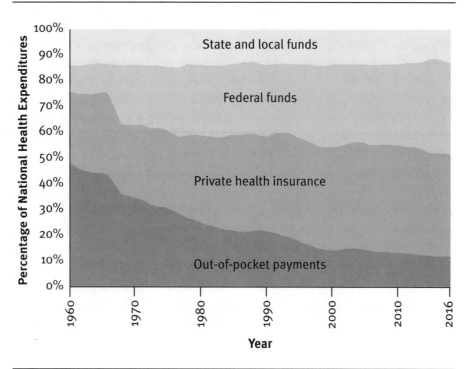

Note: The private health insurance category includes other private funds.

Source: Data from Centers for Medicare & Medicaid Services (2017).

the use or cost of services. Comprehensive health insurance results in a "moral hazard" problem; patients use more services because their insurance has greatly reduced the price they must pay. The additional benefit of using more services is much less than it would be if the patient had to pay more of the cost. Exhibit 21.1 illustrates how payment for medical services has changed since 1960.

Private insurance and government now pay for most medical services; out-of-pocket payments by patients have declined from almost 50 percent of total medical expenditures to just 10.6 percent. Furthermore, physicians, because they are paid on a fee-for-service basis, have a financial incentive to provide more services. Given the lack of patient and provider incentives to be concerned about the cost and use of services, too many services are delivered. Wide variations in care occur because factors other than clinical value are used to decide whether the services should be provided, and rapid increases have occurred in the growth of medical spending.

To control rapidly rising medical costs from the late 1960s to the early 1980s, federal and state governments used regulatory approaches. The medical sector was placed under wage and price controls from 1971 to 1974, health-planning legislation placed controls on hospital investment, many states used hospital rate regulations, and Medicare instituted hospital utilization review and limited physicians' fee increases. Medicaid simply reduced payments to hospitals and physicians. These regulatory approaches failed to slow rising medical costs.

Managed Care

Managed care was the reaction of large employers to an out-of-control healthcare system that brought about rapidly rising health insurance premiums. Under pressure from large employers and unions, health insurers and providers became adversaries. Health plans negotiated price discounts with providers and instituted cost-containment measures that reduced use of services (gatekeepers, prior authorization for specialist and hospital services, and coverage for care in settings less expensive than the hospital). These cost-reduction measures achieved large savings in insurance premiums, as shown in exhibit 20.3. When employees were offered a choice of health plans and given an opportunity to save on monthly premiums, they switched plans. Price competition penalized high-cost plans.

However, a backlash against managed care and its cost-containment methods occurred by the end of the 1990s. As more low-risk users switched to HMOs because of less expensive premiums, those remaining in traditional indemnity plans (patients with chronic illnesses and those with established primary care physician and specialist relationships) faced high premiums. (Adverse selection caused premiums to rise more in traditional indemnity plans.) They joined HMOs to reduce their premiums but were dissatisfied with the restrictions on access to providers. The backlash against managed care was likely driven by those who felt compelled to join HMOs.

Managed care was, at most, an example of partial market competition. Although managed care competition achieved large private-sector cost savings for a limited time, much of the previous regulatory and economic framework under which competition occurred was unchanged. Any market framework includes a set of consumer and supplier incentives, and market performance responds to these incentives. When these incentives influence consumers and suppliers to consider the full costs and benefits of their decisions, market outcomes are efficient. At times, however, the legal and economic framework within which consumers and producers make their choices distorts the costs and benefits of these incentives, in which case markets perform inefficiently.

The following sections provide examples of how the medical care market's legal and economic framework has distorted consumer and producer incentives—and, hence, their choices—and led to inefficient market outcomes.

Demand-Side Market Failures

These market failures on the demand side have limited the expansion of greater competitive forces.

Tax-Exempt Employer-Paid Health Insurance

When an employer purchases health insurance on behalf of employees, these contributions are not considered taxable income to the employee. Compared with other employee purchases paid for with after-tax income, the purchase of insurance is subsidized; thus, employees pay less for insurance than they would if they had to buy the same amount with after-tax income. When the price of a good or service is reduced, consumers will purchase a greater quantity of that service (known as the *law of demand*).[2] The price of insurance, when purchased by the employer, is not the same for all employees. Those in the highest income-tax brackets receive the largest tax subsidies. On average, changes in the out-of-pocket price of health insurance result in a proportional change in the quantity of insurance demanded.[3] (A 5 percent decrease in price leads to an increase of about 5 percent in the quantity demanded.) The tax subsidy for health insurance results in employees purchasing more comprehensive coverage with lower deductibles and lower cost sharing (and additional benefits, such as vision and dental care) than they would if they had to pay the entire premium themselves.

Incentives have been distorted because consumers do not pay the full cost of health insurance or of their medical services. When consumers pay, out of pocket, only a small fraction of the provider's price, they are less aware of and concerned with the prices charged by medical providers.

Health Plan Choices

Health plan competition could have been stronger for several reasons. First, many employers limited their employees' choice to only one health plan.[4] For competition to occur among plans, employees must be offered a choice. Yet throughout the 1990s and still today, about 80 percent of firms providing health benefits offer employees only one choice of health plan. Large firms are more likely than small firms to offer a choice of plans (55 percent compared with 17 percent) (Kaiser Family Foundation and Health Research & Educational Trust 2017, 65). When employees are unable to choose among substitutes, the single plan being offered has less incentive to respond to employees' preferences.

Second, many employers that offer employees a choice of health plans either contribute more to the higher-cost health plan or contribute a fixed percentage of the premium to the plan the employee chooses. A fixed-percentage contribution provides a greater dollar subsidy to the more expensive plan, thereby reducing the employee's incentive to select the less costly plan. (If the employer pays 80 percent, the employee opting for the more expensive plan pays only 20 percent of the price difference, not 100 percent.) The more efficient health plan is at a competitive disadvantage because the more expensive competitor is more heavily subsidized. When employees have a choice of plans, and the employer contributes a fixed-dollar amount, most employees will select a more restrictive plan—such as an HMO. "For example, 70–80 percent of active employees and dependents covered by the University of California, CalPERS, and Wells Fargo in California [each company makes a fixed-dollar contribution] choose HMOs" (Enthoven and Tollen 2005, w5-429).

Third, when competing managed care plans offer broad networks with overlapping providers, the plans are not sufficiently differentiated and do not offer employees real choices. Overlapping provider networks make it difficult for the plan to control costs (because it cannot exclude providers) and for employees to identify quality differences. The plans are not competing on their providers' ability to manage care, on the quality of their providers, or on patient satisfaction, and they have little incentive to invest resources to do so, because all plans with the same providers will benefit. Consumers should be able to select among health plans that vary in premiums, quality of care, access to providers, provider network, and so on.

Fourth, few employers pay insurers risk-adjusted premiums for their employees. Paying the same premium for an employee who is older and has more risk factors than a younger employee, who is less likely to incur a large medical expense, gives insurers an incentive to engage in risk selection by seeking out younger employees. Paying risk-adjusted premiums gives insurers an incentive to compete on price for higher-risk employees. Insurers also must compete on how well they can manage the care of high-risk enrollees rather than on how well they can entice low-risk employees to join their plans.

Lack of Information

Historically, healthcare providers have been opposed to being compared with one another. The Federal Trade Commission's (FTC) antitrust suit against the American Medical Association—affirmed by the US Supreme Court in 1982—involved the association's prohibitions on advertising. A consumer seeking information on a provider's prices and quality was unable to find it. (Consumers with limited cost sharing also had little incentive to search for a lower price.) Lack of information on how well one provider compares with another enables each competitor to charge higher prices or produce lower-quality care than they could if consumers were informed about both providers' prices and quality.

Wide price variations—unrelated to quality or other attributes of the service—are unlikely to persist in a price-competitive market. Knowledgeable purchasers will shun overpriced suppliers of a service. Currently, price information for medical services is difficult to obtain, and the services included in the stated price are not transparent. For example, a study by Rosenthal, Lu, and Cram (2013) tried to determine elective pricing data (bundled payment that includes hospital and physician fees) for total hip arthroplasty, a common elective surgical procedure. The authors experienced difficulty obtaining price information and observed a wide variation in the prices quoted.

One of the tenets of a competitive market is that consumers not only bear the cost of their choices but also are informed purchasers. If consumers do not have access to information about provider quality, providers have little incentive to invest in higher-quality care because they receive the same fee as those who do not. In recent years, provider quality and patient satisfaction measures have been collected on report cards and disseminated to employees during open enrollment.[5] One study found that two years after publication of a report card, "more than 20 percent of bottom-quartile surgeons stopped practicing [coronary artery bypass grafting] surgery in New York . . . whereas only about 5 percent of surgeons in the top three quartiles did so" (Jha and Epstein 2006).

Tax subsidies for purchasing health insurance have led to a demand for more comprehensive insurance—with lower out-of-pocket payments and larger employer subsidies for more expensive health plans—and have lessened consumer incentives to choose more efficient health plans. Tax subsidies, combined with a lack of information on health plans and providers, have resulted in a healthcare market where purchasers have insufficient incentives and limited opportunity to make informed choices.

Medicare and Medicaid

About half of all medical expenditures are made by federal and state governments. Incentives for beneficiaries and Medicare and Medicaid's provider payment policies have an important effect on the market's performance, similar to the impact of tax subsidies. Most Medicare beneficiaries have supplementary health insurance to cover their Medicare cost-sharing requirements. Because those with low income are covered by Medicaid, there is no cost sharing. Thus, neither Medicare nor Medicaid beneficiaries have any incentive to be concerned about provider prices or their use of medical services.

Although Medicare allows beneficiaries a choice of health plans, the elderly have not had a strong financial incentive to choose lower-cost, restrictive Medicare Advantage plans. Only if Medicare were to provide a fixed dollar contribution, with beneficiaries paying the additional cost of a more expensive health plan, would enrollees have an incentive to switch from the more costly, traditional fee-for-service plan. Medicaid enrollees, on the other hand, are not given a choice of health plans. Medicaid may enroll some of its enrollees (young, low-cost) in a health plan, but most Medicaid expenditures on behalf of the aged and disabled are paid on a fee-for-service basis to hospitals, physicians, and nursing homes.

Supply-Side Market Failures

Provider Consolidation

The greater the number of healthcare providers in a market, the greater the competition among them to respond to purchaser demands. Conversely, when only one provider is in a market, the patient has no choice but to go to that provider. Providers respond when the purchaser has a substitute provider from which to choose. A monopolist provider has no incentive to innovate, improve quality, respond to patients' needs, or offer lower prices.

Considerable provider consolidation has been occurring. When hospitals in a market merge, insurers have fewer to negotiate with. The antitrust laws are meant to prevent suppliers, such as hospitals and physicians, from gaining market power. Unfortunately, the FTC had been unsuccessful in preventing hospital mergers that decrease competition. Federal judges, ruling in the merged hospitals' favor, believed that merged nonprofit hospitals would not exercise their market power as for-profit hospitals would. Consolidated hospitals and single-specialty groups dominate certain markets (Berenson, Ginsburg, and Kemper 2010). One consequence of the movement toward accountable care organizations (ACOs) and hospitals employing physicians has been further consolidation of the provider market in many areas. As the number of competitors has declined, health plans have been forced to pay higher prices, which are passed on to consumers in the form of higher insurance premiums (Ginsburg 2016).

Federal and State Regulations

The federal and state governments have enacted a number of anticompetitive regulations that limit price competition and result in higher health insurance premiums. These regulations address such areas as the training of health professionals and the tasks they are permitted to perform, entry into medical markets, pricing of health insurance policies, health insurance benefit coverage, and rules covering provider networks.

More than 2,200 state mandates (as of 2017) have been enacted that specify the benefits, population groups, and healthcare providers that must be included in health insurance policies (National Conference of State Legislatures 2018). Large business firms are legally exempt from these state mandates since they self-insure their employees, which most large organizations do. The higher cost burden of these state mandates falls predominantly on individuals and small businesses, raising the cost of insurance and thereby making health insurance unaffordable to those who prefer less expensive health plans.

The Affordable Care Act (ACA) substituted its own insurance requirements; it specified 10 "essential" benefits that must be included in any qualified health plan. Many of these mandated benefits exceed the insurance coverage people previously purchased. Many of these essential benefits, such as maternity and newborn care as well as pediatric coverage, are not applicable to certain population groups, such as single and older men. These additional benefits have increased the cost of insurance, and the higher premiums have led many to decide the benefit of having health insurance is outweighed by its cost; being uninsured is preferable.

Although some of these state and ACA mandates may be beneficial, many individuals and small businesses would rather have insurance they can afford than no insurance at all. Insurers are unable to compete by offering insurance benefits preferred by many.[6]

When community rating was required in state individual insurance markets, such as New York and Vermont, all types of individuals or small businesses were placed in a common risk pool, and all were charged the same premium. Firms whose employees were engaged in high-risk jobs were charged the same as organizations whose employees had low-risk jobs. Firms that provide incentives to employees to engage in healthy lifestyles were charged the same premium as those that do not. Community rating eliminates price competition among insurers. Instead, insurers have an incentive to engage in favorable risk selection. Community rating increases the price of insurance to low-risk individuals, thereby leading many to drop their insurance.

The ACA regulates the pricing of health insurance. A modified form of community rating is required in federal and state health insurance exchanges. The medical costs of caring for individuals in their 50s and 60s (up to 65 years of age) are higher than those for younger individuals. The ratio is 5 or 6 to 1. The ACA requires insurers to use a ratio that is 3:1. The effect of using a smaller ratio is that younger enrollees incur higher premiums to subsidize older enrollees, even though younger individuals may have much less income. Price competition by insurers to sell insurance according to an age group's actuarial experience is unlawful. These higher premiums have reduced the demand for insurance by younger individuals.

State certificate-of-need (CON) laws prohibit competitors from entering a market. The CON process protects existing providers from competition, thereby giving monopoly power to the existing hospital, home health agency, hospice, and nursing home. Training of healthcare professionals emphasizes process measures of quality (e.g., years of education) as a prerequisite for licensure. Reexamination for relicensure is not used, and physicians have rarely been evaluated on outcomes-based measures of quality. Innovative methods of training healthcare professionals are inhibited when rigid professional rules specify training requirements. State practice acts specify the tasks that healthcare professionals are permitted to perform; these regulations are based on political competition among health associations over which profession is permitted to perform certain tasks. A greater supply of health manpower is available, and care can be delivered less expensively when performance is monitored and flexibility is allowed in the tasks that healthcare professionals are permitted to perform.

Any willing provider (AWP) laws limit price competition among physicians (and dentists). Health plans had been able to negotiate large price discounts from physicians by offering them exclusivity over their enrollees. The 13 states with AWP laws that apply to physicians enable any physician to have access to a health plan's enrollees at the negotiated price. As a result of AWP laws, physicians have no incentive to compete on price for a health plan's enrollees because they cannot be assured of receiving a higher volume of patients in return for a lower price.

Lack of Physician Information

Competitive markets assume that demand-side and supply-side participants are well informed. Physicians, who act as the patient's agent and as a supplier of a service, are considered to be knowledgeable about their patients' diagnoses and treatment. Further, physicians are assumed to act in their patients' best interests. If these assumptions are incorrect, medical services are not being provided efficiently, quality of care is lower, and the cost of medical services is higher than it otherwise would be.

Wide variations exist in the medical services provided by physicians in the same specialty, to patients with the same diagnosis, and across geographic regions (Institute of Medicine 2013). These variations in medical services are likely attributable to two factors. First, physicians are not equally proficient in their diagnostic ability or in their knowledge of the latest treatment methods. These wide variations have given rise to evidence-based medicine, whereby large insurers analyze the results of well-designed research as well as large data sets to determine best practices and disseminate clinical guidelines to their network physicians.

Second, physicians have a financial interest in the quantity and type of care they provide. Most physicians are paid fee-for-service; thus, the more they do, the more they earn. *Supplier-induced demand* is the term economists use to explain physicians' financial incentive to increase their services. When combined with the lack of consumer incentives regarding prices and use of medical services, as well as consumers' lack of knowledge regarding physicians' practice methods, both the use and cost of medical services are greatly increased. Medicare—under which most aged have supplementary insurance to cover their cost sharing—is a prime example of how the lack of patient price sensitivity and medical information, together with some physicians' lack of knowledge and the incentives inherent in fee-for-service, have resulted in large variations in the cost and number of services provided.

As the preceding discussion illustrates, market forces have been greatly weakened. Given the lack of effective competition in medical markets, one cannot claim that competition has been tried and has failed.

How Can Medical Markets Be More Competitive?

Markets always exist, but, depending on government rules, they can be efficient or inefficient. To improve market efficiency in medical care, several changes are needed in government regulations and in the private sector.

Government tax policy that excludes employer-paid health insurance from an employee's taxable income should be changed. Employer contributions should be treated as regular income; however, it is more politically feasible to limit the amount that is tax free.[7] This change will affect the amount of insurance consumers buy, which health plans they choose, and how much medical care they use. Additional needed government reforms include removing restrictions on market entry and repealing laws promoting anticompetitive behavior, such as CON and AWP laws; overriding mandates that raise health insurance costs; eliminating insurance regulations requiring modified community rating; enforcing antitrust laws; and reforming Medicare and Medicaid so that beneficiaries pay the additional cost of more expensive health plans, thereby giving these beneficiaries incentives to choose health plans on the basis of costs and benefits.[8] These policies should stimulate greater competition in the private and public medical sectors.

In the private sector, employers that subsidize their employees' health insurance should be encouraged to offer a choice of plans, give fixed-dollar contributions, and use risk-adjusted premiums in making such payments. With more plan choices and employee incentives to focus on the costs and benefits of a health plan, information is more accessible to help employees choose a plan. When consumers can choose, information has value, and private sources (e.g., Healthgrades) will provide that information, as has occurred in other markets.

For competitive markets to work, not all purchasers must be informed or switch plans in response to changes in prices and quality.[9] In competitive medical markets, as in other markets, a small percentage of knowledgeable consumers who switch is sufficient to drive the market toward greater efficiency.

Are the Poor Disadvantaged in a Competitive Market?

Opponents of competitive medical care markets claim that the poor will be unable to afford medical services. Competitive markets produce the most goods and services (with a given amount of resources) and sell them at the lowest possible price to consumers willing to buy. By doing so, competitive markets make goods and services more affordable to those with low income. However, competitive markets should not be evaluated on whether the poor receive all the medical services needed.

Achieving market efficiency has little to do with ensuring that everyone's needs are met or that everyone receives the same quantity of services. It is the role of government, based on voters' preferences, to subsidize healthcare for the poor—just as is done with food and housing. Providing the poor with subsidies (e.g., vouchers for a health plan) to be exercised in a competitive market is more likely than any other approach to ensure that they receive the greatest value for those subsidies.

Competitive medical markets may be considered unfair because those with high income are able to buy more than those with low income. The wealthy always have been, and always will be, able to buy more goods and services than can the poor. Even in the Canadian single-payer health system, patients with more money can skip the waiting lines and travel to the United States for diagnostic services and surgery.

Patient Incentives Drive Price Competition in Government and Private Markets

The following examples illustrate how a change in patient incentives resulted in a price-competitive healthcare market.

Medicare Part D Prescription Drug Benefit

In 2004, the Congressional Budget Office projected that the federal budgetary cost of the Medicare prescription drug benefit—Part D—for 2012 would be $122 billion. In 2012, the actual federal cost was $55 billion. Unlike any other government entitlement programs, the estimated federal cost of the drug benefit had been constant for more than 10 years, and cost much less than many anticipated.

The design of the Part D benefit differs from that of Medicare Parts A and B in that Part D makes the beneficiary responsible for the additional cost of choosing a more expensive drug plan. Under Part D, drug plans submit bids to the federal government for providing the basic prescription drug benefit to a beneficiary. The federal government calculates a national average bid and pays 75 percent of the national average bid to the drug plan chosen by the beneficiary, who is then responsible for the remaining 25 percent of the monthly premium. If a beneficiary enrolls in a plan that submitted a higher bid than the national average, the beneficiary pays the difference in addition to the base premium.

Plans understand that any difference between a plan's bid and the national average bid translates directly into a price difference that will be paid by beneficiaries.[10] Beneficiaries have access to a wide variety of drug plans and must choose among lower premium plans or costlier plans that may offer greater benefits, such as a more desirable drug formulary. Because competing plans vary in the brand-name drugs offered in their formulary, a person can choose the plan that covers their preferred drug. Under Medicare Part D, beneficiaries have an incentive to make a trade-off between additional plan benefits and the additional costs of a higher-priced plan.

Drug plans compete for enrollees by offering lower premiums. By relying on a drug formulary, rather than including all brand-name drugs within a disease category, the plan is able to negotiate discounted prices with a pharmaceutical firm by including only its drug in the formulary. Drug plans also encourage enrollees to use less costly generics when appropriate by using lower cost sharing for generics than for brand-name drugs. The drug plans pass on these cost-saving strategies to beneficiaries in the form of lower premiums and cost sharing.

Negotiating with drug manufacturers and encouraging generic substitution when appropriate are the direct result of plans competing for price-sensitive enrollees who must pay out of pocket the additional cost of higher-priced drug plans.

The ACA made changes to the Medicare Part D drug benefit that caused an increase in the number of Medicare drug prescriptions and in expenditures. First, the Part D "donut hole" was reduced, thereby reducing a Medicare beneficiary's out-of-pocket payments for his prescription drugs. Second, successful lobbying by the pharmaceutical association reduced competition between pharmaceutical firms and the private drug plans. Private drug plans now are required to include more than one drug per class in their formulary; this change reduced private drug plans' ability to negotiate lower drug prices with a pharmaceutical firm.

Value-Based Purchasing and Reference Pricing

In recent years, employers and insurers have begun to provide patients with financial incentives to choose higher-quality, lower-priced hospitals for their surgeries. Several employers (e.g., Walmart, Safeway, Lowe's) and insurers (e.g., WellPoint) have used value-based purchasing or reference pricing to give their employees a financial incentive to choose among competing providers (Robinson and MacPherson 2012). Under these approaches, the employer or insurer contracts for a fixed price with several centers of excellence (e.g., the Cleveland Clinic) for elective surgical procedures (e.g., orthopedic joint replacement, interventional cardiology, cardiac surgery). These are expensive procedures, whose prices vary widely, and differences in outcomes when performed by different providers are relatively small. Patients are given a fixed amount (e.g., $30,000) to cover the cost of their surgery. A patient can go to providers other than those on the employer's preferred list, but if the price is greater than $30,000, the patient pays the additional cost himself.

Robinson, Brown, and Whaley (2017) found that when patients were provided with a financial incentive, reference pricing resulted in significant savings. The most dramatic price reductions occurred in higher-priced hospitals. Also interesting is that when patients went to providers other than those on their employers' or insurers' preferred list, and when they had only $30,000 to spend, the patients were able to negotiate large price reductions. The insurer did not negotiate with these providers; the patients did. The authors stressed the importance of changing patients' financial incentives and not just relying on direct price negotiations between insurers and providers. When patients are responsible for the additional cost of their care, healthcare markets become price competitive.[11]

What Might Competitive Medical Markets Look Like?

If healthcare markets were to become more like a competitive market, what might one observe? As consumers (including Medicare and Medicaid enrollees) must pay the additional cost of more expensive health plans and become more cost conscious, the variety and number of available plans will increase. Plans will attempt to match purchasers' preferences and willingness to pay. Some people would prefer to choose among health plans, which is less expensive and time consuming than evaluating different providers.

Competitive markets may evolve in several ways. Integrated delivery systems, as articulated by Enthoven (2004), are organizations with their own provider networks that offer coordinated care to their enrollees. These integrated delivery systems may be built around large multispecialty medical groups with relationships to hospitals and other care settings, and they may be paid a risk-adjusted annual capitation amount per enrollee (similar to Medicare Advantage plans). Health plans would compete for consumers on the basis of risk-adjusted premiums. These systems would select healthcare providers, be responsible for monitoring quality, examine large data sets to develop evidence-based medicine guidelines, reduce widespread variations in physicians' practice patterns, provide coordinated care across different care settings (the physician's office, hospital, ambulatory care facility, and patient's home), have incentives to be innovative in caring for patients with chronic conditions, and minimize total treatment costs (not just the costs of providing care in one setting while shifting costs to other settings). In addition, health plans would be responsible for evaluating new technologies and, in turn, would be evaluated by how well they perform in improving the health of their enrolled populations, as well as how they perform with regard to premiums and patient satisfaction.

At the other end of the spectrum of financing and delivering medical services are consumer-directed health plans (CDHPs). Under the CDHP model, consumers purchase a high-deductible (catastrophic) plan, which provides them with the incentive to be concerned about the use of medical services and the prices of different healthcare providers. The health savings account (HSA) approach combines a high-deductible plan with a savings account; money saved in the HSA belongs to the individual and can accumulate year after year.

Health plans preferred by consumers will expand their market share, while others will decline. Health plans and large multispecialty medical groups will be motivated to innovate to reduce costs, improve quality and treatment outcomes, and achieve better patient satisfaction. By doing so, they will differentiate themselves from competitors and gain a competitive advantage. Other health plans will copy the methods used by successful competitors, and the process of innovation and differentiation will start over again. (Economist Joseph Schumpeter referred to this as the process of *creative destruction*.)

Summary

Antitrust authorities evaluate markets on the basis of how closely they approximate a competitive market. The closer the approximation, the more likely the market will produce products efficiently and be responsive to consumer demands. Medical markets are not inherently different from other markets in their ability to efficiently allocate resources. It is the regulatory framework of medical markets that leads to inefficient outcomes.

Medical markets differ from competitive markets in significant ways. The tax treatment of health insurance lessens consumer incentives to be concerned about the price and use of medical services. Consumers lack the necessary information to make economic and medical decisions; often, they are not offered choices. Competition among suppliers is limited by laws barring market entry, restricting the tasks healthcare professionals are permitted to perform, preventing price competition, and regulating market prices.

These market failures have resulted in inefficiency, inappropriate care, less-than-optimal medical outcomes, and rapidly rising medical costs. Increased government regulation has been shown to worsen rather than improve market performance. Several of the major inefficiencies in medical care markets are the result of government intervention. Regulation to limit rising medical prices was tried in the 1970s and failed. Medicare, which controls hospital and physician fees, fails to limit overuse of services and gaming of the system; upcoding and unbundling of services are common.[12] Under a system of government regulation of prices, budgets, and market entry, interest groups—such as hospitals, physicians, unions, and large employers—are more effective in representing their own economic interests than are consumers. Organized interest groups also are more effective than consumers in the political marketplace. Consumer interests are best served in competitive economic markets.

Government has an important role to play. It sets the rules for competitive markets, such as eliminating practices that result in anticompetitive behavior, monitoring inaccurate information, and enforcing antitrust laws. The government also is responsible for raising the funds to subsidize those unable to afford medical care; these subsidies can be provided at lower cost and higher quality in a competitive market.

Market competition has not failed in medical care. It just has not had a full opportunity to work. Consumer incentives must be changed so that individuals consider the costs and benefits of their healthcare choices. When Medicare beneficiaries had to pay the additional cost of more expensive drug plans, drug plan competition responded by greatly lowering the projected cost of the Medicare drug benefit. Similarly, when employees were provided with a fixed amount for their surgeries (reference pricing) and had to pay the additional cost themselves, they were able to negotiate reduced prices. Medicare enrollees should be offered a choice of health plans and given the option to pay the additional cost of a more expensive plan. In addition, restrictions on providers' ability to compete on price should be removed. Without competition, providers have no incentive to be efficient or to innovate, invest in new facilities and services, improve quality, develop best practices and clinical guidelines, or lower prices.

Discussion Questions

1. Why is it said that competition in medical care has failed?
2. What are the criteria for a competitive market?
3. How well does medical care meet the criteria of a competitive market?
4. Is it the responsibility of a competitive market to subsidize care for those with low income?
5. Explain why the cost of the Medicare Part D drug benefit has been lower than its projections.
6. What changes are required for medical care to more closely approximate a competitive market?

Notes

1. Growth of demand may result in temporary increases in prices (high price markups over cost), which equilibrate demand and supply so that shortages do not occur while signaling suppliers to raise their production to meet the greater demand. Over time, as supply grows, prices will again reflect the cost of providing those services.
2. Not every consumer purchases more when the price is reduced, but, on average, the quantity demanded will rise.
3. The tax exclusion for employer-purchased health insurance is unfair because employees in a higher tax bracket receive a greater subsidy

(see exhibit 6.2). It is also unfair to individuals who are not part of an employer group, because they do not qualify for the same tax exclusion. Individual coverage is more expensive, not only because of higher marketing costs and insurers' concern about adverse selection, but also because it is paid for with after-tax dollars.

4. Many small and medium-sized businesses were unable to offer their employees a choice of health plans; the indemnity plan was concerned that it would receive a higher-risk group. Thus, small businesses were typically offered only one plan for all of their employees.

5. Data on hospital quality—and to a lesser degree physician quality—have become available from more public sector and private sector sources. Such sources include Medicare's Hospital Compare (www.medicare.gov/hospitalcompare), the New York State Hospital Report Card (www.myhealthfinder.com), California's Office of Statewide Health Planning and Development (www.oshpd.ca.gov/HID/), Agency for Healthcare Research and Quality's Healthcare Cost and Utilization Project (www.ahrq.gov/research/data/hcup/index.html), and Healthgrades (www.healthgrades.com).

6. Exchange enrollees are exempt from these state mandates. Many individuals, however, buy insurance in nonexchange private markets and they continue to be subject to these mandates.

7. Starting in 2022, the ACA will impose a 40 percent tax on insurers of employer-sponsored health plans on the amount of employer-paid health insurance that exceeds $10,200 for individuals and $27,500 for family coverage.

8. Recent unsuccessful legislative proposals seeking to lower insurance premiums in the individual and small-group markets included permitting association health plans—organizations, such as nonemployer groups, ethnic organizations, and small business associations—to form and negotiate with insurers on behalf of their members. These associations will have stable insurance pools and greater bargaining power with insurers.

9. In some markets, such as rural areas, competition among health plans is unlikely to be strong enough to achieve the same efficiency as that in large urban areas. Rural populations do not have the same choices regarding other services either.

10. When a Medicare Advantage plan's bid is below the benchmark premium, the plan must provide additional benefits rather than pass the price difference on to the enrollee in the form of lower premiums. This difference results in Medicare Part D drug plan enrollees paying lower premiums, whereas Medicare Advantage plan enrollees must

receive more benefits rather than have a choice of benefits versus lower premiums.

11. Goodman (2011) discusses how price competition also leads to quality competition.

12. Unbundling occurs when a provider charges separately for each of the services previously provided together as part of a treatment. Upcoding occurs when the provider bills for a higher-priced diagnosis or service than was provided.

References

Berenson, R., P. Ginsburg, and N. Kemper. 2010. "Unchecked Provider Clout in California Foreshadows Challenges to Health Reform." *Health Affairs* 29 (4): 699–705.

Centers for Medicare & Medicaid Services. 2017. "National Health Expenditure Data." Accessed December. www.cms.gov/Research-Statistics-Data-and-Systems/Statistics-Trends-and-Reports/NationalHealthExpendData/index.html.

Enthoven, A. 2004. "Market Forces and Efficient Health Care Systems." *Health Affairs* 23 (2): 25–27.

———. 1993. "Why Managed Care Has Failed to Contain Health Costs." *Health Affairs* 12 (3): 27–43.

Enthoven, A., and L. Tollen. 2005. "Competition in Health Care: It Takes Systems to Pursue Quality and Efficiency." *Health Affairs* 24 (Suppl. 1): W5-420–W5-433. www.ncbi.nlm.nih.gov/pubmed/16148024.

Ginsburg, P. 2016. "Health Care Market Consolidations: Impacts on Costs, Quality and Access." Testimony before the California Senate Committee on Health. Brookings Institution. Published March 16. www.brookings.edu/testimonies/health-care-market-consolidations-impacts-on-costs-quality-and-access/.

Goodman, J. 2011. "Will Price Competition Lead to Quality Competition?" *Health Affairs Blog*. Published April 21. http://healthaffairs.org/blog/2011/04/21/will-price-competition-lead-to-quality-competition/.

Institute of Medicine. 2013. *Variation in Health Care Spending: Target Decision Making, Not Geography*. Washington, DC: National Academies Press.

Jha, A., and A. Epstein. 2006. "The Predictive Accuracy of the New York State Coronary Artery Bypass Surgery Report-Card System." *Health Affairs* 25 (3): 844–55.

Kaiser Family Foundation and Health Research & Educational Trust. 2017. *Employer Health Benefits: 2017 Annual Survey*. Accessed April 2018. http://files.kff.org/attachment/Report-Employer-Health-Benefits-Annual-Survey-2017.

National Conference of State Legislatures. 2018. "State Insurance Mandates and the ACA Essential Benefits Provisions." Published April 12. www.ncsl.org/research/health/state-ins-mandates-and-aca-essential-benefits.aspx.

Robinson, J., T. Brown, and C. Whaley. 2017. "Reference Pricing Changes the 'Choice Architecture' of Health Care for Consumers." *Health Affairs* 36 (3): 524–30.

Robinson, J., and K. MacPherson. 2012. "Payers Test Reference Pricing and Centers of Excellence to Steer Patients to Low-Price and High-Quality Providers." *Health Affairs* 31 (9): 2028–36.

Rosenthal, J., X. Lu, and P. Cram. 2013. "Availability of Consumer Prices from US Hospitals for a Common Surgical Procedure." *JAMA Internal Medicine* 173 (6): 427–32.

COMPARATIVE EFFECTIVENESS RESEARCH

As part of the $787 billion stimulus bill passed in 2010, Congress allocated $1.1 billion for comparative effectiveness research (CER). The Affordable Care Act (ACA) of 2010 included an additional $3 billion for studies to compare the effectiveness of different treatments for the same illness. The different treatments include drugs, medical devices, surgery, and other ways of treating a specific medical condition (Emanuel, Spiro, and Huelskoetter 2016).

CER and the Role of Government

What Is CER?

The scope of CER includes conducting, supporting, and synthesizing research that compares the clinical outcomes, effectiveness, and appropriateness of services and procedures used to prevent, diagnose, and treat diseases and other health conditions. CER involves three major areas: (1) comparing new treatments for an illness with the best available alternatives for treating that illness, (2) using the information from CER to improve joint physician and patient decision making, and (3) basing the data on which these comparative studies are to be conducted on a sufficiently large population.

Physicians lack information on the effectiveness of alternative treatments for many diseases. For some illnesses, the relative effectiveness of alternative treatments has not been studied; for others, the results of effectiveness studies have not been disseminated to all physicians. The CER's federal coordinating council has developed a priority list of diseases and is awarding grants to study the comparative effectiveness of alternative treatments for diseases highest on the priority list. CER is a continuing process that is conducted on more conditions as new treatments become available for illnesses whose alternative treatments previously were studied (Conway and Clancy 2009).

Why Is the Government Supporting CER?

Public insurance programs, such as Medicare, and private health insurance pay for medical treatments regardless of how small the benefit or how large the cost. Under fee-for-service payment, neither insured patients nor their physicians have any incentive not to seek the most advanced medical treatments in search of a cure. Further, many policy experts acknowledge that insufficient information exists on which treatments work best for different diseases. New drugs are typically compared with a placebo rather than with a drug already on the market.

Given the soaring cost of healthcare and the belief that each year hundreds of billions of dollars are spent on care that is of no value, more accurate information on which treatments perform better will improve quality of care and reduce the wide variations in treatment methods, thereby reducing rising medical expenditures. Few people are opposed to providing consumers, physicians, and insurers with additional information on treatments that are more effective.

As shown in exhibit 22.1, several well-known academic medical centers were compared according to their total reimbursements per decedent, hospital days per decedent, and reimbursement per day for treating a patient during the last two years of his or her life. Wide variations existed among these medical centers in each of these measures. The study authors also showed that wide variations existed in the underlying resources, such as nurse staffing and physician hours, used to treat these patients in the institutions. The federal government can play a crucial role in aggregating information about the effectiveness of various medicines and treatments and disseminating that information to physicians and their patients.

EXHIBIT 22.1
Medicare Spending per Decedent During the Last Two Years of Life (Deaths Occurring in 2014), Selected Academic Medical Centers

Academic Medical Center	Inpatient Reimbursements per Decedent	Hospital Days per Decedent	Reimbursements per Day
Johns Hopkins Hospital	$93,233	26.5	$3,520
Ronald Reagan UCLA Medical Center	$79,182	29.1	$2,721
University of Maryland Medical Center	$78,753	25.3	$3,109
Hahnemann University Hospital	$63,932	26.7	$2,397
Massachusetts General Hospital	$53,159	25.6	$2,080
Cleveland Clinic Foundation	$41,769	21.9	$1,904
Mayo Clinic-St. Mary's Hospital	$40,978	16.9	$2,429
Scott & White Memorial Hospital	$32,707	15.4	$2,118

Source: Data from Dartmouth Institute for Health Policy and Clinical Practice (2017).

Advocates of public funding for CER claim that such information has the characteristics of a public good—that is, everyone benefits from the information generated and that information cannot be denied to anyone once it becomes available. Because the information cannot be restricted to those who pay for it, the private sector (health plans) will invest too little to collect such information. Many, therefore, want government to fund CER and assist in the dissemination of such information.

Concerns over How CER Will Be Used

Using CER for Reimbursement

Funding for CER generated a great deal of controversy when it was enacted in 2010. Critics were concerned that once the effectiveness of two treatments or drugs was determined, the relative costs of the two treatments would also be used to determine which drugs should be used. Fearful of being accused of promoting "death panels," Congress prohibited the use of information based on CER for mandating coverage, reimbursement, or treatment decisions for public and private payers. However, many remain concerned that under the fiscal pressures of rising medical costs, use of CER results will eventually move closer to the way in which European countries use their findings on comparative effectiveness (Nix 2012).

Some opponents of government-funded CER believe that the government would ultimately use the findings from such research to establish medical practice guidelines, limit access to treatments, and refuse to pay for expensive new drugs. This concern was reinforced by a book by Tom Daschle, who was nominated by President Obama to become secretary of the US Department of Health and Human Services. (He subsequently withdrew his name amid a growing controversy over his failure to accurately report and pay income taxes.) Daschle had proposed a federal health board that would promote high-value medical care by recommending coverage of drugs and procedures based on the board's research (Daschle, Greenberger, and Lambrew 2008).

Differences in Patient Responses to the Same Treatment

CER is a one-size-fits-all approach to medicine; however, patients' responses to different drugs vary widely. Those who do not respond well to the recommended treatment are at a disadvantage. For example, for most patients, a generic drug is cheaper and works as well as a brand-name drug. However, for some patients the generic version may cause serious side effects or have little effect. Thus, although a branded and a generic drug may be equally effective on average, not paying for the newer, more expensive drug may lead to increased hospitalization costs and worse health outcomes for those patients who do not respond well to the cheaper drug.

The problem with a one-size-fits-all approach is illustrated by a CER analysis of antipsychotic drugs, which found little difference between the effectiveness of older, less costly antipsychotic drugs and newer, more costly drugs. Using the older drugs could have saved Medicaid $1.2 billion (out of the $5.5 billion spent on these drugs in 2005). However, Basu, Jena, and Philipson (2011) concluded that the mental health of thousands of patients would have been worse and societal costs would have been greater than any savings from using the less costly drugs.

Variations in Medical Practice

While most agree that wide variation occurs in medical practice, huge amounts of money are wasted on ineffective treatments and testing, and more information would be beneficial, there is opposition to moving from information generation and dissemination to basing payment on CER. Zuckerman and colleagues (2010) attempted to explain why wide variations in medical spending occur. Using data on Medicare beneficiaries, they found that unadjusted Medicare spending per beneficiary was 52 percent greater in the highest-spending geographic region than in the lowest-spending region. The authors then adjusted the regions based on demographics, baseline health characteristics, and changes in health status. The difference between the highest and lowest regions then decreased to 33 percent. Health status was found to explain an important part of this variation. Although inefficiency in spending per Medicare beneficiary exists, wide cost differences across geographic areas are not the result of inefficiency alone.

Policies to decrease spending differences per beneficiary between high- and low-cost areas by reimbursing physicians only for treatments that follow certain protocols or guidelines should not ignore the legitimate reasons for some of these variations.

Accuracy and Timeliness of Comparative Effectiveness Studies

One study generally does not provide a definitive answer; several studies likely will have to be undertaken. For example, bone marrow transplantation for breast cancer was widely accepted as beneficial, and patients won lawsuits because some health plans refused to cover it. Subsequently, researchers found that this treatment was ineffective.

Comparative effectiveness studies may not adequately evaluate alternative treatments for patients with multiple chronic diseases or rare illnesses. Similarly, CER often does not include sufficient numbers of women, African Americans, and Hispanics. Some drugs appear to be more effective in women than in men, while other medicines are more likely to cause serious complications in women. CER must include larger numbers of patients in clinical trials so that gender and minority differences can be considered. As CER studies are expanded to account for such differences, the time and money needed to complete these clinical trials will increase (Chandra, Jena, and Skinner 2011).

Because it takes time to complete CER and for guidelines to be approved by the government, physicians and their patients may be willing to try untested therapies, as occurred for AIDS patients. Will they be permitted to do so? Will providers be reimbursed for these therapies?

CER and Innovation

An additional concern is that CER might lead to slower adoption of new, more effective treatments. As new treatments and prescription drugs are developed, will reimbursement for them be delayed until their comparative effectiveness has been determined? Physicians might be willing to try new surgical techniques that offer the possibility of improved patient outcomes; will they and the hospital have to forgo payment because these techniques have not undergone CER? Will the healthcare system become more rigid and less innovative because physicians fear repercussions if their treatments differ from the official guidelines? Will health plans refuse to reimburse for procedures and treatments that are not within the federal recommendations?

Medical device and pharmaceutical companies are also likely to face another layer of government approval that will increase their cost to bring a product to market, thereby decreasing their incentive for innovation.

Dissemination of CER Findings

CER results must be disseminated. Will dissemination of information, which often is slow and may go against the financial interest of some physicians, be sufficient to lead to adoption of the CER? Or will financial incentives and reporting requirements be necessary? A concern with providing information to physicians is that their rate of adoption of new practices is very slow. If information is to change medical practice, lower costs, and improve quality, physician practice behavior will have to change more rapidly. However, without appropriate incentives, new information often takes years to change physician behavior.

Exhibit 22.2 provides several examples of the time from dissemination of information to treatment adoption by physicians. In 1988, the Food and Drug Administration approved the use of aspirin for treatment of heart attacks, which resulted in an increase in use from 20 percent to 62 percent. However, by the mid-1990s, aspirin use had only increased to 75 percent. After studies were published indicating the potential harmful effects of calcium-channel blockers, their use declined but remained above 30 percent ten years later.

Possible Stages in Use of CER

Again, the legislation providing government funding for CER states that CER will not be used for reimbursement or coverage decisions. However, some people

EXHIBIT 22.2
Use of Acute
Interventions
(Pharma-
ceuticals) for
Myocardial
Infarction

Pharmaceuticals	Year of Innovation	Pharmaceutical Use[a]				
		1973–1977	1978–1982	1983–1987	1988–1992	1993–1996
Beta blockers	1962	20.6	41.5	47.5	47.3	49.8
Calcium channel blockers[b]	1971	0	0	63.9	59.0	31.0
Angiotensin-converting enzyme (ACE) inhibitors	1979	0	—	—	—	56.0
Aspirin	1988[c]	15.0	14.1	20.1	62.0	75.0

[a]In hospital or 30-day use.

[b]Calcium channel blocker use increased rapidly in the early 1980s and then fell, following the publication of studies documenting potentially harmful effects of their use in acute management.

[c]In 1988, the Food and Drug Administration (FDA) proposed the use of aspirin for reducing the risk of recurrent myocardial infarction (MI), or heart attack, and preventing first MI in patients with unstable angina. The FDA also approved the use of aspirin for the prevention of recurrent transient ischemic attacks, or "mini-strokes," in men and made aspirin standard therapy for previous strokes in men.

Source: Adapted from Cutler, McClellan, and Newhouse (1999, tables 3 and 5).

believe that government funding of CER is just the first stage in its evolution. CER opponents foresee the following stages. First, CER provides information about the clinical effectiveness of different treatments and drugs for a disease. Second, their cost-effectiveness is compared. Third, given the rising costs of medical care and the increasing burden on the federal deficit, the government only pays for those drugs and other treatments that are cost-effective, even though the effects may differ among people or population groups. Fourth, instead of deciding which drug it will pay for on the basis of cost-effectiveness, the government decides which drugs and treatments it will pay for by comparing the cost of the drug with the value of an additional year of life (as occurs in Great Britain).

The following sections examine cost-effectiveness, how CER might be used for reimbursement, and how CER is used in Great Britain.

Cost-Effectiveness Analysis

Cost-effectiveness analysis compares the additional costs of alternative approaches to achieve a specific outcome designed to improve health. For example, an organization interested in decreasing hip fractures would want to know the different programs that can reduce hip fractures, the cost of expanding each program, and the extent of reduction in hip fractures each would achieve. Results from a cost-effectiveness analysis are typically presented in the form of a cost-effectiveness ratio, where the numerator of the ratio is the additional cost of the intervention and the denominator is some measure of the outcome of interest.

Alternative approaches for decreasing hip fractures are likely to differ in costs and effectiveness. Thus, they can be compared according to their cost-effectiveness ratio, which is the additional cost per averted hip fracture. (For an example of cost-effectiveness analysis, see exhibit 3.3.)

Calculating the cost-effectiveness ratio for each alternative method of achieving a given health outcome allows a comparison of the trade-offs from choosing one alternative over another. Decision makers—whether they are administrators in government agencies such as Medicaid or health maintenance organization managers—can make better-informed choices about the relative costs and effectiveness of alternative interventions by using cost-effectiveness analysis. When selecting among alternative expenditures to improve health, alternative interventions can be ranked according to their cost-effectiveness ratios (e.g., cost per death averted), giving the intervention with the lowest ratio the highest priority. Choosing interventions on the basis of the lowest cost-effectiveness ratio maximizes the outcome for a given budget.

Many cost-effectiveness studies have been conducted on the relative effectiveness of a new drug compared with existing drugs for treating the same disease. The originators of such studies include health plans seeking to determine which drugs to include in their formularies and pharmaceutical firms hoping to use the results to demonstrate to large purchasers the greater effectiveness of their new drugs compared with those of competitors.

A concern with cost-effectiveness analysis if used for reimbursement by the government is that, as discussed earlier, patients may differ in their response to a drug or other treatment. Medical costs could be higher if patients respond poorly to certain drugs and must be hospitalized. Further, the government's cost-effectiveness ratio may be different from the patient's cost or evaluation of the treatment's effectiveness.

Quality-Adjusted Life Years

A specific type of cost-effectiveness analysis uses quality-adjusted life years (QALYs) as an outcome measure. QALYs indicate the increased utility achieved as the result of an intervention, such as comparing a new drug to an existing one. The cost-effectiveness ratios are in terms of the cost per QALYs gained. The advantage of using QALYs rather than, for example, life expectancy is that QALY incorporates multiple outcomes—increase in length of life and quality of life. Using QALYs as an outcome measure also enables comparisons to be made across different disease conditions.

QALY is calculated as follows: Each additional year of perfect health for an individual is assigned a value of 1.0, which is the highest value of a complete QALY. The assigned value decreases as health decreases, with death equal to 0.0. If the patient has various limitations—such as a disability, physical pain, or receipt of kidney dialysis—the extra life years are assigned a value between 1.0 and 0.0. Thus, if new intervention A enables a person to live an additional five years, but with a quality of life weight of 0.7, then the QALY score for that intervention is 5 × 0.7 = 3.5 QALYs. If intervention B extends life for four years with a quality of life weight of 0.6, the additional QALYs provided are 4 × 0.6 = 2.4. The net benefit of intervention A over intervention B is 3.5 QALYs – 2.4 QALYs = 1.1 QALYs.

When comparing alternative interventions according to their additional cost per QALY, those with a lower cost per QALY are preferred to those with a higher cost per QALY. A common approach for developing QALYs involves the use of an activities of daily living (ADL) scale. Patients are asked to rate their ability to function independently, such as dressing, bathing, and walking. Patient responses range from unable to perform the function to able to perform the function without difficulty. These scores are summed over all the ADL categories to arrive at a patient's overall functional status.

The calculation of QALYs is the same regardless of a person's income, wealth, or age; however, QALYs that occur in later years may be valued less than QALYs occurring earlier in life.[1]

QALYs have several drawbacks. For example, QALY does not include the effects of a patient's disability on the quality of life of others, such as family members. Assigning a quantitative value to a disability may not be accurate because people differ in their perceptions of the severity of various limitations on their normal activity. Further, applying these utility measures across a large, diverse population is unlikely to reflect many individuals' utility preferences. Yet using QALYs for a large population is necessary if alternative medical treatments are to be compared.

Applications of QALYs

QALYs have been used in two types of policy analysis. First, they are used as an outcome measure in cost-effectiveness analysis to compare alternative interventions in determining which intervention offers the lowest cost per QALY. Second, and more controversial, cost per QALY has been used to determine benefit coverage—for example, to decide whether a costly treatment, such as an expensive new drug, should be provided to a breast cancer patient (Baumgardner and Neumann 2017).

Exhibit 22.3 shows the results of several cost-effectiveness studies examining different drug therapies potentially applicable to the Medicare population. Each study describes an intervention compared with the alternative of no

Intervention vs. Base Case in Target Population	Dollars per QALY Gained
Captopril therapy vs. no captopril in 80-year-old patients surviving myocardial infarction	$4,000
Treatment with mesalazine vs. no treatment to maintain remission in Crohn's disease	$6,000
One-year course of isoniazid (INH) chemoprophylaxis vs. no INH chemoprophylaxis in 55-year-old white male tuberculin reactors with no other risk factors	$18,000
Treatment to reduce the incidence of osteoporotic hip fracture vs. no treatment in 62-year-old woman with established osteoporosis	$34,000
Ticlopidine vs. aspirin in 65-year-old with high risk of stroke	$48,000
Chemotherapy vs. no chemotherapy in 75-year-old with breast cancer	$58,000
Captopril vs. propranolol in persons in the US population aged 35–64 years without the diagnosis of coronary heart disease but with essential hypertension	$150,000
Antiemetic therapy with ondansetron vs. antiemetic therapy with metoclopramide in 70-kg patient receiving cisplatin chemotherapy who had not been previously exposed to antineoplastic agents	$460,000

EXHIBIT 22.3
Selected Cost-Effectiveness Ratios for Pharmaceuticals, with a Focus on the Medicare Population

Note: QALY = quality-adjusted life year.

Source: Adapted from Neumann and colleagues (2000, exhibit 3).

treatment. The results, in the form of cost per QALY gained, are ranked from lowest to highest cost per QALY. Therapies whose cost per QALY is relatively low (e.g., $4,000) are very favorable. Therapies with a relatively high cost per QALY (e.g., $460,000) are considered unfavorable and less likely to be adopted.

The National Institute for Health and Care Excellence

Great Britain established the National Health Service (NHS) in 1948 as a single-payer system, administered by the government, funded through taxation, and provided by public institutions. The British government has a long history of underfunding the NHS, resulting in long waiting lines and failure to provide certain types of treatments. To limit expenditures on expensive innovative medical technology and drugs and to attempt to rationalize its limited budget, in 1999 the government formed the National Institute for Clinical Excellence (NICE)—now called the National Institute for Health and Care Excellence—a private, independent organization in the Department of Health, to provide guidance on health technology, clinical medicine, and new prescription drugs. Its decisions are based on clinical efficacy and cost-effectiveness (NICE 2018; Rawlins 2013).

NICE uses QALYs to determine which treatments to cover in the NHS. Given that budget constraints exist on the amount the government can spend for medical services, NICE undertakes cost-effectiveness analysis for new drugs and treatments in an attempt to provide patients, health professionals, and the public with scientifically based guidance on current best practices. A NICE committee consisting of medical and other professionals, such as health economists, statisticians, managers, patient advocates, and manufacturer representatives, assists in its decision making.

Before NICE was established, the availability of costly treatments varied greatly throughout the country, as did the level of medical services. NICE has made the availability of drugs and treatments more uniform throughout the NHS. Decisions by NICE are transparent to all, and the information on which it bases its decisions is also publicly available. Further, when NICE believes that a treatment or drug is cost-beneficial, it attempts to ensure that the treatment or drug becomes widely available.

The main criticism of NICE is that it bases its recommendations primarily on cost-effectiveness rather than on clinical effectiveness (Hope 2011; Steinbrook 2008). The criticism that NICE is coldhearted stems from the fact that it uses cost per QALY to determine cost-effectiveness. One of NICE's most contentious issues is how much should be spent per additional year of life that a drug is expected to provide. NICE's general threshold is about $66,000 per QALY. If a treatment's cost per QALY is higher, NICE will generally deny the treatment. (In 2016, NICE set the cost per QALY threshold for treatment of rare diseases at $132,000.)

The following example illustrates how NICE uses its cost per QALY to determine approval for costly treatments. A *New York Times* article tells the story of Bruce Hardy, a patient fighting kidney cancer that was spreading throughout his body (Harris 2008). His physician wanted to prescribe a new drug from Pfizer called sunitinib malate (Sutent), which delays cancer progression for six months at a cost of $54,000. NICE, however, decided that the drug was too costly to be offered free to all those who needed it. According to NICE, the cost of extending life for six months should be no more than $22,750; therefore, Hardy could not receive the drug. When NICE rejected Sutent, some patients mortgaged their homes to pay for the drug on their own. After much protest, NICE reversed its decision and approved the drug. NICE has also limited the use of certain breast cancer drugs, such as trastuzumab (Herceptin), and drugs for osteoporosis and multiple sclerosis.

Great Britain has been explicit in recognizing that resources are scarce and choices must be made on how to allocate those scarce resources. At some point, with rising medical costs and a huge government deficit, will the United States become as explicit or, more likely, make such decisions implicitly by limiting healthcare provider reimbursement, thereby limiting the resources available for new technology and expensive drugs?

Summary

CER should provide additional information to physicians and their patients regarding the effectiveness of alternative treatments. To the extent that wide variations in medical practice are the result of lack of information, CER should improve patient outcomes and reduce medical costs. However, if the CER findings are used for reimbursement or coverage decisions, some patients may suffer adverse health consequences, and the medical system could become less innovative.

Some policy experts are concerned that federal funding for CER is but the first step toward limiting government payment for treatments considered less effective than others or too expensive with respect to their return in extending life expectancy. If CER studies demonstrate that a new drug for $1,000 a year usually provides greater benefits than a $50,000 surgical procedure, but the financial incentive for many surgeons is to continue performing the more expensive procedure, will insurers and the government continue to pay for both treatments? Great Britain's NICE is often cited as an example of a government agency that determines which medical treatments will be covered based on cost-effectiveness. Using cost-effectiveness, NICE covers only those treatments that do not exceed a certain threshold, such as the cost per QALY not exceeding the value of a life. Although the ACA states that CER shall not be used as a basis for payment, some are concerned that the United States may eventually use cost-effectiveness in reimbursement of medical services.

Society cannot spend an infinite amount of money to extend each person's life; choices must be made. Economics requires trade-offs because resources are scarce and can be spent on enhancing life in other ways. The opportunity cost of spending $100,000 on a new drug that extends the life of a terminally ill patient by three months is that those same funds could be spent on prenatal care or to increase the life expectancy of very-low-birthweight infants. Spending resources on additional medical services to extend one person's life involves having fewer resources to spend on extending the lives of others. States and the federal government, faced with higher limits on their expenditures and increasing demands for costly medical services, will have to make difficult choices in coming years.

The proposal to create a separate federal health board to make difficult political decisions regarding which medical services and prescription drugs to fund insulates legislators from making these difficult choices, such as denying expensive but potentially life-extending services to a patient whose need for the treatment has been discussed in the media.

Discussion Questions

1. What are the advantages of CER?
2. What are disadvantages of using CER for federal payment?
3. What are QALYs?
4. How are QALYs used in cost-effectiveness analysis?
5. How does NICE use QALYs in determining whether to approve a new drug?

Note

1. When interventions produce QALYs over different periods, discounting may be used to convert them into equivalently valued units at the present period, similar to discounting future income streams (as is done in a cost–benefit analysis). To determine the present value of future QALYs, the number of QALYs in each future year should be multiplied by $(1/1 + rt)$, where r is the discount rate—such as 0.05—and t represents the number of years from the future to the present.

Additional Readings

Health Affairs. 2012. "Current Challenges in Comparative Effectiveness Research." Published October. www.healthaffairs.org/toc/hlthaff/31/10.

———. 2010. "Comparative Effectiveness Research." Published October. www.health affairs.org/toc/hlthaff/29/10.

Neumann, P. J., J. T. Cohen, and M. C. Weinstein. 2014. "Updating Cost-Effectiveness: The Curious Resilience of the $50,000-per-QALY Threshold." *New England Journal of Medicine* 371 (9): 796–97.

References

Basu, A., A. Jena, and T. Philipson. 2011. "Impact of Comparative Effectiveness Research on Health and Healthcare Spending." *Journal of Health Economics* 30 (4): 695–706.

Baumgardner, J., and P. J. Neumann. 2017. "Balancing the Use of Cost-Effectiveness Analysis Across All Types of Health Care Innovations." *Health Affairs Blog*. Posted April 14. www.healthaffairs.org/do/10.1377/hblog20170414.059610/full/.

Chandra, A., A. Jena, and J. Skinner. 2011. "The Pragmatist's Guide to Comparative Effectiveness Research." *Journal of Economic Perspectives* 25 (2): 27–46.

Conway, P., and C. Clancy. 2009. "Comparative-Effectiveness Research: Implications of the Federal Coordinating Council's Report." *New England Journal of Medicine* 361 (4): 328–30.

Cutler, D., M. McClellan, and J. Newhouse. 1999. "The Costs and Benefits of Intensive Treatment for Cardiovascular Disease." In *Measuring the Prices of Medical Treatments*, edited by J. Triplett, 34–71. Washington, DC: The Brookings Institution.

Dartmouth Institute for Health Policy and Clinical Practice. 2017. "Care of Chronically Ill Patients During the Last Two Years of Life." Dartmouth Atlas of Health Care. Accessed April 2018. www.dartmouthatlas.org/tools/downloads.aspx?tab=40.

Daschle, T., S. Greenberger, and J. Lambrew. 2008. *Critical: What We Can Do About the Health-Care Crisis.* New York: Thomas Dunne Books.

Emanuel, Z., T. Spiro, and T. Huelskoetter. 2016. "Re-evaluating the Patient-Centered Outcomes Research Institute." Center for American Progress. Posted May 31. www.americanprogress.org/issues/healthcare/reports/2016/05/31/138242/re-evaluating-the-patient-centered-outcomes-research-institute/.

Harris, G. 2008. "British Balance Benefit vs. Cost of Latest Drugs." *New York Times.* Published December 2. www.nytimes.com/2008/12/03/health/03nice.html.

Hope, J. 2011. "Breakthrough MS Pill Rejected as Too Expensive by NHS Watchdog (but You Can Get It in U.S. and Germany)." *Mail Online.* Published August 5. www.dailymail.co.uk/health/article-2022767/Miracle-MS-pillrejected-expensive-NHS-watchdog-available-U-S-Germany.html.

National Institute for Health and Care Excellence (NICE). 2018. "About." Accessed April. www.nice.org.uk/aboutnice/.

Neumann, P. J., E. A. Sandberg, C. M. Bell, P. W. Stone, and R. H. Chapman. 2000. "Are Pharmaceuticals Cost-Effective? A Review of the Evidence." *Health Affairs* 19 (2): 92–109.

Nix, K. 2012. "Comparative Effectiveness Research Under Obamacare: A Slippery Slope to Health Care Rationing." Heritage Foundation. *Backgrounder* No. 2679. Published April 12. http://thf_media.s3.amazonaws.com/2012/pdf/bg2679.pdf.

Rawlins, M. 2013. "NICE—Moving Onward." *New England Journal of Medicine* 369 (1): 3–5.

Steinbrook, R. 2008. "Saying No Isn't NICE—the Travails of Britain's National Institute for Health and Clinical Excellence." *New England Journal of Medicine* 359 (19): 1977–81.

Zuckerman, S., T. Waldman, R. Berenson, and J. Hadley. 2010. "Clarifying Sources of Geographic Differences in Medicare Spending." *New England Journal of Medicine* 363 (1): 54–62.

WHO BEARS THE COST OF EMPLOYEE HEALTH BENEFITS?

Many health policies affect employees directly and indirectly. Employer-paid health insurance is tax exempt to the employee; the Affordable Care Act (ACA) employer mandate requires employers to offer and pay a portion of the employee's health insurance or pay a penalty; the ACA permits employees to keep their children on their employer-paid health insurance until age 26; many employees receive employer-paid health benefits when they retire; and employers complain that their employees' rising medical costs make them less price competitive.

Employees appear to be the beneficiary of these health policies while employers and others seemingly bear the costs. However, many misconceptions arise as to who really pays for employee health benefits. To understand who benefits and who bears the costs of policies affecting employees, it is necessary to review how competitive labor markets work.

How Labor Markets Function

The market for labor is competitive. Firms compete for different types of labor, and employees compete for jobs. This competition results in similar prices for specific types of labor. For example, if a hospital pays its nurses less than other hospitals in the area, the nurses will move to the hospital that pays the highest wages. Not all nurses have to change jobs to bring about similar pay among hospitals. Some nurses will move, and the hospital will find it difficult to replace them. The hospital will soon realize that its pay levels are below what nurses are receiving elsewhere. In reality, not all firms have the same working conditions, and they are not all located near one another. Employees are willing to accept lower pay for more pleasant conditions, and they require higher pay to travel longer distances. The greater the similarity in how firms treat their employees, and the more closely located they are, the more quickly wage differences disappear.

When an employer hires an employee, the cost of that employee cannot exceed his value to the firm; otherwise, the firm will not profit from hiring the employee. The total cost to the firm of an employee consists of two parts: cash wages and noncash fringe benefits. The cost of hiring an additional worker is the total compensation—cash and noncash benefits—that the firm will have to pay to that employee. The employer does not care whether employees want 90 percent of their total compensation in cash and 10 percent in noncash fringe benefits or a cash–noncash ratio of 60 to 40. The employer is interested only in an employee's total cost.

Employees working in high-wage industries typically prefer a higher ratio of fringe benefits to cash wages because of the tax advantages of having benefits purchased with pretax income. Low-wage industries typically provide their employees with few benefits; most of their compensation is in cash income. The combination of cash and noncash income reflects the preferences of employees, not employers. If an employer compensates its low-wage employees with a high proportion of fringe benefits, the employees will seek the same total compensation at another firm that pays them a higher percentage of cash wages.

Who Bears the Cost of Rising Employee Medical Costs?

What happens when the fringe benefits portion of total compensation rises sharply, as occurs when health insurance premiums increase? For example, assume that employees in a particular industry are expected to receive a 5 percent increase in compensation the following year, but health insurance premiums, which are paid by the employer and represent 10 percent of the employees' total compensation, are expected to rise by 20 percent. The employer is always concerned with the total cost; thus, cash wages in that industry would rise by only 3.3 percent. A trade-off occurs between fringe benefits and cash wages.

If one firm in the industry gave its employees a 5 percent wage increase plus paid the 20 percent increase in insurance premiums, that firm would incur higher labor costs than all other firms in the industry. What are the consequences to the firm? To incur above-market labor costs, the firm would have to make less profit or increase the prices of the products it sells. If the firm were to make less profit, it would earn a lower return on invested capital. This lower return would lead investors to move their capital to other firms in the industry, to other industries, or to other countries where they can earn a higher return.

Capital knows no loyalties or geographic boundaries; it will move to receive the highest return (consistent with a given level of risk). Thus, higher labor costs cannot impose a permanently lower return to a firm; otherwise, the firm will shrink as it loses capital. The same would be true if labor costs among all firms in the industry increased and profits declined.

What if the firm or industry passes the higher labor costs on to consumers by raising prices? As long as the firm competes with others in the industry or with manufacturers in other countries, and consumers are price sensitive to the firm's product, the firm will lose sales.[1] Good substitutes to any firm's (or industry's) product are generally available, either other products or the same product from other manufacturers. Thus, large price differences for the same or similar products cannot be maintained. The failure to keep prices in line with a competitor's prices will reduce sales, with a consequent flight of capital from that firm or industry.

As long as competition with other firms or foreign competitors (or both) exists, and capital can move to other industries and countries, rising medical costs will not result in lower profits or higher prices but will be borne by employees in the form of lower cash wages.

Short-Term Effects of Rising Employee Medical Costs

Although rising medical costs typically are carried by the employee in the form of lower cash wages, an employer could experience a short-term effect on profits. Shifting the cost of health insurance back to employees is difficult in the short run. For example, if an employer did not anticipate how rapidly medical costs would increase and, perhaps because of a long-term labor agreement, the firm is unable to lower its employees' wages to compensate for the higher-than-expected medical costs, profitability could decline.

Few firms, however, have been unaware of how rapidly medical costs have been increasing. Thus, rising costs are built into labor agreements. However, medical costs also could rise less rapidly than anticipated, increasing profitability. In any case, unanticipated cost increases will be reflected in future wage agreements and will not affect profitability over time.

An Example of Who Bears the Cost of Rising Medical Costs

Automobile executives have long complained that their competitors in other countries have lower healthcare costs per employee, enabling them to sell their products at a lower price than US manufacturers.[2] After labor costs, healthcare is often the largest cost for many firms and employees' healthcare expenses have been increasing faster than any other single cost incurred in producing a vehicle. Unless healthcare costs can be controlled, the executives claim, US business will be priced out of international markets and foreign producers will increase their market share in the United States.

Do rising employee healthcare costs really make US industries less competitive than their foreign counterparts?

The following example illustrates why labor, not the firm, bears the burden of higher insurance premiums. Automobiles can be produced in Michigan or in the southern part of the United States. Unless the prices of cars produced in Michigan and in the South are the same, consumers will purchase the least expensive cars, assuming their quality is similar. In addition, unless labor costs and productivity are similar in both places, the automobile manufacturers would move their production facilities to the less costly location. Yet we observe that within the automobile industry, employees' medical costs and insurance premiums are higher in Detroit than in the South. How can cars produced in the North compete with cars produced in the South?

Medical costs per employee can be higher in the North as long as northern employees' cash wages are lower. Unless total compensation per employee is the same in both places, the cars produced in Michigan and in the South cannot be sold at the same price, and manufacturers will shift their production facilities to the lower-cost site.

The Effect of Unions

What if an industry were strongly unionized and the firms in that industry were not permitted to hire nonunion labor? Could the union then shift its higher medical costs to the firm or consumers? The extent to which a union can increase labor costs is always limited by the potential loss of its members' jobs. If US manufacturers increase their prices relative to those of their competitors, foreign competition and price-sensitive consumers will lead to declines in sales and profits. Even when foreign competitors are prevented from competing with US manufacturers, consumers will demand fewer automobiles as prices rise, although the declines will be lower than they would be if greater competition were permitted. Firms facing decreased demands for their products would hire fewer employees. A powerful union that is willing to accept a certain loss of its members' jobs by forcing firms to raise its members' compensation would do so regardless of whether the increase was for medical benefits or wages. Thus, increased medical benefits to the union members still come at the expense of higher wages.

For this reason, unions have been strong advocates of using government controls to limit rising healthcare costs.

The Growing Divergence Between Wages and Total Compensation

Exhibit 23.1 illustrates the effect of rising medical costs on employees' wages. After 1973, total employee compensation rose less rapidly than it had previously because of a slowdown in employee productivity. The difference between total compensation and wages increased as a greater portion of employees' total compensation went to pay for fringe benefits. Between 1973 and 1990, employers' contributions to their employees' health insurance premiums "absorbed more than half of workers' real (adjusted for inflation) gains in compensation, even though health insurance represented 5 percent or less of total compensation" (Congressional Budget Office 1992, 5).

EXHIBIT 23.1

Inflation-Adjusted Compensation and Wages per Full-Time Employee, 1965–2016

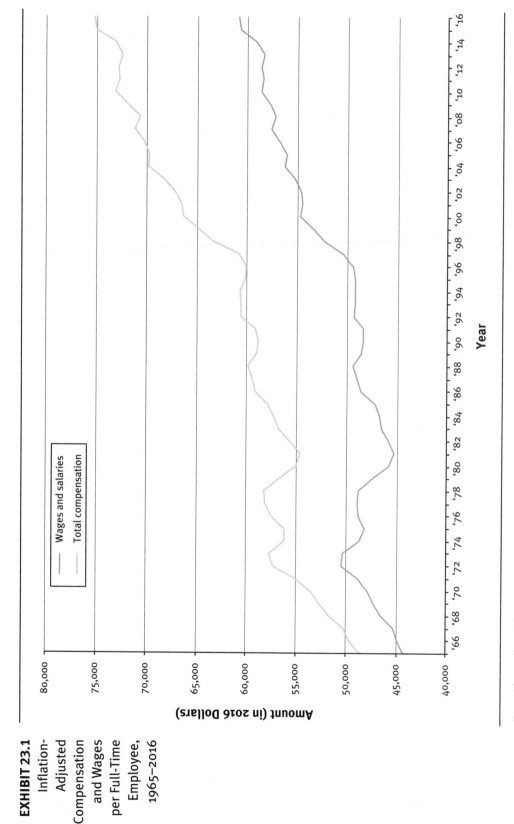

Note: Values adjusted for inflation using the consumer price index for all urban consumers.
Source: Data from Bureau of Economic Analysis (2017).

Total employee compensation increased in the 1990s, reflecting increased productivity. However, wages and salaries remained relatively constant from the late 1980s until the mid-1990s, reflecting the increasing importance of health insurance and retirement plans in employee compensation. Until the mid-1990s, employees' wages rose very slowly because most of the increase in compensation went to pay for higher health and retirement benefits.

From the late 1990s to 2000, total employee compensation and wages increased substantially, again reflecting increased productivity. However, in contrast to the earlier period of the late 1980s to the mid-1990s, wages increased at a slightly faster rate than total compensation; cost-containment activities by managed care plans resulted in a slower growth in premiums and greater wage increases for employees (see exhibit 20.3).

The late 1990s, however, saw a backlash against restrictive managed care plans; consequently, between 2001 and 2016, total compensation once again increased faster than wages. Rising medical costs have had a large negative effect on employees' take-home pay; employees have had less to spend on other goods and services.[3]

Tax-exempt employer-paid health insurance disguises the cost of health insurance to the employee. Because the federal government taxes wages and not health benefits, many employees are unaware of how much they have forgone in wages as a result of rising health benefit costs. When employees believe that their employer is paying for their healthcare benefits, they have little incentive to be concerned about their health plan choices or out-of-pocket medical expenses. If employees were more aware of the trade-off between wages and healthcare benefits, they would become more cost conscious in choosing health plans. They will weigh the greater benefits of choosing a health plan that offers broader provider networks, more comprehensive benefits, and lower out-of-pocket medical expenses against their cost, in terms of lower cash wages.

The misconception regarding who is paying the costs of employee health benefits has led to higher medical costs.

Who Pays for Retiree Medical Costs?

During labor negotiations in the past, many employers agreed to provide their employees with medical benefits when they retire in return for wage concessions.[4] In 2017, 25 percent of large firms (200 or more workers) that offered health benefits to employees also offered retiree coverage (down from 66 percent in 1988 and 34 percent in 2000) (Kaiser Family Foundation and Health Research & Educational Trust 2017, figure 11.1). Only about 5 percent of small firms (3 to 199 workers) offer retiree health benefits. When employers agreed to provide their employees with retiree medical benefits, retiree medical costs were much lower than they are today, and employers undoubtedly underestimated how costly they could become. Instead of setting aside funds to pay these retiree obligations, as one would do with a pension obligation, firms paid their retirees' medical costs on a "pay-as-you-go" basis; that is, they paid retirees' medical costs when they were incurred, out of current operating income.

As a result of a Financial Accounting Standards Board ruling, starting in 1993, firms had to set aside funds for such benefits as they were earned. Thus, retiree medical benefits must be treated similarly to pension benefits; as employees earn credit toward their retirement, the firm must set aside funds to pay for those employees' medical costs when they retire. Furthermore, the unfunded liability for current and future retirees must be accounted for on the firm's balance sheet. Firms were shocked by the size of their unfunded obligations. For example, in 2005, General Motors (GM) had an unfunded liability for its current and future retirees' medical costs of $77 billion (Seider and Williamson 2005). This liability had to be recorded on its balance sheet, and an equivalent amount had to be deducted from the firm's net worth. Consequently, GM's stockholders' equity decreased by $77 billion. In addition, GM had to expense part of that liability each year. For 2005, GM's earnings were reduced by $5.6 billion.

How did firms such as GM pay off these huge unfunded liabilities? Did they raise the prices of their products, harming US competitiveness? If they had done so, they would have lost sales to competitors, both in the United States and overseas, that did not make such commitments to their employees. That evidently did not happen. Thus, US competitiveness is not harmed by requiring firms to list unfunded retiree medical benefits on their balance sheets. (In view of the auto industry's deteriorating financial condition, in 2008 GM, together with Ford and Chrysler, reached an agreement with the United Automobile Workers [UAW] to form a union-run retiree healthcare fund, Voluntary Employee Beneficiary Association. GM was released from UAW retiree healthcare claims incurred after 2009. The total value of the healthcare trust was about $60 billion, with GM providing around $33 billion, Ford roughly $15 billion, and Chrysler about $9 billion [Smerd 2008].) A Towers Watson (2015, 9) survey of large employers found that one-half of Fortune's largest 1,000 firms estimated that, as of 2013, they had a liability of $285 billion for retiree health benefits; 67 percent of these firms reported they had no assets to cover the liability.

Employers also cannot reduce the wages of current employees to pay for unfunded obligations to current retirees. If they were to do so, the firms would lose their employees. The labor market is competitive. If a firm decides to reduce its employees' wages, those employees will move to firms whose retirees have not been promised medical benefits. Instead, firms have used current and future profits to pay off this liability, and the stockholders have been the losers.

Some firms have reneged on their promises to retirees by either reducing benefits or requiring retirees to pay part of the cost; in other words, these firms have tried to shift these obligations from their stockholders back to their retirees. Retirees responded by bringing lawsuits against their former employers. Court rulings, however, have generally allowed employers to reduce or eliminate the benefits for salaried, nonunion retirees, even years after they retired. (The employer may also reduce benefits to union employees unless the collective bargaining agreement explicitly prohibits it.)

When a firm declares bankruptcy and is reorganized, it can reduce its obligations to its unionized employees and retirees. If firms with large retiree liabilities declare bankruptcy, the stockholders, bondholders, employees, and retirees must make some sacrifice for the firm to become viable again. Another option is for the firm and its union to agree to reduce medical costs to prevent the firm from having to declare bankruptcy, in which case the retirees, current employees, and stockholders would likely suffer greater losses. GM's renegotiation of retiree health benefits with its union and the formation of a union-run fund is an example of this approach.

Reducing the Visibility of a Health Policy's Costs

Political objectives often determine who bears the burden of paying for health policies. Legislators' actions should be viewed in terms of whether they improve or hurt their chances for re-election. When a group is provided with legislative or regulatory benefits, legislators expect to receive the group's votes. Others, however, must bear the cost of those benefits. When it becomes necessary to impose costs on a population, legislators try to make them less visible—and reduce the risk of not being re-elected—by spreading the costs over a large number of people.

Another approach for reducing the visibility of a policy's costs is to make the costs indirect, by levying them on others, who are then able to shift those costs to the intended group. Thus, to understand a policy's actual, rather than stated, effect, it is necessary to realize not only who benefits but who ends up bearing the costs.

When an employer buys tax-exempt health insurance for its employees, the employee bears the cost through a reduction in wages. Similarly, rising employee medical costs that increase the premiums paid by employers on behalf of their employees reduce employee wages.

The following examples from the ACA illustrate how the cost of policies affecting employees is shifted onto the employees themselves.

The Health Insurance Tax
The ACA imposes a tax on health insurers' premiums to be paid by the health insurer. Although the tax is imposed on insurers' premiums and paid by the

insurer to the government, insurers do not have to reduce their profits to pay the tax.

Insurers respond to the health insurance tax (HIT) in the same way they respond to an increase in medical costs; they increase their premiums. Health insurers are in a price-competitive industry; they earn a competitive profit, not excess profits. If insurers were to absorb the tax increase and reduce their profit, they would have to leave the market. Their capital could earn a higher (risk-adjusted) return (a competitive profit) elsewhere. Thus, the HIT, affecting insurers in a competitive market, will result in the tax being shifted to those buying the product, namely employees and other enrollees.

Increased premiums, whether caused by the HIT or rising medical costs, will also result in some enrollees deciding the premium has become too expensive and not renewing their coverage.[5]

The ACA's Dependent Care Mandate

The Dependent Care Mandate allows children up to age 26 to be included on their parents' employer-based health insurance. Previously, many family insurance plans limited coverage of children up to 19 years of age. This aspect of the ACA has been very popular for parents able to take advantage of this change in the law.

Additional medical costs are associated with allowing children up to age 26 to remain on their parent's health insurance. These additional costs must be borne by someone. The health insurer does not bear that cost in terms of lower profits. Instead, the additional medical costs and resulting higher premiums are shifted; they are borne by the firm's employees in the form of slightly higher health insurance premiums and, consequently, in reduced employee wages. A recent study found that "workers at firms with employer-based coverage—whether or not they have dependent children—experience an annual reduction in wages of approximately $1,200." The additional costs of the dependent mandate are borne not only by those benefitting from it, but also by other employees, including those whose children are older than 26 years (Goda, Farid, and Bhattacharya 2016).

The benefits of this policy are publicized, while the wage reduction costs to those not benefitting are not; therefore, they are less visible.

Employer Health Insurance Mandate

The ACA imposed an "employer mandate" on businesses with 50 or more full-time employees. The employer is required to pay a penalty of about $2,000 per employee per year for each employee (excluding the first 30 employees) not offered an ACA-qualified health plan. The tax penalty is imposed on the *employer*, not on the employee. The public has generally favored mandating employers to buy health insurance for their employees. The public believes that employers are better able to pay the additional cost, and that the public will not have to incur higher taxes to bear that cost.

An employer mandate to buy insurance for employees is the same as imposing a tax on each of the firm's uninsured employees. When the cost of labor rises, the firm will demand fewer employees. The firm will have to compare the higher cost of that employee with the value of his or her output. Over time, the firm will employ fewer people. The firm will also have to increase prices for products and services. In addition, over time firms will attempt to substitute capital (e.g., robots) for costlier employees.

An employer mandate to buy health insurance is, however, different from an increase in the cost of labor. An employer could shift the cost of the health insurance onto employees by reducing their wages. The firm's cost of labor would not change (Antwi and Maclean 2017).[6] The employee would gain health insurance but suffer a loss in wages. In an earlier example, employees could have bought health insurance with part of their wages but preferred not to do so because they valued wages more highly than insurance. (The employer would have bought tax-exempt health insurance for employees if they preferred noncash benefits.)

For employees whose wages are near the government's minimum level, the employer is unable to reduce wages sufficiently to cover the cost of the mandated health insurance. It is likely that some of these low-wage employees would have to be let go. Interestingly, the ACA's employer mandate has had little effect on increasing employee health insurance coverage or in decreasing employers' demand for labor.

Many large employers offered their uninsured employees an ACA-qualified health plan, but employees generally refused the offer (Goodman 2015). The employer would have had to pay part of the premium, based on a percentage of the employee's income, and the employee would have had to pay the rest of the premium. The ACA-qualified Bronze plan was for single coverage and included a large deductible. Most employees believed that the out-of-pocket expense for their share of the premium and a large deductible was not worth the decrease in wages. In addition, married employees would have had to pay the entire premium for a separate family plan, which also included a very large deductible. The two deductibles (for the employee and for the family plan) would have been as high as $12,000. Many low-wage employees did not believe the health insurance was worth the expenditure of their limited income.

Imposing mandates on employers gives the appearance that employers will bear the cost of those mandates. Mandates, however, are shifted to consumers, who pay higher prices, or to the firm's employees. These indirect effects, however, are less visible to the public and, therefore, more politically feasible to legislators. In the case of the ACA's employer mandate, because employees generally thought the insurance wasn't worth the loss of cash wages, the mandate was ineffective in decreasing the number of uninsured employees.

Summary

A great deal of confusion exists regarding who bears the cost of employee health benefits, and whether employee health costs affect US firms' competitiveness. Some confusion occurs among employees themselves because many are unaware that when their employer pays part of their premium, it results in a reduction of their wages. The employee's total compensation consists of two parts: cash wages and fringe benefits. An employer is concerned with the total cost of employees, not its components. Typically, employees decide how their compensation should be divided between wages and benefits. Low-wage employees prefer a high percentage of wages, whereas high-income employees prefer a significant portion going into tax-exempt benefits, particularly employer-paid health insurance.

Rising medical costs do not directly affect US competitiveness by forcing firms to increase their prices. Instead, these higher costs are borne by the employees, who receive lower cash wages. The growing divergence between wages and total employee compensation, shown in exhibit 23.1, has mainly been the result of rising medical costs.

Unfunded retiree medical liabilities also do not affect US competitiveness because these liabilities are not paid by raising prices or reducing wages, but are shifted to the firm's stockholders in the form of reduced equity.

Politicians are concerned about the visibility of imposing costs on various voting groups. Being forthright about which groups, such as employees or enrollees, bear the actual costs of governmental policies, lessens their political attractiveness. Thus, while the benefits of health policies are publicized, the burden of financing employee health benefits often is indirect and less visible. In each of the examples presented earlier, someone *other than the employee* or enrollee is *nominally* paying the cost of an added benefit, tax, or regulation. The costs, however, are shifted. The ACA HIT is imposed on health insurers but shifted to the enrollee in the form of higher health insurance premiums; the cost of including children up to age 26 years on their parents' health insurance plan is borne by all the firm's employees or the parents themselves; and the ACA's employer mandate, whereby the employer is required to offer and pay for an employee's health insurance or pay a tax, is typically shifted to the employee or to the firm's customers in higher prices. When uninsured low-income employees were given an opportunity to accept their employer's offer to pay part of their premium, most rejected the offer, believing that the insurance was not worth the loss of wages.

Explicitly stating the costs of health policies and which population groups are likely to bear the costs will force legislators to weigh the political support of those who benefit against that of those who incur the expense.

Discussion Questions

1. What determines the ratio of cash to noncash (fringe benefits) compensation that an employer will pay its employees?
2. What are the consequences if an employer raises its prices to pay for its employees' rising medical costs?
3. How can automobile employees in Michigan receive more costly health benefits than those in the South when automobiles produced in both locations sell for the same price?
4. Even if employees bear the entire cost (in terms of lower cash wages) of rising medical expenses, why should employers still be concerned with cost containment?
5. Why do government health policies impose the cost of an employee benefit on employers (or insurers) when economists claim that the employer's (or insurer's) cost generally is shifted to the employee (or insured person)?

Notes

1. The following is an example of how global competitiveness affects a firm's sales and its labor costs. Delphi, a US firm that sells automotive components, was forced into bankruptcy because of its high labor costs. To emerge from bankruptcy, it had to reduce its US labor costs. The firm paid its US unionized employees $27 an hour, but when health and retirement benefits were included, its labor costs rose to $65 an hour. Delphi's Asian operations were highly profitable. In China, it paid its workers about $3 an hour, about a third of which was for medical and pension benefits (Sapsford and Areddy 2005).
2. At a meeting of the National Governors Association, former Ford Motor Company vice chairman Allan Gilmour stated that high healthcare costs could force Detroit automakers to invest overseas rather than in the United States to remain profitable. Ford spent $3.2 billion on healthcare in 2003 for 560,000 employees, retirees, and dependents. These costs added $1,000 to the price of every Ford vehicle built in the United States, up from $700 three years previously. Gilmour stated that the company's foreign competitors do not share these problems, and if healthcare costs are not controlled, investment

will be driven overseas. He called on the states' governors to pass legislation to control healthcare costs (Mayne 2004).

3. The fact that employees rather than employers bear the cost of rising healthcare benefits should not mean, however, that employers are absolved of the responsibility to ensure that these funds are well spent. Uwe Reinhardt (1989, 20) stated that

> even if every increase in the cost of employer-paid healthcare benefits could immediately be financed by the firm with commensurate reductions in the cash compensation of its employees—so that "competitiveness" in the firm's product market is not impaired—it would leave employees worse off unless the added health spending is valued at least as highly as the cash wages they would forgo to finance these benefits. Because it is the perceived value of a firm's compensation package that lures workers to the firm and away from competing opportunities, the typical business firm has every economic incentive to maximize this perceived value per dollar of healthcare expenditure debited to the firm's payroll expense account. Therein, and not in "competitiveness" on the product side, lies the most powerful rationale for vigorous healthcare cost containment on the part of the American business community.

4. Early retirees who are not eligible for Medicare are costlier than those who are. Early-retiree health benefits cost, on average, $14,988 in 2010, whereas Medicare-eligible retirees cost firms $7,848 on average (more recent data are unavailable). For retirees on Medicare, the firm usually pays for the portion of the retiree's medical expenses not covered by Medicare, such as deductibles and copayments (Towers Perrin 2009).

5. The HIT does not affect all employees buying health insurance. Larger firms that self-insure, namely, the firm's employees—not the insurer—bear the risk of medical costs themselves. Insurers are used to administer claims and are exempt from the HIT, as are self-insured employers and their employees. The cost of the HIT generally is borne by those who buy insurance themselves and employees working in smaller firms whose employers do not self-insure.

6. An earlier study by Gruber (1994) found that when states mandated employers to cover maternity benefits, the employers shifted the cost of the mandate to married women of child-bearing age who were the intended beneficiaries of the mandate.

References

Antwi, Y. A., and J. C. Maclean. 2017. "State Health Insurance Mandates and Labor Market Outcomes: New Evidence on Old Questions." National Bureau of Economic Research Working Paper No. 23203. Published February. www.nber.org/papers/w23203.

Bureau of Economic Analysis. 2017. "National Data: GDP and Personal Income." Accessed November. www.bea.gov/.

Congressional Budget Office. 1992. *Economic Implications of Rising Health Care Costs.* Washington, DC: US Congressional Budget Office.

Goda, G. S., M. Farid, and J. Bhattacharya. 2016. "The Incidence of Mandated Health Insurance: Evidence from the Affordable Care Act Dependent Care Mandate." National Bureau of Economic Research Working Paper No. 21846. www.nber. org/papers/w21846.

Goodman, J. C. 2015. "The Employer Mandate Is Having No Effect on the Percent with Health Insurance at Work." *Forbes.* Published October 22. www.forbes. com/sites/johngoodman/2015/10/22/the-employer-mandate-is-having-no-effect-on-the-percent-with-health-insurance-at-work/.

Gruber, J. 1994. "The Incidence of Mandated Maternity Benefits." *American Economic Review* 84 (3): 622–41.

Mayne, E. 2004. "Ford: Health Costs Could Drive Investment Overseas." *The Detroit News,* July 20.

Kaiser Family Foundation and Health Research & Educational Trust. 2017. *Employer Health Benefits: 2017 Annual Survey.* Published September. http://files.kff.org/ attachment/Report-Employer-Health-Benefits-Annual-Survey-2017.

Reinhardt, U. E. 1989. "Health Care Spending and American Competitiveness." *Health Affairs* 8 (4): 5–21.

Sapsford, J., and J. Areddy. 2005. "Why Dephi's Asia Operations Are Booming." *Wall Street Journal,* October 17, B1.

Seider, M. A., and B. L. Williamson. 2005. "Pension and OPEB Obligations in U.S. Bankruptcies: Answers to the Most Frequently Asked Questions." Accessed May 2018. www.lw.com/upload/pubContent/_pdf/pub1410_1.pdf.

Smerd, J. 2008. "UAW's VEBA Board: Autoworkers' Health Care Benefits in Peril." Published November 10. www.workforce.com/2008/11/10/uaws-veba-board-autoworkers-health-care-benefits-in-peril/.

Towers Perrin. 2009. *2010 Retiree Health Care Cost Survey Shows Continuing Affordability and Access Concerns.* Published November 18. www.thefreelibrary.com/ Towers+Perrin's+2010+Retiree+Health+Care+Cost+Survey+Shows+Continui ng...-a0212259649.

Towers Watson. 2015. *Emerging Opportunities for Retiree Health Care Programs: Insights from the 2015 Survey on Retiree Health Care Strategies.* Published February. www.towerswatson.com/en-US/Insights/IC-Types/Survey-Research-Results/2015/02/2015-survey-on-retiree-health-care-strategies.

WILL A SHORTAGE OF REGISTERED NURSES REOCCUR?

Since World War II, concerns over a national shortage of registered nurses (RNs) have recurred. At times, the shortage seems particularly acute; at other times, it appears to have been resolved, only to reassert itself several years later. Government and private commissions have attempted to quantify the magnitude of the shortage and have proposed remedies. Since 1964, the federal government has spent billions of dollars to alleviate the nursing shortage. The Great Recession during the period between 2007 and 2009 (and the subsequent slow recovery) eliminated the RN shortage and resulted in an RN surplus (National Bureau of Economic Research 2010). Once the economy fully recovers, will a shortage of RNs occur again?

Given the concern over a possible future shortage and the large federal subsidies that have supported nursing education, it is useful to examine why shortages of nurses arise, whether they are likely to occur again, and what, if anything, should be done about it.

Measuring Nursing Shortages

The measure commonly used to indicate a shortage of nurses is the nurse vacancy rate in hospitals—the percentage of unfilled nursing positions for which hospitals are recruiting. The vacancy rate reached a high of 23 percent in 1962, steadily declined throughout the 1960s, and reached single digits by the early 1970s. It rose again in the late 1970s, reaching 14 percent in 1979; however, by 1983, it had fallen to approximately 4.4 percent. By the mid-1980s, the vacancy rate was climbing again. It shot up to 12.7 percent by 1989, sank to 4 percent in 1998, and then rose sharply to 13 percent in 2001. Once again, it declined to 4 percent in 2009. In the last several years (2013–2017), the vacancy rate has been increasing (Nursing Solutions Inc. n.d.). See exhibit 24.1.

Each of these periods of high or rising RN vacancy rates brought forth commissions to study the problem and make recommendations. The high vacancy rates in the early 1960s led to the Nurse Training Act of 1964, which provided federal support for nursing education and has been renewed many times.

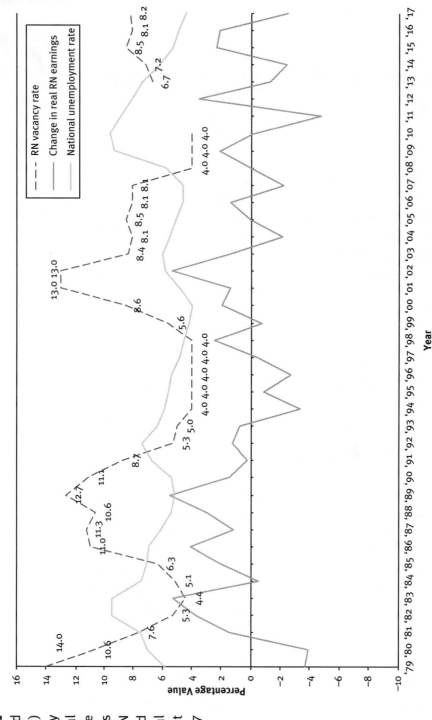

EXHIBIT 24.1
Registered Nurse (RN) Vacancy Rates, Annual Percentage Changes in Real RN Earnings, and the National Unemployment Rate, 1979–2017

Note: Estimated data for 1997–1998, 2006, and 2008–2009.

Sources: 1979–2008 data on RN vacancy rates and the national unemployment rates compiled in 2009 by Peter I. Buerhaus, Vanderbilt University School of Nursing, Douglas O. Staiger, Dartmouth College, and research associate, National Bureau of Economic Research; 2009 data on RN vacancy rate from American Hospital Association (2010); 2013–2017 data from Nursing Solutions Inc. (n.d.); data on real RN earnings and national unemployment rates from Bureau of Labor Statistics (2018).

Nursing Shortages in Theory

What are the reasons for a shortage of RNs? The definition of a nurse shortage is hospitals' inability to hire all the nurses they want at the current wage. In other words, the demand for nurses exceeds the number of nurses willing to work at the existing market wage. However, economic theory claims that if the demand for nurses exceeds the supply, hospitals will compete for nurses and nurses' wages will increase. As nurses' wages rise, nurses who are not working will seek employment, and part-time nurses will be willing to increase the hours they work. Those hospitals willing to pay the new, higher wage will be able to hire additional nurses and will no longer have vacancies.[1]

Thus, economic theory predicts that once shortages begin, we observe rising wages for nurses followed by declining vacancy rates. Nurse employment will expand (more nurses will enter the labor force and others will work longer hours), and as nurses' wages increase, hospitals will not hire as many nurses at the higher wage as they initially wanted. Shortages could arise again if the demand for nurses grows more rapidly than the supply. With higher demand, the process starts over. Hospitals find they cannot hire all the nurses they want at the current wage, and so on. Clearly, wages are not the only reason nurses work or increase the number of hours of work. The nurse's age, whether she has young children, and overall family income are also important determinants. A change in the nurse's wage, however, will alter the benefits of working versus not working and affect the number of hours the nurse chooses to work.

Nursing Shortages in Practice

How well does economic theory, which relies on increased demand for nurses, explain the recurrent shortages of nurses? These shortages must be divided into two periods: (1) before the 1965 passage of Medicare and Medicaid and (2) after their passage.

Before Passage of Medicare and Medicaid

Before Medicare, the RN vacancy rate kept rising, exceeding 20 percent by the early 1960s. Hospital demand for nurses continued to exceed the supply of nurses at a given wage. Surprisingly, however, nurses' wages did not rise as rapidly as wages in comparable occupations, which were not even subject to the same shortage pressures. Worsening shortages of nurses and limited growth of nurse wages over a period of years could only have resulted from interference with the process by which wages were determined.

Working on the hypothesis that nurse wages were being held down artificially, economist Donald Yett (1975) found that hospitals were colluding to prevent nurses' wages from rising. The hospitals believed that competing for nurses would merely result in large wage hikes and, hence, a large increase in hospital costs without a large increase in the number of employed nurses. This collusive behavior by hospitals in setting nurses' wages prevented the shortage from being resolved.

After the Passage of Medicare and Medicaid

With enactment of Medicare and Medicaid, hospitals were reimbursed according to their *costs* of treating Medicare and Medicaid patients. Consequently, hospitals were more willing to raise nurses' wages, which they did rapidly in the mid- to late 1960s. The vacancy rate declined from 23 percent in 1962 to approximately 9 percent by 1971. The nurses' wage hike brought about a large increase in the number of employed nurses, contrary to hospitals' earlier expectations. Trained nurses who were not working decided to reenter the profession. The percentage of all trained nurses who were working rose from 55 percent in 1960 to 65 percent in 1966 and 70 percent in 1972. Higher wages were an important factor in expanding nurse participation rates.

The artificial shortages created by hospitals before the mid-1960s are no longer possible. Antitrust laws make collusion illegal. Therefore, the recurrent shortage of nurses since that time has been of a different type.

Limited information lengthens the time to resolve nursing shortages. For example, if a hospital experiences growth in its admissions or a higher acuity level in patients, it will try to hire more nurses. The hospital may, however, find that its human resources department cannot hire more nurses at the current wage. The hospital's vacancy rate goes up. Other hospitals in the community may experience the same problem. The hospital then has to decide whether and by how much to raise the wage to attract additional nurses. If the hospital decides to raise nurses' wages, it will have to pay the higher wage to its existing nurses as well. The hospital must then decide how many additional nurses it can afford to hire at the higher wage.

The hospital may decide that other recruiting approaches, such as providing childcare and a more supportive environment, are less costly than raising wages. Thus, a lag exists between the decision to hire more nurses, consideration of the additional cost of more nurses, and the point at which the hospital is satisfied with the number of nurses it employs.

A lag also exists before the supply of nurses responds to changed market conditions. Once nurses' wages are increased, it takes time for this information to become widely disseminated. Nurses who are not working may decide to return to nursing at the higher wage; this change is indicated by a greater nurse participation rate. Other nurses who are working part time may decide to increase the number of hours they work, and higher wages may persuade more high school graduates to undertake the educational requirements to become a nurse. The most rapid response to higher wages will come from those who work part time, followed by those who are trained but not working as nurses. The supply of nurses in the long run is determined by those who decide to enter nursing schools (and by the immigration of foreign-trained nurses). Short- and long-run supply responses to an increase in nurses' wages (and other benefits) thus occur.[2]

Let us now return to an examination of how well economic theory explains the recurrent shortage of nurses. Throughout the late 1960s and early 1970s, nurses' wages rose more rapidly than wages in comparable professions, such as teaching. This scenario resulted in lower vacancy rates and a higher nurse participation rate. Within several years, enrollments in nursing schools (offering a bachelor's, an associate, or a diploma degree) increased (a lag of several years always exists before the information about wages is transmitted to high school graduates and nursing school enrollments change). See exhibit 24.2 for nursing school enrollments (data after 2012 have not been published).

By the late 1970s, concerns surfaced about a new shortage of nurses. The basis of this shortage began in 1971 when President Nixon imposed wage and price controls on the economy. Although these controls were removed from all other industries in 1972, they remained in effect for medical care until 1974. The wage controls, together with the increased supply of nursing school graduates, began to have an effect by the late 1970s—well after the controls were lifted because of the lag in transmission time mentioned earlier. Demand for nurses continued to grow throughout the 1970s, while the wage controls led to lower relative wages for nurses and, by the late 1970s, declining nursing school enrollments. By 1979, the vacancy rate reached 14 percent.

Trends in the 1980s

The shortage in 1979 and 1980, however, was short lived. As shown in exhibit 24.1, nurses' wages rose sharply at the same time the economy entered a severe recession in the early 1980s. The rising unemployment rate led more nurses to seek employment and increase their hours of work. Because the majority of RNs are married, the loss of a spouse's job or even the fear of it is likely to result in greater participation by nurses in the labor force to maintain their family's income (Arevalo 2008).

Higher wages and the rising unemployment rate increased nurse participation rates from 76 percent in 1980 to 79 percent by 1984. Consequently, vacancy rates dropped to 4.4 percent by 1983. The nursing shortage had once again been resolved through a combination of a wage hike, a greater nurse participation rate, and a high national unemployment rate. RN wages remained stable (and actually decreased in real dollars) between 1983 and 1985 and the vacancy rate fell, and nursing school enrollments began a sharp decline that lasted throughout the late 1980s.

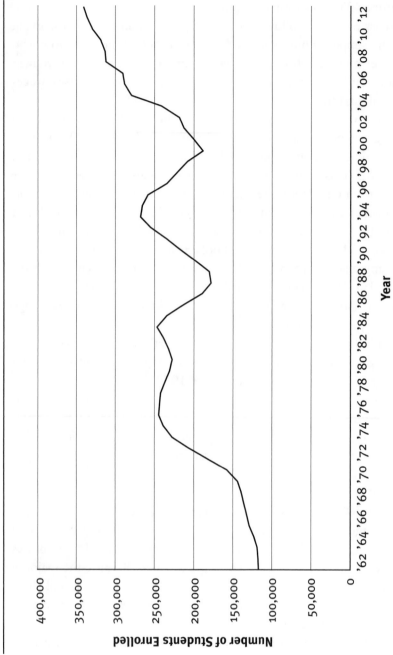

EXHIBIT 24.2
Nursing School
Enrollment,
1961–2012

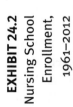

Note: Data for 1997 and 2009–2012 are unavailable and are based on author's extrapolations.
Sources: Data from American Nurses Association (n.d.); National League for Nursing (2009); US Census Bureau (n.d.); National Center for Health Statistics (n.d.).

In the 1980s, the market for hospital services underwent drastic changes, which affected the market for nurses. Medicare changed hospital payment from cost based to a fixed price per admission, and private insurers started utilization management. The trend by government and private insurers to reduce use of the hospital resulted in shorter hospital stays. Patients required more intensive treatment for the shorter time they were in the hospital. Hospitalized patients were sicker, more transplants were being performed, and the number of low-birth-weight babies increased. The recovery period, which requires less intensive care, was occurring outside the hospital. As a result, hospitals began to use more RNs per patient.

In 1975, there were 0.65 RNs per patient; this figure climbed to 0.88 by 1980, to 1.31 by 1990, and to 1.6 by 2000. The percentage increase in RNs per patient exceeded the decline in patient days due to shorter hospital stays.

The demand for nurses also rose in outpatient and nonhospital settings. As use of hospitals decreased, use of outpatient care, nursing homes, home care, and hospices for terminally ill Medicare patients increased. From 1980 to 2015, annual outpatient visits (ambulatory care visits to physicians' offices, hospital outpatient departments, and emergency departments) skyrocketed from 262 million to 1.85 billion (Centers for Disease Control and Prevention 2014, 2015; American Hospital Association 2017). Use of skilled nursing homes by Medicare patients grew from 8.6 million days in 1980 to 67.2 million days in 2015 (Centers for Medicare & Medicaid Services 2017). In addition, cost-containment companies increased their demand for RNs to conduct utilization review and case management activities.

Although the demand for nurses in these settings increased faster than the supply in the mid- to late 1980s, nurses' wages were slow to respond. Nursing school enrollments had been falling, and the national unemployment rate dropped as the economy began to improve. Consequently, vacancy rates began to rise once more—from 5.1 percent in 1984 to 12.7 percent in 1989. By the late 1980s, concern emerged again over a shortage of nurses. Hospitals again lobbied Congress for subsidies to increase nurse education programs and to ease immigration rules on foreign-trained nurses. The nursing shortage of the late 1980s resulted in enactment of the Nursing Shortage Reduction and Education Extension Act of 1988 and the Immigration Nursing Relief Act of 1989, which made it easier for foreign nurses to receive working visas.

Trends in the 1990s

Neither of these legislative acts was needed, however, as economic incentives again eliminated the shortage. As the economy weakened in the early 1990s and the unemployment rate began to rise, nurse participation rates increased to 82 percent by 1992. Nursing school enrollment had continued to grow in the early 1990s as a result of prior wage hikes. With the growth in the supply of new nurses and the higher participation rate, vacancy rates dropped to 4 percent by 1994. The nursing shortage ended.

One could have forecasted that another shortage would occur by the end of the decade. As shown in exhibit 24.1, nurses' real wages (adjusted for inflation) started to decline in 1994 and did not rise again until 1998. During this time, hospitals were trying to be more price competitive by reducing their costs to be included in managed care's provider networks. Only by 1998 did nurse wage increases finally begin to grow faster than inflation. The national unemployment rate also declined throughout the late 1990s, as the US economy performed well.

Nursing school enrollments typically decrease several years after a decline in wages and vacancy rates. As shown in exhibit 24.2, nursing school enrollments peaked at 270,000 in 1994 and then slumped for the remainder of the 1990s. The reduction in nurses' wages during the mid- to late 1990s led to a large decline in nursing school enrollments and, consequently, in the number of nursing school graduates.

The Period 2000–2010

After years of declining (adjusted for inflation) nurse wages during the latter part of the 1990s, shrinking nursing school enrollments, and the aging of the nurse population, one might have expected to read newspaper articles about a new shortage of nurses, as well as hospitals once again paying bonuses to attract nurses. After years of low vacancy rates, the vacancy rate increased from 4 percent in 1998 to 5.6 percent in 1999, and quickly rose to 13 percent by 2001.

As hospitals recognized the difficulty in attracting nurses in the beginning of the decade, nurses' real wages rose. With the wage hike, RN supply started to expand faster. Nursing school enrollments grew, part-time RNs increased their hours of work, trained RNs rejoined the workforce, immigration of RNs from other countries escalated, and more men entered the nursing profession. Further stimulating the greater supply of nurses in the beginning of the decade was the economic slowdown in 2001, leading to growth in unemployment. States that experienced the greatest spikes in unemployment saw the largest number of married RNs reentering the workforce (Buerhaus, Auerbach, and Staiger 2009). In fact, almost all of the increase in RNs in 2002 (94 percent) occurred among married nurses. The nurse vacancy rate then declined, but it was still relatively high (at 8.1 percent) by the middle of the decade.

In 2002, the Health Resources and Services Administration of the US Department of Health and Human Services projected that by 2020 there would be a shortage of 1 million nurses, mainly as a result of the medical needs of retiring baby boomers. These warnings led to the establishment of more nurse education programs and apprehension about a projected shortage of nursing instructors.

In 2007, not long after these shortage warnings, the United States slipped into a severe recession. A sharp rise in the unemployment rate resulted;

the number of uninsured patients multiplied, as did hospital bad debts; and the number of elective procedures performed in hospitals decreased. The Great Recession led to a large growth in the supply of nurses. As in previous periods of high unemployment, the need to maintain family income resulted in more nurses entering or reentering the nursing workforce. In addition, part-time RNs increased the number of hours they worked. As a result of earlier increases in nursing school enrollments, large numbers of graduates started their nursing careers. The nurse vacancy rate fell to 4 percent in 2010. The shortage of RNs was once again resolved. Not only did the shortage end, but a nursing *surplus* occurred, and many recent graduates could not find a job.

The Current Decade

The current decade started with the country in a severe recession. By 2015, the nurse participation rate was 81.1 percent, and 62 percent of these nurses were employed full time (Budden et al. 2016). This high participation rate prompted a great deal of concern that a severe RN shortage would occur as baby boomer nurses anticipated retiring. However, the steep recession during the first part of the decade led many RNs to postpone retirement, and the supply of nurses grew faster than expected. The number of RNs who did retire was partly offset by the surprisingly large increase in millennials entering the nursing profession (Auerbach, Buerhaus, and Staiger 2017).

Driving this increased demand is the aging of baby boomers, as more become eligible for Medicare and their out-of-pocket expenses to pay for care decline. Along with living longer, they have increased demands for chronic care, as well as treatment for cancer and diabetes.

For the remainder of this decade, it is likely that demand for RNs will continue to grow faster than supply. An indication of this trend is that RN wages have been rising faster than those for comparable professions. According to the Bureau of Labor Statistics (2018), RN wages increased from an average of 0.33 percent per year from 2012 to 2014 to 1.4 percent in 2016 (unadjusted for inflation).

The Outlook for Registered Nurses

Factors Affecting the Demand for Nurses

The demand for RNs is expected to continue to increase. The Bureau of Labor Statistics (2017) projects that the growth in RN employment will be 15 percent greater over the period from 2016 to 2026 than it is currently, which is much faster than the average growth of all other occupations.

The population is increasing, and a greater percentage of the population is older than 65 years; the oldest of the baby boomers began to retire in 2011.

Medical advances will continue to stimulate the demand for expensive services provided by hospitals, increasing the demand for hospital RNs. As more severely ill patients are admitted to hospitals, and the complexity of their treatment increases, the number of RNs per patient also should increase.

Payment trends, from fee-for-service to managed care and capitation, are driving the organization of care delivery to provide more care out of the hospital and to decrease rising costs. The institutional settings in which care is provided are changing rapidly, as are the employment locations for RNs. As hospital use has declined, outpatient care has increased. Hospital lengths of stay have decreased, resulting in recently discharged patients often needing additional care in skilled nursing facilities and home healthcare. The diseases of an aging population also include more chronic conditions such as Alzheimer's disease, as well as stroke and cancer. Many patients will require care in specialized facilities, as well as in their homes. As greater emphasis is placed on population health, more medical services will be provided in outpatient settings and in patients' homes. The demand for RNs in these settings will become substantial.

RN roles are also changing. In addition to hospitals, RNs are employed in urgent care centers; outpatient services, as care coordinators; in home health care; long-term care; and skilled nursing facilities. The role of advanced practice nursing is also growing, as RNs provide primary and preventive care.

In discussing the future role of RNs, Auerbach and colleagues (2013, 1470) stated,

> The importance of RNs is expected to increase in the coming decades, as new models of care delivery, global payment, and a greater emphasis on prevention are embraced. These and other changes associated with healthcare reform will require the provision of holistic care, greater care coordination, greater adherence to protocols, and improved management of chronic disease—roles that are inherently aligned with the nursing model of care.

New payment systems, such as episode-based payment and capitation, and cost-containment efforts are expanding the use of less expensive in-home and outpatient settings. Further, the shortage of primary care physicians will increase the need for nurse practitioners.[3]

These increased care requirements will increase the demand for RNs of all specialties, including nurse practitioners and nurse administrators. The shortage of primary care services will be reduced by the increased use of nursing personnel in new roles and by the increased reliance on medical technology.

Buerhaus, Auerbach, and Staiger (2017) estimated that the retirement of a large number of baby boomer RNs will significantly reduce the rate of growth in RN supply. The authors caution, "It is imperative that healthcare leaders recognize that as the retirement of RNs ramps up, a different type of nursing shortage will emerge—one of knowledge, skill, experience, and judgment, all attributes that contribute to the successful clinical and administrative operations of complex healthcare delivery systems."

Factors Affecting the Supply of Nurses

Important to determining whether shortages will reoccur is the question of whether RN supply will grow faster than demand. On the negative side, the RN workforce is aging; the average age is now 45. As these nurses retire, the supply will be reduced. Second, as healthcare has become more complex, hospitals have developed a preference for nurses with a four-year degree. In the past 10 years, the number of nurses with a bachelor's degree has sharply increased, while the number of nurses graduating with a two-year degree has leveled off. However, nurses with two-year degrees continue to represent a significant portion of the supply of nurses; in addition, such degrees, which are less costly and time consuming, are a path to the middle class for many.

Two-year graduates can take additional courses to receive a bachelor's degree (many universities offer Bachelor of Science in Nursing completion programs), and both two-year and four-year graduates can receive additional training to become a specialist, such as a nurse practitioner. If a bachelor's degree were required to become a nurse, as some nursing organizations have proposed, the supply of nurses and job prospects for many would be affected.

The supply of nursing school graduates has been increasing. The increased enrollment in nursing schools (exhibit 24.2) has been the basis for the greater number of new RNs passing the licensing exam. Over the five-year period from 2005 through 2009, 117,141 took the licensing examination, and the average annual increase over the previous five years (2000–2004) was 58 percent. During the more recent 2010 to 2013 period (for which data are available), 143,809 took the examination, which represented a 23 percent average annual increase over the previous period (American Nurses Association 2014).

About 15 percent of RNs in this country are foreign born and trained (Altorjai and Batalov 2017). Foreign-trained RNs have strong financial incentives to immigrate to the United States. They have opportunities to earn much higher pay (allowing them to send money home to assist their families), better working conditions, and the opportunity to learn and practice. In 2017, the median annual wage for RNs in the United States was $70,000, which is 20 times greater than the median annual wage for RNs in the Philippines (Bureau of Labor Statistics 2017; Payscale.com 2018). (These higher wages in the United States have even led physicians in the Philippines to train as RNs to be able to immigrate.)

In several countries, including the Philippines, RNs are trained for the purpose of immigrating to the United States, and their remittances are a major source of hard currency for their countries of origin (Aiken et al. 2004, 72). To facilitate the immigration of nurses to the United States, for-profit firms have emerged to serve as brokers between US hospitals and foreign-trained RNs.[4] An increase in supply of foreign-trained RNs will depress RN wages (wages will not increase as high as they would with a smaller supply). Lower wages will eventually affect the demand for a nursing education and, hence, reduce the future supply of graduates of US nursing schools.

Men also could become a major source of RN supply. In 1960, male RNs represented 2.2 percent of the RN workforce. By 2015, the percentage of men increased to 10 percent (Bureau of Labor Statistics 2018). The stereotype of nursing as a female-dominated profession is an important reason men have not chosen to become nurses. Also underrepresented in the nursing profession are Hispanics, who, in 2016, accounted for 6.6 percent of RNs. Increases in the proportion of both groups would lead to large increases in the supply of RNs (Buerhaus, Auerbach, and Staiger 2009).

Federal Subsidies to Nursing Schools and Students

The supply of RNs is affected by the number of nurses retiring and the number of new nursing school graduates. Each time a nursing shortage occurs, various bills are introduced in Congress to address different aspects of the shortage, such as more funding for nurse scholarships, financial support for nurses seeking advanced degrees, and funding for increasing faculty in nursing schools. Since the enactment of the Nurse Training Act of 1964, several proposals have been made to expand the supply of nurses. These recommendations ignore the important role played by higher wages in increasing the short-and long-run supply of nurses.

Federal subsidies to nursing schools and students cannot be directed only to those students who would otherwise have chosen a different career. Nurse education subsidies take years to affect the supply of nurses. More important, to the extent that federal programs are successful in increasing the number of nursing school graduates, nurses' wages rise more slowly. A larger supply of new graduates causes a lower rate of growth in nurses' wages, which, in turn, results in a smaller increase in the nurse participation rate. Nurses would be more reluctant to return to nursing or to work more hours if their wages did not rise.

The supply of US-trained RNs has been limited by the inadequate response by nursing schools to the high demand for nursing education. In 2014, only 44.9 percent of applicants were admitted to baccalaureate programs (American Association of Colleges of Nursing 2015). Nursing programs complain that they cannot admit more students because they do not have enough faculty members. Colleges and universities attempting to expand their nursing faculties operate in a highly competitive market for RNs with graduate degrees who can receive much higher salaries from hospitals and health systems. A significant factor in the shortage of nursing school faculty members is the salary, which is lower than the market wage for practicing nurses. It is surprising that nursing schools are unable to resolve the problem of attracting new faculty, a problem that other academic programs must contend with and appear to have resolved. The not-for-profit market for nursing education does not appear to be performing efficiently.

Greater reliance on market mechanisms would negate the need for federal nurse education subsidies. For example, higher wages will bring about an increase in the number of hours of work by part-time nurses; about 25 percent of all employed nurses work part time. Higher wages also attract qualified RNs from other countries, such as the Philippines. Higher wages will cause hospitals and other employers to rethink how they use their nurses. As nurses become more expensive, hospitals will assign them higher-skilled tasks and delegate certain housekeeping and other tasks currently performed by RNs to less-trained personnel, such as licensed practical nurses. Higher wages and new roles for nurses would make nursing a more attractive profession, thereby boosting the demand for a nursing career. Finally, nursing is predominantly a female profession. Higher wages and new roles will increase the attractiveness of nursing to men.

Since the mid-1960s, the recurrent shortages of nurses have been caused by greater demands for nurses and the failure of hospitals to immediately recognize that, at the higher demand, nurses' wages must be increased. Once hospitals realize that market conditions for nurses have changed, the process once again brings equilibrium to the market. The supply of nurses is responsive to changes in wages and economic conditions.

Uncertainty exists regarding how the factors affecting the demand for and supply of nurses are likely to change. Will the very large increase in nurse graduates offset the number of retiring nurses? Will the economic recovery continue? Will more states adopt higher minimum nurse-staffing ratios? Will more care be shifted outside the hospital, the predominant setting for nurse employment? Will government payments to hospitals be so reduced as to limit their ability to pay nurses market wages? Will nurses adapt to the new payment and delivery systems by undertaking new roles with greater responsibilities in caring for patients? Will states relax scope-of-practice laws to enable nurses to take on additional roles for which they are trained? (Markowitz et al. 2016). Finally, how will changing practice patterns and new technology affect the demand for and supply of RNs? The remainder of the decade should clarify the direction of each of these forces.

Summary

The nursing profession faces challenges and opportunities in coming years. The major reason for recurrent RN shortages has been the cyclical pattern of nurse wages. As wages stagnated, the rate of return on a nursing career fell and enrollments in nursing schools declined, as did the number of graduates. With a smaller supply of nurses and greater acuity level of patients, hospitals eventually realized that they could not attract as many nurses as they wanted at the current wage rate, and RN vacancy rates increased. Each of these shortages was resolved when nurses' wages rose; nursing school enrollments grew, older RNs reentered the workforce, and more foreign-trained RNs immigrated to the United States.

To forestall future shortages and enable the nurse market to function more smoothly, better information must be provided to the demanders and suppliers of nursing services. Information will facilitate the market's adjustment process by eliminating the delays in wage increases and enrollments that have caused these cyclical shortages. Hospitals and other demanders of nursing services must be made aware of approaches that increase nurses' productivity and improve the wages and working conditions necessary to attract more well-qualified nurses. To realize the full potential of nursing as a profession and enlarge the supply of nurses, potential nursing students need to be provided with timely information that allows them to make informed career choices. Nurses—particularly those who are not employed or are working part time—must be informed about opportunities in nursing, as well as wages and working conditions. Efforts to disseminate more information are more likely to eliminate shortages and lead to a greater supply of nurses than are policies that merely rely on large federal subsidies to nursing education.

Both public policy and private initiatives are directed at reducing the rising costs of medical care. If the outcome of public policy is to place arbitrary budget limits on hospitals and total medical expenditures, nurses' wages will not rise as rapidly as wages for comparably trained professionals in the nonregulated healthcare sector, and a permanent nurse shortage will occur. Innovation in the use of RNs and provision of new medical services will be stifled for lack of funds.

If, however, public policy reinforces what is occurring in the private sector—namely, competition among managed care organizations on the basis of premiums and quality of care—the demand for RNs will be determined by their productivity, the tasks they are permitted to perform, the improved patient outcomes to which they contribute, and their wages relative to the wages of other nursing personnel. To the extent that RNs are able to perform more highly valued tasks—such as assuming responsibility for more primary care services, utilization management, and management of home health care—as is currently the case in many competitive organizations, they become more valuable. In competitive markets, organizations will be willing to broaden the tasks assigned to RNs and raise their wages to reflect the higher value of services rendered. The future roles, responsibilities, and income of RNs will be affected by the incentives created by a competitive healthcare system.

Discussion Questions

1. Why was the demand for RNs rising faster than the supply during the 1980s?
2. How have the last several shortages of nurses been resolved?
3. How does an increase in nurses' wages affect hospitals' demand for nurses and the supply of nurses?
4. Why was the shortage of nurses that occurred before Medicare different from subsequent shortages?
5. Contrast the following two approaches for eliminating the shortage of nurses:
   a. Providing federal subsidies to nursing schools
   b. Providing more information about nurse demand and supply to prospective nursing students and demanders of nursing services, such as hospitals

Notes

1. Even when hospitals are able to hire all the nurses they want at the prevailing wage, a nurse vacancy rate will still exist because of normal turnover.
2. Hanel, Kalb, and Scott (2014) estimated the responsiveness of nurses to increased wages. They found that the average wage elasticity of hours worked by nurses with respect to nurses' wages is 1.3 (i.e., a 10 percent increase in wages results in a 13 percent increase in hours worked). Their elasticity estimate is affected by nurses' entry into and exit from the nursing profession in response to wage increases.
3. Nurses, in their new roles, may be less costly in providing care than are primary care physicians. Perloff, DesRoches, and Buerhaus (2016) found that the cost of care for patients whose primary care provider was a nurse practitioner was between 11 and 29 percent less than that for patients whose primary care provider was a physician.
4. US immigration and licensure policies limit the entry of foreign-trained RNs to the United States. According to Aiken and colleagues (2004, 72),

   > All US nurses must pass the National Council Licensure Examination (NCLEX-RN) to practice as RNs. To take the exam, foreign applicants must demonstrate that their education meets US standards—most notably, that their education was at the postsecondary level. Also, nurses trained in countries in which English is not the primary language must also pass an English proficiency test (the Test

of English as a Foreign Language, or TOEFL). The Commission on Graduates of Foreign Nursing Schools (CGFNS) offers an exam in many countries that is an excellent predictor of passing the NCLEXRN. The CGFNS exam reduces the number of foreign-trained nurses who travel to the United States expecting to work as RNs who cannot pass the licensing exam.

References

Aiken, L., J. Buchan, J. Sochalski, B. Nichols, and M. Powell. 2004. "Trends in International Nurse Migration." *Health Affairs* 23 (3): 69–77.

Altorjai, S., and J. Batalov. 2017. "Immigrant Health-Care Workers in the United States." Migration Policy Institute. Published June 28. www.migrationpolicy.org/article/immigrant-health-care-workers-united-states.

American Association of Colleges of Nursing. 2015. *Leading Excellence and Innovation in Academic Nursing: 2015 Annual Report.* Accessed May 2018. www.aacnnursing.org/Portals/42/Publications/Annual-Reports/AnnualReport15.pdf.

American Hospital Association. 2017. *Hospital Statistics.* Chicago: American Hospital Association.

———. 2010. *The State of America's Hospitals—Taking the Pulse.*

American Nurses Association. 2014. "The Nursing Workforce 2014: Growth, Salaries, Education, Demographics & Trends." Published August. www.nursingworld.org/~4afac8/globalassets/practiceandpolicy/workforce/fastfacts_nsgjobgrowth-salaries_updated8-25-15.pdf.

———. n.d. *Facts About Nursing.* Various editions. Silver Springs, MD: American Nurses Association.

Arevalo, J. D. 2008. "RN-to-Patient Hospital Staffing Ratios Update." AMN Healthcare. Accessed May 1, 2018. www.amnhealthcare.com/latest-healthcare-news/rn-to-patient-hospital-staffing-ratios-update/.

Auerbach, D., P. Buerhaus, and D. Staiger. 2017. "Millennials Almost Twice as Likely to Be Registered Nurses as Baby Boomers Were." *Health Affairs* 36 (10): 1804–7.

Auerbach, D., D. Staiger, U. Muench, and P. Buerhaus. 2013. "The Nursing Workforce in an Era of Health Care Reform." *New England Journal of Medicine* 368 (16): 1470–72.

Budden, J. S., P. Moulton, K. J. Harper, M. L. Brunell, and R. Smiley. 2016. "The 2015 National Nursing Workforce Survey." *Journal of Nursing Regulation.* Published April. www.ncsbn.org/2015ExecutiveSummary.pdf.

Buerhaus, P., D. Auerbach, and D. Staiger. 2017. "How Should We Prepare for the Wave of Retiring Baby Boomer Nurses?" *Health Affairs Blog.* Published May 3. http://healthaffairs.org/blog/2017/05/03/how-should-we-prepare-for-the-wave-of-retiring-baby-boomer-nurses/.

———. 2009. "The Recent Surge in Nurse Employment: Causes and Implications." *Health Affairs* (web exclusive) 28 (4): w657–68.

Buerhaus, P., D. Staiger, and D. Auerbach. 2009. *The Future of the Nursing Workforce in the United States: Data, Trends, and Implications.* Boston: Jones and Bartlett.

Bureau of Labor Statistics. 2018. "Labor Force Statistics from the Current Population Survey." Modified February 9. www.bls.gov/cps/tables.htm.

———. 2017. "Registered Nurses." In *Occupational Outlook Handbook, 2016–17 Edition.* Modified October. www.bls.gov/ooh/healthcare/registered-nurses.htm.

Centers for Disease Control and Prevention. 2015. "National Ambulatory Medical Care Survey: 2015 State and National Summary Tables." Accessed January 2018. www.cdc.gov/nchs/data/ahcd/namcs_summary/2015_namcs_web_tables.pdf.

———. 2014. "National Hospital Ambulatory Medical Care Survey: 2014 Emergency Department Summary Tables." Accessed January 2018. www.cdc.gov/nchs/data/nhamcs/web_tables/2014_ed_web_tables.pdf.

Centers for Medicare & Medicaid Services. 2017. "CMS Program Statistics 2015: Medicare Utilization Section, Medicare Skilled Nursing Facilities, MDSR SNF 1." Modified June. www.cms.gov/Research-Statistics-Data-and-Systems/Statistics-Trends-and-Reports/CMSProgramStatistics/2015/Downloads/UTIL/2015_CPS_MDCR_SNF_1.pdf.

Hanel, B., G. Kalb, and A. Scott. 2014. "Nurses' Labour Supply Elasticities: The Importance of Accounting for Extensive Margins." *Journal of Health Economics* 33: 94–112.

Markowitz, S., E. K. Adams, M. J. Lewitt, and A. Dunlop. 2016. "Competitive Effects of Scope of Practice Restrictions: Public Health or Public Harm?" National Bureau of Economic Research Working Paper No. 22780. Published October. www.nber.org/papers/w22780.

National Bureau of Economic Research. 2010. "Business Cycle Dating Committee." Published September 20. www.nber.org/cycles/sept2010.html.

National Center for Health Statistics. n.d. *Health United States.* Various editions. Hyattsville, MD: National Center for Health Statistics.

National League for Nursing. 2009. "Nursing Education Statistics." Accessed March 2014. www.nln.org/newsroom/nursing-education-statistics.

Nursing Solutions Inc. n.d. *National Health Care Retention & RN Staffing Report.* Various years (2015–2018 reports). East Petersburg, PA: Nursing Solutions Inc.

Payscale.com. 2018. "Registered Nurse (RN) in Manila Salary (Philippines)." Accessed May. www.payscale.com/research/PH/Job=Registered_Nurse_(RN)/Salary/08faaf74/Manila.

Perloff, J., C. M. DesRoches, and P. Buerhaus. 2016. "Comparing the Cost of Care Provided to Medicare Beneficiaries Assigned to Primary Care Nurse Practitioners and Physicians." *Health Services Research* 51 (4): 1407–23.

US Census Bureau. n.d. *Statistical Abstract of the United States.* Various editions. Washington, DC: Census Bureau.

US Department of Health and Human Services, Health Resources and Services Administration. 2002. "Projected Supply, Demand, and Shortages of Registered Nurses: 2000–2020." Published July. www.ahcancal.org/research_data/staffing/Documents/Registered_Nurse_Supply_Demand.pdf.

Yett, D. 1975. *An Economic Analysis of the Nurse Shortage*. Lexington, MA: D.C. Heath.

THE HIGH PRICE OF PRESCRIPTION DRUGS

Spending on prescription drugs has greatly increased since 1990, when drug expenditures were $40 billion. As of 2016, drug expenditures reached $328 billion (Centers for Medicare & Medicaid Services 2018). In the late 1990s and the early part of the past decade, drug expenditures rose more rapidly than did other medical expenditures. After reaching a peak of 18 percent in 1999, the annual rate of increase in drug expenditures has been declining; in 2016, the rate of increase was 4.8 percent compared with 4.8 percent and 5.4 percent in hospital and physician expenditures, respectively. The annual percentage increases in prescription drug expenditures and drug prices since 1980 are shown in exhibit 25.1. Prescription drug expenditures represent a smaller percentage of total health expenditures (9.8 percent) than do hospital or physician services (32.4 percent and 19.9 percent, respectively).

Despite drug expenditures being a smaller percentage of total health expenditures than expenditures for hospitals and physicians services, drug prices for innovative drugs are a continuing cause for concern in the public and private sectors. Higher drug expenditures are a growing burden to state Medicaid programs, the federal deficit, and private insurance premiums. Further, patients pay a higher percentage of drug expenditures out of pocket than they do for other major health expenditures. Not surprisingly, patients are more likely to complain about paying $50 for a prescription drug than about $20,000 to stay in the hospital, which is covered by insurance.

Reasons for the Increase in Pharmaceutical Expenditures

The major factors causing the high drug expenditures are the surge in drug prescription use, the rise in drug prices, and the changes in the types of drugs prescribed.

Surge in Drug Prescription Use

As shown in exhibit 25.2, the total number of prescriptions filled (including refills) has been sharply increasing—from 1.9 billion in 1992 to 4.5 billion in 2016. On a per capita basis, the average number of retail prescriptions increased from 7.3 in 1992 to 10.4 in 2000, to 12.9 in 2010, and to 13.8 in 2016. The two important reasons for this escalation over time are (1) the growth in the number of seniors and (2) the proliferation of insurance coverage for prescription drugs.

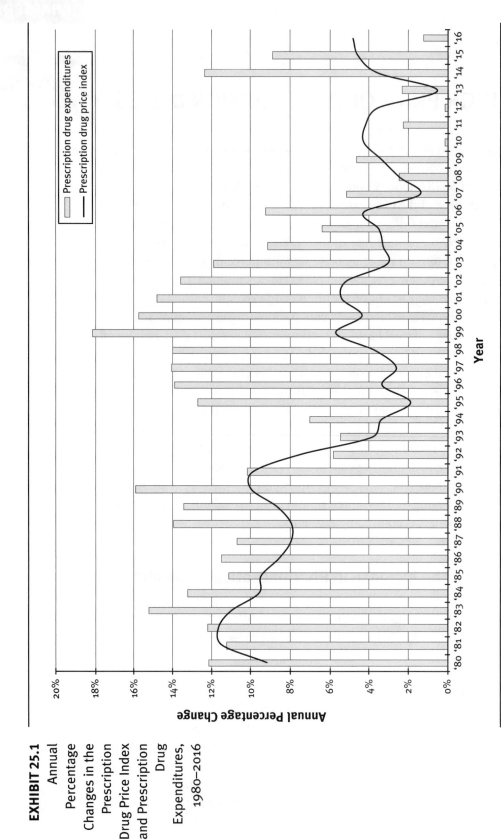

EXHIBIT 25.1
Annual
Percentage
Changes in the
Prescription
Drug Price Index
and Prescription
Drug
Expenditures,
1980–2016

Sources: Data from Bureau of Labor Statistics (2018); Centers for Medicare & Medicaid Services (2018).

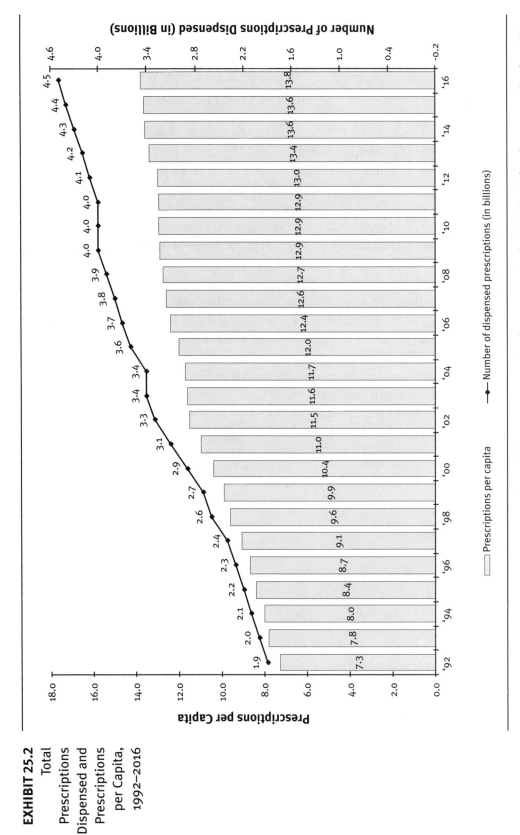

EXHIBIT 25.2
Total
Prescriptions
Dispensed and
Prescriptions
per Capita,
1992–2016

Sources: 1992–2001 data from the National Institute for Health Care Management (2002); 2002–2012 data from IMS Health (2013); 2013–2016 data from IQVIA Institute for Human Data Sciences (2017) and US Census Bureau (2017).

Although population growth is about 1 percent per year, the number of elderly individuals has been rising even faster, and their use of prescription medication is the highest among the US populace. With regard to prescriptions, including refills, purchased in an outpatient setting only, those between the ages of 18 and 44 years use, on average, 4.9 prescriptions per year, while those between the ages of 45 and 64 years use an average of 15.9 prescriptions per year. In contrast, for those between the ages of 65 and 74 years, the average number of prescriptions in 2013 was 25.9 per person, and those between the ages of 75 and 84 years received an average of 28.5 prescriptions during the year (see exhibit 25.3). As the elderly population continues to grow and their age levels increase, the volume of prescriptions is expected to rise. Given the greater number of seniors and prescriptions per aged person, drug expenditures in general (and among the aged in particular) will continue to expand.

The growth in private and public insurance coverage for prescription drugs is the second reason that drug expenditures have grown. The percentage of the population with some form of third-party payment for prescription drugs has been increasing for some time. Conversely, out-of-pocket expenditures for these medicines have been decreasing. As shown in exhibit 25.4, in 1990, 57 percent of drug expenditures were paid out of pocket, 27 percent were covered by private insurance, and the remaining 16 percent were covered by public funds (primarily Medicaid). As of 2016, only 14 percent of drug expenditures were paid out of pocket by consumers, 43 percent were paid by private insurance, and 43 percent were paid by public funds (primarily Medicaid and Medicare). A drug benefit in which the patient's copayment is only $5 per

EXHIBIT 25.3

Average Number of Prescription Drug Purchases by Age, 2013

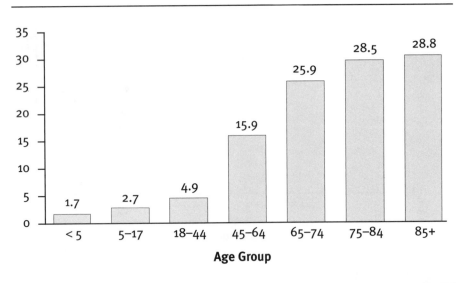

Note: Average number of prescriptions, including refills.

Source: Data from Agency for Healthcare Research and Quality (2018).

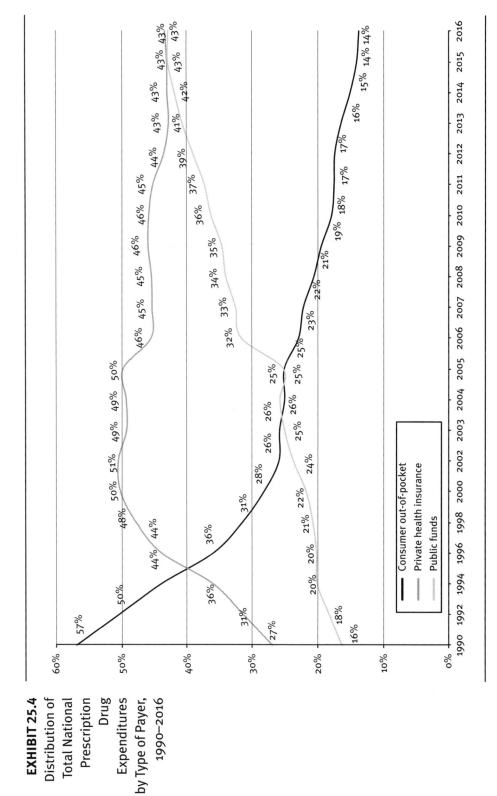

EXHIBIT 25.4
Distribution of
Total National
Prescription
Drug
Expenditures
by Type of Payer,
1990–2016

Source: Data from Centers for Medicare & Medicaid Services (2018).

prescription represents a steep price decrease, and the growth of drug plans offered by health plans led to large increases in the use of prescription drugs.

The Medicare prescription drug benefit (Part D), which became effective in 2006, stimulated greater use of prescription drugs among the elderly. (As shown in exhibit 25.4, public expenditures for drugs jumped in 2006.) With Part D, Medicare became the primary payer for many of the aged who were on Medicaid. Medicare drug expenditures rose more slowly than expected because of the way in which the drug benefit was organized; it relied on competition among private drug plans.

Private drug plans submit bids to the federal government for providing the basic prescription drug benefit to a beneficiary. The federal government calculates a national average bid and pays 75 percent of the national average bid to the drug plan chosen by the beneficiary. The beneficiary is then responsible for the remaining 25 percent of the monthly premium. If a beneficiary enrolls in a plan that submitted a higher bid than the national average, he or she pays the difference—in addition to the base premium. Any difference between a plan's bid and the national average bid translates directly into a price difference that becomes the responsibility of beneficiaries. Beneficiaries choose between plans with a low premium and plans that are more expensive but offer more benefits (e.g., inclusion of the beneficiary's drugs in the insurer's formulary).

Drug plans compete for enrollees by offering low premiums, and the premiums are held down through several cost-containment approaches. One example is the use of formularies (which exclude multiple drugs within a class as well as certain drugs) requiring prior authorization for approval of certain drugs and tiered cost sharing, such as 25 percent (or $10) copayment for generic drugs, 30 percent (or $25) for branded drugs in the formulary, and 40 to 50 percent (or $50) for branded drugs not in the formulary. Prices and expenditures would have increased more rapidly without the financial incentive for beneficiaries to choose among competing drug plans, the competition among firms providing the benefit, and the ability of these firms to negotiate price discounts from pharmaceutical companies to include their branded drugs in the plans' formularies.

Unlike other government entitlement programs, the estimated federal cost of the drug benefit has been constant for more than 10 years, and it has cost much less than many anticipated.

The Affordable Care Act made two changes to the Medicare Part D drug benefit that have resulted in an increase in Medicare drug prescriptions and expenditures. First, the Part D "donut hole" was reduced, thereby reducing Medicare beneficiaries' out-of-pocket payments for prescription drugs. Second, successful lobbying by the pharmaceutical association resulted in private drug plans having to include more than one drug per class in their formulary; this change reduced private drug plans' ability to negotiate lower drug prices with a pharmaceutical firm.

Exhibit 25.5 illustrates both the changing share of spending on prescription drugs and the growth in drug expenditures over time. Before enactment of Medicare Part D, private health insurance and health plans had the largest share of drug expenditures. After Part D became available, the share of total drug expenditures by private health plans shrank and the number of firms serving Medicare beneficiaries grew.

Rise in Drug Prices

Drug prices (which are less of a contributing factor to expenditure increases than is drug utilization) rose at double-digit rates annually during the 1980s but moderated at between 4 and 5 percent annually in recent years. Annual drug price increases have been lower than the price hikes for hospital and physician services, and they (as measured by the Bureau of Labor Statistics) appear to be less of a contributing factor to the higher drug expenditures today than in the past. An important reason for the slowdown in drug price increases is that patents for many top-selling drugs have expired, and these drugs have been subject to competition from cheaper generics, resulting in lower prices (and profits). Health plans have tried to control drug expenditure growth by creating stronger financial incentives for their enrollees to choose generic or cheaper brand-name drugs.

Several studies (e.g., Goodell and Swartz [2010]) have examined the relationship between the out-of-pocket drug price (copayments) and drug expenditures. They found that more cost sharing leads to more adverse health events, such as emergency department visits and inpatient admissions. Conversely, the use of newer drugs results in less inpatient care. The effect of price on drug use has important consequences for both drug and total medical expenditures.

A substitution effect occurs between drug use and use of other medical services. Raising the copayments for certain drugs not only reduces the demand for those drugs but also likely encourages the use of expensive medical services, thereby increasing medical expenditures.[1] Health plans, aware of the high price sensitivity between copayments and drug use, have lowered the copayments for patients taking prescription drugs for chronic illnesses (and have also used various methods to remind these patients to take their medications) to reduce costly hospitalizations.

Changes in Types of Drugs Prescribed

Over time, the types of prescription drugs used change, which, in turn, affects how fast drug expenditures grow. When a new, innovative drug enters the market, its price is higher than that of the drug it replaces. When a "me-too" drug enters the market, it becomes a good substitute for an innovative drug, which, in turn, lowers the price of both drugs. Similarly, when the patent on a drug expires and a generic version of the drug enters the market, many patients switch from the expensive brand-name drug to the cheaper generic.

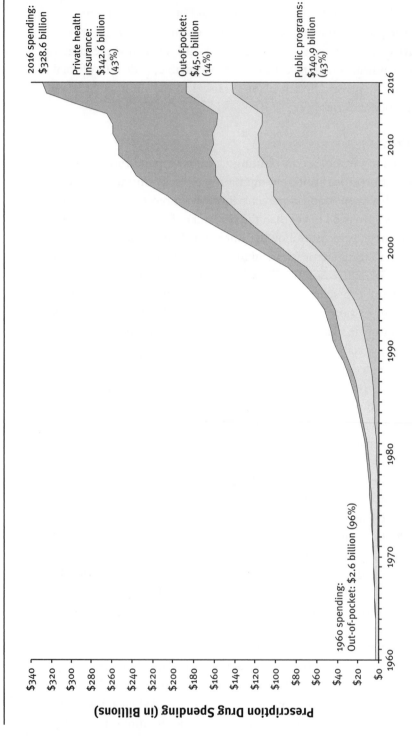

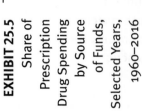

EXHIBIT 25.5
Share of
Prescription
Drug Spending
by Source
of Funds,
Selected Years,
1960–2016

Note: Public programs cover federal, state, and local spending for prescription drugs, including Medicare, workers' compensation, temporary disability, public assistance (Medicaid and Children's Health Insurance Program [CHIP]), Department of Defense, maternal/child health, Veterans Affairs, and Indian Health Services.

Source: Data from Centers for Medicare & Medicaid Services (2018).

Drug expenditures may increase more or less rapidly depending on the number of innovative, high-priced drugs brought to market, the entry of me-too drugs, whether (and how many) branded drugs lose their patent protection, and how rapidly generic substitutes become available.

The 1990s saw a large introduction to the market of innovative but costly drugs that have preventive and curative effects. These drugs can be used to treat previously untreatable illnesses and have substituted for expensive invasive medical procedures, which lowered overall treatment costs. New drugs reduce nonpharmaceutical medical costs, such as antidepressants that have minimized costly psychotherapy, as well as beta-blockers and blood pressure drugs that have lessened expensive cardiovascular-related hospital admissions and surgeries. Lichtenberg (2007, 2012) concluded that replacing older drugs with newer drugs has resulted in greater life expectancy at birth and in lower mortality, morbidity (as indicated by fewer days lost from work), and total treatment costs (particularly for inpatient care). New drugs have brought about large reductions in hospital expenditures because their use resulted in shortened lengths of stay and a decreased number of admissions. The total reduction in nondrug medical expenses is about seven times the increase in drug costs. Some new drugs also have fewer adverse effects.

Many lifestyle drugs—such as sildenafil citrate (Viagra) (treatment of male impotence), loratadine (Claritin) (relief from allergies), omeprazole (Prilosec) (relief from stomach upsets), and pain relievers—improve the quality of life. However, they may be much more expensive than older drugs. For example, new pain relievers treat severe arthritis, but they cost $150 a month, nearly 20 times more than older pain relievers. Enbrel (etanercept), a biotech drug used to treat rheumatoid arthritis, can cost $1,500 or more a month. Whereas drugs such as penicillin are prescribed for a brief period to cure an infection, some modern drugs (including lifestyle drugs) can be taken for decades. The prospect of better health and improved quality of life has led to a proliferation of prescriptions and boosted the price of new drugs.

Over the past several years, many well-known brand-name prescription drugs, such as Lipitor (atorvastatin) (an anticholesterol drug), lost their patent protection. As generic substitutes entered the market, prices for these drugs declined along with the growth rate of drug expenditures.

In coming years, additional innovative specialty drugs will become available. These specialty drugs—referred to as *biologics*—are "complex proteins that are made in living cells that treat a range of diseases, from various types of cancer to rare hereditary diseases" (Thomas 2013). The drugs are extremely expensive. Sovaldi (sofosbuvir), a pill for hepatitis C, costs about $100,000 for a course of treatment, but cures the disease in most patients and is less expensive than previous treatments, which can run as high as $500,000 for an organ transplant. Other new drugs are even more expensive; Actimmune (interferon gamma-1b), which is used to treat life-threatening osteopetrosis, a relatively rare disease, can cost between $250,000 and $500,000 per year. Although specialty drugs make up only 2 percent of all drug prescriptions, they account for 39.6 percent of total drug expenditures.

Between 2010 and 2015, expenditures on specialty drugs doubled and contributed 70 percent of the expenditure increase in drugs over that period. Although many patients relying on traditional prescription drugs will have smaller out-of-pocket costs, the expense of specialty drugs will be a financial hardship for patients who must incur large copayments to use these drugs. Insurers, as well as Medicare and Medicaid, will also face a major financial expense as the use of specialty drugs becomes common. Rising drug expenditures should be viewed favorably when innovative drugs become available to extend life, substitute for more costly treatments, and improve the quality of life. Further, a greater number of prescriptions per person (particularly for the aged) may indicate that chronic diseases can be better managed, the elderly can live longer, and their quality of life can be enhanced.

Pricing Practices of US Pharmaceutical Companies

Drug manufacturers sell their drugs to different purchasers (intermediaries), who, in turn, sell them to patients. Retail (independent and chain) pharmacies sell about 42 percent of all prescription drugs; healthcare organizations such as health maintenance organizations (HMOs), hospitals, long-term care facilities, home health care agencies, federal facilities, and clinics sell 28 percent; mail-order pharmacies sell 23 percent; and food stores sell 7 percent (see exhibit 25.6). (Patients enrolled in HMOs and insurance company plans rely on mail-order and retail pharmacies that are in their insurers' networks for their drugs.)

Pharmaceutical companies sell the same prescription drug to different purchasers at different prices. An HMO pays less for its drugs than does an independent retail pharmacy, although the latter sells a much greater volume of drugs. Similarly, patients without any prescription drug coverage (often the poor and sick) pay more for the same drug at a retail pharmacy than patients who are part of a managed care plan.

Two aspects of the pricing practices of pharmaceutical companies have been criticized as unfair and have led to proposals for government intervention. First, different purchasers are charged different prices for the same drug. Second, prescription drugs have a high price markup.

Pricing According to Cost
A new prescription drug is priced many times higher than its actual costs of production. This high markup over cost has generated a great deal of criticism. If the drug were priced closer to its production cost, the financial burden would

EXHIBIT 25.6
Prescription
Sales by Outlet,
US Market,
2016

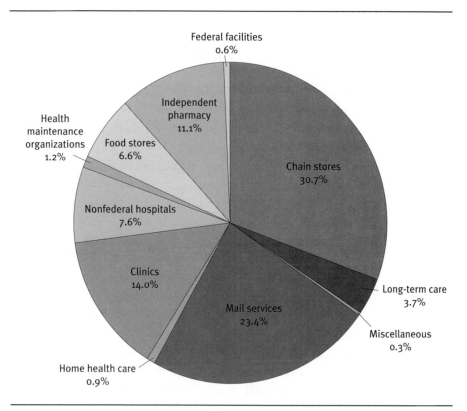

Federal facilities
0.6%

Independent
pharmacy
11.1%

Health
maintenance
organizations
1.2%

Food stores
6.6%

Chain stores
30.7%

Nonfederal hospitals
7.6%

Clinics
14.0%

Long-term care
3.7%

Mail services
23.4%

Miscellaneous
0.3%

Home health care
0.9%

Source: Data from IQVIA Institute for Human Data Sciences (2017).

lessen for those with low income, those without prescription drug coverage, and state Medicaid budgets.

Drug manufacturers often claim that their prices are determined by the high costs of developing the drugs. High research and development (R&D) costs, however, are not the reason for high or rising drug prices. Large fixed (or sunk) costs are those that have already been incurred; hence, they are not relevant for setting a drug's price. Fixed costs must eventually be recovered or the drug company will lose money; however, a new drug that is no different from drugs already on the market could not sell for more than these competing drugs—regardless of how much that drug cost to develop.

Pricing According to Demand

When price differences for the same drug cannot be explained entirely by cost variations, according to economic theory, the reason must be related to the differences in the purchaser's price sensitivity or willingness to pay. Purchasers who are not price sensitive will be charged higher prices than those who are. A purchaser who is willing to buy a lower volume or switch to another drug when the price increases is more price sensitive than one who is not.

The higher price charged to one purchaser is not meant to make up for the lower price charged to another purchaser. Instead, the reason for different prices is that the seller can simply make more money by charging according to each purchaser's willingness to pay (Frank 2001).

The ability to shift market share rather than just the volume purchased drives discounts. Not all large-volume purchasers receive price discounts. Retail pharmacies in total sell a large volume of drugs, but they do not receive the same price discounts that managed care plans receive. When an HMO negotiates with a drug company on one of several competing brand-name drugs within a therapeutic class, the HMO's willingness to place the drug on its formulary while excluding a competitor's drugs can result in substantial discounts for the HMO.[2] Medicare prescription drug plans use the same strategy as HMOs use. Similarly, pharmacy benefit managers (PBMs), who manage health plans' drug benefits for drugs sold through retail pharmacies, can promote brand-name substitution and thereby receive large discounts.[3]

Retail pharmacies pay the highest prices for prescription drugs because they must carry all branded drugs. Furthermore, the pharmacy cannot promote substitution between branded drugs because the physician may be prescribing according to a health plan's formulary. Because pharmacies cannot shift volume, drug manufacturers see no need to give them a price discount.[4] (To receive price discounts, government entities have resorted to price regulation; see chapter 28, "The Pharmaceutical Industry: A Public Policy Dilemma.") For a pharmacy to be included in a health plan or a PBM network, it must charge lower dispensing fees, which also results in lower prices to the PBM and to health plan enrollees.

Price discrimination, whereby a seller charges different prices to different purchasers, occurs in many other areas of the economy. For example, seniors and students pay lower prices at the movies and other events. Prices may differ by time of day, such as early-bird dinner specials and drinks, and airlines charge business travelers more than they do vacationers because the former group books flights on short notice. Those who are less likely to switch are less price sensitive and are charged more for the same service.

Price discrimination actually promotes price competition between drug manufacturers for more price-sensitive purchasers, which results in lower prices for purchasers and consumers. To price discriminate, a seller must prevent low-price buyers from reselling the product to those who are charged more. A 1987 federal law prevented resale of prescription drugs on the basis of preserving the safety and integrity of those drugs.

Pricing Innovative Drugs

Pharmaceutical manufacturers are strategic in how they mark up the price of their drugs (price-to-cost ratio) and negotiate price discounts. A drug's price markup is determined by demand. New drugs are priced according to their therapeutic value and the availability of good substitutes. When a new drug for which there is no close substitute comes on the market and is clearly therapeutically superior to existing drugs, it will have a higher price markup. Sometimes a drug is priced according to some concept of value, such as comparing it with the surgical procedure it replaces. Approving an existing drug for a new use also raises its value, as its therapeutic effects for that new use are greater than the effects of existing drugs; thus, the drug company is able to increase its price.

The greater the price markup over costs, the more innovative the drug and the fewer the close substitutes. Innovative drugs command higher price markups than do imitative drugs. Ultimately, the price of a new drug is determined by a purchaser's willingness to pay for its greater therapeutic benefits. A new breakthrough drug is priced much higher than any other drug in its therapeutic class (typically, more than three times the price) because no good substitutes are available. New drugs with modest therapeutic gains are priced about two times the average price for available drug substitutes. New drugs with little or no gain over existing drugs are priced at about the same level as existing substitutes. Once the patent has expired on a branded drug, generic drugs are introduced and are typically priced at 30 to 70 percent of the branded drug's price before the patent expired. As more generic versions become available, the prices of generic drugs drop.

New, higher-priced drugs will fail commercially if their therapeutic benefits are similar to those of existing drugs. As health plans evaluate drugs (on the basis of therapeutic benefits and price) for inclusion in their formularies, differences in drug prices will reflect differences in therapeutic benefits. Knowledgeable purchasers evaluating a more expensive new drug will pay a higher price only if its therapeutic benefits are greater than those of the older drug.

A new drug that is similar to an existing drug (a me-too drug) cannot be priced much higher than the existing drug because purchasers will switch to a good substitute (the existing drug) at a lower price. Although drug companies have been criticized for producing me-too drugs, their availability contributes to price competition. (Me-too drugs also provide value in that they may have fewer adverse effects than the existing drugs.)

Once competitors enter the market originally served by an innovative drug, prices decline. Interestingly, when generic versions enter the market after the patent on a branded drug has expired, the branded drug loses market share to the generic drug, but the price of the branded product actually increases; the price-sensitive customers switch to the generic drug, and those who do not switch are not price sensitive. Therefore, the seller of the branded drug is able to raise its price. Some physicians (and consumers) have strong preferences for the branded drug and do not want it substituted with the generic version; they are willing to pay more for the perceived efficacy of the brand-name drug.[5] Drug manufacturers have determined that serving a smaller market at a higher price is more profitable than reducing the price of the branded drug to compete with generic versions.

Thus, the pricing strategy of pharmaceutical companies is based on two principles. First, the greater the price sensitivity of the purchaser—such as an HMO willing to shift its drug purchases to a competitor's drug—the lower the price. Second, the more innovative the drug, the higher the price markup will be. These pricing strategies are designed to maximize profits for the drug manufacturer.

Drug Companies' Marketing Response to Managed Care Plans

Purchaser decision making regarding pharmaceuticals has changed. Up until the late 1990s, physicians chose a patient's prescription drug. As a result, drug manufacturers spent a great deal of money marketing directly to physicians. With the growth of managed care and its use of closed formularies, drug companies began to develop new marketing strategies. As the purchasing decision for prescription drugs shifted from the individual physician to the committee overseeing the organization's formulary, sending sales representatives to individual physicians caring for an HMO's patients was less useful than marketing to the HMO itself. Drug companies have had to demonstrate that their drugs are not only therapeutically superior to competing drugs but also cost-effective—namely, that the additional benefits of their drug are worth its higher price. Physicians continue to be important in prescribing drugs to their patients, but PBMs and health plans determine which brand-name drugs the physician is able to prescribe and the prices paid for those drugs.

To counteract the closed formularies, drug manufacturers started direct-to-consumer television and newspaper advertising to generate consumer demand for certain drugs from their physicians. Direct-to-consumer advertising—the cost of which increased from about $600 million in 1997 (the first year such advertising was permitted by the Food and Drug Administration [FDA]) to $2.5 billion in 2000 and to $6.4 billion in 2016—initially proved effective in boosting sales of advertised prescription drugs (Swallen 2017).

Physicians almost never wrote prescriptions for drugs requested by patients because most patients did not know enough to demand drugs by name or therapeutic class. As more medical information has become available to patients, they have begun demanding more input into the therapeutic decisions that affect their lives. Drug companies claim that ads are meant to inform the patient and stimulate a discussion between the patient and her physician. Critics claim that the ads do not inform patients about who is most likely to benefit from that drug, its possible side effects, or other treatment options.[6]

Prescription drug plan formularies include a tiered set of copayments for a drug—a small copayment for a less costly generic version of the drug and a higher copayment for the branded version. Brand-name drug firms have made coupons available to patients at the physician's office and on their websites. The coupons cover the difference in the patient's copayment between the generic and branded version. These coupons equalize the out-of-pocket costs to patients, regardless of whether they choose the generic or branded version of the drug. The coupons are subsidized by the drug firm when the patient redeems the coupon at the pharmacy (Ross and Kesselheim 2013).

Brand-name drug firms benefit from the use of coupons through increased sales of branded drugs, given that the patient's out-of-pocket price is the same as that for the generic version. Further, coupons are generally available for branded drugs that are used for long periods, such as for chronic diseases. The availability of coupons, however, is limited, typically for several months and less than a year, at which time the patient's out-of-pocket copayment for the branded drug rises. Presumably, after the patient has become used to the branded drug, he may be less likely to switch to the generic version.

Dafny, Ody, and Schmitt (2017) estimated that coupons increase the sales of branded drugs by more than 60 percent, resulting in $30 to $120 million more in sales per branded drug. By issuing coupons, drug firms have been able to undercut insurers' tiered formularies in which patients are shifted to cheaper generics through the use of different copayments. Although the cost of the branded drug to the patient has been reduced, insurers must pay the higher price of the branded drug. The cost to the drug plan is passed on to all of the plan's enrollees through higher premiums.

Although drug costs have become a large expense for health plans, and health plans have introduced tiered copayments to provide enrollees with an incentive to use less costly drugs, health plans have also reduced or eliminated copays for certain drugs. Given the inverse relationship between price and use of drugs, health plans are lowering drug copayments to encourage the use of drugs that reduce expensive medical episodes. If decreasing copayments—or even providing the drug for free—makes a patient more likely to follow the recommended drug regimen and thereby prevent recurrence of a heart attack or stroke, the health plan can reduce its cost and benefit the patient.

The Shortage of Generic Drugs

Shortages of generic drugs have been occurring for the past 15 years, and the prices of some of these drugs have increased dramatically. Because generics are inexpensive copies of drugs that have lost their patent protection, one would think that new supplies of such drugs could be quickly produced, thereby preventing any shortages or large price increases. However, a rapid market adjustment to these shortages has not occurred. Why have these shortages occurred and what are the appropriate policies to ensure they don't occur again?

There are two types of generic drugs: injectable and noninjectable. Injectable drugs, such as some cancer drugs, are generally administered by the physician, who buys them and then bills Medicare. The most critical shortages have occurred with sterile injectable drugs, whose lack of availability can have serious health consequences because few, if any, substitutes have been available. When these cancer drugs became unavailable, patients had to wait as long as 6 months before being able to continue their treatment. In the meantime, many cancer patients reliant on these drugs experienced a relapse.

The 2003 Medicare Prescription Drug, Improvement, and Modernization Act reduced payments for physician-administered outpatient drugs. These lower payments resulted in physicians and drug manufacturers shifting to more expensive drugs for which they could earn greater profit.

The profit on generic drugs is very low, particularly for older generics. Thus, manufacturers have little incentive to maintain production facilities for these drugs when they can shift to production of generics that have a higher profit margin. Given capacity constraints, manufacturing the low-margin generics decreased. Manufacturing of generic drugs has also become highly concentrated, with a few firms producing most of the generic drugs (Berndt, Conti, and Murphy 2017). Thus, if life-saving drugs become scarce, little excess capacity exists to quickly shift production.

FDA regulatory actions have also affected the supply of generic drugs. More stringent inspections of manufacturers' plants have resulted in the closure of a number of facilities. Further, the FDA made it difficult for new generic manufacturers to quickly enter the market when a shortage developed. The cost to a generic firm for filing a new abbreviated drug application increased sharply, and it took many months for the FDA to approve a generic drug, making it difficult for new firms to enter the market.

Yurukoglu, Liebman, and Ridley (2017) demonstrated that lower Medicare payments for these shortage drugs lowered the investment return to manufacturers, which consequently reduced their capacity for producing these drugs. Further, drugs used largely by Medicare patients, such as sterile injectable drugs, were most affected by shortages when Medicare reduced its payment for those drugs.

Some firms took advantage of the entry barriers imposed by the FDA's high cost of filing a drug application and the FDA's approval delays by sharply increasing the price of their generic noninjectable drugs. The most publicized case was that of Turing Pharmaceuticals, which purchased the rights to Darapriam, a 60-year-old drug. The drug, used to treat cancer and AIDS patients, was previously priced at $13.50 per pill; after renaming the drug, the firm increased the price of each pill to $750. Turing was the sole supplier of the drug. Because it was a generic drug, other firms should have been able to enter the market and drive the price down. However, doing so would have cost a new supplier about $15 million for the filing process and taken several years before it would have received FDA approval. The publicity of Turing's huge price increase for an old generic drug and the inordinate amount of time for a competitor to enter the market prompted the FDA to hire more staff and reduce the approval time for new generic drugs.

The appropriate public policy to reduce shortages of injectable and noninjectable generic drugs is not to impose price controls but to reduce the barriers to enable new suppliers of generic drugs to quickly enter the market. This can be achieved, not by the FDA's reducing quality standards, but by reducing the cost and time for drug approvals. With a new director in 2017, the FDA also is likely to try to anticipate problems that may arise with manufacturers' production, given the high concentration of generic producers, so that capacity constraints do not cause any shortages.

Summary

Prescription drug expenditures will continue to grow, partly because of greater drug use, which results from the introduction of new, costly drugs. New drugs have a high markup in relation to the cost of production. To those without drug coverage and to large purchasers of drugs, such as health plans, Medicare drug plans, and state Medicaid agencies, these facts are a cause for concern. However, the public should view rising drug expenditures and even high price markups favorably. Rising drug prices are often an indication that new drugs are more effective than existing drugs or alternative treatments. (When new drugs are of higher quality—that is, when they provide greater benefits than the drugs they replace—their quality-adjusted price may well be lower than the price of older drugs.) Moreover, when new drugs replace old drugs, purchasers place greater value on the therapeutic benefits of the new drugs and are willing to pay the cost for that value. Clearly, consumers are better off.

Replacing old drugs with new drugs is just one important factor in the growth of drug expenditures. Other contributing factors are the increase in third-party payment for prescription drugs, population growth, and the aging of the population. All of these factors will likely cause drug expenditures to remain enormous in the future.

Drug manufacturers charge different prices to different buyers for the same drug (price discrimination); they give price discounts to purchasers who are willing to switch their drug purchases and charge higher prices to those who are less price sensitive (unwilling to switch). The cost-containment strategies of health plans and PBMs have caused pharmaceutical firms to compete on price to have their drugs included in the formularies of large purchasers and to emphasize the cost-effectiveness of their drugs. These firms have rolled out direct-to-consumer advertising to encourage patients to pressure their physicians to demand the firms' drugs.[7] To limit the effect of such tactics, health plans have instituted tiered copayment systems that give consumers incentives to use drugs on the health plan's formulary.

Discussion Questions

1. Which factors have contributed most to the increase in drug expenditures?
2. Are rising drug expenditures necessarily bad?
3. Is the high price of drugs determined by the high cost of developing a new drug?
4. Why do drug manufacturers charge different purchasers different prices for the same prescription drug?
5. What methods have managed care plans used to limit their enrollees' drug costs?
6. What are the likely consequences of the Affordable Care Act's closing the "donut hole"?

Notes

1. The relationship between the out-of-pocket price of drugs and drug expenditures has been estimated to be −1.13; that is, a 1 percent *increase* in price will result in a 1.13 percent *decrease* in drug expenditures over time (Gaynor, Li, and Vogt 2006).
2. As HMOs and health plans seek volume discounts from drug companies, they are willing to limit their subscribers' choice of drugs in return for lower drug prices. Drug formulary committees focus on drugs for which therapeutic substitutes exist and evaluate different drugs according to their therapeutic value and price; higher-priced drugs are used only when justified by greater therapeutic benefits. Restrictions are then placed on their physicians' prescribing behavior. These organizations are also using computer technology to conduct drug utilization review; each physician's prescription is instantly checked against the formulary, and data are gathered on the performance of each physician and the health plan's use of specific drugs.
3. PBMs are firms that provide administrative services and process outpatient prescription drug claims for health insurers' prescription drug plans. To control growth in prescription drug expenditures, PBMs also contract with a network of pharmacies, negotiate pharmacy payments, negotiate with drug manufacturers for drug discounts and rebates, develop a drug formulary listing preferred drugs for treating an illness, encourage use of generic drugs instead of high-priced

brand-name drugs, operate a mail-order pharmacy, and analyze and monitor patient compliance programs. Some PBMs have been very aggressive in switching physicians' prescriptions; they may telephone a physician and tell her that a less expensive drug is available for the same medical condition and suggest that the physician switch to a drug on which the PBM receives a large price discount or rebate.

4. In 1993, an antitrust suit was filed by 31,000 retail pharmacies against 24 pharmaceutical manufacturers, claiming that the drug companies conspired to charge HMOs, PBMs, and hospitals lower prices while denying price discounts to retail pharmacies. Most of the drug companies settled by paying a relatively small average amount per retail pharmacy, and said they would give the same discounts to retail pharmacies if the pharmacies could demonstrate that they were able to shift the market share of their drugs. Five drug companies refused to settle. The retail pharmacies had to prove that price discrimination harmed competition and that the discounts were not a competitive response to another drug firm's lower prices. At the trial in 1998, the judge dismissed the lawsuit; the decision was upheld on appeal (Culyer and Newhouse 2000).

5. The drug companies claimed they did not offer a price discount to retail pharmacies because the discounts would not increase the drug companies' market share. Retail pharmacies had to carry a wide selection of drugs because they merely filled orders of prescribing physicians. The greater the ability of the buyer to switch market share away from one drug manufacturer to a competitor's drug, the greater the discount. The drug companies claimed that retail pharmacies were unable to switch volume from one drug company to another; therefore, there was no reason to give them a discount.

6. When the patent on a branded drug expires, the first generic version of that drug has a six-month period of exclusivity over other generics; the first generic can capture up to 90 percent of the market from the branded drug. Typically, the branded drug manufacturer does not produce the generic version when its patent expires.

7. Direct-to-consumer advertising has recently declined. Advertisers believe that such advertising is effective only for new brand-name drugs and for new drug categories (Pharma Marketing Network 2013).

References

Agency for Healthcare Research and Quality. 2018. "Medical Expenditure Panel Survey (MEPS) Household Component, 2015." MEPSnet/HC Trend Query. Accessed May. http://meps.ahrq.gov/mepsweb/data_stats/MEPSnetHC.jsp.

Berndt, E. R., R. M. Conti, and S. J. Murphy. 2017. "The Generic Drug User Fee Amendments: An Economic Perspective." National Bureau of Economic Research Working Paper No. 23642. Published August. www.nber.org/papers/w23642.

Bureau of Labor Statistics. 2018. "Consumer Price Index." Accessed May. www.bls.gov/cpi/home.htm.

Centers for Medicare & Medicaid Services. 2018. "National Health Expenditure Data." Modified January. www.cms.gov/Research-Statistics-Data-and-Systems/Statistics-Trends-and-Reports/NationalHealthExpendData/NationalHealthAccountsHistorical.html/.

Culyer, A., and J. Newhouse. 2000. *Handbook of Health Economics*, vol. 1B. New York: North-Holland.

Dafny, L., C. Ody, and M. Schmitt. 2017. "When Coupons Raise Cost: The Effect of Copay Coupons on Generic Utilization." *American Economic Journal: Economic Policy* 9 (2): 91–123.

Frank, R. G. 2001. "Prescription Drug Prices: Why Do Some Pay More Than Others Do?" *Health Affairs* 20 (2): 115–28.

Gaynor, M., J. Li, and W. Vogt. 2006. "Is Drug Coverage a Free Lunch? Cross-Price Elasticities and the Design of Prescription Drug Benefits." National Bureau of Economic Research Working Paper No. 12758. Published December. www.nber.org/papers/w12758.

Goodell, S., and K. Swartz. 2010. "Cost Sharing: Effects on Spending and Outcomes." Robert Wood Johnson Foundation Policy Brief No. 20. Published December. www.rwjf.org/content/dam/farm/reports/issue_briefs/2010/rwjf402103.

IMS Health. 2013. *Top-Line Industry Data*. www.imshealth.com.

IQVIA Institute for Human Data Science. 2017. *Medicines Use and Spending in the U.S.: A Review of 2016 and Outlook to 2021*. Published May. www.iqvia.com/institute/reports/medicines-use-and-spending-in-the-us-a-review-of-2016.

Lichtenberg, F. 2012. "Pharmaceutical Innovation and Longevity Growth in 30 Developing and High-Income Countries, 2000–2009." National Bureau of Economic Research Working Paper No. 18235. Published July. www.nber.org/papers/w18235.

———. 2007. "The Benefits and Costs of Newer Drugs: An Update." *Managerial and Decision Economics* 28 (4–5): 485–90.

National Institute for Health Care Management. 2002. "Prescription Drug Expenditures in 2001: Another Year of Escalating Costs." Revised May 6. www.nihcm.org/pdf/spending2001.pdf.

Pharma Marketing Network. 2013. "Spending on Direct-to-Consumer Advertising Takes a Nosedive." *Pharma Marketing News*. Published March 18. www.pharma-mkting.com/news/pmn1203-article03.pdf.

Ross, J., and A. Kesselheim. 2013. "Prescription-Drug Coupons: No Such Thing as a Free Lunch." *New England Journal of Medicine* 369 (13): 1188–89.

Swallen, J. 2017. "Drug Advertising Booms to $6.4 Billion." *Kantar US Insights.* Published May 8. https://us.kantar.com/business/health/2017/drug-advertising-booms/.

Thomas, K. 2013. "U.S. Drug Costs Dropped in 2012, but Rises Loom." *New York Times.* Published March 18. www.nytimes.com/2013/03/19/business/use-of-generics-produces-an-unusual-drop-in-drug-spending.html.

US Census Bureau. 2017. "Population Estimates." Accessed November. www.census.gov.

Yurukoglu, A., E. Liebman, and D. Ridley. 2017. "The Role of Government Reimbursement in Drug Shortages." *American Economic Journal: Economic Policy* 9 (2): 348–82.

26

ENSURING SAFETY AND EFFICACY OF NEW DRUGS: TOO MUCH OF A GOOD THING?

Innovative new drugs have decreased mortality, increased life expectancy, and improved the quality of life for many millions of people. New drugs have also reduced the cost of medical care, substituting for more costly surgeries and long hospital stays. At the time of discovery, however, the effects of new drugs are not fully known. Powerful drugs that have the potential for curing cancer may also have harmful side effects. Some drugs may cause illness or even death in some people but may be beneficial for others. New drugs offer a trade-off: improvements in the quality and length of life versus possible serious adverse consequences.

Approval by the Food and Drug Administration (FDA) is required before any new drug may be marketed in the United States. The FDA's objective should be to achieve a balance between the concerns of drug safety and the potential benefits of pharmaceutical innovation. Ensuring that a new drug does not harm anyone delays the introduction of a potentially beneficial drug that may save many lives. This delay may result in the deaths of thousands of people whose lives could have been saved had the new drug been approved earlier. On the other hand, introducing potential breakthrough drugs immediately may cause the deaths of many individuals, as the full effects of the new drug are not completely understood.

How should this trade-off be evaluated? Are all lives—those potentially saved by early introduction of a new drug versus those who might die as a result of premature approval—valued equally? Regulatory delay increases the time and cost of bringing a new drug to market. Thus, both excessive caution and excessive expediency incur risks. This chapter discusses the FDA and its history and performance regarding the drug-approval process.

History of Regulation of Prescription Drugs

The Pure Food and Drug Act of 1906 was the federal government's first major effort at regulating the pharmaceutical industry. The supporters of this act, however, were primarily concerned with the quality of food, not drugs. Pure food acts had been submitted to Congress for at least ten years before one was finally passed. Media publicity on the ingredients of food and drugs generated popular support for legislative action. A great deal of publicity was generated by newspapers, magazine articles, and Upton Sinclair's 1906 book *The Jungle*, with its graphic descriptions of the contents of the foods the public was eating. Public outrage resulted, and Congress responded by passing the Pure Food and Drug Act.

The act required drug companies to provide accurate labeling information, including whether the drug was addictive. (A number of medicines contained alcohol, opium, heroin, and cocaine, which were legal at the time.) The government could verify the accuracy of the stated drug contents. Subsequent court cases resolved that therapeutic claims made by the sellers of a drug would not be considered fraudulent if the sellers believed their therapeutic claims. Thus, the drug-related portion of the act was quite limited and reflected the public's concern with the contents of food.

In the 1930s, the modern drug era began with the development of sulfa drugs. As these drugs were introduced, a tragedy provided the impetus for new legislation. A company seeking to make a liquid form of sulfanilamide for children dissolved it with diethylene glycol (a component of antifreeze), unaware of the toxic effects. As a result, more than 100 children died before the drug was recalled. Responding to the public outcry, Congress passed the Food, Drug, and Cosmetic Act in 1938. This law, which created the FDA, was intended to protect the public from unsafe, potentially harmful drugs. A company had to seek approval from the FDA before it could market a new drug. Drug companies determined the necessary amount and type of premarketing testing to prove to the government that the drug was safe for its intended use.

A 1950 amendment to the 1938 act authorized the FDA to distinguish prescription from nonprescription drugs by stating that some types of drugs could be sold only by prescription, as they could be harmful to the individual if bought on one's own.

The 1962 Amendments to the Food, Drug, and Cosmetic Act

In 1959, Senator Estes Kefauver held hearings on the drug industry. Critics of the industry believed that drug prices were too high, drug companies undertook unnecessary and wasteful advertising expenditures, and the drug industry earned excessive profits.

In the late 1950s, a new drug was introduced in Europe to treat morning sickness for pregnant women. After the introduction of thalidomide in Europe, an FDA staff member expressed doubts about the safety of the drug because of reported side effects and delayed its approval. An American drug company, however, was able to introduce it into the United States on an experimental basis. (The 1938 FDA amendments permitted such limited distribution to qualified experts if the drug was labeled as being under investigation.) As soon as reports began to appear in Europe that deformed babies were born to mothers who had taken the drug during pregnancy, the American company withdrew the drug.

The resulting media attention given to thalidomide and its effects in Europe shifted Congress's concern about high drug prices, wasteful expenditures, and excessive profits to concern with public safety. Congress responded to the public's fears about drug safety by passing the 1962 amendments to the Food, Drug, and Cosmetic Act. (Harris [1964] provides a history of the 1962 amendments.)

The 1962 amendments resulted in a major change in the regulation of pharmaceuticals. Drug companies were now required to prove the safety of their new drugs and their efficacy (beyond a placebo effect) for the indications claimed in treating a particular disease or condition. (Effectiveness must be determined by a controlled study in which some patients are given the new drug and others are given a placebo, an inactive substance such as a salt or sugar pill.) Once the FDA approves a new drug for marketing, the drug is approved only for specific claims. If the drug company wants to broaden those claims, it must file a new application with the FDA and provide evidence to support the new uses of that drug. (Physicians may, however, prescribe a drug for a use that has not received approval from the FDA.)

The steps that a drug company must take to meet the FDA's safety and efficacy standards are costly and time consuming. The FDA specifies the type of premarketing tests that must be conducted. Before undertaking clinical trials using humans, animal trials are used to determine whether the drug is sufficiently safe and promising to justify human trials. Based on this evidence from animal trials, the FDA will approve clinical trials using humans. The stages of clinical trials involve increasingly more subjects so that more dangerous drugs are identified before they can affect many patients. Stage 1 introduces the drug to 20 to 80 healthy individuals to evaluate its safety and identify adverse effects. Stage 2 involves 100 to 300 individuals with the disease to determine appropriate medication dosage and preliminary effectiveness. Stage 3 involves 1,000 to 3,000 patients, half of whom take a placebo, and is designed to confirm the drug's effectiveness, demonstrate efficacy, and provide additional evidence of safety. Clinical trials take, on average, six years to complete once animal and laboratory studies have been undertaken. Once the clinical trials are completed, the drug firm must receive FDA approval, which can take an additional several years.[1] Once approved by the FDA, the new drug must be manufactured according to specified standards.

Easier Entry for Generic Drugs

After the 1962 amendments were enacted, generic and patented drugs were treated in the same manner. Both had to meet the same stringent FDA requirements as a new drug seeking a patent. Manufacturers of generic drugs had to independently prove the safety and efficacy of their products to receive FDA approval. Because the research for generic drugs had to be undertaken according to the same process as that for the patented drug, the cost and time to develop generic drugs increased. Once a new drug received its patent and was approved by the FDA, the drug had no competition for a longer period than had been the case, and the price could be kept high for a longer time. Consumers continued to face high prices for prescription drugs for which the patents had expired because of FDA requirements that delayed the entry of generic substitutes.

The Drug Price Competition and Patent Term Restoration (Hatch-Waxman) Act of 1984 simplified and streamlined the process for FDA approval of generic drugs in exchange for granting patent extensions to innovative drugs. Generic drugs no longer had to replicate many of the clinical trials performed by the original manufacturer to prove safety and efficacy. Instead, the generic-drug manufacturer was required only to demonstrate that the generic drug was bioequivalent to the already approved patented drug, which was much less costly than proving safety and efficacy. (Bioequivalence means the active ingredient in the generic drug is absorbed at the same rate and to the same extent as that for the patented drug.) The effect of the Hatch-Waxman act was to reduce the delay between patent expiration and generic entry from more than three years to less than three months. Generic substitutes for branded drugs with expired patents are now quickly available at much lower prices. Previously, only 35 percent of top-selling drugs whose patents expired had generic copies; currently, almost all do.[2]

Although the Hatch-Waxman act made entry of generic drugs easier and less costly once a patent expired, it also extended the patent life of branded drugs to compensate for patent life lost during the long FDA approval process. (Effective patent life is measured from the time the FDA approves a new drug to the end of the patent.) The act permitted drugs that contained a new chemical entity to qualify for a patent life extension. These patent extensions postpone generic entry by an average of 2.8 years. The act was a compromise between the generic-drug manufacturers, which wanted easier entry, and the brand-name drug manufacturers, which wanted a longer patent life.[3]

State legislation in the 1970s and 1980s also enabled generic drugs to rapidly increase their market share. Through the early 1970s, pharmacists in many states could not legally dispense a generic drug when a prescription specified a brand-name drug. By 1984, all states had enacted drug substitution legislation that permitted a pharmacist to substitute a generic drug even when a brand-name drug was specified, as long as the physician had not indicated otherwise on the prescription.

Accelerated Approval for Lifesaving Drugs

During the 1980s and 1990s, AIDS activists were critical of the FDA's approval process. AIDS patients were dying of the disease and wanted promising new drugs to be immediately available. Approval would be too late for many if these drugs were delayed for years because of research protocols required by the FDA. Giving half of terminally ill AIDS patients a placebo was believed to be immoral, as they would be denied a possible lifesaving drug. Many terminally ill AIDS patients were willing to bear the risk of taking drugs that might prove to be unsafe or to have adverse effects.

AIDS activists pressured Congress and the FDA for an accelerated approval process. As a result, new laws and regulations were enacted between 1987 and 1992 that enabled seriously ill patients to have access to experimental drugs. These types of drugs were provided with a "fast-track" approval process. For other serious or life-threatening diseases, drugs in the clinical trial stages that were shown to have meaningful therapeutic benefit compared with existing treatments also were given an expedited review. In return for early approval of these new drugs, the drug firm had to periodically notify the FDA about any adverse reactions to the drug that were not detected during the clinical trial periods.

In 1992, Congress enacted the Prescription Drug User Fee Act (renewable every five years), which authorized the FDA to collect fees from drug manufacturers seeking a drug approval. The revenues from these fees were to be used to increase the number of FDA staff members reviewing drug approvals. Consequently, the approval process took less time and the number of new drugs approved rose compared with figures in previous years.[4]

Both the fast-tracking approval process and the funds from user fees reduced the time for FDA approvals of new drugs. As shown in exhibit 26.1, in the late 1980s, the FDA took about 32 months to approve a new drug. By 1998, the average approval time was less than 12 months. Unfortunately, over the past decade, the average FDA approval time has increased, reaching 16.9 months in 2015. In 2016, however, the time decreased to 10.1 months; hopefully, the faster approval time represents the start of a trend.

The FDA's Stringent Guidelines for Safety and Efficacy

It is difficult to oppose greater drug safety. As a consequence of FDA regulatory requirements, physicians and the public are better informed about approved drug uses and possible side effects. However, FDA regulation has had some adverse consequences.

The US Drug Lag
One measure of the FDA's performance is how long it takes to approve a drug in the United States versus in other countries. After the 1962 amendments were enacted, a long lag developed between the time drugs were available for use in other countries and the time they could be used in the United States.

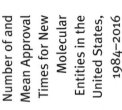

EXHIBIT 26.1
Number of and
Mean Approval
Times for New
Molecular
Entities in the
United States,
1984–2016

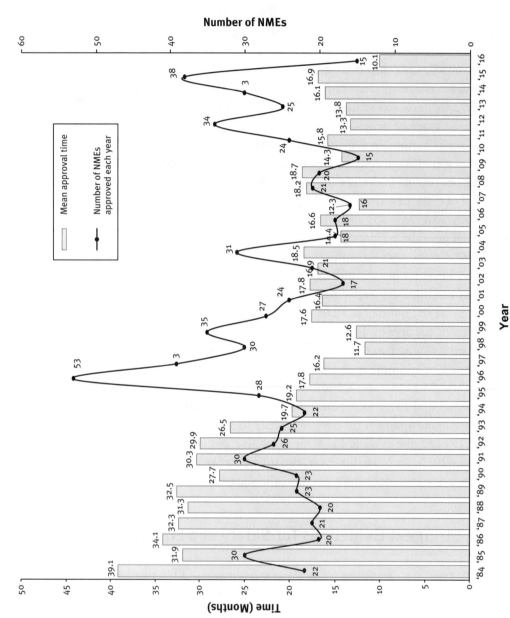

Note: NME = new molecular entity. NMEs are new medicines that have never been marketed. They include diagnostic and nondiagnostic drugs.

Source: Data from PAREXEL International (2017, 393).

For example, drugs proven effective for treating heart disease and hypertension were used in Great Britain as early as 1965, but they were not fully approved for use in the United States until 1976. Approximately 7,500 to 15,000 people died in 1988 alone from gastric ulcers while waiting for the FDA to approve misoprostol, which was already available in 43 countries. Furthermore, about 20,000 people are estimated to have died between 1985 and 1987 while waiting for approval of streptokinase, the first drug that could be administered intravenously to reopen the blocked coronary arteries of heart attack victims (Gottlieb 2004).

The drug lag—the time it takes for a new drug to be approved in the United States after it has been approved in another country—has two effects. First, the longer the time to approval, the greater the cost of producing a new drug and the fewer years that remain on the patent life of that drug; both of these factors reduce research and development (R&D) profitability and the number of new drugs likely to be developed. Second, and perhaps most important, the longer it takes to approve a new drug, the greater the harm to patients who would have benefited by having access to that drug sooner.[5]

Studies examining data through the 1970s concluded that a drug lag existed. Researchers compared drugs approved in the United Kingdom and the United States and concluded that approval in the United States lagged behind that in the United Kingdom by about two years. However, in more recent years, the US drug lag has decreased. As shown in exhibit 26.1, the approval rate of new drugs by the FDA was 50 percent faster in the mid-1990s than in the previous decade. Since then, approval times have increased: Between 2000 and 2016, the average approval time has varied from 10.1 to 18.7 months. Understanding changes in the FDA's drug approval rate requires knowledge of the FDA's decision-making process.

The FDA's Incentives

The two main criticisms of FDA regulation are the long delays before new drugs are approved (currently reduced to 10.1 months) and the increasing R&D cost imposed on drug companies to bring a new drug to market. The FDA makes a choice when it decides how much emphasis to place on drug safety and efficacy versus approval delays and increased R&D cost. It is important to understand the political incentives that the FDA faces in making this trade-off.

Politically, a large difference exists between statistical (or invisible) persons who could have been saved and identifiable persons who died as a result of a new drug. When the FDA approves a drug that subsequently results in the deaths of a number of individuals, these deaths will be publicized in the media. Congress is likely to become involved as the publicity increases. The congressional committee that has oversight of the FDA will hold hearings at which the relatives of the deceased patients testify. The FDA staff will have to explain why they approved an unsafe drug. As then–FDA commissioner Schmidt stated in 1974 (Grabowski 1976):

> In all of the FDA's history, I am unable to find a single instance where a Congressional Committee investigated the failure of the FDA to approve a new drug. But, the times when hearings have been held to criticize our approval of new drugs have been so frequent that we aren't able to count them. . . . The message to FDA staff could not be clearer. Whenever a controversy over a new drug is resolved by its approval, the Agency and the individual involved likely will be investigated. Whenever such a drug is disapproved, no inquiry will be made.

Deaths caused by a drug are "visible" or "identifiable" deaths because the individuals affected can be readily identified. Minimizing identifiable deaths, however, delays the FDA approval process. Each day a lifesaving drug is unavailable is a day someone may die because of the unavailability of that drug. Individuals who die because a potentially lifesaving drug is unavailable are referred to as *statistical deaths.*[6]

People who die because a lifesaving drug has not yet received FDA approval, although it may be available in Europe, are difficult to identify and are not as visible. The media do not publicize the nameless people who may have died because a new drug was too costly to be developed or was slow in receiving FDA approval. No media attention is given to the thousands of individuals in need of the drug and their families. Deaths that can be attributed to drug lag, particularly with the early beta-blockers that prevent heart attacks, number in the tens of thousands. The large number of these statistical deaths has greatly outweighed the number of victims of all drug tragedies before the 1962 amendments, including those deaths caused by elixir sulfanilamide in the 1930s.

Statistical lives and identifiable lives are not politically equal. The media and members of Congress place considerably more pressure on the FDA when a loss of identifiable lives results from a prematurely approved drug than when a much greater loss of statistical lives occurs as a result of the FDA's delaying approval of a new drug. The FDA's incentives are clearly to minimize the loss of identifiable lives at the expense of a greater loss of statistical lives. The FDA can make one of two types of errors, as shown in exhibit 26.2. Type I error occurs when the FDA approves a drug that is found to have harmful effects; type II error occurs when the FDA either delays or does not approve a beneficial drug. These types of errors are not weighted equally by the FDA. The FDA places greater emphasis on preventing type I errors.

The decision maker's calculation of the costs and benefits of early versus delayed approval is on the side of delayed approval. The political pressure on FDA staff to justify their decisions causes them to be overly cautious in approving new drugs until they can be sure no loss of life will occur.

	Drug Is Beneficial	Drug Is Harmful
FDA approves drug	Correct decision	Type I error
		Allowing a harmful drug; victims are identifiable and FDA staff must explain to Congress
FDA does not approve drug	Type II error	Correct decision
	Disallowing a beneficial drug; victims are not identifiable	

EXHIBIT 26.2
The FDA and Type I and Type II Errors

However, the cost–benefit decision to the FDA regarding when to approve a drug has undergone change in the past decade. Previously, the FDA bore little cost by delaying approval of a drug, while it benefited by gathering more and more information about the drug's safety; the FDA minimized the chances that Congress would criticize it for endangering the public's safety. Under these cost–benefit calculations, it was in the FDA's interest to delay approval until it was much more confident about the drug's safety. In recent years, the cost to the FDA of delaying approval has increased. Patient advocacy groups, at times allied with the company whose drug is being reviewed, have pressured the FDA for accelerated approval of drugs. Advocacy groups for AIDS patients were among the first to publicize the cost of delays in drug approval. Pharmaceutical firms supported these patient advocacy groups because they wanted to start earning revenues sooner.

The effect of patient advocacy groups' efforts and media publicity on drug approval times is illustrated by data on approval times for different types of cancer drugs (Carpenter 2004). Although lung cancer has a higher mortality rate than breast cancer and is costlier to treat (requiring more hospitalizations and longer hospital stays), breast cancer has more advocacy groups that were able to generate greater media attention. Consequently, breast cancer drugs were approved more quickly than lung cancer drugs. The same relationship between media publicity and drug approval times exists for other drugs as well.

Patient advocacy groups that can generate a great deal of media attention have increased the visibility of the consequences of delay. In doing so, they have raised the political cost to the FDA of drug approval delays (type II errors). However, whenever an approved drug is shown to be less safe than originally believed—as occurred with the arthritis drug rofecoxib (Vioxx), which was traced to a small but higher risk of heart attacks among patients who used it (type I error)—the FDA staff comes under much criticism and will revert toward excessive caution in approving new drugs.

Increased Cost of Drug Development

Stringent FDA guidelines and lengthy approval times have greatly raised the cost of developing new drugs. After the 1962 amendments required more rigorous clinical testing, proof of efficacy, and safety criteria for FDA approval, the cost and time to bring a new drug to market increased sharply. Before the 1962 amendments, the cost of a new drug (including the cost of failed drugs) was $7.9 million in 2013 dollars. The median time between starting clinical testing and receiving FDA approval has increased from 4.7 years on average during the 1960s (after the 1962 amendments) to 6.7 years in the 1970s, to 8.5 years in the 1980s, and to 9 years in 2010. In the past decade, the average time from research idea to marketing a drug was between 10 and 15 years (Pharmaceutical Research and Manufacturers of America 2018).

The cost of developing a new drug has increased dramatically. Fifteen years ago, the estimate was $800 million (DiMasi, Hansen, and Grabowski 2003). A 2012 estimate indicated that the R&D costs for a new prescription drug can go as high as $1.5 billion to $1.8 billion (Mestre-Ferrandiz, Sussex, and Towse 2012). DiMasi, Grabowski, and Hansen (2016) estimated that the postapproval R&D cost of a new drug was $2.558 billion (in 2013 dollars).

An important reason for the rapidly rising cost of drug development is the cost of human trials. Since about 2010, the typical clinical trial has taken more years and involved thousands more people than it did previously. Managed care companies are demanding that drug companies prove the value of their drugs in larger and longer clinical trials.

Included in the costs of drug development are actual expenditures as well as the opportunity cost of the interest forgone on these investment costs. For example, only about half of the cost of drug development represents actual out-of-pocket costs. The rest is the estimated cost of capital, or the amount that would have been earned over time if the same amount of money were invested and earned interest. This opportunity cost of capital is significant, because long time lags exist between investment expenditures and revenues generated by new drugs.

These investment costs include expenditures on many drugs that will never make it to market (failures). Of every 5,000 potential new drugs tested in animals, only five are likely to reach human clinical trials; of those five, only one will eventually be marketed.

Also important to a drug firm's profitability is the fact that the longer it takes to meet the FDA's stringent research guidelines and receive FDA approval, the shorter the remaining patent life on the drug and the period in which to make profits. Profit is the principal motivating factor behind drug companies' willingness to assume risk and invest large amounts in R&D. The pharmaceutical manufacturers' profitability over time is determined by their investment in R&D. As shown in exhibit 26.3, R&D expenditures as a percentage of US sales are 24 percent of revenue (as of 2016). This rate of investment is one of the highest of any industry.

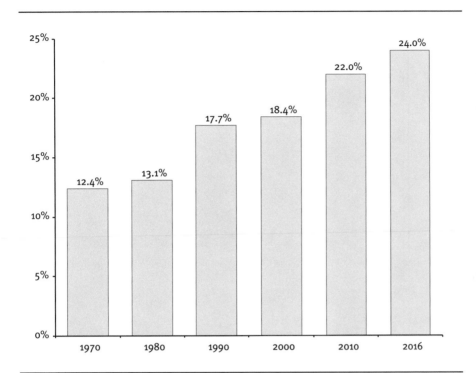

EXHIBIT 26.3

Domestic R&D Expenditures as a Percentage of US Domestic Sales, Pharmaceutical Companies, 1970–2016

Source: Data from Pharmaceutical Research and Manufacturers of America (2018).

Profitability over time (as a percentage of revenue) for pharmaceutical firms has also been higher than that for companies in any other industry. Although profits are high, so are the risks. The high rates of profit earned by drug manufacturers to finance R&D result from the few breakthrough drugs discovered. Even those that are marketed may not be financially successful; about three of ten drugs marketed make a profit, and about 10 percent of all drugs marketed provide 52 percent of the industry's profits.

Exhibit 26.4 shows the percentage of drugs for which the profits exceed average R&D costs. As can be seen, the distribution of profits is skewed. Very few drugs offer a profitable return, but for the 10 percent of drugs considered "blockbuster" drugs, the profits are substantial. Thus, a drug company needs a few "winners"—especially blockbusters—to cover the costs for the majority of drugs that do not even bring in enough revenue to pay for their R&D investments. Patent protection is essential for protecting a drug manufacturer's investments in R&D. Once a new drug is discovered, it can be reproduced relatively easily. Without the period of market exclusivity that patents provide, drug manufacturers could not recover their R&D investments.

Patents provide a drug manufacturer with market power, the ability to price above costs of production. Breakthrough drugs have a great deal more market power than does a "me-too" drug. Although a new breakthrough drug

EXHIBIT 26.4

Decile Distribution of Net Present Values of Postlaunch Returns for the Sample of 1990–1994 New Chemical Entities

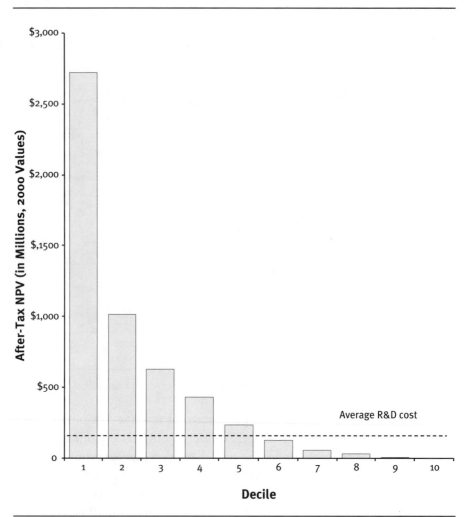

Source: Adapted from Grabowski, H., J. Vernon, and J. A. DiMasi. 2002. Figure 7. In "Returns on Research and Development for 1990s New Drug Introductions." *Pharmacoeconomics* 20 (Suppl. 3): 11–29. With permission from Springer Science and Business Media.

(the first drug to treat an illness) may initially have a great deal of market power, other companies can eventually patent drugs that use the same mechanism to treat the illness. Once patent protection expires, generic versions priced much lower than the branded drug quickly take a large part of the market. For example, in 1997, the patent on Zantac (ranitidine) expired, and the generic version captured 90 percent of the market served by Zantac within two years (Berndt 2001). Currently, about 89 percent of all prescription drugs dispensed are off-patent generic drugs (Association for Accessible Medicine 2017).

Public policy with respect to the drug industry must deal with the following trade-off. To increase R&D investments, drug manufacturers must earn high profits on innovative drugs that provide significant increases in therapeutic value. However, the cost of producing these drugs is but a small fraction of their selling price. If prices on these breakthrough drugs were made more affordable (closer to their production costs) to alleviate the large burden on those with low income, the high profits that provide the incentive to invest in R&D would disappear. Lower drug prices that benefit today's patients mean fewer innovative drugs in the future.

Orphan Drugs

As R&D costs and the time for drug approval have increased, long and costly clinical trials to develop *orphan drugs*—those that benefit only small population groups—became unprofitable. The potential revenue for a new orphan drug may be small because these drugs are designed to treat diseases that affect only a small number of people (or treat the small percentage of people who do not respond to standard treatments for common illnesses). Congress enacted the Orphan Drug Act in 1984 to provide drug companies with a financial incentive (tax incentives or exclusive marketing rights) to develop drugs that provide therapeutic benefits for fewer than 200,000 patients.

Divino and colleagues (2016) examined the drugs developed as a result of the Orphan Drug Act. They concluded that the drugs produced were highly innovative and provided important advances in care for patients with rare diseases.

Similar to the orphan drug issue is the concern that drug development is targeted toward people living in wealthy countries. Only 5 percent of global R&D is directed toward health problems unique to developing nations, although 90 percent of the global disease burden is in the developing world (Hotez et al. 2013). Private-sector R&D is determined by prospective demand conditions. For example, malaria is a parasitic disease that has a global incidence of 200 to 300 million cases annually. About 1 million deaths are caused by malaria each year, and the majority of these deaths involve children younger than five years living in sub-Saharan Africa (Bloom et al. 2006). Drug development aimed at health problems of people in poor countries needs to be subsidized by government entities.

Summary

The rationale for FDA regulation of drugs is presumably to provide a remedy for the lack of information among physicians and consumers when buying drugs. Lack of information about a drug's safety could cause serious harm to patients. Given this potentially serious consequence, what should be the FDA's role? Should the FDA continue to be the sole decision maker regarding the availability of new drugs? Or should the FDA play a more passive role by merely providing information about the safety and efficacy of new drugs and leave the decision about whether to use a new drug to the physician and the patient?

What is the optimum trade-off between statistical and identifiable deaths? Who should make that decision? Decreased identifiable deaths mean more testing, high R&D costs, delays in FDA approval, and a consequent increase in statistical deaths. Clearly, for saving lives and treating serious illnesses, the choice should be less concern with drug safety and efficacy and quicker approval to minimize the number of statistical deaths. The costs of delay vary depending on the seriousness of the illness. Even two patients with the same disease will differ in the types of risks they are willing to accept. Under the current system, the FDA is determining the level of risk acceptable to society, while some patients would be willing to bear greater risk.

Proponents of strengthening the FDA's current role are concerned that physicians and patients would have incomplete information on which to base their decisions about new drugs. Physicians may be too busy or unwilling to invest the time needed to fully understand the safety and efficacy information on new drugs, and they may even be influenced by drug company advertising. Changing the FDA's role from that of a decision maker to primarily a provider of information does not appear to have much public support. Instead, public policy is focused on speeding up the FDA's approval process. Various proposals have been made to accomplish this, such as having the FDA also rely on evidence gathered from other countries that have high approval standards, dropping the proof-of-efficacy requirement, and requiring less evidence of a lifesaving drug's safety when there is no alternative therapy.

Speeding up the FDA's approval process will require greater postmarketing surveillance of drug interactions and safety. Evidence of the effects of a new drug may not be known for several years. The long preapproval process continues to miss dangerous drugs. For example, Trovan, an antibiotic drug, had to be withdrawn because of unforeseen liver injuries. Only after a drug has been on the market and used by many people can its safety and efficacy be truly evaluated.

In addition to speeding up the FDA's approval process and expanding postmarketing surveillance, concerns exist about the time and cost required to bring a new drug to market. High R&D costs (e.g., longer times for approval that shorten patent life) decrease the profitability of an investment in new drugs. Low profitability leads to a smaller investment and results in fewer new drugs being discovered. As the costs of drug discovery increase, drug companies are less likely to develop drugs that have small market potential. An additional consequence of the high cost and lengthy time requirements to introduce a new drug is that, with fewer new drugs being introduced, drug prices are higher because there is less competition than would be the case if the process were easier. (Also, by having the FDA base its drug approval decision solely on drug safety, and not also on efficacy, the cost and time to approve a new drug will decrease. Determination of efficacy could be left to the market.)

High R&D costs also have a great effect on small drug firms. Large drug firms have many new drugs in the discovery pipeline and on the market. Small firms invest their capital in the particular drug that is going through the R&D and approval process. The longer the delay in being able to market a drug, the greater the firm's capital requirement. To minimize the chance of running out of money, a small firm with a promising new drug will merge or partner with a large firm that has greater capital resources and experience with the drug approval process.

Economics is concerned with trade-offs. Choosing one policy (namely, increased drug safety and efficacy) entails a "cost" (namely, fewer new drugs being developed). More statistical deaths will occur, the drug industry will become more consolidated, and drug prices will be higher because fewer new drugs will compete with existing drugs. Thus, favoring increased drug safety and efficacy is not a simple choice without consequences. The issue is how to strike an appropriate balance between these choices.

Discussion Questions

1. How have the 1962 amendments to the Food, Drug, and Cosmetic Act affected the profitability of new drugs?
2. What is the consequence of the FDA's providing the public with greater assurance that a new drug is safe?
3. What is the difference between identifiable death and statistical death?
4. What are orphan drugs, and why are drug firms less likely to develop such drugs today?
5. Why has the FDA's drug approval process sped up in recent years?
6. What are the advantages and disadvantages of greater reliance on premarketing test versus postmarketing surveillance?

Notes

1. Once the FDA approves a new drug as being safe and efficacious for its intended use, the new drug must also pass the health plan's review process to show that it is also cost-effective. Unless the new drug can pass this review, it may not be added to the health plan's drug formulary.

2. The Federal Trade Commission has been investigating anticompetitive behavior in the drug industry. Drug companies that hold patents on brand-name drugs have been accused of making special deals with generic-drug manufacturers to keep the generic drugs off the market (thereby not competing with the branded drug) for longer than the Hatch-Waxman Act intended. Specifically, drug manufacturers have been accused of paying generic-drug firms to delay introducing their products. Congress and the FDA are also examining whether changes to the Hatch-Waxman Act are required to close loopholes in the law. Industry critics claim that another tactic drug firms use to delay the entry of generic drugs is to sue the generic-drug manufacturers, allowing the branded drugs several more months of lucrative, exclusive sales.

3. Olson (1994) described why, after several years of failure, the Hatch-Waxman legislation was ultimately enacted. Her analysis included the proposals of various interest groups, turnover in key Senate committees, and a change in the majority party.

4. In 1994, federal legislation (called the Uruguay Round Agreements Act) changed the patent life of prescription drugs and all types of inventions from 17 years from the date a patent is granted to 20 years from the date the application is filed. Between two and three years elapse from the time an application is filed until a patent is granted. The average period during which a new drug can be marketed under patent protection has risen from about 9 years to 12.4 years (Grabowski et al. 2011).

5. One analyst who examined the 1962 amendments concluded that they left the public worse off. Sam Peltzman (1974) attempted to quantify the benefits of the 1962 amendments by comparing the estimated effect of the new regulations in keeping ineffective and dangerous drugs (of which there were very few before 1962) off the market with the costs of having fewer new drugs, higher prices for existing drugs (because of less competition from new drugs), and reduced availability of drugs because of the time lag. The decline in the development of new drugs was the greatest disadvantage of the amendments; this factor alone, according to Peltzman, made the costs of the new amendments greatly exceed the potential benefits.

6. Statistical deaths are calculated as follows. Assume that a new drug is introduced in Europe and two years elapse before the same drug receives FDA approval to be marketed in the United States. Further assume that the new drug is more effective than the drug currently on the market to treat the same disease, such that the new drug is able to decrease mortality from 5 percent to 1 percent. Suppose 100,000

persons each year are affected by the illness. The number of lives that would have been saved by earlier FDA approval is 8,000. The percentage difference in mortality rate (0.05 − 0.01 = 0.04) multiplied by the two-year lag when the drug could have been on the market (0.04 × 2 = 0.08) multiplied by the number of people at risk each year (0.08 × 100,000) equals 8,000 statistical deaths because of the two-year delay.

References

Association for Accessible Medicine. 2017. *2017 Generic Drug Access & Savings in the U.S.* Accessed May 31, 2018. http://accessiblemeds.org/sites/default/files/2017-07/2017-AAM-Access-Savings-Report-2017-web2.pdf.

Berndt, E. 2001. "The U.S. Pharmaceutical Industry: Why Major Growth in Times of Cost Containment?" *Health Affairs* 20 (2): 100–14.

Bloom, B., C. Michaud, J. Montagne, and L. Simonsen. 2006. "Priorities for Global Research and Development of Interventions." In *Disease Control Priorities in Developing Nations*, 2nd ed., edited by D. T. Jamison, J. G. Breman, A. R. Measham, G. Alleyne, M. Claeson, D. B. Evans, P. Jha, A. Mills, and P. Musgrove, 103–18. New York: Oxford University Press.

Carpenter, D. 2004. "The Political Economy of FDA Drug Review: Processing, Politics, and Lessons for Policy." *Health Affairs* 23 (1): 52–63.

DiMasi, J. A., H. G. Grabowski, and R. W. Hansen. 2016. "Innovation in the Pharmaceutical Industry: New Estimates of R&D Costs." *Journal of Health Economics* 47: 20–33.

DiMasi, J. A., R. W. Hansen, and H. G. Grabowski. 2003. "The Price of Innovation: New Estimates of Drug Development Cost." *Journal of Health Economics* 22 (2): 151–85.

Divino, V., M. DeKoven, M. Kleinrock, R. L. Wade, and S. Kaura. 2016. "Orphan Drug Expenditures in the United States: A Historical and Prospective Analysis, 2007–18." *Health Affairs* 35 (9): 1588–94.

Gottlieb, S. 2004. "The Price of Too Much Caution." *New York Sun.* Published December 22. www.nysun.com/opinion/price-of-too-much-caution/6666/.

Grabowski, H. 1976. *Drug Regulation and Innovation: Empirical Evidence and Policy Options.* Washington, DC: American Enterprise Institute Press.

Grabowski, H., M. Kyle, R. Mortimer, G. Long, and N. Kirson. 2011. "Evolving Brand-Name and Generic Drug Competition May Warrant a Revision of the Hatch-Waxman Act." *Health Affairs* 30 (11): 2157–66.

Grabowski, H., J. Vernon, and J. A. DiMasi. 2002. "Returns on Research and Development for 1990s New Drug Introductions." *Pharmacoeconomics* 20 (Suppl. 3): 11–29.

Harris, R. 1964. *The Real Voice*. New York: MacMillan.

Hotez, P., R. Cohen, C. Mimura, T. Yamada, and S. Hoffman. 2013. "Strengthening Mechanisms to Prioritize, Coordinate, Finance, and Execute R&D to Meet Health Needs in Developing Countries." Institute of Medicine. Published January 15. http://nam.edu/wp-content/uploads/2015/06/GlobalHealthRD.pdf.

Mestre-Ferrandiz, J., J. Sussex, and A. Towse. 2012. *The R&D Cost of a New Medicine*. Office of Health Economics. Published December. www.ohe.org/publications/rd-cost-new-medicine#.

Olson, M. K. 1994. "Political Influence and Regulatory Policy: The 1984 Drug Legislation." *Economic Inquiry* 32 (3): 363–82.

PAREXEL International. 2017. *PAREXEL Biopharmaceutical R&D Statistical Sourcebook, 2017/2018 Edition*. Waltham, MA: PAREXEL International.

Peltzman, S. 1974. *Regulation of Pharmaceutical Innovation*. Washington, DC: American Enterprise Institute.

Pharmaceutical Research and Manufacturers of America. 2018. *2017 PhRMA Annual Membership Survey*. Accessed May. http://phrma-docs.phrma.org/files/dmfile/PhRMA_membership-survey_2017.pdf.

27

WHY ARE PRESCRIPTION DRUGS LESS EXPENSIVE OVERSEAS?

necdotes abound about people traveling to Canada or Mexico to buy a prescription drug at a much lower price than that offered by retail pharmacies in the United States. In addition, studies by the US Government Accountability Office (formerly the General Accounting Office) (GAO 1992, 1994) have shown that branded prescription drugs are more expensive in the United States than in other countries. The studies concluded that US prices were 32 percent higher than prices in Canada and 60 percent higher than prices in the United Kingdom. A 2015 report found that the average price of Humira (adalimubab), a drug commonly prescribed to treat rheumatoid arthritis, was $2,669 in the United States but only $552 in South Africa and $1,362 in the United Kingdom (see exhibit 27.1) (International Federation of Health Plans 2015).

Cross-national comparison studies of branded (prescription) drug prices generally concluded that lower prices in other countries are a result of regulatory

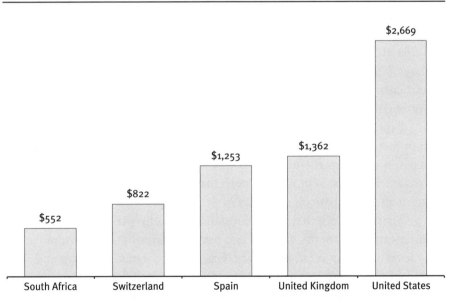

EXHIBIT 27.1
Prices for Humira, Selected Countries, 2015

Note: Humira (adalimubab) is prescribed to treat rheumatoid arthritis.
Source: Data from International Federation of Health Plans (2015).

price controls, which implies that the United States can similarly lower drug prices by implementing price controls. The following sections discuss the accuracy of cross-national drug price studies, the reason higher prices for prescription drugs in the United States are not surprising, and the implications of requiring US drug manufacturers to charge a single uniform price overseas and in this country.

Accuracy of Studies on International Variations in Drug Prices

The methodology used in the 1994 GAO studies and in similar studies concluding that prescription drug prices are higher in the United States than in other countries has been widely criticized. What these studies purport to analyze and the methods used should be subject to greater examination before their implications for the United States are accepted.

Retail Price Comparisons

Typically, cross-national studies compare the retail prices of selected prescription drugs that are bought by cash-paying patients in the United States with the retail prices of the same drugs in another country. (The GAO studies used listed wholesale prices in the United States, which were intended to approximate prices charged to retail pharmacies.)

These comparisons greatly overstate US drug prices because they assume that all purchasers of the same prescription drug in this country pay the same price. Using retail (or even wholesale) prices as the prescription drug price in the United States does not account for the large discounts and rebates received by large US purchasers such as managed care organizations (MCOs), pharmacy benefit managers, mail-order drug firms, private drug plans, and federal government programs such as Medicaid.

Patients in these organizations only pay a copayment that is a small fraction of the price the organizations pay for the drug. Not only do these large purchasers make up the majority of the US prescription drug market, large purchasers also represent a larger percentage of the purchasers in the United States than in comparison countries.

These large purchasers pay substantially less for prescription drugs than cash-paying US patients who do not have prescription drug insurance and buy directly from a retail pharmacy. Cash-paying patients represent a small segment of the prescription drug buyers in the United States, so comparisons using these patients greatly overstate prices. Rather than assuming a single US retail price, a more appropriate approach would be to compare the prices paid on average by all drug purchasers in the United States with the prices paid by overseas patients.[1]

Cost of Drug Therapy

Given the public policy implications of cross-national studies, the purpose of these comparisons must be clarified so that an appropriate study design can be determined. One objective of such studies might be to estimate the cost of drug therapy (by disease) in different countries, not just the differences in prices for specific prescription products. To accurately examine differences in drug therapy costs across countries, such studies should adjust for the use of generic substitutes and weighting of the different drugs used in a country's drug price index.

Cross-national studies have excluded generic drugs, which are priced between 40 and 80 percent lower than branded drugs. Furthermore, US purchasers rely on generic drugs much more heavily than do patients in other countries. (Generics accounted for 84 percent of prescriptions in the United States in 2012 [IMS Health 2013], whereas use of generics in countries with strict drug price regulation, such as France and Italy, is very low.) If generic drugs are more frequently substituted for expensive branded drugs in the United States than they are in other countries, a comparison based solely on branded drugs overstates the cost of a prescription for US patients.

Another important issue in cross-national comparisons is the mix or consumption pattern of drugs used in different countries. Comparisons of drug prices between countries rely on a simple average of the prices paid for several leading brand-name drugs. For example, the 1992 GAO study compared US prices with Canadian prices for a number of branded drugs. (The Canadian prices were added up and compared with the sum of the US retail prices for the same drugs. Dividing the sum of the prices in one country by the sum of the prices in the other country resulted in a ratio of prices between the two countries.) In doing so, the researchers gave an equal weight to each branded drug being compared. Whether some branded drugs were widely or infrequently used did not matter; each received an equal weight.

Because the United States and other countries have different drug consumption patterns, any price index should reflect these differences by weighting the volume of different branded drugs used. Some branded drugs represent a greater percentage of purchased branded drugs than others; these percentages differ by country.

Cross-national comparisons also should use a weighted average of the prices of branded drugs. In addition, the index should include the use of generic drugs and the average prices paid for all drugs, including the discounted prices paid by MCOs and other large purchasers in the United States, as well as the volume purchased. Doing so would result in a much lower weighted average price than simply using the price of the branded drug (and its volume) sold to retail customers. Further, for some branded drugs, a great deal of generic substitution occurs. A weighted average price of the drug would include the branded and generic versions, resulting in a much lower price than simply using the price of the branded version. Each drug also should be assigned a weight in the index according to its use in that country.

Drug Price Index

Research conducted by Danzon and Chao (2000) determined that when a drug price index is constructed for each country using average prices paid by different purchasers and weighting drug prices by the drugs' (including generic drugs) frequency of use, the index might be no higher in the United States than in other countries. Although individual prescription drugs may be more expensive in the United States, the costs of drug therapy across countries (based on an accurately constructed drug price index) are not much different. (For a detailed discussion of cross-national comparisons, including additional limitations such as the unit of measurement and the availability of branded drugs, as well as appropriate methodologies and results, see Danzon and Furukawa [2008].)

Why Prescription Drugs Are Expected to Be Priced Lower Overseas

Numerous examples can be found of prescription drugs that are less expensive in other countries than in the United States. Why would a manufacturer of a patented prescription drug be willing to sell the same drug at greatly reduced prices overseas? This pricing behavior is based on two characteristics of the drug industry: its cost structure and differences in each country's bargaining power.

The costs of developing and bringing to market an innovative drug are high; 15 years ago, the estimate was $800 million (DiMasi, Hansen, and Grabowski 2003). A 2012 estimate indicated the research and development (R&D) costs for a new prescription drug can be as high as $1.5 billion to $1.8 billion (Mestre-Ferrandiz, Sussex, and Towse 2012). DiMasi, Grabowski, and Hansen (2016) estimated that the postapproval R&D cost of a new drug was $2.558 billion (in 2013 dollars). Compared with the results of their previous study, these costs increased at an annual rate that was 8.5 percent more rapid than general price inflation.

Experimental trials must be conducted, and the Food and Drug Administration's (FDA's) approval is required. Developing a new drug and receiving FDA approval may take seven to ten years. The R&D costs—including the interest that could have been earned on those funds and the costs involved in receiving FDA approval—are known as *fixed costs*. These development costs are the same regardless of how much of the patented new drug is produced and sold. The actual costs of producing the new drug, once its chemical entities have been determined through the R&D process and it has received FDA approval, are relatively small. Thus, patented drugs are characterized by large fixed costs and relatively small variable costs (the actual costs of producing the drug).

The drug manufacturer would like to receive the highest possible price for a new drug. For some purchasers, however, the manufacturer would be willing to accept any price that exceeds its variable costs. A price in excess of variable costs contributes to the large fixed costs and to profit. The manufacturer is better off receiving $5 even if it costs $4 to produce the drug; the $1 revenue from some purchasers is better than nothing.

The drug industry is sophisticated in its pricing of the same medicine across different countries. A drug manufacturer would like to add new users (i.e., sell the drug in more countries) because the variable costs of producing the drug are so low, but it is not willing to add new users if it has to reduce the price and, in turn, the revenues it earns in higher-priced markets. The single largest market for innovative drugs is the United States, which accounts for 35.7 percent of the world pharmaceutical market (the United States and Canada combined represent 38.4 percent; see exhibit 27.2). People in the United States are, on average, wealthier than those in other countries and want access to innovative drugs as soon as possible; therefore, they are less price sensitive. In 2012, about 85 percent of the US population had insurance for prescription drugs (Rowan 2012). Not surprisingly, drug manufacturers charge higher prices when consumers are less price sensitive.

EXHIBIT 27.2
World Pharmaceutical Market, 2015

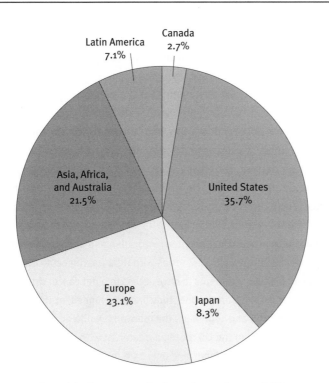

Latin America 7.1%

Canada 2.7%

Asia, Africa, and Australia 21.5%

United States 35.7%

Europe 23.1%

Japan 8.3%

Total world pharmaceutical market = $1,057 billion

Source: Data from IMS Health (2015).

In countries that regulate the price of drugs, the same manufacturer is willing to sell the same drug at a lower price as long as the regulated price exceeds the manufacturer's variable cost of producing that drug. The drug manufacturer would be concerned if purchasers in the lower-priced countries were to resell the drug in the higher-priced markets. If resale from the lower-priced countries to the higher-priced countries were possible, a differential pricing system could not persist.

As long as the manufacturer is able to prevent resale of the same drug from low- to high-priced markets, this system of differential pricing allows markets that otherwise would be neglected to be served. Differential pricing—whereby a drug manufacturer charges different prices to different countries for the same medicine—results in the greatest number of people gaining access to a drug. The manufacturer is willing to reduce its price to countries that regulate drugs and to poor countries that cannot afford to pay much for drugs, not because it has a social conscience but because any sales at a price that exceeds the drug's variable cost contribute to profits. By trying to increase profits, however, the drug manufacturer also provides the greatest number of people with access to its drug.

Canadian and European governments, which pay for most of their populations' health expenditures, keep drug prices down because they have limited budgets for healthcare. These tight budgets for drug expenditures have had unintended consequences. The introduction of innovative and cost-effective drugs has been delayed, and restrictions have been placed on patients' eligibility for new prescription drugs because the costs exceed the budget for drugs (Kanavos et al. 2013). Consequently, surgical and hospital expenditures have been higher than they would have been if costly innovative drugs had been used. In addition, delays have occurred in approving lifesaving drugs for citizens of these countries. For example, "Herceptin, which was considered to be a breakthrough drug for about a third of all breast cancer patients . . . was approved two years [earlier] by regulators in the US, where it benefited from an accelerated review offered to novel cancer therapies" (Moore 2000, A1, A4). Further,

> Many European countries also attempt to restrict demand after new medicines reach pharmacy shelves. European . . . countries with tight pharmaceutical budgets have made it difficult for cancer patients to have access to older cancer drugs (Taxol) that were top selling anti-cancer drugs. One study (industry funded) examining prescribing patterns between 1996 and 1998 finds the following: while 99.9% of patients with advanced breast cancer in the US received treatment with taxane, the comparable [rate] was 48% for the Netherlands and only 25% for Britain.

Another consequence of regulated lower drug prices overseas is that total drug expenditures represent a higher portion of total medical expenditures in those countries than in the United States (see exhibit 27.3) because the prices

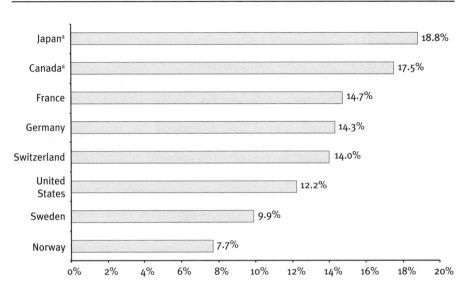

EXHIBIT 27.3
Pharmaceutical
Expenditures
as a Percentage
of Total Health
Expenditures,
Selected
Countries, 2015

[a] 2014 data.

Note: Pharmaceuticals include prescription and nonprescription drugs.

Source: Data from Organisation for Economic Co-operation and Development (2017).

for drugs overseas are quite low (generally for older molecules), and neither patients nor their physicians have any incentive to use fewer drugs. For example, to reduce drug expenditures, the German government imposed financial penalties on physicians to limit their prescriptions. The United States spends a smaller portion on drugs (12.2 percent of total healthcare expenditures) than France (14.7 percent), Japan (18.8 percent), Canada (17.5 percent), or Germany (14.3 percent).

Public Policy Issues

Cross-national studies that have found that the United States has higher prescription drug prices imply that the United States should institute a price-control system similar to those of countries that have lower drug prices. By publicizing these cross-national study findings, along with examples of patients who cannot afford to pay high retail drug prices, advocates of price controls hope to build political support for imposing controls on US prescription drugs.

Two methods for equalizing US and overseas prices on prescription drugs are favored by proponents of a regulatory approach. Under the first method, the US government would require that the retail price of prescription drugs sold in the United States be no different from the price at which the same drugs are sold in other countries, such as Canada and Mexico. The second approach is to allow pharmacists to import FDA-approved US prescription drugs to the United States from countries where they sell for substantially less. Each of these proposals has short-term effects as well as indirect, or unintended, long-term consequences.

A Single Price for Prescription Drugs Across Countries

What would happen to prescription drug prices in the United States and overseas if US drug manufacturers were required to price US-branded drugs at the same price at which they are sold to other countries? Proponents of a single price for the same medicine assume that the uniform price will be the lowest of the different prices charged for the same drug. Assume that a prescription drug, called ABC, sells for $10 in the United States and $5 in Canada. Further assume that the United States enacts a law requiring the manufacturer of ABC to charge the same price regardless of the country in which ABC is sold. Would the price of ABC be reduced to $5 and US consumers receive a $5 benefit?

The answer is no.

The manufacturer of ABC would have to determine which single price would result in the greatest amount of profit. Because the United States is the largest single market for innovative branded drugs and its consumers are less price sensitive, greatly reducing ABC's price in the US market would not result in a large increase in the number of ABC users. Consequently, a large decrease in price (without a correspondingly large increase in volume) would cause a large drop in revenue.[2] Given the substantial profits earned in the United States (the price markup over variable cost multiplied by the large number of users), the uniform price of ABC would likely be closer to the US price than to the lower prices paid in other countries. The drug company would lose less money if it raised the prices in other countries by a greater amount than the amount it lowered the US price.

Setting the uniform price closer to the US price for a drug would result in a price increase in other countries, which likely would cause a decrease in use. These countries typically have limited government budgets for healthcare, and a large increase in the price of drugs would cause the government to restrict their use. Whether total revenue to the US manufacturer from sales of the drug in other countries increases or decreases depends on whether the percentage increase in price exceeds the percentage decrease in use in those countries.

In either case, requiring a uniform price for ABC in the United States and other countries means overseas patients who need the drug will be worse off. Whereas formerly they (or the government on their behalf) paid $5, they will now have to pay a higher price. Some patients will no longer have access to ABC. If close substitute drugs are available, patients will buy these other drugs (assuming the price of these other drugs had not similarly increased). If close substitutes are not available for innovative drugs, patients or the government will have to spend more of their income on ABC. If patients cannot afford to buy ABC or their government restricts its use because of its higher price, adverse health consequences will occur.

Thus, requiring a uniform pricing policy in the United States and other countries would likely lead to a small reduction in the US price of a drug and a large increase in the drug's overseas price. This policy would inflict harm on many patients in other countries because they would have to forego innovative drugs.

Reimportation

The second regulatory approach to reducing US retail prices for prescription drugs is to allow US pharmacists and drug wholesalers to buy lower-priced supplies of FDA-approved medicines in Canada and other nations for resale in the United States. Drugs reimported into the United States from Canada would likely be less expensive than the same drugs sold in the United States because of Canadian price controls. The presumed effect of this policy would be to reduce the US retail price of drugs to prices comparable to those in the countries from which they are reimported.

A federal law permitting reimportation was enacted in October 2000. This law overturned a 1988 law that permitted only pharmaceutical manufacturers to reimport prescription drugs based on the concern that drugs were being improperly stored and repackaged overseas. Although reimportation was vigorously opposed by the pharmaceutical industry, senators and congressional candidates from both political parties running for reelection in 2000 voted for the bill, which was then signed into law by President Clinton. Because the two political parties could not agree on a Medicare prescription drug benefit at that time, legislators running for reelection believed that voting for reimportation would be viewed by the public as being in favor of helping the aged with their prescription drug costs.

In December 2000, Donna Shalala, then-secretary of the US Department of Health and Human Services (HHS), refused to implement the new law, claiming that it was unworkable and would not lower drug costs (Kaufman 2000). (Since then, no HHS secretary under Republican or Democratic administrations has agreed to implement the law.) At the time of the debate, the FDA said it could oversee the drug reimportation system, but only at considerable cost. Unless funding was provided ($93 million a year), the safety of the reimported drugs could not be monitored; full funding was not included in the legislation. Further, the Clinton administration believed the bill had several fatal flaws that would deter reimportation—namely, that the drug companies would retaliate against reimporters by not providing them with the necessary package labeling inserts.

A US manufacturer of a branded prescription drug would be unlikely to increase its sales to a country that resells the drug in the United States. Drug manufacturers could easily monitor sales to each country to determine whether sales of a particular drug had suddenly increased. (If the drug importer resold the country's limited supply of that drug to the United States, patients in that country would be harmed by not having access to the drug.)

Thus, to be able to reimport drugs into the United States, US pharmacists and wholesalers would have to buy the chemical entities from a foreign producer of the drugs. When a drug is manufactured in the United States, the manufacturer must adhere to strict FDA guidelines to ensure that the drug meets certain quality standards. If a drug is manufactured in another country without extensive monitoring of the reimported drug by the FDA, no guarantee can be given that the drug will meet the same quality standards. The concern over drug safety resulted in 11 former FDA commissioners opposing the reimportation bill (Dalzell 2000).

Thousands of illegal shipments of prescription drugs enter the United States each month through the postal service. This growth in overseas sales to US patients has dramatically increased because of the Internet. The sheer volume of these shipments has overwhelmed the ability of the FDA and customs officials to verify the safety of the imported drugs. Finally, on June 7, 2001, the FDA proposed stopping overseas drug products from being mailed to individuals unless the products met certain strict conditions. The FDA claimed that these products could be counterfeit or even dangerous and that the volume is so large that it no longer has the ability to inspect them.

Reimportation is unlikely to be effective in reducing US prescription drug prices for several reasons. First, US drug manufacturers would be unwilling to sell large quantities of their drugs at greatly reduced prices to other countries so that these countries could sell the same drugs back to US pharmacists at lower prices.[3] Second, if foreign drug manufacturers are permitted to produce a drug patented by a US manufacturer and sell that drug to customers in the United States, those foreign producers would be violating US patent laws, and the imports would be prohibited. Third, if countries were unable to receive sufficient supplies of US-produced drugs to sell back to the United States, counterfeit drugs likely would be produced and sold to US patients, resulting in significant safety issues, which would eventually halt mail-order drug sales from overseas.

The pressure to enact a stronger drug importation law that would permit reimportation without the consent of the secretary of HHS (as some in Congress have proposed) decreased once Medicare beneficiaries were provided with a prescription drug benefit as part of the Medicare Modernization Act, which lowered their out-of-pocket costs for prescription drugs. However, in recent years, the very high price of innovative drugs has again resulted in legislative proposals prohibiting the secretary of HHS from preventing reimportation.

Summary

Cross-national comparison studies that claim drug prices are lower in other countries have been seriously misleading. Although the retail prices of certain prescription drugs may be lower overseas than in the United States, the more relevant comparison is the cost of drug therapy in different countries. Only a small percentage of the US population pays retail prices for drugs. The majority of the US population receives some form of third-party payment for drugs, and these large purchasers buy their drugs at discounted prices. Generic drugs are also used much more widely in the United States than in other countries. Absent from these cross-national comparisons is any discussion of the availability of innovative drugs overseas.

Prices of branded drugs are lower overseas because drug development costs are very high but the cost of producing a drug is very low. Drug manufacturers price their drugs according to purchasers' willingness to pay. Being able to prevent resale of their drugs permits a drug firm to sell its drug overseas at any price above its variable cost. The ability of drug firms to price discriminate, set their prices in each country according to that country's willingness to pay and prevent drug resales, results in the greatest amount of profit for that drug firm and also the largest distribution of that drug.

Public policy affecting prescription drugs should be evaluated on the basis of its effect on R&D expenditures. The incentive for drug manufacturers to invest large sums in R&D and develop breakthrough drugs is based on the prospect of earning large profits. Once a drug has been developed and approved by the FDA for marketing, the actual cost of producing that drug is low. Not surprisingly, therefore, countries can regulate the price of drugs and still have access to US drugs. (Evidence exists that regulation of drug prices resulted in a decline in R&D by drug firms in those countries.) These countries can receive a free ride with respect to the large R&D expenditures by US drug firms. However, if the United States were to regulate its drug prices as do other countries or permit reimportation by foreign drug producers, R&D investment would decline, as would the supply of innovative drugs. Without government enforcement of patent rights and pricing freedom, the drug industry would decrease its investment in R&D—as drugs are easy to copy but expensive to develop. Consumers in the United States and other countries benefit from differential pricing policies. In other countries, more consumers benefit by having access to lower-priced drugs, whereas in the United States, the higher prices generate greater profits for the drug companies and provide them with an incentive to invest more in R&D.

If the objective of cross-national studies is to pressure legislators to lower the retail prices of drugs so that cash-paying seniors can buy them at lower prices, a better approach has become available. Seniors received a prescription drug benefit as part of the 2003 Medicare Modernization Act; they have a financial incentive to choose among competing drug plans based on the premiums charged and the plan's drug formulary. The competing plans negotiate lower drug prices from the drug manufacturer, substitute generic drugs when appropriate, and manage the drug benefit to reduce the total cost of drug therapy. The cost to the government of this Medicare drug benefit was much lower than projected. Seniors now have better access to needed drugs, and competition has reduced their prescription drug prices as well as their monthly premiums (Congressional Budget Office 2017; Hoadley, Cubanski, and Neuman 2016). Further, for those younger than 65 years, the Affordable Care Act has mandated the inclusion of drug coverage in all health insurance plans.

Discussion Questions

1. What are some criticisms of cross-national studies of drug prices?
2. Although some prescription drugs are priced lower in other countries, is the cost of drug treatment also lower in those countries?
3. Why would a drug manufacturer be willing to sell a drug that is priced high (in relation to its variable costs) in the United States at a low price overseas?
4. What would be the consequences—in terms of drug prices and drug users—if prices of prescription drugs sold in the United States had to equal the prices at which the same drugs are sold in other countries?
5. Why would a policy of reimportation of prescription drugs be ineffective?

Notes

1. A number of other issues are involved in examining retail drug prices, such as dosage form, strength, and pack size—for example, price per gram of active ingredient or price per dose (standard unit), which may be one tablet, one capsule, or 10 milliliters of a liquid. Differences in prescription drug prices also occur because of differences in dosage form, strength, and pack size used in the comparison countries.
2. When consumers are less price sensitive, changes in price cause smaller proportionate changes in volume. By increasing price, total revenue increases because the percentage change in price is greater than the percentage decrease in volume. Similarly, lowering price when consumers are not price sensitive will result in a decrease in total revenue. Conversely, when consumers are price sensitive, the percentage

decrease in price is less than the percentage increase in volume. With price-sensitive consumers, total revenue increases when prices are reduced, up to a certain point.

3. In an effort to eliminate drug shipments to Canadian Internet pharmacies that sell lower-cost US-produced drugs to US consumers, Pfizer notified all Canadian drug retailers of its policy to halt all sales of Pfizer drugs to them if they sell Pfizer drugs to US consumers. Pfizer receives information on all drug orders from individual drug stores from its distributors (Carlisle 2004).

Additional Readings

Congressional Budget Office. 2004. "Would Prescription Drug Importation Reduce US Drug Spending?" Published April 29. www.cbo.gov/sites/default/files/108th-congress-2003-2004/reports/04-29-prescriptiondrugs.pdf.

Downing, N. S., J. A. Aminawung, N. D. Shah, J. B. Braunstein, H. M. Krumholz, and J. S. Ross. 2012. "Regulatory Review of Novel Therapeutics: Comparison of Three Regulatory Agencies." *New England Journal of Medicine* 366 (24): 2284–93.

US Government Accountability Office (GAO). 2012. "Drug Pricing: Research on Savings from Generic Drug Use." Published January 31. www.gao.gov/assets/590/588064.pdf.

References

Carlisle, T. 2004. "Pfizer Pressures Canadian Sellers of Drugs to U.S." *Wall Street Journal,* January 14, A6.

Congressional Budget Office. 2017. "Medicare—Congressional Budget Office's June 2017 Baseline." Published June 29. www.cbo.gov/sites/default/files/recurringdata/51302-2017-06-medicare.pdf.

Dalzell, M. 2000. "Prescription Drug Reimportation: Panacea or Problem?" Published December 1. www.managedcaremag.com/archives/2000/12/prescription-drug-reimportation-panacea-or-problem.

Danzon, P. M., and L. W. Chao. 2000. "Cross-National Price Differences for Pharmaceuticals: How Large, and Why?" *Journal of Health Economics* 19 (2): 159–95.

Danzon, P. M., and M. F. Furukawa. 2008. "International Prices and Availability of Pharmaceuticals in 2005." *Health Affairs* 27 (1): 221–33.

DiMasi, J. A., H. G. Grabowski, and R. W. Hansen. 2016. "Innovation in the Pharmaceutical Industry: New Estimates of R&D Costs." *Journal of Health Economics* 47: 20–33.

DiMasi, J. A., R. W. Hansen, and H. G. Grabowski. 2003. "The Price of Innovation: New Estimates of Drug Development Cost." *Journal of Health Economics* 22 (2): 151–85.

Hoadley, J., J. Cubanski, and T. Neuman. 2016. *Medicare Part D in 2016 and Trends over Time*. Kaiser Family Foundation. Published September. http://files.kff. org/attachment/Report-Medicare-Part-D-in-2016-and-Trends-over-Time.

IMS Health. 2015. *Total Unaudited and Audited Global Pharmaceutical Market by Region, 2014–2019*. Published May. http://quintilesimsconsultinggroup. com/files/web/Corporate/News/Top-Line%20Market%20Data/Global%20 Prescription%20Sales%20Information5%20World%20figures%20by%20 Region%202015-2019.pdf.

———. 2013. "IMS Health Study Points to a Declining Cost Curve for U.S. Medicines in 2012." Press release. Published September. www.imshealth.fr/en_AU/ about-us/news/ims-health-study-points-to-a-declining-cost-curve-for-u.s.- medicines-in-2012.

International Federation of Health Plans. 2015. *2015 Comparative Price Report: Variation in Hospital and Medical Prices by Country*. Accessed May 2018. http://static1.squarespace.com/static/518a3cfee4b0a77d03a62c98/t/57d 3ca9529687f1a257e9e26/1473497751062/2015+Comparative+Price+Rep ort+09.09.16.pdf.

Kanavos, P., A. Ferrario, S. Vandoros, and G. F. Anderson. 2013. "Higher US Branded Drug Prices and Spending Compared to Other Countries May Stem Partly from Quick Uptake of New Drugs." *Health Affairs* 32 (4): 753–61.

Kaufman, M. 2000. "Shalala Halts Bid to Lower Drug Costs." *Washington Post*, December 27, 1.

Mestre-Ferrandiz, J., J. Sussex, and A. Towse. 2012. *The R&D Cost of a New Medicine*. Office of Health Economics. Published December. www.ohe.org/publications/ rd-cost-new-medicine.

Moore, S. D. 2000. "Battle over Cancer Care in Europe May Offer Example for U.S. Debate." *Wall Street Journal*. Published July 21. www.wsj.com/articles/ SB964129134252374661.

Organisation for Economic Co-operation and Development. 2017. *OECD Health Statistics 2017*. Updated November 10. www.oecd.org/els/health-systems/ health-data.htm.

Rowan, K. 2012. "Why Americans' Prescriptions Are Going Unfilled." Live Science. Posted September 13. www.livescience.com/23179-why-americans- prescriptions-are-going-unfilled.html.

US Government Accountability Office (GAO). 1994. *Prescription Drugs: Companies Typically Charge More in the United States Than in the United Kingdom*. Washington, DC: US Government Printing Office.

———. 1992. *Prescription Drugs: Companies Typically Charge More in the United States Than in Canada*. Washington, DC: US Government Printing Office.

THE PHARMACEUTICAL INDUSTRY: A PUBLIC POLICY DILEMMA

The pharmaceutical industry is subject to a great deal of criticism regarding the high prices charged for its drugs, its large (some would say "wasteful") marketing expenditures, and its emphasis on "lifestyle" and "me-too" drugs over drugs to treat infectious diseases and chronic conditions. However, the industry has developed important drugs that have saved lives, reduced pain, and improved the lives of many. Public policy that attempts to respond to industry critics may at the same time change the industry's incentives for research and development (R&D), thereby reducing the number of potentially blockbuster drugs. To evaluate the criticisms of this profitable industry and the consequences of public policy directed toward it, an understanding of the structure of the pharmaceutical industry is needed.

The pharmaceutical industry is made up of two distinct types of drug manufacturers: (1) pharmaceutical manufacturers, which engage in R&D (or buy newly developed drugs from small R&D firms) and market brand-name drugs, and (2) generic manufacturers. Pharmaceutical manufacturers invest large sums in R&D, whereas generic manufacturers do not. Consequently, the former group develops innovative branded drugs for new therapeutic uses, while generic firms sell copies of branded drugs (when their patents expire) at greatly reduced prices. These two types of manufacturers differ in their economic performance and in the public policies directed toward them. Most public policy is directed at pharmaceutical manufacturers.

Understanding the distribution channel for prescription drugs is also essential in understanding the structure of the industry. Manufacturers produce the drugs and, for the most part, sell them to wholesalers, which then sell them to pharmacies, where the drugs are purchased by patients; manufacturers also sell to pharmacy benefit managers (PBMs), who manage prescriptions for insurers and employers. Pharmacies can take many forms and are found in various places, including chain drugstores such as Walgreens, mass merchandisers such as Walmart and Target, grocery store pharmacies such as Kroger, mail-order and retail pharmacies, and pharmacy websites. Over time, the number of independent retail pharmacies has declined. Wholesalers and retail pharmacies are each competitive industries.

Public Policy Dilemma

An important characteristic of the drug industry is the low cost of actually producing a drug once it has been discovered. Very large costs are incurred by the pharmaceutical manufacturer in the R&D phase and in marketing the new drug once it has been approved by the Food and Drug Administration (FDA). A new drug's price is not determined by its R&D costs, however, because these costs have already been incurred. Instead, the price is based on the demand for that drug, which is determined by its therapeutic value and whether it has close substitutes. Because the production costs of a drug (marginal costs) are low, a drug with great therapeutic value and few, if any, substitutes will command a high price. The resulting markup of price over production costs will therefore be high, leading to criticism of the drug company that the drug is priced too high for those who need it.

Grabowski and colleagues (2012) estimated the economic value of statins, a breakthrough drug used for the treatment of cardiovascular disease. The authors estimated that between 1987 and 2008, the economic value was $1.25 trillion. The use of statins resulted in fewer deaths, and it reduced heart attacks and strokes and their associated costs. Subtracting the actual payments made for the drug, $300 billion, over that period from the economic benefits results in a net benefit (social value) to society of about $950 billion. The social value (which economists refer to as "consumer surplus") represents the amount people who benefited would have been willing to pay, but did not, to receive the benefits of statin drugs. The net benefits of statins would have been much greater if the analysis had been extended for more years, if all those in the United States who could have benefited from the drug actually took it, and if the analysis were extended to other countries.

The public policy dilemma is that if the high price markups over cost are decreased so that more people can buy the drug, profits will also be lowered, thereby reducing future R&D investment and the discovery of new drugs with great therapeutic value.

Structure of the Pharmaceutical Industry

The structure of the pharmaceutical industry, together with regulatory restraints and government payment policies, affects drug prices and the rate of investment in innovative drugs. Industry performance is generally measured by the number of blockbuster drugs produced. High price markups for innovative, high-value drugs with no existing substitutes appear justified; high price markups on older drugs are simply an indication of the lack of price competition, because the industry is unable (or lacks the incentive) to produce innovative drugs to take their place. Industry performance is also affected by regulations that raise the cost of developing new drugs, the time it takes for a new drug to receive FDA approval, and whether the government establishes the prices it will pay for new drugs; each of these government policies affects the profitability of new drugs and, hence, incentives for R&D investment.

The growth in regulatory requirements over the past several decades has adversely affected the discovery of new drugs by increasing the cost of developing them. The costs of enrolling patients in phase 3 clinical trials (representing about 90 percent of the total cost of clinical trials), as well as the length of time spent in clinical trials, have been increasing; bringing a new drug to market can take about 12 years and cost as much as $2.5 billion (in 2013 dollars) (DiMasi, Grabowski, and Hansen 2016). Given the time to bring the drug to market and the size of the investment required, little time is available to recoup the investment because the patent expires in 20 years.

Drug firms are also experiencing a more difficult reimbursement climate. The patent periods on several blockbuster drugs (e.g., Lipitor) have expired, and the drugs have been replaced by generic substitutes. Medicare Part D drug plans use formularies, forcing drug firms to compete on price to have their drug included in the formulary. Managed care plans use similar approaches to reduce their enrollees' pharmacy costs.

Mergers and Acquisitions

Since the mid-1990s, many mergers have taken place among pharmaceutical companies. These mergers have been of two types.

The first type is a vertical merger, whereby a firm diversifies into another product line. The growth of managed care and the greater importance of PBMs led several large drug manufacturers to spend many billions of dollars to buy PBMs in the early 1990s. (Merck, for example, paid $6.6 billion for the PBM Medco in 1993.) These drug firms believed that, by buying PBMs, they could gain more control over the market for their drugs; the PBMs would presumably substitute their drugs for those of their competitors, increasing their market share and drug sales. PBMs, however, were unable to simply include their owners' drugs to the exclusion of others because their credibility in serving health plans would have been adversely affected.

The drug firms' PBM strategy does not appear to have been worthwhile. Pharmaceutical companies that did not buy PBMs were also able to increase drug sales, and some companies that bought PBMs sold them. The growth of managed care turned out to be a benefit rather than a threat to drug manufacturers. As more people enrolled in managed care, they received prescription drug coverage, use of prescription drugs grew, and sales at all drug firms sharply increased.

The second type is horizontal merger, in which one drug manufacturer purchases another. There are several reasons for horizontal mergers. First, by becoming larger, firms expect that economies of scale will increase efficiency and decrease costs. Merging two companies can lower administrative costs and raise the efficiency of the two companies' sales forces, which is critical to the success of any drug firm. Drug firms with distinctive products are able to use a single distribution system and sales force when they merge, which results in significant cost savings. Consolidating research units can eliminate competing efforts, and mergers can reduce duplicative manufacturing costs.

Second, for some large firms, mergers are a response to patent expirations and gaps in a firm's product pipeline (Danzon, Epstein, and Nicholson 2007). A wider array of prescription drugs diversifies the financial risk of a firm that produces only a few best-selling drugs. Third, for small pharmaceutical firms, mergers are primarily an exit strategy, an indication of financial trouble. Fourth, horizontal mergers can improve the combined drug firms' market power. However, few mergers have occurred between firms with drugs in the same therapeutic category. Instead, the drugs offered by the combined drug firms are in different therapeutic categories, offering a broader range of prescription drugs across many therapeutic categories to large purchasers.

Pharmaceutical Firms' New Research Strategy

The pharmaceutical industry has undergone major changes in the past several decades. Previously, most pharmaceutical firms were large, able to take advantage of economies of scale, and vertically integrated—that is, most activities were performed in-house, from drug discovery to clinical trials to regulatory approval processes to marketing. The firm's investments in R&D were financed by internally generated funds. Large drug firms' drug development relied on having very large research staffs to screen millions of compounds to discover the next blockbuster drug that would be used by large population groups. This strategy, however, resulted in finding very few new blockbuster drugs.

Revolutionary discoveries in biologic sciences in the 1970s changed the structure of the industry. Thousands of new biotechnology firms emerged. Venture capital funded many of these startups, which were not expected to be profitable for a number of years. Although the risk was high, the profit potential from new drug discoveries was believed to be so high that investors were willing to risk substantial sums on these new firms. The biotechnology industry became a major source of drug innovation (Cockburn, Stern, and Zausner 2011).

Scientific advances in genetics and biology enabled drug discovery to become more focused, targeting the particular pathway that causes a disease in relatively small population groups. Biotechnology firms attempt to discover genetically targeted drugs that treat relatively small populations, but because of the effectiveness of these new drugs, the drug's price can be as high as $100,000 a year. Because there are no close substitutes, insurers are willing to pay higher prices compared with what they would pay for drugs for common diseases, such as high cholesterol, for which there are many generic substitutes. These specialty drugs are generally able to receive regulatory approval in a shorter period; the time required to bring a new drug to market is reduced from 12 years to about 6 years.

Large drug firms were concerned that they had fallen behind small bio-technology firms in their ability to develop innovative drugs. Small companies were more likely to take greater scientific risks and devote a greater number of researchers to a particular idea, whereas large companies became more bureau-cratic in their scientific decision making. Large drug firms began to depend on small biotechnology firms to fill their drug pipelines.

The new approach to drug discovery also changed the size of a drug manufacturer's research efforts. Large research staffs have been downsized and reorganized. The firm's research team has been greatly reduced to only 20 to 40 focused teams. Drug companies believe that smaller research units may be willing to take greater risks and be more innovative than large bureaucracies.

Another major change in drug firms' research strategy has been to become venture capitalists. Rather than investing $1 billion to find the next blockbuster drug, large drug firms are minimizing their financial risks by devel-oping contractual relationships with and investing in a number of small bio-technology companies to find promising new drugs (Walker and Loftus 2013).

Most of the small, new biotechnology firms did not possess the large drug firms' capabilities to bring a new product to market. At the same time, large drug firms recognized the profit potential of the drug research being undertaken by these small firms. Both types of firms realized that developing relationships would enable them to capitalize on each other's strengths. These small firms face large risks and huge investment costs before their products can be marketed. The process of discovery, clinical trials, and drug approval is lengthy and costs several billion dollars. Larger firms are able to bear these costs and have the expertise to navigate the drug-approval process. Greater risk pooling also occurs when many drugs are in the discovery and development phase, as only a few of the many drugs developed will be successful. Only a large firm can afford to undertake these large research efforts. Small firms may not have the financial resources to complete the long drug-approval process or the expertise to perform all of the steps required (Golec and Vernon 2009; Lazonick and Tulum 2011).

Although the research innovation is being generated by small firms, large firms have an advantage when it comes to marketing and selling their drugs. They are able to offer drugs to health plans and PBMs (which contract with large employers and medical plans) for almost all therapeutic categories at a package discount. Providing a full line of drugs for different therapeutic areas at a discount lowers the cost to the PBM by removing the need to negotiate with multiple firms, while enabling the large pharmaceutical firm to include drugs in its package that the PBM might not otherwise select. The Medicare Part D drug benefit reinforces these marketing advantages for the large firm; they are better able to provide the range of drugs in the restricted formularies used by the drug plans offering the Part D benefit to Medicare beneficiaries.

Scientific advances have changed the structure of the pharmaceutical industry by stimulating the growth of many small biotechnology firms, shifting the direction of drug research, downsizing research teams, and creating a new role for large drug firms as venture capitalists.

Industry Competitiveness

The pharmaceutical industry appears to be relatively competitive, as measured by the degree of market concentration. Concentration—which is measured by the combined market share of the top four firms—was only about 21 percent in 2016, based on data from PAREXEL International (2017, 36). However, when therapeutic categories are used, the degree of market concentration is much higher (in some cases, 100 percent) as a therapeutic category may include only one drug. Thus, the competitiveness of the pharmaceutical industry depends on the definition of the market.

Markets that are less concentrated (i.e., have more competitors) are typically more price competitive. The higher the degree of market concentration and the fewer the substitutes available for a particular drug, the greater the firm's market power—that is, the ability to raise the price without losing sales. Thus, the manufacturer of the first breakthrough drug in a therapeutic category has a great deal of market power. As additional branded drugs are developed in that therapeutic category, substitutes become available and price competition increases. When the patents on those drugs expire and generic versions are introduced, a great deal of price competition occurs. At each of these stages, purchasers are able to buy the prescription drug at a lower price.

Development of New Drugs by the US Pharmaceutical Industry

Several measures are used to indicate the productivity of the US pharmaceutical industry. One measure is designation as a global *new chemical entity* (NCE), a drug that is marketed to a majority of the world's leading purchasers of drugs; this designation is preferred over total NCEs as an indicator of a drug's commercial and therapeutic importance. *First in* (a therapeutic) *class* is another designation that reveals the innovativeness of a drug. In addition, the introduction of biotechnology and orphan drugs is examined, as both are major sources of industry growth and innovation.

Grabowski and Wang (2006) analyzed all NCEs introduced worldwide between 1982 and 2003. During that period, 919 NCEs were introduced; 42 percent were global NCEs, 13 percent were first in class, 10 percent were biotechnology drugs, and 8 percent were orphan drugs. Over this period, the total number of NCEs introduced each year exhibited a downward trend. However, measures of the drugs' importance (global NCEs, first in class, biotechnology drugs, and orphan drugs) increased during the same period. Grabowski and Wang (2006) concluded that although the trend in total NCEs declined, the relative quality of new drugs increased, and most of the biotechnology and orphan drugs were introduced from 1993 to 2003. The number of NCEs considered global or first in class varied by therapeutic category, with the highest number being oncology drugs, which are emphasized by the biotechnology industry. (The United States is the dominant source of biotechnology drugs.)

When Grabowski and Wang (2006) analyzed the introduction of drugs by country, the United States was found to be a leader in the development of innovative drugs, particularly from 1993 to 2003. As shown in exhibit 28.1, 30 of 62 first-in-class drugs (48 percent), 37 of 71 biotechnology products (52 percent), and 27 of 49 orphan drugs (55 percent) are manufactured in the United States. Further, when these authors examined the countries in which important new drugs were first introduced (as opposed to developed), the United States was again a strong leader compared with the rest of the world in the most recent period for which data are available (i.e., 1993 to 2003). Both foreign and domestic drug firms preferred to introduce their important new drugs first in the US market. US patients benefit from having earlier access to important new drugs (although there is an associated risk with being the first users of such drugs).

Country	All NCEs		Global NCEs		First-in-Class NCEs		Biotech NCEs		Orphan NCEs	
	82–92	93–03	82–92	93–03	82–92	93–03	82–92	93–03	82–92	93–03
EU total	230	183	99	112	23	27	6	23	9	20
France	35	18	9	11	2	3	0	3	0	4
Germany	53	42	21	27	5	5	2	6	2	5
Italy	29	14	4	1	1	0	0	0	0	0
Switzerland	42	41	26	30	8	11	3	8	1	8
U.K.	34	36	23	27	6	7	0	3	5	2
Others	38	33	17	16	2	2	1	3	1	2
Japan	125	88	12	12	5	3	5	9	1	0
U.S.	120	152	66	81	24	30	9	37	10	27
ROW	7	13	3	1	0	2	0	2	0	2
Total	482	437	179	206	53	62	19	71	20	49

EXHIBIT 28.1 Country-Level Output of New Chemical Entities (NCEs) by Category and Time Period, 1982–1992 and 1993–2003

Notes: EU is European Union. ROW is rest of world.

Source: Reprinted with permission as it appeared in Henry G. Grabowski and Y. Richard Wang, "The Quantity and Quality of Worldwide New Drug Introductions, 1982–2003," *Health Affairs*, 25 (2), March/April 2006: 425–60, Exhibit 4. © 2006 Project HOPE-The People-to-People Health Foundation, Inc.

Unfortunately, no updates to these figures are available. However, although the data in exhibit 28.2 are not comparable to those in exhibit 28.1, they are more recent and indicate that the United States still leads in the discovery of new chemical or biological entities. Biotechnology drugs, in which the United States is a leader, have been a source of important new drugs and industry productivity growth.

The US market provides greater incentives to drug firms than do other countries for developing important new drugs and for first introducing innovative drugs. Whether the predominance of the United States in drug innovation and in being the first place of introduction will continue depends on government payment policies to reduce the costs of new drugs.

The Political Attractiveness of Price Controls on Prescription Drugs

For many years, the high price of prescription drugs was a major concern of the elderly. When Medicare was enacted in 1965, prescription drugs were not included as a benefit. Many elderly beneficiaries, who are the highest users of prescription drugs, could not afford to buy needed drugs; attaining a prescription drug benefit became their highest political priority. In 2003, the Medicare Modernization Act was enacted. It included a new voluntary Medicare Part D prescription drug benefit, which became effective in 2006 (see chapter 8).

Part D increased seniors' demand for prescription drugs, and pharmaceutical manufacturers benefited from higher revenues. However, increased revenues to the pharmaceutical companies meant higher federal expenditures for prescription drugs. Part D, similar to Medicare Part B, became another unfunded federal entitlement; no matter how much was spent on drugs by the elderly, Medicare was committed to paying 75 percent of those expenditures. (As part of the 2010 Affordable Care Act [ACA], Part D beneficiaries' cost sharing for prescription drugs is reduced over time, leading to greater use of prescription drugs and higher drug expenditures.)

EXHIBIT 28.2
Output of New Chemical or Biological Entities by Region of Origin and Time Period

Region	1997–2001	2002–2006	2007–2011	2012–2016
Europe	79	46	52	75
United States	84	67	65	88
Japan	29	21	20	32
Other	4	14	12	38

Source: Data from STATISTA (2017).

The Medicare Modernization Act and the ACA prohibited the federal government from negotiating drug prices with pharmaceutical firms. Elderly individuals enroll in a private drug plan, which then negotiates prices with the drug manufacturer. The cost of the Medicare drug benefits has been much less than expected, which generally has been attributed to the use of formularies by competing drug plans, which enable them to negotiate lower prices from pharmaceutical firms. Pharmaceutical companies are, however, concerned that Congress will change the law and have the government regulate drug prices because of the high prices of specialty drugs, which can exceed $100,000 a year. (Several legislators have proposed changing the law to allow the federal government to negotiate directly with pharmaceutical companies.) As long as the government is ultimately responsible for paying for the drug expenses of Part D enrollees, regardless of who administers the benefit, there is concern that drug expenditures will eventually be regulated, as the government currently regulates payment for each type of provider participating in Medicare.

Proponents of government regulation of drug prices claim that in addition to reducing federal expenditures, the aged would also benefit by lowering their out-of-pocket drug expenses and their premium for the Medicare drug benefit, which equals 25 percent of total Medicare drug expenditures. As evidence of the benefits of price controls, proponents claim that prices on branded drugs are as much as 30 percent higher in the United States than they are in Canada, which uses price controls.

Price controls on new breakthrough drugs are politically attractive. Politicians try to provide their constituents with short-term visible benefits, seemingly at no cost. In the short run, drug prices would be reduced and there would be no decrease in access to drugs currently on the market. Because the costs of R&D have already been incurred, the only cost to produce an existing drug is its relatively small variable cost. As long as the regulated drug price is greater than the drug's variable costs, the firm will continue selling the drug. Profits from that drug will be lower, but the firm will make more money by continuing to sell the drug, even at the regulated price, than by not selling it.

Consequences of Price Controls on Prescription Drugs

Price controls would not decrease access to innovative drugs currently on the market or even to those currently in the drug-approval process. Those who would benefit include patients who cannot afford expensive drugs, states with rapidly increasing Medicaid expenditures, and the federal government, which is responsible for bearing 75 percent of the cost of the prescription drug benefit. The aged (who have the highest voting-participation rate), state Medicaid programs, and legislators interested in decreasing federal drug expenditures are likely to favor legislation to reduce drug prices. The only apparent loser would be drug companies.

The real problem with price controls is their effect not on current drugs but on R&D for future drugs. Price controls reduce the profitability of new drugs. With lower expected profits, drug companies will be less willing to risk hundreds of millions of dollars on R&D. Most new drugs (70 to 80 percent) are not therapeutic breakthroughs and, although their price may exceed their variable costs, do not generate sufficient profit to cover their R&D investments. Thus, the drug company loses money on these drugs (see exhibit 26.4).

The small percentage of drugs that are considered blockbuster drugs have high price markups over their variable costs. The large profits generated by these blockbuster drugs provide the funding for the drugs that lose money. Although there is a short-term visible benefit to price controls, they impose a long-term cost on patients. This long-term cost is not obvious because it occurs in the future, and the public would be unaware of breakthrough drugs that were never developed.

Blockbuster drugs, with their high price markups, would be targeted by price controls. With price controls, profit would be insufficient to provide R&D funding for new drugs. Fewer breakthrough drugs would lead to more costly treatment for a disease, whereas such drugs might make surgical intervention unnecessary or even prevent the disease from developing. Through R&D and the development of new drugs, the total cost of medical treatment is lowered, such as has occurred with Sovaldi (sofosbuvir) for treatment of hepatitis C. With price controls, R&D investments would decline. Drug companies would also redirect their R&D efforts away from diseases affecting the elderly (where price controls limit profits) and toward diseases affecting other population groups (where profits are not limited).

Exhibits 28.3 and 28.4 illustrate the effects of price controls on the product life cycle of a blockbuster drug (Helms 2004). During the beginning phases of R&D, including clinical trials, the company incurs a negative cash flow. Once the FDA approves the drug and the drug company markets the drug, the cash flow is positive—until other branded drugs (substitutes) enter the market, and eventually the patent expires and generics enter the market.

If price controls are imposed on a drug after it is approved by the FDA and marketed, the positive cash flow from the new drug is greatly diminished, as shown by the black, dotted curve in exhibit 28.4. To illustrate the financial effects of imposing price controls in the previous example, one would have to examine the present value of both the cash outlay and the positive cash return.

Money received in the future is worth less than the same amount of money received today. These money outflows (before the drug is sold) and inflows occur at different times. The cost of developing a new drug includes all the costs of bringing it to market, such as research expenditures, the cost of clinical trials, the cost of having the drug approved by the FDA, and marketing

EXHIBIT 28.3
Life Cycle of a
New Drug

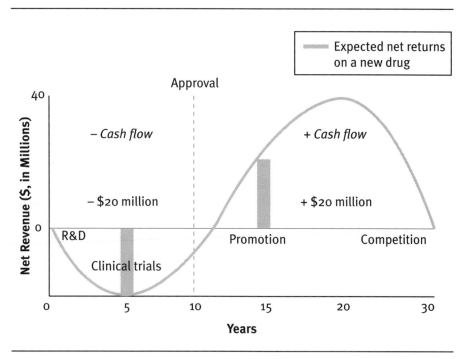

Note: R&D = research and development.
Source: Helms (2004).

EXHIBIT 28.4
Effect of Price
Controls on
Drug Returns

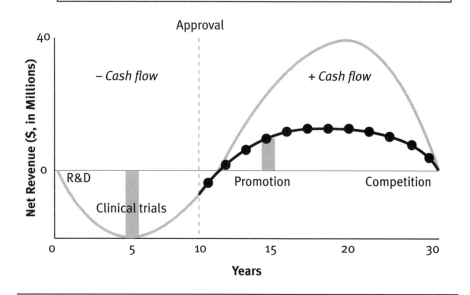

Note: R&D = research and development.
Source: Helms (2004).

costs once it is approved. A company would calculate what it could have earned on that investment if the funds were instead invested in a corporate bond and gained interest. For example, if $10 were invested today and earned 6 percent interest per year, in five years that initial investment would grow to $13.38. Thus, in calculating the cost of developing a new drug, the firm calculates both its cash outlay and what it could have earned on that money (the opportunity cost). Similarly, in calculating the return received from that new drug, which generates a positive cash flow in the future, it is necessary to discount (using the same interest rate) the positive cash flow and determine what the money received in the future is worth in today's dollars (the present value).

Using the example shown in exhibits 28.3 and 28.4, if a firm invests $20 million in year 5, the present value of that investment equals $14.95 million. (In other words, $14.95 million invested today would be worth $20 million in five years.) If, after 15 years, a new drug earns $20 million, the present value of that return is only $8.35 million. Clearly, the $20 million spent and the $20 million earned are not equal. In this example, the drug firm would lose $6.6 million on its investment. Thus, the longer it takes to bring a drug to market, the longer the negative cash flow and the smaller the present value of the positive cash flow once the drug is marketed.

If price controls are imposed on a drug once it is marketed, as shown by the dotted line in exhibit 28.4, both its positive cash flow and the present value of that reduced cash flow will be lower. Thus, if the firm earns only $10 million in year 15, the present value equals only $4.17 million. The present value of the cash outflow remains at $14.95 million (Helms 2004).

In the previous example, a drug firm would change its investment strategy. It would decrease its overall investment in R&D, invest in drugs with a quicker payoff, seek drugs with less risky profitability outcomes, and invest in drugs whose market potential is very large and profitable, thereby abandoning research on drugs for diseases affecting relatively few people.

Examples of Price Controls on US Prescription Drugs

The debate over President Clinton's health plan, introduced in the fall of 1993, provides an indication of the likely effect of price controls on prescription drugs. Included in the plan was the Advisory Council on Breakthrough Drugs, whose purpose was to review prices of new drugs. If the proposed council believed that a new drug's price was excessive, it would try to have it reduced or, failing that, have the drug excluded from health insurance payment. The targeted drugs were those that were the most profitable and had high price markups—namely breakthrough drugs.

The pharmaceutical industry was concerned that if the plan were enacted, price controls would be imposed on prescription drugs and the profitability of new drugs would be decreased. As a result, the annual rate of increase in

R&D expenditures declined sharply, falling from 18.2 percent in 1992 to 5.6 percent by 1994, the smallest annual rate of increase in 30 years (see exhibit 28.5). Once it became clear that the Clinton health plan would be defeated and price controls would not be imposed on new drugs, the annual rate of increase in pharmaceutical R&D spending rose again.

The next threat to the drug companies occurred in 2002 when the firms believed Congress was going to legalize reimportation of drugs from Canada and Europe (without the approval of the secretary of the US Department of Health and Human Services). As a result, in 2002 R&D expenditures grew by only 4.2 percent, after having increased by 14.4 percent in 2001. Once the threat of reimportation did not materialize, R&D expenditures again rose—to 11.1 percent in 2003.

In 2008 and 2009, R&D expenditures sharply decreased over concerns that the newly elected Democratic president and large Democratic majorities in Congress would pass legislation that adversely affected the industry by requiring reductions in Medicare and Medicaid prescription drug prices. In the fee-for-service section of Medicaid, drug firms pay a rebate to Medicaid for each drug the program purchases on behalf of its beneficiaries. President Obama's 2010 budget proposed an increase in that rebate (ultimately lowering the price that drug firms charged). Proposals were also made to require a rebate on drugs purchased by Medicare Part D beneficiaries. As the data indicate, R&D expenditures are sensitive to possible legislative changes that would reduce drug firms' profits (Congressional Budget Office 2009).

History does not offer much hope for drug manufacturers evading price controls. Governments in other countries have used various approaches to lower their drug expenditures. In a study of 19 OECD (Organisation for Economic Co-operation and Development) countries, Sood and colleagues (2008) found various forms of regulation that decreased pharmaceutical revenues. The types of controls used by these countries included fixing the price of drugs, delaying approval for expensive new drugs for several years, restricting the use of a drug once it has been approved, establishing global (country) budget caps, setting annual budget limits for physicians' prescriptions, applying profit controls, and setting the price of all drugs within a specific therapeutic category at the cost of the lowest-priced drug. While a majority of the regulations decrease pharmaceutical revenues, direct price controls have the largest negative effect on revenues. If similar price controls were imposed in the United States, pharmaceutical revenues would fall as much as 20 percent. Further, the longer the regulations are in place, the greater their impact on revenues.

Several approaches have already been used in the United States to reduce government expenditures for prescription drugs (Vernon and Golec 2009). Because of their tight budgets, state Medicaid programs have more restrictive formularies than do managed care plans. Newer drugs that are more expensive

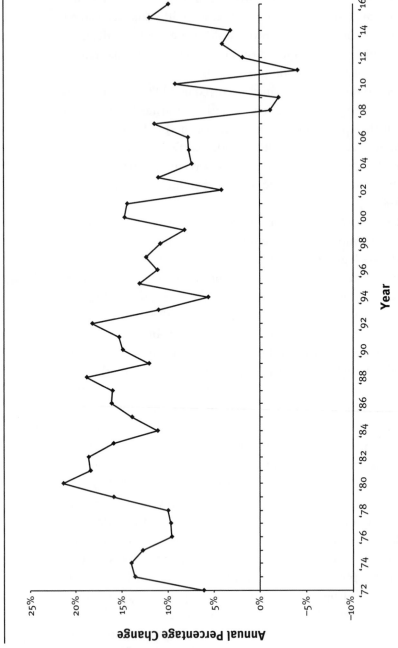

EXHIBIT 28.5
Annual Percentage Change in US R&D, Pharmaceutical Companies, 1971–2016

Note: R&D = research and development. Domestic US R&D includes expenditures within the United States by all Pharmaceutical Research and Manufacturers of America (PhRMA) member companies. R&D abroad includes expenditures by US-owned PhRMA companies outside the United States and R&D conducted abroad by the US divisions of foreign-owned PhRMA member companies. R&D performed abroad by the foreign divisions of foreign-owned PhRMA member companies is excluded. Data for 1995 R&D were affected by merger and acquisition activity.

Source: Data from Pharmaceutical Research and Manufacturers of America (2018).

but more effective are more likely to be excluded in favor of less expensive generics. Further, Medicaid programs delay inclusion of expensive innovative drugs in their formularies for several years. Studies have shown that the effect of limiting access to preferred drugs results in a shift toward more costly settings, higher nursing home admissions, and greater risk of hospitalization among Medicaid populations (Soumerai 2004). Further, the savings in drug costs were offset by increases in the costs of hospitalization and emergency department care (Hsu et al. 2006).

A price-control approach that has been used by the federal government requires the drug manufacturer to sell the drug to the government at its "best" price. In the 1980s, as a result of price competition among drug companies to persuade health maintenance organizations (HMOs) and group purchasing organizations (GPOs) to include their drugs in HMO and GPO drug formularies, drug manufacturers gave large price discounts to certain HMOs and GPOs. In 1990, the federal government, in an attempt to reduce Medicaid expenditures, enacted a law that required drug manufacturers to give state Medicaid programs the same discounts they gave their best customers. Consequently, the drug companies gave smaller discounts to HMOs and GPOs. A study by the Congressional Budget Office (1996) found that the best (largest) price discount given to HMOs and GPOs declined from 24 percent and 28 percent, respectively, in 1991 to 14 percent and 15 percent, respectively, in 1994, the minimum amount required by the government.

The study concluded that drug companies were much less willing to give steep discounts to large purchasers when they had to give the same discounts to Medicaid. Drug prices and expenditures consequently increased for many private buyers.

Summary

Two important characteristics of the pharmaceutical industry are (1) the low costs of actually producing a drug and (2) the high cost of developing a new drug. The price at which a new drug is sold is determined not by its cost of production or the R&D investment in that drug, but by its value to purchasers and whether any close substitutes to that drug are available. Valuable drugs that have no close substitutes (blockbuster drugs) will be priced high relative to their costs of production. Lowering the price of these blockbuster drugs to make them more affordable will decrease pharmaceutical companies' incentive to invest hundreds of millions of dollars in drugs that may have great value to society. That is the public policy dilemma.

The pharmaceutical industry has been changing over time from large, vertically integrated organizations to an industry that still consists of large firms but also has many small biotechnology firms (funded by venture capital) that are engaged in developing new blockbuster drugs. A great deal of private money is invested in these highly risky ventures in the hope of developing a valuable (and profitable) new drug.

Compared with the rest of the world, the United States has been a leader in developing important new drugs, and it is the country of first choice for introducing innovative drugs. Government payment policies to reduce drug expenditures threaten both the US industry's leadership and patients' access to innovative drugs.

A growing concern is that the federal government, which has become a large indirect purchaser of prescription drugs as a result of including Part D in Medicare, will attempt to lower its drug expenses by "negotiating" the price of prescription drugs. Direct government negotiations with drug companies over the price of their drugs will be tantamount to the government fixing the price of drugs.

Implementing price controls will not have any immediate effect on seniors' access to drugs. However, over time, drug companies will invest less in R&D and redirect their R&D toward population groups and diseases that offer greater profitability.

In coming years, enormous scientific progress is likely. The mapping of the human genome and advances in molecular biology are expected to lead to drug solutions for many diseases. Drug prices and expenditures will also likely be higher to reflect the increased willingness of people to pay for these new discoveries. It would be unfortunate if the desire to reduce the cost of drugs through price controls decreased the availability of breakthrough drugs.

Any public policy must deal with trade-offs: reducing the high price markup of breakthrough drugs versus maintaining incentives for investing in R&D. It is important to distinguish between the short- and long-term effects of public policy. Using price controls to lower drug prices results in a visible short-term benefit, but it comes at a less visible longer-term cost of fewer breakthrough drugs. Patients in the future would be willing to pay for lifesaving breakthrough drugs that were not developed because the government removed the incentives to do so. Given the trade-off between instituting regulation to reduce the cost of drugs and having innovative drugs to cure disease, reduce mortality, and lower the overall cost of medical treatment, society would likely choose the full benefits that scientific discovery will offer.

Discussion Questions

1. How has the structure of the pharmaceutical industry changed over time?

2. What are alternative ways of judging whether the pharmaceutical industry is competitive?

3. Why are price controls on prescription drugs politically attractive?

4. Why would price controls not limit access to blockbuster drugs that are either currently on the market or have almost completed the FDA approval process?

5. What are the expected long-term consequences of price controls on R&D investments, quality of life, mortality rates, and the cost of medical care?

References

Cockburn, I., S. Stern, and J. Zausner. 2011. "Finding the Endless Frontier: Lessons from the Life Sciences Innovation System for Energy R&D." In *Accelerating Energy Innovation: Insights from Multiple Sectors*, edited by R. Henderson and R. Newell, 113–57. Chicago: University of Chicago Press.

Congressional Budget Office. 2009. "Pharmaceutical R&D and the Evolving Market for Prescription Drugs." Published October 26. www.cbo.gov/ftpdocs/106xx/doc10681/10-26-DrugR&D.pdf.

———. 1996. *How the Medicaid Rebate on Prescription Drugs Affects Pricing in the Pharmaceutical Industry*. Washington, DC: US Government Printing Office.

Danzon, P., A. Epstein, and S. Nicholson. 2007. "Mergers and Acquisitions in the Pharmaceutical and Biotech Industries." *Managerial and Decision Economics* 28 (4–5): 307–28.

DiMasi, J. A., H. G. Grabowski, and R. W. Hansen. 2016. "Innovation in the Pharmaceutical Industry: New Estimates of R&D Costs." *Journal of Health Economics* 47: 20–33.

Golec, J., and J. A. Vernon. 2009. "Financial Risk of the Biotech Industry Versus the Pharmaceutical Industry." *Applied Health Economics and Policy* 7 (3): 155–65.

Grabowski, D. C., D. N. Lakdawalla, D. P. Goldman, M. Eber, L. Z. Liu, T. Abdelgawad, A. Kuznik, M. E. Chernew, and T. Philipson. 2012. "The Large Social Value Resulting from Use of Statins Warrants Steps to Improve Adherence and Broaden Treatment." *Health Affairs* 31 (10): 2276–85.

Grabowski, H. G., and Y. R. Wang. 2006. "The Quantity and Quality of Worldwide New Drug Introductions, 1982–2003." *Health Affairs* 25 (2): 452–60.

Helms, R. 2004. "The Economics of Price Regulation and Innovation." *Managed Care* 13 (6 Suppl): 10–12.

Hsu, J., M. Price, J. Huang, R. Brand, V. Fung, R. Hui, B. Fireman, J. Newhouse, and J. Selby. 2006. "Unintended Consequences of Caps on Medicare Drug Benefits." *New England Journal of Medicine* 354 (22): 2349–59.

Lazonick, W., and O. Tulum. 2011. "US Biopharmaceutical Finance and the Sustainability of the Biotech Business Model." *Research Policy* 40 (9): 1170–87.

PAREXEL International. 2017. *PAREXEL Biopharmaceutical R&D Statistical Sourcebook, 2017/2018 Edition*. Waltham, MA: PAREXEL International.

Pharmaceutical Research and Manufacturers of America (PhRMA). 2018. *2017 PhRMA Annual Membership Survey*. Accessed May. http://phrma-docs.phrma.org/files/dmfile/PhRMA_membership-survey_2017.pdf.

Sood, N., H. deVries, I. Gutierrez, D. Lakdawalla, and D. Goldman. 2008. "The Effect of Regulation on Pharmaceutical Revenues: Experience in Nineteen Countries." *Health Affairs* 28 (1): w125–w135.

Soumerai, S. 2004. "Benefits and Risks of Increasing Restrictions on Access to Costly Drugs in Medicaid." *Health Affairs* 23 (1): 135–46.

STATISTA. 2017. "Number of New Chemical or Biological Entities Developed Between 1992 and 2016, by Region of Origin." Accessed May 2018. www.statista.com/statistics/275262/pharmaceutical-industry-new-entities-by-region/.

Vernon, J., and J. Golec. 2009. *Pharmaceutical Price Regulation: Public Perceptions, Economic Realities, and Empirical Evidence*. Washington, DC: American Enterprise Institute Press.

Walker, J., and P. Loftus. 2013. "Merck to Cut Staff by 20% as Big Pharma Trims R&D." *Wall Street Journal*. Published October 2. www.wsj.com/articles/merck-plans-further-cuts-in-revamp-of-commercial-rampd-arm-1380630165.

SHOULD KIDNEYS AND OTHER ORGANS BE BOUGHT AND SOLD?

B etween 1995 and 2017, 154,381 people on waiting lists for an organ died. During this period, the number of people waiting for a transplant rose 200 percent (from 43,937 to 126,478), while the number of organs donated increased by just 78 percent (from 23,255 in 1995 to 42,601 in 2017) (see exhibit 29.1). More than 80 percent (83 percent as of 2017) of those waiting for organ transplants are waiting for kidneys; the remainder are waiting for a heart, liver, lung, intestine, or pancreas. The number of people who die each year while waiting for an organ transplant is increasing: In 2017, the number was 5,818, up from 3,722 in 1995.

Although the total number of transplants has increased (see exhibit 29.2), the gap between those waiting for organ transplants and the supply of organs has also been growing rapidly as more patients are recommended for such transplants. Improved transplant techniques and the development of better immunosuppressive drugs to reduce the risk of rejection have greatly increased the success rate of organ transplants; success rates for kidney transplants have increased from approximately 60 percent in the late 1950s to 97 percent in 2017 (one-year survival based on 2012–2015 transplants). Unfortunately, the number of organs is insufficient to keep up with the growing demand. Consequently, many of those waiting for a transplant die before an organ becomes available.

Patients waiting for a kidney transplant must rely on kidney dialysis, which is costly. Kidney transplantation is a lower-cost form of treatment and provides a better quality of life for the patient. The cost to Medicare of a kidney transplant is about one-third of the cost per year for dialysis (United States Renal Data System 2017). If all patients on dialysis who are waiting for a transplant could receive a kidney, the federal government, which pays for kidney dialysis and kidney transplants under Medicare, could save approximately $30 billion (in 2017 dollars) over a five-year period.[1] In addition to being costlier, dialysis takes time—up to seven hours per day for several days a week. In addition, kidney dialysis patients have a reduced quality of life as well as lower productivity.

Sources of Organs for Transplantation

The two sources of supply for organ transplants are (1) living donors, such as family members who donate one of their kidneys, and (2) cadavers. Approximately

EXHIBIT 29.1
Demand for
Organs and
Total Number
of Organs
Donated,
1995–2017

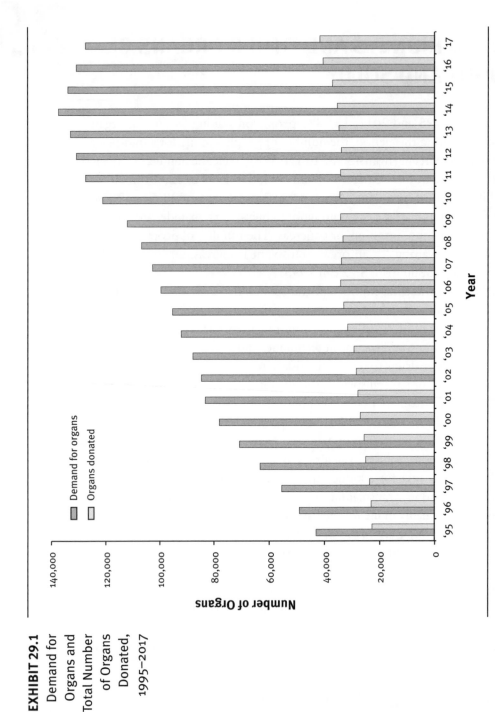

Source: Data on the number of organs demanded are based on the waiting list of the Organ Procurement and Transplantation Network (OPTN) on the last day of each year. Data for the number of organs donated are from OPTN as of January 31, 2018 (see http://optn.transplant.hrsa.gov).

EXHIBIT 29.2

Number of Organ Transplants, Selected Years, 1981–2017

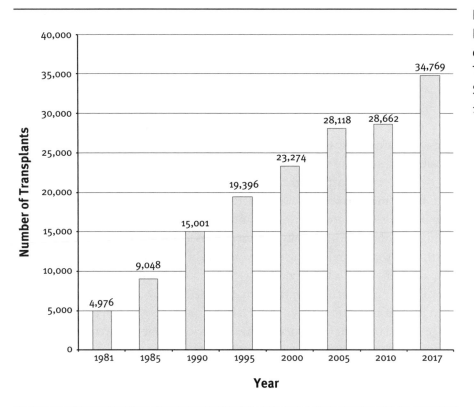

Source: Based on Organ Procurement and Transplantation Network data as of January 31, 2018 (see https://optn.transplant.hrsa.gov/data/view-data-reports/national-data/#).

72 percent of kidneys—as well as most other organs used for transplants (96 percent of livers, 99 percent of lungs, and 100 percent of pancreases and hearts)—come from victims who have just been killed in an accident. A total of 82 percent of all organs come from accident victims (OPTN n.d.).

The motivating force on which transplant patients have long depended is altruism. According to the National Organ Transplant Act of 1984, purchase or sale of human organs is illegal. Current efforts to increase the supply of organs rely on approaches to stimulate voluntary donations by the family members of those who die in accidents.

Kidney exchanges are an innovative approach currently being used. Previously, what often occurred is that a person was willing to donate a kidney to an intended recipient but was unable to do so because of an incompatibility, such as blood type, between the donor and the recipient. The kidney donation did not take place, and the recipient had to wait his turn on the waiting list. Many patients on the waiting list died before receiving a donated kidney. Using a kidney exchange, a data system of donors and their intended recipients is developed so that two incompatible patient–donor pairs exchange kidneys, with each patient receiving a compatible kidney from the other's donor. In a three-way exchange, a donor's kidney is transplanted into a patient from the second donor–recipient pair, while the kidney from the second donor is transplanted into a patient in the third donor–recipient pair, and the third donor's kidney is transplanted into the patient in the first donor–recipient pair (Roth, Sonmez, and Unver 2005). The data collection efforts of kidney exchanges have enabled much higher donor–recipient matches, such as four-way and five-way match chains. Thousands of additional kidney transplants have been possible as a result of these kidney exchanges.[2]

Currently, shortly after they have been notified of the death of their loved one, family members are asked by medical personnel to donate the deceased's organs. Physicians are often reluctant to make such a request to a grieving family, and the grieving family is reluctant to agree while still shocked by the death. For some families, the sorrow might be somewhat offset by the belief that another person's life might be saved. About 30 percent of families are still unwilling to give permission for their deceased family member's organs to be used for transplantation (Goldberg, Halpern, and Reese 2013). For psychological (e.g., the thought of dismemberment of a loved one) and religious reasons, families of the deceased are often unwilling to donate the organs. The period in which such a request can be made is short; tissues must be recovered from donors no longer than 24 hours after cessation of a heartbeat as the organ will quickly deteriorate. The family must be located, permission must be received, a recipient must be located through the national organ network, and a tissue match must be made between the recipient and the deceased.

Various approaches have been proposed to increase voluntary organ donations. One is to use improved "marketing" techniques on how to approach (and who should talk to) grieving families, whose sorrow may be lessened by the knowledge that they have saved another person's life by donating the deceased's organs. Another approach is to provide greater publicity and education to the public on registering to become a donor, which makes a person's organs available to potential recipients. (Each US state has a donor registry and specific instructions for potential donors.) Although education and publicity are likely to increase the number of people registering to become an organ donor, the organ transplant community still seeks permission from the donor's family before harvesting organs. In some states, such as Texas, medical authorities have been legally granted permission to harvest organs from bodies if the family has not been identified within four hours. This authority, however, has rarely been used. Fear of lawsuits and unfavorable publicity, as well as the desire to maintain the public's trust prevent physicians from immediately harvesting a deceased donor's organs.

Presumed consent laws have been proposed that would make the deceased's organs available unless the deceased or her family had previously opposed it. (Presumed consent laws are also referred to as an opt-in system whereby a person who is unwilling to donate her organs must opt out.) These laws, which are in force in many European countries, have increased organ donation rates by 25 to 30 percent over those in the United States; however, in most countries with presumed consent laws, such as Spain (which has the highest organ donation rate in the world), medical authorities do not authorize the removal of organs without an explicit family approval. Thus, while presumed consent would alleviate the organ shortage in the United States, it would not eliminate it (Abadie and Gay 2006). Waiting for permission from the deceased's family often results in the organs being lost. Although about 20,000 people who die each year in the United States have organs suitable for harvesting, only 15 to 20 percent of those organs are actually donated. Under the current system of altruism, the supply of living and deceased donors has increased slowly—from 5,909 in 1988 to 9,220 in 1996 to 16,466 in 2017.

An organ donation approach used in Israel has resulted in an increase in voluntary organ donations. In 2010, Israel changed its law regarding organ donations by giving priority to patients whose family members donated an organ or if the patient himself had previously donated an organ. The 2010 law provided an incentive for individuals to register as kidney donors in case they or a family member eventually needed a kidney transplant. The change in the law resulted in a sharp decrease in the number of patients waiting for an organ transplant and a very large increase in the number of registered donors. "More than 35 percent of those who actually got organs after the law was passed got them because of the prioritizing system" said the director of the transplantation center (Wen 2014).[3]

Donor Compensation Proposals

The growing imbalance between supply and demand for organs has led some to advocate compensating donors to increase the supply of donated organs. Paying donors (or their families) is highly controversial and would require a change in current legislation prohibiting the purchase or sale of body organs. Organ payment proposals cover the spectrum from mild (paying family members for organs of their kin before or after death) to strong (paying a living donor for a kidney). The following discussion covers three such proposals.

Compensating Families After the Donor's Death
One approach proposes that the burial costs of the deceased be paid if the family permits harvesting of the deceased's organs. Similarly, the family of the deceased could be paid an amount varying between $1,000 and $5,000. A potential problem with these proposals is that negotiating a financial transaction with a family traumatized by the death of a loved one may be awkward. Another possible

problem is that purchases of organs, which presumably would be directed toward those with low income, might offend low-income minority families, who may feel that they are being exploited to benefit wealthy white people.

Compensating Donors Before Death

Allowing people to sell their organs in advance of their death has the advantage that family members would not be subject to the psychological and social pressure to make a quick decision at a very difficult time. Thus, a second approach is to allow people to sell the rights to their organs in return for reducing their health or auto insurance premiums. Health or automobile insurance companies might offer lower annual premiums to those who are willing to donate their organs if they die during the coming year. The insurance company would then have the right to harvest the deceased's organs during the period of the insurance contract. Each potential donor would be listed in a central computer registry, which a hospital would check when a patient died. Transplant recipients would also be listed in a national registry, and their health insurer or the government would reimburse the deceased's automobile or health insurance company for a previously stated price.

For example, if the value of all of a deceased's organs is $100,000 at the time of death, and the probability of dying during the year is 10,000:1 (the current average chance of dying during a year), the annual premium reduction would be $10. If the value of all the organs is greater than $100,000, or the probability of death is lower than 10,000:1, the premium reduction would be greater. Young drivers and motorcyclists, who are more likely to die in accidents, presumably would be offered larger automobile insurance reductions.

The price of organs could be established competitively or by the government—for example, $10,000 for a kidney. These prices would be used by insurance companies, together with the probability that a subscriber would die during the next year, to establish the annual premium reduction for a potential donor. If too few insurance subscribers are willing to accept the premium reduction, the price of the organ (if established by the government) could be increased until the likely supply is sufficient to satisfy the estimated demand for organs.

Compensating Living Kidney Donors

The most controversial approach is to pay living donors a sufficiently high price for them to part with one of their kidneys. Paying a market price to bring forth an increase in supply already takes place in other highly sensitive areas of human behavior, such as use of sperm banks and surrogate mothers, who are willing to be impregnated with another couple's fertilized egg in return for a fee. Compensating bone marrow donors recently became legal (Bergstrom et al. 2013). In the past, 2,000 to 3,000 people with cancer and blood diseases died each year while waiting for a bone marrow transplant.[4]

Market transactions consist of a voluntary exchange of assets between two parties. People engage in voluntary exchange because they differ in their valuation of the asset, and both parties expect to benefit from the transaction. If sales of kidneys were permitted, the person selling the kidney would receive a fee that she believes would compensate her for the loss of a kidney. The purchaser believes the kidney is worth at least what he is willing to pay for it. The purchaser is likely to be the government rather than an individual, as kidney transplants are covered under Medicare; in this case, paying for the kidney would be similar to paying the surgeon for the operation. No one is worse off by voluntary trade. Thus, the first major advantage of legalizing the sale of kidneys is that both parties are likely better off with the voluntary exchange than when it is prohibited.

Permitting a commercial market for kidneys has other important advantages. Organs that would save the lives of all those waiting for a kidney could be purchased. No longer would they have to endure the suffering that occurs while waiting for a kidney donation, possibly dying before one becomes available. Further, the government would save a great deal of money by substituting kidney transplants for kidney dialysis, as a transplant is a lower-cost method of treatment. Finally, the quality of donated kidneys would increase, improving the success rate of transplants. Currently, donated kidneys that are not good tissue matches are used because of the severe shortage of organs. Paying living donors for their kidneys would result in a greater choice of donors, enabling tissue matches between recipient and donor to be made in advance.

Opposition to Using Financial Incentives

Opposition to using financial incentives to increase the supply of organs is based on several factors. First, some believe that offering financial incentives would discourage voluntary organ donations, further reducing the supply of organs. When financial incentives were used to augment the blood supply, voluntary donations of blood decreased, but the decline was more than offset by the growth of paid donations (Dunham 2008).

Second, some claim that paying living donors for their organs would exploit the poor to benefit the wealthy. The poor are likely to be the sellers of organs, whereas those with higher income are likely to be the beneficiaries. The poor, it is claimed, would be forced to sell their organs to provide for their families. However, the reason the poor have inadequate funds is that society is unwilling to provide them with sufficient subsidies or education to enable them to increase their productivity and income. Prohibiting the poor from selling an asset would leave them worse off, and they would be prevented from doing something they believe will improve their situation. Although little risk is involved in selling one's kidney, a donor would be accepting a slightly higher risk of dying in return for greater financial rewards. Many people seek additional compensation by choosing to work in higher-risk occupations. Working in a coal mine, in a skyscraper, or on an offshore drilling platform carries occupational risks, yet society does not interfere with these voluntary transactions. Someone willing to make the trade-off between greater compensation and the loss of a kidney is not "forced" to sell her organs.

Third, some are concerned that those selling their kidneys might be subject to fraud and then regret selling their kidneys. Various protections could be included in legislation legalizing the sale of kidneys. A waiting period (e.g., six months) could be implemented to give the donor time to change his mind. In addition, the donor could be required to be of a minimum age (at least 18 years). A panel that includes a psychiatrist or social worker could also be put in place to assess the donor's ability to make rational choices.

When demand exceeds supply in a market, prices rise. When prices are not permitted to rise or sales are illegal, the potential for a black market exists. Although the sale of kidneys in the United States is illegal, a wealthy patient has access to an international black market, particularly from donors from less developed countries, such as India and China. Demand for organs is lower when the activity is illegal than when it is legal. On the black market, the search for an organ donor is more expensive, purchasers are less certain of the organ's quality, no legal remedies are available if fraud occurs, and the purchaser has to pay the hospital's and surgeon's costs out of pocket. However, this option is available only to the wealthy. Therefore, prohibiting the sale of organs discriminates against the poor, who do not have access to the international black market in kidneys.

If a legal market in organs were permitted, would only the wealthy be able to afford kidney transplants once the price of a kidney is included in the already high price of a transplant? The answer is "no." The federal government currently pays for kidney transplants; the higher cost would not be a deterrent to any patient needing a transplant. Most of the transplant costs are for hospital and physician services, so the price of the organ would not add substantially to these costs. Everyone associated with the transplant benefits—the patient receives a new kidney, and the surgeon and hospital are paid for the transplantation. Why shouldn't the donor also benefit?

What if a low-income person desperate for money sells his kidney and subsequently develops kidney disease? Because the government currently pays for all kidney transplants as part of Medicare, that donor would become eligible for a free transplant. A new donor would be paid for a kidney to be used for the previous donor's transplant.

Would the opponents of a compensation system be inclined to support it if the poor—defined, for example, as those with income below the federal poverty level—were prohibited from selling their organs? Would the poor be better off if they were denied the right to sell one of their assets? A belief that society helps the poor when those with higher income limit their choices is paternalistic.

Additional Considerations

The poor and minority groups are placed at a disadvantage by the present altruistic system for securing and allocating organs. Many of those waiting for transplants have low incomes. Further, although African Americans are statistically more likely to suffer from kidney disease than are whites, they are less likely to receive an organ transplant. In fact, while African Americans make up 13.1 percent of the population, they make up 34 percent of those on the waiting list for kidney transplants. The relatively higher proportion of African Americans on the waiting list is due to three factors: (1) They need proportionately more kidneys than whites, (2) their tissue match rate with whites is low, and (3) they are not as likely to receive donations from African-American families as they are from white families. (The refusal rate for organ donations among African-American families is 45 percent, compared with 23 percent for white families [Goldberg, Halpern, and Reese 2013].)[5]

As Epstein (2006, 15) wrote, "Only a bioethicist would prefer a world in which we have 1,000 altruists per annum and more than 6,500 excess deaths over one in which we have no altruists and no excess deaths." Markets and altruism offer differing approaches for increasing the number of organ donations; they should be evaluated on the basis of which approach produces less loss of life.

Summary

The demand for organ transplantations will continue to grow as the incidence of obesity-driven diabetes and high blood pressure—the two main causes of end-stage kidney failure—rises; as the feasibility of transplantations increases; and as more hospitals and surgeons find status and profit in performing such operations. However, without any financial incentives for donors, the waiting times for transplants will increase and the shortage of organs will become more severe. As Cohen (2005, 33) said, "If the benefits of an organs market are so clear, then why do we still . . . condemn people to death and suffering while the organs that could restore them to health are instead fed to worms?"

Perhaps the strongest objections to compensating donors for their organs are the ideological and moral beliefs of some people. Financial incentives would replace altruism as a person's motivating force for donating her organs, an idea that is deeply offensive to many people. However, a trade-off must be considered. Although the thought of having people sell their organs may be offensive, thousands of people die each year because they did not receive the organ transplant they needed, and this number will rise. Which choice is more offensive—violating the strongly held beliefs of some people who view a market for human organs as repugnant or watching the suffering and subsequent loss of life of thousands of people who need an organ transplant?

Discussion Questions

1. Why have voluntary methods for increasing the supply of human organs been unsuccessful?
2. Evaluate the following proposal: People would be permitted to sell the rights to their organs (in the form of reduced health or auto insurance premiums) if they die in an accident in the coming year.
3. Would government expenditures for kidney disease (currently covered as part of Medicare for all persons) be higher or lower under a free-market system for kidneys?
4. Would the poor be disadvantaged to the benefit of the wealthy under a free-market system for selling kidneys?
5. Would it be equitable to prohibit the poor from selling their kidneys in a free market that otherwise permitted the sale of kidneys?

Notes

1. The following is a rough calculation of Medicare's five-year savings: $90,000 is the annual cost of kidney dialysis, and $59,000 is the one-time cost of a kidney transplant (the annual cost of $25,000 for immunosuppressive drugs is included in the $59,000). According to the United Network for Organ Sharing, about 103,000 patients are currently waiting for kidney transplants. Assuming that these patients receive a kidney transplant this year, Medicare costs over a five-year period will equal ($59,000 × 103,000 + 4 × $25,000 × 103,000) = $16,377,000,000 (or $16.4 billion). However, if these patients undergo dialysis for the next five years, Medicare will have spent 103,000 × $90,000 × 5 = $46,350,000,000 (or $46.4 billion). Therefore, if all patients on dialysis who are waiting for a transplant could receive a kidney, the federal government would save $46.4 billion – $16.4 billion = $30 billion over a five-year period. Data on the annual cost of kidney dialysis and on the average cost of kidney transplants are

from the United States Renal Data System (2017). The 2014 annual cost estimates in these sources were updated to 2017 dollar costs.

2. For a more general discussion of the development of kidney exchanges, see Alvin E. Roth, *Who Gets What—and Why*, chapter 3, "Lifesaving Exchanges" (New York: Houghton Mifflin Harcourt, 2015). Roth also discusses the development of matches for physician residency programs, school applications, and other programs.

3. Basing their research on an experimental game, Kessler and Roth (2012) found that giving priority on waiting lists to those who previously registered as organ donors (if they were to die) increased the number of registered donors.

4. Australia started a two-year experimental trial (to be reviewed in 2015) to compensate living kidney donors as a means of reducing the gap between the number of kidney donors and the number of patients needing kidneys. Donors will be offered up to six weeks of paid leave. On May 8, 2017, the Australian Government announced that the program would continue for four years from July 1, 2017, with some important changes. From July 1, 2017, the program was expanded to allow donors who are undergoing surgery on or after this date to claim reimbursement for some out-of-pocket expenses, enabling donors who are not employed to participate. The program provides a payment of up to nine weeks, based on a 38-hour week (a maximum of 342 hours), at up to the National Minimum Wage (Australian Government, Department of Health. 2017. *Supporting Living Organ Donors Program*. Accessed May 2018. www.health.gov.au/internet/main/publishing.nsf/content/leave-for-living-organ-donors).

5. In December 2014, the United Network for Organ Sharing began a new kidney allocation system that improved the allocation of kidneys to blacks and Hispanics. Previously, kidneys were allocated according to who waited longest. The new system allocates kidneys according to the earliest of when a patient received their first dialysis treatment or the date he or she was placed on the waiting list. Black and Hispanic patients were more likely than white patients to receive dialysis before being placed on the waiting list (Melanson et al. 2017).

Additional Readings

Becker, G., and J. Elias. 2007. "Introducing Incentives in the Market for Live and Cadaveric Organ Donations." *Journal of Economic Perspectives* 21 (3): 3–24.

Howard, D. 2007. "Producing Organ Donors." *Journal of Economic Perspectives* 21 (3): 25–36.

References

Abadie, A., and S. Gay. 2006. "The Impact of Presumed Consent Legislation on Cadaveric Organ Donation: A Cross-Country Study." *Journal of Health Economics* 25 (4): 599–620.

Bergstrom, T., S. DellaVigna, J. J. Elias, R. Garratt, M. Gibbs, J. Kessler, N. Lacetera, S. Leider, J. List, M. Macis, D. McFadden, M. Rabin, A. Roth, D. Sheehan-Connor, R. Slonim, and A. Tabarrok. 2013. "Comment on Change to the Definition of 'Human Organ' Under Section 301 of the National Organ Transplant Act of 1984. Health Resources and Services Administration, HHS. RIN 0906–AB02." Letter. Published December 2. http://everything.movie/wp-content/uploads/2016/06/Comment_Economists.pdf.

Cohen, I. 2005. "Directions for the Disposition of My (and Your) Vital Organs." *Regulation* 28 (3): 32–38.

Dunham, C. 2008. "'Body Property': Challenging the Ethical Barriers in Organ Transplantation to Protect Individual Autonomy." *Annals of Health Law* 17 (1): 39–65.

Epstein, R. 2006. "Kidney Beancounters." *Wall Street Journal*, May 15, 15.

Goldberg, D., S. Halpern, and P. Reese. 2013. "Deceased Organ Donation Consent Rates Among Racial and Ethnic Minorities and Older Potential Donors." *Critical Care Medicine* 41 (2): 496–505.

Kessler, J., and A. Roth. 2012. "Organ Allocation Policy and the Decision to Donate." *American Economic Review* 102 (5): 2018–47.

Melanson, T. A., J. M. Hockenberry, L. Plantinga, M. Basu, S. Pastan, S. Mohan, D. H. Howard, and R. E. Patzer. 2017. "New Kidney Allocation System Associated with Increased Rates of Transplants Among Black and Hispanic Patients." *Health Affairs* 36 (6): 1078–85.

Organ Procurement and Transplantation Network (OPTN). n.d. "Data Reports." Various years. Accessed May 2018. https://optn.transplant.hrsa.gov/data/view-data-reports/national-data/.

Roth, A., T. Sonmez, and M. Unver. 2005. "A Kidney Exchange Clearing House in New England." *American Economic Review* 95 (2): 376–80.

United States Renal Data System. 2017. "Economic Costs of ESRD." In *2016 USRDS Annual Data Report,* tables K.7, K.9, and K.12. Accessed May 2018. www.usrds.org/reference.aspx.

Wen, T. 2014. "Why Don't More People Want to Donate Their Organs?" *The Atlantic.* Published November 10. www.theatlantic.com/health/archive/2014/11/why-dont-people-want-to-donate-their-organs/382297/.

SHOULD PROFITS IN HEALTHCARE BE PROHIBITED?

Statements such as the following are often made as reasons for prohibiting the profit motive in healthcare.

It is fundamentally wrong to make a profit on somebody's illness. Patients' healthcare decisions should not be based on making money. Profit maximization might be an appropriate goal for other areas of the economy, such as cars and housing, but not where people's health is concerned. Should people make a profit from others' need for life-saving treatments? Profit incentivizes people to provide unnecessary care, decrease quality, raise prices, and reduce care to the sick.

The policy prescription that usually follows from such comments is a single-payer healthcare system or government price controls; in both scenarios, the government determines the allocation of capital.

Trade-offs always exist. Eliminating profits must be weighed against the "costs" of doing so. Under which approach would enrollees and patients be better off? Would substituting altruism for the incentive to earn profits achieve greater efficiency, lower healthcare costs, improved care coordination, higher quality, and more rapid innovation? Does empirical evidence exist to show that government bureaucrats are wiser than entrepreneurs in their allocation of capital and in deciding which innovations should be funded? Which approach would be subject to less interference from politicians?

Definition of Profits

Accounting Definition of Profits

What is the appropriate definition of profits? Accountants define profit as the difference between revenues (net of discounts) and the amount that is spent to earn those revenues. In addition to the direct costs of production, costs include administration, depreciation of capital, marketing, interest expense on loans, and taxes. These are "explicit" costs. Earnings and net income are sometimes used as substitute terms for profits.

Net profit margin is an indicator of a company's profitability and is calculated by dividing net profit by net revenue, converting that number into a percentage, and multiplying it by 100. The result is a measure of the net income (profit) generated from each dollar of revenue. For example, if a firm has $100,000 in revenue and its net profit is $10,000, then its profit margin is 10 percent. Profit margins are often used to compare profitability between firms in an industry.

According to the accounting definition of profit, any firm with positive net income is profitable.

Economic Definition of Profits

Economists, however, disagree with this definition. A firm might be making a positive profit, yet economists would conclude the firm is losing money. Unless the firm can increase its profit, it may go out of business.

How can a profitable firm, according to generally accepted accounting principles, be losing money according to economists? More important, whose definition of profit is a more accurate predictor of whether the firm will be able to attract more capital and expand or perhaps be forced to merge with stronger competitors if it is to survive?

To get started in business, a firm needs capital to build a facility, hire employees, buy supplies and equipment, and so forth.[1] To raise the necessary capital, the firm's management must attract investors by promising them a return on their money. Investors are only willing to provide the firm with money if they can earn a greater return than that in comparable investments. Investors can earn a return on their capital in various ways; they can invest in other businesses, either directly or through the stock exchanges, as well as buy government bonds. Because investing in a business is riskier than buying government bonds, investors would require a greater return on their capital than the interest on government bonds. The return to investors must be commensurate with the risk involved.[2]

The return to stockholders in the form of dividends is not a business expense that is deducted from revenues. The amount of money remaining after all of the firm's expenses are deducted from the firm's revenues, which accountants consider to be profit, is used to pay dividends to the firm's shareholders.[3]

Thus, if the firm earns some profit, but not enough to pay the dividends expected by investors, the accounting statement will still show that the firm has earned a profit. However, unless these "implicit" (as well as explicit) costs are covered, capital will leave the firm and seek a higher return elsewhere. The firm will not have covered all its costs and will be unable to secure the necessary capital to enable it to grow and compete with more profitable firms.

The rate of return to investors is considered to be the *cost of capital*; it is a cost and is not, according to economists, part of the firm's profit. It is the rate of return on what the firm's capital could have earned if it had been invested in its next best use, after adjustment for risk. (This is referred to as the *opportunity* cost of capital.)[4]

A firm that makes a positive accounting profit that is insufficient to pay an adequate return to its investors is considered to be losing money.

When a firm earns enough money to cover all its costs, including its cost of capital, economists consider the firm to be making *zero economic profit*. (For simplicity, this term can be referred to as a *normal profit*.) Revenue will equal the firm's explicit and implicit costs, thereby earning a normal profit. There would be no reason for capital to leave the firm or for investors to want to invest more funds in the firm. The firm is in equilibrium.

Firms require a normal profit to remain in business. Each of the firm's resources is paid what they are worth in their next best use. If they do not receive that return, those resources will move to where they can earn it, likely a different firm or industry. Normal profits typically occur in competitive industries in which no firm has a comparative advantage over other firms in the industry.

Excess Profits (Economic Profit)

Firms may earn more than a normal profit, more than is necessary to pay its cost of capital. The firm is then earning "economic profit," or simply "excess profits."

If a firm earns excess profits, is it greedy and should those excess profits be taken away?

Healthcare providers are able to earn excess profits for one of three reasons; the first is beneficial for consumers and should be encouraged, whereas the other two are disadvantageous to patients and taxpayers.

Excess Profits Based on Differentiation and Innovation

When the iPhone was invented, it was unique; nothing like it existed. A new product was made available to consumers that they were willing to buy because they valued it highly. Apple earned excess profits. Similarly, purchasers are willing to pay higher prices for innovative blockbuster drugs that treat previously untreatable diseases because the benefit they receive is worth the higher cost.

Some hospitals are able to attract a greater volume of patients (and charge insurers higher rates) because insured enrollees value those hospitals more highly than others; they have a better perceived reputation, they may offer services their competitors do not, or their location may be more convenient. These attributes differentiate them from their competitors. The same is true for some physicians. They may earn excess profits because of their reputation, their professional manner, and so on.

Hospitals, physicians, other healthcare providers, and insurers who are able to differentiate themselves in a positive manner from their competitors may be able to earn excess profits. The additional value provided to consumers justifies these excess profits.

Excess profits, earned as a result of innovation or differentiation, are temporary. Competitors begin to emulate those who earn excess profits. Over time, the differentiation between firms decreases. As imitators enter the market, prices are driven down, as are excess profits. Under competition, firms must continually strive to differentiate themselves to earn excess profits. Patients benefit when firms continually strive to develop better services to earn excess profits.

Excess Profits Based on Anticompetitive Actions

Excess profits have adverse effects on consumers when they are generated by anticompetitive behavior. For example, if two hospitals, each with large market shares in a community, merge, thereby decreasing the number of hospital competitors, the merged hospitals will be able to raise their prices and make excess profits. As generally occurs with hospital mergers, the merged hospitals have not improved services or provided a higher-quality product, although that is often the reason given by hospital executives for the merger. With fewer hospital competitors in the market, health insurers have less negotiating power and must pay higher prices to the merged hospitals.

Consumers have not benefited from the merger and, in fact, are worse off because they must pay higher insurance premiums and have fewer choices for their care. Even if hospital prices are fixed by Medicare, mergers provide hospitals with greater market power. The merged hospitals have less incentive to innovate, improve quality and care coordination, or be responsive to their patient population. Patients have fewer choices with respect to the providers from whom they can seek care.

Similarly, merged health insurers that achieve market power are likely to charge higher premiums. Medical groups, or other healthcare provider organizations, that merge do so to become dominant in their market and increase their profits. Merged organizations do not necessarily improve their services; instead, consumers are made worse off by having to pay higher prices from fewer providers.

Only when organizations have to compete are they more responsive to their purchasers. The higher the degree of monopoly power, achieved through anticompetitive actions, the less responsive the firm will be toward those it serves.

The federal antitrust agencies, the Federal Trade Commission, and the Department of Justice investigate mergers and other potential anticompetitive actions to determine whether consumers are harmed. These government agencies have investigated and brought to trial numerous cases, such as mergers between not-for-profit hospitals to gain monopoly power, boycotts by medical and dental societies against health insurers, and attempts by medical societies to engage in price fixing.

Not-for-profit healthcare organizations generally have not behaved any differently from for-profit counterparts in their search for excess profits through anticompetitive actions.

Excess Profits Based on Third-Party Payment and Lack of Patient Incentives

Another reason why healthcare providers can make excess profits is health insurance. For example, a person enrolled in Medicaid or a Medicare patient with Supplement Part B coverage pays little out of pocket when seeking medical care. When an insured person bears little of the cost of care, he has less incentive to be concerned about use of medical services, to search for lower-priced providers, or to check whether the provider has billed accurately for the services received. In these situations, providers do not need to have a better reputation, provide higher-quality care, or be the only provider to make excess profits.

Fraud is particularly rampant in Medicare and Medicaid because government oversight is less vigorous than oversight by private health insurers. The US Government Accountability Office (2015) estimates that in 2015 Medicare made improper and fraudulent payments of approximately $60 billion, 10 percent of Medicare's annual provider payments.

Excess profits generated through lack of patient and/or purchaser incentives to pay attention to the cost of care or inadequate monitoring of provider billings by the government have negative effects on rising medical costs, quality of care, and taxpayers, who pay for government-funded programs such as Medicare and Medicaid.

Do Not-for-Profit Hospitals and Insurers Generate "Profits"?

All firms require capital to get started. Not-for-profit hospitals relied heavily on charitable capital donations from members of the community to finance their development. These charitable donors did not seek a financial return on their donation. Instead, their "return" was to ensure that their community would have a hospital that improved the health of those it served. (The "return" to some donors, similar to donors in the fields of arts and education, is a degree of immortality by having their names inscribed on a specific capital project.)

Not-for-profit Blue Cross plans were begun by not-for-profit hospitals in their region that provided the initial capital. These hospitals controlled Blue Cross plans until the 1980s. In return for their capital, Blue Cross plans sold a type of hospital insurance designed to advance the self-interest of those hospitals.[5]

A not-for-profit company is supposed to provide services for the benefit of the general public, and it has restrictions on how surpluses (net income or earnings) can be distributed. Further, a not-for-profit company does not have stockholders, and its primary motive is not to increase its profit.

Legal distinctions between for-profit and not-for-profit firms are less important than any behavioral differences between the two types of organizations. Currently, many not-for-profit hospitals and insurers exist. They have expanded in size, developed new services, bought physician practices, and gained excellent reputations. How have they been able to achieve all this without earning profits? Where did the capital originate for these investments?

In reality, healthcare not-for-profits earn (or try to earn) a profit. However, the excess of their revenues over cost is not called *profit*; *net margin* or *margin* is used to refer to the difference between revenues and expenses.

If healthcare profit were eliminated, would that also include the net margins of not-for-profit hospitals and "reserves" for insurers? A statement heard repeatedly from not-for-profits is this: "no margin, no mission." Thus, even not-for-profit hospitals must earn more money than their costs if they are to expand, innovate, develop new services, buy physician practices, and even survive in a competitive environment.[6]

Even if the funds were donated to a not-for-profit healthcare provider, those funds have a "cost." That cost, however, is not included on the provider's income and expense statements. The real cost of those subsidies is their "opportunity cost," which is the value the subsidies could have produced if they were spent on another government project, such as infant nutrition or preventive health programs. Government subsidies should have a yardstick by which to judge the value of the expenditures.

The financial return to private capital is a measure of what that private capital could have earned if invested elsewhere. Donations to not-for-profits should include a market return on the subsidy as a cost on their income and expense statements. Failing to include that return understates the true cost of the not-for-profit hospital's efficiency in producing healthcare.

Not-for-profit institutions also raise capital by borrowing. Debt markets and banks try to ensure that their loans can be repaid. To demonstrate their creditworthiness, the borrower has to show that its earnings are several times greater than the interest payments on the debt. The additional earnings—above what is required to pay interest on the debt—would be considered profit or net margin.

Some not-for-profit healthcare organizations report substantial "profits." For example, not-for-profit Kaiser Foundation Health Plan and Hospitals reported a six-month net income of $1.2 billion in 2016.[7] Similarly, Blue Shield of California was reported as having a reserve or profit of $4.2 billion in 2015. Not-for-profit health insurers can use their profits in several ways, one of which is to increase the size of the reserves. Insurers' reserves are essential if they are to pay medical claims when expenses exceed premium revenues. (State insurance regulators are often concerned regarding whether those reserves are excessive, and premiums should instead be reduced.[8])

Generally, little difference exists between for-profit and not-for-profit healthcare providers in their pricing strategies, which are based on what the market will bear.[9] Both types of hospitals generally set their prices to maximize profits. For example, purchasers, such as health maintenance organizations (HMOs), who are more willing than other insurers to shift their patients to competing hospitals, receive greater not-for-profit hospital discounts than insurers who are less able to shift their use of the hospital. Automobile insurance companies typically do not have prenegotiated contracts with hospitals for insured enrollees who are hurt in auto accidents. Hospitals will charge these insurers much higher rates than insurers who have negotiated contracts.

The main cost advantage that not-for-profits have over for-profits is not that they don't earn profits, but that they are exempt from federal and state income taxes and state sales taxes. One might expect that this competitive advantage would enable them to charge lower prices than their for-profit competitors and drive them from the market. Yet, this has not occurred.

What Are the Consequences of Eliminating "Profit" from Healthcare?

If healthcare profits were prohibited, would healthcare costs and premiums be lower and healthcare more affordable? The history of not-for-profit firms provides some indication of what would likely occur if all healthcare organizations had to be not-for-profit and government were responsible for the allocation of capital.

Goals and Behavior of Not-for-Profits in Noncompetitive Markets

The difference between for-profit and not-for-profit ownership lies in what each type of hospital (or insurer) does with its profits. When only normal profits are earned, each type of institution must use such profits to pay the full costs of the enterprise, including a return to capital and debt.

When excess profits are earned, either in the short or long run, shareholders in for-profit firms receive a greater return after taxes are paid. Not-for-profit hospitals may spend their excess profits in several ways. They may invest in new facilities and services (some of which may not be profitable but may increase the hospital's prestige); they may subsidize certain unprofitable services; or they may increase employee benefits and salaries.

What the not-for-profit hospital or insurer does with its excess profits depends on management and its board of directors' objectives. When not-for-profit hospitals are not subject to competitive pressures, their actions have greatly varied. Some not-for-profits have used their "profits" to benefit their communities. Others have used their "profits" for ends that are less noble.[10] Once hospitals no longer have to compete, and they cannot distribute their profits to stakeholders, their production costs will rise faster than they would otherwise.

Lack of Incentives to Respond to Purchasers

Prohibiting, or even limiting, profits in healthcare will similarly reduce the public benefits that profits provide. The public, and patients, benefit from the profit motive among healthcare providers and insurers in the following ways.

Profits are the incentive for firms to be responsive to the desires of purchasers. Firms try to gain a competitive advantage by providing better amenities, achieving a better reputation, improving the quality of care, providing better patient services and improved access to care, and achieving greater efficiencies. Firms that are more successful in meeting the needs of purchasers are able to increase their market share. Patients, enrollees, and purchasers (with an incentive and information to make appropriate choices) will switch to firms that are better able to meet their needs. Firms that do not adapt are driven out of business.

Only firms that have gained monopoly power through anticompetitive actions, such as monopolization of the market through mergers, price fixing, legal barriers to entry, or lack of consumer information, can continue to earn a profit while neglecting the preferences of buyers. Patient satisfaction and quality of care are lower when patients cannot choose and are unable to shift to other healthcare providers and payers.

Lack of Incentives for Innovation

Patents on blockbuster drugs result in monopolies, but pharmaceutical company profits are the incentive for developing innovative drugs. Without the opportunity to earn excess profits, firms would have no incentive to devote the huge amounts of capital and incur the large risk involved to develop innovative drugs that the public values and is willing to buy.

The search for profits has led to innovations in the delivery and financing of health services. Until the late 1940s, not-for-profit Blue Cross plans were the dominant insurers, offering only one type of health plan. Commercial insurers entered the health insurance market by offering greater choice of insurance plans, using deductibles and copayments to lower premiums. These for-profit insurers also based their premiums on the actuarial risk group of the enrollee (experience rating), rather than on the average risk of all insured enrollees (community rating). Blue Cross had to adapt to remain competitive.

In the 1980s and 1990s, entrepreneurs saw a great opportunity to profit if they could reduce rising healthcare costs. Hospitals were inefficient and costly, and patients were being hospitalized who could be treated in less costly settings. The pursuit of profits led to major changes in the delivery and payment of care. For-profit entrepreneurs innovated in the use of lower-cost (and patient preferred) outpatient surgery centers, forcing not-for-profit hospitals and (hospital-controlled) Blue Cross to similarly expand their use of outpatient surgery.

The growth of HMOs and the managed care revolution continue today. Utilization was reduced and hospitals were forced to compete to join HMO networks. Hospitals had to become efficient to survive, and many went out of business. Lower HMO premiums forced existing insurers to adopt the same managed care techniques to survive. Consumers benefited through lower premiums (see exhibit 20.3).

High-deductible health plans, health savings accounts, retail medical clinics, reference pricing, clinical apps for smartphones, virtual and digital access to physicians, and large data analyses are among the many examples of ongoing private sector innovations that are lowering costs and increasing patient access to care.

The prospect of excess profits continues to change the healthcare financing and delivery system. Patients are being moved to less costly and patient-preferred settings. They have an increased choice of health plans, lower premiums than would otherwise be the case, and greater access to care through the use of digital technology.

The profit motive has led to the entry of innovative firms that were able to lower medical costs and be more responsive to the public's interests. Without the profit incentive, why would firms be willing to risk their capital to try and innovate to the benefit of purchasers? How would the medical sector be able to attract high-quality medical personnel and healthcare executives? If profit were prohibited, who would perform the functions of for-profit and not-for-profit firms?

Other mechanisms have been tried, such as command and control systems, price regulation, and government control and allocation of capital. However, historically, these alternative approaches have not been nearly as successful in improving consumer welfare as has the profit incentive.

Inefficient Allocation of Capital

Government regulators are unable to allocate capital better than the private market. Without profits as a measure of success in meeting the public's demand, where would government regulators get the information necessary to allocate capital to healthcare projects and to healthcare organizations? Profits (and expected profits) are necessary information to guide the allocation of resources.

What incentive do regulators have to take on risk and innovate? They cannot legally earn more money, and if they take any risk in allocating capital and their project fails, they might get fired or demoted. Government regulators' incentive is to play it safe and not undertake risky innovations or upset politically powerful organizations. Politics often takes precedence in regulatory policy and in the allocation of federal capital subsidies. The following are examples of how government has allocated capital.

Certificate of Need: In 1974, Congress enacted a law, referred to as Certificate of Need (CON), to limit rising medical expenditures by controlling hospital capital expenditures. Government regional planning agencies were established to review all hospital capital expenditures exceeding $100,000. Not only did CON fail to limit hospital expenditure increases, but existing hospitals "captured" the CON planning agency and used the controls on capital investment to limit competition by preventing new hospitals from entering their market (Mitchell 2016, 22–24). The law, and hospitals' self-interest, was used to prevent competitive free-standing outpatient surgery centers from being established. Although the federal law was repealed in 1979, many states still have a CON agency, which is used to benefit existing healthcare firms by serving as an entry barrier to competitive healthcare firms.

Medicare Demonstration Project: A government demonstration project showed that Medicare could lower the cost of acquiring durable medical equipment (DME), but the program was not implemented. The DME providers, who would have lost revenues, objected to their legislators, and the program was cancelled (Newman et al. 2017).

Solyndra: Solyndra was a solar-panel start-up that failed, leaving taxpayers liable for $535 million in federal guarantees. Despite studies expressing doubt about the potential for success, administration officials allocated large sums of capital to Solyndra and other similar companies based on a political agenda (Leonnig and Stephens 2012).

Consumer Operated and Oriented Plans (CO-OPs)
The ACA provided loans to 23 not-for-profit health insurance CO-OPs ($2.4 billion was eventually spent). The justification for establishing the CO-OPs was based on the faulty premise that the CO-OPs, being not-for-profit, would have lower costs and could charge lower premiums, thereby promoting competition on the health insurance exchanges. The CO-OPs received subsidized loans. Although the government expected that one-third of the CO-OPs would fail, the interest rate charged to the CO-OPs did not reflect the very high risk of failure. Government is less concerned about risk when taxpayer funds are used than are private investors using their own funds.

Not-for-profit health plans, such as Blue Cross and Blue Shield, and for-profit insurers were already competing on the health insurance exchanges. These plans had achieved economies of scale. How were the newly established CO-OPs expected to compete against these large Blue plans?

Of the 23 CO-OPs, only 4 were expected to offer plans in 2018. The other CO-OPs failed because of large financial losses and operational problems (Norris 2017). CO-OPs exist and can even prosper in many areas of the economy, but they have grown very slowly and require sufficient capital to do so. Typically, CO-OPs accumulate reserves (profits) to finance their growth and to offset losses until they can achieve economic efficiency. The health insurance CO-OPs made many mistakes, such as hiring unqualified managers and pricing their premiums too low relative to the risk level of their enrollees; in addition, they tried to expand too rapidly (Harrington 2016). As occurs in many new businesses, their projections were inaccurate, they suffered large losses, and they required more capital but didn't have investors who could provide additional risk capital.

An important role of private investors (for which they require a profit commensurate with their investment risk) is to evaluate the quality of the management of a start-up business. Private investors will also provide sufficient capital to sustain the start-up when it incurs losses. When hospitals started Blue Cross plans, they provided the capital to ensure that these plans succeeded.

The CO-OPs are cooperatives, owned by their enrollees. They had no backup source of capital. Consequently, once they started to incur losses, they failed. Evergreen, a Maryland co-op, stated on its website, "For far too long, health insurance carriers have put profits ahead of people. We were founded by healthcare leaders who believe there's a better way forward—for the health of Maryland and for future of healthcare in America." Subsequently, as its losses mounted and to prevent bankruptcy, Evergreen changed to a for-profit company to attract private investors who provided the risk capital needed to keep the co-op in business (Goldstein 2016).

Summary

Agreeing on an appropriate definition of "profit" is necessary to understand the consequences of eliminating profit from healthcare. The accounting definition of profit is the difference between revenues and explicit costs, as commonly used in financial statements. The economists' definition differs in that it considers the rate of return on capital as a cost to the firm. It is an implicit cost, not a profit, because if capital does not earn its return, it will leave and be invested elsewhere.

The economic definition of profit leads to better predictions of the firm's behavior. If the firm's revenues cover all of the firm's costs, including the rate of return on capital (adjusted for the riskiness of the investment), then the firm is making a "normal" profit. The consequence of earning less than normal profits is that the firm has not covered its cost of capital. Capital will leave and the firm will eventually go out of business.

Not-for-profit healthcare providers and insurers must also generate a profit or margin (the excess of revenues minus explicit costs); otherwise, they would not have the necessary capital to expand, invest in new equipment and technology, purchase physicians' practices, hire staff, or even survive.

Eliminating a firm's accounting "profit" or "margin" will cause for-profit firms to exit the healthcare industry and limit the ability of not-for-profit providers and insurers to innovate or provide additional services to patients. Patients will be worse off under such a policy.

Allowing healthcare firms to earn "excess" profits is also essential to incentivize them to innovate, improve services, reduce costs, and be responsive to patient preferences. Patients benefit when firms compete on the basis of service and quality. When a firm achieves excess profits through anticompetitive mergers or through lack of patient information or incentives to choose among less costly and higher-quality providers, these concerns should be addressed separately through antitrust actions and changing patient incentives so that cost of care is considered as well as benefits.

Access to capital is essential for innovations to occur, for firms to grow, and for patients to benefit from medical research. Without investors' expectation of profit, capital would shift to other sectors of the economy, and healthcare would remain as it was 50 years ago.

The alternative to relying on profit (or private donations) to allocate capital is to rely on government and its regulators to decide which firms are more deserving, who should expand, what services should be provided, by which type of provider, and what innovations should be financed. When for-profit firms fail, investors lose money, not taxpayers. Government is less able than private investors (using their own funds) to properly evaluate the investment prospects and management ability of healthcare firms. Government allocation of capital is often based on politics rather than on potential economic performance. Examples of misallocation of capital are numerous in the healthcare field and other areas, such as the failed ACA CO-OPs and the Solyndra scandal.

Patients' best interests are not served by removing profit from healthcare. The fact that a firm is not-for-profit does not guarantee that its costs are lower, its quality is higher, or it will act more in the interests of its patients than will for-profit firms. The Federal Trade Commission has successfully sued not-for-profit hospitals that have merged to gain market power and then raised their prices. Medical schools have failed to innovate in their curricula, despite many efforts to do so (Nutter and Whitcomb 2005).

The Department of Veterans Affairs healthcare system acquired a notorious reputation for falsifying waiting lists and denying care to veterans, resulting in the deaths of many patients (Slack 2017). Not-for-profit firms without competition will act no differently from for-profit monopolies.

The best guarantor of efficiency and responsiveness to the consumer is price-competitive markets with informed purchasers, regardless of whether providers are for-profit or not-for-profit firms.[11] The role of government in a profit-driven system is to remove the impediments to competition, eliminate barriers to entry that are meant to protect incumbents, promote dissemination of information so purchasers can be informed, and subsidize those with low incomes so they have the same choices among competitive healthcare firms as everyone else.

Discussion Questions

1. What is the difference between the accounting and economic definitions of profit?
2. What is the difference between normal and excess profit?
3. Under what circumstances does excess profit benefit consumers?
4. Under what circumstances does excess profit harm consumers?
5. What remedies are available when excess profits occur because of anticompetitive actions, lack of patient information, or comprehensive insurance coverage (because patients have little incentive to be concerned with prices)?
6. What functions do profits serve in healthcare?

Notes

1. Firms cannot start, grow, and survive on only loans. Banks and the debt markets lend money based on the risk that the loan will be repaid with interest. A firm without any assets is an extremely poor risk. As the firm has greater amounts of invested capital and improved earnings prospects, loans become less risky. Once a firm has incurred too much debt (in relation to its capital), loans again become very risky.
2. Physicians, and other healthcare professionals, also must earn a profit based on their large investment in the cost of their medical education. The capital outlay for their investment includes, in addition to tuition, cost of books, and other supplies, the opportunity cost of not earning an income comparable to other college graduates during their additional years of training. Their higher income represents the return on their education investment and their fewer working years. Physicians

in some specialties earn excess profits because entry into those residency programs is limited.

3. Instead of paying dividends, firms may reinvest their dividends and provide a return to investors in the form of a higher stock price. The tax consequences of dividends and capital gains on a higher stock price differ.

4. When a firm has both debt and investor capital (equity), then the expected cost of debt and return to equity, adjusted for risk, must be calculated to determine the firm's overall cost of capital.

5. For example, Blue Cross sold only inpatient hospital insurance. A Blue Cross patient was entitled to a 30-day hospital stay and was not responsible for any out-of-pocket payments. Because patients did not have to pay a deductible or copays, hospitals did not have to compete on price for such patients. A Blue Cross insurer had to sign up at least 75 percent of the hospitals in its market; therefore, hospitals did not have to compete to be included in the Blue Cross provider network. Also, when outpatient surgery centers opened, Blue Cross, controlled by hospitals, refused to cover care in centers unaffiliated with existing hospitals. It was more expensive for a Blue Cross patient to go to an unaffiliated surgery center than to go to a hospital for surgery. Hospitals' self-interest was an important reason why Blue Cross insurance was more costly than commercial insurance, which offered broader coverage and included patient copays and deductibles. Blue Cross plans eventually had to break away from hospital control to survive in a price-competitive insurance market.

6. Relying on 2013 Medicare Cost Reports and Final Rule Data from the Centers for Medicare & Medicaid Services, Bai and Anderson (2016) used the measure of net income from patient care services per adjusted discharge to calculate the profitability of acute care hospitals. They determined that seven of the ten most profitable hospitals were not-for-profit, and each of those hospitals earned more than $163 million in total profits from patient care services.

7. For the six months ending June 30, 2016, Kaiser Foundation Health Plan Inc., Kaiser Foundation Hospitals, and their respective subsidiaries reported net income of $1.2 billion, compared with $2.1 billion for the same period in 2015 (Kaiser Permanente 2016). Kaiser also reported that year-to-date capital spending was $1.28 billion, which reflects continued investments in facilities and technology to support care delivery. These investments in facilities are to ensure that Kaiser Permanente can meet the needs of its growing membership and communities.

8. The California Franchise Tax Board removed the tax exemption of Blue Shield of California in 2015 (Cohen 2015). Blue Shield has appealed that decision. One reason given for the state's action is that Blue Shield maintains a reserve of $4.2 billion, which critics claim is four times greater than the amount Blue Shield requires for potential future claims. Given the large reserve, greater than the amount that Blue Shield claimed it needed to meet losses and future claims, critics wondered why Blue Shield needed the rate increases it requested.

9. Little difference also exists between for-profit and not-for-profit healthcare providers in how much charity care is provided, although not-for-profit teaching hospitals provide a greater degree of charity care. (See chapter 15, "Do Nonprofit Hospitals Behave Differently Than For-Profit Hospitals?") Congress revoked Blue Cross's federal tax exemption in 1986. The General Accounting Office concluded that the difference between Blue Cross and Blue Shield and for-profit insurers was not sufficient to justify the Blues' federal tax-exempt status (*New York Times* 1986).

10. When Medicare began, hospitals were reimbursed according to their costs of caring for the aged. Cost-based payment resulted in hospitals paying higher wages to their executives and staff. Cost reimbursement enabled hospitals to invest in the latest technology, facilities, and services. Costs increased and quality of care declined in many of these hospitals. Studies found that hospital open-heart surgery units that performed few surgeries cost more and had worse outcomes than units that performed a large number of surgeries (Robinson and Luft 1987).

11. In 1776, Adam Smith wrote, "It is not from the benevolence of the butcher, the brewer, or the baker that we can expect our dinner, but from their regard to their own interest."

References

Bai, G., and G. Anderson. 2016. "A More Detailed Understanding of Factors Associated with Hospital Profitability." *Health Affairs* 35 (5): 889–97.

Cohen, R. 2015. "CA Pulls Tax-Exempt Status of Blue Shield of California." *Nonprofit Quarterly*. Published March 19. https://nonprofitquarterly.org/2015/03/19/ca-pulls-tax-exempt-status-of-nonprofit-blue-shield-of-california/.

Goldstein, A. 2016. "Maryland's ACA Health Co-op Will Switch to For-Profit to Save Itself." *Washington Post*. Published October 3. www.washingtonpost.com/news/health-science/wp/2016/10/03/marylands-aca-health-co-op-will-switch-to-for-profit-to-save-itself/.

Harrington, S. 2016. "Review of the Affordable Care Act Health Insurance CO-OP Program." Statement Before the Permanent Subcommittee on Investigations, Committee on Homeland Security and Government Affairs, US Senate, March 10, 2016. www.hsgac.senate.gov/download/harrington-testimony_-psi-2016-03-10.

Kaiser Permanente. 2016. "Kaiser Foundation Health Plan and Hospitals Report Second Quarter 2016 Financial Results." Posted August 5. https://share.kaiserpermanente.org/article/kaiser-foundation-health-plan-hospitals-report-second-quarter-2016-financial-results/.

Leonnig, C. D., and J. Stephens. 2012. "Energy Dept. E-mails on Solyndra Provide New Details on White House Involvement." *Washington Post.* Published August 9. www.washingtonpost.com/politics/energy-dept-e-mails-on-solyndra-provide-new-details-on-white-house-involvement/2012/08/08/668dc042-e162-11e1-a25e-15067bb31849_story.html.

Mitchell, M. D. 2016. "Do Certificate-of-Need Laws Limit Spending?" Mercatus working paper. Published September. www.mercatus.org/system/files/mercatus-mitchell-con-healthcare-spending-v1a.pdf.

Newman, D., E. Barrette, and K. McGraves-Lloyd. 2017. "Medicare Competitive Bidding Program Realized Price Savings for Durable Medical Equipment Purchases." *Health Affairs* 36 (8): 1367–75.

New York Times. 1986. "Blue Cross Tax Status Is Challenged." Published July 4. www.nytimes.com/1986/07/04/us/blue-cross-tax-status-is-challenged.html.

Norris, L. 2017. "CO-OP Health Plans: Patients' Interests First." Healthinsurance.org. Published August 27. www.healthinsurance.org/obamacare/co-op-health-plans-put-patients-interests-first/.

Nutter, D., and M. Whitcomb. 2005. "The AAMC Project on the Clinical Education of Medical Students." Association of American Medical Colleges. Accessed May 2018. www.aamc.org/download/68522/data/clinicalskillsnutter.pdf.

Robinson, J., and H. Luft. 1987. "Competition and the Cost of Hospital Care, 1972–1982." *Journal of the American Medical Association* 257 (23): 3241–45.

Slack, D. 2017. "VA Still in Critical Condition, Secretary David Shulkin Says." *USA Today.* Published May 31. www.usatoday.com/story/news/politics/2017/05/31/veterans-affairs-secretary-david-shulkin-state-of-va/102333422/.

Smith, A. 1776. *An Inquiry into the Nature and Causes of the Wealth of Nations.* Edited by E. Cannan (London: Methuen, 1904). Accessed May 2018. http://oll.libertyfund.org/titles/smith-an-inquiry-into-the-nature-and-causes-of-the-wealth-of-nations-cannan-ed-vol-1.

US Government Accountability Office. 2015. *Medicare Program: Additional Actions Needed to Improve Eligibility Verification of Providers and Suppliers.* Published June. www.gao.gov/assets/680/671021.pdf.

THE ROLE OF GOVERNMENT IN MEDICAL CARE

G overnment intervention in the financing and delivery of medical services is pervasive. On the financing side, the Affordable Care Act (ACA) provides subsidies and tax credits to individuals, small businesses, and low-income employees, and employers are required to provide health insurance benefits to their employees. Further, hospital and physician services for the aged are subsidized (Medicare), and a separate payroll tax pays for those subsidies. Medicaid, a federal/state matching program, pays for medical services for the poor and near-poor. Further, a large network of state and county hospitals is in place; health professional schools are subsidized; loan programs for students in the health professions are guaranteed by the government; employer-paid health insurance is excluded from taxable income; military members, retirees, and their families have access to a separate healthcare program called TRICARE; and medical research is subsidized. In all, government pays for more than 50 percent of total health expenditures.

In addition to these financing programs, extensive government regulations influence the financing and delivery of medical services. For example, state licensing boards determine the criteria for entry into different professions, and practice regulations determine which tasks can be performed by which professional groups. In some states, hospital investment is subject to state review, hospital and physician prices under Medicare are regulated, health insurance companies are regulated by the states, and each state mandates which benefits (e.g., in Minnesota, hair transplants) and providers (e.g., in Washington, naturopaths) should be included in health insurance sold in that state (Bunce 2013).

The role of government in the financing and delivery of medical services (and through federal and state regulations) is extensive. To understand the reasons for these different types of government intervention, and at times seemingly contradictory policies, it is necessary to understand the two theories that underlie the government's objectives.

Public-Interest Theory of Government

The public-interest, or traditional, theory of government can be classified according to its policy objectives and the policy instruments used to achieve those objectives. The objectives of government in the healthcare field are twofold: (1) to redistribute medical resources to those least able to purchase medical services and (2) to improve the economic efficiency by which medical services are purchased and delivered. These traditional objectives of government—redistribution and economic efficiency (also referred to as *market failure*)—can be achieved by using one or more of the following policy instruments: expenditure, taxation, and regulation. (Government provision of services, such as in Veterans Affairs hospitals, is rarely proposed as a policy instrument in the United States.)

These policy instruments—expenditure, taxation, and regulation—can be applied to the purchaser (demand) side or the supplier (provider) side of the market. For example, expenditure policies on the demand side are Medicare and Medicaid, and on the supply side are subsidies for hospital construction and health manpower training programs. Taxation policies on the demand side cover tax-exempt employer-paid health insurance, and on the supply side are tax-exempt bonds for nonprofit hospitals. The individual mandate to buy health insurance is a regulation policy on the demand side; on the supply side are licensing requirements, restrictions on the tasks various healthcare professionals can perform, entry barriers to building a hospital or a new hospice in a region, and regulated provider prices for hospitals and physicians under Medicare.

These policy objectives and instruments—which can be used to classify each type of government health policy according to objectives, the type of policy instrument used, and whether the policy instrument is directed toward the demand side or supply side of the market—are shown in exhibit 31.1. According to the public-interest theory, each policy should achieve one of the two government objectives.

Redistribution

Redistribution causes a change in wealth. According to the public-interest theory of government, society makes a value judgment that medical services

		Government Objectives	
Government Policy and Instruments		**Redistribution**	**Efficiency Improvement**
Expenditure {	Demand side		
	Supply side		
Taxation (+/−) {	Demand side		
	Supply side		
Regulation {	Demand side		
	Supply side		

EXHIBIT 31.1
Health Policy Objectives and Interventions

should be provided to those with low income and should be financed by taxing those with high income. Redistributive programs typically lower the cost of services to a particular group by enabling members of that group to purchase those services at below-market prices. These benefits are financed by imposing a cost on some other group. Two large redistributive programs are Medicare for the aged and Medicaid for the medically indigent. Any redistributive medical program such as Medicaid should have the redistributive effects shown in exhibit 31.2.

Efficiency Improvement

The second traditional objective of government is to improve the efficiency with which society allocates resources. Inefficiency in resource allocation can occur, for example, when firms in a market have monopoly power or when externalities exist. A firm has monopoly power when it is able to charge a price that exceeds its cost by more than a normal profit. Monopoly is inefficient because it produces a level of service (output) that is too small. The additional benefit to purchasers from consuming a service (as indicated by its price) is greater than the cost of producing that benefit; therefore, more resources should flow into that industry until the additional benefit equals the additional cost of producing it.

Several bases of monopoly power exist: (1) The market may have only one firm, as with a natural monopoly such as an electric company; (2) barriers to entry into a market may exist; (3) firms may collude on raising their prices; and (4) a lack of information may mean consumers are unable to judge the differences in price, quality, and service among suppliers. In each of these situations, the prices charged will exceed the costs of producing the product (which include a normal profit). The appropriate government remedy for decreasing monopoly power is to eliminate barriers to entry into a market, prevent price collusion, and improve dissemination of information among consumers.

The other situation in which the allocation of resources can be improved is when externalities occur—that is, when someone undertakes an action and in so doing affects others who are not part of that transaction. The effects on others could be positive or negative. For example, a utility company using high-sulfur coal to produce electricity also produces air pollution. As a result of the air pollution, residents in surrounding communities may have a higher-than-average incidence of respiratory illness. Resources are misallocated because the cost

	Low Income	High Income
Benefits	X	
Costs		X

EXHIBIT 31.2
Determining the Redistributive Effects of Government Programs

of producing electricity excludes the costs imposed on others. As a result, too much electricity is being generated. If the costs of electricity production also include the costs imposed on others, the price of electricity would be higher and its demand lower. The allocation of resources would be improved if the utility's costs include production and external costs. The appropriate role of government in such a situation is to determine the costs imposed on others and to tax the utility company an equivalent amount. (This subject is discussed more completely in chapter 33.)

According to the public-interest theory, if a policy does not have redistribution as its objective, then its goal should be to achieve greater economic efficiency.

Economic Theory of Regulation

Dissatisfaction with the public-interest theory occurred for several reasons. Instead of simply regulating natural monopolies, government has also regulated competitive industries (e.g., airlines, trucks, taxicabs), as well as various professions. Further, unregulated firms always want to enter regulated markets. To prevent entry into regulated industries, the government establishes entry barriers. If the government supposedly reduces prices in regulated markets—hence, the firm's profitability—why should firms seek to enter a regulated industry?

To reconcile these apparent contradictions with the public-interest theory of government, an alternative theory of government behavior—the economic theory of regulation—was developed (Stigler 1971). (For a more complete discussion of this theory and its applicability to the healthcare field, see Feldstein [2006].) The basic assumption underlying the economic theory is that political markets are no different from economic markets; individuals and firms seek to further their self-interest. Firms undertake investments in private markets to achieve a high rate of return. Why would the same firms not invest in legislation if it also offered a high rate of return? Organized groups are willing to pay a price for legislative benefits. This price is political support, which brings together the suppliers and demanders of legislative benefits.

The Suppliers: Legislators

The suppliers of legislative benefits are legislators, and their assumed goal is to maximize their chances for reelection. As the late Senator Everett Dirksen said, "The first law of politics is to get elected; the second law is to be reelected." To be reelected requires political support, which consists of campaign contributions, votes, and volunteer time. Legislators are assumed to be rational—that is, to make cost–benefit calculations when faced with demands for legislation. However, the legislator's cost–benefit calculations are not the costs and benefits to society of enacting particular legislation. Instead, the benefits are the additional political support the legislator would receive from supporting the legislation, and the costs are the political support she would lose as a result of supporting the legislation. When the benefits to the legislators exceed the costs, they will support the legislation.

The Demanders: Those with a Concentrated Interest

Those who have a concentrated interest—that is, those for whom the legislation will have a large economic effect—are more likely to be successful in the legislative marketplace. It becomes worthwhile for the group to incur the costs to organize, represent its interests before legislators, and raise political support to achieve the profits that favorable legislation can provide. For this reason, only those with a concentrated interest will demand legislative benefits.

Diffuse Costs

When legislative benefits are provided to one group, others must bear the costs. When only one group has a concentrated interest in the legislation, that group is more likely to be successful if the costs to finance those benefits are not obvious and can be spread over a large number of people. When this occurs, the costs are said to be diffuse. For example, assume that ten firms are in an industry, and if legislation is enacted that limits imports that compete with their products, they will be able to raise their prices, thereby receiving $300 million in legislative benefits. These firms have a concentrated interest ($300 million) in trying to enact such legislation. The costs of these legislative benefits are financed by a small increase in the price of the product amounting to $1 per person.

Often, the fact that legislation raises their costs is not obvious to consumers. Further, even if consumers were aware of the legislation's effect, it would not be worthwhile for them to organize and represent their interests to forestall a price increase of only $1 a year. The costs of trying to prevent the price increase would exceed the potential savings.

It is easier (less costly) for providers than for consumers to organize, provide political support, and impose a diffuse cost on others. For this reason, much legislation has affected entry into the healthcare professions, which tasks are reserved for certain professions, how (and which) providers are paid under public medical programs, why subsidies for medical education are given to schools and not to students (otherwise, schools would have to compete for students), and so on. Most health issues have been relatively technical, such as the training of health professionals, certification of their quality, methods of payment, controls on hospital capital investment, and so forth. The higher medical prices resulting from regulations that benefit physicians, for example, by successfully placing limits on nurses' scope of practice, have been diffuse and not visible to consumers.

Entry Barriers to Regulated Markets

The economic theory of regulation provides an explanation for these dissatisfactions with the public-interest theory. Firms in competitive markets seek regulation to earn higher profits than would be available without regulation. Prices in regulated markets (e.g., interstate air travel) were always higher than those in unregulated markets (e.g., intrastate air travel), enabling regulated firms to earn greater profits. These higher prices gave unregulated firms an incentive to try to enter regulated markets. Government, on behalf of the regulated industry, imposed barriers to prevent low-priced competitors from gaining entry. Otherwise, the regulated firms could not earn more than a competitive rate of return.

Through legislation, firms try to receive the monopoly profits they are unable to achieve through market competition.

Opposing Concentrated Interests

When only one group has a concentrated interest in the outcome of legislation and the costs are diffuse, legislators will respond to the political support provided by the group that seeks to have favorable legislation enacted. When there are opposing groups, each with a concentrated interest in the outcome, legislators are likely to reach a compromise between the competing demanders of legislative benefits. Rather than balancing the gain in political support from one group against the loss from the other, legislators prefer to receive political support from both groups and impose diffuse costs on those offering little political support.

Visible Redistributive Effects

When the beneficiaries are specific population groups, such as the aged, the redistributive effects of legislation are meant to be visible. Medicare is an example. By making clear which population groups will benefit, legislators hope to receive their political support. The costs (taxes) of financing such visible redistributive programs, however, are still designed to be diffuse so as not to generate political opposition from others.

A small, diffuse tax imposed on many people, such as a sales or a payroll tax, is the only way large sums of money can be raised to finance visible redistributive programs with little opposition. These taxes are regressive; the tax represents a greater portion of income from low-income employees and consumers. Economists have determined that payroll taxes, even when imposed on the employer, are borne mostly by the employee. (The employer is only interested in the total cost of an employee; thus, the employee eventually receives a lower wage than he would have received if these costs had not been imposed.) Imposing part of the tax on the employer, however, gives the impression that employees are paying a smaller portion of it than they really are. The remainder of the tax is shifted forward to consumers in the form of higher prices for the goods and services they purchase, which is also regressive.

Medicare: A Case Study of the Success of Concentrated Interests

The concentrated interests of medical providers and the subsequent diffuse (small) costs imposed on consumers explain much of the legislative history of the financing and delivery of medical services until the early 1960s. The enactment and design of Medicare illustrate the real purpose of visible redistribution policy: to redistribute wealth—that is, increase benefits to politically powerful groups without their paying the full costs of those benefits by shifting the costs to the less politically powerful.

Throughout the 1950s and early 1960s, the American Federation of Labor and Congress of Industrial Organizations (AFL-CIO) unions had a concentrated interest in their retirees' medical costs that placed them in opposition to the American Medical Association (AMA). Employers had not prefunded union retirees' medical costs, but instead paid them as part of current labor expenses. If union retirees' medical expenses could be shifted away from the employer, those funds would be available to spend as higher wages to union employees.

To ensure that their union retirees would be eligible for Medicare, AFL-CIO insisted that eligibility be based on having paid into the Social Security system while working, and that the new Medicare program (hospital services) be financed by a separate Medicare payroll tax to be included as part of the Social Security tax. Although the current retirees had not contributed to the proposed Medicare program, they were to become immediately eligible because they had paid Social Security taxes. The use of the Social Security system to determine eligibility became the central issue in the debate over Medicare (Feldstein 2006).

The AMA was willing to have government assistance go to those unable to afford medical services, which would have increased the demand for physicians. Thus, the AMA favored a means-tested program funded by general tax revenues because it was concerned that including the nonpoor in the new program would merely substitute government payment for private payment. The AMA believed such a program would cost too much, leading to controls on hospital and physician fees.

With the landslide victory of President Johnson in 1964, AFL-CIO achieved its objective. Once Social Security financing was used to determine Medicare eligibility, Medicare Part B (physician services) was added, financed by general tax revenues. Although AFL-CIO won on the financing mechanism, Congress acceded to the demands of the AMA (as well as the American Hospital Association) on all other aspects of the legislation. The system of payment to hospitals and physicians promoted inefficiency (cost-plus payments to hospitals), and restrictions limiting competition were placed on alternative delivery systems.

This historic conflict between opposing concentrated interests in medical care left both sides victorious, and it illustrates how the power of government can be used to benefit politically important groups. As a result of Medicare, a massive redistribution of wealth took place in society. The beneficiaries were the aged, union members, and medical providers, and the benefits were financed by a diffuse, regressive tax (the Medicare payroll tax) on a large group—the working population, who also paid higher prices for their medical services and more income taxes to finance Medicare Part B. Medicare was designed to be both inefficient and inequitable simply because it was in the economic interests of those with concentrated interests.

Medicaid and Medicare

To understand the two main redistributive programs in the United States, one must recognize the differences in the sources of political support. Medicaid is a means-tested program for the poor funded from general tax revenues. Because the poor (who have low voting participation rates) are unable to provide legislators with political support, the support for Medicaid comes from the middle class (who must agree to higher taxes to provide the poor with medical benefits). The inadequacy of Medicaid in every state, the conditions necessary to achieve Medicaid eligibility, the low levels of eligibility, and beneficiaries' lack of access to medical providers are related to the generosity (or lack thereof) of the middle class. The beneficiaries of Medicare, on the other hand, are the elderly (who generally have the highest voting participation rate of any age group). The aged, together with their adult children, provide the political support for the program. As the cost of Medicare has risen, government has raised the Medicare payroll tax and lowered payments to providers rather than reduce benefits to this politically powerful group.[1]

The political necessity of keeping costs diffuse explains why Medicare and producer regulation were financed using regressive taxes—either payroll taxes or higher prices for medical services. Spreading the costs over large populations keeps those costs diffuse, with the net effect being that low-income people pay the costs and high-income people (e.g., physicians, well-to-do elderly) receive the benefits. Determining who receives the benefits and who bears the costs, according to the economic theory, is not based on income (see exhibit 31.2), but rather on which groups are able to offer political support (the beneficiaries) and which groups are unable to do so (those who bear the costs). Regressive taxes typically are used to finance producer regulation and provide benefits to specific population groups.

Changes in Health Policies

Health policies change over time because groups who previously bore a diffuse cost develop a concentrated interest. Until the 1960s, medical societies were the main groups with a concentrated interest in the financing and delivery of medical services. Thus, the delivery system was structured to benefit physicians. The physician-to-population ratio remained constant for 15 years (until the mid-1960s) at 141 per 100,000 (see exhibit 4.1), state restrictions were imposed on health maintenance organizations (HMOs) to limit their development, advertising was prohibited, and restrictions were placed on other health professionals to limit their ability to compete with physicians. Financing mechanisms also benefited physicians; until the 1980s, capitation payment for HMOs was prohibited under Medicare and Medicaid, and competitors to physicians were excluded from reimbursement under public and private insurance systems.

As the costs of medical care continued to increase rapidly for government and employers, their previously diffuse costs became concentrated. Under Medicare, the federal government was faced with the choice of raising taxes or reducing benefits to the aged, both of which would have cost the Johnson administration political support. Successive administrations developed a concentrated interest in lowering the rate of increase in medical expenditures. Similarly, large employers worried that rising medical costs were making them less competitive internationally. The pressures for cost containment increased as the costs of an inefficient delivery and payment system grew larger. Rising medical expenditures are no longer a diffuse cost to large purchasers of medical services.

Other professional organizations, such as the associations for psychologists, chiropractors, podiatrists, nurse practitioners, and nurse anesthetists, saw the potentially greater revenues their members could receive if they were better able to compete with physicians. These groups developed a concentrated interest in securing payment for their members under public and private insurance systems and in expanding their scope of practice. The increase in opposing concentrated interests weakened the political influence of organized medicine.

Political Markets Compared with Economic Markets

The usefulness of the different theories of government should be judged by their predictive ability. While it is unlikely that any one theory can explain all or even a high percentage of all legislation, a theory is necessary to try to understand why certain types of legislation are passed and why others are not, unless one believes that all legislation is ad hoc. Organizing our observations in some meaningful manner is natural. The criteria for selecting one theory over another should be based on pragmatic grounds; which approach is better at explaining events under a broad range of circumstances? To reject a theory, it is necessary to have a better theory.

Similarities Between Political and Economic Markets
The economic theory of government assumes that human behavior is no different in political markets than in private markets. Individuals, groups, firms, and

legislators seek to enhance their self-interests; they are assumed to be rational in assessing the benefits and costs of their actions. This behavioral assumption enables us to predict that firms in competitive markets will try to produce their products and services as efficiently as possible to keep their costs down, and that they will set their prices to make as much profit as possible. They will be motivated to enter markets in which the profit potential is greatest and, similarly, to leave markets in which the profit potential is low.

Including political markets is merely an extension of the earlier discussion. Individuals and firms attempt to use the power of the state to further their own interests. Firms try to gain competitive advantages in private markets by investing in technology and advertising. Why shouldn't they also make political investments to use the powers of government to increase or maintain profit?

The actions of groups of individuals are no different from those of firms. Many people would like to use the power of the state to assist them in accomplishing what they cannot otherwise achieve. For some, this may mean using the state to help them impose their religious or social preferences on others. Still other groups would like to use the state to provide them with monetary benefits—such as low-cost education for their children, pension payments in excess of their contributions, and subsidized medical benefits—that they could not earn in the market and that others would not voluntarily provide to them.

It is usually with regard to our public servants that the assumption of acting in one's self-interest becomes difficult to accept. After all, why would a person run for office if not to serve the public interest? However, success in the electoral process requires legislators to behave in a manner that enhances their reelection prospects. Political support, votes, and contributions are the bases for reelection. Legislators must therefore understand the sources of such support and the requirements for receiving it. A hungry man quickly realizes that if money buys food, he must have money to eat. Legislators act no differently from others.

Differences Between Political and Economic Markets

Political markets have several characteristics that differentiate them from economic markets. These differences make it possible for organized interests to benefit at the expense of majorities. First, individuals are not as informed about political issues as they are about the goods and services on which they spend their own funds.

Second, in private markets individuals make separate decisions regarding each item they purchase. They do not have to choose between sets of packages, such as different combinations of automobile models and home sizes. Yet in political markets, their choices are between two sets of votes by competing legislators on a wide variety of issues.

Third, voting participation rates differ by age group. The young do not vote; however policies are enacted that impose costs on them. Future generations depend on current generations and voters to protect their interests. However, as has been the case many times, such as with respect to the federal deficit, Social Security, and Medicare, their interests have been sacrificed to current voters.

Fourth, legislators use different decision criteria from those used in the private sector. A firm or an individual making an investment considers both the benefits and the costs of that investment. Legislators, however, have a different time horizon, which not only affects the emphasis they place on costs and benefits but also affects when each is incurred. Because members of the House of Representatives run for reelection every two years, they are likely to favor programs that provide immediate benefits (presumably just before the election) while delaying the costs until after the election or years later.

Fifth, from the legislator's perspective, the program does not even have to meet the criterion that the benefits exceed the costs, only that the *immediate benefits exceed any immediate costs*. Future legislators can worry about future costs.

For these reasons, organized groups are able to receive legislative benefits while imposing the costs of those benefits on the remainder of the population. For those bearing the costs, it may be perfectly rational not to oppose such legislation. As long as the cost of changing political outcomes exceeds the lost wealth imposed by the legislation, it is rational for voters to lose some wealth rather than to organize and bear the cost of trying to change the legislative outcome.

At times, self-interest legislation may be in the public interest. When this occurs, however, it is a by-product of the outcome rather than its intended effect.

Summary

The public-interest theory of government and economic theory of regulation provide opposing predictions of the redistributive and efficiency effects of government legislation, as shown in exhibit 31.3. To determine which of these contrasting theories is a more accurate description of government, we must match the actual outcomes of legislation to each theory's predictions. Do the benefits of redistributive programs go to those with low income, and are they financed by taxes that impose a larger burden on those with higher income? Does the government try to improve the allocation of resources by reducing barriers to entry and, in markets in which information is limited, by monitoring the quality of physicians and other medical services and making this information available to the public?

The economic theory of regulation provides a better explanation of why health policies are enacted and why they have changed over time. An

EXHIBIT 31.3
Health Policy
Objectives
Under Different
Theories of
Government

Theories of Government	Objective of Government	
	Redistribution	**Efficiency Improvement**
Public-interest theory	Assist those with low income	Remove (and prevent) monopoly abuses and protect environment (externalities)
Economic theory of regulation	Provide benefits to those able to deliver political support and finance it from those offering little political support	Efficiency objective unimportant; more likely to protect industries to provide them with redistributive benefits

indication of the inadequacy of the public-interest theory is the difficulty in placing demand-side and supply-side policies for each of the three policy instruments—expenditure, taxation, and regulation (described in exhibit 31.1)—into a redistribution or efficiency improvement framework. The economic theory predicts that government is not concerned with efficiency issues. Redistribution is the main objective of government, but the purpose is to redistribute wealth to those who are able to offer political support from those who are unable to do so. Thus, medical licensing boards are inadequately staffed, have never required reexamination for relicensure, and have failed to monitor practicing physicians because organized medicine has been opposed to any approaches seeking to increase quality that would adversely affect physicians' income. Regressive taxes are used to finance programs such as Medicare and the ACA's employer mandate, not because legislators are unaware of their regressive nature, but because the taxes are designed to be diffuse and not obvious to those with low income (who actually bear the burden of the benefits provided to those who have a concentrated interest).

The structure and financing of medical services is rational; the participants act according to their calculations of costs and benefits. Viewed in its entirety, however, health policy is uncoordinated and seemingly contradictory. Health policies are inequitable and inefficient; low-income people end up subsidizing those with higher income. These results, however, are the consequences of a rational system. The outcomes were the result of policies enacted by legislators.

Discussion Questions

1. What were the dissatisfactions with the public-interest theory of government?

2. Contrast the benefit–cost calculations of legislators under the public-interest theory of government and the economic theory of regulation.

3. Why are concentrated interests and diffuse costs important in predicting legislative outcomes?

4. Contrast the predictions of the public-interest and economic theories regarding redistributive policies.

5. Evaluate the following policies according to the two differing theories:

   a. Medicare and Medicaid beneficiaries, taxation, and generosity of benefits

   b. The performance of state licensing boards in monitoring physician quality

6. In what ways are political and economic markets similar?

7. In what ways are political and economic markets different?

Note

1. The political support offered by providers, such as hospitals and physicians, is important in determining how such redistributive legislation is designed. Providers benefit because such programs increase demand by those with low income. However, medical societies have opposed government coverage of entire population groups (e.g., the aged) regardless of income level because government payment would merely substitute for private payment for those who are not poor. Physicians were concerned that if government covered everyone or all of the aged, regardless of income, the cost of such programs would rise and the government would eventually control physician fees. This was the AMA's basic reason for opposing Medicare. To gain the political support of physicians, Congress acceded to physicians' preferences when Medicare was established by permitting them to decide whether or not to accept the government payment for treating Medicare patients. Medicaid was not controversial because it covered those with low income; hospitals were paid for their costs, and physicians were paid fee-for-service and could allocate their time as they wished. As the federal and state governments experienced large expenditure increases under each of these programs, government developed a concentrated interest in controlling hospital and medical spending.

References

Bunce, V. 2013. *Health Insurance Mandates in the States 2012*. Alexandria, VA: Council for Affordable Health Insurance.

Feldstein, P. J. 2006. *The Politics of Health Legislation: An Economic Perspective*, 3rd ed. Chicago: Health Administration Press.

Stigler, G. J. 1971. "The Theory of Economic Regulation." *Bell Journal of Economics* 2 (1): 3–21.

HEALTH ASSOCIATIONS AND THE POLITICAL MARKETPLACE 32

Healthcare providers and payers, whether they are for-profit or not-for-profit, compete in two different markets: an economic market and a political market. In the economic market, hospitals compete against other hospitals, physicians compete against other physicians, insurers compete against other insurers, and so on. Being a successful competitor in the economic marketplace requires an economic strategy, which includes increasing the demand for the organization's services and gaining market power to be able to charge higher prices.

The political market, at both the federal and state levels, determines the legislation and regulations that define the rules of competition in the economic marketplace. Barriers to entry have been established in different geographic markets, and licensing and scope-of-practice laws determine who can practice in different professions, including required years of training and which tasks various healthcare professionals are permitted to perform. Further, the government is a major payer of healthcare and establishes how different professionals, hospitals, and insurers may be paid for services provided under public programs. These are but a few of the ways in which the government affects the roles and incomes of healthcare professionals, hospital revenues, and insurer payments.

Given the enormous impact that legislation and regulations have on incomes and revenues of every healthcare provider and insurer, they must be involved in the political marketplace to ensure their survival and (hopefully) gain an economic advantage.

The Role of Health Associations

To be successful in the political market, a political strategy is required. First, a hospital must ally itself with its economic competitors to successfully compete in the political market. Each type of provider or insurer must join with its economic rivals to form a health association that represents their common economic interests. Otherwise, they may be excluded from public programs, receive disadvantageous public payments, be unable to enter certain markets, and so forth.

Second, and the focus of this chapter, is to understand the types of legislative and regulatory approaches successful health associations have favored in the political marketplace.

Each type of healthcare provider and insurer has its own trade association. These associations have a concentrated interest in health legislation and regulations that enhance their members' economic interests.[1] The American Medical Association (AMA) serves physicians, and each physician specialty also has its own association. The American Hospital Association (AHA) serves hospitals, as do hospitals' respective state associations, and health insurers belong to the Health Insurance Association of American (HIAA). Midlevel health practitioners have their own associations, as do pharmaceutical firms, and everyone else involved in healthcare.

Health associations serve an important function for their members. The association's lobbyists promote their members' economic interests before legislators and congressional staff. They strive to structure legislation so that it is advantageous to their members. For example, almost all legislation that provides additional insurance benefits (e.g., Medicare Part D) includes a section on how providers will be reimbursed. Pharmaceutical firms successfully excluded the government from "negotiating" prescription drug prices directly with the pharmaceutical firms. Once legislation has been enacted, association lobbyists try to influence those in the administration responsible for drafting the legislation's regulations.

Legislators and their staff often rely on an association's lobbyist to find out which aspects of the legislation or regulation will benefit or be opposed by the association's members. Legislators need to determine the gains and losses of political support as a result of their actions. AARP has often been viewed as the agent representing the economic interests of Medicare beneficiaries.

Lobbyists often are called upon by legislators and their staff to explain how a certain health policy will affect the economic market. For example, if the pre-existing condition exclusion is prohibited, what further actions are needed to ensure that adverse selection does not result? Congressional and administration staff are not necessarily knowledgeable about how all aspects of the healthcare system interact.

Health associations hold meetings with their membership to develop legislative priorities. They must also report back to membership regarding their success (or lack thereof) in advancing the association's interests.

Health associations are not equally successful in serving their members. In addition to differing in their ability to generate political support for legislators, associations differ in several other ways. When an association's membership represents the vast majority of those in the profession or industry, it carries more weight with legislators when it claims to be speaking on behalf of those affected by the legislation. Merely having a common economic interest is insufficient for a professional to pay dues to join her association. Physicians can be "free riders" and still benefit from the association's legislative activities. Overcoming the free rider problem is an important determinant of an association's legislative success. Unless the professionals can be coerced into joining (e.g., unions requiring membership to become a plumber), the association will sell goods such as health insurance and educational programs that are discounted for members.

The political influence of some health associations has changed over time. For example, for many years the AMA was the dominant health association, able to negotiate large economic benefits for its members. Over time, competitive associations, such as the AHA, HIAA, and American Nurses Association (ANA), with economic interests contrary to those of the AMA, developed, thereby lessening the AMA's political influence.

Health associations are competitors in the political market, which also includes organizations whose members are not healthcare providers or insurers, such as AARP and employer coalitions striving to reduce their employees' medical costs.

Producer-type legislation and regulation have affected the financing, payment, structure, and efficiency of the healthcare market. Although the legislative results of health associations have not been as visible as redistributive legislation, such as Medicare, Medicaid, and the ACA, health associations have influenced the costs of these programs. They also have affected the performance of each of the medical markets.

The remainder of this chapter explores the different types of legislation demanded by health associations and provides examples in which those approaches have been applied. Understanding the types of legislation demanded by health associations on behalf of their members provides insights into the types of legislation that health associations likely will favor or oppose in the years ahead.

The Five Types of Legislation Favored by Health Associations

Members of the various health associations differ in their ultimate goals, such as higher income (healthcare professionals and for-profit health firms) and greater prestige (medical schools renowned for training specialists, academic researchers, and academic faculty; not-for-profit hospitals seeking to become or remain prestigious by having the latest technology; world-class surgeons and specialists; and not-for-profit insurers whose increased market share will bring higher executive salaries). Although each of their goals may differ, associations' legislative approaches to achieving their goals are similar. These associations all strive to help their members earn as much money as possible. Members can then retain the profits for themselves (healthcare professionals) or spend them to achieve prestige goals. Executives of prestigious hospitals and medical centers have higher reputations and incomes than those of executives in less prestigious institutions.

Thus, the overall objective underlying all health associations' demand for legislation and regulation is the same, regardless of whether their members are for-profit or not-for-profit.

Each association attempts to achieve through legislation what cannot be achieved through a competitive market, namely, a monopoly position. Increased monopoly power and the ability to price as a monopolist are the best ways for association members to achieve their goals.

Five types of legislation are demanded by health associations on behalf of their members. As government policy shifted over time from increasing to limiting rising health expenditures, the emphasis placed on each type of legislation has changed.

Increasing Demand

An association favors demand-increasing legislation because an increase in demand, with a given supply, will result in an increase in price, an increase in total revenue, and, consequently, an increase in incomes or net revenues for its members.

The most obvious way to increase the demand for services is to have the government pay everyone's medical bills. Healthcare providers, however, are opposed to such a proposal. Instead, to increase the demand for their services, providers favor government subsidies for only those with lower incomes.

The reason for selective government subsidies is twofold. First, people with higher incomes presumably have private insurance coverage or can afford to purchase the provider's services. The greatest increase in demand would result from extending coverage to those unable to pay. Second, extending government subsidies to those currently able to pay would greatly increase the government's cost, which would result in the government developing a concentrated interest in controlling the provider's prices, utilization, and expenditures. Thus, when health associations favored demand subsidies, they were always in relation to specific population groups or services rather than to the population at large.

The following are examples of demand-increasing legislation.

The AMA has favored government subsidies (e.g., Medicaid) to cover those with low incomes. It opposed Medicare because it covered all aged, regardless of income level. The AMA also supported an employer mandate, whereby employers are required to purchase health insurance on behalf of their employees. Providing subsidies to those with low incomes and private coverage to the working uninsured increased the demand for physician services.

The American Dental Association (ADA) has opposed any legislative "cap" on tax-exempt employer-paid health insurance. If a tax cap were passed, employees would continue with hospital and medical insurance but choose to forego dental insurance because it would have to be bought with after-tax dollars. Consumers would then have to pay the full price of dental care, which would decrease the demand for it.[2]

To increase the demand for registered nurses (RNs), the ANA has promoted minimum nurse-to-patient staffing ratios (higher than existing staffing ratios) in hospitals, nursing homes, and home health agencies.

Nursing associations have tried to expand the nurse's role (i.e., increase the number of tasks nurses are legally able to perform). The nurses' value to the institution increases as they are permitted to perform more, and higher-valued, tasks. The demand for their services will increase, with a consequent rise in incomes. The AMA, fearful that the demand for physicians would decrease, has opposed state laws that increase the scope of practice for nurses with advanced training (Priest 1993).

The association that is successful in enabling its members to expand their role, while preventing other health professionals from encroaching on their own turf, will be able to increase the demand for, and hence the incomes of, its members. Examples of the legislative conflict over state practice acts are the attempts by optometrists to increase their role at the expense of ophthalmologists, as well as the struggles of psychologists versus psychiatrists, obstetricians versus nurse midwives, and podiatrists versus orthopedic surgeons.

The AHA has favored government subsidies to stimulate the demand for hospital services by the aged (Medicare) and the poor (Medicaid), which would decrease hospital bad debts for caring for the uninsured. The AHA also has favored an employer mandate, which would increase the demand for private health insurance (and hospitals) by the working uninsured. The AHA and state hospital associations have been important advocates of the ACA's Medicaid state expansions.

America's Health Insurance Plans has favored the employer mandate, which requires employers to provide their employees with health insurance, and the individual mandate, which requires every individual to buy health insurance or pay a financial penalty.

Achieving the Highest Price

The method of reimbursement, or the method used by the provider to charge for services, has been crucial to understanding provider economic and political behavior.

Health associations have used two basic approaches to achieve the highest possible reimbursement for their members.

Elimination of Price Competition

The first approach has been to try to eliminate price competition. The ability to engage in price competition is more important for new practitioners or firms desiring to enter a market. New competitors need to let potential patients know (through advertising) they are available, and new surgeons have to provide primary care physicians with an incentive (fee splitting) to switch their surgical referrals away from established surgeons.

Before the applicability of the antitrust laws (1982), health associations referred to advertising, price competition, and fee splitting as *unethical behavior* and prohibited such behavior in their state practice acts.[3] To prevent price competition from occurring, medical and dental professions used strong sanctions (suspended licenses and removal of hospital privileges) against practitioners who engaged in unethical behavior (Kessel 1958).

An example of the AMA's attempt to eliminate price competition among physicians was its lobbying of Congress for an exemption from the antitrust laws to allow competing physicians to collectively negotiate prices for their services with insurers. If the AMA had been successful, independent physicians would have been able to collude and agree on their prices, just as a cartel does. For example, all the anesthesiologists in a market could get together and decide on the prices they wanted to charge.

The AMA has favored any willing provider (AWP) laws. Rather than being procompetitive, AWP laws have been used to eliminate price competition among physicians and weaken "closed" provider panels. Health maintenance organizations (HMOs) and preferred provider organizations could not negotiate volume discounts with physicians who become part of a closed provider panel if they had to offer their enrollees free choice of any provider.

Since the enactment of Medicare, the AHA has successfully eliminated any incentive for hospitals to compete on price for Medicare patients. Under both cost-based hospital payment and, subsequently, diagnosis-related group payment, Medicare patients were responsible only for paying a large hospital deductible. Hospitals were prohibited from competing for Medicare patients by offering to reduce the hospital deductible.

When the Medicare Prescription Drug Act was passed, insurers were required to cover at least one drug in each class. Pharmaceutical firms had to compete on price to have their drug be the one drug included in an insurer's formulary. Pharmaceutical Research and Manufacturers of America (PhRMA) was successful in having that rule changed in the Affordable Care Act (ACA). An insurer's formulary had to include as many drugs in a class as were required in a state's "benchmark" insurance plan, which was usually two or more drugs in a class. Price competition decreased as the number of drugs included in an insurer's formulary increased.

The Association of American Medical Colleges has been successful in ensuring that government medical education subsidies are given to medical schools rather than given directly to students. If government subsidies went directly to the student, the schools would have to compete for students. Similarly, medical and dental schools distribute loans and scholarships rather than have students apply directly to the government for such financial assistance. If students received the subsidies and loans directly from the government, they would have an incentive to shop around and select a school based on its tuition rates and reputation.

Price Discrimination

The second approach used by healthcare providers to secure the highest possible payment for their services is to engage in price discrimination, which entails charging different prices to patients or payers for the same service. These price differences do not result from differences in costs, but from the patients' or their payers' willingness to pay. Charging according to ability to pay results in greater revenues than would be generated by a pricing system that charges everyone the same price.

The AMA's desire to maintain a system in which physicians could price-discriminate influenced the financing and delivery of medical services for many years. The initial Medicare payment for physicians was modeled after Blue Shield payments. Medical societies started and controlled Blue Shield, which would only pay the physician's fee in full for patients with low incomes. Physicians could then charge higher-income Blue Shield patients an additional fee, referred to as *balance billing*. Further, by having the option of participating in Medicare (and Blue Shield) when they wanted to, physicians were assured of payment from low-income patients, while still being able to charge a higher price to higher-income patients. This method of pricing and flexibility in physician participation under Blue Shield and Medicare was crucial to physicians' acceptance of these plans. More recent Medicare physician payment methods have changed physicians' ability to price discriminate (see chapter 10).

The ADA has taken political positions similar to those of the AMA, such as regarding prohibitions on advertising, price competition, and balance billing.

Pharmaceutical firms sell the same prescription drug at a higher price in the United States than in other countries. The two conditions enabling a firm to price discriminate are that the two markets must have a different willingness to pay (price elasticity) and the two markets must be kept separate; otherwise, buyers in the low-priced market would resell the drug to the higher-priced market, resulting in similar prices for the two markets. For this reason, pharmaceutical firms have opposed legislation permitting reimportation. If reimportation were permitted, drug firms would no longer be able to price discriminate. The drug would have to be sold at the same price in every country. In addition to concerns that fake drugs would be sold in the United States from overseas, the higher overseas price would decrease demand for the drug because other countries are less able to pay for such drugs than the United States is, and drug firm revenues would decline.

The methods used by health professionals and health organizations to price their services have enabled them to maximize their revenues. In negotiating with the government, in establishing their own insurance organizations, and in proposing legislation, the health associations representing provider groups have developed a clear appreciation for which pricing strategies are in their members' economic interest.

Reducing the Price of Complements and/or Increasing the Quantity

A nurse practitioner (NP) may be a substitute or a complement to the physician. However, it is difficult to determine when a health professional, such as an NP, is a complement or a substitute based only on the task performed. An NP may be as competent as a physician in performing selected tasks. If the NP works for the physician, and the physician receives the fee for performance of that task, the NP is a complement; the NP has increased the physician's productivity. If, however, the NP performs the same task and bills independently of the physician, the NP is a substitute for the physician. The essential element in determining whether an input is a complement or a substitute is who receives payment for the services provided by that input.

The state practice acts were the legal basis for determining which tasks each health profession can perform and under whose direction health professionals must work. A major legislative activity for each health association was to ensure that the state practice acts worked to serve their members' interests. Health associations that represent complements (e.g., nurses and denturists) attempt to have their members become substitutes. Health associations whose members control complements seek to retain the status quo.

In the past, almost all health professions and health institutions were complements to the physician; the physician either billed for the service or, in the case of a hospital as a complement, the hospital provided the facilities and staff to increase the physician's productivity. That situation has changed. The physician is no longer the sole entry point in the delivery of medical services. HMOs (and retail clinics), for example, may use NPs to serve their enrollees. The AMA has continued to oppose the use of independent NPs and has lobbied against state laws that allow advance practice nurses to provide medical care without the supervision of a physician. The American Academy of Family Physicians (2017) (which would be most adversely affected by independent NPs) has stated that such nurses should only be paid by insurers when they work in a "collaborative" relationship with physicians.

Providers can increase their incomes if an increase in demand for their services is met through greater productivity rather than through an increase in the number of competing providers. Providers' incomes can be increased further if their increases in productivity are subsidized, and they do not have to pay the full cost of the increased productivity.

Legislative Examples

The following are examples of legislation to subsidize health professionals' complements.

The AMA has favored internship and residency programs in hospitals, which are excellent complements for physicians; interns and residents can take care of the physician's hospitalized patients and relieve the physician from serving in the hospital emergency department and from being on call. The more advanced the resident, the closer the resident is to being a potential substitute for the physician. Residents, however, are complements because the resident cannot bill for the service. The AMA has also favored the use of foreign medical graduates (FMGs) to serve as interns and residents. Once FMGs graduate, however, they become substitutes to existing practitioners. Therefore, the AMA has favored requiring FMGs to return to their home country once their residencies are completed. (The AMA advocated a time limit on how long FMGs can remain in the United States, as well as the requirement that they be out of the country for two years before returning.)[4]

The AMA (2016) has favored subsidies for the training of RNs but not for graduate or advanced training for RNs because they might become substitutes for physicians.

The AMA's main concern with regard to emerging health professionals, such as physician assistants (PAs), is to ensure that these types of personnel become complements to, not substitutes for, the physician. Thus, whether there is direct or indirect supervision of the PA by the physician is less important to the AMA's political position than who receives the fee for the PA's services.

Before the 1980s, demand for dentists was high, so state dental practice acts were relaxed to permit dentists to delegate more of their tasks to dental auxiliaries. In the 1980s, as demand for dental care decreased, dental societies opposed further delegation of tasks. Growth in dentists' productivity (paid on a fee-for-service basis) was related more to demand conditions facing dentists than to the competency of dental auxiliaries.

The AHA lobbied for passage of the Nurse Training Act in the belief that federal educational subsidies would increase the supply of RNs available to hospitals. With a larger supply of nurses, hospitals would be able to pay RNs lower wages than otherwise would have been possible. The AHA called for a moratorium on the separate licensing of each health professional. (Separate licensing limits the hospital's ability to substitute different health professionals in the tasks they perform; hospital costs are greater if licensed personnel cannot be used more flexibly.) Conversely, professional associations insist on separate licensing to increase the demand for their members' services by restricting the tasks that other healthcare professionals can perform.

Increasing the Price and/or Decreasing the Availability of Substitutes

All health associations try to increase the prices charged by their substitutes. (Similar to increasing the price of a substitute is decreasing its availability.) Higher prices for a substitute translate into lower demand for the substitute and increased demand for the association's members.

Professional associations use two general approaches to accomplish this objective. The first is to simply have the substitute declared illegal. If substitute health professionals are not permitted to practice, or if substitutes are severely restricted in the tasks they are legally permitted to perform, there will be a shift in demand away from the substitute's service.

The second approach, used when the first approach is unsuccessful, is to exclude the substitute service from payment by any third party, including government health programs. By covering only physician services, the prices of substitute providers are effectively increased relative to those of physicians. A Medicare Part B patient pays only a copayment for a physician's services, but pays the full fee for a nonphysician.

The following examples illustrate the behavior of associations with respect to these approaches.

Dentistry's actions toward denturists illustrate the legislative behavior of associations in having substitute competitors declared illegal. *Denturism* is the term applied to the fitting and dispensing of dentures directly to patients by individuals not licensed as dentists. Independently practicing denturists are a threat to dentists' incomes because they provide dentures at lower prices. Denturists are legal in most of Canada. As a result of their political success in Canada, denturists in the United States, although strongly opposed by dental societies, lobbied for changes in the state practice acts. Currently, denturism has been legislated and is practiced in six states: Maine, Arizona, Washington, Oregon, Idaho, and Montana.

The ADA would like dental hygienists to remain as complements to dentists, not to become substitutes for them. Dentistry was successful in opposing state dental hygienist associations when they tried to change the state practice act to permit hygienists to practice without a dentist's supervision and to become independent practitioners. Currently, only Colorado allows licensed hygienists to operate independent practices without dentist supervision. Other states allow dental hygienists to practice unsupervised in nursing homes, schools, community centers, and other underserved institutions.

In the past several years, teeth whitening has become very popular. Various whitening kits have been developed and are sold by nondentist firms. Most dentists believe only they should be the providers of teeth whitening services; their fees for such services are generally several times higher than those of substitute providers. Dentists in a number of states have lobbied against others selling these services. The Connecticut State Dental Commission ruled that only dentists can perform teeth whitening, and violators of state dental laws in that state can go to jail. The Federal Trade Commission (2015) has ruled that these actions by state dental associations are anticompetitive. The US Supreme Court ruled that, although state actions are generally immune from the antitrust laws, when dentists controlled the state board and prevented nondentists from whitening teeth, the action was illegal.

Medical societies have been very successful in restricting the tasks that substitute health professionals can perform by preventing changes in a state's scope of practice laws. For example, chiropractors' ability to compete with physicians is limited by the fact that they are prohibited from prescribing drugs (Markowitz et al. 2016).

The AHA was concerned about the growth of physician-owned specialty hospitals. Physician specialists, such as cardiovascular and orthopedic surgeons, would invest in a specialty hospital and refer some of their patients to their own facility for surgery. Hospitals claimed that these specialty hospitals decreased the demand for their own facilities. As part of the ACA, the AHA was able to eliminate this competition by having the construction of new physician-owned specialty hospitals declared illegal.

In negotiations over the ACA, the health insurance industry (HIAA) was opposed to competing in the health insurance exchanges with a proposed government public option health insurance plan. The HIAA was successful in that no such plan was included in the ACA.

The ACA specifically prevents the government from negotiating with pharmaceutical firms over Medicare Part D prescription drug prices. PhRMA was concerned that the government would regulate the prices of high-priced blockbuster drugs, thereby reducing profits. Congress acceded to the pharmaceutical industry's demand.

Medicare has been the vehicle for much legislative action pertaining to substitute providers. The AMA lobbied to cover only physician services under Medicare Part B and to exclude nonphysician providers, thereby raising their prices relative to those of physicians. For example, optometrists are potential substitutes for ophthalmologists, nurse anesthetists for anesthesiologists, and nurse practitioners for primary care physicians.

Blue Cross, Blue Shield, and private health plans also have used these approaches to exclude hospital and physician substitutes from payment.

Limiting Increases in Supply

Essential to the creation of a monopoly is a limit on the number of suppliers. Health associations, however, have justified supply control policies on the grounds of quality. Restrictions on entry, they maintain, ensure the delivery of high-quality care. These same health associations, however, oppose quality measures that would have an adverse economic effect on existing providers (their members). This apparent anomaly—stringent entry requirements and then virtually no quality assurance programs directed at existing providers—is consistent with a policy that seeks to establish a monopoly for existing providers.

If health associations were consistent in their desire to establish and maintain high quality standards, they should favor all policies that ensure quality of care, regardless of the effect on their members' incomes. Quality-control measures directed at existing providers, such as re-examination, relicensure, and outcome measures, would adversely affect the incomes of some providers. More important, such outcome measures of quality would make entry or process measures less necessary, thereby permitting entry of more providers.

Does the health association favor quality measures, regardless of the effect on its members' incomes, or does it favor only those quality measures that enhance or do not affect their members' incomes? If the answer is the latter, then one can conclude that the real intent of the quality measures is the improvement of its members' competitive position rather than the assurance of high-quality care delivered in the most efficient manner.

Existing healthcare providers in a market, such as hospitals, outpatient surgical centers, home health agencies, hospices, and nursing homes, have favored state certificate-of-need (CON) laws because they make it very difficult for a new provider to enter their market. In CON states, new providers must receive approval from the state CON agencies and are opposed by existing providers. CON approval is required in 37 states. Various economic studies have found that CON is a barrier to entry, protecting existing providers and resulting in less price competition, higher prices, and less choice. CON has had no observed effect on reducing the rate of increase in hospital or other provider expenditures.[5]

The AMA and other health associations have relied on educational requirements, generally from approved schools, before a student can take a professional qualifying examination. Few healthcare professionals are subject to re-examination. As educational requirements are heightened, existing members of the profession are grandfathered, so they do not have to meet the additional requirements. Among the most well-known entry barriers in healthcare have been limits on the number of professional schools, such as medical and dental schools. The history of AMA and ADA control over the number and size of medical and dental schools can be traced to the early 1900s (Kessel 1958).

Believing there were too many dentists in the 1980s, the ADA proposed that the "ADA encourage and assist constituent societies in preparing legislation that may be used to petition state legislatures and governmental bodies with respect to private schools to adjust enrollment in dental schools."[6] At times, the dental profession imposed requirements on new entrants that were blatant barriers. For example, foreign dental school graduates were required to be US citizens before they were allowed to practice in some states.[7] Further, a dentist desiring to practice in Hawaii, for example, no matter how well trained or how long in practice in another state, was required to complete a one-year residency before being allowed to practice.[8] Forgoing income for a year before one can practice is a high cost for entering a new market. Such requirements cannot be remotely related to the profession's focus on quality.

The ADA and the American Dental Education Association have increased the time requirements for a foreign-trained dentist wishing to practice in the

United States; thus, it is very costly for foreign-trained dentists (both US and non-US citizens) to fulfill these requirements. A minimum number of years of training in the foreign country is required, as well as a license to practice in that country. (A US citizen studying in an overseas dental school would have to learn a foreign language.) Once foreign-trained dentists enter the United States, additional requirements are then imposed on them. They are required to take the last two years of dental school in an accredited US dental school. They may also be required to take additional examinations before the licensing examination. In 2016, only 5.9% of US dentists were foreign trained (Vujicic 2017).

The ANA has lobbied state legislatures to decree that nursing education should be provided only in colleges that offer a Bachelor of Science degree.[9] Only graduates of four-year programs would be referred to as professional nurses; others would be technical nurses. As of 2015, only 42 percent of nurses are graduates of a four-year college. Increasing the educational requirement would result in a *decrease* in the number of nurse graduates and an increase in the incomes of *existing* nurses, who would be grandfathered in as professional nurses. The ANA also has tried to decrease the number of foreign-trained RNs from entering the United States by changing its immigration preferences.

Summary

Healthcare professionals and health institutions cannot achieve a monopoly position through the normal competitive process. Therefore, they seek to achieve it through legislation. The first step toward increasing their monopoly power is to erect barriers to entry. The next step is to limit competition among their members. They then attempt to improve their monopoly position by lobbying for legislation that will increase the demand for their services, permit them to set prices as would a price-discriminating monopolist, lower their costs of doing business, and disadvantage their competitors by causing them to become illegal providers or by forcing them to raise their prices.

Exhibit 32.1 lists the five types of legislative behavior and examples of each type of legislation discussed earlier.

It is unlikely that a health association would ever propose increased educational requirements that are then applied to its existing members. Health associations do not favor relicensure or re-examination requirements for their current members, even though increased knowledge is the basis for requiring additional training for those entering the profession. Re-examination and relicensure would lower the members' incomes, because they would have to take the time to study for and could possibly fail the exam. On the other hand, no professional association proposes reducing the time required to prepare a person to enter the profession.

EXHIBIT 32.1

Five Types of Health Legislation Favored by Health Associations

Type of Legislation	Examples
1. Increasing demand	AMA: Employer mandate, Medicaid ADA: Opposed to tax "cap" on health insurance ANA: Minimum RN-to-patient staffing ratios, expanded RN role AHA: Employer mandate, Affordable Care Act Medicaid expansion AHIP: Employer mandate, individual mandate
2. Achieving highest price	
Elimination of price competition	AMA: Sanctions for price competition, collectively negotiate prices, any willing provider laws AHA: No competition on Medicare deductible, no competition on diagnosis-related group prices PhRMA: Two or more drugs for Medicare Part D AAMC: Subsidies to schools, not students
Price discrimination	AMA and ADA: Balance billing, prohibitions on advertising PhRMA: Opposition to reimportation laws
3. Reducing price or increasing quantity of complements	AMA: Favored residency programs for foreign medical graduates if they then return home, favored educational subsidies for RNs, but not for advanced training AHA: Favored educational subsidies for RNs, moratorium on separate licensing of each health professional
4. Increasing price or decreasing availability of substitutes	
Making substitutes illegal	AMA: Restrictions on scope of practice ADA: Denturists, hygienists, teeth whitening AHA: Physician-owned specialty hospitals HIAA: No government public option insurer PhRMA: No government negotiation on Medicare Part D drugs
Excluding substitutes from third-party payment	AMA: Excluding chiropractors, nurse anesthetists, etc.
5. Limiting increases in supply	AMA and ADA: Increased educational requirements, approved schools, increased training times AHA: Certificate-of-need laws ANA: Four-year bachelor's degree, foreign-trained RNs

Notes: AAMC = Association of American Medical Colleges; ADA = American Dental Association; AHA = American Hospital Association; AHIP = America's Health Insurance Plans; AMA = American Medical Association; ANA = American Nurses Association; HIAA = Health Insurance Association of America; PhRMA = Pharmaceutical Research and Manufacturers of America; RN = registered nurse.

The determination of which tasks a health professional is able to perform is related more to the economic effects on another health profession than to the professional's qualifications and training.

Much of the structure of the healthcare delivery and payment systems has been influenced by the concentrated interests of health associations. However, the success of these associations has resulted in costs being imposed on the rest of society.

First, the more successful a health association is at achieving its members' anticompetitive goals, the higher the price of its members' services. Second, successful legislative behavior by health associations has given the public a false assurance with respect to the quality of the medical care it receives. In all likelihood, an association would only support additional requirements, such as continuing medical education, for its members in order to forestall more stringent requirements pertaining to quality improvement. In addition, states have delegated their responsibility for protecting the public to the individual licensing boards, which, in turn, have been controlled by the providers themselves.[10]

Third, health associations have delayed innovation in the delivery of medical care. Innovation benefits consumers, providing greater choice, higher quality, and lower costs. The introduction of alternative delivery systems, such as HMOs and preferred provider organizations, as well as greater reliance on midlevel healthcare professionals, such as nurse midwives and nurse practitioners, have been opposed because innovation threatens the monopoly power of a protected provider group.

Discussion Questions

1. Why would a health association, such as the AMA, favor having the government subsidize healthcare for those with low incomes but object to a government single-payer system that subsidizes everyone?
2. How can a nurse practitioner be considered either a complement or a substitute?
3. Predict which organizations would oppose and support:
   A. Subsidies for the training of nurse midwives
   B. State mandates requiring all health insurers to include chiropractic services in their benefits.
   C. Inclusion of psychologists as a covered provider under Medicare
4. Pharmaceutical firms have set up charitable foundations to assist those with low incomes to pay the deductibles and/or copayments for the prescription drugs. Other than charity, what is an alternative hypothesis for their actions?
5. What are some practices in medical care that are purported to result in higher standards of quality but are, in fact, restrictive devices intended to confer monopoly power on the profession's practitioners? What are alternative ways of achieving the goal of higher quality without the restrictive element?

Notes

1. In 1975, the Federal Trade Commission (FTC) charged the AMA and two medical societies with restricting the ability of their members to

advertise. The AMA claimed that the antitrust laws did not apply to the AMA because the AMA was a not-for-profit organization. The approach used in this chapter, which is a condensed and updated version of an earlier book (Feldstein 1977), was the basis for my testimony on the jurisdictional issue, on behalf of the FTC, to demonstrate that the AMA acted in the economic interests of its members. The FTC prevailed on both the jurisdictional and advertising issues. The lower court's decision was upheld in 1982 by the US Supreme Court and led to the applicability of the antitrust laws to healthcare.

2. One demand-increasing proposal is reputed to have had an adverse effect on patients' oral health. In 1974, the Federal Social Court in Germany ruled that false teeth should be included in the country's compulsory health insurance programs. "Fillings went out of fashion and prevention was ignored as vast quantities of teeth were pulled and replaced. By 1980, German dentists were using 28 tons of tooth gold a year, one third of the world total." Dentists' incomes soared, exceeding those of physicians by 30 percent. The sickness funds reported a huge deficit, forcing them to raise the level of compulsory contributions (Gumbel 1985, 11).

3. Fee splitting occurred when a physician referred a patient to a surgeon and in return received part of the surgeon's fee; surgeons competed among themselves on the size of their fee to be given to the referring physician. The state practice acts permitted surgeons to act as a cartel by preventing them from engaging in this form of price competition. Surgeons opposed to fee splitting considered it unethical because the referring physician has a monetary incentive to select the surgeon. Any concern the medical profession had with the quality of surgeons or with the ethical behavior of physicians should have been addressed directly through examination and monitoring procedures and not by prohibiting price competition. For a more complete discussion of fee splitting, see Pauly (1979).

4. For a review of immigration policies toward FMGs during this period, see Mejia, Pizurki, and Royston (1980).

5. The classic study in this area was conducted by Salkever and Bice (1979). For a literature review and FTC study, see Sherman (1988).

6. 1984 House of Delegates Resolutions, October 25, p. 537. This resolution follows a previous resolution (124H-1981) in which the ADA (1984) was to encourage its "constituent dental societies to utilize these reports (on dentist supply) in petitioning their legislative bodies to consider by lawful means the number of dentists that should be trained."

7. Many states adopted the citizenship requirement for foreign medical graduates after the AMA's House of Delegates passed such a resolution in 1938. Five states continued such a requirement as late as 1975. Citizenship is no longer required in any state.

8. Restrictions on interstate mobility are another entry barrier used in dentistry. Various studies have shown that dentists graduating from a dental school within a state have a greater chance of passing that state's licensing exam than dentists from other states. Unlike medicine, most states do not permit reciprocal licensing for dentists. See, for example, Shepard (1978), as well as Friedland and Valachovic (1991).

9. For a more complete discussion of this proposal, see Dolan (1978).

10. For an excellent discussion of licensure, quality, and the production of information regarding comparative performance of physicians and hospitals, see Benham (1991).

References

American Academy of Family Physicians. 2017. "Nurse Practitioners." Accessed May 2018. www.aafp.org/about/policies/all/nurse-practitioners.html.

American Dental Association (ADA). 1984. *Transactions of the 125th Annual Session, October 20–25, 1984.* Chicago: American Dental Association.

American Medical Association (AMA). 2016. "AMA Statement on VA Rule on Advanced Practice Nurses." Published December 13. www.ama-assn.org/ama-statement-va-rule-advanced-practice-nurses.

Benham, L. 1991. "Licensure and Competition in Medical Markets." In H. E. Frech III, *Regulating Doctors' Fees: Competition, Benefits, and Controls Under Medicare*, 75–90. Washington, DC: American Enterprise Institute.

Dolan, A. K. 1978. "The New York State Nurses Association 1985 Proposal: Who Needs It?" *Journal of Health Politics, Policy and Law* 2 (4): 508–30.

Federal Trade Commission (FTC). 2015. *North Carolina State Board of Dental Examiners.* Updated February 25. www.ftc.gov/enforcement/cases-proceedings/north-carolina-state-board-dental-examiners.

Feldstein, P. 1977. *Health Associations and the Demand for Legislation: The Political Economy of Health.* Lexington, MA: Ballinger Publishing Company.

Friedland, B., and R. W. Valachovic. 1991. "The Regulation of Dental Licensing: The Dark Ages." *American Journal of Law and Medicine* 17 (3): 249–70.

Gumbel, P. 1985. "Dentists Gnashing Teeth in West Germany." *Wall Street Journal*, December 26.

Kessel, R. A. 1958. "Price Discrimination in Medicine." *Journal of Law and Economics* 1: 20–53.

Markowitz, S. E., K. Adams, M. J. Lewitt, and A. Dunlop. 2016. "Competitive Effects of Scope of Practice Restrictions: Public Health or Public Harm?" National Bureau of Economic Research Working Paper No. 22780. Published October. www.nber.org/papers/w22780.

Mejia, A., H. Pizurki, and E. Royston. 1980. "Immigration and Licensure Policies (Appendix)." In *Foreign Medical Graduates*. Lexington, MA: Lexington Books.

Pauly, M. V. 1979. "The Ethics and Economics of Kickbacks and Fee Splitting." *Bell Journal of Economics* 10 (1): 344–52.

Priest, D. 1993. "Doctors Group Denounces Nurses' Demand for Power." *Washington Post*. Published December 7. www.washingtonpost.com/archive/politics/1993/12/07/doctors-group-denounces-nurses-demand-for-power/39e89452-50dd-41f1-88f8-0dc1fb89a9fa/?utm_term=.7f87a986eaf4.

Salkever, D. S., and T. W. Bice. 1979. *Hospital Certificate-of-Need Controls: Impact on Investment, Costs, and Use*. Washington, DC: American Enterprise Institute.

Shepard, L. 1978. "Licensing Restrictions and the Cost of Dental Care." *Journal of Law and Economics* 21 (1): 187–201.

Sherman, D. 1988. *The Effect of State Certificate-of-Need Laws on Hospital Costs: An Economic Policy Analysis*. Washington, DC: Federal Trade Commission.

Vujicic, M. 2017. "Will We See More Foreign-Trained Dentists in the United States?" *Journal of the American Dental Association* 148 (7): 538–40.

MEDICAL RESEARCH, MEDICAL EDUCATION, ALCOHOL CONSUMPTION, AND POLLUTION: WHO SHOULD PAY?

An important role of government is to improve the way markets allocate resources. When markets perform poorly, fewer goods and services are produced, and incomes are lower than they would be otherwise. The usual policy prescription for improving the performance of markets is for the government to eliminate barriers to entry and increase information. Competitive markets, in which no entry barriers are in place and purchasers and producers are fully informed, are likely to produce the correct (or optimal) rate of output. The correct rate occurs if individuals benefiting from the service pay the full cost of producing that service.

Resources are optimally allocated when the additional benefits from consuming the last unit equal the cost of producing that last unit. When still more units are consumed, the costs of those additional units exceed the benefits provided, and the resources would be better used to produce other goods and services whose benefits exceed their costs. As shown in exhibit 33.1, when the costs are C_1 and benefits are B_1, the correct rate of output is Q_1. The benefit curve is declining because the more one has of a good, the lower the value of an additional unit will be.

Under certain circumstances, however, even a competitive market may not allocate resources correctly. The optimal rate of output in a market occurs when *all* costs and benefits are included. Private decision makers consider only their *own* costs and benefits and exclude the costs or benefits imposed on others, if any. The effect may be that some services are underproduced, while others are overproduced.

The quantity of medical and health services may not be optimal because costs and benefits may be imposed on individuals other than those who purchase and provide the service. What happens when costs or benefits are imposed on someone *who is not a voluntary participant in that private transaction*? Such external costs and benefits must be included; otherwise, too much or too little of the service is produced and purchased. For example, when external costs are imposed on others, as shown by C_2 in exhibit 33.1, the correct rate of output declines from Q_1 to Q_2, where both private (C_1) and external (C_2) costs equal the benefits (B_1) from consuming that good or service.

When such external costs or benefits exist, government should calculate their magnitude and use subsidies and taxes to achieve the "right" rate of output

EXHIBIT 33.1
Optimal Rate of
Output

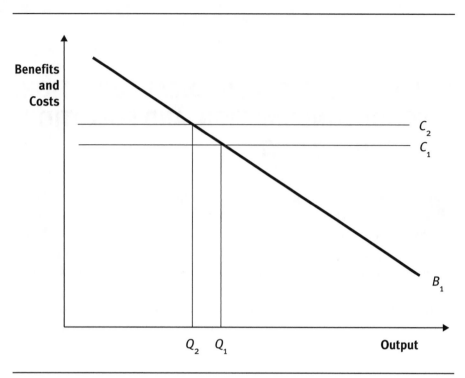

in the affected industry. Subsidies or taxes on the producers in that industry will change the costs of producing a service so that producers will adjust their levels of output. The difference between C_1 and C_2, the external cost, is also the size of the tax to be imposed on each unit of the product.

External Costs and Benefits

Pollution

One reason externalities, such as pollution, exist is that no one owns the resource being exploited. When a resource such as air or water is scarce and no one owns it, a firm may use it as though it were free; it does not become a cost of production as it would if the firm were charged a fee for its use. The lack of property rights over scarce resources is the basis for government intervention. For example, when a firm pollutes a stream in the process of producing its product, those who use the stream for recreational purposes are adversely affected; they bear a cost not included in the firm's calculation of its costs of producing the product. Because the firm has not had to include the external costs of production, it sells the product at a lower price, and the user pays less for that product than the product actually costs society. Because of its lower price, a greater quantity of the product is purchased and produced.

When no property rights over a scarce resource exist, and that resource is used by large numbers of people and firms, negotiations among the parties over use of that resource are likely to be difficult and costly. Government intervention is needed to calculate the external costs and, in the case of pollution, to impose a tax on each unit of product sold based on the proportional amount of pollution emitted. The product's higher price would include both the cost of production and the unit tax; therefore, less of the product would be sold. If all costs and benefits—both private and external—are part of the private decision-making process, the industry will produce the right rate of output.

A pollution tax could not be expected to eliminate all pollution, but it would reduce it to the correct level; the tax revenues received by the government would go toward cleaning up the pollution or compensating those who were adversely affected. If the government attempted to eliminate all of the pollution, it would have to stop production of that product completely. Eliminating all pollution could adversely affect many people if the total benefits derived from that product outweigh its costs, including the costs of pollution. Consider, for example, the effect of eliminating all air pollution originating from automobiles or electricity production. Clearly, people prefer some quantity of these products to zero air pollution, which means it becomes necessary to determine the correct amount of air pollution.

Imposing a tax on pollution has another important consequence. The producer of the product will attempt to lower the tax by devising methods to reduce pollution.[1] The firm may move to an area where the costs of pollution (hence, the tax) are lower, or the firm may innovate in its production process to reduce pollution. The tax creates incentives for producers to lower their production costs, which include the tax.

Imposing a tax directly on pollution is preferable to such indirect methods of controlling pollution as allowing existing firms to continue polluting but not permitting others to enter the market or mandating that all firms use a particular production process to reduce pollution. Such indirect approaches eliminate incentives for producers to search for cheaper ways to reduce pollution.

Based on the example of the external costs of pollution, the role of government seems straightforward: When widespread external costs exist, the government should calculate the extent of those costs and assess a tax on each unit of output produced. The purchasers of that product will base their decision about how much to purchase on all of the costs and benefits (external as well as private) of that product.

Medical Research

The analysis is similar when applied to external benefits. If a university medical researcher develops a new method of performing open-heart surgery that reduces the mortality rate for that procedure, other surgeons will copy the technique to benefit their own patients. An individual researcher or surgeon cannot declare ownership over all possible uses of that technique. However, if the university medical researcher were not compensated for all those who would eventually benefit, she would not find it feasible or worthwhile to invest time and resources to develop new medical techniques.

Similarly, if medical researchers were not properly compensated in some fashion, they would underproduce basic scientific discoveries because, presumably, they would not be able to charge all those who would eventually benefit from their research. Although difficult, the government should attempt to calculate the potential benefits of scientific discoveries and subsidize medical research. Unless the external benefits are assessed and the costs are shared by potential beneficiaries, the costs of producing medical research will exceed the private benefits.

An alternative to offering a subsidy to private firms is to give them property rights or ownership over their discoveries in the form of patent protection. Drug companies need to be compensated for the risks taken and investments made in research and development. Patent protection, however, is not possible for all basic research or for new surgical techniques. Unpatented medical research or new drug discoveries can be copied by others who then benefit from the discoveries.

Immunization

Another example of external benefits involves protection from contagious diseases. Individuals who decide to be immunized against contagious diseases base their decisions primarily on the costs and benefits to themselves of immunization. However, those who are not immunized also benefit because their chances of catching the disease are lowered. If immunization were solely a private decision, not enough individuals would be immunized. The costs incurred by those who choose to be immunized should be subsidized by imposing a small tax on those who are not immunized but who also benefit. In this manner, the "right" numbers of people become immunized. The immunization decision thus encompasses private benefits, external benefits, and the costs of immunization.

When transaction costs—that is, the administrative costs of monitoring people, collecting taxes, and subsidizing individuals—are substantial, it may be less costly to simply require everyone to be immunized against certain diseases.

Subsidies to the Medically Indigent

Externalities are also the rationale for providing subsidies to the medically indigent. If voluntary contributions were the only means through which the poor received medical care, many people who did not make such contributions would benefit by knowing that the poor were cared for through the contributions of others. Too little would be provided to the medically indigent because those who did not contribute receive a free ride; they benefit without having to pay. Government intervention would be appropriate to tax those who benefit by knowing the poor receive medical care.

Government Policies When Externalities Exist

In the examples described, the subsidies and taxes are related to the size of the external benefits and costs. Furthermore, the taxes imposed on products that pollute are to be spent for the benefit of those adversely affected. When external benefits exist, the subsidies are financed by taxes on those who receive the external benefit. Patents are an attempt to recover the external benefits of research. In each case, taxes and subsidies are matched according to external costs and benefits.

Recognizing how externalities affect the correct rate of output in an industry is useful for understanding which government policies would be appropriate in a number of additional areas. For example, when a motorcyclist has an accident and suffers a head injury as a result of not wearing a helmet, government (society) pays the medical expenses if the cyclist does not have insurance or sufficient personal funds. Fines for not wearing helmets are an attempt to make motorcyclists bear the responsibility for external costs that they would otherwise impose on others. At times, imposing requirements (e.g., helmet use, immunizations, grade school education) may be the least costly approach for achieving the correct output.

The same analogy can be used to describe those who can afford to buy health insurance but refuse to do so. When they incur catastrophic medical expenses for which they cannot pay, they become a burden on society. Requiring everyone who can afford it to have catastrophic medical coverage is a way of preventing individuals from imposing external costs on others.[2]

Similarly, drunk drivers frequently impose costs on innocent people. Penalties, such as jail terms, forfeiture of driver's licenses, fines, and higher alcohol taxes, have been used in an attempt to shift the responsibility for these external costs back to those who drink and drive. One study concluded that federal and state alcohol taxes should be increased (from an average of 11 cents to 24 cents a drink) to compensate for the external costs imposed on others by drunk drivers (Manning et al. 1989).

However, some people might misapply the externalities argument to justify intervention by the government in all markets. For example, if you admire someone's garden, should you be taxed to subsidize the gardener? Should the student who asks a particularly clever question in class be subsidized by a tax on other students? These examples, although simple, illustrate several important points about externalities. First, when only a few individuals are involved, the parties concerned should be able to reach an accommodation among themselves without resorting to government intervention. Second, even when ownership of the property is clear, high transaction costs may make it too costly to charge for external benefits or costs. The owner of the garden can decide whether it is worthwhile to erect a fence and charge a viewing fee. Chances are the cost of doing so will exceed the amount others are willing to pay. Thus, many individuals may receive external benefits simply because excluding them or collecting payment from them is too costly. Only when the external benefits (or costs) become sufficiently large relative to their transaction costs does it pay for the provider of the external benefits to exclude others or charge them for the benefits.

Another point these examples illustrate pertains to the relative size of private benefits compared with external benefits. Would the gardener's output be too small if neighbors did not contribute? Although many goods and services provide external benefits to others, excluding these external benefits does not result in a rate of output that is too small. In markets in which the external benefits are sufficiently small relative to the total private benefits, excluding external benefits does not affect the optimal rate of output. This type of externality, referred to as an *inframarginal* externality, occurs within the market. Thus, gardeners may receive so much pleasure from their gardens that they put forth the same level of effort with or without their neighbors' financial contribution.

The concept of inframarginal benefit is important to understanding the issue of financing education for health professionals. We all benefit from knowing that we have access to physicians, dentists, and nurses if we become ill. However, if their educations were not subsidized, would too few physicians be available? The education of physicians is heavily subsidized. The average four-year subsidy for a medical education exceeds $500,000. One reason this cost is so high is that medical schools have little incentive to reduce their costs. Given the continual excess demand for a medical education, large subsidies that go to the school rather than directly to prospective medical students, and entry barriers established by the accrediting commission, nonprofit medical schools have little incentive to be efficient or innovative. This would change if medical schools had to compete for students who bore more of the cost themselves. For example, some medical educators claim that medical students could be admitted to medical school after two years of college, medical education could be reduced by at least one year, the residency period could be shortened, and innovations in teaching methods and curricula could reduce the cost still more.

Even if physicians had to pay their entire educational costs themselves, however, the economic return on the costs of becoming a physician has been estimated to be sufficiently attractive that we would have had no fewer physicians than the current number. Over time, these economic returns on a medical (or dental) education have varied according to specialty status; returns were higher in the 1950s to 1970s than they are currently. Thus, the concept of external benefits as it relates to the number of physicians is more likely a case of infra-marginal benefits; sufficient private benefits to individuals from becoming a physician would ensure a sufficient supply in a tuition-competitive education market even if no subsidies were provided.

A separate issue is whether low-income individuals could afford a medical education if subsidies were removed. Yet making medical and dental education affordable to all qualified individuals could be accomplished more efficiently by targeting subsidies and loan programs based on economic need than by equally subsidizing everyone who attends medical school regardless of income level. The rationale for large subsidies for a health professional education should be reexamined. (See this chapter's appendix for a more complete discussion of this issue.)

Divergence Between Theoretical and Actual Government Policy

Correcting for external costs and benefits creates winners and losers. Taxes and subsidies have redistributive effects; taxpayers have lower income, whereas subsidy recipients have higher income. Every group affected by external costs and benefits desires favorable treatment and has incentives to influence government policy. For example, an industry that pollutes the air and water has a concentrated interest in forestalling government policy that would increase its production costs. All who benefit from environmental protection must organize and provide legislators with political support if anything more than symbolic legislation is to be directed at imposing external costs on those who pollute. The growth of the environmental movement was an attempt to offset the imbalance between those with concentrated interests (polluters) and those bearing the diffuse costs (the public).

The Clean Air Act (1977 amendments) illustrates the divergence between the theoretical approach for resolving external costs and the real-world phenomenon of concentrated and diffuse interests. A greater amount of air pollution is caused when electric utilities burn high-sulfur coal rather than low-sulfur coal. Imposing a tax on the amount of sulfur dioxides (air pollution) emitted would shift the external costs of air pollution to the electric utilities, which would then have an incentive to search for ways to reduce this tax and, consequently, the amount of air pollution. One alternative would be for the utilities to switch to low-sulfur coal.

Low-sulfur coal, however, is produced only in the West (of the United States); furthermore, mining low-sulfur coal is less expensive than mining high-sulfur coal. Low-sulfur coal is therefore a competitive threat to the Eastern coal interests that produce high-sulfur coal. Faced with taxes based on the amount of air pollution emitted, Midwestern and Eastern utilities would find it less expensive to pay added transportation costs to have low-sulfur coal shipped from the West. However, the concentrated interests of the Eastern coal mines, their heavily unionized employees, and the Senate majority leader at that time (who was from West Virginia, which would have been adversely affected) succeeded in having legislation enacted that was directed toward the *process* of reducing pollution rather than the *amount* of pollution emitted.

Requiring utilities to merely use specified technology for reducing pollution eliminated the utilities' incentives to use low-sulfur coal. When specific technology is mandated, the utility loses its incentive to maintain that technology in good operating condition and to search for more efficient approaches to reducing pollution. Western utilities that used low-sulfur coal bore the higher costs of using mandated technology, although they could have achieved the desired outcomes by less expensive means (Ackerman and Hassler 1981; Crandall 1983).

Summary

Even if medical care markets were competitive, the "right" quantity of output might not occur because of external costs and benefits. With regard to personal medical services, externalities are likely to exist related to medical services for the poor and for those who can afford catastrophic medical insurance but refuse to buy it. Why should medical and dental education be so heavily subsidized? A tuition-competitive education market would produce more physicians than the number demanded by including additional external benefits. Any such external benefits are likely to be inframarginal, thereby not affecting the optimal number of health professionals. Imposing taxes on personal behaviors (or products), such as excessive alcohol consumption, that may result in external costs will also serve as an incentive to reduce these external costs. Most externalities in healthcare in the United States derive from medical research, medical services for the poor, lack of catastrophic insurance for those who can afford it, alcohol consumption, and pollution.

Implicit in discussions of externalities is the assumption that government regulation can correct these failures of competitive markets. Politicians, however, may at times be even less responsive to correcting external costs and benefits than are producers and consumers. When externalities are present, a theoretical framework for determining appropriate government policy provides a basis for evaluating alternative policies. The divergence between theoretical and actual policies can often be explained by a comparison of the amounts of political support offered by those with concentrated and diffuse interests.

Discussion Questions

1. What is the economist's definition of the correct, or optimal, rate of output?
2. Why do externalities, such as air and water pollution, occur?
3. Why do economists believe there can be an optimal amount of pollution? What would occur if all pollution were eliminated?
4. Explain the rationale for requiring everyone who can afford it to purchase catastrophic health insurance.
5. The number of medical school spaces in this country is limited. Would fewer people become physicians if government subsidies for medical education were reduced?

Notes

1. Another approach to reducing pollution that also provides incentives for polluters to search for the most efficient method of reducing pollution is to establish a market for pollution rights. The 1990 Clean Air Act Amendments established the first large-scale use of the tradable permit approach to pollution control. A market for transferable sulfur dioxide emission allowances among electric utilities was established. Along with a cap on annual emissions, electric utilities had an opportunity to trade rights to emit sulfur dioxide. Firms facing high abatement costs had an opportunity to purchase the right to emit pollution from firms with lower costs.

2. The ACA included an individual mandate (the penalty was repealed in 2017). The penalty tax for not buying health insurance is small—$95 in 2014 and increasing to $695 (for a single adult) by 2016 and beyond (indexed for inflation). The tax might alternatively be calculated as a percentage of income—1 percent in 2014 and up to 2.5 percent of income in 2018. A person earning $50,000 a year would have to pay a tax of only $1,250. Because the cost of health insurance for single adults is likely to be about $3,000 plus a deductible of $6,000, an out-of-pocket payment of $9,000 before receiving any insurance benefits, it is likely that many young adults will find it preferable to pay the tax for being uninsured rather than buy insurance whose cost exceeds its perceived value. The low penalty tax does not shift back to the free riders the external cost that is imposed on the insured by those who can afford to buy insurance but choose not to do so.

Additional Readings

Goulder, L. 2013. "Markets for Pollution Allowances: What Are the (New) Lessons?" *Journal of Economic Perspectives* 27 (1): 87–102.

Joskow, P., R. Schmalensee, and E. Bailey. 1998. "The Market for Sulfur Dioxide Emissions." *American Economic Review* 88 (4): 669–85.

References

Ackerman, B., and W. T. Hassler. 1981. *Clean Coal/Dirty Air: Or How the Clean Air Act Became a Multibillion-Dollar Bail-Out for High Sulfur Coal Producers and What Should Be Done About It.* New Haven, CT: Yale University Press.

Crandall, R. W. 1983. "Air Pollution, Environmentalists, and the Coal Lobby." In *The Political Economy of Deregulation*, edited by R. G. Noll and B. M. Owen, 84–96. Washington, DC: American Enterprise Institute.

Manning, W., E. Keeler, J. Newhouse, E. Sloss, and J. Wasserman. 1989. "The Taxes of Sin: Do Smokers and Drinkers Pay Their Way?" *Journal of the American Medical Association* 261 (11): 1604–9.

APPENDIX: INFRAMARGINAL
EXTERNALITIES IN MEDICAL EDUCATION

An externality argument for medical education subsidies claims that in addition to the private benefits gained by the student receiving a medical education, the public at large benefits from having a greater number of physicians. Consequently, basing the demand for a medical education on just the private benefits to be received by students would result in too few physicians. Adding the external benefits received by individuals other than students to the private demand by students would result in a greater demand for a medical education. (The fact that medical school spaces do not respond to increases in demand for a medical education is neglected by proponents of subsidies based on an externality argument.)

As shown in exhibit 33.2, MPB represents the marginal private benefits received by students from a medical education. MPC represents the marginal private costs of producing additional physicians (for simplicity, the MPC curve is assumed to be horizontal). The intersection of these marginal private benefit and cost curves results in Q1 number of physicians, which some believe is too small, because the external benefits to others from having physicians (MEB) are excluded from this calculation. Adding the external benefits to the private benefits, shown by the line MTB, intersects the MPC curve at a point to the right of Q1 physicians; Q2 would then be the optimal quantity of physicians.

To achieve the increased output, the government could provide a subsidy to the suppliers sufficient to shift the MPC curve down so that it intersects the MPB curve below the point at which MTB intersects the MPC curve; the MPB and the subsidized MPC curve result in output Q2. This government subsidy could be distributed either to prospective medical students, which would lower their tuition costs and increase the quantity of medical education demanded, or, in a competitive market, the subsidy could be provided to the medical schools, thereby lowering their cost and, consequently, tuition.

It is not enough to assert that there are external benefits to having a greater number of physicians and then to call for massive government support for medical schools. Not all externalities require government intervention. Even assuming that there are some external benefits of having a minimum number of physicians (we all benefit by having physicians available in case we need them), this does not justify government subsidies. The private market is likely to produce this minimum number.

EXHIBIT 33.2
Illustration
of External
Benefits
in Medical
Education

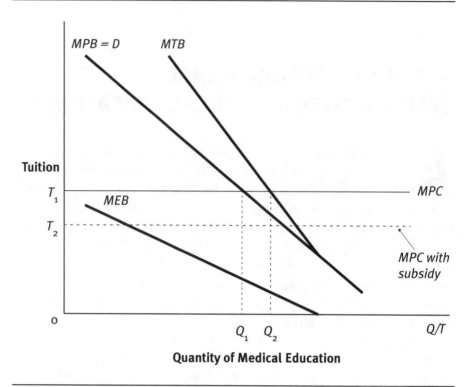

Note: MPB = marginal private benefits; MPC = marginal private costs; MTB = marginal total benefits.

As shown in exhibit 33.3, the externalities may be relatively small. When the MEB is added to the MPB curve, the sum of the two curves intersect at a point to the left of where MPB intersects MPC. The optimal output is unaffected by adding MEB to MPB. Thus, the private market will produce the optimal rate of output; it will produce more than the amount demanded by the addition of MEB. When the private market produces the optimal quantity, even though external benefits exist, it is referred to as *inframarginal* externalities.

Because neither clear evidence nor strong arguments exist that sufficient external benefits occur in medical, dental, or veterinary education to exceed the number of physicians that would be produced by a competitive market in medical education, the case for public subsidies to the health professions' educational institutions on grounds of externalities should be reexamined.

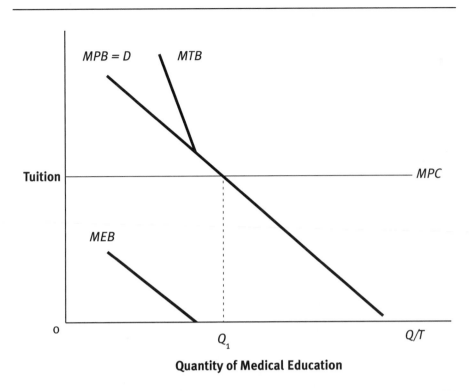

EXHIBIT 33.3
Inframarginal
Externalities
in Medical
Education

Note: MEB = marginal external benefits; MPB = marginal private benefits; MPC = marginal private costs; MTB = marginal total benefits.

THE CANADIAN HEALTHCARE SYSTEM

The Canadian healthcare system, a single-payer system, has been suggested as a model for the United States. Starting in the late 1960s, the Canadian government established the basic guidelines for the system, and each province was provided with federal funds contingent on its adherence to them. Under these guidelines, everyone has access to hospital and medical services, and there are no deductibles or copayments. Patients have free choice of physician and hospital. Unlike the single-payer system in Great Britain, it is not possible to buy out of the system; private health insurance is not permitted for these basic hospital and medical services.

The basic cost-control mechanism used in Canada is expenditure limits on healthcare providers. Each province sets its own overall health budget and negotiates a total budget, which it cannot exceed, with each hospital. The province also negotiates with the medical association to establish uniform fees for all physicians, who are paid on a fee-for-service basis and must accept the province's fee as payment in full for their services.[1] In some provinces, physicians' income is also subject to controls; once physicians' revenues exceed a certain level, further billings are paid at 25 percent of their fee schedule.

These cost-containment measures have limited the increase in Canadian health expenditures, although providers complain about their budgets and, occasionally, physicians go on strike. Because each province finances its services through an income tax, receives federal funds, and pays all medical bills, the need for insurance companies is eliminated. The province controls the adoption and financing of high-technology equipment.

According to its proponents, the Canadian system offers higher life expectancy, universal coverage, comprehensive hospital and medical benefits, no out-of-pocket expenses for hospital and medical services,[2] and lower administrative costs, while devoting a smaller percentage of the gross domestic product (GDP) to healthcare and spending less per capita than the United States. Would the United States be better off if it adopted the Canadian single-payer health system?

Comparing the Canadian System with the US System

Life Expectancy and Lower Infant Mortality Rate

Proponents of the Canadian system claim that for less money they can achieve better health outcomes than can the US healthcare system. Life expectancy at birth for Canadians is about three years higher than that for US residents and little more than one year higher at age 65. Canada also has a lower infant mortality rate per 1,000 live births (Organisation for Economic Co-operation and Development 2017).

Life expectancy and infant mortality rates, however, are inappropriate measures of the output of each country's medical care system. Many factors other than medical services affect these measures, such as lifestyle factors (diet, exercise, smoking, homicides, and so on). For example, the obesity rate among males and females is much greater in the United States than it is in Canada; the mortality rate among those younger than 40 years due to accidents and homicides is also much higher in the United States than in Canada, as is the mortality rate due to heart disease among those older than 45 years (O'Neill and O'Neill 2008).

Treatment Outcomes and Prevention

More relevant to a comparison of each country's medical system are the treatments and outcomes for people who are ill. The percentage of low-birth-weight infants (under 1,500 grams) is higher in the United States than in Canada (which is likely related to lifestyle factors); however, the mortality rate for these infants is lower in the United States than in Canada (which is an outcome of the medical system).

An examination of the percentage of individuals with a specific medical condition, such as high blood pressure or heart disease, who receive treatment shows that whites in the United States are more likely to be treated than are white Canadians. Similarly, rates of preventive screening for various types of cancer, such as mammograms for breast cancer, Pap smears for cervical cancer, prostate-specific antigen tests for prostate cancer, and colonoscopies for colorectal cancer, are much higher in the United States than in Canada (O'Neill and O'Neill 2008; Preston and Ho 2010).

Another important indication of the performance of a country's medical system is the survival rate of those with cancer. (Relative survival is the ratio of survival among patients with cancer to patients subjected to normal mortality.) As shown in exhibit 34.1, overall cancer survival rates are higher in California (with a similar-size population) than in Canada. In addition, cancer survival rates in California and the United States are among the highest in the world. Although cancer survival rates vary among regions in the United States, the variation in survival rates is much greater in Europe and among Canadian provinces.

	Year of Diagnosis	Breast	Prostate	Colorectum	Lung
Canadian registries	1996–1998	86	91	60	16
	2006–2008	88	95	65	18
California registries	1996–1998	88.9	97.7	63.6	14.6
	2006–2008	91.5	99.7	67.1	17.9

EXHIBIT 34.1
Age-Standardized Five-Year Relative Survival Rates for Cancer in Canada and California, 1996–1998 and 2006–2008

Sources: Data for Canada from Canadian Cancer Society (2007, table 16; 2017, table 5.2). Data for California from Kwong (2013).

The discussion thus far is not meant to imply that the current US medical system does not need important reform changes to make it more equitable and efficient, just that, contrary to the beliefs of single-payer proponents, the Canadian system does not have better medical outcomes than those in the United States.

Universal Coverage

According to proponents, the Canadian system has two major advantages. The first is universal coverage. However, as adoption of the Canadian system is but one proposal for reform, it should be compared not with the current US system but with other healthcare reform proposals to achieve universal coverage (see chapter 36). Thus, adopting the Canadian system solely to achieve universal coverage is not necessary. The second advantage is that, to many, the Canadian system is based on its presumed ability to control the rising costs of healthcare.

Controlling Healthcare Costs in Canada

Proponents of the Canadian system point to two cost savings. The first is lower administrative costs, and the second is a slower rate of increase in healthcare costs. Each is discussed in the sections that follow.

Administrative Costs

Advocates of the Canadian system have claimed that if the United States adopted the Canadian system, it could greatly reduce its administrative costs, as health insurance companies would no longer be necessary; therefore, universal access could be financed at no additional cost (Woolhandler, Campbell, and Himmelstein 2003). Many agree that administrative costs in the United States could be lowered somewhat with standardization of claims processing and billing.

Simple comparisons of administrative expenses between the two countries, however, are misleading.[3] Administrative and marketing costs could be reduced if the United States eliminated choice of health plans and decreed a standardized set of health benefits. The United States has a wide variety of health plans—such as health maintenance organizations (HMOs), point-of-service plans, and preferred provider organizations—that offer different benefits, cost-sharing levels, and access to providers. Competition among health plans offers consumers greater choice at different premiums.

Choice is costly. However, without choice, there would be less innovation in benefit design, patient satisfaction would be lower, and there would be less competition on health plan premiums. The diversity of insurance plans reflects differences in enrollees' preferences and how much they are willing to pay for those preferences.

Lower administrative costs are not synonymous with greater system efficiency. One can imagine very low administrative costs in a system in which physicians and hospitals send their bills to the government and the government simply pays them. These lower administrative costs cause higher healthcare expenditures because they do not detect or deter inappropriate use or overuse of services.

A trade-off occurs between lower administrative costs and higher health expenditures caused by insufficient monitoring of physician and hospital behavior. If higher administrative cost resulting from utilization management did not pay for itself by reducing medical expenses and overutilization, managed care plans would not use these measures. For example, the US Medicare system, which has a similar design to that of the Canadian system, seemingly has much lower administrative costs than do private managed care plans. However, the US Government Accountability Office (GAO) criticized Medicare for having administrative costs that are "too low," noting that billions of dollars could be saved "by adopting the healthcare management approach of private payers to Medicare's public payer role" (GAO 1995).

This concern has not changed over time. The Centers for Medicare & Medicaid Services (2012) reported that Medicare payment for durable medical equipment had an error rate of 66 percent for improper or fake claims. In 2015, the GAO (2017) estimated that Medicare made improper and fraudulent payments of approximately $60 billion a year, 10 percent of Medicare's annual provider payments. Fraud is particularly rampant in Medicare and Medicaid where government oversight is less vigorous than oversight by private health insurers. Medicare's lack of scrutiny (it automatically pays 95 percent of all claims) results in lower overhead costs but makes the program highly vulnerable to fraud.

The private health insurance industry in the United States is very competitive and would only increase administrative costs if the benefits from doing so exceeded its costs. Studies have shown that cost-containment approaches, such as catastrophic case management and physician profiling for appropriateness of care, save money (National Conference of State Legislatures 2011). Any savings in administrative costs by eliminating cost-containment techniques and patient cost sharing would be more than offset by higher utilization. Medicare and the Canadian system are forgoing substantial savings by not raising their administrative costs, investing more in cost-containment programs, and developing mechanisms to monitor physicians' practice patterns.

Rising Healthcare Costs

An oft-cited measure of the Canadian system's cost-containment success is that healthcare costs make up a smaller percentage of the country's GDP than that in the United States. Although correct, this information can be misleading. At different times, GDP may increase faster in one country than in another, distorting any conclusion regarding which country's healthcare costs are rising faster.

A more accurate indication of which country's healthcare costs have grown more slowly is the rise in per capita health expenditures. Again, one must be careful in making such comparisons, as 40 percent of US medical expenditures are by the government, for Medicare, Medicaid, and health insurance exchange subsidies, which have limited cost controls. Some regions of the United States also have greater managed care penetration than others. The US medical system has evolved from one that, until the 1980s, provided limited, if any, incentives for efficiency to one in which the private sector (in some states more than others) emphasizes managed care delivery systems. Thus, it is more relevant to compare the performance of the US system, starting in the 1990s—particularly in states with a great portion of the population under managed care—with the Canadian system.

As shown in exhibit 34.2, since the 1980s, per capita health expenditures (adjusted for inflation) have risen at a slower rate in Canada than in the United States. However, during some periods, Canada's rate has been higher to compensate for the serious lack of funding in previous years. The effect of managed care can be seen by the lower rate of increase in the United States during the mid-1990s than in prior years. (As a result of the backlash against managed care in the late 1990s, managed care's cost-containment methods were loosened and premiums rose more rapidly.) Between 2004 and 2009, Canada had a *higher* average annual rate of increase in per capita health expenditures than that in the United States.

Since 2011, Canada's per capita healthcare expenditures, adjusted for inflation, have actually *decreased*. This decrease in real spending per capita is the result of slower economic growth and greater fiscal restraint, as the federal and provincial governments sought to reduce budget deficits following the 2009 recession. (Rather than being an indicator of greater efficiency, this reduction in Canadian healthcare spending has become a source of great concern, which will be apparent when access to care is discussed later.) It is highly likely that,

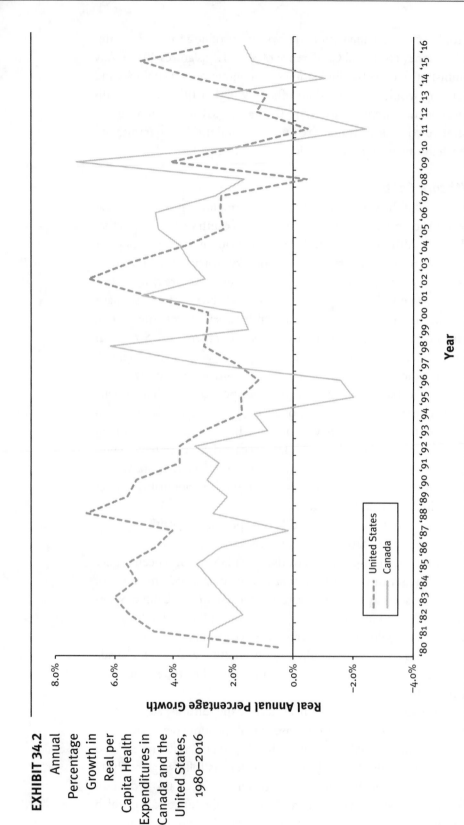

EXHIBIT 34.2
Annual Percentage Growth in Real per Capita Health Expenditures in Canada and the United States, 1980–2016

Note: Values adjusted for inflation using the consumer price index for each country.

Source: Health expenditures per capita data from the Organisation for Economic Co-operation and Development (2017); consumer price index data from Bureau of Labor Statistics (2017) and Statistics Canada (2017).

similar to earlier periods, future spending will increase more rapidly to alleviate such concerns.

Canada's lower per capita healthcare costs and lower percentage of GDP devoted to healthcare compared with the US system are not the result of greater efficiency in producing medical services.

Difference in Hospital Length of Stay

Although efficiency studies would have to control for many differences between the two countries, such as populations served, distribution of illnesses, outcomes of care, staffing patterns, wage rates, and so on, one simple, although partial, measure of efficiency is the difference in lengths of hospital stay.

Managed care systems in the United States have a financial incentive to use the least costly combination of medical services. Hospitals are the most expensive setting for providing care. Use of the hospital is subject to review. Outpatient diagnostics and surgery are used whenever possible, and catastrophic case management may involve renovating a patient's home to make it a lower-cost and more convenient setting in which to care for the patient.

The efficiency gains from managed care are evident in a comparison of utilization data between the United States and Canada. As shown in exhibit 34.3, Canadian hospitals have a higher average length of stay (LOS) than that in hospitals in the United States, but the difference is decreasing. In 1980, the LOS in Canada was 10.0 days, compared with 7.6 days in the United States.

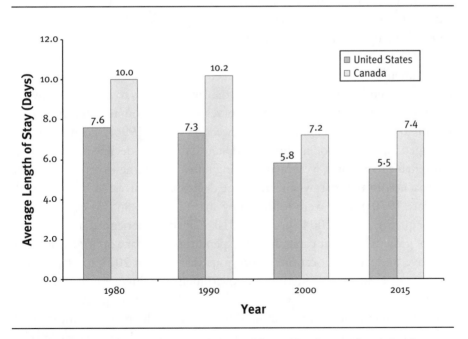

EXHIBIT 34.3
Average Length of Hospital Stay in Canada and the United States, 1980–2015

Sources: Data from Organisation for Economic Co-operation and Development (2017); American Hospital Association (2017).

In 2015, the respective LOS in Canada and the United States were 7.4 days and 5.5 days, respectively. In California, a state with high managed care penetration, the average LOS was 5.1 days (2015). The average LOS for those 65 years and older is very high in Canada because few alternatives are available. Canadian hospitals are used inefficiently; many services could be provided in an outpatient setting, the physician's office, or the patient's home.

Annual hospital budgets in Canada also provide administrators with an incentive to fill a portion of their beds with elderly patients, who stay many days. If more surgical patients were admitted, hospitals would not receive additional funds to purchase the necessary supplies and nursing personnel to serve them. Thus, as inflation diminishes the real value of Canadian hospitals' budgets with which to purchase resources, they admit fewer acutely ill patients and prolong their stays.

If the lower rate of increase in Canada's healthcare expenditures is not a result of greater efficiency, to what is it attributable?

Consequences of Strict Limits on Per Capita Costs

In the late 1980s, Canada was experiencing rising healthcare costs and a deep recession. As a result, the federal government reduced its financial commitment to the provinces. Initially, the federal government paid for 50 percent of each province's health spending; this figure was reduced to an average of about 24 percent (in 2016 to 2017) (Allin and Rudoler 2017). As these federal cash and tax transfers fell, the growing cost of the Canadian health system placed a greater financial burden on each province.

The consequence of these costs for both the federal and provincial governments has been periods of reduced healthcare spending, followed by increased spending to compensate for the lack of access to care. As shown in exhibit 34.2, the annual percentage increase in inflation-adjusted per capita health expenditures fell dramatically between 1994 and 1996. In contrast to the managed care revolution in the United States, this steep decline in Canada was attributable to cuts in government funding rather than to new cost-containment approaches. In the past, when such large decreases occurred (e.g., in the early and late 1970s), they were followed by sharp increases in subsequent years. Consequently, from 2004 through 2010, Canada experienced a more rapid rate of growth in its per capita health expenditures to make up for the low and negative budgetary allocations in previous years. From 2011 to 2016 (most recent data available), reductions in government funding were the reason for the decrease in real Canadian per capita expenditures. This pattern—years of slow growth in expenditures followed by years of high growth—repeats itself.

Government expenditure limits are the inevitable consequence of an unlimited demand for medical services. No government can fund all of the medical care that is demanded at zero price. Because expenditure limits result in less care being provided than is demanded at zero price, choices must be made about how scarce healthcare resources are to be allocated. Scarce resources must be rationed either by price or by waiting times. Lacking a price system, Canada must make many trade-offs—for example, between preventive care, acute care, access to new technology, and patient waiting times to receive treatment. With limited dollars, providing more of one choice means less money is available to fulfill other choices.

The inevitable consequences of tight per capita expenditure limits, as have occurred in Canada, are more shortages in medical services and less access to new technology. Further, because the beneficial effects of preventive care are realized in the future, existing resources are allocated to acute services for patients whose needs are immediate.

Access to Technology

One of the distinguishing features of the US medical system is the rapid diffusion of technologic innovation. Major advances in diagnostic and treatment procedures have occurred. Imaging equipment has improved diagnostic accuracy and minimized the need for exploratory surgery. New technology has resulted in less invasive procedures, quicker recovery times, and better treatment outcomes. Technologic advances have increased the survival rate of low-birth-weight babies and permitted a growing number and type of organ transplants. Any comparison of the Canadian and US health systems should consider the rate at which new technology is diffused and made available to patients.

Managed care, which is characteristic of the private US healthcare system, uses different criteria from those used in Canada for adopting and diffusing new technology. Two types of technologic advances occur. The first type, and simplest to evaluate under managed care, is when new technology reduces costs and improves patient satisfaction. A competitive managed care system invests the necessary capital to bring about these technologic savings. The second type is when new technology improves medical outcomes, but the treatment is much more costly than existing treatment. Particularly troublesome is new technology that may have only a low probability of success—for example, 10 to 20 percent. In such cases, the patient would like access to the expensive treatment, while the insurer may believe it is not worth the expenditure given the low success rate.

Technology that is clearly believed to be beneficial is highly likely to be adopted. If one health plan decided not to adopt the technology when its competitors did, it would lose enrollees. Competition among health plans forces the adoption of highly beneficial technology. The costs of such technology are eventually passed on to enrollees in the form of higher premiums.

New technology that offers small benefits (e.g., a new method of conducting Pap smears that increases cancer detection by 5 percent or experimental breast cancer treatments for patients with late-stage disease) has caused problems for managed care firms. Several health plans that have denied such treatments incurred penalties of up to $100 million as a result of lawsuits. To reduce their liability, more health plans have delegated such decisions to outside firms made up of ethicists and physicians who have no financial stake in the decision.

In Canada, the availability of capital to invest in cost-saving and outcome-enhancing technology is determined by the government, not the hospital. Given its budget constraints and reluctance to raise taxes, the government is less likely to provide capital for new technology (and for as many units) than are firms that compete for enrollees. Outpatient diagnostic and surgical services are less available in Canada, denying patients the benefits (and society the cost savings) of such technologic improvements. Costly outcome-enhancing technology, such as that for transplants and experimental treatments, is also less available to Canadians.

A competitive managed care system may adopt technology too soon and have excess technologic capacity. Excess capacity, however, means faster access and lower patient risks. Enrollees may be willing to pay higher premiums to have that excess capacity available. If so, excess technologic capacity is appropriate; the benefits to enrollees are at least equal to their willingness to pay for it. The adoption of new technology under managed care competition is different from that by a government (or quasigovernmental agency), as the government would be concerned about losing political support if it had to raise taxes or incur large budget deficits to increase access to new technology.

Exhibit 34.4 provides examples of differences in the availability of technology between Canada and the United States. Twice as many gamma cameras per person are available in the United States than in Canada, four times as many magnetic resonance imaging (MRI) units and positron emission tomography scanners, and almost three times as many computed tomography (CT) scanners and mammography units. Clearly, the likelihood of a patient in the United States receiving any of the services shown in exhibit 34.4 is much greater than that of a patient in Canada with equal or similar needs. How successful would an HMO be in the United States if it used access criteria similar to those used in Canada?

The Technological Change in Healthcare (TECH) Research Network is an international group of researchers who examine differences in technologic change across countries in the treatment, resource costs, and health outcomes for common health problems (Bech et al. 2009; TECH Research Network 2001). Because knowledge of heart attack treatment has greatly changed in recent years, and data from various studies have shown that improvements in outcomes may be the result of differences in medical practices, variations among countries in adopting technology for inpatient care are likely to occur.

The researchers found different patterns of technologic change in adopting more intensive cardiac procedures. The United States adopted an "early

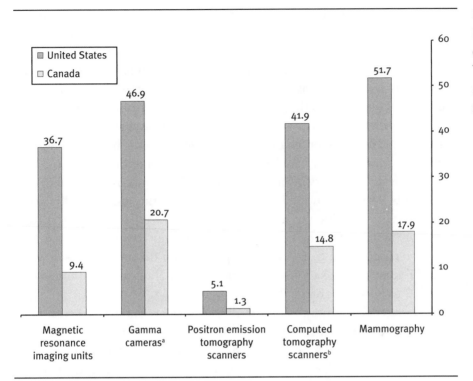

EXHIBIT 34.4

Indicators of Medical Technology per Million People, 2016

[a]2013 data for United States, 2012 data for Canada.

[b]2015 data for United States.

Source: Data from Organisation for Economic Co-operation and Development (2017).

start and fast growth" pattern, which resulted in relatively high treatment rates in the overall population, as well as in the elderly population. Conversely, in Canada, the adoption of new technology begins later, its diffusion is slower (as well as lower than in the United States), and both the elderly and general populations have lower treatment rates. The TECH Research Network (2001, 37) attributed these variations in the adoption and diffusion of technology for care of heart attack patients to differences in funding and decision making, "such as global budgets for hospitals and central planning of the availability of intensive services" in Canada. The researchers further stated, "It is clear that if high-quality care requires rapid innovation and diffusion of valuable high-cost as well as low-cost treatments, quality of care may differ greatly around the world, and national health policy may influence quality in important ways" (TECH Research Network 2001, 38).

Patient Waiting Times

As demand for services exceeds available supply, waiting time is used to ration nonemergency care. For some types of care, the quantity demanded increases because patients have no copayments. Facing a zero price, patients demand a high volume of physician visits. Consequently, to see more patients, physicians spend less time per visit. The physician then asks the patient to return for multiple short visits rather than provide all the needed services during one visit. Patient time costs are, therefore, high under a "free" system with tight fee controls because each visit requires the same patient travel and waiting time regardless of the length of the visit.[4] The cost of waiting is also high for the poor and those with low incomes (Goodman 2015). The decrease in Canada's real per capita healthcare spending over the past several years has caused waiting times to increase, and they have become the longest ever recorded (Barua 2017).

Expenditure limits invariably result in high time costs being imposed on patients. However, not all care rationed by waiting time is of low value to the patient. According to a 2017 Fraser Institute report on the Canadian healthcare system, patients had to wait, on average, 10.8 weeks for an MRI scan (the range was 6 to 24 weeks, depending on the province), 4.1 weeks for a CT scan (range, 3 to 6 weeks), and almost 3.9 weeks for an ultrasound (range, 2 to 8 weeks) (Barua 2017).

Longer wait times to confirm diagnosis can mean delayed treatment, which often prolongs stress for the individual and can impact outcomes. For example, for colorectal cancer screening, wait times for a follow-up colonoscopy after an abnormal fecal test result for the majority of patients ranged from 104 to 151 days in nine reporting provinces. The national target states that the delay should not exceed 60 days, which is in itself a long time (Canadian Partnership Against Cancer 2017).

Acknowledging these long waits and their adverse effects on patients, several Canadian provinces pay for heart surgery and radiation oncology treatment in the United States, which is Canada's safety valve. Ontario has contracted with hospitals in Buffalo, New York, and Detroit, Michigan, for MRI services. Quebec has sent hundreds of cancer patients to the United States for treatment, because they waited more than eight weeks for radiation treatment or chemotherapy (more than four weeks of waiting time is considered medically risky) (Druzin 2016).

The Fraser Institute administers annual surveys on waiting times from referral by the general practitioner (GP) to an appointment with a specialist, as well as on the waiting time from an appointment with a specialist to treatment. These surveys are conducted by medical specialty for each Canadian province. Exhibit 34.5 describes the waiting time for treatment by specialty. For example, for orthopedic surgery (e.g., hips and knees), a person would have to wait, on average, 41.7 weeks to receive treatment; in some provinces, however, the wait for surgery may be as short as 30.9 weeks or as long as 90.9 weeks. (In 1991, aged patients in some provinces had to wait up to four years for a hip or knee replacement.) Ophthalmological surgery (e.g., cataract removal) requires an average wait of 31.4 weeks, but it can vary from 13.1 to 63.9 weeks depending

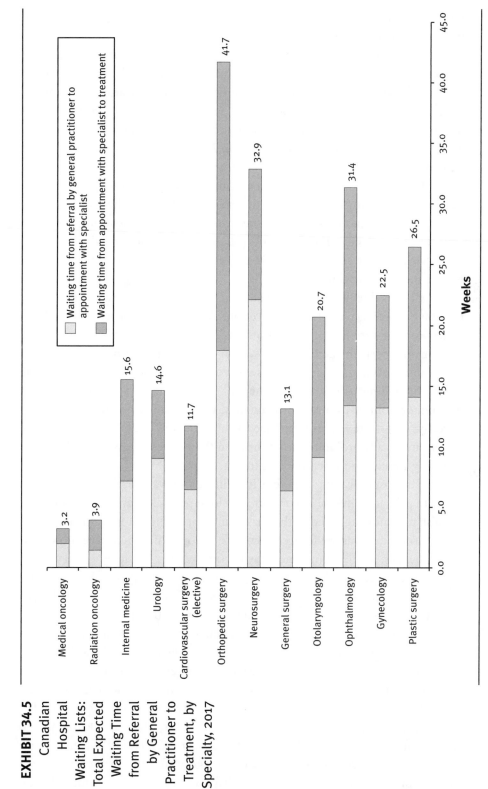

EXHIBIT 34.5
Canadian Hospital Waiting Lists: Total Expected Waiting Time from Referral by General Practitioner to Treatment, by Specialty, 2017

Waiting time from referral by general practitioner to appointment with specialist

Waiting time from appointment with specialist to treatment

Medical oncology — 3.2
Radiation oncology — 3.9
Internal medicine — 15.6
Urology — 14.6
Cardiovascular surgery (elective) — 11.7
Orthopedic surgery — 41.7
Neurosurgery — 32.9
General surgery — 13.1
Otolaryngology — 20.7
Ophthalmology — 31.4
Gynecology — 22.5
Plastic surgery — 26.5

Weeks

0.0   5.0   10.0   15.0   20.0   25.0   30.0   35.0   40.0   45.0

Source: Data from Barua (2017).

on the province. For neurosurgery, the average waiting time is 32.9 weeks, but it varies by province between 11.1 and 64.7 weeks.

The Fraser Institute also asks specialists how long a patient *should* wait before receiving the recommended treatment. For example, in Nova Scotia the actual waiting time for urgent cardiovascular surgery after a patient has seen a specialist is more than four weeks, whereas specialists believe the waiting time should not exceed one week. For elective cardiovascular surgery, the actual waiting time is much longer (Barua 2017). There have been reports of patients dying while waiting for heart surgery.

Clearly, access to care depends on the province in which one lives. Furthermore, in any one province, the waiting time is not the same for every procedure. Waiting times from referral by the GP to treatment in Ontario are almost one-third shorter (15.4 weeks) than those for someone living in New Brunswick (41.7 weeks). Exhibit 34.6 presents these waiting times from GP to treatment by province.

Canada does not have an egalitarian system. Access to care depends not only on the province in which one lives but also on whether a person can afford to pay for her care in the United States. The failure to consider the higher patient time costs in the Canadian system *understates* health expenditures in that country. As demand for services exceeds the available supply, many people would be willing to pay more rather than incur the cost of multiple trips, waiting, or doing without. Unfortunately, the Canadian system prohibits the purchase of private health insurance for hospital and medical services. Thus, people are legally prohibited from insuring themselves against the risks of not receiving timely care when they require it.

The cost of waiting manifests itself in various ways. Patients may have to live with pain and physical discomfort for a long period. They may suffer mental anguish not knowing whether they have cancer and whether it is growing inside them. Prolonged waiting for treatment of a serious illness may have substantial consequences; medical outcomes may become worse. An older person waiting for cataract surgery may be unable to drive for a prolonged period. While waiting for treatment, patients may be unable to work or perform their job, leading to unemployment. These burdens fall more heavily on those with low incomes.

Wealthy individuals can skip the queues and purchase medical services in the United States, as did the then-premier of Newfoundland and Labrador. When he learned that he needed heart surgery in 2010, instead of waiting his turn, he went to the United States for his operation at his own expense (CBC News 2010). Similarly, the politically powerful are able to jump to the head of the queue, as happened with Canada's health minister, who was able to undergo surgery after being diagnosed with prostate cancer in 2001. Other patients with prostate cancer were angered by his quick surgery after they had to wait much longer, some as long as a year between diagnosis and surgery (Rupert 2001).

EXHIBIT 34.6
Canadian Hospital Waiting Lists: Total Expected Waiting Time from Referral by General Practitioner to Treatment, by Province, 2017

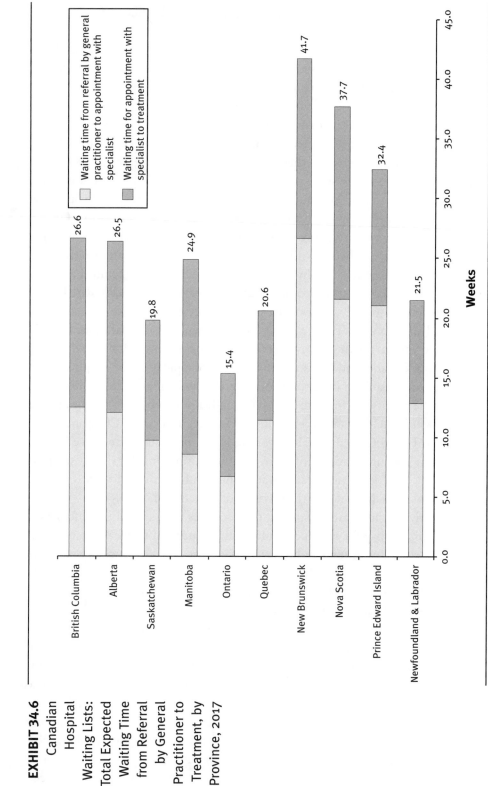

Legend:
- Waiting time from referral by general practitioner to appointment with specialist
- Waiting time for appointment with specialist to treatment

Weeks

Province	Total
British Columbia	26.6
Alberta	26.5
Saskatchewan	19.8
Manitoba	24.9
Ontario	15.4
Quebec	20.6
New Brunswick	41.7
Nova Scotia	37.7
Prince Edward Island	32.4
Newfoundland & Labrador	21.5

Source: Data from Barua (2017).

Is Canada Abandoning Its Single-Payer System?

A Quebec patient, forced to wait a year for a hip replacement and prohibited from paying privately for his operation, brought a lawsuit against the Quebec government to the Canadian Supreme Court. In a surprise ruling, the Supreme Court concluded that the wait for medical services had become so long that the health system and its ban on private practice violated patients' "life and personal security, inviolability and freedom," which are part of Quebec's Charter of Rights and Freedoms. Further, "the evidence in this case shows that delays in the public healthcare system are widespread, and that, in some serious cases, patients die as a result of waiting lists for public healthcare. . . . In sum, the prohibition on obtaining private health insurance is not constitutional where the public system fails to deliver reasonable services" (Krauss 2005). The ruling applied only to Quebec; in other provinces, the sale of private health insurance to cover hospital and physician services is still illegal. One must pay cash to use a private physician or other outpatient services, such as MRIs. Private diagnostic and special surgery clinics have rapidly expanded.

The amount of private care now available across Canada varies widely from province to province. Privately funded primary and surgical care in British Columbia, Ontario, and Quebec have experienced rapid growth, but private care remains unavailable in other parts of the country, such as in New Brunswick, although patients can travel to British Columbia or Quebec. Private healthcare firms include such organizations as Regal Healthcare Services, Cleveland Clinic Canada, HealthCare 365, Medisys, Medcan Clinic, and Executive Health Centre in Toronto. Patients often bypass the waiting time for diagnostic tests by having them done at these private clinics and then wait for treatment at Canada's public hospitals (Cribb, Isai, and Shakeel 2017).

Private clinics are expanding their services, and several provinces contract with and pay for treatments in privately operated surgical clinics. As in the United States, Canadian physicians have also started concierge practices for those willing to pay for better access.

Out-of-pocket expenses for the 30 percent of healthcare not covered by Canada's healthcare system have increased rapidly over time and are estimated to be about $1,800 per person annually (Have and Brown 2016). Several factors have led to these increased costs: an aging population, increased use of private services, and higher prices. These costs will continue to increase sharply, particularly as personalized medicine expands and new innovative drugs become available. Many employers provide private insurance to cover the majority of these costs; however, for those who are self-employed or unemployed, these costs will become significant. Further, private insurers may limit or deny individual coverage to those with a preexisting condition.

In addition, a new industry consisting of medical travel agents has been created to assist Canadian patients seeking medical treatment in other countries.

These agents, such as MedSolution, specialize in out-of-country hospital care to places such as France, Turkey, and India. Other medical travel agents, such as Vancouver-based Timely Medical Alternatives, offer package deals on hotels and operations at US clinics not more than a two-hour drive from the border. Private health insurance and private clinics have been expanding in Canada and will likely reduce medical tourism to other countries.

Supporters of the single-payer system are opposed to a two-tier medical system, believing the private sector will draw physicians and nurses away from the public system, where a severe physician shortage already exists, making waiting times even longer. The dam has already broken, however. As of 2017, at least 136 for-profit clinics were in operation across Canada, offering surgeries, MRI scans, and access to physician services (Ontario Health Coalition 2017). Patients must pay with cash, but the wait time is short.[5] Stopping the trend toward privatization and a two-tier medical system, which already exist in other countries, will be difficult.

Should the United States Adopt the Canadian System?

Canada has been the only Westernized country with a single-payer system. Other countries that started with a single-payer system, such as Great Britain, moved to a two-tier system that permits private medical markets. Canada is also moving in this direction. Governments find that it eventually becomes too expensive to fund all the new technology and medical services its population demands when they do not have to pay any out-of-pocket costs. Inequities develop in a single-payer system; the wealthy can reduce their waiting time by traveling to another country, and the politically powerful are able to jump the queue. A two-tier medical system recognizes that there are people willing to spend more of their money in return for quicker access to medical services and the latest medical technology.

Alternative approaches exist to achieve the objectives of a single-payer system. With regard to the equity criterion—namely, how to provide for the uninsured—the Canadian system should not be compared with the current US system, but with a system in which the goal is universal coverage. This goal can be achieved in alternative ways, such as by providing income-related subsidies to those with low income (see chapter 36).

A single-payer system, as evidenced by the Canadian system, does not provide everyone with equal access to medical care. We should acknowledge that every health system has multiple tiers; those who can afford to will be able to purchase more medical services or have quicker access to care. Unequal access to care exists in Canada depending on the province in which people live or whether they can afford to pay for their care in the United States or in other countries.

Arbitrarily limiting the growth in medical expenditures, the cost-containment method used in single-payer systems, will not increase efficiency. Efficiency incentives on the part of patients or medical providers are not used in the Canadian system. Efficiency incentives are important because they affect the cost of any national health insurance plan and the willingness of the public to provide subsidies to those less fortunate than themselves. To whom are government decision makers accountable? What information do they have on which to base their decisions? In a competitive market, people can leave a health plan when they are dissatisfied with that plan; in a monopolized system (single payer), they have no similar way in which to express their dissatisfaction with the system. In a single-payer system, information on waiting times and access problems is either unavailable or dated, making it difficult for decision makers to make adjustments based on changes in demand or supply conditions. Also important in deciding which national health insurance plan to adopt are the criteria used for access to and investment in new medical technology. Efficiency, innovation, and capital investment are determined by incentives; a government bureaucracy is highly unlikely to outperform competitive markets in this regard.[6]

Political versus private decision making will result in differences in access to care, technology adoption, efficiency, equity, and even health outcomes. Before the United States places its healthcare system (which accounts for almost one-fifth [17.9 percent of GDP in 2016] of its economy) under complete government control, single-payer advocates should provide evidence (more than just opinion) showing why a single-payer system will not suffer the same fate experienced by every other country that has tried and subsequently abandoned its own single-payer system.

Further, why would the problems of a national single-payer system differ from those experienced by the two single-payer systems that currently exist in the United States: Medicare, in which low-income aged must fall back on Medicaid to pay their medical bills, and which will have to undergo reform to prevent bankruptcy of the Hospital Trust Fund; and Medicaid, which offers poor access to care (see chapter 9)?

Summary

Proposals to achieve universal access to care in the US healthcare system should not be evaluated solely against the Canadian single-payer system, but against other national health insurance proposals also aiming to achieve universal coverage and limit rising healthcare expenditures. Further, single-payer advocates should not dismiss the flaws of the Canadian system by claiming that the United States would be able to devote more money to a single-payer system. Given growing medical costs, advancements in medical technology, and no limits on patients' access to care, the evidence, based on the experience of every country that has tried a single-payer system, suggests that such a system in the United States would eventually suffer the same fate as the Canadian system. It would eventually resemble Medicaid.

Before the United States emulates another country's medical system, it should know all the facts—good and bad—about the performance of that country's medical system and the criteria by which a system should be evaluated. Controlling the percentage of GDP devoted to medical care or the rise in per capita expenditures should not be the overriding objectives of a medical system; if they were, the United States could use Great Britain's National Health Service, which performs better than the Canadian system on these criteria, but is clearly unacceptable on other grounds.

Adopting another country's health system without understanding the differences in its history and social values would likely result in a great deal of dissatisfaction.

Patient preferences differ regarding how much they are willing to spend for faster access to care and for the latest advances in medical science. Single-payer systems disregard such differences in preferences. The Canadian system places greater emphasis on primary care than on specialist care and complex and costly procedures. The United States spends a great deal more on cancer care and achieves better outcomes. Similarly, older adults are able to undergo hip and knee replacement surgery and other orthopedic procedures sooner—without sacrificing their quality of life—than is possible in Canada.

The appropriate rate of growth in medical expenditures should be based on how much people are willing to pay (directly and through taxes). There are legitimate reasons for increased medical expenditures—such as an aging population, more chronic illness, new technology that saves lives and improves the quality of life, new diseases, shortages of personnel (thereby resulting in wage increases), and so on. Arbitrary expenditure limits would result in reduced access to medical services and technology.

Discussion Questions

1. Describe the Canadian healthcare system and the methods used to control costs.
2. What are the consequences of making medical services free to everyone?
3. Why is the size of administrative expenses (as a percentage of total medical expenditures) a poor indication of a healthcare system's efficiency?
4. What are the costs (negative effects) of expenditure limits?
5. Contrast the criteria used in Canada with those used in competitive managed care systems for deciding whether an investment should be made in new technology.

Notes

1. Hutchison and Glazier (2013) discussed changes in primary care payment to physicians in Ontario using fee-for-service, capitation, and pay-for-performance. See also Lewis (2015) for background on the Canadian system.

2. As of 2016, provincial governments pay, on average, only about 70 percent of total medical expenses—mainly for hospital and physician services. Canadian patients pay the remaining 30 percent, which includes outpatient prescription drugs, dental care, vision care, and other hospital and professional services. Many Canadians, or employers on their behalf, buy private insurance to cover these services. Despite first-dollar public coverage for hospital and physician services, Canadians spend more privately on healthcare than citizens of most European countries (Allin and Rudoler 2017).

3. The criticism of high administrative costs in the US private health insurance market is often made in comparison with Medicare because the ratio of administrative costs to total expenditures for private insurers is much larger than that for Medicare. It is fallacious to use these expense ratios as an indication of differences in efficiency. Medicare's per capita claim costs are much higher than those of privately insured patients; thus, Medicare's administrative expenses represent a smaller proportion of total costs.

   Further, Medicare administrative costs are artificially lower because other agencies incur some of those costs. The Centers for Medicare & Medicaid Services, which performs administrative services for Medicare, is generally excluded from the calculation of Medicare's administrative costs. Additional costs necessary for the operation of Medicare, such as enrollment and billing, are included in the Social Security Administration's costs. The collection of Medicare payroll taxes by the Internal Revenue System is not attributed to Medicare. Medicare also has lower costs because it relies on price controls and thus does not negotiate with providers or undertake cost-containment and quality improvement functions (e.g., medical management); in addition, it spends too little to reduce fraud and abuse. Medicare is also exempt from paying state premium taxes, and it does not incur regulatory and compliance costs that affect insurance companies.

4. The value to the patient of additional physician visits when there are no out-of-pocket payments is low. Generally, the approaches used to limit use of services whose value is worth less than their costs of production are cost-containment techniques and requiring patients to wait longer.

Cost containment is included as an explicit administrative expense, whereas implicit patient waiting cost is not.

5. One physician who opened private medical clinics said, "This is a country in which dogs can get a hip replacement in under a week and in which humans can wait two to three years" (Krauss 2006). Dogs also have received preferential treatment with regard to diagnostic tests. The government provides funding for hospitals to operate its MRIs only eight hours a day. In 1998, a Canadian hospital offered MRIs to pets in the middle of the night in an effort to make money. After an outcry from angry people, who were waiting up to a year for nonurgent scans, the hospital was forced to stop this practice (Walkom 2002).

6. For a brief critique of single-payer plans, see Emanuel (2008).

References

Allin, S., and D. Rudoler. 2017. "The Canadian Health Care System." Commonwealth Fund. Accessed December 12. http://international.commonwealthfund.org/countries/canada/.

American Hospital Association. 2017. *Hospital Statistics, 2017 Edition*. Accessed May 2018. www.aha.org/2016-12-27-aha-hospital-statistics-2017-edition.

Barua, B. 2017. *Waiting Your Turn: Wait Times for Health Care in Canada, 2017 Report*. Fraser Institute. Accessed May 2018. www.fraserinstitute.org/sites/default/files/waiting-your-turn-2017.pdf.

Bech, M., T. Christiansen, K. Dunham, J. Lauridsen, C. H. Lyttkens, K. McDonald, A. McGuire, and TECH Investigators. 2009. "The Influence of Economic Incentives and Regulatory Factors on the Adoption of Treatment Technologies: A Case Study of Technologies Used to Treat Heart Attacks." *Health Economics* 18 (10): 1114–32.

Bureau of Labor Statistics. 2017. "Consumer Price Index." Accessed December. www.bls.gov/cpi/home.htm.

Canadian Cancer Society. 2017. *Canadian Cancer Statistics, 2017*. Published June. www.cancer.ca/~/media/cancer.ca/CW/publications/Canadian%20Cancer%20Statistics/Canadian-Cancer-Statistics-2017-EN.pdf.

———. 2007. *Canadian Cancer Statistics, 2007*. Published April. www.cancer.ca/~/media/cancer.ca/CW/cancer%20information/cancer%20101/Canadian%20cancer%20statistics/Canadian-Cancer-Statistics-2007-EN.pdf.

Canadian Partnership Against Cancer. 2017. "Screening Reports Show Many Canadians Still Waiting Too Long for Final Diagnosis of Breast and Colorectal Cancer." Published July 10. www.partnershipagainstcancer.ca/screening-reports-show-many-canadians-still-waiting-long-final-diagnosis-breast-colorectal-cancer/.

CBC News. 2010. "Danny Williams Going to US for Heart Surgery." Posted February 1. www.cbc.ca/news/canada/newfoundland-labrador/dannywilliams-going-to-u-s-for-heart-surgery-1.878492.

Centers for Medicare & Medicaid Services. 2012. "Fiscal Year 2012 Improper Payment Rates for CMS Programs." Accessed May 2018. www.cms.gov/Newsroom/MediaReleaseDatabase/Fact-sheets/2012-Fact-sheets-items/2012-11-21.html.

Cribb, R., V. Isai, and M. Shakeel. 2017. "Should the Wealthy Be Allowed to Buy Their Way to Faster Health Care at Private Clinics?" *Toronto Star*. Published March 18. www.thestar.com/news/canada/2017/03/18/should-the-wealthy-be-allowed-to-buy-their-way-to-faster-care-at-private-clinics.html.

Druzin, R. 2016. "Crossing the Border for Care." *US News & World Report*. Published August 3. www.usnews.com/news/best-countries/articles/2016-08-03/canadians-increasingly-come-to-us-for-health-care.

Emanuel, E. J. 2008. "The Problem with Single-Payer Plans." *Hastings Center Report* 38 (1): 38–41.

Goodman, J. C. 2015. "What Everyone Should Know About Rationing by Waiting." *Forbes*. Published November 9. www.forbes.com/sites/johngoodman/2015/11/09/what-everyone-should-know-about-rationing-by-waiting/.

Have, J., and R. Brown. 2016. "Private Health Insurance Coverage in Canada Needs a Review." *Huffington Post*. Published September 16. www.huffingtonpost.ca/john-have/private-health-insurance-canada_b_12032150.html.

Hutchison, B., and R. Glazier. 2013. "Ontario's Primary Care Reforms Have Transformed the Local Landscape, but a Plan Is Needed for Ongoing Improvement." *Health Affairs* 32 (4): 695–703.

Krauss, C. 2006. "Canada's Private Clinics Surge as Public System Falters." *New York Times*, February 28, A3.

———. 2005. "In Blow to Canada's Health System, Quebec Law Is Voided." *New York Times*, June 10, A3.

Kwong, S. 2013. Personal correspondence with the author, December 23.

Lewis, S. 2015. "A System in Name Only: Access, Variation, and Reform in Canada's Provinces." *New England Journal of Medicine* 372 (6): 497–500.

National Conference of State Legislatures. 2011. *Health Cost Containments and Efficiencies*. Accessed May 2018. www.ncsl.org/documents/health/introandbrief-scc-16.pdf.

O'Neill, J. E., and D. M. O'Neill. 2008. "Health Status, Health Care and Inequality: Canada vs. the U.S." *Forum for Health Economics & Policy*. Published April 3. www.degruyter.com/view/j/fhep.2008.10.1/fhep.2008.10.1.1094/fhep.2008.10.1.1094.xml.

Ontario Health Coalition. 2017. *Private Clinics and the Threat to Public Medicare in Canada*. Published June 10. http://healthcoalition.ca/wp-content/uploads/2017/06/Private-Clinics-Report.pdf.

Organisation for Economic Co-operation and Development. 2017. *OECD Health Statistics 2017.* Updated November 10. www.oecd.org/els/health-systems/health-data.htm.

Preston, S., and J. Ho. 2010. "Low Life Expectancy in the United States: Is the Health Care System at Fault?" In *International Differences in Mortality at Older Ages: Dimensions and Sources*, edited by E. Crimmins, S. Preston, and B. Cohen, 268–308. Washington, DC: National Academies Press.

Rupert, J. 2001. "Man Protests Rock's Speedy Surgery." *Ottawa Citizen*, February 17, D3.

Statistics Canada. 2017. "Consumer Price Index, Historical Summary (1998 to 2017)." Accessed May 2018. www.statcan.gc.ca/tables-tableaux/sum-som/l01/cst01/econ46a-eng.htm.

Technological Change in Health Care (TECH) Research Network. 2001. "Technological Change Around the World: Evidence from Heart Attack Care." *Health Affairs* 20 (3): 25–42.

US Government Accountability Office (GAO). 2017. *High-Risk Series: Progress on Many High-Risk Areas, While Substantial Efforts Needed on Others.* Published February. www.gao.gov/assets/690/682765.pdf.

———. 1995. *Medicare: Rapid Spending Growth Calls for More Prudent Purchasing.* Published June 28. www.gao.gov/assets/110/106132.pdf.

Walkom, T. 2002. "No Pets Ahead of People." *Toronto Star*, January 11, A6.

Woolhandler, S., T. Campbell, and D. Himmelstein. 2003. "Costs of Health Care Administration in the United States and Canada." *New England Journal of Medicine* 349 (8): 768–75.

EMPLOYER-MANDATED NATIONAL HEALTH INSURANCE

An employer mandate for health insurance has had a great deal of political support. President Nixon proposed it, as did President Clinton; Hawaii and Massachusetts instituted it; and it was included as part of President Obama's 2010 Affordable Care Act (ACA). Starting in 2014, employers were required to offer their employees a qualified health plan or pay a tax per employee. Before the ACA, about 75 percent of the uninsured were either employed full time or in a family with an employed member. Therefore, mandating employers to provide their employees with health insurance could cover a large percentage of the uninsured at small cost to the government.

Several variations on the basic approach have been proposed. Mandated employer proposals have generally required the employer to pay 80 percent and the employee 20 percent of the cost of the insurance. And instead of a fixed tax per employee, President Clinton proposed requiring employers to spend a fixed percentage of wages for health insurance. Employer mandate proposals generally exclude firms with fewer than 50 employees, with the understanding that, although small firms have a high rate of uninsured workers, the additional cost to such firms would represent a financial hardship.

Under the ACA, employers (with 50 or more employees working 30 or more hours a week) were required to *offer* their employees a "qualified" and "affordable" health plan for single coverage only. If they did not, they had to pay a new payroll tax of $2,000 per employee—hence, the name "play-or-pay" national health insurance. A qualified plan consisted of one of four types of plans, each having the same comprehensive benefits, but whose premiums varied according to the size of the deductible. The insurance coverage had to be affordable, defined as not costing employees more than 2.5 to 9.66 percent of their family income, depending on the size of the income.

Before analyzing the politics and economic consequences of mandating employers to provide health insurance to the working uninsured, it is useful to examine who the uninsured are and why they do not have insurance.

Characteristics of the Employed Uninsured

As shown in exhibit 35.1, 75 percent of the nonelderly uninsured are members of a family with one or more full-time workers. Proponents of an employer mandate therefore assume that requiring employers to cover their employees

EXHIBIT 35.1
Characteristics of the Nonelderly Uninsured, 2016

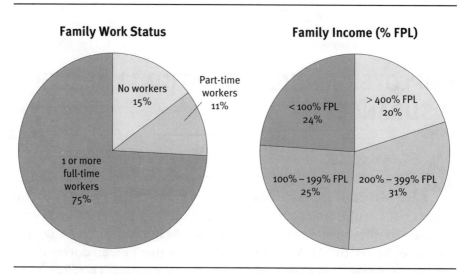

Family Work Status

No workers 15%

Part-time workers 11%

1 or more full-time workers 75%

Family Income (% FPL)

< 100% FPL 24%

> 400% FPL 20%

100% – 199% FPL 25%

200% – 399% FPL 31%

Notes: Includes nonelderly individuals aged 0–64 years. The US Census Bureau's poverty threshold for a family with two adults and one child was $19,318 in 2016. FPL = federal poverty level.
Source: Kaiser Family Foundation (2017a, figure 4).

would result in a large decrease in the number of uninsured. This assumption, however, fails to consider whether the employer, particularly small employers, can afford to pay for their employees' insurance. Further, can the employee afford his share of the premium and deductible?

Half of the uninsured workers make less than 200 percent of the federal poverty level (FPL), which, in 2016, was $23,760 per year for a single person and $48,600 for a family of four.

To better understand the characteristics of uninsured workers, it is useful to examine their ages, sizes of firms, and wages per hour.

As shown in exhibit 35.2, those in older age groups (35 to 64 years) represent 55.4 percent of the employed uninsured, while those younger than

EXHIBIT 35.2
Uninsured Workers by Age Group, 2015

Age in Years	Working Population, in Thousands	% Distribution of Workers	% Uninsured Within Each Group	% Distribution of All Uninsured
16–18	4,387	2.7	6.3	1.6
19–24	19,639	12.1	12.5	13.7
25–34	38,847	23.9	13.5	29.4
35–44	34,747	21.4	12.6	24.4
45–64	64,825	39.9	8.6	31.0

Source: Data from Rhoades (2017).

35 years make up 44.7 percent of all the employed uninsured. The older age groups represent a greater portion of uninsured employees because they make up 61.3 percent of all employees. However, a higher proportion of younger employees than older employees are uninsured.

To reduce the number of uninsured young adults, the ACA permitted them to join or remain on a parent's health insurance policy until they reach age 26, as long as they are not eligible for coverage under their own employer's policy. The cost of this policy is borne by parents and other employees in those firms through higher premiums.

The second important characteristic of the employed uninsured is the size of the firm in which they work. The fewer the number of employees, the greater the likelihood that the employer does not provide health insurance (see exhibit 35.3). About 60 percent of all uninsured employees work in firms with fewer than 50 employees. When we include the self-employed, the total percentage of all uninsured workers increases to about 80 percent.

An employer mandate that excludes those in firms with fewer than 50 employees is directed at only 20 percent of the employed uninsured.

The third important characteristic of the employed uninsured is their low wages. As shown in exhibit 35.4, as of 2015, 36 percent of the employed uninsured earned less than $10 an hour, and another 38.1 percent earned between $10 and $15 per hour. Thus, 74 percent earned less than $15 per hour. Employees who earn more than $20 an hour represent only 12 percent of uninsured workers. (These data exclude those whose wages and hours of work are unknown.) With respect to hours worked, 80 percent of the employed uninsured work more than 30 hours a week. Thus, the general picture of the uninsured worker that emerges is one of young adults who work in small firms and earn low wages.

Characteristic	Working Population, in Thousands[a]	% Distribution of Workers	% Uninsured Within Each Group	% Distribution of All Uninsured
Self-employed	15,501	10.4	19.3	18.7
< 10 workers	27,087	18.1	18.2	30.9
10–24 workers	24,091	16.1	13.2	19.9
25–49 workers	16,337	10.9	10.7	11.0
50–99 workers	17,425	11.7	6.1	6.7
100–499 workers	28,786	19.3	4.8	8.6
≥ 500 workers	20,221	13.5	3.3	4.2

EXHIBIT 35.3
Uninsured Workers by Size of Firm, 2015

[a]Excludes persons with unknown self-employment status and size of establishment.
Source: Data from Rhoades (2017).

EXHIBIT 35.4
Percentage
Distribution
of Uninsured
Workers by
Wage Rate and
Hours Worked,
2015

Characteristic	Working Population, in Thousandsª	% Distribution of Workers	% Uninsured Within Each Group	% Distribution of All Uninsured
Hours of work				
< 20	11,224	7.1	9.2	6.0
20–29	15,822	10.0	14.1	13.0
≥ 30	131,347	82.9	10.6	81.0
Hourly wage				
< $5.00	1,638	1.1	25.9	2.9
$5.00–$9.99	23,606	16.3	20.4	33.1
$10.00–$14.99	37,317	25.7	14.9	38.1
$15.00–$19.99	23,860	16.5	8.4	13.8
≥ $20.00	58,526	40.4	3.0	12.1

ªExcludes persons with unknown hours of work and unknown hourly wages.
Source: Data from Rhoades (2017).

Why the Uninsured Do Not Have Health Insurance

The employed uninsured have not had health insurance for three important reasons.

First, the price of insurance has generally been higher (relative to its perceived benefits) for low-income workers employed in small firms. Before the ACA, small firms were unable to take advantage of economies of scale in administering and marketing health insurance, which resulted in higher insurance costs per employee. Insurance companies also charged small firms higher premiums to make allowance for adverse selection, believing many employees would join a company just to take advantage of health benefits. For example, an owner might hire a sick relative so that her medical costs could be paid. In large firms with lower turnover rates, employment for the primary purpose of receiving health benefits is less likely. Finally, many states mandated various benefits, such as in vitro fertilization and hair transplants, that had to be included in any health insurance plan sold in the state, which resulted in higher premiums. Large firms, however, were able to self-insure, exempting them from the costs of these additional mandates. Small firms are too small to self-insure and, therefore, had to pay the higher premiums, which lessened the demand for health insurance.

The ACA required insurers to have minimum medical loss ratios (premiums could not exceed the plan's benefits by more than a certain percentage), but for small firms, premiums relative to benefits were still higher than those for larger firms.

Second, the demand for health insurance is low among employees in small firms because of their low incomes. The uninsured in small firms (fewer than 50 employees) account for about 62 percent of all uninsured employees. Further, because 74 percent of the employed uninsured earn less than $15 per hour, their share of health insurance premiums plus the deductible (before insurance pays for any care) substantially reduces their funds available for other necessities. For example, an employee earning $15 an hour makes $31,000 a year. Requiring her to purchase health insurance and pay the deductible would significantly reduce her income. In 2013, before implementation of the ACA, health insurance cost an average of $5,884 per person per year and $16,351 per year for a family of four (Kaiser Family Foundation and Health Research & Educational Trust 2013).

In 2016, after implementation of the ACA, insurance cost an average of $6,435 per person per year and $18,142 per year for a family of four, plus a large deductible (Kaiser Family Foundation and Health Research & Educational Trust 2016). Consequently, the ACA exchanges provide both premium tax credits and cost-sharing subsidies to those with low incomes. Those whose incomes are above 250 percent up to 400 percent of the FPL receive only premium tax credits, based on their income. Those with incomes above 400 percent of the FPL do not qualify for subsidies (see chapter 38). About 45 percent of the uninsured believe cost is still a problem.

Third, Medicaid is a low-cost substitute for private insurance for those with low incomes, particularly in the ACA's Medicaid expansion states that have higher income eligibility limits. Also, when low-wage employees or their families become ill, they are likely to become eligible for Medicaid, which does not cost them anything. Thus, for low-wage workers and their families, Medicaid is their health insurance plan.

The ACA's Employer Mandate

The ACA employer mandate was designed differently from previous employer mandates. Large employers only had to *offer* to buy an affordable and ACA-qualified health plan, with single coverage, for their employees. (The mandate only applied to firms with 50 or more employees who worked full time, defined as at least 30 hours a week.) An affordable plan was defined as one in which the employee did not have to spend more than 2.5 to 9.66 percent of their wages (depending on their income) on the plan. This approach was more equitable than mandate proposals that required employees to spend a fixed dollar amount or a percentage of the plan's cost.

The minimum qualified health plan was a Bronze plan that included a $6,000 deductible and cost-sharing expenses. The uninsured employee could choose not to accept the employer's offer. Once the employer made the offer, the employer was no longer subject to the employer mandate tax. Many single uninsured employees believed the value of the Bronze plan, with its large out-of-pocket payments, was not worth the cost. An employee with a family who accepted the employer's offer would have to pay the full premium to buy an additional Bronze plan for his family (at least $2,700 for the spouse plus the per-child cost); the plan also would have a $6,000 deductible and cost-sharing expenses. Many uninsured employees declined their employer's offer because they would have had to pay two deductibles amounting to $12,000 and the additional premium before they could receive any insurance benefits. The health insurance was not worth the decrease in their already limited income.

Another significant problem with the ACA employer mandate was that by declining the employer's offer of single coverage, the employee and family members then became ineligible for the tax credit and cost-sharing subsidies offered on the health insurance exchanges. Further, they then became subject to the ACA's individual mandate penalty for not having health insurance.

The ACA exempted employers with fewer than 50 employees from the employer mandate. To encourage these employers to buy insurance for their employees, the ACA offered firms with 25 or fewer employees (who had an average annual wage of $50,000 or less) a tax credit good for two years, equal to 50 percent of the premium. The employer would have to pay the other half of their employees' health insurance premium and buy the insurance through an ACA small business exchange. The tax credit was apparently an insufficient incentive for small employers to buy insurance for their uninsured employees. The insurance imposed too great an administrative and financial burden on these small firms.

Exhibit 35.5 shows insurance coverage for those younger than 65 years before (2013) and after (2016) the ACA was implemented, according to five categories: employer, nongroup, Medicaid, other public, and uninsured. As a result of the ACA, decreases in the uninsured occurred because of subsidies in the health insurance exchanges (nongroup market) to those with low incomes and from the Medicaid expansions.

The ACA's employer mandate does not appear to have had any discernable effect on decreasing the number of uninsured employees. The percentage of insured employees was the same before and after implementation of the ACA employer mandate.

Consequences of Employer-Mandated Health Insurance

Failure to Achieve Universal Coverage

Employer-mandated health insurance by itself cannot achieve universal coverage. Even if all working uninsured were covered by an employer mandate, those

EXHIBIT 35.5
Health
Insurance
Coverage for
Nonelderly,
2013 and 2016

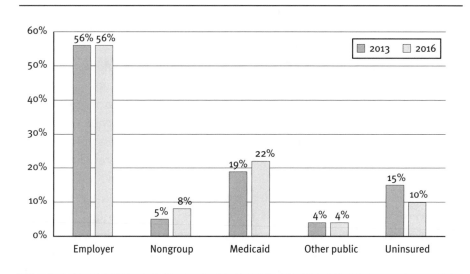

Employer: Includes those covered by employer-sponsored insurance, either through their own job or as a dependent in the same household.

Nongroup: Includes individuals and families who purchased or are covered as a dependent by nongroup insurance.

Medicaid: Includes those covered by Medicaid or the Children's Health Insurance Program (CHIP), as well as those who have both Medicaid and another type of coverage, such as dual eligibles who are also covered by Medicare.

Other public: Includes those covered under the military or Veterans Affairs, as well as nonelderly Medicare enrollees.

Uninsured: Includes those without health insurance and those who have coverage under the Indian Health Service only.

Source: Kaiser Family Foundation (2017b).

employed part time and those not employed, together with their dependents, would still not have insurance coverage. This would leave approximately 25 percent of the uninsured without coverage. To achieve universal coverage, the ACA combined an employer mandate with an individual mandate, together with an expansion of Medicaid eligibility and insurance subsidies for other low-income population groups, such as the self-employed. Although the ACA decreased the number of uninsured by about 14 million, it was unable to achieve universal coverage. In 2016, 10.1 percent of those younger than 65 years, or 27.5 million individuals, were still uninsured.

Who Pays for Employer Mandates?

Proposals for an employer mandate have always required the employer to pay for a significant part of the cost of health insurance and the employee to pay for a small part. The ACA required employers with 50 or more employees to offer uninsured employees health insurance and pay between 90.34 and 97.5 percent of the employees' premium (the employees' contribution was not to exceed 2.5 to 9.66 percent of their income). Employers who did not make this offer were required to pay a $2,000 tax for each employee who had no health insurance (excluding the first 30 employees).

Thus, most of the cost of an employer mandate would appear to be borne by the firm. However, whether the employer or the employee actually bears the burden of the tax does not depend on whom the tax is imposed. In competitive industries, firms do not make excess profits; otherwise, other firms (including foreign firms) would enter that industry until excess profits ceased to exist. When employers are earning a competitive rate of return, they are unable to bear the burden of an additional tax themselves, or they eventually go out of business. Instead, faced with a new employee tax, within a short period employers shift the cost of that tax to others by increasing prices, decreasing employees' cash wages, or discharging employees whose incomes are near or below the minimum wage and, therefore, are unable to bear part of the tax.

Imposing a per-employee tax on the employer is likely to result in one of several possible outcomes (Blumberg 1999). Exactly which outcome occurs depends on the particular labor and product markets in which the firm competes, because the nature of these markets determines how much of the higher labor cost is shifted back to the employee and how much is shifted forward in the form of higher consumer prices.

Changes in the Composition of Employee Compensation

Employers are concerned with the employees' total compensation, not how the compensation is divided between cash wages and fringe benefits (including health insurance). The cost of labor to the employer is unchanged if wages or fringe benefits become a greater portion of total compensation. A tax on employers to pay for their employees' insurance would be shifted to employees in the form of lower wages.[2] Although employees receive more health insurance, they clearly value the insurance less than the cash wages it takes to purchase it, because they could have purchased the insurance before the ACA but chose not to. Thus, the first effect of an employee tax is that uninsured low-wage employees become worse off by being forced to change how they spend their limited income.

Increased Cost of Labor

The cost of labor to the firm will be increased because the mix between wages and health insurance is not perfectly flexible, particularly right away. With higher labor costs, the firm will have to increase the prices of its goods and services. These higher prices will lead consumers to purchase fewer goods and services. To the extent that labor costs are increased, part of the employee tax is shifted forward in the form of higher consumer prices. This second effect of the tax is a regressive form of consumer taxation because all consumers, regardless of their income, pay higher prices. The higher prices represent a greater portion of the income of low-income consumers than of high-income consumers. Such a tax is an inequitable method of financing universal health insurance.

Decreased Demand for Employees

A major concern with an employer mandate is its effect on firms' demand for labor. Regardless of whether the firm buys health insurance for its employees or pays the penalty for not doing so, the firm's cost of labor is increased, at least in the short run. When part of the cost of labor is passed on to consumers in the form of higher prices, the demand for the firm's output decreases; with less demand for its output, the firm will need fewer employees. Many employees near the minimum wage whose wages cannot be reduced to offset the cost of insurance or the employer tax will likely be let go. The Congressional Budget Office (2012) estimated that the ACA employer mandate would result in employment decreases of approximately one-half of 1 percent. This percentage is equivalent to about 700,000 people losing their jobs. Those at greatest risk of losing their jobs are low-income workers.

Employers with fewer than 50 employees are exempt from paying a per-employee penalty of $2,000. Anecdotal evidence suggests that many small employers have refused to hire more than 49 employees.[3] Firms also decreased flexible working hours for those who work between 30 and 39 hours a week because, under the ACA, the employer had to buy insurance for employees working 30 or more hours a week. Part-time employees (and some full-time employees who were shifted to part-time status) often had to work two part-time jobs to make up for their decreased hours. Thus, another effect of a health insurance tax per employee is that fewer full-time workers may be employed, small firms may be reluctant to increase hiring above 49 employees, and more part-time employees are likely to be hired.

The ACA tried to make the employer mandate more equitable than previous employer mandate proposals by varying the employee's premium contribution according to her income. However, financing national health insurance through an employer mandate relies on a hidden and inequitable method of financing health insurance for the uninsured. Imposing the cost of health insurance or the tax on the employer makes it appear as though the employer bears the cost. These costs, however, are shifted to both consumers and employees. In both cases, the costs are regressive. For example, consumers, regardless of the size of their incomes, pay the same higher prices. Low-income consumers have to pay a higher percentage of their income than those with higher incomes. This hidden tax on consumers and employees also understates its budgetary effects on the government. Federal and state governments lose tax revenues as more employees are insured through employer-paid tax-exempt health insurance.

Political Consequences of Employer-Mandated Health Insurance

Advantages

Given the inequities and inefficiencies associated with an employer mandate, why has it received so much political support? The political advantages received by various interest groups outweigh the inequities and inefficiencies that an employer mandate imposes on others. The employer mandate is attractive to government because it would appear that government does not have to raise a large amount of tax revenues for an employer-mandated national health insurance plan; such a plan could even reduce Medicaid expenditures by shifting the cost of low-wage labor from Medicaid to employees and their employers. Thus, employer-mandated national health insurance offers the illusion that federal expenditures are little affected. States, whose Medicaid expenditures are increasing faster than any other expenditure, are reluctant to raise taxes. If the states are able to shift the medical costs of low-wage employees and their dependents from Medicaid to employees and their employers, the states' own fiscal problems would be alleviated.

However, an employer mandate is more costly to the government than it appears. First, because employer-paid health insurance is not considered to be taxable income, the change in compensation from cash wages to health insurance decreases Social Security taxes as well as state and federal income taxes. Second, government welfare expenditures will be higher as a consequence of the increase in unemployment resulting from layoffs of low-wage workers and the reduction in employee income as more are shifted from full-time to part-time work. Third, if an employer mandate is used to achieve universal coverage, additional federal subsidies and taxes will be necessary to finance care for approximately one-third of the uninsured who are not employed or are dependents of an employee.

Hospital and physician organizations have favored an employer mandate because it would provide insurance to those previously without it, increasing the demand for hospital and physician services. Payment levels to healthcare providers would be higher than Medicaid payment levels.

Health insurance companies also would benefit because the demand for their services would grow. Health insurers favored the ACA's employer mandate and the health insurance exchanges but opposed the final bill when the individual mandate penalty for not buying insurance was weakened. With the elimination of the preexisting condition exclusion and an inadequate penalty for not having insurance, insurers were rightfully concerned that adverse selection would occur on the exchanges.

Large employers and their unions, which thought they would be unaffected because they already provided health benefits in excess of the mandated minimum, believed they would benefit competitively from employer-mandated insurance because the labor costs of their low-wage competitors would increase, making them less price competitive. More than two decades ago, Robert Crandall, the then-chair of American Airlines, stated that as a result of the difference between the medical costs of American employees and those of Continental Airlines employees, "Continental's unit cost advantage vs. American's is enormous—and worse yet, is growing! . . . which is why we're supporting ... legislation mandating minimum [health] benefit levels for all employees" (*Wall Street Journal* 1987).

Opposition

The major political opposition to an employer mandate has come from small businesses, which believed that the entire tax could not be shifted to the low-wage workers who typically work in small firms. These firms are aware of the consequences of an employee tax on the prices they would have to charge, on demand for their goods and services, and on their demand for labor.

Opposition by small businesses was an important reason the Clinton administration's legislation failed. In an attempt to buy off the political opposition to the ACA by the powerful small-business lobby, the Obama administration treated small businesses (those with fewer than 50 employees) differently: They were exempt from the employer mandate and were provided with partial tax subsidies to offset their higher costs if they purchased health insurance for their employees. The tax subsidies, however, proved to be an insufficient incentive for many small firms to buy health insurance for their employees.

Summary

An employer-mandated national health insurance plan has numerous political advantages. Previous employer mandate proposals imposed most of the cost of the employees' health insurance on the employer. Although an employer mandate statutorily imposes most of the cost on employers, in reality a large portion of the cost is shifted to the employee in the form of lower wages. The ACA's employer mandate differed in two ways from previous proposals. First, to assist the lowest-wage employees, the employee share was based on income levels, up to a maximum percentage of income. Second, rather than requiring the employer to buy health insurance for its uninsured employees, the employer merely had to offer to buy it for the employee. The employee could reject the offer, which many did, because they believed the insurance was not worth their loss of income.

The ACA's employer mandate is not equitable because it treats individuals with the same income differently. A low-income employee who chooses not to accept the employer's offer of health insurance cannot buy insurance on the health insurance exchange (and must pay a penalty for being uninsured), whereas a low-income employee who works for a small firm or is self-employed can buy subsidized insurance on the health insurance exchange. The mandate increases the cost to employers of low-wage workers and imposes a financial burden on those least able to afford it. An important reason for low-wage employees' lack of insurance coverage is that they have more pressing needs for their limited income, and Medicaid is available to them as a substitute to buying private health insurance.

An employer mandate does not achieve universal coverage because not all of the uninsured are employed. To remedy this, the ACA added an individual mandate, health insurance exchanges with income-related federal subsidies, and an expansion of Medicaid eligibility to the employer mandate to achieve universal coverage. Unintended consequences of an employer mandate are decreases in demand for low-wage labor and a reduction in employee work hours. Employers could avoid the tax imposed for not offering health insurance by limiting the work hours of their employees to less than 30 hours per week. To avoid these labor market distortions, alternative approaches for achieving national health insurance need to be examined, such as separating health insurance from the workplace.

Discussion Questions

1. What are the characteristics of the uninsured?
2. Would it be equitable to provide all employees in small firms with a subsidy to purchase health insurance?
3. What is the likely effect of employer-mandated health insurance on the employer's demand for labor?
4. Does an employer-mandated health insurance tax have a regressive, proportional, or progressive effect on the income of employees and consumers?
5. Which groups favor and which groups oppose an employer mandate for achieving national health insurance? Why?
6. How does the ACA employer mandate differ from previous employer mandate proposals?

Notes

1. The Medical Expenditure Panel Survey–Household Component produces estimates of the uninsured for three periods within a year: one

or more months, one to four months, and the entire year. In 2013—the latest year for which all three measures are available—27.1 percent of the population younger than 65 years (nonelderly) were uninsured one or more months, 5.8 percent were uninsured one to four months, and 15.6 percent were uninsured the entire year (Rhoades 2015).

2. Kolstad and Kowalski (2012) estimated that the employer mandate instituted in Massachusetts decreased wages by an average of $6,058 annually, which was only slightly smaller than the average cost of the mandate to employers.

3. If an employer hires a fiftieth employee, the ACA's employer mandate creates a huge tax on that additional employee. The employer would have to pay a penalty of $2,000 per employee, minus the first 30 employees; thus, the additional cost of the fiftieth employee, excluding her wages, is $40,000 (50 − 30 = 20 employees × $2,000). This high marginal tax on a fiftieth employee is a disincentive for the employer to hire that additional employee.

Additional Reading

Krueger, A., and U. Reinhardt. 1994. "Economics of Employer Versus Individual Mandates." *Health Affairs* 13 (2 Part II): 34–53.

References

Blumberg, L. 1999. "Who Pays for Employer-Sponsored Health Insurance?" *Health Affairs* 18 (6): 58–61.

Congressional Budget Office. 2012. "CBO and JCT's Estimates of the Effects of the Affordable Care Act on the Number of People Obtaining Employment-Based Health Insurance." Posted March. http://cbo.gov/sites/default/files/cbofiles/attachments/03-15-ACA_and_Insurance_2.pdf.

Kaiser Family Foundation. 2017a. "Key Facts About the Uninsured Population." Published November. http://files.kff.org/attachment/Fact-Sheet-Key-Facts-about-the-Uninsured-Population.

———. 2017b. "State Health Facts: Health Insurance Coverage of Nonelderly 0–64." Accessed May 2018. www.kff.org/other/state-indicator/nonelderly-0-64/.

Kaiser Family Foundation and Health Research & Educational Trust. 2016. *Employer Health Benefits: 2016 Annual Survey.* Published September. http://files.kff.org/attachment/Report-Employer-Health-Benefits-2016-Annual-Survey.

———. 2013. *Employer Health Benefits: 2013 Annual Survey.* Published August. http://files.kff.org/attachment/full-report-ehbs-2013-abstract.

Kolstad, J., and A. Kowalski. 2012. *Mandate-Based Health Reform and the Labor Market: Evidence from the Massachusetts Reform.* National Bureau of Economic Research Working Paper No. 17933. Published March. www.nber.org/papers/w17933.

Rhoades, J. 2017. Personal correspondence with the author, October 17.

———. 2015. "Spells of Uninsurance: Estimates for the U.S. Civilian Noninstitutionalized Population Under Age 65, 2013." Agency for Healthcare Research and Quality Statistical Brief No. 476. Published June. https://meps.ahrq.gov/data_files/publications/st476/stat476.pdf.

Wall Street Journal. 1987. "Notable and Quotable." *Wall Street Journal*, August 8, 16.

36

NATIONAL HEALTH INSURANCE: WHICH APPROACH AND WHY?

National health insurance is an idea whose time has often come and then gone. However, in 2010 President Obama, with the Democrats controlling both Houses of Congress, signed the Affordable Care Act (ACA) over the opposition of all House and Senate Republicans. The legislation was intended to provide medical coverage for 95 percent of the population by covering an additional 32 million people. The legislation is complex; it expands coverage by increasing eligibility for Medicaid, provides insurance subsidies on government health insurance exchanges, includes an employer mandate, and requires everyone to have insurance (individual mandate). Also included are financial penalties if people are not insured, a series of different types of taxes, and reductions in Medicare provider reimbursement to pay for the program. Regulations were imposed on the insurance industry, and state-based insurance exchanges were established (a federal health insurance exchange also is available for states that couldn't establish or didn't want to establish their own exchanges). Most of the legislation's benefits were phased in at the beginning of 2014, with the last ones to be implemented in 2019.[1]

The ACA turned out not to be the final word on national health insurance. Various aspects of the ACA have not performed as expected, such as the employer and individual mandates; the premiums on the health insurance exchanges have been sharply higher than expected; many states have refused to expand Medicaid eligibility; large numbers of people remain uninsured; the long-term care program (CLASS Act) has already been repealed because it is unworkable; and the individual mandate penalty and the Independent Payment Advisory Board (IPAB) also have been repealed. Further, the dramatic Medicare payment reductions to hospitals (based on assumed productivity adjustments) will need to be changed to prevent many hospital bankruptcies.

A new Republican president and a Republican-controlled Congress are committed to drastically revising, if not repealing, legislation that they had opposed. Thus, national health insurance is back on the political agenda.

To have a basis by which new legislation can be evaluated, different proposals for national health insurance are examined. The previous system was a mixture of private and public financing with elements of market competition and regulation; the ACA continued this mix of public and private aspects. In contrast, general national health insurance proposals rely on one approach to financing and delivery. For political reasons, however, any plan enacted will likely have elements from several models.

A variety of national health insurance plans have been proposed—from replicating the Canadian (single-payer) system to expanding existing public programs for the poor, to mandating employers to provide coverage for their employees, to providing tax credits for the purchase of health insurance. The proponents of each approach claim different virtues of their plans. One plan is more likely to limit the growth of medical expenditures, one will require a smaller tax increase, another will allow individuals greater choice, and still another may be more politically acceptable.

Unless some commonly accepted criteria are established for what national health insurance should accomplish, evaluating and choosing among these plans will be difficult.

Criteria for National Health Insurance

Economists are concerned with two issues: efficiency and equity. Efficiency has two parts: production efficiency and consumption efficiency. The equity criterion is focused on equitable redistribution.

Production Efficiency

Production efficiency, as the first criterion, determines whether the services (for a given level of quality) are produced at the lowest cost. Efficiency in production not only includes whether the hospital portion of a treatment is produced at the lowest cost but also whether the treatment itself is produced at the minimum cost. Unless the treatment is provided in settings, such as hospitals, outpatient care, and home care, with the lowest cost mix, the overall cost of providing the care will not be as low as possible. Production efficiency also should consider how a healthcare organization can combine medical and nonmedical resources (e.g., preventive and lifestyle services), and can best maintain and/or improve a person's health for a given annual medical expenditure.

Ensuring that each component of the treatment (e.g., hospital services) as well as the entire medical treatment is produced efficiently requires appropriate financial incentives. These incentives are usually placed on the providers of medical services; however, they could also be placed on consumers, as occurs when enrollees choose among competing health plans and pay out of pocket the additional cost of more expensive plans (or under a health savings account approach). On whom to place the incentives is a controversial issue, but whether the plan includes appropriate incentives for efficiency in production is not.

Consumption Efficiency

Consumption efficiency is controversial. In other sectors of the economy, consumers make choices regarding the amount of income to allocate to different goods and services. Consumers have incentives to consider the costs and benefits of their choices. Spending their funds on one good or service means forgoing the benefits of another good or service. When consumers allocate their funds in this manner, resources are directed to their highest-valued uses, as perceived by consumers.

Some people are opposed to having consumers decide how much should be spent on medical services. They would prefer to have the government decide how much is allocated to medical care, as is done in the Canadian healthcare system. Yet Canadians are unable to purchase additional private health insurance to forgo waits for open-heart surgery, hip replacements, or treatment for other illnesses. Inherent in the concept of consumption efficiency is that the purpose of national health insurance is to benefit the consumer, and that the consumer will be free to purchase more medical services than the minimum offered in any health insurance plan.

Even if one accepts the concept of consumer-based decision making, concern has arisen that the costs of consumers' choices may be distorted. If the cost of one choice is subsidized but the costs of other choices are not, consumers will demand more of the subsidized choice, resulting in consumption inefficiency. For example, the government does not consider employer-purchased health insurance to be taxable income to the employee. Consumers purchase more health insurance because health insurance is paid with before-tax dollars, whereas other choices (e.g., education, housing) must be paid for with after-tax dollars. The tax-free status of employer-paid health insurance, therefore, causes inefficiency. Thus, this second criterion for national health insurance plans is whether consumers are able to decide how much of their income they want to spend on medical services and whether any subsidies distort the costs of their choices.

When production and consumption efficiency are achieved through the use of appropriate incentives, the rate of increase in medical expenditures is considered to be appropriate. Having a national health insurance objective of limiting the rate of increase in total medical expenditures to, for example, 18 percent of the gross domestic product (GDP) would be inappropriate if achieving this objective meant sacrificing the goals of consumption and production efficiency.

Equitable Redistribution

Presumably, an important (and some would say the only) objective of national health insurance is to provide additional medical services to the poor. When evaluating national health insurance plans on how those with low income are to be subsidized, one must determine which population groups benefit (or are subsidized) and which bear the costs (or pay higher taxes). For *equitable redistribution* to occur, those with higher income are expected to incur net costs (their taxes are in excess of their benefits), whereas those with low income should receive net benefits (benefits in excess of costs). When an individual's costs are not equal to the benefits he receives, redistribution occurs. Thus, if redistribution is the goal, high-income groups should subsidize the care of those with low income. Therefore, the third criterion for evaluating alternative national health insurance plans is whether equitable redistribution occurs.

Crucial in determining whether redistribution goes from high- to low-income groups is the definition of beneficiaries and how the plan is financed. Ideally, those with the lowest income should receive the largest subsidy (which would decline as income rises), and the subsidy should be financed by a tax that is either proportional or progressive to income. If the tax is proportional to income (e.g., a flat tax of 5 percent regardless of income), those with the lowest income will receive a net benefit because the subsidy they receive (sufficient to purchase a minimum-benefit package) will exceed the taxes they pay. When a progressive tax such as an income tax (with a rate that increases as one's income level increases) is used to finance benefits for those with low income, the redistribution from those with high income to those with low income is even greater.

An income tax is the most equitable method of financing a redistributive program because it is either a proportional tax or a progressive tax and places the greatest cost burden on those with high income. The disadvantages of an income tax are that it is highly visible and therefore likely to generate political opposition from middle- and high-income groups. Further, while income tax financing is generally regarded as being more equitable, it is a tax on work effort and may therefore cause a decrease in the supply of such effort.

Payroll taxes are imposed on the employer and employees. A regressive payroll tax (a certain dollar amount per employee or a percent of the employee's income up to a certain amount of income), such as a Social Security tax or a sales tax, takes a higher portion of income from low-income employees than from high-income employees (because a greater portion of the latter group's income is above the threshold for taxation). Because regressive taxes require low-income employees to pay a higher percentage of their income than is required of high-income employees, such taxes are a less desirable method of financing redistributive programs. A sales tax—particularly if it does not exclude such basic expenditures as food—could be regressive in that those with low income pay a higher percentage of their income than do those with high income. A small increase in a sales tax typically generates a great deal of tax revenue and is not as visible as a tax on income or property taxes; property taxes are paid in a lump sum, making their magnitude very visible to voters. So-called sin taxes—taxes on alcohol and cigarettes, for example—are also regressive, but they are economically efficient when the beneficiaries of such goods are required to pay the full costs of their consumption.

In fact, when a regressive tax is used, the tax paid by many low-income people may exceed the value of the benefits they receive. For example, if everyone is eligible to receive the same set of benefits, but those with high income use more medical services—perhaps because they are located closer to medical providers or their attitudes toward seeking care are different from those with less education (who also may have low income)—the taxes paid by low-income individuals may exceed the benefits they receive. Perversely, those with low income may end up subsidizing the care received by those with high income. (This also occurs when low-income nonelderly workers subsidize the healthcare benefits of high-income elderly.)

A user tax is imposed when those receiving the benefits incur their full cost. An example is a tax on cigarettes, which is used to pay the additional medical costs incurred by smokers. An individual mandate, whereby everyone must purchase a minimum or a defined health insurance policy (discussed later in the chapter), may also be considered similar to a user fee; everyone pays for expected medical costs.

Deficit financing—whereby the government borrows the money to subsidize different population groups—shifts the cost burden to future generations. Therein lie both its political advantage and its inequity. Deficit financing from a legislator's perspective is ideal; future generations do not vote on current policies, so politicians can provide benefits without imposing any costs on current voters. Deficit financing is regressive in that current populations, including those with high income, receive the benefits while their costs are subsidized by future generations, including those with low income (depending on the type of tax used for financing the deficit). As the federal deficit becomes too large, however, macroeconomic effects may occur, and the public is likely to view a presidential administration that greatly increases the deficit as being reckless.

An examination of the size of the benefits received according to income level in relation to the amount of tax paid is important. Income tax financing is the preferred way to achieve redistribution because it results in greater net benefits to those with low income.

Exhibit 36.1 shows the different types of taxes that have been used to finance Medicaid, Medicare, and the ACA, as well as additional types of taxes that might be used. Included with each type of tax are its visibility and equitability.

Based on our discussion of efficiency and equitable redistribution thus far, a national health insurance plan should provide incentives for efficiency in production; should enable consumers to decide how much of their income they want to spend on medical care; and should be redistributive—those with low income should receive net benefits, whereas those with high income should bear costs in excess of their benefits. All national health insurance proposals should be judged by how well they fulfill these criteria.

EXHIBIT 36.1
Taxes for
Financing
Redistributive
Healthcare
Programs

Type of Tax	Visibility	Equitability	Medicaid	Medicare	Affordable Care Act (ACA)
Income tax	High	Progressive	State Medicaid	Parts B and D	Those with high income pay higher Medicare payroll and unearned income tax
Sales tax	Low	Regressive	—	—	Insurer, medical devices, etc.
Sin tax	Low	Regressive	—	—	Higher premiums on smokers
Payroll tax	Low	Regressive (becoming progressive)	—	Part A, ACA	Employer mandate
User fee	High	B = C	—	—	Individual mandate
Deficit financing	Low	Regressive B = current generation C = future generation	Federal Medicaid	Parts B and D	—

Notes: Property taxes are not considered as a source for financing healthcare services. B = benefits; C = costs.

An important reason national health insurance plans fail to meet these efficiency and equitable redistribution criteria is that proposals have objectives other than improving efficiency or achieving equitable redistribution. These other objectives become obvious when the explicit efficiency and redistributive criteria are used.

National Health Insurance Proposals

Many types of national health insurance plans have been proposed. Some proposals are incremental in that they build on the current system and do not propose changes in the delivery of medical services. Others are more radical, and dramatic changes are proposed in the financing and delivery of medical services. In general, however, the types of national health insurance plans proposed can be classified into three broad categories: (1) a single-payer (Canadian) system, (2) employer-mandated health insurance with an individual mandate, and (3) income-related tax credits. Although separate chapters are devoted to the Canadian approach and an employer mandate, we present a brief description of each, together with an evaluation of how well they achieve the three criteria.

Single-Payer System

Under a single-payer system, the entire population is covered; benefits are uniform for all; no out-of-pocket expenses are incurred for basic medical services; and, most important, private insurance for hospital and medical services is not permitted (one cannot opt out of the single-payer system). The method of financing may be a combination of income taxes and other sources of funds, such as payroll taxes on the employer and employee, Medicare and Medicaid payments, "sin" taxes (on alcohol and tobacco), or even a sales tax.

The major advantage of a single-payer system is its apparent simplicity in achieving universal coverage. Proponents claim that access to care for those with low income and the uninsured is improved. Single-payer proponents also claim that less would be spent per capita on medical services, and total medical expenses would account for a smaller percentage of GDP.

The major disadvantages of a single-payer approach pertain to consumption and production efficiency (see chapter 34). Global budget caps are used to limit total medical expenditures. Fixed budgets are imposed on hospitals, their capital outlays are controlled by a central authority, and annual limits are placed on the amount each physician can earn. These arbitrarily determined budget levels limit the amount that consumers can spend on medical services, forcing them to wait inordinate lengths of time for services or do without. Higher-income individuals are able to skip the queue by traveling outside the country for their medical services. The result is consumer inefficiency. Incentives to achieve production efficiency are lacking in a single-payer system, as are incentives for prevention and innovation.

Expansion of Public Programs

Somewhat similar to a single-payer system is the proposal to expand existing public programs, such as Medicaid, by increasing the income limits to allow more low-income individuals and the uninsured to become eligible. Medicaid is funded by general income taxes, and beneficiaries are those with low income; thus, the equitable redistribution goal would be appropriate. Advocates of expanding public programs claim that no major changes in the financing or delivery system are required; the only changes needed are in the eligibility criteria. Similarly, more uninsured children could be covered by the Children's Health Insurance Program (CHIP) simply by expanding its eligibility levels, which was done in the 2010 renewal of CHIP.

Some people also have proposed that uninsured adults aged 55 to 65 years be allowed to buy into Medicare. Expanding Medicare to include these younger adults and increasing Medicaid and CHIP eligibility to include those with higher income would eventually bring more people into a single-payer–type system (often the goal of such proponents). Although differences between traditional Medicare and Medicaid exist, the programs have the same characteristics as a single-payer system. Beneficiaries of these programs pay little if anything for use of medical services (particularly when the Medicare patient has Medigap supplementary coverage) and have free choice of provider (except for those enrolled in a Medicaid health maintenance organization), providers are paid on a fee-for-service basis, and the government controls expenditures by limiting provider fees. These programs have none of the cost-containment and quality initiatives—such as utilization management and care coordination—used by the private sector, nor do they have any incentives for provider efficiency.

Some who advocate for expanding public programs view "Medicare for All" as an approach to achieving a single-payer system in the United States. Many people would prefer becoming part of traditional Medicare with its unlimited access to providers, ability to self-refer to any provider, and heavily subsidized costs. However, Medicare has large deductibles (particularly for hospitals) and out-of-pocket expenses for Part B (physician and outpatient services) and Part D prescription drugs. Medicare does not have an out-of-pocket limit on how much an enrollee may spend during the year. Those with low incomes cannot afford these expenses; thus, many aged are forced to rely on Medicaid. Those with higher incomes buy supplemental coverage for these expenses.

Thus, "Medicare for All" would have to be drastically changed to become a truly single payer system.[2] Further, expanding Medicare to include all those younger than 65 years would merely hasten the time before the inefficient and fraud-ridden Medicare system goes bankrupt. The federal deficit for Medicare Parts A, B, and D would soar beyond its total deficit of $10.5 trillion, and payroll and income taxes would have to sharply increase (Boards of Trustees, Federal Hospital Insurance and Federal Supplementary Medical Insurance Trust Funds 2017, tables V.G2, V.G4, and V.G6). Eventually, price controls would be placed on providers, severely limiting access to care, as occurs under any single-payer system, including the Canadian system and Medicaid.[3]

In 2016, the Urban Institute analyzed Senator Sanders's single-payer plan and estimated that federal expenditures would increase by $32 trillion between 2017 and 2026 (Holahan et al. 2016). The large increase in federal spending includes the current amounts spent by states, local governments, employers, and households, as well as expenditures for the uninsured. The additional spending also covers more benefits and the cost-sharing currently paid by the private sector. The sources of additional financing proposed by Senator Sanders would be inadequate to fund the increased federal expenditures, and new revenue sources (taxes) would be required.

The problem with expanding Medicaid to care for a greater portion of the uninsured (up to 138 percent of the federal poverty level, as enacted in the ACA) is that many states cannot afford their share of the matching funds required to include more of the uninsured. Particularly in times of recession, states lack the funds and are reluctant to increase taxes to expand eligibility limits. In fact, many states have been reducing enrollment in CHIP as their tax revenues have fallen and they face budget deficits. Medicaid and CHIP do not have a stable source of funding, and many states are reluctant to commit themselves to expanding these programs.

Many states expanded their Medicaid eligibility with the understanding that the federal government would pay 90 percent of their additional costs. Given the federal government's increasing deficit, in excess of $20 trillion and an increasing percentage of GDP, how long will it be before these costs are shifted back to the states?

The Veterans Affairs (VA) healthcare system is another publicly funded single-payer system. However, in light of the relatively recent scandals in the VA system, in which veterans have died waiting for care, employees have destroyed waiting lists, and administrators have been unable to fire employees responsible for the system's poor performance, the system has not been promoted as a single-payer model for the rest of the country (Slack 2016).

Employer-Mandated Health Insurance

An employer mandate usually requires employers to purchase health insurance for their employees or pay a specified amount (tax) per employee. Although the financial burden for purchasing health insurance is placed on the employer, studies have found that the burden would be shifted back to the employee in the form of lower wages (see chapter 23, "Who Bears the Cost of Employee Health Benefits?"). In effect, a tax is imposed on low-wage workers (who are typically without health insurance), requiring them to buy health insurance. Under the ACA, the employer mandate is somewhat different from previous employer mandates. The employer must *offer* to buy a qualified ACA health plan for an employee and pay the premium (less the income-related employee contribution) or pay a per-employee tax of $2,000. In either case, if the employer purchased a health plan for the employee or paid the tax, these costs would be shifted back to the employee in the form of lower wages (or slower raises). Many employees earning close to the minimum wage whose wages cannot be reduced to offset the employer costs would likely be let go.

The ACA employer mandate was largely ineffective in increasing employees' coverage (Duggan, Goda, and Jackson 2017). The employer was required to offer a qualified and affordable health plan (employee coverage only) that covers the ACA's ten essential health benefits.[4] To lower the cost of such comprehensive coverage, the lowest-cost ACA Bronze health plan includes a $6,000 deductible. If the employee desires to buy a separate health plan for family members, she would have to pay the full premium, and that plan also would include a $6,000 deductible. Low-wage employees determined that the second out-of-pocket premium cost along with the two $6,000 deductibles exceeded their expected benefit from such coverage.

If the employee rejected the employer's offer, the employer does not have to pay the employer mandate tax. But, having rejected the offer, according to the ACA, the low-wage employee becomes ineligible for subsidized insurance on the health insurance exchange. Further, the employee then became subject to the individual mandate tax penalty.

Consumption efficiency cannot be achieved by the ACA employer mandate. The employee cannot choose a health plan that contains fewer benefits and is less costly. Production efficiency can be achieved under an employer mandate by having health plans compete for employees. However, the inability to achieve equitable redistribution (the employer's costs are shifted to low-wage employees) is another disadvantage of the ACA's employer mandate.

Individual Mandate

An employer mandate cannot, by itself, achieve universal coverage. To achieve universal coverage, the government must ensure that the two groups without health insurance—those who can afford insurance but refuse to purchase it and those who cannot afford insurance—have coverage. It is for this reason (and to ensure a larger risk pool) that the ACA imposed an individual mandate. Everyone whose income was above a minimum level was required to have health insurance; the remainder (except for undocumented people) became eligible for Medicaid.

Many uninsured are financially able to purchase a high-deductible health insurance plan but choose not to do so. If someone who can afford insurance does not have catastrophic coverage and suffers a large medical expense that has to be subsidized by the community, the person is shifting the risk—hence, the cost of catastrophic coverage—to the rest of the community.[5] Thus, for an employer mandate to achieve universal coverage, the ACA combined it with an individual mandate.

The ACA's individual mandate had three serious problems. First, the penalty for not buying insurance was too low. Second, the ACA permitted a large number of exemptions from the individual mandate tax, which many people took advantage of. Third, insurers complained that a number of people bought health insurance, and once they received treatment, dropped their insurance. (This behavior caused adverse selection and higher premiums.)

The Internal Revenue Service (IRS) reported that of the 23 million uninsured in 2015, 6.5 million paid the individual mandate tax, 12.7 million claimed an exemption, and 4.3 million did not check the box indicating whether they had insurance or paid the penalty tax. The IRS did not follow up with those who had not checked the box (Koskinen 2017).

The individual mandate penalty, which was politically unpopular, was repealed in 2017 by the Republican-controlled Congress.

Income-Related Tax Credits

Various income-related tax credit approaches have been proposed over the years. The following proposal attempts to achieve universal coverage in an equitable manner while providing incentives for efficiency in the use and delivery of medical services.

Refundable Tax Credits

A refundable tax credit would replace the current, inequitable system whereby the employer purchases tax-exempt health insurance on behalf of employees. As shown in exhibits 6.2 and 6.3, high-wage employees benefit more than low-wage workers from tax-exempt, employer-paid health insurance because they are in a higher tax bracket. An additional inequity is that employees whose employer does not buy health insurance and those who are self-employed are not eligible for the same tax-free benefit when they buy insurance.

As part of the refundable tax credit proposal, the current exclusion of employer-purchased health insurance from an employee's taxable income would be removed, as the tax credit is substituted for it. The lost revenues from this open-ended subsidy would be an important revenue source to be made available for a refundable tax credit (in 2016 dollars, this amounted to an annual loss of federal revenues of $275 billion) (Congressional Budget Office 2016).[6]

A refundable tax credit of $5,000 would be provided to individuals, and $10,000 would be provided to families. Everyone would receive a refundable tax credit (age-adjusted) for the purchase of health insurance. Taxpayers would be allowed to subtract the tax credit to purchase health insurance from their income taxes. Individuals whose tax credits exceed their tax liabilities would receive a refund for the difference. Thus, if a person's income were too low for her to pay taxes, the full amount of the credit would be used to provide her with a voucher for a managed care plan. As a person's income increases to the point where she has an income tax liability, the tax credit would offset part of the liability, leaving her with the remainder of the tax credit to be used toward purchasing a health insurance voucher.

The tax credit would have to be refundable, or the benefits would go only to those who pay taxes, which would exclude many low-income people.

The full tax-credit subsidy would be equal to the premium of a managed care plan. (These refundable tax credits essentially would be vouchers for a health plan for those with little or no tax liability.) The tax credit could be an equal dollar amount for all families, such as $10,000, or could be lower for those with higher income. Under a refundable tax credit that declines with higher income, the subsidy would go to those with the lowest income. However, providing a tax credit of an absolute dollar amount would be more politically acceptable in that those with middle and high incomes also would benefit.

The value of the voucher could be determined in several ways. First, the government could take bids from managed care plans, as occurs under Medicare Advantage. Second, the voucher could equal the premium of the second-lowest-cost managed care plan in the market; this approach is used by more and more employers. In this manner, the preferences of the nonpoor regarding what they want to purchase from a managed care plan would determine the benefits to be offered to those with low income. (Those receiving a full or partial voucher could choose a more expensive health plan by paying the additional cost themselves.)

To achieve universal coverage, a refundable tax credit could also be combined with an individual mandate. However, the individual mandate has been politically unpopular. Alternatively, the tax credit could slowly decline in value the longer a person delays purchasing insurance; this would be an incentive to buy insurance when it is offered rather than waiting until one is sick, which would cause adverse selection. (A similar approach is used to encourage seniors to enroll in Medicare Parts B and D when they turn 65 years by increasing their premiums each year they delay.)

The refundable tax credit would also replace the current Medicaid program, and Medicaid expenditures would be used to partially offset the cost of the refundable credit.[7] Medicaid-eligible adults and children would receive the same refundable tax credit as others and have greater choice in their selection of health plans. Eventually, because Medicare must be restructured to become financially viable, it also could be included in a refundable tax credit plan. There is little reason to have different financing systems for different population groups—those who work, those who are retired, and those who are uninsured because of their low income.

Consumption efficiency would be achieved by permitting individuals to choose among competing health plans and allowing them to purchase greater coverage or policies with fewer restrictions on access to providers by paying the additional premium themselves for such plans. Production efficiency presumably would occur as health plans compete for enrollees based on price, quality of services, and access to care. By providing a refundable tax credit, financed from general income taxes, redistributive equity would be achieved.

Health Savings Accounts

A proposal that places greater responsibility for medical expenses on the individual is a health savings account (HSA) used in conjunction with a high-deductible, catastrophic health insurance policy. HSAs could be an option under the employer mandate and the refundable tax credit proposals.

The basic idea behind an HSA is to combine an inexpensive high-deductible insurance policy with a tax-free savings account. An HSA plan works as follows: An individual (or his employer acting on his behalf) purchases a high-deductible health plan and then annually contributes a specified tax-free amount to the HSA. (A high-deductible catastrophic policy has a much lower premium than a comprehensive health insurance policy.) In 2018, the maximum that could be contributed each year to an HSA account was $3,450 for an individual and $6,900 for a family—or the amount of the deductible of the high-deductible health plan, whichever is lower. The maximum out-of-pocket expenses for which the person is liable can be as high as $6,650 a year for an individual or $13,300 for a family. A person would be at risk for the difference between the out-of-pocket maximum ($6,650) and his annual contribution to the HSA ($3,450), which is $3,200.[8]

HSA proponents claim that an HSA reduces the monthly insurance premium and provides individuals with a financial incentive to be concerned about the prices they pay for medical services, and consider which services they really need. (Most high-deductible health plans also include several preventive visits.) Proponents believe that if consumers have a greater financial incentive, medical expenditures will increase at a lower rate.

The funds in the HSA account can be invested, grow tax free, and can be used later for long-term care expenses (or any other uses, as the funds belong to the individual).

Opponents of HSAs claim that any savings would be relatively small because once the out-of-pocket maximum is reached, the patient has no incentive to spend less. Critics also claim that the adoption and availability of new technology, which is typically used in an inpatient setting, determine expenditure increases, not spending for outpatient services. HSA critics further claim that HSAs would split the insurance risk pools; healthier, lower-risk persons would choose HSAs (thereby gaining financially), and higher-risk persons would remain in more comprehensive plans.

In response, HSA proponents argue that higher-risk individuals would also benefit from and choose HSAs because their total medical out-of-pocket expenses, including prescription drugs, would be subject to a limit. Under Medicare, for example, out-of-pocket expenses are *not* limited.

HSAs include financial incentives for consumption efficiency. (If consumers are to become informed purchasers, however, more information on provider performance and prices is needed.) Presumably, production efficiency would result as providers compete on price and as managed care plans become responsible for providing catastrophic services. Government subsidies would be needed to enable those with low income to establish HSAs (Fronstin and Roebuck 2016; Haviland et al. 2016).

Health Insurance Exchanges with a Refundable Tax Credit

With a refundable tax credit, the health insurance would belong to the individual. If the individual changes jobs, she would not have to worry about what type of coverage the new employer offered or whether she would have a waiting period for a preexisting medical condition. Further, employers—particularly small employers—would not have to be concerned with administering a health insurance plan or bearing any costs if they hire low-wage employees. Health insurance would no longer be connected to the workplace.

In the past, employers purchased health insurance for their employees because employer-paid health insurance was tax exempt. Under this proposal, everyone could use the health insurance exchanges. Everyone would be able to choose among competing insurers offering different benefits (unlike the ACA exchanges in which only four types of plans with the same comprehensive benefits are permitted).

Under the age-adjusted refundable tax credit proposal, people buying insurance on the exchanges would be classified into risk categories by age and family status. The current cross-subsidies that are part of the ACA, such as young adults subsidizing older individuals, would be eliminated; each risk group's premium would reflect its actuarial cost, thereby lowering the cost of insurance for those who are young and have lower income.

Preexisting condition exclusions have long been a concern of those unable to purchase health insurance. In the past, many states established high-risk pools to provide subsidized insurance for those with a preexisting condition. The ACA prohibits insurers from excluding those with preexisting conditions, under the assumption that the individual mandate would provide insurers with a sufficiently large insurance pool to negate any effects of adverse selection. Unfortunately, the ACA's individual mandate penalty for not having insurance was so low that many people who decided to remain uninsured were not deterred by it, and many took advantage of the ACA's many exemptions to remain uninsured. Thus, the exchange risk pools were more costly than expected.

Possible alternatives for those with a preexisting condition include a federal high-risk pool, reinsurance for insurers, and charging a higher premium the longer they delay buying insurance (see chapter 38 for more discussion of this issue).

Advantages of Income-Related Tax Credits

The income-related, age-adjusted tax credit meets the efficiency and equitable redistribution criteria in the following ways:

Everyone would have a minimum set of health insurance benefits. Those with the lowest income would be assured of adequate health insurance and would receive the largest net benefits under the proposed plan.

The size of the subsidy would decline as income grows and increase with age. Employer-purchased health insurance would no longer be tax exempt, and the employee's taxable income would increase. The higher tax revenues, together with funds from the income tax system and Medicaid, would then provide the funding for the income-related subsidies. Thus, the financing source is based on progressive taxation.

Having the value of the tax credit decline the longer the delay in purchasing insurance would likely achieve near-universal insurance coverage. Thus, the cost shifting to the remaining population that occurs when those who can afford insurance do not buy it would be decreased.

The refundable tax credit is based on the *individual*, not the employer; thus, the individual would be able to change jobs without fear of losing insurance or being denied coverage because of a preexisting condition. Because everyone would have a tax credit for insurance, an employer should be willing to hire someone who is older, is less healthy, or has a preexisting condition because no additional health insurance cost would be incurred by the employer or other employees.

Employees would have incentives to make cost-conscious choices, and a competitive health insurance market would help achieve efficiency and quality. The greater out-of-pocket liability for employees purchasing more expensive health plans would increase their price sensitivity to different managed care plans. Price (premium) sensitivity by employees (and employers acting on their behalf) would provide incentives for managed care plans and providers, such as hospitals and physicians, to be as efficient as possible. Unless health plans were responsive to consumers at a premium the consumer was willing to pay, the health plans would not be able to compete in a price-competitive market.

A brief description and comparison of the three national health insurance proposals is presented in exhibit 36.2.

Fundamental Differences in Perspectives Regarding Government's Health Policy Role

The reason it is so difficult to achieve compromise when discussing health policy is that fundamental differences exist regarding the role of government and the private sector. These differences are ideological and reflect differences in constituents' interests. For example, there are those who distrust the profit motive in healthcare and individuals' ability to make appropriate healthcare choices. Others disagree, placing greater trust in market competition than in government monitoring to achieve efficiency and to respond to consumer preferences.

These different beliefs in the role of government and the private sector also reflect the economic interests of important constituencies. Unions would like to shift their members' healthcare costs to the government (the taxpayer), thereby resulting in higher take-home wages for their members. Unions believe a single-payer system would achieve this goal, as they were able to shift their retirees' healthcare costs by having these retirees enroll in Medicare. Hospitals, physicians, insurers, and pharmaceutical companies believe they would be more profitable under a private system in which the government's main role is to subsidize those with low income to enable them to buy healthcare in a privately operated system.

Exhibit 36.3 describes these differences in values, cost-containment approaches, and types of health plans preferred by those with opposing ideologies and constituent interests.

EXHIBIT 36.2
A Comparison
of Three
National Health
Insurance
Proposals

Feature	Employer Mandate	Single-Payer System	Refundable Tax Credit (With or Without an Individual Mandate)
How does it work?	Requires all employers to buy health insurance for their employees or pay into a pool	Provides comprehensive coverage with no out-of-pocket payments; private insurance not permitted	Everyone is provided with a refundable tax credit to purchase health insurance; those with low income receive a voucher
Does it provide universal coverage?	Excludes those who work part time and those who are not working; achieves universal coverage when an individual mandate and subsidies are included	Achieves universal coverage	Achieves universal coverage when an individual mandate is included; the insurance belongs to the individual and is not tied to the workplace
Is there consumption efficiency?	Partially: Minimum mandated benefits are greater than low-income workers prefer, and employer may not provide choice of health plans	No: Individuals are not permitted to buy medical services or private insurance for services covered by the basic health plan	Yes: Participants can choose among different health plans and can purchase additional medical services and insurance above minimum-required catastrophic insurance
Is there production efficiency?	Plan relies on market-based competition to achieve production efficiency	No consumer or provider incentives are included to encourage efficiency, to minimize the cost of a treatment, or to provide preventive care	Plan includes consumer and provider incentives for efficiency; relies on market-based competition to achieve production efficiency
Is it equitably financed?	Regressive: The plan retains tax-exempt employer coverage, and a tax is imposed on employers and employees, including low-income employees without insurance	Partially regressive: There is pooling of funds from employers, Medicare, Medicaid, and increased payroll taxes	Progressive: Tax-exempt employer-paid insurance is replaced with a refundable tax credit for everyone; those with low income receive income-related subsidies
What are the administrative costs?	High costs: Because of multiple health plans, monitoring and enforcement of mandate	Low costs: Too low to detect fraud and abuse or to institute disease management and other types of cost-containment programs	High costs: Because of multiple health plans, monitoring and enforcement of mandate
How are healthcare costs controlled?	Plan relies on the market to achieve appropriate rate of increase in costs	Plan relies on arbitrary budget caps and regulated fees	Plan relies on market to achieve appropriate rate of increase in costs

Summary

National health insurance proposals should be judged according to their production efficiency, consumption efficiency, and equitable redistribution (whether those with low income receive a net benefit). A market-based system, in contrast to a single-payer system, has demonstrated its ability to achieve the goals

Ideology	Values	Cost Containment	Redistribution
Left	• Trust in government as regulator • Distrust of profit motive • Distrust of consumers' ability to make choices	• Fee and price controls (IPAB) for hospitals and physicians • Government negotiation with pharmaceutical companies • Comparative/cost-effectiveness	• Expand existing public programs • Expand eligibility for Medicare (age ≥ 55) • Expand eligibility for Medicaid (by income and age) • Maintain employer-paid system • Single-payer program (by combining above programs)
Right	• Trust in market competition • Belief in necessity of financial incentives • Values consumer sovereignty and choices	• Markets and competition • FEHB for Medicare • Individual choice (HSAs) • Eliminate state mandates	• Income-related refundable tax credits • Medicare should be a fixed contribution program (premium support) • Income-related public programs • Cap amount of health insurance premiums that are tax exempt

EXHIBIT 36.3
Constituent/
Ideological
Differences on
Health Policy

Notes: FEHB = Federal Employees Health Benefits; HSA = health savings account; IPAB = Independent Payment Advisory Board (Affordable Care Act).

of production efficiency and consumption efficiency. Subsidies to those with low income, such as through a refundable tax credit, are a direct method of improving equity and can provide greater choices (consumption efficiency) and result in production efficiency when provided through a market-based system.

An important role of government under national health insurance is to monitor quality and access to care received by those with low income. Government has not adequately performed this function for Medicaid (and Veterans Health Administration) patients. However, Medicaid can be eliminated by providing everyone with a refundable tax credit. Allowing those with low income to enroll in managed care plans that also serve other population groups and to buy health insurance on exchanges would provide consumers with greater choice of health plans and achieve greater competition among insurers.

Information on health plans, their prices, and the quality and access they provide are important in achieving a competitive market. In addition to states providing information on each plan's performance, other organizations and websites likely would develop and offer information to assist consumers in making informed choices. These reporting and monitoring activities would benefit all enrollees, including those subsidized by the government.

Under a market-based national health insurance system, the rate of increase in medical expenditures would be based on what consumers decide is appropriate by balancing cost and use of services. The government would not need to set arbitrary limits on total medical expenditures as occurs in a single-payer system and the ACA. Instead, the rate of increase in medical expenditures would be the "correct" rate because consumers, through their choices, would make the trade-off between access to care and premiums to pay for that level of access.

Discussion Questions

1. Discuss the criteria that should be used for evaluating alternative national health insurance proposals.
2. Evaluate the desirability of the following types of taxes for financing national health insurance: payroll, sales, and income tax.
3. What is the justification for requiring everyone (all those who can afford it) to purchase a minimum level of health insurance?
4. Outline (and justify) a proposal for national health insurance. As part of your proposal, discuss the benefits package, beneficiaries, method of financing, delivery of services, and role of government. How well does your proposal meet the criteria discussed in the chapter?
5. What are alternative ways for treating Medicare under national health insurance?

Notes

1. One stated objective of the administration in designing the new legislation was that it would not contribute to the federal deficit over a ten-year period. To achieve this goal, the new taxes and the reductions in Medicare expenditures used to finance the new benefits started at the beginning of the ten-year period, whereas the benefits (expenditures) became effective in only the last six of the ten years.
2. Senator Bernie Sanders's proposed legislation, "Medicare for All Act of 2017," (Sanders 2017, 62) actually repeals Medicare.
3. Allowing just the uninsured to buy into Medicare would result in adverse selection; sicker individuals—those without employment-based health insurance—would pay a premium that is below their expected costs.
4. The ACA requires insurers to cover a broad range of mandated "essential" benefits, the scope of which is greater than typical individual policies previously sold. Mandated benefits include preventive services with no copayments, behavioral health, contraceptives, maternity care

(even for single men and women past child-bearing age), outpatient prescription drugs, and pediatric dental and vision care; annual lifetime limits on health benefits are prohibited. The more comprehensive and generous the insurance, the more expensive it is.

5. The ACA permits those younger than 30 years to buy a catastrophic health plan.

6. The ACA imposes a 40 percent tax on health coverage that exceeds $10,200 for individuals and $27,500 for families, thereafter indexed for inflation, starting in 2022.

7. Medicaid for those with long-term care needs would not be included in the refundable tax credit program.

8. Additional information on HSAs can be found at www.treasury.gov/resource-center/faqs/Taxes/Pages/Health-Savings-Accounts.aspx.

Additional Readings

Baicker, K., and A. Chandra. 2010. "Uncomfortable Arithmetic: Whom to Cover Versus What to Cover." *New England Journal of Medicine* 362 (2): 95–97.

Fuchs, V. 2009. "The Proposed Government Health Insurance Company: No Substitute for Real Reform." *New England Journal of Medicine* 360 (22): 2273–75.

Furman, J. 2008. "Health Reform Through Tax Reform: A Primer." *Health Affairs* 27 (3): 622–32.

References

Boards of Trustees, Federal Hospital Insurance and Federal Supplementary Medical Insurance Trust Funds. 2017. *2017 Annual Report of the Boards of Trustees of the Federal Hospital Insurance and Federal Supplementary Medical Insurance Trust Funds.* Published July. www.cms.gov/Research-Statistics-Data-and-Systems/Statistics-Trends-and-Reports/ReportsTrustFunds/Downloads/TR2017.pdf.

Congressional Budget Office. 2016. *Options for Reducing the Deficit: 2017 to 2026.* Published December 8. www.cbo.gov/publication/52142.

Duggan, M., G. S. Goda, and E. Jackson. 2017. "The Effects of the Affordable Care Act on Health Insurance Coverage and Labor Market Outcomes." National Bureau of Economic Research Working Paper No. 23607. www.nber.org/papers/w23607.

Fronstin, P., and M. C. Roebuck. 2016. "The Impact of an HSA-Eligible Health Plan on Health Care Services Use and Spending by Worker Income." Employee Benefit Research Institute Issue Brief No. 425. Published August. www.ebri.org/pdf/briefspdf/EBRI_IB_425.Aug16.HSAs.pdf.

Haviland, A., M. D. Eisenberg, A. Mehrotra, P. J. Huckfeldt, and N. Sood. 2016. "Do 'Consumer-Directed' Health Plans Bend the Cost Curve over Time?" *Journal of Health Economics* 46: 33–51.

Holahan, J., M. Buettgens, L. Clemans-Cope, M. M. Favreault, L. J. Blumberg, and S. Ndwandwe. 2016. "The Sanders Single-Payer Health Care Plan: The Effect on National Health Expenditures and Federal and Private Spending." Urban Institute. Published May 9. www.urban.org/research/publication/sanders-single-payer-health-care-plan-effect-national-health-expenditures-and-federal-and-private-spending.

Koskinen, J. A. 2017. "Letter to Congress Regarding 2016 Tax Filings Related to Affordable Care Act Provisions." Published January 9. www.irs.gov/pub/newsroom/commissionerletteracafilingseason.pdf.

Sanders, B. 2017. "Medicare for All Act of 2017." 115th Congress, September 13. Accessed May 2018. www.sanders.senate.gov/download/medicare-for-all-act.

Slack, D. 2016. "VA Bosses in 7 States Falsified Vets' Wait Times for Care." *USA Today*. Published April 7. www.usatoday.com/story/news/politics/2016/04/07/va-wait-time-manipulation-veterans/82726634/.

37

FINANCING LONG-TERM CARE

S pending for long-term care (LTC) services is expected to increase sharply over the next several decades. For the elderly (and their families), LTC expenditures represent a large uninsured financial risk; only a small percentage of the elderly protect themselves against possibly catastrophic LTC expenses by buying private LTC insurance. Federal and state governments also face huge financial pressures in paying for the LTC needs of the growing number of elderly. Medicaid, the primary government insurance program for LTC, pays for the majority of all LTC services (Reaves and Musumeci 2015).

How federal and state governments can limit their financial burden in paying for LTC for the aged, while ensuring that the elderly are protected from possibly catastrophic expenditures, is a major public policy dilemma. More generally, how should LTC services be financed, and by whom?[1]

The population is aging, as shown in exhibit 37.1. The number of seniors is expected to increase from 51.1 million in 2017 (15.6 percent of the population) to 74.1 million in 2030 (20.6 percent of the population) and to 88.0 million in 2050 (22.1 percent of the population). An aging population that is living longer increases the number at risk of needing LTC services. The fastest-growing group in the elderly population are those 85 years or older. This older group is expected to increase from 12.7 percent of all aged in 2017 (the oldest of the baby boomers started to retire in 2011) to 21.6 percent in 2050. As the impaired elderly demand more services to assist them with necessary daily activities, the cost of providing those services is rising at a faster rate than is general inflation.

The Nature of Long-Term Care

LTC consists of a range of services for those who are unable to function independently, including services that can be provided in the home, such as shopping, preparing meals, and housekeeping; in community-based facilities, such as adult day care; and in nursing homes for those who are unable to perform most activities of daily living (ADLs), such as bathing, toileting, and dressing. A nursing home is but the end of a spectrum for those with physical and mental impairments.

EXHIBIT 37.1

Percentage of
US Population
Aged 65 Years
or Older,
1980–2050

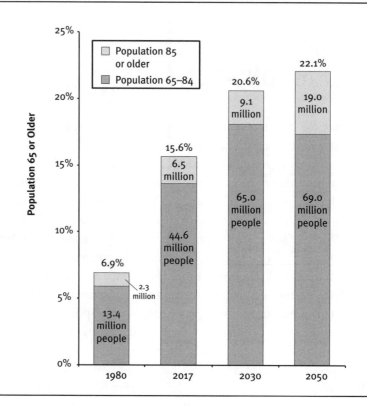

Source: Data from US Census Bureau (2017).

The need for LTC increases with age. As shown in exhibits 37.2 and 37.3, the group most in need makes up 50 percent of those 85 years and older. The need for nursing home care also increases with age. At any point in time (as of 2014), approximately 3.0 percent of the aged (about 1.4 million) are in a nursing home. An estimated 0.84 percent of those aged 65 to 74 years are in nursing homes, compared with 2.7 percent of those aged 75 to 84 years and 9.3 percent of those 85 years and older (Administration on Aging 2016). The main reasons for nursing home use are severe functional deficiencies, mental disabilities (e.g., Alzheimer's disease), and lack of a family member to provide services in the elderly person's own home. As shown in exhibit 37.3, the number of functional limitations increases with age.

Most LTC is provided in the home rather than in an institutional setting. Informal caregivers are predominantly family members or other close relatives. Older men with a disability are more likely to have a surviving spouse to provide them with LTC than are older women. However, as those requiring LTC age, it becomes increasingly difficult for their spouse to provide the care or services they need. In 2011, about 9 million people older than 65 years were cared for by about 18 million informal caregivers (Freedman and Spillman 2013). Of the informal caregivers, about 20 percent were spouses,

	Adult Day Services Center	Home Health Agency	Hospice	Nursing Home	Residential Care Community
No. of users (including younger than 65 years)	282,200	4,934,600	1,340,700	1,369,700	825,200
Age	**Percentage of Users**				
< 65	36.4	17.5	5.6	15.1	7.2
65 and older	63.7	82.6	94.4	84.9	92.9
65–74	20.0	25.5	17.1	16.1	10.4
75–84	27.5	31.1	30.0	27.2	29.9
≥ 85	16.2	26.0	47.3	41.6	52.6

EXHIBIT 37.2
Users of Long-Term Care Services by Provider Type and Age, 2014

Source: Data from Harris-Kojetin et al. (2016, table 4).

	All Medicare Beneficiaries				
	Total	< 65	65–74	75–84	≥ 85
Beneficiaries (thousands)	53,574	9,058	25,165	13,258	6,093
	Beneficiaries as a Percentage of Column Total				
Functional limitation					
None	50.5	20.0	67.0	51.5	25.4
IADL only	13.4	21.8	10.1	13.1	15.2
One to two ADLs	22.6	33.7	16.2	23.3	30.7
Three to six ADLs	13.5	24.5	6.7	12.1	28.8

EXHIBIT 37.3
Medicare Beneficiaries by Age and Disability Level, 2013

Notes: ADL = activities of daily living; IADL = instrumental activities of daily living.
Source: Data from Centers for Medicare & Medicaid Services (2013, table 2.1).

29 percent were daughters, 18 percent were sons, and about 22 percent were other relatives. Almost half of the spouses were the only informal caregiver. Daughters provided about 30 percent of the total amount of informal care, while sons provided about 15 percent (Spillman et al. 2014).

Children provide a great portion of the informal care to their parents. Women more often than men provide this uncompensated care. When the impaired person is a woman, typically a widow, children and other relatives are the most common caregivers. These services by family members, although uncompensated, are costly to the caregivers in terms of added strain and reduced hours at work.

Current State of Long-Term Care Financing

LTC is expensive and represents a significant financial risk to the elderly. In 2017, the national average annual cost for a private room in a nursing home was $97,455 (Genworth Financial Inc. 2017), and this figure is expected to almost double by 2037 (Genworth Financial Inc. 2017). A person turning 65 years in 2000 had a 44 percent chance of entering a nursing home at some point in his life. Most of the aged who enter a nursing home stay for a short period, but 19 percent stay longer than five years and incur 89 percent of all nursing home costs. Because women have a longer life expectancy, a 65-year-old woman has a 51 percent chance of entering a nursing home during her lifetime and, on entering, has an expected average stay of two years.

A person turning 65 during the period from 2015 to 2019 can be expected to live another 20.9 years. About half will likely develop a serious disability requiring LTC services (i.e., assistance with the basic personal tasks of everyday life, which include bathing, dressing, toileting, and eating). About 19 percent will need such care for less than a year , and about 14 percent will need care for more than five years (Favreault and Dey 2016). The costs of such care can be expensive.

In 2017, the average cost for a home health aide was $20.50 per hour (American Elder Care Research Organization 2017). Thus, LTC services in a nursing home or from an aide who comes to the home are too costly for most elderly on a fixed income and with limited assets. The uneven expenditures for LTC services and the very large financial risk for about 20 percent of the elderly suggest that there would be a large demand for private LTC insurance. Yet, this has not occurred.

Many aged mistakenly believe Medicare will pay for their LTC needs. In fact, Medicare pays for certain, limited LTC expenses, such as home health care for those who need part-time skilled nursing care or therapy services and are under the care of a physician. A limited number of post-acute care days (100) in a skilled nursing home are covered for those discharged from a hospital. Medicare spending on these services accounted for about 29.4 percent of total LTC spending in 2016 (about $74.9 billion).

However, when an aged person has decreased ability to care for himself because of chronic illness, a disability, or normal aging, Medicare does not cover the services needed.

In 2016, spending from all public and private sources for LTC (for all ages) totaled $255 billion, which represented about 7.6 percent of total healthcare expenditures. The largest component of LTC services is for nursing homes, which represents 63.8 percent of such expenditures; home care represents 36.2 percent. The major sources of LTC financing are public programs—primarily Medicaid and Medicare—at 66.3 percent. Individuals pay for about 24.1 percent of the costs out of pocket, and the remainder (about 9.6 percent) is covered by private LTC insurance. These percentages differ according to whether the LTC is provided in a nursing home or in the patient's home. LTC insurance covers 9.1 percent of nursing home costs and 10.4 percent of home health care costs. Private LTC insurance is beginning to become prevalent, but very few of the aged have such insurance. See exhibit 37.4.

On average, 32 percent of all nursing home care costs ($52.1 billion) are paid out of pocket and are a significant financial burden for many. In addition, $9.4 billion is paid out of pocket for long-term home health care costs, for a total out-of-pocket cost of $61.5 billion. These costs do not include the substantial nonfinancial burden imposed on families and relatives who are unpaid caregivers. The Congressional Budget Office (2013) estimated that the economic value of family caregiving in 2011 for those 65 years and older was $234 billion. Reinhard and colleagues (2015) estimated that the economic value of family caregiving for people of all ages in 2013 was $470 billion.

Payment Source	Nursing Home Care	Home Health Care	Total
	Billions of Dollars		
Total	**$162.7**	**$92.4**	**$255.0**
Medicare	37.5	37.4	74.9
Medicaid	50.0	34.0	84.0
Other federal	5.1	0.7	5.8
Other state and local	3.3	1.2	4.5
Private insurance	14.8	9.6	24.5
Out-of-pocket and other sources	52.1	9.4	61.5
	% of Total		
Total	**100.0**	**100.0**	**100.0**
Medicare	23.0	40.5	29.3
Medicaid	30.7	36.8	32.9
Other federal	3.1	0.8	2.3
Other state and local	2.0	1.4	1.8
Private insurance	9.1	10.4	9.6
Out-of-pocket and other sources	32.0	10.2	24.1

EXHIBIT 37.4
Estimated Spending on Long-Term Care Services by Type of Service and Payment Source, 2016

Source: Data from Centers for Medicare & Medicaid Services (2017a).

Medicaid LTC Expenditures

Medicaid is a joint federal–state financing program for those with low income. Total Medicaid expenditures were $566 billion in 2016, of which $84 billion was for payment of long-term services and supports; the remainder was for acute-care services (Centers for Medicare & Medicaid Services 2017a; Eiken et al. 2017). States vary greatly in their per capita (per person within the state) annual expenditures for LTC, with amounts range from $1,190 in the District of Columbia and $1,157 in New York to $192 in Utah (Eiken et al. 2017, table Y).

Medicaid is a major payer of nursing home care (30.7 percent) and pays 36.8 percent of in-home care. Medicaid is the payer of last resort, covering LTC expenses only after the elderly person has exhausted her own financial resources. To qualify for Medicaid, an individual must first spend down his assets, and is allowed to keep only $2,000. Current law permits a spouse to retain half of the couple's financial assets up to a maximum of $120,900 (inflation adjusted) in addition to a private home of any value if it is the principal residence (Centers for Medicare & Medicaid Services 2017b).

To limit their Medicaid expenditures, states have restricted the availability of nursing home beds, paid nursing homes low rates, and provided limited in-home services to those eligible for Medicaid. The consequence of these policies has been a continual excess demand for nursing home beds by the impaired aged. Because demand exceeds supply and states set low payment rates, the quality of services provided is often poor. Few states pay nursing homes according to the level of care needed by the patient; thus, nursing homes have an incentive to admit Medicaid patients who have lower care needs. When a private-pay patient seeks nursing home care, he will be admitted before the Medicaid patient because his payment exceeds Medicaid reimbursement. As nursing home demand by private patients rises, the excess demand by Medicaid patients will become greater in those states that continue to limit the number of nursing home beds.

Home care costs have become a growing share of Medicaid LTC expenditures. From 2000 to 2016, Medicaid spending on home care rose from $6.8 billion to $34 billion, an average annual rate of 25 percent, compared with an annual rate of increase of 4 percent on nursing homes (Centers for Medicare & Medicaid Services 2017a). States have also attempted to reduce their nursing home spending by substituting less costly in-home and community-based LTC services.[2]

The potential financial risk of needing LTC suggests a role for private LTC insurance. Among people turning 65 in the period from 2015 to 2019, about 31.5 percent will incur more than $75,000 of LTC costs during the rest of their life. Half of these people, or 15 percent, will incur more than $250,000 of LTC costs (Nordman 2016).

The probability of needing long-term support and services for 65-year-old men is 47 percent and for 65-year-old women is 58 percent (Favreault and Dey 2016). Nursing homes cost about $100,000 per year. Although the lifetime risk of a person's entering a nursing home and having to spend down her assets is relatively low, the fear of incurring this financial burden is the basis of the demand for LTC insurance and government subsidies.

Why Do So Few Aged Buy Private Long-Term Care Insurance?

When people are at risk for a large unexpected expense but only a few will actually incur such catastrophic costs, private insurance is a solution—for those who can afford it. A private insurance market enables people to reduce their financial risk in exchange for a premium. Given the growing number of aged at such risk, the potential market for LTC insurance is huge. Dependence on Medicaid and government LTC subsidies would diminish if more of the elderly purchased LTC coverage; however, less than 14 percent (7.2 million people) have done so.

Why has private LTC insurance not grown more rapidly? How feasible is it to expect this insurance to alleviate the middle-class elderly's concerns that their LTC needs will be provided for without burdening their family caregivers or spending down their estates?

Characteristics of LTC Insurance Policies

About 70 percent of LTC insurance is sold to individuals, in contrast to medical insurance, which is mainly sold to groups. This is so, even though group LTC insurance is eligible for the same tax subsidy as is employer-purchased health insurance. Given the predominance of individual LTC coverage, our discussion focuses on this market. Most LTC insurance policies cover all forms of LTC needs, including nursing homes, home care, and assisted-living facilities. Case management services, medical equipment in the home, and training of caregivers may also be included. Most plans also have a deductible in the form of days of care for which the individual must pay (30 to 100 days) before the policy is effective. These deductible provisions ensure that the policy is for a chronic condition and does not cover acute medical or rehabilitative services, which are the responsibility of Medicare or private medical insurance.

LTC plans also contain benefit maximums. Policies may limit lifetime benefits to five years in a nursing home. In addition, most policies contain a maximum daily payment for care in a nursing home or for reimbursement for care in the home. These maximum daily benefits are either fixed over time or (for an additional premium) increased by an annual percentage amount. Further, to qualify for LTC benefits, the individual must meet certain criteria, such as requiring substantial assistance to perform specific ADLs for an extended period, such as 90 days.

Premiums for LTC insurance reflect the cost of providing the services and the risk that the person will need the services as he ages. In 2017, the average annual premium (with 5 percent inflation protection) was $4,184 at age 65 years, $7,117 at age 75 years, and $13,420 at age 85 years. If a policy is purchased at age 30 years, the premium is only $2,140 per year; this rate reflects both the lower risk of the young enrollee and the assumption that the person will be paying the premium over a greater number of years (Federal Long Term Care Insurance Program n.d.).

The type of benefits included in an LTC policy greatly affect the premiums charged. For example, the premium on a policy sold in 2017 to a 70-year-old will vary from a low of about $2,685 to a high of $7,775 per year, depending on the benefits included. Premiums are also higher if the purchaser wishes to protect herself against inflation in LTC costs. Because most policies provide specified cash benefits in the event that the purchaser requires LTC, a policy that pays $100 per day for care in a nursing home is not sufficient if nursing home costs continue to increase at 4.4 percent annually, which is greater than the rate of inflation (Genworth Financial Inc. 2017). Protection against these additional financial risks raises the premium.

LTC policies are guaranteed renewable, and premiums vary by age and risk class, of which there are usually three: preferred, standard, and extra risk. Once a person has purchased a plan, she is not charged an additional amount as her age or health condition changes (Nordman 2016).

Possible explanations for why less than 15 percent of the elderly population has LTC insurance can be classified according to (1) the factors that limit the demand for LTC insurance and (2) the possible market imperfections in the supply of LTC insurance.

Factors Limiting the Demand for LTC Insurance

Elderly individuals' income and ability to pay for insurance vary. The oldest old—those most in need of LTC services—generally have lower incomes than do younger seniors and are in a high-risk group, which makes their insurance premiums much higher.

A great deal of misinformation exists among the aged. Many believe Medicare and Medigap insurance (private insurance that pays Medicare's deductibles and copayments) cover LTC, but they do not. Additionally, the elderly may be unaware of their potential LTC risks and the financial consequences of those risks. Further, the number and types of policies available, with their differing copayments and benefits, may be confusing to some elderly people.

Publicly funded or family-provided LTC decreases the demand for private insurance. Many elderly do not buy (or are less likely to buy) private LTC insurance because of the availability of Medicaid. They (and perhaps their family members) view Medicaid as a low-cost substitute to LTC insurance. To those elderly who wish to bequeath their assets to their children or other loved ones,

Medicaid is a poor substitute to purchased private insurance because they would have to spend down most of their assets before qualifying for Medicaid. In effect, Medicaid imposes a high implicit tax on the assets of the aged.

Expectations that family members will provide financial and nonfinancial support to them if they require LTC also affects elderly individuals' demand for private insurance (Brown, Goda, and McGarry 2012).

Possible Market Imperfections in the Supply of LTC Insurance

Supply-side concerns relate to whether LTC plans are priced significantly above their actuarial fair value (their pure premium), in which case the premiums would greatly exceed the policy's expected benefits. The greater the difference between the premium and the expected benefits (referred to as the *loading charge*), the lower the demand for such insurance.

Premiums for LTC plans may be much higher than the expected benefits for several reasons. When LTC insurance policies are sold to individuals, the marketing and administrative costs are much higher than when they were sold to large employer groups. The loading charges for individually sold LTC insurance are estimated to be 32 to 50 percent, but loading charges for group purchasers are only 10 percent (Brown and Finkelstein 2011).

Also increasing the loading charge is insurers' concern about adverse selection.[3] Individual LTC insurance is bought on a voluntary basis, whereas employer-paid health insurance includes everyone in a group, which eliminates the chance that only sick employees will buy the insurance. Because insurance premiums are based on the average expected claims experience (use rate multiplied by the price of the service) of a particular age group, insurers are concerned that a higher proportion of the impaired aged will purchase LTC insurance. If the premium is based on an expected higher-risk group than that of the general population of elderly desiring to buy insurance, those elderly who are at an average risk level will find the premium greatly in excess of their expected benefits. (Delay-of-benefits provisions, indemnity coverage with a large deductible, and copayments are usually included in policies to discourage adverse selection.)

Insurers are also concerned that as insurance becomes available to pay for in-home LTC services, the demand for such services will sharply increase beyond the amount believed necessary. To the extent that such moral hazard occurs and is not controlled by the insurer, the premium will reflect these higher use rates. These higher premiums will greatly exceed the expected benefits for those seniors who would not increase their use of services once their insurance starts paying for them.[4]

Conclusions About the Small Market for Private LTC Insurance

The size of the loading charge does not seem to be the determining factor in the small demand for LTC insurance.[5] Such policies charge the same premiums for men and women of the same age. Brown and Finkelstein (2008) estimated the loading charge for a 65-year-old man to be 44 percent—that is, he would expect to receive $56 worth of benefits in return for paying a $100 premium. However, because premiums are the same regardless of sex, the loading charge for a 65-year-old woman was estimated to be negative—that is, her expected benefits are greater than the premium paid: $104 in expected benefits in return for a $100 premium. Despite the favorable pricing for women, only about 10 percent of elderly women purchase LTC policies, which is no different from the percentage of men purchasing such policies. These findings suggest that market-supply imperfections, reflected by the loading charge, are insufficient to explain the limited demand for LTC insurance.

Demand factors are, therefore, more likely explanations for the limited insurance demand. Brown and Finkelstein (2011) believed that the availability of Medicaid is critical in explaining the small demand, as Medicaid crowds out the demand. For an elderly person with median wealth, most of the premiums for a private LTC policy pay for the same benefits that are covered by Medicaid. Further, women are more likely than men to end up on Medicaid—regardless of whether they have private LTC insurance—because of their much greater expected lifetime utilization of LTC services. Thus, even though they might be able to buy a policy with a zero loading charge, women still would not buy it because of the availability of Medicaid. As long as Medicaid exists in its present form, expanding the demand for private LTC insurance will be difficult.

To learn more about the factors affecting this demand, Brown and colleagues (2012) administered a survey and concluded that if the demand for LTC insurance is to increase, public policy should address multiple factors, such as the high cost of insurance, the availability of Medicaid and unpaid care from family members, the existence of a person's savings to pay for his care, and the limited knowledge of the risk of needing such care.

Approaches to Financing Long-Term Care

The LTC needs of the older aged, their fear of having to spend down their assets, and the high cost of private LTC insurance form the basis of the demand for government LTC subsidies. Providing the aged with a range of services—from in-home services to nursing home care—without financially burdening them or their children requires huge government subsidies. Given the rapid increase in the number and proportion of elderly individuals in the United States, federal and state subsidies for LTC would be a very large financial burden on the nonelderly, who already face the financial burden of paying for the enormous federal deficit.

Federal spending on programs benefiting the aged—Medicare, Medicaid, and Social Security—consumed 10.6 percent of gross domestic product (GDP) in 2017. By 2027, inflation-adjusted expenditures on these programs will rise to 13.3 percent of GDP (Congressional Budget Office 2017, table 1). Federal spending on the elderly will absorb a larger and ultimately unsustainable share of the federal budget and economic resources.

Thanks in part to medical advances, people are living longer and spending more time in retirement, which places greater demands on these three federal programs. The aged are a growing proportion of the total population, the oldest baby boomers have already started to retire, and the number of workers per aged to finance the costs of Medicaid, Medicare, and Social Security is declining. These demographic, technologic, and economic pressures have profound implications for the US economy and the continued funding of these entitlement programs.

Medicaid is the fastest-growing and second-largest program in state spending. About 55 percent of Medicaid expenditures are on behalf of the aged and those with disabilities. The growing number of aged will place a greater burden on state budgets in coming years. Expanding public subsidies for LTC would not only exacerbate federal and state fiscal pressures but also serve as a disincentive to purchase private LTC insurance.

Given these trends in both the number and percentage of aged and the likely inability of government to continue financing these benefits, subsidies for LTC are likely to be curtailed rather than expanded. The public policy dilemma centers on the role of government in financing LTC.

Stimulating the Demand for Private LTC Insurance

Increasing the demand for private LTC insurance would, over time, decrease the demand for Medicaid subsidies for LTC services. To stimulate the insurance demand, it is necessary to make Medicaid a less attractive substitute. Government subsidies for buying private LTC insurance could offset the low-cost advantage of Medicaid (once the spend-down requirement is met) if an individual requires LTC.

One type of government subsidy is a tax subsidy that is similar to tax-exempt employer-paid health insurance. Since 1996, employees do not have to pay income taxes on their employer's contributions toward their LTC insurance premiums; however, most private LTC insurance is sold on the individual market, where the premiums are not tax exempt. Even if the law were changed to make such premiums tax exempt, the benefits would primarily accrue to those in high marginal tax brackets, who otherwise are not eligible for Medicaid.

Under the Affordable Care Act, a voluntary federal insurance program for LTC was established—the Community Living Assistance Services and Supports (CLASS) Act. The federal government would serve as the insurer and would sell private LTC insurance directly to the public. As an insurer, the government—rather than private insurers—would bear the liability if premiums fell short of the program's outlays. Those purchasing the insurance would have to wait a minimum of five years before they became eligible to collect benefits. Once eligible, if a person had two or more functional limitations—that is, unable to perform certain ADLs (e.g., eating, bathing)—and a healthcare practitioner certified that he continued to suffer these limitations for more than 90 days, the person would receive a cash benefit of not less than $75 per day (adjusted for inflation) for the rest of his life, assuming his limitations continued. These funds could be used to purchase nonmedical services and supports necessary to maintain a community residence, such as hiring an aide (or a family member) to bathe the person or prepare meals at his home.

Proponents of the CLASS Act claimed that the new program, which was to be privately financed by premiums, would reduce Medicaid expenditures because care in the home is less expensive than living in a nursing home.

In 2011, the federal government claimed the program could not be implemented because it would be fiscally unsustainable. In addition to permitting those below the federal poverty level to enroll at below actuarial rates, there was the problem of adverse selection.

Enrollment in the CLASS Act was voluntary, and after only a short period an enrollee could become eligible for benefits. A voluntary program was more likely to attract those who expected to benefit from it, particularly because the premiums were adjusted for age but not for health status. As more high-risk people enrolled, the premiums would have increased, and those at low risk would either not have enrolled or would have dropped out. As proportionately more high-risk people enrolled, benefit payouts would have exceeded premiums. As the unfunded deficit for this program increased over time, there would be pressure for the federal government to support the program, which would further increase the already large federal deficit. The CLASS Act was subsequently repealed by Congress.

The Government as a Safety Net

Given the fiscal pressures on the federal and state governments, the government is likely to (1) become a safety net for low-income aged and (2) develop approaches for improving the effectiveness of how those subsidies are spent. When government acts as a safety net, primary responsibility for paying LTC expenses is placed on the individual and the family. The government fills the gap between the needs of the elderly and what their families and financial resources can provide. Availability of government assistance, such as Medicaid, is based on an elderly person's income and assets, and it is financed from general taxes; those with high income bear the financial burden of subsidizing those with low income. Because states differ in their generosity and financial capacity, the availability of LTC services (access to nursing homes and in-home care) varies greatly among state Medicaid programs.

Most states now have provisions that prevent people from qualifying for Medicaid within three years of voluntarily impoverishing themselves through bequests of their assets to family members. (States are going after middle- and high-income individuals who have adopted estate-planning strategies that permit them to qualify for Medicaid by transferring their assets just before they need nursing home care.) Further, because some assets are excluded for purposes of determining Medicaid eligibility—such as a house, assets spent on home improvements, an automobile, and assets placed in certain types of trusts—tightening Medicaid requirements would further reduce eligibility and increase public subsidies for those most in need.

Lengthening the period for asset transfers from three to five years (which is opposed by AARP), limiting excludable assets, and enforcing these requirements would reduce Medicaid expenditures; make Medicaid a less desirable substitute for insurance for middle- and high-income elderly; and, consequently, increase the demand for private LTC plans. Even if all these actions were undertaken, however, a majority of the elderly would still be unlikely to buy private LTC coverage.

Given that Medicaid will continue to be the major source of LTC funding for a majority of elderly individuals needing such services, and that government expenditures for LTC are expected to rise significantly in coming years, how can Medicaid be made more effective?

Improving the Effectiveness of Government LTC Programs

Several states have developed innovative LTC programs with the expectation that Medicaid's LTC expenditures will decrease. These states also hope to improve patient satisfaction with the care they receive. Several states use consumer-directed "cash and counseling" programs, for example. Under this approach, Medicaid beneficiaries living in the community are provided with funds to purchase LTC services rather than rely on Medicaid-provided services. Beneficiaries are given more choice regarding providers and the type of LTC services they use. Medicaid beneficiaries currently have no financial incentive to use LTC efficiently. Cash and counseling programs give beneficiaries an incentive to shop for lower-priced services and obtain more care for their budgets. Preliminary evidence from these demonstration projects indicates that participants are more satisfied with the care received and have fewer unmet needs than beneficiaries in traditional Medicaid (Doty, Mahoney, and Sciegaj 2010).

Other innovative programs integrate acute and LTC. Social health maintenance organizations (S/HMOs) receive a monthly premium in return for providing acute and LTC services to their enrollees. The S/HMO is at financial risk for the cost of all the medical and LTC services required by enrollees. Both healthy and impaired aged are eligible to enroll in the S/HMO, which has an incentive to improve efficiency by coordinating care and reducing unnecessary services.

The Program of All-Inclusive Care for the Elderly (PACE) model is directed toward Medicare- and Medicaid-eligible beneficiaries who qualify for nursing home care but want to continue living at home. PACE organizations receive a monthly capitation payment; use a multidisciplinary team of providers, such as physicians, nurses, and case managers; and provide services to enrollees in adult day care centers. Preliminary evaluations indicate that PACE enrollees use less nursing home and hospital care. These results may be biased, however, by favorable selection. PACE enrollees may be less impaired than nursing home patients, which is their comparison group.

Public subsidies affect the demand for private LTC insurance. The lower the responsibility for LTC expenses, the lower the likelihood of buying insurance. Appropriate public policy should do two things: (1) encourage those who can afford it to purchase private LTC insurance, and (2) stipulate that limited public funds be used for those unable to afford LTC insurance.

Summary

Fewer than 40 percent of elderly people are likely able to afford private LTC insurance. Although this percentage indicates that the private insurance market can grow substantially, it also indicates that a sizable number—mainly the older aged—will be unable to purchase insurance for the LTC services they need, forcing them to rely on Medicaid.

As the number of elderly people increases and they make up a greater percentage of the US population, another concern pertains to the supply of LTC services. Patients prefer to remain in their homes, and in-home LTC services are less costly than nursing home care. There is a trade-off between paying home health care providers sufficient wages to attract them to this profession and the out-of-pocket cost to the patient to be able to afford home health care.

A fundamental issue concerns the extent to which the government should provide LTC subsidies to the aged. LTC policy requires making choices. The elderly have greater needs for care, do not wish to be a burden on family members, do not want to spend down their hard-earned assets, and would like to be assured of having access to a high-quality nursing home (should the need arise). Yet, given the projected number of aged, government subsidies would be very costly. Such subsidies would require large tax hikes at a time when Medicare taxes will also need to be increased to keep it from going bankrupt. These tax increases would represent a huge financial burden on workers because the number of workers per aged person is declining.

Subsidies also reduce the incentive for many aged to rely on their children or to purchase private LTC insurance. To reduce the cost of LTC subsidies, subsidies should be targeted to those with the lowest income. Estate-planning strategies that enable middle- and high-income aged to transfer their assets shortly before qualifying for Medicaid are inequitable in that they shift their costs to others. To the extent that Medicaid rules are enforced and Medicaid becomes a less desirable substitute for private insurance, the demand for LTC insurance will grow. Greater growth in demand will reduce Medicaid LTC expenditures. Educating both workers and the aged about the need to protect themselves against catastrophic LTC costs also is important.

Discussion Questions

1. Describe the demographic and economic trends affecting the outlook for LTC.
2. What should be the objectives of an LTC policy? How do these objectives differ from the LTC goals of the middle class?
3. Why has the market for LTC insurance grown so slowly?
4. How can Medicaid be changed so it is not a low-cost substitute for private LTC insurance for the middle-income aged?
5. Why does private LTC insurance, when sold to the aged, have such a high loading charge relative to the pure premium?
6. Why did the government decide not to implement the CLASS Act?

Notes

1. Although many nonelderly have disabilities requiring LTC services, the expected large growth in the number of elderly (particularly the oldest old, who are much greater users of LTC services) and the financing of their care have been the main focus of LTC policy.
2. States cover nonmedical and social support services to allow people to remain in the community. These services include personal care, homemaker assistance, adult day care, chore assistance, and other services shown to be cost-effective and necessary to avoid nursing home institutionalization. To control costs, however, states limit eligibility and the scope of services covered.
3. Since the late 1980s, insurers have marketed LTC insurance to large employee groups. Group policies have lower loading charges because of their lower administrative and marketing costs. Adverse selection is also less of a concern when everyone in a group participates, particularly when they are at low risk for LTC. Further, because employees would not be at risk for many years, group policies could be sold at very low premiums. Employer-sponsored policies are a more useful financing source for future than for current aged.

4. To lower the cost of providing LTC, insurers provide comprehensive services—both in-home assistance and nursing home care. In-home services are less expensive (and are preferred by the impaired aged) when they reduce use of the more expensive nursing home. Case managers ideally would evaluate the elderly's needs and determine the mix of services to be provided. In-home services could be substituted for nursing home care, and the discretionary use of in-home assistance could be minimized. Controlling adverse selection and discretionary use of services is essential to keeping private LTC insurance premiums low. Currently, greater reliance is placed on financial incentives (deductibles and copayments) than on the use of case managers to control costs.

5. The importance of price on the demand for LTC insurance has been estimated to be between –0.23 and –0.87; that is, if the price of insurance were to decrease by 1 percent, demand would increase by less than 1 percent (Stevenson, Frank, and Tau 2009).

References

Administration on Aging. 2016. *A Profile of Older Americans: 2016.* Accessed November 2017. www.giaging.org/documents/A_Profile_of_Older_Americans__2016. pdf.

American Elder Care Research Organization. 2017. *Home Care Financial Assistance and Payment Options.* Accessed November. www.payingforseniorcare.com/ longtermcare/paying-for-home-care.html.

Brown, J., and A. Finkelstein. 2011. "Insuring Long Term Care in the United States." *Journal of Economic Perspectives* 25 (4): 119–42.

———. 2008. "The Interaction of Public and Private Insurance: Medicaid and the Long Term Insurance Market." *American Economic Review* 98 (3): 1083–102.

Brown, J., R. G. Goda, and K. McGarry. 2012. "Long-Term Care Insurance Demand Limited by Beliefs About Needs, Concerns About Insurers, and Care Available from Family." *Health Affairs* 31 (6): 1294–302.

Centers for Medicare & Medicaid Services. 2017a. "National Health Expenditure Data." Accessed December. www.cms.gov/Research-Statistics-Data-and-Systems/ Statistics-Trends-and-Reports/NationalHealthExpendData/NationalHealth AccountsHistorical.html.

———. 2017b. "2017 SSI and Spousal Impoverishment Standards." Accessed November. www.medicaid.gov/medicaid/eligibility/downloads/spousal-impoverishment/2017-ssi-and-spousal-impoverishment-standards.pdf.

———. 2013. "2013 Characteristics and Perceptions of the Medicare Population." Accessed November 2017. www.cms.gov/Research-Statistics-Data-and-Systems/ Research/MCBS/Data-Tables-Items/2013CNP.html.

Congressional Budget Office. 2017. "An Update to the Budget and Economic Out-look: 2017 to 2027." Published June. www.cbo.gov/system/files/115th-congress-2017-2018/reports/52801-june2017outlook.pdf.

———. 2013. *Rising Demand for Long-Term Services and Supports for Elderly People.* Published June. www.cbo.gov/sites/default/ files/cbofiles/attachments/44363-LTC.pdf.

Doty, P., K. Mahoney, and M. Sciegaj. 2010. "New State Strategies to Meet Long-Term Care Needs." *Health Affairs* 29 (1): 49–56.

Eiken, S., K. Sredl, B. Burwell, and R. Woodward. 2017. *Medicaid Expenditures for Long-Term Services and Supports (LTSS) in FY2015.* Truven Health Analytics report. Published April 14. www.medicaid.gov/medicaid/ltss/downloads/reports-and-evaluations/ltssexpendituresffy2015final.pdf.

Favreault, M., and J. Dey. 2016. *Long-Term Services and Supports for Older Americans: Risks and Financing Research Brief.* Office of the Assistant Secretary for Planning and Evaluation. Revised February. https://aspe.hhs.gov/basic-report/long-term-services-and-supports-older-americans-risks-and-financing-research-brief.

Federal Long Term Care Insurance Program. n.d. "Monthly Premium Rates." Various years. Accessed May 2018. www.ltcfeds.com/programdetails/monthlyrates chart.html.

Freedman, V. A., and B. C. Spillman. 2013. "Residential Care Estimates from the National Health and Aging Trends Study." Presentation at the NHATS Early Results Workshop and Annual Disability TRENDS Network meeting, Ann Arbor, MI, April 25–26.

Genworth Financial Inc. 2017. *Genworth 2017 Cost of Care Survey.* Published June. www.genworth.com/dam/Americas/US/PDFs/Consumer/corporate/cost-of-care/179703_2017CofC_Annual_092717.pdf.

Harris-Kojetin, L., M. Sengupta, E. Park-Lee, and R. Valverde. 2016. "Long-Term Care Providers and Services Users in the United States: Data from the National Study of Long-Term Care Providers, 2013–2014." *Vital and Health Statistics.* Accessed November 2017. www.cdc.gov/nchs/data/series/sr_03/sr03_038. pdf.

Nordman, E. C. 2016. *The State of Long-Term Care Insurance: The Market, Challenges and Future Innovations.* National Association of Insurance Commissioners and Center for Insurance Policy and Research. Published May. www.naic.org/documents/cipr_current_study_160519_ltc_insurance.pdf.

Reaves, E. L., and M. Musumeci. 2015. *Medicaid and Long-Term Services and Supports: A Primer.* Kaiser Family Foundation. Published December 15. www.kff.org/medicaid/report/medicaid-and-long-term-services-and-supports-a-primer/.

Reinhard, S., L. F. Feinberg, R. Choula, and A. Houser. 2015. "Valuing the Invalu-able: 2015 Update. Undeniable Progress, but Big Gaps Remain." AARP Public Policy Institute. Published July. www.aarp.org/content/dam/aarp/ppi/2015/valuing-the-invaluable-2015-update-new.pdf.

Spillman, B. C., J. Wolff, V. A. Freedman, and J. Kasper. 2014. *Informal Caregiving for Older Americans: An Analysis of the 2011 National Study of Caregiving*. Office of Disability, Aging and Long-Term Care Policy, Office of the Assistant Secretary for Planning and Evaluation, US Department of Health and Human Services. Published April. https://aspe.hhs.gov/report/informal-caregiving-older-americans-analysis-2011-national-study-caregiving.

Stevenson, D., R. Frank, and J. Tau. 2009. "Private Long-Term Care Insurance and State Tax Incentives." *Inquiry* 46 (3): 305–21.

US Census Bureau. 2017. "International Data Base." Updated August. www.census.gov/data-tools/demo/idb/informationGateway.php.

THE AFFORDABLE CARE ACT: DID IT ACHIEVE ITS GOALS?

When President Obama was elected in 2008, the Democrats achieved majority control of the House of Representatives and a filibuster-proof majority in the US Senate. The Affordable Care Act (ACA) was enacted in 2010 without the support of a single Republican in either the House or Senate. Given the partisan nature of the vote, Republicans have continually opposed the ACA, while Democrats have felt obliged to support it.

Leading up to the debate over the ACA, the middle class became anxious about changes to their healthcare. To alleviate their concerns, President Obama made a series of promises to the American public. In doing so he raised expectations as to what the ACA would accomplish. Among his promises, "If you like your healthcare plan, you'll be able to keep your healthcare plan, period. No one will take it away, no matter what."[1] "That means that no matter how we reform healthcare, we will keep this promise to the American people: If you like your doctor, you will be able to keep your doctor, period."[2] And, "In an Obama administration, we'll lower premiums by up to $2,500 for a typical family per year."[3]

Given the partisan nature of the ACA, it became a major issue in the 2012 congressional elections. The controversial legislation cost the Democrats control of their House majority, but they maintained their majority in the Senate, although several incumbent Democrats lost their seats. The divided Congress meant that Democrats could not fix problems that had arisen with the ACA because Republicans only favored repealing it.

Republicans brought several lawsuits questioning the ACA's constitutionality. The US Supreme Court upheld the ACA's individual mandate but ruled that states could not be penalized if they didn't participate in the Medicaid eligibility expansion. When the Congress failed to appropriate additional funds after 2014 for cost-sharing subsidies on the health insurance exchanges, the Obama administration continued to pay the subsidies to health insurers. The Republican-controlled House of Representatives sued, claiming only Congress has the authority to appropriate federal funds. In 2016, a federal judge ruled that these subsidies were illegal.

The ACA is the most significant health legislation enacted since Medicare and Medicaid in 1965. While members of both political parties supported Medicare and Medicaid, the fact that the ACA did not receive similar bipartisan support meant that the ACA would be less durable.

In 2017, the Trump administration continued the cost-sharing subsidies, expecting that a Republican-controlled House and Senate would repeal the ACA. When that did not occur, President Trump stopped the illegal cost-sharing exchange subsidies. With only Republican votes, the Tax Reform Act, enacted in December 2017, repealed the individual mandate penalty. President Trump then permitted "short-term" health plans, which have limited benefits and lower premiums, to be extended for a year and then renewed, thereby providing individuals with a low-cost alternative to ACA health plans. This policy, expected to take effect in 2019, will significantly affect the exchange risk pools.

The ACA is being changed in important ways. Contrary to early claims, the ACA will not have finally resolved the debate over health reform. The ACA affected many aspects of the financing and delivery of medical services. The complexity of the program also included imposing new types of taxes and severe reductions in healthcare provider payments to finance government subsidies for expanding insurance coverage.

Determining the equity and efficiency aspects of the ACA's taxes would require a discussion of who actually bears the burden of the tax (compared with who is required to pay the tax) and the effects on work effort of the different taxes (e.g., employees might be less likely to work longer hours if their higher income decreases their ACA exchange subsidy or makes them ineligible for Medicaid). Similarly, analyzing the consequences of the reductions in Medicare provider payments, assuming the payment reductions are fully implemented, would necessitate an analysis of the effects on patient access to care. (Given the Medicare actuary's concern over the drastic effect the payment reductions would have on hospitals, it is unlikely that they will ever be fully implemented.)

Instead of analyzing all aspects of the ACA, this relatively brief chapter analyzes President Obama's promise to "sign a universal healthcare bill into law by the end of my first term as president that will cover every American."

How well did the ACA achieve the goal of reducing the number of uninsured? Which ACA approaches have been more successful in this regard? It is important to keep in mind that increased insurance is not synonymous with increased access to care or to high-quality care.

Reducing the Number of Uninsured

Most of the ACA's provisions became effective in 2014. In 2017, several changes occurred that likely affected the number of uninsured in 2018 unrelated to the ACA. The economy began growing faster in 2017; the rate of growth in

GDP increased to 2.5 percent compared with only 2.1 percent in previous years, and as economic activity increased, the unemployment rate decreased to 4.1 percent. Thus, any decrease in the number of uninsured late in 2017 could not be attributed solely to the ACA. Further, the new administration reduced marketing expenses and shortened the enrollment period for exchange enrollees, which might have affected enrollment.

Two types of data are available on health insurance coverage: survey and administrative data. Administrative data do not cover all the insurance categories included in survey data. The advantages of administrative data, however, are that survey data undercount Medicaid and exchange enrollment and, second, the most recent survey data from the US Census Bureau are from June 2016, while Centers for Medicare & Medicaid Services administrative data are for late 2017. Thus, the analyses of the ACA's approaches for reducing the number of uninsured compare the period 2013 to 2016 based on survey data, as well as to 2017 based on administrative data.[4]

Exhibit 38.1 presents the number and percentage of insured and uninsured in 2013 and 2016 based on the latest US Census Bureau survey data, according to the major sources of insurance coverage for those younger than 65 years.

Overall, the ACA succeeded in reducing the number of uninsured from 41.1 million in 2013 to 27.5 million in 2016; 13.6 million gained insurance. The number of uninsured as a percentage of the nonelderly population decreased from 15.3 percent to 10.1 percent during this period. Based on administrative data, Medicaid enrollment increased by 13 million as of 2017, to 74 million, and the exchanges expanded to 9.1 million (2016) and 9.9 million by 2017.

The ACA used six approaches to cover the uninsured:

1. Expand Medicaid eligibility from 100 to 138 percent of the federal poverty level (FPL).
2. Impose an employer mandate requiring employers to *offer* their employees health insurance or pay a penalty.
3. Provide tax credits to small employers to incentivize them to buy insurance for their employees.
4. Impose an individual mandate to buy insurance or pay a penalty.
5. Permit dependent children up to age 26 to be included on their parent's insurance.
6. Provide income-related tax credits for use on newly established ACA insurance exchanges to those with incomes between 138 and 400 percent of the FPL.

Each of these approaches and how well they achieved their objective is discussed.

EXHIBIT 38.1
Sources
of Health
Insurance
Coverage of
US Nonelderly
(Younger Than
65 Years), 2013
and 2016

Market Segment	2013		2016	
	Population (Millions)	Percentage of Total	Population (Millions)	Percentage of Total
Employment-based	161.1	59.9%	164.9	60.8%
Individual (direct purchase)	23.7	8.8%	37.9	14.0%
Medicaid	52.0	19.3%	58.9	21.7%
Medicare[a]	7.5	2.8%	7.5	2.8%
Military-related healthcare	10.8	4.0%	10.9	4.0%
Uninsured	41.1	15.3%	27.5	10.1%

Note: Numbers may not add up exactly to totals because individuals may receive coverage from more than one source.

[a]Those younger than 65 may be eligible for Medicare if they have end-stage kidney disease and/or are permanently disabled.

Source: Data from US Census Bureau (2017, table HI01).

Medicaid Eligibility Expansion

About 74 million people are enrolled in Medicaid (68 million in Medicaid and 6 million in CHIP), or one in five Americans. The program is funded by state and federal matching funds (Centers for Medicare & Medicaid Services 2018). The federal government and each state have different federal matching formulas, which vary between 50 and 74 percent of the state's cost.

The ACA expanded Medicaid eligibility from 100 percent of the FPL up to 138 percent of the FPL (which translates to $16,643 for an individual and $33,948 for a family of four, as of 2017). For the first time, these eligibility standards include childless adults.

The ACA committed the federal government to pay the entire Medicaid cost (100 percent) for each state's expansion population (i.e., from 100 to 138 percent of the FPL) for the first three years; the percentage was decreased to 95 percent in 2017 and then to 90 percent in subsequent years. Given that almost all of the expense is paid by the federal government, an expansion state has little incentive to monitor how well federal dollars are spent.[5]

When the US Supreme Court overturned the ACA requirement that all states expand Medicaid eligibility, only 30 states and the District of Columbia chose to expand Medicaid eligibility. By 2017, about 13 million new adults had enrolled in Medicaid (Kaiser Family Foundation 2017d). A recent study, however, estimates that only about one-third of the new enrollees became eligible as a result of Medicaid expansion. Those who had been previously eligible accounted for a much larger percentage—as high as two-thirds—of Medicaid enrollment increases in expansion states (Frean, Gruber, and Sommers 2016). Had all states chosen to expand eligibility, the decrease in the number of uninsured would have been greater. Medicaid expansion states experienced a much greater increase in enrollment than expected.

The ACA's Impact on Medicaid

Increased Medicaid eligibility increased demand for medical services. However, the supply of physicians did not similarly increase. Concerned that Medicaid's low physician payment rates would limit access to primary care physicians, the ACA required the federal government to pay the additional cost of making Medicaid fees equal to Medicare fees for primary care physicians for just two years (covering the 2014 Congressional midterm elections). After the two years, Medicaid fees were again determined by the states, and they have returned to their previous lower levels, with a consequent decrease in access to physicians.

Several studies have been conducted to determine the effect of Medicaid expansion on the patient's health status, access to care, use of services, and financial effects (Antonisse et al. 2018; Courtemanche et al. 2018; McMorrow et al. 2017; Miller and Wherry 2017). A consistent finding in these studies is that those who became newly eligible in the Medicaid expansion states felt less stressed regarding their ability to pay for medical care, and were financially better able to pay for additional follow-up care than those in nonexpansion states. The researchers noted that in expansion states, increased waiting times were reported for appointments, which delayed receipt of medical care. These studies generally concluded that health effects have been minimal, although the study periods have only been a few years. More time is needed to determine whether significant changes in health status occurred compared with comparable groups of uninsured people.

When the ACA expanded Medicaid eligibility, proponents expected that those previously uninsured would have increased access to care, would receive coordinated care, and would not have to wait many hours in an expensive emergency department (ED) for routine medical issues. Further, having a usual source of care would result in cost savings because Medicaid enrollees would have fewer visits to the ED.

Contrary to these expectations, ED use increased by 40 percent in the first 15 months after individuals enrolled in Medicaid. In a study of Oregon's Medicaid expansion, which relied on a lottery to randomly select a limited number of new Medicaid enrollees, researchers found that the large increase in ED use by these new enrollees resulted in a greater-than-projected cost increase in the state. In a follow-up study, the authors "found no evidence that the increase in ED use due to Medicaid coverage was driven by pent-up demand that dissipated over time; the effect on ED use appears to persist over the first 2 years of coverage" (Finkelstein et al. 2016, 1506).

Interestingly, the authors found that visits to a physician's office were not a substitute for going to the ED. For these patients, ED use increased along with physician office visits. Perhaps the physician sent the patient to the ED where more could be done for the patient.

The Oregon Medicaid expansion study is also significant for estimating the health effects in those who enrolled in Medicaid and in those in the lottery who remained uninsured. Those newly enrolled in Medicaid increased their use of medical services; in addition to increased visits to the ED, the number of outpatient visits increased, as did hospitalizations and use of prescription drugs. However, the researchers did not find improvements in three measures of physical health—blood pressure, cholesterol levels, or blood sugar (for diabetes control)—relative to the control group. New enrollees, however, did report a higher level of self-reported health. Similarly, newly enrolled individuals in Medicaid reported having less medical debt, feelings of greater financial security, and lower rates of depression (Baicker et al. 2013).

The findings of the Oregon Medicaid study were disappointing to proponents of Medicaid expansion. Medicaid coverage often results in uncoordinated care that is inefficient; it is less valuable than private insurance. When the ACA's higher Medicaid fees for two years were reduced, new Medicaid patients once again experienced higher wait times for an appointment (Candon et al. 2018). Many physicians refuse to accept Medicaid's low fees, access to primary care and specialty physicians is limited, and Medicaid managed care firms rely on more restrictive provider networks than those available to privately insured people.

ACA-Mandated Benefits and Regulations

The ACA imposed strict rules regarding the purchase and sale of health insurance. These requirements on purchasers and insurers affected the insured, the uninsured, health insurers, and the performance of the health insurance markets, which are large employers, small employers, and the individual health insurance market. The following is a brief description of these ACA rules.

Ten Essential Health Benefits

ACA requires insurers to cover a broad range of mandated "essential" benefits, the scope of which is greater and more comprehensive than typical health insurance policies previously sold, particularly in the individual market. Some of the comprehensive benefits are pregnancy, maternity and newborn care, women's contraceptives (a required benefit even for single men and women past child-bearing age), preventive and wellness services with no copayment, chronic disease management, and pediatric dental and vision services.

One problem with requiring the same comprehensive benefits for everyone is that premiums are higher for those who prefer less comprehensive coverage.

Four Types of Health Plans

Enrollees must choose from among only four types of ACA health plans. All four types cover the same comprehensive ("essential") benefits, but they differ according to their premiums, deductibles, cost sharing, and maximum out-of-pocket costs. For each type of plan, the insurer is expected to pay, on average, a maximum percentage of the insured's medical costs, referred to as the "actuarial value" of the plan. A Bronze plan covers, on average, 60 percent of the insured's medical costs, a Silver plan pays 70 percent, a Gold plan pays 80 percent, and a Platinum plan pays 90 percent.

Removal of the Preexisting Condition Requirement

Preexisting condition exclusions have long been a concern of those with a health condition, such as heart disease or cancer. Many states developed high-risk pools that sold subsidized insurance to those who were rejected by health insurers for having a preexisting condition. These risk pools typically charged premiums that were about 150 percent of health insurers' premiums for those without a preexisting condition. When the ACA prohibited insurers from denying coverage because of a person's preexisting condition, states that had high-risk pools closed them.

Medical Loss Ratios

The medical loss ratio (MLR) is calculated by dividing the medical claims expense by the total premium. The ACA required health plans to have an MLR of no less than 80 percent (spending 80 percent of the premium on medical expenses) in the individual and small group markets and a minimum MLR of 85 percent in the large group market. Inability to meet the MLR required the insurer to refund the difference to enrollees. For example, if an insurer has an MLR of 70 percent in the individual market, it is required to refund the difference between 70 and 80 percent to enrollees (Kaiser Family Foundation 2012).

The remaining portion of the premium is considered administrative costs, which includes the insurance company's marketing costs, costs of establishing a provider network, administrative costs of handling insurance claims, costs of monitoring provider fraud and abuse, and profit (see exhibit 7.2). Differences in premiums and annual premium increases are primarily due to changes in the insured group's claims experience.

The following ACA requirements were particularly important in their effect on enrollment and premium increases in the individual insurance market.

Modified Community Rating

The ACA established rules governing how health insurers are permitted to price their health plans. For each type of health plan, insurers are permitted to vary their premiums by family status, county within a state, smoking status, and age. On average, the medical costs of older people, not yet eligible for Medicare, are higher than those for people in their 20s by a ratio of 5 or 6 to 1. The ACA, however, requires that differences in premiums according to age be no greater than 3:1, much less than the actuarial cost differences. (This age-rating rule was supported by AARP because it would lower premiums for older enrollees.)

Regulation of premiums by age, rather than by actuarial cost differences (as would occur in an experience-rated market), fails to consider the enrollment consequences of such a "tax" on the young.

Gender Rating

The ACA prohibits using gender rating for individuals (and employers with fewer than 100 employees). Women, on average, use more healthcare services than men of the same age. They visit the physician more often and take more prescription drugs. Because of their higher healthcare costs, a young woman's premium in the individual health insurance market would be 50 percent greater than that for a young man if gender rating were used.

Similar to age rating, gender rating replaces experience-rated premiums (based on cost differences) and relies on value judgments to determine premiums; therefore, enrollment decisions will differ for the two approaches for determining premiums.

Health Insurance Tax

The ACA imposed a health insurance provider fee on insurers. Any tax imposed on insurers is shifted to those buying insurance and will also affect their enrollment decisions. Imposing the tax on insurers is merely a way to make it less visible to enrollees. (See chapter 23, "Who Bears the Cost of Employee Health Benefits?") Large employers and their employees are unaffected by the tax because large firms self-insure and, therefore, are not subject to the tax. The new tax is not a specified fee, but is determined annually by the Treasury department to raise a certain amount of revenue. Those most affected by the tax are small employers and individuals buying insurance.

ACA's Employer Mandate

The ACA employer mandate required that employers with 50 or more employees who worked full-time (defined as at least 30 hours a week) must *offer* to buy their employees single coverage for an affordable and ACA-qualified health plan. An affordable plan was defined as one in which the employee did not have to spend more than 2.5 to 9.66 percent of her wages (depending on income) on the premium. Qualified ACA health plans consisted of four metal plans (Bronze, Silver, Gold, and Platinum). An employer failing to offer employees an affordable and qualified plan had to pay a $2,000 tax per employee.

The uninsured employee did not have to accept the employer's offer. If the employee rejected the employer's offer, the employer was no longer subject to the employer mandate tax.

Many uninsured employees believed the value of the minimum-qualified Bronze plan, with its large out-of-pocket payments, was not worth even the reduced amount they would have had to pay for it. The Bronze plan included a $6,000 deductible and cost-sharing expenses, and it paid about 60 percent of medical costs. In 2017, the average annual premium for a Bronze plan was $3,200, for which the employee was liable for only 2.5 to 9.66 percent of his income. If the employee wanted to buy a separate health plan for his family, in addition to having to pay the full $3,200 annual premium (plus child cost), the plan also included a $6,000 deductible. Many uninsured, low-income employees declined their employer's offer because they would have had to pay the additional premium of $3,200 plus two deductibles ($12,000) before they could receive any insurance benefits.

Another significant problem with the ACA employer mandate was that by declining the employer's offer of single coverage, the low-wage employee and family members became ineligible for premium tax credit and cost-sharing subsidies offered on the health insurance exchanges. Further, once the employee rejected the employer's offer, he became subject to the ACA's individual mandate penalty for not having health insurance.

Several studies concluded that the ACA's employer mandate was ineffective in decreasing the number of uninsured employees (Duggan, Goda, and Jackson 2017; Frean, Gruber, and Sommers 2016). In addition, it has been estimated that 3.7 million employees have been adversely affected by these ACA rules (Garfield et al. 2017, figure 1).

Small-Business Premium Tax Credit

The ACA exempted employers with fewer than 50 employees from the employer mandate.[6] To encourage these employers to buy insurance for their employees, the ACA offered firms with 25 or fewer employees (with an average income of $50,000 or less) a tax credit good for two years, equal to 50 percent of the premium. The employer would have had to pay the other half of the employees' health insurance premiums and buy the insurance through an ACA small business exchange.

The premium tax credit was apparently an insufficient incentive for small employers to buy insurance for their employees. The administrative and financial burden imposed on them was too great. The ACA small business premium tax credit failed to decrease the number of uninsured employees by any appreciable amount.

ACA's Individual Mandate

The individual mandate was intended to achieve two goals: first, to eliminate the "free rider" problem. Many uninsured are financially able to purchase a high-deductible health insurance plan but choose not to do so. If someone can afford insurance, but is uninsured and suffers a large medical expense, that person will still be cared for. The community will subsidize the medical treatment. That person is shifting the risk—hence, the cost of catastrophic coverage—to the rest of the community.

Second, an individual mandate was to ensure that the individual market risk pool would be larger and would include a greater number of healthy adults to offset the higher medical costs of those who are older and sicker.

To achieve universal coverage, the government must ensure that the two groups without health insurance—those who can afford insurance but refuse to purchase it and those who cannot afford insurance—gain coverage. The intent of the individual mandate was to require everyone above a minimum level of income to have health insurance, while the remainder (except for undocumented individuals) became eligible for Medicaid.

Frean, Gruber, and Sommers (2016) concluded that the individual mandate did not appear to increase insurance coverage. The authors, however, qualified their conclusion by stating that the tax penalty might have encouraged some uninsured individuals to sign up for Medicaid, even if they were previously eligible but had not done so. (The Congressional Budget Office confirms that if the individual mandate were repealed, many individuals who enrolled in Medicaid to avoid paying the tax penalty would disenroll) (Kaiser Family Foundation 2017a).

Young Adult Coverage Expansion

Starting in 2010, the ACA permitted dependent children, up to age 26, to be included on their parents' employer-based health insurance. About 2 million young adults, whose parents generally had higher incomes, took advantage of this provision (McMorrow and Polsky 2016). It is unknown whether these young adults previously had insurance.

Goda, Farid, and Bhattacharya (2016) estimated that *all* employees, regardless of whether they had children up to age 26, subsidized those with dependent children in the form of about $1,200 in reduced wages.

Health Insurance Exchanges

A New Insurance Marketplace for Individuals

The health insurance exchanges were designed to become marketplaces for individuals buying health insurance. In 2016, the individual market consisted of about 38 million people and represented about 14 percent of the total number of insured individuals younger than 65 years. Those purchasing insurance in the individual market tend to be self-employed, students, retirees not yet eligible for Medicare, unemployed, individuals between jobs, and individuals who are employed but have not been offered insurance through their employers. The individual market, although small compared with the numbers enrolled in employer-based insurance, Medicare, and Medicaid, is a major policy concern.

Before the ACA, individuals purchased health insurance through a broker, directly from a health plan, or on the internet. They were able to choose from among a variety of health plans at different premiums. Insurers used an individual's "risk-rating" to price his premiums, using the person's age group, gender, and medical benefits desired. Those with a preexisting health condition were often unable to buy insurance; they had to use state high-risk pools when they were available.

Further, premiums in the individual insurance market were higher relative to medical claims (a lower MLR) because enrolling individuals involves higher marketing and enrollment costs than those for large employer groups. MLRs in the individual market were generally between 60 and 70 percent.

The ACA's approach for decreasing the number of uninsured individuals whose incomes were too high to be eligible for Medicaid was to replace the private individual health insurance markets with federal and state health insurance exchanges based on ACA rules. Individuals, regardless of their medical conditions, can buy subsidized insurance on the exchanges. The exchanges offer a choice of ACA plans from competing insurers for citizens and legal residents whose incomes exceed the expanded Medicaid eligibility levels (138 to 400 percent of the FPL). Also eligible for federal subsidies are those who are not offered ACA-compliant insurance through their employers.[7]

Subsidies Available on the Health Insurance Exchanges

Two types of income-related subsidies are available on the exchanges. The size of each subsidy declines at higher income levels.

A premium tax credit lowers the monthly premium for those with incomes between 138 and 400 percent of the FPL; according to the ACA provisions, enrollees do not have to pay more than 2.04 percent to 9.69 percent of their income. A cost-sharing subsidy reduces the out-of-pocket liability (deductibles and copays) for those with incomes between 138 and 250 percent of the FPL. Without these cost-sharing subsidies, many low-income exchange enrollees would have difficulty paying their out-of-pocket medical expenses.

Both types of subsidies are based on the premium for the second-lowest-cost Silver ("benchmark") plan offered in the exchange.

Exhibit 38.2 shows the premium tax credits and cost-sharing subsidies available for a single person, aged 40 years, according to different income levels. Exhibit 38.3 presents the same information for a family of four. These exhibits illustrate the approximate financial burden of the premium and deductible on individuals and families at different income levels in 2017. In addition to paying the premium and deductible, enrollees are responsible for copays to providers. A Silver plan covers 70 percent of a person's expected medical expenses (deductible and copays). Thus, in 2017, the maximum liability for an enrollee with a Silver plan was $7,150 (excluding the premium); for a family of four, the maximum liability was $14,300.

After receiving a premium tax credit and a deductible cost-sharing subsidy, a single individual with an income of $30,150 (250 percent of the FPL) would still have to pay $5,342 or 17.7 percent of her income *before* receiving any insurance benefits. The financial burden increases as the enrollee's income rises. An individual with an income of $42,210 (350 percent of the FPL), who is ineligible for the cost-sharing subsidy, would have had to pay $7,638, or 18.1 percent of their income, before receiving any insurance benefits in 2017.

After receiving a premium tax credit and a deductible cost-sharing subsidy, a family of four with an income of $61,500 (250 percent of the FPL) would have to spend $10,808—or 17.6 percent of their income—out of pocket *before* receiving any insurance benefits. Further, a family of four, with an income of $86,100 (350 percent of the FPL) (ineligible for a cost-sharing subsidy), would have to pay $15,480 (18 percent of their income) out of pocket before receiving any insurance benefits.

Those with incomes below 250 percent of the FPL receive the largest subsidies and spend the smallest portion of their limited income on health insurance. Enrollees with incomes above 250 percent of the FPL must spend almost 20 percent of their income before their insurance covers any medical expenses. These out-of-pocket payments for premiums and deductibles represent a significant portion of a person's or a family's income. Someone faced with such a large expenditure for unknown medical risks must weigh the value of being insured against other necessary household expenses. It is not surprising then that many people with incomes greater than 250 percent of the FPL, who must spend nearly 20 percent of their income on insurance, have decided to remain uninsured.

Adverse Selection in the Health Insurance Exchanges

In 2010, when the ACA was enacted, the Congressional Budget Office projected that the health insurance exchanges, which became effective in 2014, would enroll about 23 million people by 2017 (Congressional Budget Office

EXHIBIT 38.2

Subsidy by Income for a Single Person, 40 Years of Age, US Averages, Silver Plan, 2017

Income	% of Federal Poverty Level	Annual Premium	Premium Tax Credit	Net Premium Cost to Person	Average Deductible (Medical and Prescription Drugs)[a]	Cost-Sharing Subsidy	Total Net Premium Cost to Person and Average Deductible	Total Net Premium Cost to Person and Average Deductible as a Percentage of Income	Total Maximum Out-of-Pocket Cost (Excluding Premium)	Total Maximum Out-of-Pocket (Excluding Premium) as a Percentage of Income
$18,090	150	$4,328	$3,601	$727	$255	94%	$982	5.4%	$2,350	12.99%
$24,120	200	$4,328	$2,800	$1,528	$809	87%	$2,337	9.7%	$2,350	9.74%
$30,150	250	$4,328	$1,890	$2,438	$2,904	73%	$5,342	17.7%	$5,700	18.91%
$36,180	300	$4,328	$875	$3,454	$3,609	0%	$7,063	19.5%	$7,150	19.76%
$42,210	350	$4,328	$299	$4,029	$3,609	0%	$7,638	18.1%	$7,150	16.94%
$48,240	400	$4,328	$0	$4,328	$3,609	0%	$7,937	16.5%	$7,150	14.82%
$54,270	450	$4,328	$0	$4,328	$3,609	0%	$7,937	14.6%	$7,150	No maximum

[a]Data for average deductible are not available from Health Insurance Marketplace Calculator; therefore, a different source was used.

Sources: Kaiser Family Foundation (2018); data on averages from Rae, Claxton, and Levitt (2017, figure 1).

EXHIBIT 38.3

Subsidy by Income for a Family of Four, US Averages, Silver Plan, 2017 (Adults 40 Years of Age and Children Younger Than 20 Years)

Income	% of Federal Poverty Level	Annual Premium	Premium Tax Credit	Net Premium Cost to Family	Average Deductible (Medical and Prescription Drugs)[a]	Cost-Sharing Subsidy	Total Net Premium Cost to Family and Average Deductible	Total Net Premium Cost to Family and Average Deductible as a Percentage of Income	Total Maximum Out-of-Pocket Cost (Excluding Premium)	Total Maximum Out-of-Pocket (Excluding Premium) as a Percentage of Income
$36,900	150	$12,957	$11,466	$1,491	$510	94%	$2,001	5.4%	$4,700	12.74%
$49,200	200	$12,957	$9,824	$3,133	$1,618	87%	$4,751	9.7%	$4,700	9.55%
$61,500	250	$12,957	$7,957	$5,000	$5,808	73%	$10,808	17.6%	$11,400	18.54%
$73,800	300	$12,957	$5,876	$7,081	$7,218	0%	$14,299	19.4%	$14,300	19.38%
$86,100	350	$12,957	$4,695	$8,262	$7,218	0%	$15,480	18.0%	$14,300	16.61%
$98,400	400	$12,957	$3,515	$9,442	$7,218	0%	$16,660	16.9%	$14,300	14.53%
$110,700	450	$12,957	$0	$12,957	$7,218	0%	$20,175	18.2%	$14,300	No maximum

[a]Data for average deductible are not available from Health Insurance Marketplace Calculator; therefore, a different source was used.

Sources: Kaiser Family Foundation (2018); data on averages from Rae, Claxton, and Levitt (2017, figure 1).

2010, table 4). Many health insurers viewed the exchanges as a new business opportunity and eagerly entered the exchange markets.

The Failure of the Individual Mandate to Expand the Risk Pool

The elimination of the preexisting medical condition requirement was expected to increase the number of high-cost enrollees. The individual mandate, however, was expected to expand the risk pool to include young and healthy individuals whose lower medical costs would offset the higher medical costs of other enrollees. The ACA anticipated that the higher costs of those with a preexisting condition would be small when spread over a large number of healthy enrollees.

The individual mandate, however, failed to expand the risk pool for three important reasons. First, the penalty for not buying insurance was too low. In 2014, the penalty was the greater of $95 a year for an individual or 1 percent of income. By 2016 (and into the future), the tax penalty increased modestly to $695 (or 2.5 percent of taxable income), which is only $1,250 for a person with an annual income of $50,000. Someone buying the lowest-cost ACA-qualified Bronze plan in 2017 would have had to spend $3,200 for the premium plus $6,000 for the deductible before she would receive any insurance benefits. Many healthy individuals concluded that the value of being insured did not exceed the penalty for being insured.

Second, the Internal Revenue Service failed to enforce the already low penalty for being uninsured. In 2015, 23 million people lacked health insurance; 6.5 million tax filers paid the individual mandate tax, 12.7 million uninsured claimed an exemption from the mandate on their federal income tax forms (Norris 2018), and 4.3 million did not check the box indicating whether they had insurance or paid the penalty tax. The federal government processed these tax forms as usual, and the IRS did not follow up with those who had not checked the box (Internal Revenue Service 2017).

Third, the size of the exchange risk pool decreased as a result of an administrative ruling to reduce opposition to the ACA. When the ACA exchanges started, millions of individuals who previously purchased individual health insurance received cancellation notices from their insurers because their coverage did not meet the ACA's mandated benefits. To continue being insured, they would have had to buy more expensive insurance on the new exchanges. Many people did not want to change their health plans, and their anger at no longer being able to keep their health plan and their physician, as President Obama promised, created a great deal of adverse publicity for the ACA. In response, President Obama "grandfathered" these health plans, with the stipulation that insurers could not reduce the plans' benefits. About 2 million individual enrollees preferred to remain in their grandfathered plans than switch to the new ACA plans (American Academy of Actuaries 2017, 8).

The inability of the exchanges to enroll a greater number of young and healthy adults resulted in an older and sicker risk pool than insurers had estimated. Adverse selection occurred; the risk pool was more heavily weighted toward higher-cost enrollees. Insurers suffered large losses, many exited the exchanges, and those remaining sharply increased their premiums.[8] The ACA exchanges failed to achieve the projected decrease in the number of uninsured. In 2017, 9.9 million people enrolled in the exchanges, fewer than the projected 23 million (Centers for Medicare & Medicaid Services 2017).

The Use of Cross Subsidies in the Health Insurance Exchanges

The ACA rules provided a disincentive for the young and healthy to enroll in the exchanges. The ACA relied on cross subsidies among the insured, increasing premiums on young enrollees, instead of using federal subsidies to lower the premiums of higher-cost exchange enrollees. The purpose of using redistribution among enrollees was to lower the federal cost of the ACA.

The ACA exchanges require that a form of community rating be used to narrow the differences in premiums between young and older adults. Age-rated premiums could not be greater than 3:1 for different age groups, even though the medical costs incurred by older adults are five to six times greater than those incurred by adults in their 20s and 30s. The increasing divergence between the premiums and actuarial cost for young adults was an important reason for many to remain uninsured.

Similarly, gender rating was prohibited in determining an enrollee's premium. Because women have higher medical costs on average than men, the rule resulted in increased premiums for men to subsidize women.

Insurers are required to include more comprehensive benefits in all insurance plans. These "essential benefits" exceeded what many were willing to purchase. For example, older men and women and young single men are required to buy coverage for maternity care.

Finally, the ACA imposed a new health insurance tax (HIT) on insurers, which, when shifted to enrollees, serves as a further disincentive for those not receiving premium tax credits to remain uninsured (Burton 2013).

The overall effect of these rules, which increase premiums on all or some segments of the individual market, is higher premiums and a lower demand for insurance. Many individuals, even those eligible for exchange subsidies (7.9 million), preferred to be subject to the penalty for being uninsured rather than buy insurance whose cost exceeded its perceived value (Kaiser Family Foundation and Health Research & Educational Trust 2016).

Consequences of the ACA Legislation on the Health Insurance Exchanges

Health Insurers

The individual mandate's low penalty, IRS's lack of enforcement of the penalty, retention of grandfathered plans for 2 million people, ACA rules that increased premiums, and imposition of cross subsidies on younger adults reduced much of the demand for insurance and decreased the size of the risk pool. Further, about 7 million people preferred to purchase ACA-compliant individual insurance outside the exchanges. Consequently, the exchange risk pools became more heavily weighted with costlier enrollees. Premiums, based on insurers' expectations of a larger risk pool with a lower average risk level, failed to cover the medical costs of enrollees.

Insurers incurred large financial losses, and many exited the exchanges. Competition among insurers decreased as many geographic areas had few remaining insurers. Many exchanges were left with only one insurer. Sharply increased premiums after 2014 reflected insurers' realization that the risk pools would be more costly (Cox et al. 2016).

As fewer healthy people enrolled and the risk pool consisted of a greater proportion of higher-risk enrollees, insurers complained that some enrollees bought health insurance and then stopped paying premiums once they received treatment. This behavior exacerbated adverse selection on the exchanges and contributed to higher medical costs and premiums.

Exchange Enrollees

The consequences of sharply higher premiums differ for the three income groups enrolled on the exchanges. Those with incomes at or below 250 percent of the FPL and those with incomes up to 400 percent of the FPL (groups 1 and 2) are not affected by rising premiums because the premium tax credit is based on income; enrollees in these groups contribute no more than 2.04 to 9.5 percent of their income for a benchmark plan (Kaiser Family Foundation 2017b).

However, the insurer offering the benchmark (second-lowest cost) Silver plan often changed each year. Thus, to be unaffected by rising premiums, the individual had to keep switching insurers (and their provider network and physician) to enroll in the benchmark plan. Doing so is troubling for many people, who may be in a higher-risk group and receive care for chronic conditions. If they stayed with their previous year's plan, they would have had to pay a higher premium.

Although average actual premiums increased by 21 percent in 2017, those with incomes of less than 400 percent of the FPL were able to pay the same after-tax credit premium that they paid in 2016, as long as they enrolled in the benchmark plan.

The financial burden of sharply increasing premiums has been especially difficult for those with incomes above 400 percent of the FPL. In some communities, premium increases have exceeded 100 percent. For many middle-class individuals and families who rely on the individual insurance market, the high premiums, together with large deductibles and copayments, have become a financial hardship that has made health insurance unaffordable. This middle-class group faces the choice of paying sharply higher premiums and deductibles (which consume about 20 percent of their income) or being uninsured (Pear 2016). The high cost of insurance was the reason given by 45 percent of uninsured adults for being uninsured (Kaiser Family Foundation 2017c).

In 2017, the ACA exchanges enrolled about 9.9 million; 70 percent were in group 1, with incomes up to 250 percent of the FPL. These enrollees received both premium tax credits and cost-sharing subsidies. They benefit the most from the ACA exchanges.

Proposed Changes to the ACA to Further Reduce the Uninsured

Decreases in the number of uninsured resulted from ACA subsidies in the health insurance exchanges to those with low incomes and from Medicaid expansions. It is unlikely, however, that the health insurance exchanges will be able to further reduce the 28 million uninsured. Several approaches are available that can expand coverage by lowering premiums and reducing adverse selection in the exchanges. Implementing any of these approaches requires legislative changes to the ACA.

Increasing the individual mandate penalty would incentivize more uninsured to buy insurance. However, public opinion polls show that the penalty was very unpopular, and it was repealed by the Republican-controlled Congress as part of a tax bill in 2017.

To reduce the cost of insurance for young adults and increase their enrollment, Congress should replace the exchange cross subsidies (requiring young adults to subsidize older adults [age rating]) with refundable tax credits, which would be based on age and income. Older adults would still receive a subsidy, but it would come from the federal government (taxpayers), not from young adults. (The same approach should be used to eliminate the gender rating.) Insurers would then base their premiums on the expected medical costs of different age groups.

The HIT is another example of redistribution. All exchange enrollees pay the tax, and the government uses the proceeds to subsidize those with low incomes. Similar to age and gender ratings, removing the tax would lower premiums; the subsidies could then be funded on a more equitable basis.

ACA-qualified health plans include the same "essential" benefits, but vary according to premiums and the percentage of out-of-pocket expenses. Exchange enrollees differ in many ways, among them being the amount they are willing to pay for a plan and the degree of financial risk they are willing to bear. Decreasing the number of "essential" benefits would lower premiums and provide more choices. The type of health insurance demanded would then reflect enrollees' preferences.[9]

The ACA regulates health insurers' MLR. If the intent of the ACA was to force insurers to reduce their administrative costs, then establishing the MLR as a percentage of premiums is unnecessary. Insurers are unlikely to waste administrative dollars if their goal is to maximize profits. They would only increase administrative costs, such as fraud detection or marketing, up to the point at which the additional revenue gained equals the additional cost incurred (i.e., marginal revenue equals marginal cost).

If the purpose of the MLR was to limit an insurer's profit, the best way to achieve this is to ensure that insurers compete. The unintended consequence of using the MLR to limit an insurer's profit is that it provides insurers with an incentive to raise their premiums. An insurer can only increase the absolute size of its profit by applying the MLR to a higher premium. If insurers are less forceful in curbing providers' prices, enrollees' medical costs increase and, consequently, premiums, along with insurers' profit. Most exchange enrollees are unaffected by higher premiums because their premium payments cannot exceed a certain percentage of their income.

Providing care for those with a preexisting condition is a necessary requirement for health insurance reform. The issue is how that coverage should be provided. Allowing those with a preexisting condition to buy insurance, combined with a weak individual mandate, causes adverse selection. The risk pools are more heavily weighted with older and sicker individuals than expected, and the higher premiums discourage healthy adults.

Prohibiting exclusion of preexisting conditions has not been a panacea for those with serious medical conditions. A recent study found that the ACA's ban on discriminating against those with preexisting conditions has led insurers to design their provider networks and drug formularies so that individuals with serious medical problems do not receive high-quality care. Specifically, exchange insurers have narrowed their provider networks, excluding costly cancer centers and teaching hospitals, and limiting access to costly drugs (Geruso, Layton, and Prinz 2016).

Alternative approaches would be more favorable to those with a preexisting condition and would also benefit individuals currently required to cross subsidize them. Allowing the exchange risk pools to reflect the actuarial costs of different age groups would have two positive effects. More young adults would become insured because their premiums would be lower. Second, for older adults, subsidies should be paid by the government. Moving toward experience rating with subsidies based on income and age, insurers would be less concerned with adverse selection. Subsidies and premiums for older and higher-risk groups (including those with preexisting conditions) would reflect their higher medical costs.

Alternatively, a separate, federally funded, high-risk pool could be established to subsidize those with a preexisting condition. The ACA initially established such a risk pool; it was closed when the exchanges opened. The advantages of a separately funded high-risk pool are twofold. First, premiums in the individual market would be reduced, thereby encouraging more healthy individuals to buy insurance. Second, those in the federally funded risk pool, who require more specialized medical services, would have improved access to cancer centers and teaching hospitals; they also would have a greater choice of physicians (and specialists in particular).

The federal government also could establish a reinsurance program to protect health insurers from the very high cost of covering some patients. A federal reinsurance program was established for Medicare Part D insurers to protect them from the very high drug expenses of some patients (Frank and Zeckhauser 2018). Like the other proposals discussed, a reinsurance program for the exchanges would reduce premiums and ensure high-quality care for costly patients, because those costs would be shifted from insurers to the government.[10]

Summary

Prior to implementation of the ACA, about 41.1 million nonelderly individuals (or 15 percent of the nonelderly population) were uninsured. The major accomplishment of the ACA has been the 13.6 million decrease in the number of uninsured, to 27.5 million (10 percent of the population) in 2016 (exhibit 38.1). This happened because of Medicaid eligibility expansion (13 million) and income-related subsidies to those in the nongroup health insurance exchanges (9.9 million) (Kaiser Family Foundation 2017d). The other ACA approaches to reduce the number of uninsured, namely the employer mandate, the small business tax credit, and the individual mandate, were ineffective in expanding coverage.

The employer mandate, backed by a significant penalty, failed to increase employees' coverage. Many employees chose not to accept their employer's coverage offer because their premium contribution and the deductible in the ACA-qualified plan exceeded their perceived benefits. Employees would also have had to buy separate insurance for their families and pay the full premium, plus bear an additional deductible. Once the employee rejected the employer's insurance offer, he could not purchase subsidized health insurance on the exchanges.

The temporary small-business tax credits were an insufficient incentive for many small businesses to offer health insurance to their employees. Low-income employees, whether in large or small firms, still need affordable coverage.

The ACA's removal of the prohibition against insuring people with a preexisting condition was beneficial to those with health problems. They could no longer be denied coverage in the individual insurance market. To prevent adverse selection by having a risk pool consisting of many high-risk individuals, the ACA included an individual mandate to require large numbers of healthy young adults to buy insurance. However, the penalty was too weak to be effective, exemptions from the penalty were readily available, and the IRS failed to enforce the penalty. The greater proportion of high-cost patients in the risk pool led to sharply increased exchange premiums.

After suffering large financial losses, insurers have exited the exchanges, thereby limiting competition and patient choice. Insurers that remained sharply increased their premiums to reflect the higher costs of their enrollees. Many exchange-eligible individuals (particularly young, healthy adults) decided that they preferred being uninsured to paying high premiums (greater than their actuarial value) and large deductibles, as well as being required to use narrow networks, for comprehensive insurance they didn't believe they needed.

Exchange enrollees, particularly those with incomes at or below 250 percent of the FPL, have benefited most from the premium tax credits and cost-sharing subsidies. They have not been affected by double-digit premium increases, as long as they switch to the new benchmark Silver plan each year. The exchanges will continue to provide them with affordable health insurance. However, many with serious medical conditions are limited in their choice of providers; having to switch to the lower-cost benchmark plan and change providers causes great anxiety.

Shortcomings of the ACA make it unlikely that further decreases in the 28 million uninsured will occur without significant legislative changes. Many middle-class families buying individual coverage face a financial hardship from sharply rising premiums and high deductibles.

Few of the ACA's cost-control measures have been effective in reducing costs. They have either failed to produce significant savings (accountable care organizations) or have not been implemented (a 40 percent tax on "Cadillac" plans exceeding $27,500 for family coverage and the Independent Payment Advisory Board).

The ACA is likely to be seen as an extension of Medicaid, serving those with incomes below 250 percent of the FPL and those who have preexisting medical conditions. The exchange insurers are also becoming similar to Medicaid HMOs, limiting patient access by using narrow provider networks.

Millions of middle-class individuals and families, however, whose incomes are too high for premium tax credits, those buying insurance in the off-market, and the uninsured (45 percent of whom state that cost is a reason for being uninsured) find the high premiums unaffordable (Goddeeris, McMorrow, and Kenney 2017). Premiums for 2017 increased, on average, by 21 percent; some exchanges, such as in Phoenix, reported increases as high as 145 percent (Cox et al. 2016).[11] These individuals are experiencing great anxiety and financial hardship, and many consider reducing their working hours and income to qualify for subsidies. Revisions to the ACA must address the economic insecurity of these middle-class individuals and families, which will require a bipartisan consensus.

Discussion Questions

1. What were the ACA's approaches for reducing the number of uninsured?
2. What change did the ACA institute that was of major importance in the individual market that any replacement plan would likely maintain in one form or other?
3. How effective was the individual mandate in expanding the exchange risk pools?
4. Why did adverse selection occur in the health insurance exchanges?
5. How did health insurers respond to adverse selection?
6. What are alternative approaches for subsidizing health insurance for those with a preexisting condition?

Notes

1. The ACA required that all health plans be ACA compliant, which made previous health plans, particularly in the individual market, noncompliant with the law. A public outburst occurred as many millions of individuals were shocked to find that they could not keep their health plan as promised. They were forced to buy new, more costly health plans on the ACA exchanges. PolitiFact, a nonpartisan organization, has called President Obama's "If you like your healthcare plan, you can keep it," the Lie of the Year for 2013 (National Public Radio 2013).
2. Those buying insurance on the exchanges were shocked and angered when they realized that not only could they not keep their health plan but they also could not keep their physician. To control higher-than-expected medical costs, insurers narrowed their provider networks, requiring enrollees to use network physicians and hospitals. Further, the benchmark Silver plan kept changing as insurers entered and exited the market. To avoid higher premiums, enrollees had to keep switching insurers, which also included changing their provider networks, including their physicians.
3. The Obama administration claimed that it would "bend the cost curve." Instead, the ACA *increased* the rate of growth of medical expenditures. In the years before the ACA, there was a slowdown in

the annual percentage increase in health expenditures. The slowdown was generally attributed to the recession and the growth of high-deductible health plans. The ACA's expanded coverage resulted in an increase in use of services and higher prices, both of which increased per capita and total healthcare spending (Weiner, Marks, and Pauly 2017). Health expenditures increased from 17.2 percent of the gross domestic product in 2013 to 17.9 percent in 2016. On a per capita basis, health expenditures, adjusted for inflation, increased from 1.7 percent annually in the six-year period before the ACA was enacted to 3.2 percent annually for the three-year period from 2014 to 2016. Premiums in the highly volatile nongroup market increased, on average, 8 percent in 2016 and 21 percent in 2017. Some cities experienced very high premium increases; in Phoenix, they rose 145 percent (Cox et al. 2016).

4. Enrollment data for the health insurance exchanges and for Medicaid expansion differ based on their data collection methods and time periods used. Some sources use a broad definition of the individual marketplace, such as "nongroup," while others use a narrower definition, such as "exchange enrollment." Enrollment estimates may be based on administrative data or surveys, which vary according to the methods used, such as personal or telephone interviews, sample sizes, and geographic area (e.g., state, county). Data for exhibit 38.1 are based on the US Census Bureau's Current Population Survey Annual Social and Economic Supplement because this survey is the primary source of annual health insurance information in the United States. Administrative enrollment data vary according to time of year; for example, 10.8 million enrolled in an exchange plan in 2016, but by December 2016, enrollment was only 9.1 million. Similarly, 12.2 million selected an exchange plan in January or February 2017, but as of June 2017, only 9.9 million had actually paid their first premium (Centers for Medicare & Medicaid Services 2017). The more accurate definition of exchange enrollment is the number paying their premiums.

5. Archambault (2017) stated, "When California first expanded ObamaCare, the state predicted enrollment would max out at 910,000 able-bodied adults. As of July 2017, expansion enrollment sat at 3.8 million. . . . California initially predicted that its ObamaCare expansion would cost roughly $11.6 billion in the first three fiscal years of the program. The actual cost during that time? An astounding $43.7 billion."

6. Mulligan (2017) estimated that designating a large firm by the number of full-time employees affects hiring decisions. To be exempt from the employer mandate tax, many small firms reduced the number of employees to below 50. This change resulted in the loss of approximately 250,000 employees.

7. In states that have not expanded Medicaid eligibility, the premium tax credits are for those with incomes between 100 and 400 percent of the FPL. About 2.5 million people in states that did not expand Medicaid eligibility would otherwise have fallen into a "coverage gap," having incomes between 100 and 138 percent of the FPL (Garfield and Damico 2017).

8. The ACA had already caused adverse selection in "child-only" health insurance policies. An ACA rule, which took effect in 2010, prohibited insurers from excluding children younger than 19 years who were diagnosed with a preexisting condition. Many parents purchased child-only plans because their small employers' health insurance policies did not cover children. Concerned that they would experience adverse selection (and the associated high costs) by enrolling large numbers of children with preexisting conditions, many insurers exited the market, and others stopped selling child-only policies. Parents who previously had enrolled their children faced much higher premiums and many disenrolled, while other parents were unable to buy child-only plans (Keith, Lucia, and Corlette 2012).

9. Allowing greater choice of health plans that differ in their benefits is similar to the introduction of Medicare Advantage (MA) plans. Initially, Medicare permitted MA enrollees to switch to traditional Medicare with 30 days' notice. Adverse selection occurred in traditional Medicare. When a person required a great deal of medical treatment, he would leave the MA plan and enroll in traditional Medicare, which permitted a greater choice of specialists and hospitals. Adverse selection was reduced when the 30-day period was lengthened to an annual open-enrollment period.

10. Medicare appears to have solved the problem of adverse selection in Medicare Part B (physician and outpatient services) and Part D (outpatient prescription drugs), which are both voluntary. Concerned that the aged would wait until they were sick to enroll in these programs, Medicare charges a higher premium the longer a person delays enrollment.

11. If it had not been for deductibles rising much faster than premiums in 2016, it has been suggested that premiums would have risen even more (Kaiser Family Foundation and Health Research & Educational Trust 2016).

References

American Academy of Actuaries. 2017. "An Evaluation of the Individual Health Insurance Market and Implications of Potential Changes." Published January. www.actuary.org/files/publications/Acad_eval_indiv_mkt_011817.pdf.

Antonisse, L., R. Garfield, R. Rudowitz, and S. Artiga. 2018. "The Effects of Medicaid Expansion Under the ACA: Updated Findings from a Literature Review." Kaiser Family Foundation issue brief. Published March 28. www.kff.org/medicaid/issue-brief/the-effects-of-medicaid-expansion-under-the-aca-updated-findings-from-a-literature-review-march-2018/.

Archambault, J. 2017. "The California Medicaid Rush: More Costly Than Gold." *Forbes.* Published December 20. www.forbes.com/sites/theapothecary/2017/12/20/the-california-medicaid-rush-more-costly-than-gold/.

Baicker, K., S. L. Taubman, H. L. Allen, M. Bernstein, J. H. Gruber, J. P. Newhouse, E. C. Schneider, B. J. Wright, A. M. Zaslavsky, and A. N. Finkelstein for the Oregon Health Study Group. 2013. "The Oregon Experiment: Effects of Medicaid on Clinical Outcomes." *New England Journal of Medicine* 368 (18): 1713–22.

Burton, D. 2013. "Obamacare's Health Insurance Tax Targets Consumers and Small Businesses." Heritage Foundation. Published October 31. www.heritage.org/health-care-reform/report/obamacares-health-insurance-tax-targets-consumers-and-small-businesses.

Candon, M., S. Zuckerman, D. Wissoker, B. Saloner, G. M. Kenney, K. Rhodes, and D. Polsky. 2018. "Declining Medicaid Fees and Primary Care Availability for New Medicaid Patients." *JAMA Internal Medicine* 178 (1): 145–46.

Centers for Medicare & Medicaid Services. 2018. "Monthly Medicaid & CHIP Application, Eligibility Determination, and Enrollment Reports & Data." Accessed May. www.medicaid.gov/medicaid/program-information/medicaid-and-chip-enrollment-data/monthly-reports/index.html.

———. 2017. "First Half of 2017 Average Effectuated Enrollment Report." Published December 13. www.cms.gov/Newsroom/MediaReleaseDatabase/Fact-sheets/2017-Fact-Sheet-items/2017-12-13-2.html.

Congressional Budget Office. 2010. "Manager's Amendment to Reconciliation Proposal." Letter to the Honorable Nancy Pelosi. Dated March 20. www.cbo.gov/sites/default/files/111th-congress-2009-2010/costestimate/amendreconprop.pdf.

Courtemanche, C., J. Marton, B. Ukert, A. Yelowitz, and D. Zapata. 2018. "Early Effects of the Affordable Care Act on Health Care Access, Risky Health Behaviors, and Self-Assessed Health." *Southern Economic Journal* 84 (3): 660–91.

Cox, C., M. Long, A. Semanskee, R. Kamal, G. Claxton, and L. Levitt. 2016. "2017 Premium Changes and Insurer Participation in the Affordable Care Act's Health Insurance Marketplaces." Kaiser Family Foundation. Published October 24. www.kff.org/health-reform/issue-brief/2017-premium-changes-and-insurer-participation-in-the-affordable-care-acts-health-insurance-marketplaces/.

Duggan, M., G. S. Goda, and E. Jackson. 2017. "The Effects of the Affordable Care Act on Health Insurance Coverage and Labor Market Outcomes." National Bureau of Economic Research Working Paper No. 23607. Published July. www.nber.org/papers/w23607.

Finkelstein, A. N., S. L. Taubman, H. L. Allen, B. J. Wright, and K. Baicker. 2016. "Effect of Medicaid Coverage on ED Use: Further Evidence from Oregon's Experiment." *New England Journal of Medicine* 375 (16): 1505–7.

Frank, R., and R. Zeckhauser. 2018. "High-Priced Drugs in Medicare Part D: Diagnosis and Prescription." Hutchins Center on Fiscal and Monetary Policy, Brookings Institution. Published January. www.brookings.edu/wp-content/uploads/2017/05/wp28-formatted-new_.pdf.

Frean, M., J. Gruber, and B. Sommers. 2016. "Disentangling the ACA's Coverage Effects: Lessons for Policymakers." *New England Journal of Medicine* 375 (17): 1605–8.

Garfield, R., and A. Damico. 2017. "The Coverage Gap: Uninsured Poor Adults in States That Do Not Expand Medicaid." Kaiser Family Foundation. Published November 1. www.kff.org/uninsured/issue-brief/the-coverage-gap-uninsured-poor-adults-in-states-that-do-not-expand-medicaid/.

Garfield, R., A. Damico, J. Foutz, G. Claxton, and L. Levitt. 2017. "Estimates of Eligibility for ACA Coverage Among the Uninsured in 2016." Kaiser Family Foundation. Published October 25. www.kff.org/uninsured/issue-brief/estimates-of-eligibility-for-aca-coverage-among-the-uninsured-in-2016-october-2017-update/.

Geruso, M., T. Layton, and D. Prinz. 2016. "Screening in Contract Design: Evidence from the ACA Health Insurance Exchanges." National Bureau of Economic Research Working Paper No. 22832. Published November. www.nber.org/papers/w22832.

Goda, G. S., M. Farid, and J. Bhattacharya. 2016. "The Incidence of Mandated Health Insurance: Evidence from the Affordable Care Act Dependent Care Mandate." National Bureau of Economic Research Working Paper No. 21846. Published January. www.nber.org/papers/w21846.

Goddeeris, J. H., S. McMorrow, and G. M. Kenney. 2017. "Off-Marketplace Enrollment Remains an Important Part of Health Insurance Under the ACA." *Health Affairs* 36 (8): 1489–94.

Internal Revenue Service. 2017. "IRS Commissioner John Koskinen Updated Members of Congress Regarding the 2016 Tax Filings Related to the Affordable Care Act." Internal Revenue Service. Published January 9. www.irs.gov/pub/newsroom/commissionerletteracafilingseason.pdf.

Kaiser Family Foundation. 2018. "Health Insurance Marketplace Calculator." Published November 3. www.kff.org/interactive/subsidy-calculator/.

———. 2017a. "CBO Projects 13 Million More Nonelderly Uninsured by 2025 If the Individual Mandate Is Repealed." Published November 15. www.kff.org/health-reform/slide/cbo-projects-13-million-more-nonelderly-uninsured-by-2025-if-the-individual-mandate-is-repealed/.

———. 2017b. "Explaining Health Care Reform: Questions About Health Insurance Subsidies." Published November 8. kff.org/health-reform/issue-brief/explaining-health-care-reform-questions-about-health/.

———. 2017c. "Key Facts About the Uninsured Population." Updated November 29. www.kff.org/uninsured/fact-sheet/key-facts-about-the-uninsured-population/.

_____. 2017d. "State Health Facts: Total Monthly Medicaid and CHIP Enrollment." Accessed May 2018. www.kff.org/health-reform/state-indicator/total-monthly-medicaid-and-chip-enrollment/.

_____. 2012. "Explaining Health Care Reform: Medical Loss Ratio (MLR)." Published February 29. www.kff.org/health-reform/fact-sheet/explaining-health-care-reform-medical-loss-ratio-mlr/.

Kaiser Family Foundation and Health Research & Educational Trust. 2016. *2016 Employer Health Benefits Survey*. Published September 14. http://kff.org/report-section/ehbs-2016-summary-of-findings/.

Keith, K., K. W. Lucia, and S. Corlette. 2012. "Child-Only Coverage and the Affordable Care Act: Lessons for Policymakers." Commonwealth Fund. Published October. www.commonwealthfund.org/~/media/Files/Publications/Issue%20Brief/2012/Oct/1629_Keith_child_only_coverage_ACA_ib.pdf.

McMorrow, S., J. A. Gates, S. K. Long, and G. M. Kenney. 2017. "Medicaid Expansion Increased Coverage, Improved Affordability, and Reduced Psychological Distress for Low-Income Parents." *Health Affairs* 36 (5): 808–18.

McMorrow, S., and D. Polsky. 2016. "Insurance Coverage and Access to Care Under the Affordable Care Act." Leonard Davis Institute of Health Economics, University of Pennsylvania. Published December 8. http://ldi.upenn.edu/brief/insurance-coverage-and-access-care-under-affordable-care-act.

Miller, S., and L. R. Wherry. 2017. "Health and Access to Care During the First 2 Years of the ACA Medicaid Expansions." *New England Journal of Medicine* 376 (10): 947–56.

Mulligan, C. 2017. "The Employer Penalty, Voluntary Compliance, and the Size Distribution of Firms: Evidence from a Survey of Small Businesses." National Bureau of Economic Research Working Paper No. 24037. Published November. www.nber.org/papers/w24037.

National Public Radio. 2013. "Obama's 'You Can Keep It' Promise Is 'Lie of the Year'." Published December 13. www.npr.org/sections/thetwo-way/2013/12/13/250694372/obamas-you-can-keep-it-promise-is-lie-of-the-year.

Norris, L. 2018. "Obamacare Penalty Exemptions." Healthinsurance.org. Published April 10. www.healthinsurance.org/obamacare/obamacare-penalty-exemptions/.

Pear, R. 2016. "Some Health Plan Costs to Increase by an Average of 25 Percent, U.S. Says." *New York Times*. Published October 24. www.nytimes.com/2016/10/25/us/some-health-plan-costs-to-increase-by-an-average-of-25-percent-us-says.html.

Rae, M., G. Claxton, and L. Levitt. 2017. "Impact of Cost Sharing Reductions on Deductibles and Out-of-Pocket Limits." Kaiser Family Foundation. Published March. http://files.kff.org/attachment/Issue-Brief-Impact-of-Cost-Sharing-Reductions-on-Deductibles-and-Out-Of-Pocket-Limits.

US Census Bureau. 2017. "Health Insurance Coverage Status and Type of Coverage by Selected Characteristics: 2016." *Current Population Survey (CPS) Annual Social and Economic (ASEC) Supplement.* Updated February 13, 2018. www.census.gov/data/tables/time-series/demo/income-poverty/cps-hi/hi-01.2016.html.

Weiner, J., C. Marks, and M. Pauly. 2017. "Effects of the ACA on Health Care Cost Containment." Leonard Davis Institute of Health Economics, University of Pennsylvania. Published March 2. http://ldi.upenn.edu/brief/effects-aca-health-care-cost-containment.

GLOSSARY

accountable care organization (ACO)—A network of hospitals, physicians, and other providers receiving payment incentives from Medicare for coordinating care for a defined group of Medicare patients.

actual versus list price—The difference between the fees actually collected or paid for a particular good or service and the stated price of that good or service. The differences between actual and list prices are provider discounts, which vary by type of payer.

actuarially fair insurance—Insurance whose expected payments (benefits) are equivalent to premiums paid by beneficiaries (plus a competitive loading charge).

adverse selection—A market phenomenon where high-risk individuals have more information on their health status than the insurer and are thus able to buy insurance at a premium that is based on a lower-risk group.

Affordable Care Act (ACA)—Formally named the Patient Protection and Affordable Care Act, contentious legislation passed in 2010 that expanded coverage to an additional 13.6 million people by increasing Medicaid eligibility and providing federal subsidies to those enrolled in state and federal health insurance exchanges.

all-payer system—A payment system where every payer pays the same charges for hospital and medical services.

American Medical Association (AMA)—A national organization established in 1897 to represent the collective interests of physicians.

antitrust laws—A body of legislation that promotes competition in the US economy.

any willing provider (AWP) laws—Laws that lessen price competition by permitting any physician to have access to a health plan's enrollees at the negotiated price. Because physicians cannot be assured of having a greater number of enrollees in return for discounting their prices, physicians have no incentive to compete on price to be included in the health plan's network.

assignment/participation—An agreement whereby the provider accepts the approved fee from the third-party payer and is not permitted to charge the patient more, except for the appropriate copayment fees.

balance billing—When the physician collects from the patient the difference between the third-party payer's approved fee and the physician's fee.

barriers to entry—Barriers, which may be legal (e.g., licensing laws and patents) or economic (e.g., economies of scale), that limit entry into an industry.

benefit–premium ratio—The percentage of the total premium paid out in benefits to each insured group divided by the price of insurance (also referred to as the medical loss ratio).

budget neutral—Total payments to providers under the current payment system are set equal to what was spent under the previous payment system.

Canadian-type health system—A form of national health insurance in which medical services are free to everyone and providers are paid by the government. Expenditure limits are used to restrict the growth in medical use and costs.

capitation incentive—When the provider receives a fixed payment and is therefore motivated to coordinate all medical services, provide care in the least costly manner, monitor the cost of enrollees' hospital use, increase productivity, prescribe less costly drugs, and be innovative in the delivery of medical services. Conversely, the provider also has an incentive to reduce use of services and decrease patient access.

capitation payment—A risk-sharing arrangement in which the provider group receives a predetermined fixed payment per member per month in return for providing all of the contracted services.

case-mix index—A measure of the relative complexity of the patient mix treated in a given medical care setting.

certificate-of-need (CON) laws—State laws requiring healthcare providers to receive prior approval from a state agency for capital expenditures exceeding predetermined levels. CON laws are a barrier to entry.

coinsurance—A fixed percentage of the medical provider's fee paid by the insurance beneficiary at the point of service.

community rating—An insurance pricing system that requires premiums to be the same for all of the insured, regardless of their claims experience or risk group.

competitive market—The interaction between a large number of buyers and suppliers, where no single seller or buyer can influence the market price.

complements—Healthcare providers who increase the productivity and/or lower the cost of those who use them (e.g., a physician hiring a nurse practitioner). The essential element in determining whether an input is a complement or a substitute is who receives the payment for the services provided by that input.

concentrated interest—When some regulation or legislation has a sufficiently large effect on a group to make it worthwhile for that group to invest resources to either forestall or promote that effect.

consumer-driven healthcare—Consumers purchase high-deductible health insurance and bear greater responsibility for their use of medical services and the prices they pay healthcare providers.

consumer sovereignty—Consumers, rather than health professionals or the government, choose the goods and services they can purchase with their income.

copayment—A specific dollar amount paid by the patient at the point of service.

cost-containment program—Approaches used to reduce healthcare costs, such as utilization review and patient cost sharing.

cost shifting—The belief that providers charge a higher price to privately insured patients because some payers, such as Medicaid or the uninsured, do not pay their full costs.

declining marginal productivity of health inputs—The additional contribution to output of a health input declines as more of that input is used.

deductible—A flat dollar amount that consumers pay for a medical service before their insurance picks up all or part of the remainder of the price of that service.

diagnosis-related group (DRG)—A method of reimbursement established under Medicare to pay hospitals based on a fixed price per admission according to the diagnosis for which the patient is admitted.

diffuse cost—When the burden of a tax or program is spread over a large population and is relatively small per person so that the per person cost of opposing such a burden exceeds the actual size of the burden on the person.

economic profit (zero or normal)—When a firm earns enough money to cover all its costs, including its "cost of capital" (the rate of return on what the firm's capital could have earned if it was invested in its next best use, adjusted for risk), economists consider the firm to be making "zero or normal economic profit." Revenue will equal the firm's explicit and implicit costs. The firm is in "equilibrium." A firm that earns more than "normal" profits is earning "economic profit," or simply "excess profits." A firm earning less than "normal" profits will eventually leave the industry because its resources will move to where it can earn a "normal" return.

economic theory of regulation—A theory of legislative and regulatory outcomes that assumes political markets are no different from economic markets in that organized groups seek to further their self-interests.

economies of scale—The relationship between cost per unit and size of firm. As firm size increases, cost per unit falls, reaches a minimum, and eventually rises. In a competitive market, each firm operates at the size that has the lowest per unit costs. For a given size market, the larger the firm size required to achieve the minimum costs of production, the fewer the number of firms that will be able to compete.

economies of scope—Occur when it is less costly for a firm to produce certain services (or products) jointly than if separate firms produced each of the same services independently.

employer-mandated health insurance—Effective in 2014, the requirement that employers provide health insurance to their employees and dependents or pay a tax per employee.

experience rating—Insurance premiums are based on the claims experience or risk level, such as age, of each insured group.

externality—Occurs when an action undertaken by an individual (or a firm) has secondary effects on others, and these effects are not taken into account by the normal operations of the price system (see also *inframarginal externalities*).

fee-for-service payment—A method of payment for medical care services in which payment is made for each unit of service provided.

fee-splitting—Occurs when a physician receives part of the surgeon's fee for referring a patient.

free choice of provider—Included in the original Medicare and Medicaid legislation to specify that all beneficiaries had to have access to all providers. This precluded closed provider panels and capitated HMOs. Economists consider the provision to be anticompetitive in that it limits competition; beneficiaries could not choose a closed provider panel in return for lower prices or increased benefits.

gatekeeper—In many HMOs, the primary care physician or gatekeeper is responsible for the administration of the patient's treatment and must coordinate and authorize all medical services, laboratory studies, specialty referrals, and hospitalizations.

geographic market definition—Used in antitrust analysis to determine the relevant market in which a healthcare provider competes. The broader the geographic market, the greater the number of substitutes available to the purchaser and hence the smaller the market share of merging firms.

guaranteed issue—Health insurers have to offer health insurance to those willing to purchase it.

guaranteed renewal—Requires health insurers to renew all health insurance policies, as long as premiums are paid, regardless of changes in the health of the insured. Any premium changes must be for the entire class of policyholders.

health maintenance organization (HMO)—A type of managed care plan that offers prepaid comprehensive healthcare coverage for hospital and physician services, relying on its medical providers to minimize the cost of providing medical services. HMOs contract with or directly employ participating healthcare providers. Enrollees must pay the full cost of receiving services from non-network providers.

health savings account (HSA)—Enacted as part of the Medicare Modernization Act, individuals are permitted to have a high-deductible insurance plan together with a savings account to use toward healthcare expenses. The unused portion of the savings account can accumulate over time.

horizontal merger—When two or more firms from the same market merge to form one firm.

income elasticity—The percentage change in quantity that occurs with a given percentage change in income. When the percentage change in quantity exceeds the percentage change in income, the service is income "elastic."

indemnity insurance—Medical insurance that pays the provider or the patient a predetermined amount for the medical service provided.

independent practice association (IPA)—A physician-owned and physician-controlled contracting organization comprising solo and small groups of physicians (on a nonexclusive basis) that enables physicians to contract with payers on a unified basis.

individual mandate—Under the ACA, the requirement that everyone have health insurance or pay a penalty. Subsidies to purchase insurance are to be provided to those with low income.

inframarginal externalities—When the optimal quantity is produced by a competitive private market, even though external benefits exist, these externalities are referred to as inframarginal. For example, the assumption of external benefits in having a minimum number of physicians is insufficient to justify government subsidies. A competitive, private educational market would produce more physicians than the number demanded by including additional external benefits.

insurance premium—Consists of two parts: the expected medical expense of the insured group and the loading charge, which includes administrative expenses and profit.

integrated delivery system (IDS)—A healthcare delivery system that includes or contracts with all of the healthcare providers to provide coordinated medical services to the patient. An IDS also views itself as being responsible for the health status of its enrolled population.

law of demand—States that a decrease in price will result in an increase in quantity demanded, other factors affecting demand held constant.

managed care organization (MCO)—An organization that controls medical care costs and quality through provider price discounts, utilization management, drug formularies, and profiling participating providers according to their appropriate use of medical services.

mandated benefits—According to state insurance laws, specific medical services, providers, or population groups must be included in health insurance policies.

marginal benefit—The change in total benefits from purchasing one additional unit.

marginal contribution of medical care to health—The increase in health status resulting from an additional increment of medical services.

marginal cost—The change in total costs from producing one additional unit.

Medicaid—A health insurance program financed by federal and state governments and administered by the states for qualifying segments of the low-income population.

Medicaid risk contract—A Medicaid managed care program in which an HMO contracts to provide medical services in return for a capitation premium.

medical care price index—Calculated by the Bureau of Labor Statistics and included as part of the consumer price index, it is used as a measure of the rate of inflation in medical care prices.

medical group—A group of physicians who coordinate their activities in one or more group facilities and share common overhead expenses; medical records; and professional, technical, and administrative staffs.

medical loss ratio—See *benefit–premium ratio*.

Medicare—A federally sponsored and supervised health insurance plan for the elderly. Part A provides hospital insurance for inpatient care, home health agency visits, hospice, and skilled nursing facilities. The aged are responsible for a deductible but do not have to pay an annual premium. Part B provides payments for physician services, physician-ordered supplies and services, and outpatient hospital services. Part B is voluntary, and the aged pay an annual premium that is 25 percent of the cost of the program in addition to a deductible and copayment. Part C permits private health plans to compete for serving the aged. Part D is a prescription drug benefit that includes deductibles and copayments and requires a monthly premium.

Medicare Advantage plans—Enacted as part of the Medicare Modernization Act, private health plans receive a monthly capitation payment from Medicare and accept full financial risk for the cost of all medical benefits (Part A, Part B, and Part D services) to which their enrollees are entitled. Enrollees using nonparticipating providers are responsible for the full charges of such providers. Previously referred to as Medicare+Choice plans.

Medicare risk contract—See *Medicare Advantage plans*.

Medigap insurance policy—Insurance policy privately purchased by the elderly to supplement Medicare coverage by covering deductibles and copayments.

monopoly—A market structure in which there is a single seller of a product that has no close substitutes.

moral hazard—Occurs when patients can affect the size of their loss, as when patients increase their use of medical services when the price of those services is reduced.

multihospital system—A system in which a corporation owns, leases, or manages two or more acute care hospitals.

multipayer system—A system in which reimbursement for medical services is made by multiple third-party payers.

network HMO—A type of HMO that signs contracts with a number of group practices to provide medical services.

nonprice hospital competition—Hospitals compete on the basis of their facilities and services and the latest technology rather than on price.

not-for-profit—An institution that cannot distribute profits to shareholders and is tax exempt.

nurse participation rate—The percentage of trained nurses who are employed.

opportunity cost—Relevant costs for economic decision making that include explicit and implicit costs. For example, the opportunity costs of a medical education include the forgone income the student could have earned had she not gone to medical school.

out-of-pocket price—The amount that the beneficiary must pay after all other payments have been considered by the health plan.

over-the-counter drug—A drug that is available for public purchase and self-directed use without a prescription.

patient dumping—A situation in which a high-cost patient is not admitted to or is discharged early from a hospital because the patient has no insurance or the amount reimbursed by the third-party payer will be less than the cost of caring for that patient.

pay-for-performance—Higher payments are made to those healthcare providers who demonstrate that they provide higher-quality services.

per diem payment—A method of payment to institutional providers that is based on a fixed daily amount and does not differ according to the level of service provided.

pharmacy benefit manager (PBM)—Firm that provides administrative services and processes outpatient prescription drug claims for health insurers' prescription drug plans.

physician agency relationship—The physician acts on behalf of the patient. Agency relationships may be perfect or imperfect, and the method of physician payment (fee-for-service or capitation) produces different behavioral responses among imperfect physician agents.

physician–hospital organization (PHO)—An organization in which hospitals and their medical staffs develop new types of group practice arrangements that will allow the hospitals to seek contracts from HMOs and other carriers on behalf of the physicians and hospitals together.

play or pay—Employers are required to provide medical insurance to their employees (play) or pay a certain amount of tax per employee.

point-of-service plan—A plan that allows the beneficiary to select from participating providers (the health plan) or use nonparticipating providers and pay a high copayment.

portability—Included as part of health insurance reform to enable the insured to change jobs without losing their insurance.

preexisting exclusion—To protect themselves against adverse selection by new enrollees, insurers used a preexisting exclusion clause that excluded treatment for any specified illnesses diagnosed within the previous (usually 12) months. Under the ACA, preexisting-condition exclusion can no longer be used to deny health insurance to those willing to buy insurance.

preferred provider organization (PPO)—An arrangement between a panel of healthcare providers and purchasers of healthcare services in which a closed panel of providers agrees to supply services to a defined group of patients on a discounted fee-for-service basis. This type of plan offers its members a limited number of physicians and hospitals, negotiated fee schedules, utilization review, and consumer incentives to use PPO-participating providers.

preferred risk selection—Occurs when insurers receive the same premium for everyone in an insured group and try to attract only those with lower risks, whose expected medical costs would be less than the group's average premium.

prescription drug—A drug that can be obtained only with a physician's order. It includes the following:

- breakthrough (or innovator) drug—The first brand-name drug to use a particular therapeutic mechanism (i.e., a particular method of treating a given disease).
- generic drug—A copy of a breakthrough drug that the Food and Drug Administration judges to be comparable in terms of such factors as strength, quality, and therapeutic effectiveness. Generic drugs are sold after the patent on a brand-name drug has expired and generally under their chemical names.
- "me-too" drug—A brand-name drug that uses the same therapeutic mechanism as a breakthrough drug and thus directly competes with it.
- multiple-source drug—A drug available in both brand-name and generic versions from a variety of manufacturers.
- single-source drug—A brand-name drug that is still under patent and thus is usually available from only one manufacturer.

price discrimination—An indication of monopoly power by a provider. The provider is able to charge different purchasers different prices according to the purchaser's elasticity of demand (willingness to pay) for the same or a similar service.

price elasticity—The percentage change in quantity divided by the percentage change in price. When the percentage change in quantity exceeds the percentage change in price, the service is price "elastic."

primary care physician—A physician who coordinates all of the routine medical care needs of an individual. Typically, this type of physician specializes in family practice, internal medicine, pediatrics, or obstetrics/gynecology.

process measures of quality—A type of quality assessment that evaluates process of care by measuring the specific way in which care is provided or, with respect to health manpower, the educational requirements.

product market definition—Used in antitrust cases to determine whether the product or service in question has close substitutes, which depends on the willingness of purchasers to use other services if the relative prices change. The closer the substitutes, the smaller the market share of the product being examined.

prospective payment system (PPS)—A method of payment for medical services in which providers are paid a predetermined rate for the services rendered regardless of the actual costs of care incurred. Medicare uses a PPS for hospital care based on a fixed price per hospital admission (by diagnosis).

public-interest theory of government—Assumes that legislation is enacted to serve the public interest. According to this theory, the two basic objectives of government are to improve market efficiency and, based on a societal value judgment, redistribute income.

pure premium—The expected claims experience for an insured group, exclusive of the loading charge. The pure premium for an individual is calculated by multiplying the size of the loss by the probability the loss will occur.

redistribution—When, as a result of public policy, the benefits and costs to a person are not equal, redistribution occurs. For example, based on a societal value judgment that those with higher income should be taxed to provide for those with lower income, the benefits and costs are not equal for either of the groups affected.

reference pricing—An employer (or insurer) determines the maximum price it will pay the provider for an employee's medical treatment, such as a hip replacement. The reference price is usually based on the treatment price at high-quality hospitals. If the employee goes to other hospitals for treatment, the employee pays the difference between the reference price and the hospital's price.

refundable tax credit—A proposal for national health insurance under which individuals are given a tax credit to purchase health insurance. The tax credit may be income related (i.e., declining at higher levels of income). Persons whose tax credit exceeds their tax liabilities would receive a refund for the difference. For those with little or no tax liability, the tax credit is essentially a voucher for a health plan.

regressive tax—When those with lower income pay a higher portion of their income for a given tax than do those with higher income.

report card—Standardized data representing process and outcome measures of quality that are collected by independent organizations to enable purchasers to make more informed choices of health plans and their participating providers.

resource-based relative value scale (RBRVS)—The current Medicare fee-for-service payment system for physicians, initiated in 1992, under which each physician service is assigned a relative value based on the presumed resource costs of performing that service. The relative value for each service is then multiplied by a conversion factor (in dollars) to arrive at the physician's fee.

risk-adjusted premium—The employer adjusts the insurance premium to reflect the risk levels of the employees enrolled with different insurers.

risk pool—Represents a population group that is defined by its expected claim experience.

risk selection—Occurs when insurers attempt to attract a more favorable risk group than the average risk group, which was the basis for the group's premium (preferred risk selection). Similarly, enrollees may seek to join a health plan at a premium that reflects a lower level of risk than their own (adverse selection).

rule of reason—Used in antitrust cases to determine whether the anticompetitive harm caused by a particular activity (e.g., merger) exceeds the procompetitive benefits of not permitting the particular activity.

second opinion—A utilization-review approach in which decisions to initiate a medical intervention are typically reviewed by two physicians.

self-funding self-insurance—A healthcare program in which employers fund benefit plans from their own resources without purchasing insurance. Self-funded plans may be self-administered, or the employer may contract with an outside administrator for an administrative-service-only arrangement. Employers who self-fund can limit their liability via stop-loss insurance.

single payer—A form of national health insurance in which a single third-party payer (usually the government) pays healthcare providers and the entire population has free choice of all providers at zero (or little) out-of-pocket expense.

skilled nursing facility—A long-term care facility that provides inpatient skilled nursing care and rehabilitation services.

specialty PPO—A type of PPO that offers one or more limited healthcare services or benefits, such as anesthesia, vision, and dental services.

staff-model HMO—A type of HMO that hires salaried physicians to provide healthcare services on an exclusive basis to the HMO's enrollees.

stop-loss insurance—Insurance coverage providing protection from losses resulting from claims greater than a specific dollar amount (equivalent to a large deductible).

substitutes—Personnel or facilities that decrease the demand for their competitors, such as independent nurse anesthetists (competing with anesthesiologists) and independent outpatient surgery centers (competing with hospitals).

supplier-induced demand—When physicians modify their diagnosis and treatment to favorably affect their own economic well-being.

sustainable growth rate (SGR)—Medicare's expenditure limit on physician payments consists of four elements: the percentage increase in real GDP per capita, a medical inflation rate of physician fee increases, the annual percentage increase in Part B enrollees, and the percentage change in spending for physicians' services resulting from changes in laws and regulations (e.g., expanded Medicare coverage for preventive services).

target income hypothesis—A model of supplier-induced demand that assumes physicians will induce demand only to the extent they will achieve a target income, determined by the local income distribution, particularly with respect to the relative income of other physicians and professionals in the area.

tax-exempt employer-paid health insurance—Health insurance purchased by the employer on behalf of its employees is not considered to be taxable income to the employee. By lowering the price of insurance, the quantity demanded is increased (as is its comprehensiveness). The major beneficiaries are those in higher income-tax brackets.

tertiary care—This type of care includes the most complex services (e.g., transplantation, open-heart surgery, and burn treatment) provided in inpatient hospital settings.

third-party administrator (TPA)—An independent entity that provides administrative services, such as claims processing, to a company that self-insures. A TPA does not underwrite the risk.

third-party payer—An organization (e.g., an HMO, insurance company, or government agency) that pays for all or part of the insured's medical services.

triple-option health plan—A type of health plan in which employees may choose from an HMO, a PPO, or an indemnity plan depending on how much they are willing to contribute.

unbundling—Occurs when a provider charges separately for each of the services previously provided together as part of a treatment.

uncompensated care—Services rendered by the provider without reimbursement, as in the case of charity care and bad debts.

universal coverage—When the entire population is eligible for medical services or health insurance.

upcoding—Occurs when the provider bills for a higher-priced diagnosis or service rather than the lower-cost service actually provided.

usual, customary, and reasonable fee—A method of reimbursement in which the fee is "usual" in that physician's office, "customary" in that community, and "reasonable" in terms of the distribution of all physician charges for that service in the community.

vacancy rate—The percentage of a hospital's budgeted registered nurse positions that are unfilled.

vertical integration—The organization of a delivery system that provides an entire range of services to include inpatient care, ambulatory care clinics, outpatient surgery, and home care.

vertical merger—A merger between two firms that have a supplier–buyer relationship.

virtual integration—The organization of a delivery system that relies on contractual relationships rather than complete ownership to provide all medical services required by the patient.

voluntary performance standard—An expenditure target adopted by the Medicare program in 1992 to limit the rate of increase in its expenditures for physicians' services. Replaced by the SGR formula as part of the Balanced Budget Act of 1997.

INDEX

Note: Italicized page locators refer to figures or tables in exhibits.

ABOUT THE AUTHOR

Paul J. Feldstein, PhD, has been a professor and the Robert Gumbiner Chair in Health Care Management at the Paul Merage School of Business at the University of California, Irvine, since 1987. Previously, he was a professor at the University of Michigan in both the Department of Economics and the School of Public Health. Before that, he was the director of the Division of Research at the American Hospital Association. Professor Feldstein received his PhD from the University of Chicago.

Professor Feldstein has written seven books and more than 70 articles on healthcare. His book *Health Care Economics* (Cengage, 2011) is one of the most widely used textbooks on health economics, and his book *The Politics of Health Legislation: An Economic Perspective* (Health Administration Press, 2006) uses economic analysis to explain the outcome of health legislation in terms of the interest groups affected.

During leaves from the university, Professor Feldstein worked at the federal Office of Management and Budget, the Social Security Administration, and the World Health Organization. He has been a consultant to many government and private health agencies, has served as an expert witness on health antitrust issues, and was a board member of Sutter Health (a large not-for-profit healthcare organization serving Northern California), Province Healthcare (a hospital company serving nonurban populations), and Odyssey Healthcare (a hospice company).